What's Out?

Models, concepts, and topics that don't pass a simple test:
"Does this help students analyze cases and real business situations?"

What's In?

"**VRIO**" – an integrative framework (see next page for details).

- Broad enough to apply in analyzing a variety of cases and real business settings.
- Simple enough to understand and teach.

The Results?

Provides students with the tools they need to do strateg[...]
Nothing more. Nothing less.

V R I O

"VALUE. RARITY. IMITABILITY. ORGANIZATION."

What Is It?

This book is not just a list of concepts, models, and theories. It is the first undergraduate textbook to introduce a **theory-based, multi-chapter organizing framework** to add additional structure to the field of strategic management.

"VRIO" is a mechanism that integrates two existing theoretical frameworks: the positioning perspective and the resource-based view. It is the primary tool for accomplishing internal analysis. It stands for four questions one must ask about a resource or capability to determine its competitive potential:

1. **The Question of Value:** Does a resource enable a firm to exploit an environmental opportunity, and/or neutralize an environmental threat?

2. **The Question of Rarity:** Is a resource currently controlled by only a small number of competing firms?

3. **The Question of Imitability:** Do firms without a resource face a cost disadvantage in obtaining or developing it?

4. **The Question of Organization:** Are a firm's other policies and procedures organized to support the exploitation of its valuable, rare, and costly-to-imitate resources?

What's the Benefit of the VRIO Framework?

The VRIO framework is the organizational foundation of the text. **It creates a decision-making framework for students** to use in analyzing case and business situations.

Students tend to view concepts, models, and theories (in all of their coursework) as fragmented and disconnected. Strategy is no exception. This view encourages rote memorization, not real understanding. VRIO, by serving as a consistent framework, connects ideas together. This encourages real understanding, not memorization.

This understanding enables students to better analyze business cases and situations—the goal of the course.

The VRIO framework makes it possible to discuss the formulation and implementation of a strategy simultaneously, within each chapter.

Because the VRIO framework provides a simple integrative structure, we are actually able to address issues in this book that are largely ignored elsewhere—including discussions of vertical integration, outsourcing, real options logic, and mergers and acquisitions, to name just a few.

EDITION

5

Strategic Management *and* Competitive Advantage

Concepts and Cases
Global Edition

Jay B. Barney

The University of Utah

William S. Hesterly

The University of Utah

PEARSON

Boston   Columbus   Hoboken   Indianapolis   New York   San Francisco
Amsterdam   Cape Town   Dubai   London   Madrid   Milan   Munich   Paris   Montréal   Toronto
Delhi   Mexico City   São Paulo   Sydney   Hong Kong   Seoul   Singapore   Taipei   Tokyo

Editor in Chief: Stephanie Wall
Head of Learning Asset Acquisition, Global Editions: Laura Dent
Acquisitions Editor: Daniel Tylman
Program Management Lead: Ashley Santora
Program Manager: Sarah Holle
Editorial Assistant: Linda Albelli
Acquisitions Editor, Global Editions: Vrinda Malik
Senior Project Editor, Global Editions: Vaijyanti
VP, Marketing: Maggie Moylan
Product Marketing Manager: Anne Fahlgren
Field Marketing Manager: Lenny Raper

Strategic Marketing Manager: Erin Gardner
Project Management Lead: Judy Leale
Project Manager: Karalyn Holland
Senior Manufacturing Production Controller, Global Editions: Trudy Kimber
Media Production Manager, Global Editions: M Vikram Kumar
Procurement Specialist: Michelle Klein
Cover Designer: Lumina Datamatics
Interior Illustrations: Gary Hovland
Cover Art: ©John T Takai/Shutterstock
Full-Service Project Management, Interior Design, Composition: Integra

Credits and acknowledgments borrowed from other sources and reproduced, with permission, in this textbook appear on the appropriate page within text.

Pearson Education Limited
Edinburgh Gate Harlow
Essex CM20 2JE
England

and Associated Companies throughout the world

Visit us on the World Wide Web at:
www.pearsonglobaleditions.com

© Pearson Education Limited 2015

British Library Cataloguing-in-Publication Data
A catalogue record for this book is available from the British Library

10 9 8 7 6 5 4 3 2 1
15 14

ISBN 10:   1-292-06008-5
ISBN 13: 978-1-292-06008-8

Typeset in 10/12 Palatino LT Std Roman by Integra

Printed by Courier Kendallville in the United States of America

This book is dedicated to my family: my wife, Kim; our children, Lindsay, Kristian, and Erin, and their spouses; and, most of all, our nine grandchildren, Isaac, Dylanie, Audrey, Chloe, Lucas, Royal, Lincoln, Nolan, and Theo. They all help me remember that no success could compensate for failure in the home.

Jay B. Barney
Salt Lake City, Utah

This book is for my family who has taught me life's greatest lessons about what matters most. To my wife, Denise; my daughters, sons, and their spouses: Lindsay, Matt, Jessica, John, Alex, Brittany, Austin, Julia, Ian, and Drew.; and my grandchildren, Ellie, Owen, Emerson, Cade, Elizabeth, Amelia, Eden, Asher, Lydia, and Scarlett.

William Hesterly
Salt Lake City, Utah

Brief Contents

Contents

Part 1: THE TOOLS of STRATEGIC ANALYSIS

Part 2: BUSINESS-LEVEL STRATEGIES

Part 3: CORPORATE STRATEGIES

End-of-Part 3 Cases

Appendix: Analyzing Cases and Preparing for Class Discussions   365

Preface

The first thing you will notice as you look through this edition of our book is that it continues to be much shorter than most textbooks on strategic management. There is not the usual "later edition" increase in number of pages and bulk. We're strong proponents of the philosophy that, often, less is more. The general tendency is for textbooks to get longer and longer as authors make sure that their books leave out nothing that is in other books. We take a different approach. Our guiding principle in deciding what to include is: "Does this concept help students analyze cases and real business situations?" For many concepts we considered, the answer is no. But, where the answer is yes, the concept is in the book.

New to This Edition

This edition includes many new chapter-opening cases, including:

- Chapter 1: A case on the video app "Angry Birds"
- Chapter 2: A case on the music streaming industry
- Chapter 3: A case on how Google keeps going
- Chapter 8: A case on Berkshire-Hathaway's corporate strategy
- Chapter 9: A case on the alliance between Apple and Samsung
- Chapter 10: A case on Google's acquisition strategy
- Chapter 11: A case on the infant formula business in China

All the other opening cases have been reused and updated, along with all the examples throughout the book.

Two newer topics in the field have also been included in this edition of the book: the business model canvas (in Chapter 1) and blue ocean strategies (in Chapter 5).

This edition features several new and updated cases, including:

- You Say You Want a Revolution: Soda Stream International
- True Religion Jeans: Will Going Private Help It Regain Its Congregation?
- Walmart: Walmart Stores, Inc., in 2013
- Air Asia X: Can the Low Cost Model Go Long Haul?
- RyanAir—The Low Fares Airline: Whither Now?
- Papa John's International, Inc.
- e-Bay's Outsourcing Strategy
- National Hockey League Enterprises Canada: A Retail Proposal
- Starbucks: An Alex Poole Strategy Case
- Rayovac Corporation: International Growth and Diversification Through Acquisitions

VRIO Framework and Other Hallmark Features

One thing that has not changed in this edition is that we continue to have a point of view about the field of strategic management. In planning for this book, we recalled our own educational experience and the textbooks that did and didn't work for us then. Those few that stood out as the best did not merely cover all of the different topics in a field of study. They provided a framework that we could carry around in our heads, and they helped us to see what we were studying as an integrated whole rather than a disjointed sequence of loosely related subjects. This text continues to be integrated around the VRIO framework. As those of you familiar with the resource-based theory of strategy recognize, the VRIO framework addresses the central questions around gaining and sustaining competitive advantage. After it is introduced in Chapter 3, the VRIO logic of competitive advantage is applied in every chapter. It is simple enough to understand and teach yet broad enough to apply to a wide variety of cases and business settings.

Our consistent use of the VRIO framework does not mean that any of the concepts fundamental to a strategy course are missing. We still have all of the core ideas and theories that are essential to a strategy course. Ideas such as the study of environmental threats, value chain analysis, generic strategies, and corporate strategy are all in the book. Because the VRIO framework provides a single integrative structure, we are able to address issues in this book that are largely ignored elsewhere—including discussions of vertical integration, outsourcing, real options logic, and mergers and acquisitions, to name just a few.

We also have designed flexibility into the book. Each chapter has four short sections that present specific issues in more depth. These sections allow instructors to adapt the book to the particular needs of their students. "Strategy in Depth" examines the intellectual foundations that are behind the way managers think about and practice strategy today. "Strategy in the Emerging Enterprise" presents examples of strategic challenges faced by new and emerging enterprises. "Ethics and Strategy" delves into some of the ethical dilemmas that managers face as they confront strategic decisions. "Research Made Relevant" includes recent research related to the topics in that chapter.

We have also included cases—including many new cases in this edition—that provide students an opportunity to apply the ideas they learn to business situations. The cases include a variety of contexts, such as entrepreneurial, service, manufacturing, and international settings. The power of the VRIO framework is that it applies across all of these settings. Applying the VRIO framework to many topics and cases throughout the book leads to real understanding instead of rote memorization. The end result is that students will find that they have the tools they need to do strategic analysis. Nothing more. Nothing less.

Supplements

At the Instructor Resource Center, at www.pearsonglobaleditions.com/Barney, instructors can download a variety of digital and presentation resources. Registration is simple and gives you immediate access to all of the available supplements. In case you ever need assistance, our dedicated technical support team is ready to help with the media supplements that accompany this text. Visit http://247.pearsoned.custhelp.com for answers to frequently asked questions and toll-free user support phone numbers.

The following supplements are available for download to adopting instructors:

- Instructor's Manual
- Case Teaching Notes
- Test Item File
- TestGen® Computerized Test Bank
- PowerPoint Slides

Videos

Videos illustrating the most important subject topics are available in MyLab—available for instructors and students, provides round-the-clock instant access to videos and corresponding assessment and simulations for Pearson textbooks. Contact your local Pearson representative to request access.

Other Benefits

Element	Description	Benefit	Example
Chapter Opening Cases	We have chosen firms that are familiar to most students. Opening cases focus on whether or not Rovio Entertainment, Ltd.—maker of the popular video game "Angry Birds"—can sustain its success, how Ryanair has become the lowest cost airline in the world, how Victoria's Secret has differentiated its products, how ESPN has diversified its operations, and so forth.	By having cases tightly linked to the material, students can develop strategic analysis skills by studying firms familiar to them.	24–25
Full Length Cases	This book contains selective, part-ending cases that underscore the concepts in each part. This provides a tight link to the chapter concepts to reinforce understanding of recent research. These are 1) decision oriented, 2) recent, 3) student-recognized companies, and 4) cases where the data are only partly analyzed.	Provides a tight link to chapter concepts, facilitating students' ability to apply text ideas to case analysis.	PC 1–1– PC 1–10
Strategy in Depth	For professors and students interested in understanding the full intellectual underpinnings of the field, we have included an optional Strategy in Depth feature in every chapter. Knowledge in strategic management continues to evolve rapidly, in ways that are well beyond what is normally included in introductory texts.	Customize your course as desired to provide enrichment material for advanced students.	245
Research Made Relevant	The Research Made Relevant feature highlights very current research findings related to some of the strategic topics discussed in that chapter.	Shows students the evolving nature of strategy.	69
Challenge Questions	These might be of an ethical or moral nature, forcing students to apply concepts across chapters, apply concepts to themselves, or extend chapter ideas in creative ways.	Requires students to think critically.	147
Problem Set	Problem Set asks students to apply theories and tools from the chapter. These often require calculations. They can be thought of as homework assignments. If students struggle with these problems they might have trouble with the more complex cases. These problem sets are largely diagnostic in character.	Sharpens quantitative skills and provides a bridge between chapter material and case analysis.	179–180
Ethics and Strategy	Highlights some of the most important dilemmas faced by firms when creating and implementing strategies.	Helps students make better ethical decisions as managers.	230
Strategy in the Emerging Enterprise	A growing number of graduates work for small and medium-sized firms. This feature presents an extended example, in each chapter, of the unique strategic problems facing those employed in small and medium-sized firms.	This feature highlights the unique challenges of doing strategic analysis in emerging enterprises and small and medium-sized firms.	75

Acknowledgments

Obviously, a book like this is not written in isolation. We owe a debt of gratitude to all those at Pearson who have supported its development. In particular, we want to thank Stephanie Wall, Editor-in-Chief; Dan Tylman, Acquisitions Editor; Sarah Holle, Program Manager; Erin Gardner, Marketing Manager; Judy Leale, Project Manager Team Lead; and Karalyn Holland, Senior Project Manager.

Many people were involved in reviewing drafts of each edition's manuscript. Their efforts undoubtedly improved the manuscript dramatically. Their efforts are largely unsung but very much appreciated.

Thank you to these professors who participated in manuscript reviews:

Yusaf Akbar—Southern New Hampshire University

Joseph D. Botana II—Lakeland College

Pam Braden—West Virginia University at Parkersburg

Erick PC Chang—Arkansas State University

Mustafa Colak—Temple University

Ron Eggers—Barton College

Michael Frandsen—Albion College

Swapnil Garg—University of Florida

Michele Gee—University of Wisconsin, Parkside

Peter Goulet—University of Northern Iowa

Rebecca Guidice—University of Nevada Las Vegas

Laura Hart—Lynn University, College of Business & Management

Tom Hewett—Kaplan University

Phyllis Holland—Valdosta State University

Paul Howard—Penn State University

Richard Insinga—St. John Fisher College

Homer Johnson—Loyola University Chicago

Marilyn Kaplan—University of Texas at Dallas

Joseph Leonard—Miami University

Paul Maxwell—St. Thomas University, Miami

Stephen Mayer—Niagara University

Richard Nemanick—Saint Louis University

Hossein Noorian—Wentworth Institute of Technology

Ralph Parrish—University of Central Oklahoma

Raman Patel—Robert Morris College

Jiten Ruparel—Otterbein College

Roy Simerly—East Carolina University

Sally Sledge—Christopher Newport University

David Stahl—Montclair State University

David Stephens—Utah State University

Philip Stoeberl—Saint Louis University

Ram Subramanian—Grand Valley State University

William W. Topper—Curry College

Thomas Turk—Chapman University

Henry Ulrich—Central Connecticut State (soon to be UCONN)

Floyd Willoughby—Oakland University

Reviewers of the Fourth Edition

Terry Adler—New Mexico State University

Jorge Aravelo—William Patterson University

Asli M. Arikan—The Ohio State University

Scott Brown—Chapman University

Carlos Ferran—Governors State University

Samual Holloway—University of Portland

Paul Longenecker—Otterbein University

Shelly McCallum—Saint Mary's University

Jeffrey Stone—CAL State–Channel Islands

Edward Taylor—Piedmont College

Les Thompson—Missouri Baptist University

Zhe Zhang—Eastern Kentucky University

All these people have given generously of their time and wisdom. But, truth be told, everyone who knows us knows that this book would not have been possible without Kathy Zwanziger and Rachel Snow.

Pearson would like to thank and acknowledge the following people for their work on the Global Edition.

For their contribution:

Malay Krishna—S.P. Jain Institute of Management & Research

Thum Weng-Ho—Murdoch University

And for their reviews:

S Siengthai—Asian Institute of Technology

Kate Mottaram—Coventry University

Charles Chow—Lee Kong Chian School of Business

Dr.Pardeep Kumar—MGM Institute of Management

Author Biographies

JAY B. BARNEY

Jay Barney is a Presidential Professor of strategic management and the Lassonde Chair of Social Entrepreneurship of the Entrepreneurship and Strategy Department in the David Eccles Business School, The University of Utah. He received his Ph.D. from Yale and has held faculty appointments at UCLA, Texas A&M, and OSU [The Ohio State University]. He joined the faculty at The University of Utah in summer of 2013. Jay has published more than 100 journal articles and books; has served on the editorial boards of *Academy of Management Review, Strategic Management Journal*, and *Organization Science;* has served as an associate editor of *The Journal of Management* and senior editor at *Organization Science*; and currently serves as co-editor at the *Strategic Entrepreneurship Journal*. He has received

honorary doctorate degrees from the University of Lund (Sweden), the Copenhagen Business School (Denmark), and the Universidad Pontificia Comillas (Spain) and has been elected to the Academy of Management Fellows and Strategic Management Society Fellows. He has held honorary visiting professor positions at Waikato University (New Zealand), Sun Yat-Sen University (China), and Peking University (China). He has also consulted for a wide variety of public and private organizations, including Hewlett-Packard, Texas Instruments, Arco, Koch Industries Inc., and Nationwide Insurance, focusing on implementing large-scale organizational change and strategic analysis. He has received teaching awards at UCLA, Texas A&M, and Ohio State. Jay served as assistant program chair and program chair, chair elect, and chair of the Business Policy and Strategy Division. In 2005, he received the Irwin Outstanding Educator Award for the BPS Division of the Academy of Management, and in 2010, he won the Academy of Management's Scholarly Contribution to Management Award. In 2008, he was elected as the President-elect of the Strategic Management Society, where he currently serves as past-president.

WILLIAM S. HESTERLY

William Hesterly is the Associate Dean for Faculty and Research as well as the Dumke Family Endowed Presidential Chair in Management in the David Eccles School of Business, University of Utah. After studying at Louisiana State University, he received bachelors and masters degrees from Brigham Young University and a Ph.D. from the University of California, Los Angeles. Professor Hesterly has been recognized multiple times as the outstanding teacher in the MBA Program at the David Eccles School of Business and has also been the recipient of the Student's Choice Award. He has taught in a variety of executive programs for both large and small companies. Professor Hesterly's research on organizational economics, vertical integration,

organizational forms, and entrepreneurial networks has appeared in top journals including the *Academy of Management Review, Organization Science, Strategic Management Journal, Journal of Management*, and the *Journal of Economic Behavior and Organization*. Currently, he is studying the sources of value creation in firms and also the determinants of who captures the value from a firm's competitive advantage. Recent papers in this area have appeared in the *Academy of Management Review* and *Managerial and Decision Economics*. Professor Hesterly's research was recognized with the Western Academy of Management's Ascendant Scholar Award in 1999. Dr. Hesterly has also received best paper awards from the Western Academy of Management and the Academy of Management. Dr. Hesterly currently serves as the senior editor of *Long Range Planning* and has served on the editorial boards of *Strategic Organization, Organization Science,* and the *Journal of Management*. He has served as Department Chair and also as Vice-President and President of the faculty at the David Eccles School of Business at the University of Utah.

1 THE TOOLS OF STRATEGIC ANALYSIS

1 What Is Strategy and the Strategic Management Process?

LEARNING OBJECTIVES *After reading this chapter, you should be able to:*

1. Define strategy.

2. Describe the strategic management process.

3. Define competitive advantage and explain its relationship to economic value creation.

4. Describe two different measures of competitive advantage.

5. Explain the difference between emergent and intended strategies.

6. Discuss the importance of understanding a firm's strategy even if you are not a senior manager in a firm.

MyManagementLab®

⭐ **Improve Your Grade!**
Over 10 million students improved their results using the Pearson MyLabs.
Visit **mymanagementlab.com** for simulations, tutorials, and end-of-chapter problems.

Why Are These Birds So Angry?

Rarely can the beginning on an entire industry be traced to a single event on a specific day. But this is the case with the smart phone applications industry.

On June 29, 2007, Apple first introduced the iPhone. A central feature of the iPhone was that it would be able to run a wide variety of applications, or "apps." And, most importantly for the evolution of the apps industry, Apple decided that while it would evaluate and distribute these applications—through the online Apple App Store—it would not develop them. Instead, Apple would "crowd source" most applications from outside developers.

And, thus, the smart phone applications industry began. By April 24, 2009, iPhone users had downloaded more than 1 billion apps from the Apple App Store. During 2012, more than 45.6 billion smart phone apps were downloaded from all sources, generating revenues in excess of $25 billion. Projections suggest double-digit growth in this industry for at least another five years.

Of course, much has changed since 2007. For example, Apple now has six competitors for its Apple App Store, including Amazon App Store, Google Play Store, BlackBerry World, and Windows Phone Store. Some of these stores distribute apps for non-Apple phone operating systems developed by Google (Android), BlackBerry, and Windows. But all of these distributors have adopted Apple's original model for developing applications: mostly outsource it to independent development companies.

These development companies fall into four categories: (1) Internet companies—including Google—who have developed smart phone versions of popular Internet sites—including, for

example, YouTube and Google Maps; (2) traditional video game companies—including Sega—who have developed smart phone versions of popular video games—including, for example, Sonic Dash; (3) diversified media companies—including Disney—who have built apps featuring characters and stories developed in their far-flung media operations—including, for example, Monster's University; and (4) companies who have been formed to develop entirely new apps.

There are, of course, literally thousands—maybe hundreds of thousands—of this last type of app development firm. The proliferation of these firms—sometimes no more than one person with an idea—has led to a proliferation of apps across all smart phone platforms. Currently, there are 1.5 million downloadable apps available on both the Apple App Store and Google Play Store.

Among these thousands of independent developers, a few have been unusually successful. None exemplifies this "rag to riches" dynamic more than Rovio, an app development company headquartered outside Helsinki, Finland. Rovio is best known for an amazingly simple game involving enraged avians—yes, Angry Birds.

The challenge facing Rovio, and all these successful independent app developers, is: Can they go beyond developing a single "killer app," or will they be "one-hit wonders?" Rovio is trying to avoid this fate by leveraging the Angry Birds franchise into a series of related apps—Angry Birds Star Wars, Bad Piggies; by developing apps that build on new characters—The Croods; by diversifying into related non-app businesses—Angry Birds Toons; and by licensing Angry Birds characters to toy manufactures—including Mattel.

Rovio has even begun crowd sourcing new app ideas that it can bring to market. Independent developers can pitch games and apps to Rovio online. Whether this effort will lead to the next generation of Rovio apps is not yet known.

What is known is that the smart phone applications industry—an industry that was created only in 2007—is likely to grow and evolve dramatically over the next few years. And firms as diverse as Google, Apple, Disney, Sega—and even Rovio—will have to evolve with it.

Sources: www.rovio.com accessed August 23, 2013; www.distimo.com accessed August 23, 2013; www.newrelic.com accessed August 23, 2013

Firms in the smart phone applications industry—whether they have entered this business from another media industry—like Google and Disney—or not—like Rovio—face classic strategic questions. How is this industry likely to evolve? What actions can be taken to change this evolution? How can firms gain advantages in this industry? How sustainable are these advantages?

The process by which these, and related, questions are answered is the strategic management process, and the answers that firms develop for these questions help determine a firm's strategy.

Strategy and the Strategic Management Process

Although most can agree that a firm's ability to survive and prosper depends on choosing and implementing a good strategy, there is less agreement about what a strategy is and even less agreement about what constitutes a good strategy. Indeed, there are almost as many different definitions of these concepts as there are books written about them.

Defining Strategy

In this book, a firm's **strategy** is defined as its theory about how to gain competitive advantages.[1] A good strategy is a strategy that actually generates such advantages. Disney's theory of how to gain a competitive advantage in the apps industry is to leverage characters from its movie business. Rovio's theory is to develop entirely new content for its apps.

Each of these theories—like all theories—is based on a set of assumptions and hypotheses about the way competition in this industry is likely to evolve and how that evolution can be exploited to earn a profit. The greater the extent to which these assumptions and hypotheses accurately reflect how competition in this industry actually evolves, the more likely it is that a firm will gain a competitive advantage from implementing its strategies. If these assumptions and hypotheses turn out not to be accurate, then a firm's strategies are not likely to be a source of competitive advantage.

But here is the challenge. It is usually very difficult to predict how competition in an industry will evolve, and so it is rarely possible to know for sure that a firm is choosing the right strategy. This is why a firm's strategy is almost always a theory: It's a firm's best bet about how competition is going to evolve and how that evolution can be exploited for competitive advantage.

The Strategic Management Process

Although it is usually difficult to know for sure that a firm is pursuing the best strategy, it is possible to reduce the likelihood that mistakes are being made. The best way to do this is for a firm to choose its strategy carefully and systematically and to follow the strategic management process. The **strategic management process** is a sequential set of analyses and choices that can increase the likelihood that a firm will choose a good strategy; that is, a strategy that generates competitive advantages. An example of the strategic management process is presented in Figure 1.1. Not surprisingly, this book is organized around this strategic management process.

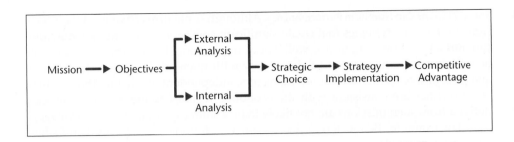

Figure 1.1   The Strategic Management Process

A Firm's Mission

The strategic management process begins when a firm defines its mission. A firm's **mission** is its long-term purpose. Missions define both what a firm aspires to be in the long run and what it wants to avoid in the meantime. Missions are often written down in the form of **mission statements**.

Some Missions May Not Affect Firm Performance.   Most mission statements incorporate common elements. For example, many define the businesses within which a firm will operate—medical products for Johnson and Johnson; adhesives and substrates for 3M—or they can very simply state how a firm will compete in those businesses. Many even define the core values that a firm espouses.

Indeed, mission statements often contain so many common elements that some have questioned whether having a mission statement even creates value for a firm.[2] Moreover, even if a mission statement does say something unique about a company, if that mission statement does not influence behavior throughout an organization, it is unlikely to have much impact on a firm's actions. After all, while Enron was engaging in wide ranging acts of fraud[3], it had a mission statement that emphasized the importance of honesty and integrity.[4]

Some Missions Can Improve Firm Performance.   Despite these caveats, research has identified some firms whose sense of purpose and mission permeates all that they do. These firms include, for example, 3M, IBM, Philip Morris, Wal-Mart, and Disney. Some of these **visionary firms**, or firms whose mission is central to all they do have enjoyed long periods of high performance.[5] From 1926 through 1995, an investment of $1 in one of these firms would have increased in value to $6,536. That same dollar invested in an average firm over this same time period would have been worth $415 in 1995.

These visionary firms earned substantially higher returns than average firms even though many of their mission statements suggest that profit maximizing, although an important corporate objective, is not their primary reason for existence. Rather, their primary reasons for existence are typically reflected in a widely held set of values and beliefs that inform day-to-day decision making. While, in other firms, managers may be tempted to sacrifice such values and beliefs to gain short-term advantages, in these special firms, the pressure for short-term performance is balanced by widespread commitment to values and beliefs that focus more on a firm's long-term performance.[6]

Of course, that these firms had performed well for many decades does not mean they will do so forever. Some previously identified visionary firms have stumbled more recently, including American Express, Ford, Hewlett-Packard, Motorola, and Sony. Some of these financial problems may be attributable to the fact that these formally mission-driven companies have lost focus on their mission.

Some Missions Can Hurt Firm Performance.   Although some firms have used their missions to develop strategies that create significant competitive advantages, missions can hurt a firm's performance as well. For example, sometimes a firm's mission will be very inwardly focused and defined only with reference to the personal values and priorities of its founders or top managers, independent of whether those values and priorities are consistent with the economic realities facing a firm. Strategies derived from such missions are not likely to be a source of competitive advantage.

For example, Ben & Jerry's Ice Cream was founded in 1977 by Ben Cohen and Jerry Greenfield, both as a way to produce super-premium ice cream and as a way to create an organization based on the values of the 1960s' counterculture. This strong sense of mission led Ben & Jerry's to adopt some very unusual human resource and other policies. Among these policies, the company adopted a compensation system whereby the highest-paid firm employee could earn no more than five times the income of the lowest-paid firm employee. Later, this ratio was adjusted to seven to one. However, even at this level, such a compensation policy made it very difficult to acquire the senior management talent needed to ensure the growth and profitability of the firm without grossly overpaying the lowest-paid employees in the firm. When a new CEO was appointed to the firm in 1995, his $250,000 salary violated this compensation policy.

Indeed, though the frozen dessert market rapidly consolidated through the late 1990s, Ben & Jerry's Ice Cream remained an independent firm, partly because of Cohen's and Greenfield's commitment to maintaining the social values that their firm embodied. Lacking access to the broad distribution network and managerial talent that would have been available if Ben & Jerry's had merged with another firm, the company's growth and profitability lagged. Finally, in April 2000, Ben & Jerry's Ice Cream was acquired by Unilever. The 66 percent premium finally earned by Ben & Jerry's stockholders in April 2000 had been delayed for several years. In this sense, Cohen's and Greenfield's commitment to a set of personal values and priorities was at least partly inconsistent with the economic realities of the frozen dessert market in the United States.[7]

Obviously, because a firm's mission can help, hurt, or have no impact on its performance, missions by themselves do not necessarily lead a firm to choose and implement strategies that generate competitive advantages. Indeed, as suggested in Figure 1.1, while defining a firm's mission is an important step in the strategic management process, it is only the first step in that process.

Objectives

Whereas a firm's mission is a broad statement of its purpose and values, its **objectives** are specific measurable targets a firm can use to evaluate the extent to which it is realizing its mission. High-quality objectives are tightly connected to elements of a firm's mission and are relatively easy to measure and track over time. Low-quality objectives either do not exist or are not connected to elements of a firm's mission, are not quantitative, or are difficult to measure or difficult to track over time. Obviously, low-quality objectives cannot be used by management to evaluate how well a mission is being realized. Indeed, one indication that a firm is not that serious about realizing part of its mission statement is when there are no objectives, or only low-quality objectives, associated with that part of the mission.

External and Internal Analysis

The next two phases of the strategic management process—external analysis and internal analysis—occur more or less simultaneously. By conducting an

external analysis, a firm identifies the critical threats and opportunities in its competitive environment. It also examines how competition in this environment is likely to evolve and what implications that evolution has for the threats and opportunities a firm is facing. A considerable literature on techniques for and approaches to conducting external analysis has evolved over the past several years. This literature is the primary subject matter of Chapter 2 of this book.

Whereas external analysis focuses on the environmental threats and opportunities facing a firm, **internal analysis** helps a firm identify its organizational strengths and weaknesses. It also helps a firm understand which of its resources and capabilities are likely to be sources of competitive advantage and which are less likely to be sources of such advantages. Finally, internal analysis can be used by firms to identify those areas of its organization that require improvement and change. As with external analysis, a considerable literature on techniques for and approaches to conducting internal analysis has evolved over the past several years. This literature is the primary subject matter of Chapter 3 of this book.

Strategic Choice

Armed with a mission, objectives, and completed external and internal analyses, a firm is ready to make its strategic choices. That is, a firm is ready to choose its theory of how to gain competitive advantage.

The strategic choices available to firms fall into two large categories: business-level strategies and corporate-level strategies. **Business-level strategies** are actions firms take to gain competitive advantages in a single market or industry. These strategies are the topic of Part 2 of this book. The two most common business-level strategies are cost leadership (Chapter 4) and product differentiation (Chapter 5).

Corporate-level strategies are actions firms take to gain competitive advantages by operating in multiple markets or industries simultaneously. These strategies are the topic of Part 3 of this book. Common corporate-level strategies include vertical integration strategies (Chapter 6), diversification strategies (Chapters 7 and 8), strategic alliance strategies (Chapter 9), merger and acquisition strategies (Chapter 10), and global strategies (Chapter 11).

Obviously, the details of choosing specific strategies can be quite complex, and a discussion of these details will be delayed until later in the book. However, the underlying logic of strategic choice is not complex. Based on the strategic management process, the objective when making a strategic choice is to choose a strategy that (1) supports the firm's mission, (2) is consistent with a firm's objectives, (3) exploits opportunities in a firm's environment with a firm's strengths, and (4) neutralizes threats in a firm's environment while avoiding a firm's weaknesses. Assuming that this strategy is implemented—the last step of the strategic management process—a strategy that meets these four criteria is very likely to be a source of competitive advantage for a firm.

Strategy Implementation

Of course, simply choosing a strategy means nothing if that strategy is not implemented. **Strategy implementation** occurs when a firm adopts organizational policies and practices that are consistent with its strategy. Three specific organizational policies and practices are particularly important in implementing a strategy: a firm's formal organizational structure, its formal and informal management control systems, and its employee compensation policies. A firm that adopts an organizational structure, management controls, and compensation policy that are consistent with and reinforce its strategies is more likely to be able to implement those strategies than a firm that adopts an organizational structure, management controls, and compensation policy that are inconsistent with its strategies. Specific organizational structures, management controls, and compensation policies used to implement the business-level strategies of cost leadership and product differentiation are discussed in Chapters 4 and 5. How organizational structure, management controls, and compensation can be used to implement corporate-level strategies, including vertical integration, strategic alliance, merger and acquisition, and global strategies, is discussed in Chapters 6, 9, 10, and 11, respectively. However, there is so much information about implementing diversification strategies that an entire chapter, Chapter 8, is dedicated to the discussion of how this corporate-level strategy is implemented.

What Is Competitive Advantage?

Of course, the ultimate objective of the strategic management process is to enable a firm to choose and implement a strategy that generates a competitive advantage. But what is a competitive advantage? In general, a firm has a **competitive advantage** when it is able to create more economic value than rival firms. **Economic value** is simply the difference between the perceived benefits gained by a customer that purchases a firm's products or services and the full economic cost of these products or services. Thus, the size of a firm's competitive advantage is the difference between the economic value a firm is able to create and the economic value its rivals are able to create.[8]

Consider the two firms presented in Figure 1.2. Both these firms compete in the same market for the same customers. However, Firm I generates $180 of economic value each time it sells a product or service, whereas Firm II generates $150 of economic value each time it sells a product or service. Because Firm I generates more economic value each time it sells a product or service, it has a competitive advantage over Firm II. The size of this competitive advantage is equal to the difference in the economic value these two firms create, in this case, $30($180 − $150 = $30).

However, as shown in the figure, Firm I's advantage may come from different sources. For example, it might be the case that Firm I creates greater perceived benefits for its customers than Firm II. In panel A of the figure, Firm I creates perceived customer benefits worth $230, whereas Firm II creates perceived customer benefits worth only $200. Thus, even though both firms' costs are the same (equal to $50 per unit sold), Firm I creates more economic value ($230 − $50 = $180) than Firm II ($200 − $50 = $150). Indeed, it is possible for Firm I, in this situation, to have higher costs than Firm II and still create more economic value than Firm II if these higher costs are offset by Firm I's ability to create greater perceived benefits for its customers.

Alternatively, as shown in panel B of the figure, these two firms may create the same level of perceived customer benefit (equal to $210 in this example) but have different costs. If Firm I's costs per unit are only $30, it will generate $180 worth of economic value ($210 − $30 = $180). If Firm II's costs are $60, it will generate only $150 of economic value ($210 − $60 = $150). Indeed, it might be possible for Firm I to create a lower level of perceived benefits for its customers than Firm II and still create more economic value than Firm II, as long

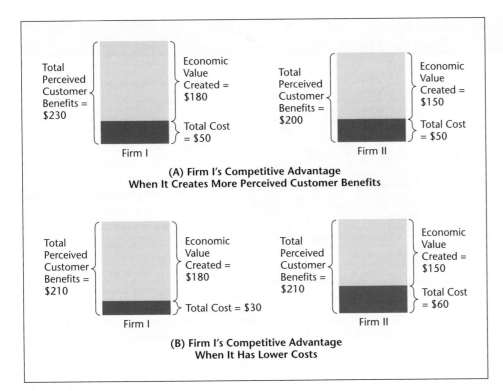

Figure 1.2   The Sources of a Firm's Competitive Advantage

as its disadvantage in perceived customer benefits is more than offset by its cost advantage.

A firm's competitive advantage can be temporary or sustained. As summarized in Figure 1.3, a **temporary competitive advantage** is a competitive advantage that lasts for a very short period of time. A **sustained competitive advantage**, in contrast, can last much longer. How long sustained competitive advantages can last is discussed in the Research Made Relevant feature. Firms that create the same economic value as their rivals experience **competitive parity**. Finally, firms that generate less economic value than their rivals have a **competitive disadvantage**. Not surprisingly, competitive disadvantages can be either temporary or sustained, depending on the duration of the disadvantage.

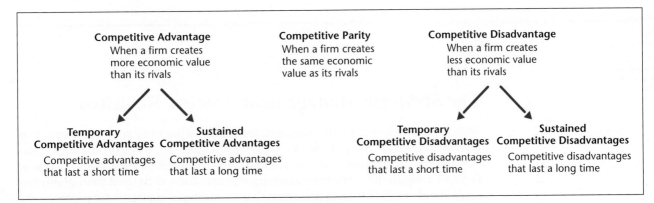

Figure 1.3   Types of Competitive Advantage

Research Made Relevant

For some time, economists have been interested in how long firms are able to sustain competitive advantages. Traditional economic theory predicts that such advantages should be short-lived in highly competitive markets. This theory suggests that any competitive advantages gained by a particular firm will quickly be identified and imitated by other firms, ensuring competitive parity in the long run. However, in real life, competitive advantages often last longer than traditional economic theory predicts.

One of the first scholars to examine this issue was Dennis Mueller. Mueller divided a sample of 472 firms into eight categories, depending on their level of performance in 1949. He then examined the impact of a firm's initial performance on its subsequent performance. The traditional economic hypothesis was that all firms in the sample would converge on an average level of performance. This did not occur. Indeed, firms that were performing well in an earlier time period tended to perform well in later time periods, and firms that performed poorly in an earlier time period tended to perform poorly in later time periods as well.

Geoffrey Waring followed up on Mueller's work by explaining why competitive advantages seem to

How Sustainable Are Competitive Advantages?

persist longer in some industries than in others. Waring found that, among other factors, firms that operate in industries that (1) are informationally complex, (2) require customers to know a great deal in order to use an industry's products, (3) require a great deal of research and development, and (4) have significant economies of scale are more likely to have sustained competitive advantages compared to firms that operate in industries without these attributes.

Peter Roberts studied the persistence of profitability in one particular industry: the U.S. pharmaceutical industry. Roberts found that not only can firms sustain competitive advantages in this industry, but that the ability to do

so is almost entirely attributable to the firms' capacity to innovate by bringing out new and powerful drugs.

The most recent work in this tradition was published by Anita McGahan and Michael Porter. They showed that both high and low performance can persist for some time. Persistent high performance is related to attributes of the industry within which a firm operates and the corporation within which a business unit functions. In contrast, persistent low performance was caused by attributes of a business unit itself.

In many ways, the difference between traditional economics research and strategic management research is that the former attempts to explain why competitive advantages should not persist, whereas the latter attempts to explain when they can. Thus far, most empirical research suggests that firms, in at least some settings, can sustain competitive advantages.

Sources: D. C. Mueller (1977). "The persistence of profits above the norm." *Economica*, 44, pp. 369–380; P. W. Roberts (1999). "Product innovation, product-market competition, and persistent profitability in the U.S. pharmaceutical industry." *Strategic Management Journal*, 20, pp. 655–670; G. F. Waring (1996). "Industry differences in the persistence of firm-specific returns." *The American Economic Review*, 86, pp. 1253–1265; A. McGahan and M. Porter (2003). "The emergence and sustainability of abnormal profits." *Strategic Organization*, 1(1), pp. 79–108.

The Strategic Management Process, Revisited

With this description of the strategic management process now complete, it is possible to redraw the process, as depicted in Figure 1.1, to incorporate the various options a firm faces as it chooses and implements its strategy. This is done in Figure 1.4. Figure 1.4 is the organizing framework that will be used throughout this book. An alternative way of characterizing the strategic management process—the business model canvas—is described in the Strategy in Depth feature.

Figure 1.4   Organizing Framework

Measuring Competitive Advantage

A firm has a *competitive advantage* when it creates more economic value than its rivals. *Economic value* is the difference between the perceived customer benefits associated with buying a firm's products or services and the full cost of producing and selling these products or services. These are deceptively simple definitions. However, these concepts are not always easy to measure directly. For example, the benefits of a firm's products or services are always a matter of customer perception, and perceptions are not easy to measure. Also, the total costs associated with producing a particular product or service may not always be easy to identify or associate with a particular product or service. Despite the very real challenges associated with measuring a firm's competitive advantage, two approaches have emerged. The first estimates a firm's competitive advantage by examining its accounting performance; the second examines the firm's economic performance. These approaches are discussed in the following sections.

Accounting Measures of Competitive Advantage

A firm's **accounting performance** is a measure of its competitive advantage calculated by using information from a firm's published profit and loss and balance sheet statements. A firm's profit and loss and balance sheet statements, in turn, are typically created using widely accepted accounting standards and principles. The application of these standards and principles makes it possible to compare the accounting performance of one firm to the accounting performance of other firms, even if those firms are not in the same industry. However, to the extent that these standards and principles are not applied in generating a firm's accounting statements or to the extent that different firms use different accounting standards and principles in generating their statements, it can be difficult to compare the accounting performance of firms. These issues can be particularly challenging when comparing the performance of firms in different countries around the world.

One way to use a firm's accounting statements to measure its competitive advantage is through the use of accounting ratios. **Accounting ratios** are simply numbers taken from a firm's financial statements that are manipulated in ways that describe various aspects of a firm's performance. Some of the most

Strategy in Depth

Recently, some strategic management scholars have developed an alternative approach to characterizing the strategic management process. Rather than starting with mission statements and objectives and then proceeding through the different kinds of analyses that need to be done to choose and implement a strategy, this approach starts by identifying activities that have an impact on the ability of a firm to create and appropriate economic value and then specifying exactly how a particular firm accomplishes these activities. That set of activities that a firm engages in to create and appropriate economic value, in this approach, is called a firm's **business model**.

Probably the most influential approach to identifying a firm's business model was developed by Alex Osterwalder and Yves Pigneur in their book *Business Model Generator*. In the book, a generic business model—not unrelated to the generic value chains that will be introduced in Chapter 3 of this book—is presented. Because this approach enables managers to see the entire landscape of their business in a single page, this model is called the *business model canvas*. This canvas is reproduced in this feature.

The center of the canvas is dominated by a box labeled *Value Propositions*. A firm's value propositions are statements about how it will attempt to create value for its customers, customer problems it is trying to solve through its business operations, which customers it will focus on, and so forth. Identifying a firm's value propositions is very close to identifying its strategy, as presented in Figure 1.4.

Once a firm's value propositions are identified, they have important

The Business Model Canvas

implications for the *Key Activities* a firm needs to engage in, the *Key Resources* it needs to control to engage in those activities, and the *Key Partners* it needs to have to gain access to those resources. The value propositions also help determine critical *Customer Relationships*, the *Channels* a firm needs to use to reach those critical customers, and which *Customer Segments* a firm will address with its products or services.

If a firm's key activities, resources, and partners, on the one hand, and its customer relationships, channels, and segments, on the other hand, all support the execution of its value propositions, then these activities—collectively—will improve a firm's cost structure and revenue streams. Consistent with the definitions presented in this chapter, the difference between a firm's revenues and costs is a measure of the economic value created by a firm.

Different business models—as summarized by the business model canvas—have been given labels to help distinguish them. For example, a "bricks and clicks" business model

(where online retail is integrated with off-line retail) implies a very different set of business activities than a "franchise" business model (where quasi-independent entrepreneurs own and operate retail outlets), which are also different from a "direct" retail model (where firms eliminate in-process inventory by having customers order each product sold), and so forth.

Some scholars have objected to the introduction of the canvas, arguing that it does not add anything fundamental to our understanding of the strategic management process. Others have suggested that some important components of that process—including, for example, organizing to implement a firm's strategy—are left out of the canvas. Others argue that competition is not well represented in the canvas—if numbers of competing firms all adopt the same business model canvas, how is that canvas supposed to enhance the competitive position of any one of those firms? On the other hand, the canvas is a convenient way to summarize a wide variety of firm activities, how those activities are related to one another, and how they ultimately affect a firm's costs and revenues. And while the framework presented in Figure 1.4 will be used to organize the material in the rest of this book, insights from the canvas approach will be incorporated throughout the book as appropriate.

Sources: A. Osterwalder and Y. Pigneur (2010). Business Model Generator. NY: Wiley. G. George and A. J. Bock (2011). The business model in practice and its implications for entrepreneurial research. *Entrepreneurship: Theory and Practice*, 35(1), 83–111. C. Zott, R. Amit, and L. Massa. (2010). The Business Model: Theoretical Roots, Recent Development, and Future Research. Working Paper 862, IESE, Barcelona, Spain.

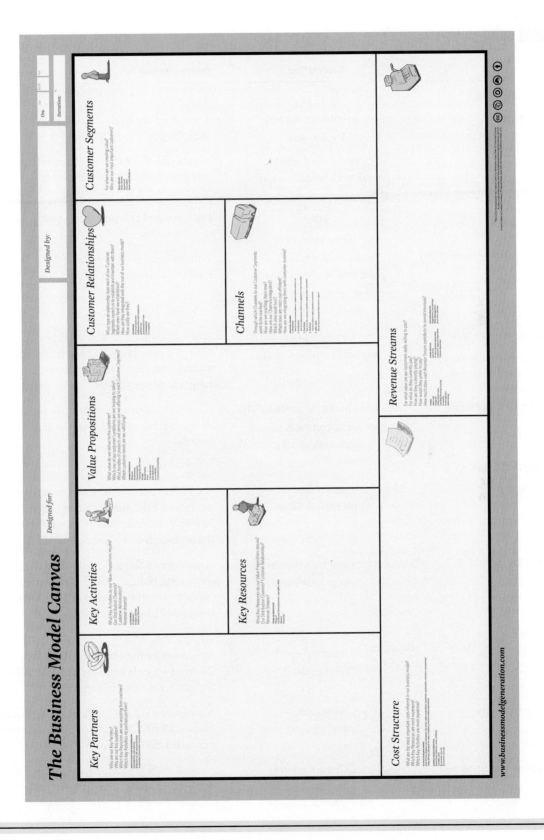

TABLE 1.1   Common Ratios to Measure a Firm's Accounting Performance

Ratio	Calculation	Interpretation
Profitability Ratios		
1. ROA	$\dfrac{\text{profit after taxes}}{\text{total assets}}$	A measure of return on total investment in a firm. Larger is usually better.
2. ROE	$\dfrac{\text{profit after taxes}}{\text{total stockholder's equity}}$	A measure of return on total equity investment in a firm. Larger is usually better.
3. Gross profit margin	$\dfrac{\text{sales} - \text{cost of goods sold}}{\text{sales}}$	A measure of sales available to cover operating expenses and still generate a profit. Larger is usually better.
4. Earnings per share (EPS)	$\dfrac{\text{profits (after taxes)} - \text{preferred stock dividends}}{\text{number of shares of common stock outstanding}}$	A measure of profit available to owners of common stock. Larger is usually better.
5. Price earnings ratio (p/e)	$\dfrac{\text{current market price/share}}{\text{after-tax earnings/share}}$	A measure of anticipated firm performance—a high p/e ratio tends to indicate that the stock market anticipates strong future performance. Larger is usually better.
6. Cash flow per share	$\dfrac{\text{after-tax profit} + \text{depreciation}}{\text{number of common shares stock outstanding}}$	A measure of funds available to fund activities above current level of costs. Larger is usually better.
Liquidity Ratios		
1. Current ratio	$\dfrac{\text{current assets}}{\text{current liabilities}}$	A measure of the ability of a firm to cover its current liabilities with assets that can be converted into cash in the short term. Recommended in the range of 2 to 3.
2. Quick ratio	$\dfrac{\text{current assets} - \text{inventory}}{\text{current liabilities}}$	A measure of the ability of a firm to meet its short-term obligations without selling off its current inventory. A ratio of 1 is thought to be acceptable in many industries.
Leverage Ratios		
1. Debt to assets	$\dfrac{\text{total debt}}{\text{total assets}}$	A measure of the extent to which debt has financed a firm's business activities. The higher, the greater the risk of bankruptcy.
2. Debt to equity	$\dfrac{\text{total debt}}{\text{total equity}}$	A measure of the use of debt versus equity to finance a firm's business activities. Generally recommended less than 1.
3. Times interest earned	$\dfrac{\text{profit before interest and taxes}}{\text{total interest charges}}$	A measure of how much a firm's profits can decline and still meet its interest obligations. Should be well above 1.

Ratio	Calculation	Interpretation
Activity Ratios		
1. Inventory turnover	$\dfrac{\text{sales}}{\text{inventory}}$	A measure of the speed with which a firm's inventory is turning over.
2. Accounts receivable turnover	$\dfrac{\text{annual credit sales}}{\text{accounts receivable}}$	A measure of the average time it takes a firm to collect on credit sales.
3. Average collection period	$\dfrac{\text{accounts receivable}}{\text{average daily sales}}$	A measure of the time it takes a firm to receive payment after a sale has been made.

common accounting ratios that can be used to characterize a firm's performance are presented in Table 1.1. These measures of firm accounting performance can be grouped into four categories: (1) **profitability ratios**, or ratios with some measure of profit in the numerator and some measure of firm size or assets in the denominator; (2) **liquidity ratios**, or ratios that focus on the ability of a firm to meet its short-term financial obligations; (3) **leverage ratios**, or ratios that focus on the level of a firm's financial flexibility, including its ability to obtain more debt; and (4) **activity ratios**, or ratios that focus on the level of activity in a firm's business.

Of course, these ratios, by themselves, say very little about a firm. To determine how a firm is performing, its accounting ratios must be compared with some standard. In general, that standard is the average of accounting ratios of other firms in the same industry. Using ratio analysis, a firm earns **above average accounting performance** when its performance is greater than the industry average. Such firms typically have competitive advantages, sustained or otherwise. A firm earns **average accounting performance** when its performance is equal to the industry average. These firms generally enjoy only competitive parity. A firm earns **below average accounting performance** when its performance is less than the industry average. These firms generally experience competitive disadvantages.

Consider, for example, the performance of Apple Inc. Apple's financial statements for 2011 and 2012 are presented in Table 1.2. Losses in this table would be presented in parentheses. Several ratio measures of accounting performance are calculated for Apple in these two years in Table 1.2.

Apple's sales increased dramatically from 2011 to 2012, from just over $108 billion to just over $156 billion. Profitability accounting ratios suggest its profitability during this same time period, from a return on total assets (ROA) of 0.217 to 0.237 and from a return on equity (ROE) of 0.33 to 0.353. Much of this increase may be attributable to Apple's increase in its gross profit margin from 0.408 to 0.439. So its sales went up, its overall profitability up, as did its gross profit margin. This pattern suggests that Apple was able to increase the prices of the products it was selling in 2012 compared with 2011, either by introducing new products or more expensive versions of its current products or both.

Apple's liquidity and leverage ratios remained largely unchanged over these two years. With current and quick ratios well over 1, it's pretty clear that Apple had enough cash on hand to respond to any short-term financial needs. And its leverage ratios suggest that it still had some opportunities to borrow money for long-term investments should the need arise.

Overall, the information in Tables 1.2 and 1.3 suggests that Apple Inc., in 2011 and 2012, was, financially speaking, very healthy.

TABLE 1.2 Apple Inc.'s Financial Statements for 2011 and 2012 (numbers in millions of dollars)

	2011	2012
Net sales	108,249	156,508
Cost of goods sold	64,431	87,846
Gross margin	43,818	68,662
Selling, general, and administrative expenses	7,599	10,040
R & D expense	2,429	3,381
Total operating expenses	10,028	13,421
Operating income (loss)	33,790	55,241
Total income (loss), before taxes	33,375	55,763
Provision for taxes	8,076	14,052
Net income, after taxes	25,299	41,711
Inventories	776	791
Total current assets	44,988	57,653
Total assets	116,371	176,064
Total current liabilities	27,970	38,542
Total debt	39,756	57,756
Total shareholders' equity	76,615	118,210
Retained earnings	62,841	

Economic Measures of Competitive Advantage

The great advantage of accounting measures of competitive advantage is that they are relatively easy to compute. All publicly traded firms must make their accounting statements available to the public. Even privately owned firms will typically release some information about their accounting performance. From these statements, it is quite easy to calculate various accounting ratios. One can learn a lot about a firm's competitive position by comparing these ratios to industry averages.

However, accounting measures of competitive advantage have at least one significant limitation. Earlier, economic profit was defined as the difference between the perceived benefit associated with purchasing a firm's products or services and the cost of producing and selling that product or service. However, one important component of cost typically is not included in most accounting measures of competitive advantage: the cost of the capital a firm employs to produce and sell its products. The **cost of capital** is the rate of return that a firm promises

TABLE 1.3 Some Accounting Ratios for Apple Inc. in 2011 and 2012

	2011	2012
ROA	$25,299/116,371 = 0.217$	$41,711/176,064 = 0.237$
ROE	$25,299/76,615 = 0.353$	$41,711/118,210 = 0.353$
Gross profit margin	$\dfrac{108,249 - 64,431}{108,249} = 0.405$	$\dfrac{156,508 - 87,846}{156,508} = 0.439$
Current ratio	$44,988/27,976 = 1.61$	$57,653/653 = 1.50$
Quick ratio	$\dfrac{44,988 - 776}{27,970} = 1.58$	$\dfrac{57,653 - 791}{38,542} = 1.48$
Debt to assets	$39,756/116.371 = 0.341$	$057,756/176,064 = 0.323$
Debt to equity	$39,756/76,615 = 0.519$	$57,756/118,210 = 0.489$

to pay its suppliers of capital to induce them to invest in the firm. Once these investments are made, a firm can use this capital to produce and sell products and services. However, a firm must provide the promised return to its sources of capital if it expects to obtain more investment capital in the future. **Economic measures of competitive advantage** compare a firm's level of return to its cost of capital instead of to the average level of return in the industry.

Generally, there are two broad categories of sources of capital: **debt** (capital from banks and bondholders) and **equity** (capital from individuals and institutions that purchase a firm's stock). The **cost of debt** is equal to the interest that a firm must pay its debt holders (adjusted for taxes) in order to induce those debt holders to lend money to a firm. The **cost of equity** is equal to the rate of return a firm must promise its equity holders in order to induce these individuals and institutions to invest in a firm. A firm's **weighted average cost of capital (WACC)** is simply the percentage of a firm's total capital, which is debt times the cost of debt plus the percentage of a firm's total capital; that is, equity times the cost of equity.

Conceptually, a firm's cost of capital is the level of performance a firm must attain if it is to satisfy the economic objectives of two of its critical stakeholders: debt holders and equity holders. A firm that earns above its cost of capital is likely to be able to attract additional capital because debt holders and equity holders will scramble to make additional funds available for this firm. Such a firm is said to be earning **above normal economic performance** and will be able to use its access to cheap capital to grow and expand its business. A firm that earns its cost of capital is said to have **normal economic performance**. This level of performance is said to be "normal" because this is the level of performance that most of a firm's equity and debt holders expect. Firms that have normal economic performance are able to gain access to the capital they need to survive, although they are not prospering. Growth opportunities may be somewhat limited for these firms. In general, firms with competitive parity usually have normal economic performance. A firm that earns less than its cost of capital is in the process of liquidating. **Below normal economic performance** implies that a firm's debt and equity holders will be looking for alternative ways to invest their money, someplace where they can earn at least what they expect to earn; that is, normal economic performance. Unless a firm with below normal performance changes, its long-term viability will come into question. Obviously, firms that have a competitive disadvantage generally have below normal economic performance.

Measuring a firm's performance relative to its cost of capital has several advantages for strategic analysis. Foremost among these is the notion that a firm that earns at least its cost of capital is satisfying two of its most important stakeholders: debt holders and equity holders. Despite the advantages of comparing a firm's performance to its cost of capital, this approach has some important limitations as well. For example, it can sometimes be difficult to calculate a firm's cost of capital. This is especially true if a firm is **privately held**—that is, if it has stock that is not traded on public stock markets or if it is a division of a larger company. In these situations, it may be necessary to use accounting ratios to measure a firm's performance. Moreover, some have suggested that although accounting measures of competitive advantage understate the importance of a firm's equity and debt holders in evaluating a firm's performance, economic measures of competitive advantage exaggerate the importance of these two particular stakeholders, often to the disadvantage of other stakeholders in a firm. These issues are discussed in more detail in the Ethics and Strategy feature.

Figure 1.5   Competitive Advantage and Firm Performance

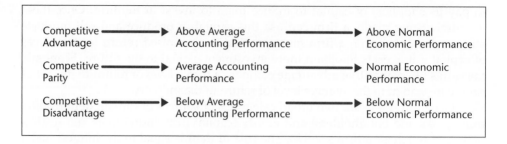

The Relationship Between Economic and Accounting Performance Measures

The correlation between economic and accounting measures of competitive advantage is high. That is, firms that perform well using one of these measures usually perform well using the other. Conversely, firms that do poorly using one of these measures normally do poorly using the other. Thus, the relationships among competitive advantage, accounting performance, and economic performance depicted in Figure 1.5 generally hold.

However, it is possible for a firm to have above average accounting performance and simultaneously have below normal economic performance. This could happen, for example, when a firm is not earning its cost of capital but has above industry average accounting performance. Also, it is possible for a firm to have below average accounting performance and above normal economic performance. This could happen when a firm has a very low cost of capital and is earning at a rate in excess of this cost, but still below the industry average.

Emergent Versus Intended Strategies

The simplest way of thinking about a firm's strategy is to assume that firms choose and implement their strategies exactly as described by the strategic management process in Figure 1.1. That is, they begin with a well-defined mission and objectives, they engage in external and internal analyses, they make their strategic choices, and then they implement their strategies. And there is no doubt that this describes the process for choosing and implementing a strategy in many firms.

For example, FedEx, a world leader in the overnight delivery business, entered this industry with a very well-developed theory about how to gain competitive advantages in this business. Indeed, Fred Smith, the founder of FedEx (originally known as Federal Express), first articulated this theory as a student in a term paper for an undergraduate business class at Yale University. Legend has it that he received only a "C" on the paper, but the company that was founded on the theory of competitive advantage in the overnight delivery business developed in that paper has done extremely well. Founded in 1971, FedEx had 2013 sales just over $44 billion and profits of $2.5 billion.[9]

Other firms have also begun operations with a well-defined, well-formed strategy but have found it necessary to modify this strategy so much once it is actually implemented in the marketplace that it bears little resemblance to the theory with which the firm started. **Emergent strategies** are theories of how to gain competitive advantage in an industry that emerge over time or that have been radically reshaped once they are initially implemented.[10] The relationship between a firm's intended and emergent strategies is depicted in Figure 1.6.

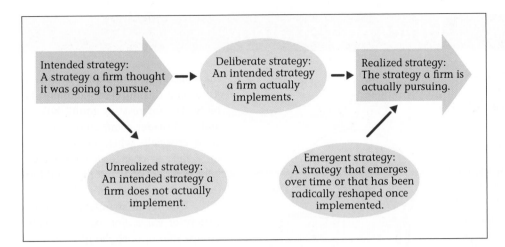

Figure 1.6 Mintzberg's Analysis of the Relationship Between Intended and Realized Strategies

Source: Reprinted from "Strategy formation in an adhocracy," by H. Mintzberg and A. McHugh, published in *Administrative Science Quarterly, 30*, No. 2, June 1985, by permission of Administrative Science Quarterly. Copyright © 1985 by Administrative Science Quarterly.

Several well-known firms have strategies that are, at least partly, emergent. For example, J&J was originally a supplier of antiseptic gauze and medical plasters. It had no consumer business at all. Then, in response to complaints about irritation caused by some of its medical plasters, J&J began enclosing a small packet of talcum powder with each of the medical plasters it sold. Soon customers were asking to purchase the talcum powder by itself, and the company introduced "Johnson's Toilet and Baby Powder." Later, an employee invented a ready-to-use bandage for his wife. It seems she often cut herself while using knives in the kitchen. When J&J marketing managers learned of this invention, they decided to introduce it into the marketplace. J&J's Band-Aid products have since become the largest-selling brand category at J&J. Overall, J&J's intended strategy was to compete in the medical products market, but its emergent consumer products strategies now generate more than 40 percent of total corporate sales.

Another firm with what turns out to be an emergent strategy is the Marriott Corporation. Marriott was originally in the restaurant business. In the late 1930s, Marriott owned and operated eight restaurants. However, one of these restaurants was close to a Washington, D.C., airport. Managers at this restaurant noticed that airline passengers would come into the restaurant to purchase food to eat on their trip. J. Willard Marriott, the founder of the Marriott Corporation, noticed this trend and negotiated a deal with Eastern Airlines whereby Marriott's restaurant would deliver prepackaged lunches directly to Eastern's planes. This arrangement was later extended to include American Airlines. Over time, providing food service to airlines became a major business segment for Marriott. Although Marriott's initial intended strategy was to operate in the restaurant business, it became engaged in the emergent food service business at more than 100 airports throughout the world.[11]

Some firms have almost entirely emergent strategies. PEZ Candy, Inc., for example, manufactures and sells small plastic candy dispensers with cartoon and movie character heads, along with candy refills. This privately held firm has made few efforts to speed its growth, yet demand for current and older PEZ products continues to grow. In the 1990s, PEZ doubled the size of its manufacturing operation to keep up with demand. Old PEZ dispensers have become something of a collector's item. Several national conferences on PEZ collecting have been held, and some rare PEZ dispensers were once

Ethics and Strategy

Considerable debate exists about the role of a firm's equity and debt holders versus its other stakeholders in defining and measuring a firm's performance. These other stakeholders include a firm's suppliers, its customers, its employees, and the communities within which it does business. Like equity and debt holders, these other stakeholders make investments in a firm. They, too, expect some compensation for making these investments.

On the one hand, some argue that if a firm maximizes the wealth of its equity holders, it will automatically satisfy all of its other stakeholders. This view of the firm depends on what is called the *residual claimants* view of equity holders. This view is that equity holders only receive payment on their investment in a firm after all legitimate claims by a firm's other stakeholders are satisfied. Thus, a firm's equity holders, in this view, only receive payment on their investments after the firm's employees are compensated, its suppliers are paid, its customers are satisfied, and its obligations to the communities within which it does business have been met. By maximizing returns to its equity holders, a firm is ensuring that its other stakeholders are fully compensated for investing in a firm.

Stockholders Versus Stakeholders

On the other hand, some argue that the interests of equity holders and a firm's other stakeholders often collide and that a firm that maximizes the wealth of its equity holders does not necessarily satisfy its other stakeholders. For example, whereas a firm's customers may want it to sell higher-quality products at lower prices, a firm's equity holders may want it to sell low-quality products at higher prices; this obviously would increase the amount of money left over to pay off a firm's equity holders. Also, whereas a firm's employees may want it to adopt policies that lead to steady performance over long periods of time—because this will lead to stable employment—a firm's equity holders may be more interested in its

maximizing its short-term profitability, even if this hurts employment stability. The interests of equity holders and the broader community may also clash, especially when it is very costly for a firm to engage in environmentally friendly behaviors that could reduce its short-term performance.

This debate manifests itself in a variety of ways. For example, many groups that oppose the globalization of the U.S. economy do so on the basis that firms make production, marketing, and other strategic choices in ways that maximize profits for equity holders, often to the detriment of a firm's other stakeholders. These people are concerned about the effects of globalization on workers, on the environment, and on the cultures in the developing economies where global firms sometimes locate their manufacturing and other operations. Managers in global firms respond by saying that they have a responsibility to maximize the wealth of their equity holders. Given the passions that surround this debate, it is unlikely that these issues will be resolved soon.

Sources: T. Copeland, T. Koller, and J. Murrin (1995). *Valuation: Measuring and managing the value of companies.* New York: Wiley; L. Donaldson (1990). "The ethereal hand: Organizational economics and management theory." *Academy of Review*, 15, pp. 369–381.

---

auctioned at Christie's. This demand has enabled PEZ to raise its prices without increases in advertising, sales personnel, and movie tie-ins so typical in the candy industry.[12]

Of course, one might argue that emergent strategies are only important when a firm fails to implement the strategic management process effectively. After all, if this process is implemented effectively, then would it ever be necessary to fundamentally alter the strategies that a firm has chosen?

In reality, it will often be the case that at the time a firm chooses its strategies, some of the information needed to complete the strategic management

Strategy in the Emerging Enterprise

Every entrepreneur—and would-be entrepreneur—is familiar with the drill: If you want to receive financial support for your idea, you need to write a business plan. Business plans are typically 25 to 30 pages long. Most begin with an Executive Summary; then move quickly to describing an entrepreneur's business idea, why customers will be interested in this idea, how much it will cost to realize this idea; and usually end with a series of charts that project a firm's cash flows over the next five years.

Of course, because these business ideas are often new and untried, no one—including the entrepreneur—really knows if customers will like the idea well enough to buy from this firm. No one really knows how much it will cost to build these products or produce these services—they've never been built or produced before. And, certainly, no one really knows what a firm's cash flows will look like over the next five years or so. Indeed, it is not unusual for entrepreneurs to constantly revise their business plan to reflect new information they have obtained about their business idea and its viability. It is not even unusual for entrepreneurs to fundamentally revise their central business idea as they begin to pursue it in earnest.

Emergent Strategies and Entrepreneurship

The truth is, most decisions about whether to create an entrepreneurial firm take place under conditions of high uncertainty and high unpredictability. In this setting, the ability to adjust on the fly, to be flexible, and to recast a business idea in ways that are more consistent with customer interests may be a central determinant of a firm's ultimate success. This, of course, suggests that emergent strategies are likely to be very important for entrepreneurial firms.

This view of entrepreneurship is different from the popular stereotype. In the popular view, entrepreneurs are assumed to be hit by a "blinding rush of insight" about a previously unexploited market opportunity. In reality, entrepreneurs are more likely to experience a series of smaller insights about market opportunities.

But, typically, these periods of insight will be preceded by periods of disappointment, as an entrepreneur discovers that what he or she thought was a new and complete business model is, in fact, either not new or not complete or both. In the popular view, entrepreneurship is all about creativity, about being able to see opportunities others cannot see. In reality, entrepreneurship may be more about tenacity than creativity because entrepreneurs build their firms step by step out of the uncertainty and unpredictability that plague their decision making. In the popular view, entrepreneurs can envision their success well before it occurs. In reality, although entrepreneurs may dream about financial and other forms of success, they usually do not know the exact path they will take, nor what success will actually look like, until after they have arrived.

Sources: S. Alvarez and J. Barney (2005). "How do entrepreneurs organize firms under conditions of uncertainty?" *Journal of Management*, 31(5), pp. 776–793; S. Alvarez and J. Barney (2004). "Organizing rent generation and appropriation: Toward a theory of the entrepreneurial firm," *Journal of Business Venturing*, 19, pp. 621–636; W. Gartner (1988). "Who is the entrepreneur? is the wrong question." *American Journal of Small Business*, 12, pp. 11–32; S. Sarasvathy (2001). "Causation and effectuation: Toward a theoretical shift from economic inevitability to entrepreneurial contingency." *Academy of Management Review*, 26, pp. 243–264.

process may simply not be available. As suggested earlier, in this setting a firm simply has to make its "best bet" about how competition in an industry is likely to emerge. In such a situation, a firm's ability to change its strategies quickly to respond to emergent trends in an industry may be as important a source of competitive advantage as the ability to complete the strategic management process. For all these reasons, emergent strategies may be particularly important for entrepreneurial firms, as described in the Strategy in the Emerging Enterprise feature.

Why You Need to Know About Strategy

At first glance, it may not be obvious why students would need to know about strategy and the strategic management process. After all, the process of choosing and implementing a strategy is normally the responsibility of senior managers in a firm, and most students are unlikely to be senior managers in large corporations until many years after graduation. Why study strategy and the strategic management process now?

In fact, there are at least three very compelling reasons why it is important to study strategy and the strategic management process now. First, it can give you the tools you need to evaluate the strategies of firms that may employ you. We have already seen how a firm's strategy can have a huge impact on its competitive advantage. Your career opportunities in a firm are largely determined by that firm's competitive advantage. Thus, in choosing a place to begin or continue your career, understanding a firm's theory of how it is going to gain a competitive advantage can be essential in evaluating the career opportunities in a firm. Firms with strategies that are unlikely to be a source of competitive advantage will rarely provide the same career opportunities as firms with strategies that do generate such advantages. Being able to distinguish between these types of strategies can be very important in your career choices.

Second, once you are working for a firm, understanding that firm's strategies, and your role in implementing those strategies, can be very important for your personal success. It will often be the case that expectations of how you perform your function in a firm will change, depending on the strategies a firm is pursuing. For example, as we will see in Part 2 of this book, the accounting function plays a very different role in a firm pursuing a cost leadership strategy versus a product differentiation strategy. Marketing and manufacturing also play very different roles in these two types of strategies. Your effectiveness in a firm can be reduced by doing accounting, marketing, and manufacturing as if your firm were pursuing a cost leadership strategy when it is actually pursuing a product differentiation strategy.

Finally, although it is true that strategic choices are generally limited to very experienced senior managers in large organizations, in smaller and entrepreneurial firms many employees end up being involved in the strategic management process. If you choose to work for one of these smaller or entrepreneurial firms—even if it is not right after graduation—you could very easily find yourself to be part of the strategic management team, implementing the strategic management process and choosing which strategies this firm should implement. In this setting, a familiarity with the essential concepts that underlie the choice and implementation of a strategy may turn out to be very helpful.

Summary

A firm's strategy is its theory of how to gain competitive advantages. These theories, like all theories, are based on assumptions and hypotheses about how competition in an industry is likely to evolve. When those assumptions and hypotheses are consistent with the actual evolution of competition in an industry, a firm's strategy is more likely to be able to generate a competitive advantage.

One way that a firm can choose its strategies is through the strategic management process. This process is a set of analyses and decisions that increase the likelihood that a firm will be able to choose a "good" strategy, that is, a strategy that will lead to a competitive advantage.

The strategic management process begins when a firm identifies its mission, or its long-term purpose. This mission is often written down in the form of a mission statement. Mission statements, by themselves, can have no impact on performance, enhance a firm's performance, or hurt a firm's performance. Objectives are measurable milestones firms use to evaluate whether they are accomplishing their missions. External and internal analyses are the processes through which a firm identifies its environmental threats and opportunities and organizational strengths and weaknesses. Armed with these analyses, it is possible for a firm to engage in strategic choice. Strategies can be classified into two categories: business-level strategies (including cost leadership and product differentiation) and corporate-level strategies (including vertical integration, strategic alliances, diversification, and mergers and acquisitions). Strategy implementation follows strategic choice and involves choosing organizational structures, management control policies, and compensation schemes that support a firm's strategies.

The ultimate objective of the strategic management process is the realization of competitive advantage. A firm has a competitive advantage if it is creating more economic value than its rivals. Economic value is defined as the difference between the perceived customer benefits from purchasing a product or service from a firm and the total economic cost of developing and selling that product or service. Competitive advantages can be temporary or sustained. Competitive parity exists when a firm creates the same economic value as its rivals. A competitive disadvantage exists when a firm creates less economic value than its rivals, and it can be either temporary or sustained.

Two popular measures of a firm's competitive advantage are accounting performance and economic performance. Accounting performance measures competitive advantage using various ratios calculated from a firm's profit and loss and balance sheet statements. A firm's accounting performance is compared with the average level of accounting performance in a firm's industry. Economic performance compares a firm's level of return with its cost of capital. A firm's cost of capital is the rate of return it had to promise to pay to its debt and equity investors to induce them to invest in the firm.

Although many firms use the strategic management process to choose and implement strategies, not all strategies are chosen this way. Some strategies emerge over time, as firms respond to unanticipated changes in the structure of competition in an industry.

Students need to understand strategy and the strategic management process for at least three reasons. First, it can help in deciding where to work. Second, once you have a job it can help you to be successful in that job. Finally, if you have a job in a small or entrepreneurial firm you may become involved in strategy and the strategic management process from the very beginning.

MyManagementLab®

Go to **mymanagementlab.com** to complete the problems marked with this icon ⭐.

Challenge Questions

1.1. Some firms publicize their corporate mission statements by including them in annual reports, on company letterheads, and in corporate advertising. What, if anything, does this practice say about the ability of these mission statements to be sources of sustained competitive advantage for a firm?

⭐ **1.2.** Why would including a corporate mission statement on company letterhead or in corporate advertising be seen as a source of sustained competitive advantage?

1.3. Little empirical evidence indicates that having a formal, written mission statement improves a firm's performance. Yet many firms spend a great deal of time and money developing mission statements. Why?

1.4. Firm 2 generates a perceived customer benefit of $200 at a cost of $50. Compare this with Firm 1's customer benefit of $220 generated at a cost of $30. What is the source of Firm 1's advantage? Provide real-life examples of firms that match Firm 1.

1.5. Both external and internal analyses are important in the strategic management process. Is the order in which these analyses are conducted important?

1.6. If the order of analyses is important, which should come first: external analysis or internal analysis?

1.7. Concerning external analysis and internal analysis, if the order of analyses is not important, why not?

1.8. Will a firm that has a sustained competitive disadvantage necessarily go out of business?

1.9. Will a firm with below average accounting performance over a long period of time necessarily go out of business?

1.10. Will a firm with below normal economic performance over a long period of time necessarily go out of business?

1.11. Can more than one firm have a competitive advantage in an industry at the same time?

✪ **1.12.** Is it possible for a firm to simultaneously have a competitive advantage and a competitive disadvantage?

Problem Set

1.13. Write objectives for each of the following mission statements.

(a) We will be a leader in pharmaceutical innovation.
(b) Customer satisfaction is our primary goal.
(c) We promise on-time delivery.
(d) Product quality is our first priority.

1.14. The following objectives need to inform a firm's strategic planning. Can you modify them to be more actionable?

(a) We will improve productivity
(b) Our product features will be enhanced every year
(c) The cost of raw materials will fall
(d) We will delight all our clients

1.15. Do firms with the following financial results have below normal, normal, or above normal economic performance?

(a) ROA = 14.3%, WACC = 12.8%
(b) ROA = 4.3%, WACC = 6.7%
(c) ROA = 6.5%, WACC = 9.2%
(d) ROA = 8.3%, WACC = 8.3%

1.16. For each of the following cases, comment on the firm's performance in relative and absolute terms.

(a) WACC < ROA < Industry Avg. ROA
(b) WACC > ROA > Industry Avg. ROA
(c) ROA > Industry Avg. ROA > WACC
(d) ROA < Industry Avg. ROA < WACC

1.17. Is it possible for a firm to simultaneously earn above normal economic returns and below average accounting returns? What about below normal economic returns and above average accounting returns? Why or why not? If this can occur, which measure of performance is more reliable: economic performance or accounting performance? Explain.

1.18. Examine the corporate Web sites of the following companies and determine if the strategies pursued by these firms were emergent, deliberate, or both emergent and deliberate. Justify your answer with facts from the Web sites.

(a) Lenovo
(b) Mercedes-Benz
(c) Airtel

1.19. Using the information provided, calculate this firm's ROA, ROE, gross profit margin, and quick ratio. If this firm's WACC is 6.6 percent and the average firm in its industry has an ROA of 8 percent, is this firm earning above or below normal economic performance and above or below average accounting performance?

Net sales	6,134	Operating cash	3,226	Net other operating assets	916
Cost of goods sold	(4,438)	Accounts receivable	681	Total assets	5,161
Selling, general administrative expenses	(996)	Inventories	20	Net current liabilities	1,549
Other current assets	0	Long-term debt	300	Other expenses	(341)
Total current assets	3,927	Deferred income taxes	208	Interest income	72
Gross properties, plant, equipment	729	Preferred stock	0	Interest expense	(47)
Retained earnings	0	Provision for taxes	(75)	Accumulated depreciation	(411)
Common stock	3,104	Other income	245	Book value of fixed assets	318
Other liabilities	0	Net income	554	Goodwill	0
Total liabilities and equity	5,161				

MyManagementLab®

Go to **mymanagementlab.com** for the following Assisted-graded writing questions:

✪ **1.20.** Describe what visionary firms may do to earn substantially higher returns than average firms.

✪ **1.21.** What is the relationship between a firm's business model and its value proposition?

End Notes

1. This approach to defining strategy was first suggested in Drucker, P. (1994). "The theory of business." *Harvard Business Review*, 75, September–October, pp. 95–105.
2. This approach to defining strategy was first suggested in Drucker, P. (1994). "The theory of business." *Harvard Business Review*, 75, September–October, pp. 95–105.
3. See www.enron.com.
4. See Emshwiller, J., D. Solomon, and R. Smith. (2004). "Lay is indicted for his role in Enron collapse." *The Wall Street Journal*, July 8, pp. A1+; Gilmartin, R. (2005). "They fought the law." *BusinessWeek*, January 10, pp. 82–83.
5. These performance results were presented originally in Collins, J. C., and J. I. Porras. (1997). *Built to last: Successful habits of visionary companies*. New York: HarperCollins.
6. Collins, J. C., and J. I. Porras. (1997). *Built to last: successful habits of visionary companies*. New York: HarperCollins.
7. See Theroux, J., and J. Hurstak. (1993). "Ben & Jerry's Homemade Ice Cream Inc.: Keeping the mission(s) alive." Harvard Business School Case No. 9-392-025; Applebaum, A. (2000). "Smartmoney.com: Unilever feels hungry, buys Ben & Jerry's." *The Wall Street Journal*, April 13, pp. B1+.

8. This definition of competitive advantage has a long history in the field of strategic management. For example, it is closely related to the definitions provided in Barney (1986, 1991) and Porter (1985). It is also consistent with the value-based approach described in Peteraf (2001), Brandenburger and Stuart (1999), and Besanko, Dranove, and Shanley (2000). For more discussion on this definition, see Peteraf and Barney (2004).
9. FedEx's history is described in Trimble, V. (1993). *Overnight success: Federal Express and Frederick Smith, its renegade creator*. New York: Crown.
10. Mintzberg, H. (1978). "Patterns in strategy formulation." *Management Science*, 24(9), pp. 934–948; and Mintzberg, H. (1985). "Of strategies, deliberate and emergent." *Strategic Management Journal*, 6(3), pp. 257–272. Mintzberg has been most influential in expanding the study of strategy to include emergent strategies.
11. The J&J and Marriott emergent strategy stories can be found in Collins, J. C., and J. I. Porras. (1997). *Built to last: Successful habits of visionary companies*. New York: HarperCollins.
12. See McCarthy, M. J. (1993). "The PEZ fancy is hard to explain, let alone justify." *The Wall Street Journal*, March 10, p. A1, for a discussion of PEZ's surprising emergent strategy.

2 Evaluating a Firm's External Environment

LEARNING OBJECTIVES *After reading this chapter, you should be able to:*

1. Describe the dimensions of the general environment facing a firm and how this environment can affect a firm's opportunities and threats.

2. Describe how the structure-conduct-performance (S-C-P) model suggests that industry structure can influence a firm's competitive choices.

3. Describe the five environmental threats and indicators of when each of these forces will improve or reduce the attractiveness of an industry.

4. Describe how rivals and substitutes differ.

5. Discuss the role of complements in analyzing competition within an industry.

6. Describe four generic industry structures and specific strategic opportunities in those industries.

7. Describe the impact of tariffs, quotas, and other non-tariff barriers to entry on the cost of entry into new geographic markets.

MyManagementLab®

⭐ **Improve Your Grade!**
Over 10 million students improved their results using the Pearson MyLabs.
Visit **mymanagementlab.com** for simulations, tutorials, and end-of-chapter problems.

---

iTunes and the Streaming Challenge

It was a normal Wednesday, February 24, 2010. Seventy-one-year-old Louie Sulce, from Woodstock, Georgia, had just finished downloading a song from one of his favorite country artists—Johnny Cash's "Guess Things Happen that Way"—from the iTunes store. Suddenly, the phone rang.

It was Steve Jobs, CEO of Apple calling to congratulate Mr. Sulce for downloading the 10 billionth song from the iTunes store. For being "Mr. 10 Billion," Mr. Sulce received a $10,000 iTunes store gift card.

This story is interesting on several dimensions. First, it signaled the remarkable growth of iTunes. Founded on April 28, 2003, iTunes grew steadily, reaching the 1 billion download mark less than three years later, on February 23, 2006. But with the growing popularity of Apple's iPod MP3 player and, later, its iPhone and iPad, iTunes downloads began to take off. It took less than a year to go from 1 billion to 2 billion downloads, less than six months to get to 3 billion, and so forth. By February 6, 2013, more than 25 billion songs had been downloaded from iTunes. By September 12, 2006, iTunes had 88 percent of the legal download market in the United States.

And this growth wasn't limited to just downloaded songs. Over the years, the range of products sold by iTunes has expanded from songs to movies, television shows, video games, and other media products.

Not surprisingly, iTunes revenues grew right along with the growth in iTunes downloads. With first-year revenues of $278 million, iTunes revenues had grown to $2.4 billion in the first *quarter* of 2013.

But Mr. Sulce's story is interesting in another way as well—a 71-year-old man was using iTunes to download music. By 2010, iTunes was no longer a Web site for technologically sophisticated young people to buy their music; it was the place where everyone bought their music. By June 2013, iTunes had more than 575 million active accounts supporting 315 million mobile devices in 119 countries. It has been the largest music vendor in the United States since April 2008 and the largest in the world since February 2010.

But such success and growth were bound to attract competition. In 2007, Amazon became an important rival for iTunes as it began selling online music downloads at a price lower than iTunes. In 2013, Amazon's share of the U.S. music download market had risen to 22 percent—still smaller than iTunes' share, but significant growth nevertheless.

© Gallo Images/Alamy

Perhaps even more importantly, some important substitutes for iTunes had begun to emerge. In particular, music streaming services—where consumers listen to but do not buy music—were beginning to grow. In 2013, two versions of these streaming services existed: subscription services—including one Spotify service, Rdio, and Rhapsody—where consumers paid a monthly fee for unlimited music access and advertising-supported services—including a second Spotify service and Pandora—that provided unlimited access for free but required consumers to listen to commercials periodically.

Streaming services had several perceived advantages over iTunes. For example, these services provided instant access to a much wider variety of music than in most people's purchased collections. Also, users of these services did not have to use so much of the memory in their devices storing music. By 2013, iTunes' share of the music download business had dropped from 69 percent to 63 percent, mostly due to the increased popularity of music streaming services.

Indeed, in 2013, iTunes announced that it would introduce an advertising-supported streaming product on the iTunes store. Whether this will be enough to enable iTunes to retain its dominant position in the download industry remains to be seen.

Sources: Andy Fixmer. April 25, 2013. "Apple's 10-Year-Old iTunes Loses Ground to Streaming," http://www.businessweek.com/articles/2013-04-25/apples-10-year-old-itunes-loses-ground-to-streaming. Accessed July 3, 2013; Apple Press Release. "iTunes Serves Up 10 Billionth Song Download," February 2010. Accessed July 3, 2013; E. Smith (2006) "Can Anybody Catch iTunes?" *Wall Street Journal*, November 27, pp. R1+.

The strategic management process described in Chapter 1 suggested that one of the critical determinants of a firm's strategies is the threats and opportunities in its competitive environment. If a firm understands these threats and opportunities, it is one step closer to being able to choose and implement a "good strategy"; that is, a strategy that leads to competitive advantage.

iTunes is clearly in this position in the music download industry. Despite its dominant position, rivals—like Amazon—and substitutes—like Spotify and Pandora—have both emerged.

Of course, it is not enough to recognize that it is important to understand the threats and opportunities in a firm's competitive environment. A set of tools that managers can apply to systematically complete this external analysis as part of the strategic management process is also required. These tools must be rooted in a strong theoretical base, so that managers know that they have not been developed in an arbitrary way. Fortunately, such tools exist and will be described in this chapter.

Understanding a Firm's General Environment

Any analysis of the threats and opportunities facing a firm must begin with an understanding of the general environment within which a firm operates. This **general environment** consists of broad trends in the context within which a firm operates that can have an impact on a firm's strategic choices. As depicted in Figure 2.1, the general environment consists of six interrelated elements: technological change, demographic trends, cultural trends, the economic climate, legal and political conditions, and specific international events. Each of these elements of the general environment is discussed in this section.

In 1899, Charles H. Duell, commissioner of the U.S. patent office, said, "Everything that can be invented has been invented."[1] He was wrong. Technological changes over the past few years have had significant impacts on the ways firms do business and on the products and services they sell.

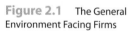

Figure 2.1 The General Environment Facing Firms

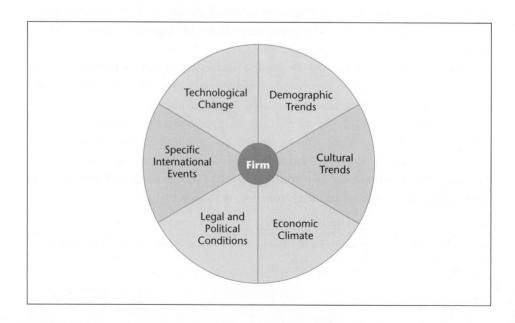

These impacts have been most obvious for technologies that build on digital information—computers, the Internet, cell phones, and so forth. Many of us routinely use digital products or services that did not exist just a few years ago. However, rapid technological innovation has not been restricted to digital technologies. Biotechnology has also made rapid progress over the past 10 years. New kinds of medicines are now being created. As important, biotechnology holds the promise of developing entirely new ways of both preventing and treating disease.[2]

Technological change creates both opportunity, as firms begin to explore how to use technology to create new products and services, and threats, as technological change forces firms to rethink their technological strategies.

A second element of the general environment facing firms is demographic trends. **Demographics** is the distribution of individuals in a society in terms of age, sex, marital status, income, ethnicity, and other personal attributes that may determine buying patterns. Understanding this basic information about a population can help a firm determine whether its products or services will appeal to customers and how many potential customers for these products or services it might have.

Some demographic trends are very well known. For example, everyone has heard of the "baby boomers"—those who were born shortly after World War II. This large population has had an impact on the strategies of many firms, especially as the boomers have grown older and have had more disposable income. However, other demographic groups have also had an impact on firm strategies. This is especially true in the automobile industry. For example, minivans were invented to meet the demands of "soccer moms"—women who live in the suburbs and have young children. The Nissan Xterra seems to have been designed for the so-called Generation Y—young men and women currently in their 20s and either just out of college or anticipating graduation shortly.

In the United States, an important demographic trend over the past 20 years has been the growth of the Hispanic population. In 1990, the percentage of the U.S. population that was African American was greater than the percentage that was Hispanic. However, by 2000, people of Latin descent outnumbered African Americans. Currently, Hispanics constitute almost 15 percent of the U.S. population, whereas the percentage of African Americans remains constant at less than 8 percent. These trends are particularly notable in the South and Southwest. For example, more than 36 percent of children under 18 in Houston are Hispanic, 39 percent in Miami and San Diego, 53 percent in Los Angeles, and more than 61 percent in San Antonio.[3]

Of course, firms are aware of this growing population and its buying power. Indeed, Hispanic disposable income in the United States jumped 29 percent, to $652 billion, from 2001 to 2003. In response, firms have begun marketing directly to the U.S. Hispanic population. In one year, Procter & Gamble spent $90 million marketing directly to Spanish-speaking customers. Procter & Gamble has also formed a 65-person bilingual team to manage the marketing of products to Hispanics. Indeed, Procter & Gamble expects that the Hispanic population will be the cornerstone of its sales growth in North America.[4]

Firms can try to exploit their understanding of a particular demographic segment of the population to create a competitive advantage—as Procter & Gamble is doing with the U.S. Hispanic population—but focusing on too narrow a demographic segment can limit demand for a firm's products. The WB, the alternative television network created by Time Warner in 1995, faced this dilemma. Initially, the

WB found success in producing shows for teens—classics such as *Dawson's Creek* and *Buffy the Vampire Slayer*. However, in 2003, the WB saw an 11 percent drop in viewership and a $25 million drop in advertising revenues. Although it did not leave its traditional demographic behind, the WB began producing some programs intended to appeal to older viewers. Ultimately, the WB merged with UPN to form a new network, the CW network. CW is a joint venture between CBS (owner of UPN) and Time Warner (owner of the WB).[5]

A third element of a firm's general environment is cultural trends. **Culture** is the values, beliefs, and norms that guide behavior in a society. These values, beliefs, and norms define what is "right and wrong" in a society, what is acceptable and unacceptable, what is fashionable and unfashionable. Failure to understand changes in culture, or differences between cultures, can have a very large impact on the ability of a firm to gain a competitive advantage.

This becomes most obvious when firms operate in multiple countries simultaneously. Even seemingly small differences in culture can have an impact. For example, advertisements in the United States that end with a person putting their index finger and thumb together mean that a product is "okay"; in Brazil, the same symbol is vulgar and offensive. Ads in the United States that have a bride dressed in white may be very confusing to the Chinese because, in China, white is the traditional color worn at funerals. In Germany, women typically purchase their own engagement rings, whereas in the United States, men purchase engagement rings for their fiancées. And what might be appropriate ways to treat women colleagues in Japan or France would land most men in U.S. firms in serious trouble. Understanding the cultural context within which a firm operates is important in evaluating the ability of a firm to generate competitive advantages.[6]

A fourth element of a firm's general environment is the current economic climate. The **economic climate** is the overall health of the economic systems within which a firm operates. The health of the economy varies over time in a distinct pattern: Periods of relative prosperity, when demand for goods and services is high and unemployment is low, are followed by periods of relatively low prosperity, when demand for goods and services is low and unemployment is high. When activity in an economy is relatively low, the economy is said to be in **recession**. A severe recession that lasts for several years is known as a **depression**. This alternating pattern of prosperity followed by recession, followed by prosperity, is called the **business cycle**.

Throughout the 1990s, the world, and especially the United States, enjoyed a period of sustained economic growth. Some observers even speculated that the government had become so skilled at managing demand in the economy through adjusting interest rates that a period of recession did not necessarily have to follow a period of sustained economic growth. Of course, the business cycle has reared its ugly head twice since the 1990s—first with the technology bubble-burst around 2001 and, more recently, in the credit crunch in 2008. Most observers now agree that although government policy can have a significant impact on the frequency and size of economic downturns, these policies are unlikely to be able prevent these downturns altogether.

A fifth element of a firm's general environment is **legal and political conditions**. The legal and political dimensions of an organization's general environment are the laws and the legal system's impact on business, together with the general nature of the relationship between government and business. These laws and the relationship between business and government can vary significantly around the world. For example, in Japan, business and the government are generally seen as having a consistently close and cooperative relationship. Indeed, some have observed that one reason that the Japanese economy has been growing so slowly over the past decade has been the government's reluctance to impose economic restructuring that would hurt the performance of some Japanese firms—especially the largest Japanese banks. In the United States, however, the quality of the relationship between business and the government tends to vary over time. In some administrations, rigorous antitrust regulation and tough environmental standards—both seen as inconsistent with the interests of business—dominate. In other administrations, antitrust regulation is less rigorous and the imposition of environmental standards is delayed, suggesting a more business-friendly perspective.

A final attribute of a firm's general environment is **specific international events**. These include events such as civil wars, political coups, terrorism, wars between countries, famines, and country or regional economic recessions. All of these specific events can have an enormous impact on the ability of a firm's strategies to generate competitive advantage.

Of course, one of the most important of these specific events to have occurred over the past several decades was the terrorist attacks on New York City and Washington, D.C., on September 11, 2001. Beyond the tragic loss of life, these attacks had important business implications as well. For example, it took more than five years for airline demand to return to pre–September 11 levels. Insurance companies had to pay out billions of dollars in unanticipated claims as a result of the attacks. Defense contractors saw demand for their products soar as the United States and some of its allies began waging war in Afghanistan and then Iraq.

A firm's general environment defines the broad contextual background within which it operates. Understanding this general environment can help a firm identify some of the threats and opportunities it faces. However, this general environment often has an impact on a firm's threats and opportunities through its impact on a firm's more local environment. Thus, while analyzing a firm's general environment is an important step in any application of the strategic management process, this general analysis must be accompanied by an analysis of a firm's more local environment if the threats and opportunities facing a firm are to be fully understood. The next section discusses specific tools for analyzing a firm's local environment and the theoretical perspectives from which these tools have been derived.

The Structure-Conduct-Performance Model of Firm Performance

In the 1930s, a group of economists began developing an approach for understanding the relationship among a firm's environment, behavior, and performance. The original objective of this work was to describe conditions under which competition in an industry would *not* develop. Understanding when competition was not developing in an industry assisted government regulators in identifying industries where competition-enhancing regulations should be implemented.[7]

Ethics and Strategy

One of the basic tenets of economic theory is that society is better off when industries are very competitive. Industries are very competitive when there are large numbers of firms operating in an industry, when the products and services that these firms sell are similar to each other, and when it is not very costly for firms to enter into or exit these industries. Indeed, as is described in more detail in the Strategy in Depth feature, these industries are said to be *perfectly competitive.*

The reasons that society is better off when industries are perfectly competitive are well known. In such industries, firms must constantly strive to keep their costs low, keep their quality high, and, when appropriate, innovate if they are to even survive. Low costs, high quality, and appropriate innovation are generally consistent with the interests of a firm's customers and, thus, consistent with society's overall welfare.

Indeed, concern for **social welfare,** or the overall good of society, is the primary reason the S-C-P model was developed. This model was to be used to identify industries where perfect competition was not occurring and, thus, where social welfare was not being maximized. With these industries identified, the government

Is a Firm Gaining a Competitive Advantage Good for Society?

could then engage in activities to increase the competitiveness of these industries, thereby increasing social welfare.

Strategic management scholars turned the S-C-P model upside down by using it to describe industries where firms could gain competitive advantages and attain above-average performance. However, some have asked that if strategic management is all about creating and exploiting competitive imperfections in industries, is strategic management also all about reducing the overall good of society for advantages to be gained by a few firms? It is not surprising that individuals who are more interested in improving society

than improving the performance of a few firms question the moral legitimacy of the field of strategic management.

However, there is another view about strategic management and social welfare. The S-C-P model assumes that any competitive advantages a firm has in an industry must hurt society. The alternative view is that at least some of the competitive advantages exist because a firm addresses customer needs more effectively than its competitors. From this perspective, competitive advantages are not bad for social welfare; they are actually good for social welfare.

Of course, both perspectives can be true. For example, a firm such as Microsoft has engaged in activities that at least some courts have concluded are inconsistent with social welfare. However, Microsoft also sells applications software that is routinely ranked among the best in the industry, an action that is consistent with meeting customer needs in ways that maximize social welfare.

Sources: J. B. Barney (1986). "Types of competition and the theory of strategy." *Academy of Management Review,* 11, pp. 791–800; H. Demsetz (1973). "Industry structure, market rivalry, and public policy." *Journal of Law and Economics,* 16, pp. 1–9; M. Porter (1981). "The contribution of industrial organization to strategic management." *Academy of Management Review,* 6, pp. 609–620.

The theoretical framework that developed out of this effort became known as the **structure-conduct-performance (S-C-P) model**; it is summarized in Figure 2.2. The term **structure** in this model refers to industry structure, measured by such factors as the number of competitors in an industry, the heterogeneity of products in an industry, the cost of entry and exit in an industry, and so forth. **Conduct** refers to the strategies that firms in an industry implement. **Performance** in the S-C-P model has two meanings: (1) the performance of individual firms and (2) the performance of the economy as a whole. Although both definitions of performance in the S-C-P model are important, as suggested in Chapter 1, the strategic

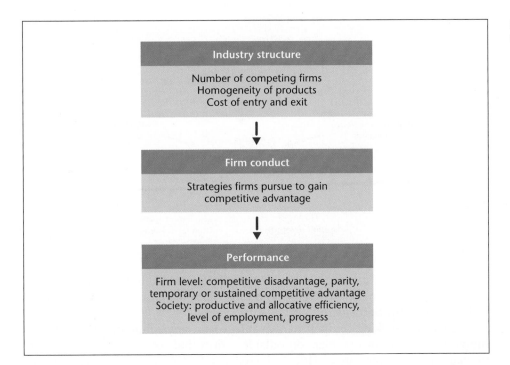

Figure 2.2   The Structure-Conduct-Performance Model

management process is much more focused on the performance of individual firms than on the performance of the economy as a whole. That said, the relationship between these two types of performance can sometimes be complex, as described in the Ethics and Strategy feature.

The logic that links industry structure to conduct and performance is well known. Attributes of the industry structure within which a firm operates define the range of options and constraints facing a firm. In some industries, firms have very few options and face many constraints. In general, firms in these industries can only gain competitive parity. In this setting, industry structure completely determines both firm conduct and long-run firm performance.

However, in other, less competitive industries, firms face fewer constraints and a greater range of conduct options. Some of these options may enable them to obtain competitive advantages. However, even when firms have more conduct options, industry structure still constrains the range of options. Moreover, as will be shown in more detail later in this chapter, industry structure also has an impact on how long firms can expect to maintain their competitive advantages in the face of increased competition.

A Model of Environmental Threats

As a theoretical framework, the S-C-P model has proven to be very useful in informing both research and government policy. However, the model can sometimes be awkward to use to identify threats in a firm's local environment. Fortunately, several scholars have developed models of environmental threats based on the S-C-P model that are highly applicable in identifying threats facing a particular firm.[8] These models identify the five most common threats, presented in Figure 2.3, faced by firms in their local competitive environments and the

Figure 2.3 Environmental
Threats and the Profit Potential
of Industries

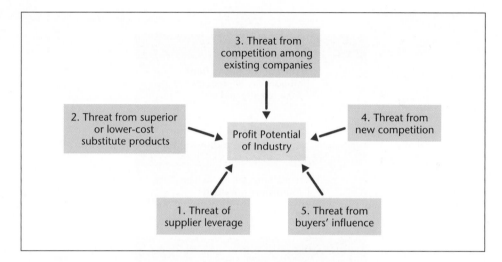

conditions under which these threats are more or less likely to be present. The relationship between the S-C-P model and the framework presented in Figure 2.3 is discussed in the Strategy in Depth feature.

To a firm seeking competitive advantages, an **environmental threat** is any individual, group, or organization outside a firm that seeks to reduce the level of that firm's performance. Threats increase a firm's costs, decrease a firm's revenues, or in other ways reduce a firm's performance. In S-C-P terms, environmental threats are forces that tend to increase the competitiveness of an industry and force firm performance to competitive parity level. The five common environmental threats identified in the literature are: (1) threat from new competition, (2) threat from competition among existing competitors, (3) threat from superior or low-cost substitutes, (4) threat of supplier leverage, and (5) threats from buyers' influence.

Threat from New Competition

The first environmental threat identified in Figure 2.3 is the threat of new competitors. **New competitors** are firms that have either recently started operating in an industry or that threaten to begin operations in an industry soon. For the music download industry, Amazon is a new competitor. For televised sports, Fox Sports, NBC Sports Network, and CBS Sports Network are new competitors.[9]

According to the S-C-P model, new competitors are motivated to enter into an industry by the superior profits that some incumbent firms in that industry may be earning. Firms seeking these high profits enter the industry, thereby increasing the level of industry competition and reducing the performance of incumbent firms. With the absence of any barriers, entry will continue as long as any firms in the industry are earning competitive advantages, and entry will cease when all incumbent firms are earning competitive parity.

The extent to which new competitors act as a threat to an incumbent firm's performance depends on the cost of entry. If the cost of entry into an industry is greater than the potential profits a new competitor could obtain by entering, then entry will not be forthcoming, and new competitors are not a threat to incumbent firms. However, if the cost of entry is lower than the return from entry, entry will occur until the profits derived from entry are less than the costs of entry.

Strategy in Depth

The relationship between environmental threats and the S-C-P model turns on the relationship between the CE threats and the nature of competition in an industry. When all five threats are very high, competition in an industry begins to approach what economists call *perfect competition*. When all five threats are very low, competition in an industry begins to approach what economists call a *monopoly*. Between perfect competition and monopoly, economists have identified two other types of competition in an industry—*monopolistic competition* and *oligopoly*—where the five threats identified in the literature are moderately high. These four types of competition, and the expected performance of firms in these different industries, are summarized in the table below.

Industries are **perfectly competitive** when there are large numbers of competing firms, the products being sold are homogeneous with respect to cost and product attributes, and entry and exit costs are very low. An example of a perfectly competitive industry is the spot market for crude oil. Firms

Environmental Threats and the S-C-P Model

in perfectly competitive industries can expect to earn only competitive parity.

In **monopolistically competitive industries**, there are large numbers of competing firms and low-cost entry into and exit from the industry. However, unlike the case of perfect competition, products in these industries are not homogeneous with respect to costs or product attributes. Examples of monopolistically competitive industries include toothpaste, shampoo, golf balls, and automobiles. Firms in such industries can earn competitive advantages.

Oligopolies are characterized by a small number of competing firms, by homogeneous products, and by high entry and exit costs. Examples of oligopolistic industries include the U.S. automobile and steel industries in the 1950s and the U.S. breakfast cereal market today. Currently, the top four producers of breakfast cereal account for about 90 percent of the breakfast cereal sold in the United States. Firms in such industries can earn competitive advantages.

Finally, **monopolistic industries** consist of only a single firm. Entry into this type of industry is very costly. There are few examples of purely monopolistic industries. Historically, for example, the U.S. Post Office had a monopoly on home mail delivery. However, this monopoly has been challenged in small-package delivery by FedEx, in larger-package delivery by UPS, and in mail delivery by e-mail. Monopolists can generate competitive advantages—although they are sometimes managed very inefficiently.

Source: J. Barney (2007). *Gaining and sustaining competitive advantage,* 3rd ed. Upper Saddle River, NJ: Pearson Higher Education.

Types of Competition and Expected Firm Performance

Type of Competition	Attributes	Examples	Expected Firm Performance
Perfect competition	Large number of firms Homogeneous products Low-cost entry and exit	Stock market Crude oil	Competitive parity
Monopolistic competition	Large number of firms Heterogeneous products Low-cost entry and exit	Toothpaste Shampoo Golf balls Automobiles	Competitive advantage
Oligopoly	Small number of firms Homogenous products Costly entry and exit	U.S. steel and autos in the 1950s U.S. breakfast cereal	Competitive advantage
Monopoly	One firm Costly entry	Home mail delivery	Competitive advantage

TABLE 2.1 Possible Barriers to Entry into an Industry	1. Economies of scale 2. Product differentiation 3. Cost advantages independent of scale 4. Government regulation of entry

The threat of new competitors depends on the cost of entry, and the cost of entry, in turn, depends on the existence and "height" of barriers to entry. **Barriers to entry** are attributes of an industry's structure that increase the cost of entry. The greater the cost of entry, the greater the height of these barriers. When there are significant barriers to entry, potential new competitors will not enter into an industry even if incumbent firms are earning competitive advantages.

Four important barriers to entry have been identified in the S-C-P and strategy literatures. These four barriers, listed in Table 2.1, are (1) economies of scale, (2) product differentiation, (3) cost advantages independent of scale, and (4) government regulation of entry.[10]

Economies of Scale as a Barrier to Entry

Economies of scale exist in an industry when a firm's costs fall as a function of its volume of production. **Diseconomies of scale** exist when a firm's costs rise as a function of its volume of production. The relationship among economies of scale, diseconomies of scale, and a firm's volume of production is summarized in Figure 2.4. As a firm's volume of production increases, its costs begin to fall. This is a manifestation of economies of scale. However, at some point a firm's volume of production becomes too large and its costs begin to rise. This is a manifestation of diseconomies of scale. For economies of scale to act as a barrier to entry, the relationship between the volume of production and firm costs must have the shape of the line in Figure 2.4. This curve suggests that any deviation, positive or negative, from an optimal level of production (point X in Figure 2.4) will lead a firm to experience much higher costs of production.

Figure 2.4 Economies of Scale and the Cost of Production

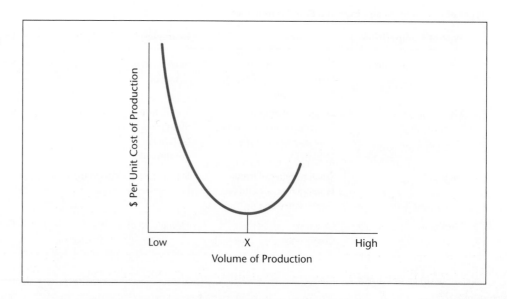

To see how economies of scale can act as a barrier to entry, consider the following scenario. Imagine an industry with the following attributes: The industry has five incumbent firms (each firm has only one plant); the optimal level of production in each of these plants is 4,000 units (X = 4,000 units); total demand for the output of this industry is fixed at 22,000 units; the economies-of-scale curve is as depicted in Figure 2.4; and products in this industry are very homogeneous. Total demand in this industry (22,000 units) is greater than total supply (5 × 4,000 units = 20,000). Everyone knows that when demand is greater than supply, prices go up. This means that the five incumbent firms in this industry will have high levels of profit. The S-C-P model suggests that, absent barriers, these superior profits should motivate entry.

However, look at the entry decision from the point of view of potential new competitors. Certainly, incumbent firms are earning superior profits, but potential entrants face an unsavory choice. On the one hand, new competitors could enter the industry with an optimally efficient plant and produce 4,000 units. However, this form of entry will lead industry supply to rise to 24,000 units (20,000 + 4,000). Suddenly, supply will be greater than demand (24,000 > 22,000), and all the firms in the industry, including the new entrant, will earn negative profits. On the other hand, the new competitor might enter the industry with a plant of smaller-than-optimal size (e.g., 1,000 units). This kind of entry leaves total industry demand larger than industry supply (22,000 > 21,000). However, the new competitor faces a serious cost disadvantage in this case because it does not produce at the low-cost position on the economies-of-scale curve. Faced with these bleak alternatives, the potential entrant simply does not enter even though incumbent firms are earning positive profits.

Of course, potential new competitors have other options besides entering at the efficient scale and losing money or entering at an inefficient scale and losing money. For example, potential entrants can attempt to expand the total size of the market (i.e., increase total demand from 22,000 to 24,000 units or more) and enter at the optimal size. Potential entrants can also attempt to develop new production technology, shift the economies-of-scale curve to the left (thereby reducing the optimal plant size), and enter. Or potential new competitors may try to make their products seem very special to their customers, enabling them to charge higher prices to offset higher production costs associated with a smaller-than-optimal plant.[11]

Any of these actions may enable a firm to enter an industry. However, these actions are costly. If the cost of engaging in these "barrier-busting" activities is greater than the return from entry, entry will not occur, even if incumbent firms are earning positive profits.

Historically, economies of scale acted as a barrier to entry into the world-wide steel market. To fully exploit economies of scale, traditional steel plants had to be very large. If new entrants into the steel market had built these efficient and large steel-manufacturing plants, they would have had the effect of increasing the steel supply over the demand for steel, and the outcome would have been reduced profits for both new entrants and incumbent firms. This discouraged new entry. However, in the 1970s, the development of alternative mini-mill technology shifted the economies-of-scale curve to the left by making smaller plants very efficient in addressing some segments of the steel market. This shift had the effect of decreasing barriers to entry into the steel industry. Recent entrants, including Nucor Steel and Chaparral Steel, now have significant cost advantages over firms still using outdated, less efficient production technology.[12]

Product Differentiation as a Barrier to Entry

Product differentiation means that incumbent firms possess brand identification and customer loyalty that potential new competitors do not. Brand identification and customer loyalty serve as entry barriers because new competitors not only have to absorb the standard costs associated with starting production in a new industry; they also have to absorb the costs associated with overcoming incumbent firms' differentiation advantages. If the cost of overcoming these advantages is greater than the potential return from entering an industry, entry will not occur, even if incumbent firms are earning positive profits.

Numerous examples exist of industries in which product differentiation tends to act as a barrier to entry. In the brewing industry, for example, substantial investments by Budweiser, Miller, and Coors (among other incumbent firms) in advertising (will we ever forget the Budweiser frogs?) and brand recognition have made large-scale entry into the U.S. brewing industry very costly.[13] Indeed, rather than attempting to enter the U.S. market, InBev, a large brewer headquartered in Belgium, decided to purchase Anheuser Busch.[14]

E. & J. Gallo Winery, a U.S. winemaker, faced product differentiation barriers to entry in its efforts to sell Gallo wine in the French market. The market for wine in France is huge—the French consume 16.1 gallons of wine per person per year, for a total consumption of more than 400 million cases of wine, whereas U.S. consumers drink only 1.8 gallons of wine per person per year, for a total consumption of less than 200 million cases. Despite this difference, intense loyalties to local French vineyards have made it very difficult for Gallo to break into the huge French market—a market where American wines are still given as "gag gifts" and only American theme restaurants carry U.S. wines on their menus. Gallo is attempting to overcome this product differentiation advantage of French wineries by emphasizing its California roots—roots that many French consider to be exotic—and downplaying the fact that it is a U.S. company; corporate origins that are less attractive to many French consumers.[15]

Cost Advantages Independent of Scale as Barriers to Entry

In addition to the barriers that have been cited, incumbent firms may have a whole range of cost advantages, independent of economies of scale, compared to new competitors. These cost advantages can act to deter entry because new competitors will find themselves at a cost disadvantage vis-à-vis incumbent firms with these cost advantages. New competitors can engage in activities to overcome the cost advantages of incumbent firms, but as the cost of overcoming them increases, the economic profit potential from entry is reduced. In some settings, incumbent firms enjoying cost advantages, independent of scale, can earn superior profits and still not be threatened by new entry because the cost of overcoming those advantages can be prohibitive. Examples of these cost advantages, independent of scale, are presented in Table 2.2; they include (1) proprietary technology, (2) managerial know-how, (3) favorable access to raw materials, and (4) learning-curve cost advantages.

Proprietary Technology. In some industries, **proprietary** (i.e., secret or patented) **technology** gives incumbent firms important cost advantages over potential entrants. To enter these industries, potential new competitors must develop their own substitute technologies or run the risks of copying another firm's patented technologies. Both of these activities can be costly. Numerous firms in a wide variety of industries have discovered the sometimes substantial economic costs

Proprietary technology. When incumbent firms have secret or patented technology that reduces their costs below the costs of potential entrants, potential new competitors must develop substitute technologies to compete. The cost of developing this technology can act as a barrier to entry.

Managerial know-how. When incumbent firms have taken-for-granted knowledge, skills, and information that take years to develop and that is not possessed by potential new competitors. The cost of developing this know-how can act as a barrier to entry.

Favorable access to raw materials. When incumbent firms have low-cost access to critical raw materials not enjoyed by potential new competitors. The cost of gaining similar access can act as a barrier to entry.

Learning-curve cost advantages. When the cumulative volume of production of incumbent firms gives them cost advantages not enjoyed by potential new competitors. These cost disadvantages of potential entrants can act as a barrier to entry.

TABLE 2.2 Sources of Cost Advantage, Independent of Scale, That Can Act as Barriers to Entry

associated with violating another firm's patented proprietary technology. Indeed, the number of patent infringement suits continues to increase, especially in industries—such as consumer electronics—where products apply technologies developed by many different companies. In the past few years, Intertrust has sued Apple, Yahoo! has sued Facebook, Google has sued BT, Boston University has sued Apple, Nokia has sued HTC, Samsung has sued Apple, and Apple has sued Samsung.[16] In 2012, a total of 5,778 patent infringement suits were filed in the United States.[17]

Managerial Know-How. Even more important than technology per se as a barrier to entry is the managerial know-how built up by incumbent firms over their history.[18] **Managerial know-how** is the often-taken-for-granted knowledge and information that are needed to compete in an industry on a day-to-day basis.[19] Know-how includes information that it has taken years, sometimes decades, for a firm to accumulate that enables it to interact with customers and suppliers, to be innovative and creative, to manufacture quality products, and so forth. Typically, new entrants will not have access to this know-how, and it will often be costly for them to build it quickly.

One industry where this kind of know-how is a very important barrier to entry is the pharmaceutical industry. Success in this industry depends on having high-quality research and development skills. The development of world-class research and development skills—the know-how—takes decades to accumulate. New competitors face enormous cost disadvantages for decades as they attempt to develop these abilities, and thus entry into the pharmaceutical industry has been quite limited.[20]

Favorable Access to Raw Materials. Incumbent firms may also have cost advantages, compared to new entrants, based on favorable access to raw materials. If, for example, only a few sources of high-quality iron ore are available in a specific geographic region, steel firms that have access to these sources may have a cost advantage over those that must ship their ore in from distant sources.[21]

Learning-Curve Cost Advantages. It has been shown that in certain industries (such as airplane manufacturing) the cost of production falls with the cumulative volume of production. Over time, as incumbent firms gain experience in manufacturing, their costs fall below those of potential entrants. Potential new competitors, in this context, must endure substantially higher costs while they gain experience, and thus they may not enter the industry despite the superior profits being earned by incumbent firms. These learning-curve economies are discussed in more detail in Chapter 4.

Government Policy as a Barrier to Entry

Governments, for their own reasons, may decide to increase the cost of entry into an industry. This occurs most frequently when a firm operates as a government-regulated monopoly. In this setting, the government has concluded that it is in a better position to ensure that specific products or services are made available to the population at reasonable prices than competitive market forces. Industries such as electric power generation and elementary and secondary education have been (and, to some extent, continue to be) protected from new competitors by government restrictions on entry.

Threat from Existing Competitors

New competitors are an important threat to the ability of firms to maintain or improve their level of performance, but they are not the only threat in a firm's environment. A second environmental threat comes from the intensity of competition among a firm's current direct competitors. Amazon and iTunes are direct competitors. ESPN, CBS, NBC, Fox, USA Networks, and TNN—to name a few—are all direct competitors in televised sports.

Direct competition threatens firms by reducing their economic profits. High levels of direct competition are indicated by such actions as frequent price cutting by firms in an industry (e.g., price discounts in the airline industry), frequent introduction of new products by firms in an industry (e.g., continuous product introductions in consumer electronics), intense advertising campaigns (e.g., Pepsi versus Coke advertising), and rapid competitive actions and reactions in an industry (e.g., competing airlines quickly matching the discounts of other airlines).

Some of the attributes of an industry that are likely to generate high levels of direct competition are listed in Table 2.3. First, direct competition tends to be high when there are numerous firms in an industry and these firms tend to be roughly the same size. Such is the case in the laptop personal computer industry. Worldwide, more than 120 firms have entered the laptop computer market, and no one firm dominates in market share. Since the early 1990s, prices in the laptop market have been declining 25 to 30 percent a year. Profit margins for laptop personal computer firms that used to be in the 10 to 13 percent range have rapidly fallen to 3 to 4 percent.[22]

Second, direct competition tends to be high when industry growth is slow. When industry growth is slow, firms seeking to increase their sales must often acquire market share from established competitors. This tends to increase competition. Intense price rivalry emerged in the U.S. fast-food industry—with 99-cent Whoppers at Burger King and "dollar menus" at Wendy's and McDonald's—when the growth in this industry declined.[23]

TABLE 2.3 Attributes of an Industry That Increase the Threat of Direct Competition

1. Large number of competing firms that are roughly the same size
2. Slow industry growth
3. Lack of product differentiation
4. Capacity added in large increments

Third, direct competition tends to be high when firms are unable to differentiate their products in an industry. When product differentiation is not a viable strategic option, firms are often forced to compete only on the basis of price. Intense price competition is typical of high-competition industries. In the airline industry, for example, intense competition on longer routes—such as between Los Angeles and New York and Los Angeles and Chicago—has kept prices on these routes down. These routes have relatively few product differentiation options. However, by creating hub-and-spoke systems, certain airlines (American, United, Delta) have been able to develop regions of the United States where they are the dominant carrier. These hub-and-spoke systems enable airlines to partially differentiate their products geographically, thus reducing the level of competition in segments of this industry.[24]

Finally, direct competition tends to be high when production capacity is added in large increments. If, in order to obtain economies of scale, production capacity must be added in large increments, an industry is likely to experience periods of oversupply after new capacity comes online. This overcapacity often leads to price cuts. Much of the growing rivalry in the commercial jet industry between Boeing and AirBus can be traced to the large manufacturing capacity additions made by AirBus when it entered the industry.[25]

Threat of Substitute Products

A third environmental threat is the threat of substitute products. The products or services provided by a firm's direct competitors meet approximately the same customer needs in the same ways as the products or services provided by the firm itself. **Substitutes** meet approximately the same customer needs, but do so in different ways. Substitutes for downloaded music include Spotify, Pandora, and other music-streaming firms. Substitutes for televised sports include sports magazines, sports pages in the newspapers, and actually attending sporting events.

Substitutes place a ceiling on the prices firms in an industry can charge and on the profits firms in an industry can earn. In the extreme, substitutes can ultimately replace an industry's products and services. This happens when a substitute is clearly superior to previous products. Examples include electronic calculators as substitutes for slide rules and mechanical calculators, electronic watch movements as substitutes for pin–lever mechanical watch movements, and compact discs as substitutes for long-playing (LP) records (although some audiophiles continue to argue for the sonic superiority of LPs).

Substitutes are playing an increasingly important role in reducing the profit potential in a variety of industries. For example, in the legal profession private mediation and arbitration services are becoming viable substitutes for lawyers. Computerized texts are becoming viable substitutes for printed books in the publishing industry. Television news programs, especially services such as CNN and Fox News, are very threatening substitutes for weekly newsmagazines, including *Time* and *Newsweek*. In Europe, so-called superstores are threatening smaller food shops. Minor league baseball teams are partial substitutes for major league teams. Cable television is a substitute for broadcast television. Groups of "big box" retailers are substitutes for traditional shopping centers. Private mail delivery systems (such as those in the Netherlands and Australia) are substitutes for government postal services. Home financial planning software is a partial substitute for professional financial planners.[26]

Threat of Supplier Leverage

A fourth environmental threat is supplier leverage. **Suppliers** make a wide variety of raw materials, labor, and other critical assets available to firms. Suppliers can threaten the performance of firms in an industry by increasing the price of their supplies or by reducing the quality of those supplies. Any profits that were being earned in an industry can be transferred to suppliers in this way. In music downloading, record labels and, to a lesser extent, artists are critical suppliers. In televised sports, critical suppliers include sports leagues—such as the NFL and the NHL—as well as TV personalities.

Some supplier attributes that can lead to high levels of threat are listed in Table 2.4. First, suppliers are a greater threat if the *suppliers'* industry is dominated by a small number of firms. In this setting, a firm has little choice but to purchase supplies from these firms. These few firms thus have enormous flexibility to charge high prices, to reduce quality, or in other ways to squeeze the profits of the firms in the industry to which they sell. Much of Microsoft's power in the software industry reflects its dominance in the operating system market, where Windows remains the de facto standard for most personal computers. For now, at least, if a company wants to sell personal computers, it is going to need to interact with Microsoft. It will be interesting to see if Linux-based PCs become more powerful, thereby limiting some of Microsoft's leverage as a supplier.

Conversely, when a firm has the option of purchasing from a large number of suppliers, suppliers have less leverage to threaten a firm's profits. For example, as the number of lawyers in the United States has increased over the years (up 40 percent since 1981, currently more than 1 million), lawyers and law firms have been forced to begin competing for work. Some corporate clients have forced law firms to reduce their hourly fees and to handle repetitive simple legal tasks for low flat fees.[27]

Second, suppliers are a greater threat when what they supply is unique or highly differentiated. There is only one LeBron James. As a basketball player, as a spokesperson, and as a celebrity, his unique status gives him enormous bargaining power as a supplier and enables him to extract some of the economic profit that would otherwise have been earned by the Miami Heat and Nike. In the same way, Intel's unique ability to develop, manufacture, and sell microprocessors gives it significant bargaining power as a supplier in the personal computer industry.

The uniqueness of suppliers can operate in almost any industry. For example, in the highly competitive world of television talk shows, some guests, as suppliers, can gain surprising fame for their unique characteristics. For example, one woman was a guest on eight talk shows. Her claim to fame: She was the tenth wife of a gay, con-man bigamist.

Third, suppliers are a greater threat to firms in an industry when suppliers are *not* threatened by substitutes. When there are no effective substitutes, suppliers can

TABLE 2.4 Indicators of the Threat of Supplier Leverage in an Industry

1. Suppliers' industry is dominated by small number of firms.
2. Suppliers sell unique or highly differentiated products.
3. Suppliers are *not* threatened by substitutes.
4. Suppliers threaten forward vertical integration.
5. Firms are *not* important customers for suppliers.

take advantage of their position to extract economic profits from firms they supply. Both Intel (in microprocessors) and Microsoft (in PC operating systems) have been accused of exploiting their unique product positions to extract profits from customers.

When there are substitutes for supplies, supplier power is checked. In the metal can industry, for example, steel cans are threatened by aluminum and plastic containers as substitutes. In order to continue to sell to can manufacturers, steel companies have had to keep their prices lower than would otherwise have been the case. In this way, the potential power of the steel companies is checked by the existence of substitute products.[28]

Fourth, suppliers are a greater threat to firms when they can credibly threaten to enter into and begin competing in a firm's industry. This is called **forward vertical integration**; in this situation, suppliers cease to be suppliers only and become suppliers *and* rivals. The threat of forward vertical integration is partially a function of barriers to entry into an industry. When an industry has high barriers to entry, suppliers face significant costs of forward vertical integration, and thus forward integration is not as serious a threat to the profits of incumbent firms. (Vertical integration is discussed in detail in Chapter 6.)

Finally, suppliers are a threat to firms when firms are *not* an important part of suppliers' business. Steel companies, for example, are not too concerned with losing the business of a sculptor or of a small construction company. However, they are very concerned about losing the business of the major can manufacturers, major white-goods manufacturers (i.e., manufacturers of refrigerators, washing machines, dryers, and so forth), and automobile companies. Steel companies, as suppliers, are likely to be very accommodating and willing to reduce prices and increase quality for can manufacturers, white-goods manufacturers, and auto companies. Smaller, "less important" customers, however, are likely to be subject to greater price increases, lower-quality service, and lower-quality products.

Threat from Buyers' Influence

The final environmental threat is buyers. **Buyers** purchase a firm's products or services. Whereas powerful suppliers act to increase a firm's costs, powerful buyers act to decrease a firm's revenues. In music downloads, consumers are the ultimate buyer. In televised sports, buyers include all those who watch sports on television as well as those who purchase advertising space on networks. Some of the important indicators of the threat of buyers are listed in Table 2.5.

First, if a firm has only one buyer or a small number of buyers, these buyers can be very threatening. Firms that sell a significant amount of their output to the U.S. Department of Defense recognize the influence of this buyer on their operations. Reductions in defense spending have forced defense companies to try even harder to reduce costs and increase quality to satisfy government

1. Number of buyers is small.
2. Products sold to buyers are undifferentiated and standard.
3. Products sold to buyers are a significant percentage of a buyer's final costs.
4. Buyers are *not* earning significant economic profits.
5. Buyers threaten backward vertical integration.

TABLE 2.5 Indicators of the Threat of Buyers' Influence in an Industry

demands. All these actions reduce the economic profits of these defense-oriented companies.[29] Firms that sell to large retail chains have also found it difficult to maintain high levels of profitability. Powerful retail firms—such as Wal-Mart and Home Depot—can make significant and complex logistical and other demands on their suppliers, and if suppliers fail to meet these demands, buyers can "fire" their suppliers. These demands can have the effect of reducing the profits of suppliers.

Second, if the products or services that are being sold to buyers are standard and not differentiated, then the threat of buyers can be greater. For example, farmers sell a very standard product. It is very difficult to differentiate products such as wheat, corn, or tomatoes (although this can be done to some extent through the development of new strains of crops, the timing of harvests, pesticide-free crops, and so forth). In general, wholesale grocers and food brokers can always find alternative suppliers of basic food products. These numerous alternative suppliers increase the threat of buyers and force farmers to keep their prices and profits low. If any one farmer attempts to raise prices, wholesale grocers and food brokers simply purchase their supplies from some other farmer.

Third, buyers are likely to be more of a threat when the supplies they purchase are a significant portion of the costs of their final products. In this context, buyers are likely to be very concerned about the costs of their supplies and constantly on the lookout for cheaper alternatives. For example, in the canned food industry, the cost of the can itself can constitute up to 40 percent of a product's final price. Not surprisingly, firms such as Campbell Soup Company are very concerned about keeping the price of the cans they purchase as low as possible.[30]

Fourth, buyers are likely to be more of a threat when they are *not* earning significant economic profits. In these circumstances, buyers are likely to be very sensitive to costs and insist on the lowest possible cost and the highest possible quality from suppliers. This effect can be exacerbated when the profits suppliers earn are greater than the profits buyers earn. In this setting, a buyer would have a strong incentive to enter into its supplier's business to capture some of the economic profits being earned by the supplier. This strategy of **backward vertical integration** is discussed in more detail in Chapter 6.

Finally, buyers are more of a threat to firms in an industry when they have the ability to vertically integrate backward. In this case, buyers become both buyers and rivals and lock in a certain percentage of an industry's sales. The extent to which buyers represent a threat to vertically integrate, in turn, depends on the barriers to entry that are not in place in an industry. If there are significant barriers to entry, buyers may not be able to engage in backward vertical integration, and their threat to firms is reduced.

Environmental Threats and Average Industry Performance

The five environmental threats have three important implications for managers seeking to choose and implement strategies. First, they describe the most common sources of local environmental threat in industries. Second, they can be used to characterize the overall level of threat in an industry. Finally, because the overall level of threat in an industry is, according to S-C-P logic, related to the average level of performance of a firm in an industry, they can also be used to anticipate the average level of performance of firms in an industry.

	Industry I	Industry II	Industry III	Industry IV
Threat of new competitors	High	Low	High	Low
Threat of direct competition	High	Low	Low	High
Threat of superior or low cost product substitutes	High	Low	High	Low
Threat of supplier leverage	High	Low	Low	High
Threat of buyers; influence	High	Low	High	Low
Expected average firm performance	Low	High	Mixed	Mixed

TABLE 2.6 Estimating the Level of Average Performance in an Industry

Of course, it will rarely be the case that all five threats in an industry will be equally threatening at the same time. This can sometimes complicate the anticipation of the average level of firm performance in an industry. Consider, for example, the four industries in Table 2.6. It is easy to anticipate the average level of performance of firms in the first two industries: In Industry I, this performance will be low; in Industry II, this performance will be high; however, in Industries III and IV it is somewhat more complicated. In these mixed situations, the real question to ask in anticipating the average performance of firms in an industry is, "Are one or more threats in this industry powerful enough to appropriate most of the profits that firms in this industry might generate?" If the answer to this question is yes, then the anticipated average level of performance will be low. If the answer is no, then the anticipated performance will be high.

Even more fundamentally, this type of analysis can be used only to anticipate the average level of firm performance in an industry. This is acceptable if a firm's industry is the primary determinant of its overall performance. However, as described in the Research Made Relevant feature, research suggests that the industry a firm operates in is far from the only determinant of its performance.

Another Environmental Force: Complementors

Professors Adam Brandenburger and Barry Nalebuff have suggested that another force needs to be added to the analysis of the profit potential of industries.[31] These authors distinguish between competitors and what they call a firm's *complementors*. If you were the chief executive officer of a firm, the following is how you could tell the difference between your competitors and your complementors: Another firm is a **competitor** if your customers value your product less when they have the other firm's product than when they have your product alone. Direct competitors, new competitors, and substitutes are all examples of competitors. In contrast, another firm is a **complementor** if your customers value your product more when they have this other firm's product than when they have your product alone.

Consider, for example, the relationship between producers of television programming and cable television companies. The value of these firms' products partially depends on the existence of one another. Television producers need outlets for their programming. The growth in the number of channels on cable television provides more of these outlets and thus increases the value of these production firms. Cable television companies can continue to add channels, but those channels need content. So, the value of cable television companies depends partly on the existence of television production firms. Because the value of program-producing companies is greater when cable television firms exist and because the value of cable television companies is greater when program-producing companies exist, these types of firms are complements.

Brandenburger and Nalebuff go on to argue that an important difference between complementors and competitors is that a firm's complementors help to increase the size of a firm's market, whereas a firm's competitors divide this market among a set of firms. Based on this logic, these authors suggest that, although it is usually the case that a firm will want to discourage the entry of competitors into its market, it will usually want to encourage the entry of complementors. Returning to the television producers/cable television example, television producers will actually want cable television companies to grow and prosper and constantly add new channels, and cable television firms will want television show producers to grow and constantly create new and innovative programming. If the growth of either of these businesses slows, it hurts the growth of the other.

Of course, the same firm can be a complementor for one firm and a competitor for another. For example, the invention of satellite television and increased popularity of DirecTV and the Dish Network represent a competitive challenge to cable television companies. That is, DirecTV and, say, Time Warner Cable are competitors. However, DirecTV and television production companies are complementors to each other. In deciding whether to encourage the entry of new complementors, a firm has to weigh the extra value these new complementors will create against the competitive impact of this entry on a firm's current complementors.

It is also the case that a single firm can be both a competitor and a complementor to the same firm. This is very common in industries where it is important to create technological standards. Without standards for, say, the size of a CD, how information on a CD will be stored, how this information will be read, and so forth, consumers will often be unwilling to purchase a CD player. With standards in place, however, sales of a particular technology can soar. To develop technology standards, firms must be willing to cooperate. This cooperation means that, with respect to the technology standard, these firms are complementors. And, indeed, when these firms act as complementors, their actions have the effect of increasing the total size of the market. However, once these firms cooperate to establish standards, they begin to compete to try to obtain as much of the market they jointly created as possible. In this sense, these firms are also competitors.

Understanding when firms in an industry should behave as complementors and when they should behave as competitors is sometimes very difficult. It is even more difficult for a firm that has interacted with other firms in its industry as a competitor to change its organizational structure, formal and informal control systems, and compensation policy and start interacting with these firms as a complementor, at least for some purposes. Learning to manage what Brandenburger and Nalebuff call the "Jekyll and Hyde" dilemma associated with competitors and complementors can distinguish excellent from average firms.

Research Made Relevant

For some time now, scholars have been interested in the relative impact of the attributes of the industry within which a firm operates and the attributes of the firm itself on its performance. The first work in this area was published by Richard Schmalansee. Using a single year's worth of data, Schmalansee estimated the variance in the performance of firms that was attributable to the industries within which firms operated versus other sources of performance variance. Schmalansee's conclusion was that approximately 20 percent of the variance in firm performance was explained by the industry within which a firm operated—a conclusion consistent with the S-C-P model and its emphasis on industry as a primary determinant of a firm's performance.

Richard Rumelt identified some weaknesses in Schmalansee's research. Most important of these was that Schmalansee had only one year's worth of data with which to examine the effects of industry and firm attributes on firm performance. Rumelt was able to use four years' worth of data, which allowed him to distinguish between stable and transient industry and firm effects on firm performance.

The Impact of Industry and Firm Characteristics on Firm Performance

Rumelt's results were consistent with Schmalansee's in one sense: Rumelt also found that about 16 percent of the variance in firm performance was due to industry effects, versus Schmalansee's 20 percent. However, only about half of this industry effect was stable. The rest represented year-to-year fluctuations in the business conditions in an industry. This result is broadly inconsistent with the S-C-P model.

Rumelt also examined the impact of firm attributes on firm performance and found that more than 80 percent of the variance in firm performance was due to these firm attributes, but that more than half of this 80 percent (46.38 percent) was due to stable firm effects. The importance of stable firm differences in explaining differences in firm performance is also inconsistent with the S-C-P framework. These results are consistent with another model of firm performance called the *resource-based view*, which will be described in Chapter 3.

Since Rumelt's research, efforts to identify the factors that explain variance in firm performance have accelerated. At least nine articles addressing this issue have been published in the literature. One of the most recent of these suggests that, while the impact of the industry and the corporation on business unit performance can vary across industries and across corporations, overall, business unit effects are larger than either corporate or industry effects.

Sources: R. P. Rumelt (1991). "How much does industry matter?" *Strategic Management Journal,* 12, pp. 167–185; R. Schmalansee (1985). "Do markets differ much?" *American Economic Review,* 75, pp. 341–351; V. F. Misangyi, H. Elms, T. Greckhamer, and J. A. Lepine (2006). "A new perspective on a fundamental debate: A multi-level approach to industry, corporate, and business unit effects." *Strategic Management Journal,* 27(6), pp. 571–590.

Industry Structure and Environmental Opportunities

Identifying environmental threats is only half the task in accomplishing an external analysis. Such an analysis must also identify opportunities. Fortunately, the same S-C-P logic that made it possible to develop tools for the analysis of environmental threats can also be used to develop tools for the analysis of environmental opportunities. However, instead of identifying the threats that are common in most industries, opportunity analysis begins by identifying several generic industry structures and then describing the strategic opportunities that are available in each of these different kinds of industries.[32]

TABLE 2.7 Industry
Structure and Environmental
Opportunities

Industry Structure	Opportunities
Fragmented industry	Consolidation
Emerging industry	First-mover advantages
Mature industry	Product refinement
	Investment in service quality
	Process innovation
Declining industry	Leadership
	Niche
	Harvest
	Divestment

Of course, there are many different generic industry structures. However, four are very common and will be the focus of opportunity analysis in this book: (1) fragmented industries, (2) emerging industries, (3) mature industries, and (4) declining industries. A fifth industry structure—international industries—will be discussed later in the chapter. The kinds of opportunities typically associated with these industry structures are presented in Table 2.7.

Opportunities in Fragmented Industries: Consolidation

Fragmented industries are industries in which a large number of small or medium-sized firms operate and no small set of firms has dominant market share or creates dominant technologies. Most service industries, including retailing, fabrics, and commercial printing, to name just a few, are fragmented industries.

Industries can be fragmented for a wide variety of reasons. For example, the fragmented industry may have few barriers to entry, thereby encouraging numerous small firms to enter. The industry may have few, if any, economies of scale, and even some important diseconomies of scale, thus encouraging firms to remain small. Also, close local control over enterprises in an industry may be necessary—for example, local movie houses and local restaurants—to ensure quality and to minimize losses from theft.

The major opportunity facing firms in fragmented industries is the implementation of strategies that begin to consolidate the industry into a smaller number of firms. Firms that are successful in implementing this **consolidation strategy** can become industry leaders and obtain benefits from this kind of effort, if they exist.

Consolidation can occur in several ways. For example, an incumbent firm may discover new economies of scale in an industry. In the highly fragmented funeral home industry, Service Corporation International (SCI) found that the development of a chain of funeral homes gave it advantages in acquiring key supplies (coffins) and in the allocation of scarce resources (morticians and hearses). By acquiring numerous previously independent funeral homes, SCI was able to substantially reduce its costs and gain higher levels of economic performance.[33]

Incumbent firms sometimes adopt new ownership structures to help consolidate an industry. Kampgrounds of America (KOA) uses franchise agreements with local operators to provide camping facilities to travelers in the fragmented private campgrounds industry. KOA provides local operators with professional training, technical skills, and access to its brand-name reputation.

Local operators, in return, provide KOA with local managers who are intensely interested in the financial and operational success of their campgrounds. Similar franchise agreements have been instrumental in the consolidation of other fragmented industries, including fast food (McDonald's), muffler repair (Midas), and motels (La Quinta, Holiday Inn, Howard Johnson's).[34]

The benefits of implementing a consolidation strategy in a fragmented industry turn on the advantages larger firms in such industries gain from their larger market share. As will be discussed in Chapter 4, firms with large market share can have important cost advantages. Large market share can also help a firm differentiate its products.

Opportunities in Emerging Industries: First-Mover Advantages

Emerging industries are newly created or newly re-created industries formed by technological innovations, changes in demand, the emergence of new customer needs, and so forth. Over the past 30 years, the world economy has been flooded by emerging industries, including the microprocessor industry, the personal computer industry, the medical imaging industry, and the biotechnology industry, to name a few. Firms in emerging industries face a unique set of opportunities, the exploitation of which can be a source of superior performance for some time for some firms.

The opportunities that face firms in emerging industries fall into the general category of first-mover advantages. **First-mover advantages** are advantages that come to firms that make important strategic and technological decisions early in the development of an industry. In emerging industries, many of the rules of the game and standard operating procedures for competing and succeeding have yet to be established. First-moving firms can sometimes help establish the rules of the game and create an industry's structure in ways that are uniquely beneficial to them. In general, first-mover advantages can arise from three primary sources: (1) technological leadership, (2) preemption of strategically valuable assets, and (3) the creation of customer-switching costs.[35]

First-Mover Advantages and Technological Leadership

Firms that make early investments in particular technologies in an industry are implementing a **technological leadership strategy**. Such strategies can generate two advantages in emerging industries. First, firms that have implemented these strategies may obtain a low-cost position based on their greater cumulative volume of production with a particular technology. These cost advantages have had important competitive implications in such diverse industries as the manufacture of titanium dioxide by DuPont and Procter & Gamble's competitive advantage in disposable diapers.[36]

Second, firms that make early investments in a technology may obtain patent protections that enhance their performance.[37] Xerox's patents on the xerography process and General Electric's patent on Edison's original lightbulb design were important for these firms' success when these two industries were emerging.[38] However, although there are some exceptions (e.g., the pharmaceutical industry and specialty chemicals), patents, per se, seem to provide relatively small profit opportunities for first-moving firms in most emerging industries. One group of researchers found that imitators can duplicate first movers' patent-based advantages for about 65 percent of the first mover's costs.[39] These researchers also found that 60 percent of all patents are imitated within four years of being granted—without legally violating patent rights obtained by first movers. As we will discuss in detail in Chapter 3, patents are rarely a source of sustained competitive advantage for firms, even in emerging industries.

First-Mover Advantages and Preemption of Strategically Valuable Assets

First movers that invest only in technology usually do not obtain sustained competitive advantages. However, first movers that move to tie up strategically valuable resources in an industry before their full value is widely understood can gain sustained competitive advantages. **Strategically valuable assets** are resources required to successfully compete in an industry. Firms that are able to acquire these resources have, in effect, erected formidable barriers to imitation in an industry. Some strategically valuable assets that can be acquired in this way include access to raw materials, particularly favorable geographic locations, and particularly valuable product market positions.

When an oil company such as Royal Dutch Shell (because of its superior exploration skills) acquires leases with greater development potential than was expected by its competition, the company is gaining access to raw materials in a way that is likely to generate sustained competitive advantages. When Wal-Mart opens stores in medium-sized cities before the arrival of its competition, Wal-Mart is making it difficult for the competition to enter into this market. And when breakfast cereal companies expand their product lines to include all possible combinations of wheat, oats, bran, corn, and sugar, they, too, are using a first-mover advantage to deter entry.[40]

First-Mover Advantages and Creating Customer-Switching Costs

Firms can also gain first-mover advantages in an emerging industry by creating customer-switching costs. **Customer-switching costs** exist when customers make investments in order to use a firm's particular products or services. These investments tie customers to a particular firm and make it more difficult for customers to begin purchasing from other firms.[41] Such switching costs are important factors in industries as diverse as applications software for personal computers, prescription pharmaceuticals, and groceries.[42]

In applications software for personal computers, users make significant investments to learn how to use a particular software package. Once computer users have learned how to operate particular software, they are unlikely to switch to new software, even if that new software system is superior to what they currently use. Such a switch would require learning the new software and determining how it is similar to and different from the old software. For these reasons, some computer users will continue to use outdated software, even though new software performs much better.

Similar switching costs can exist in some segments of the prescription pharmaceutical industry. Once medical doctors become familiar with a particular drug, its applications, and side effects, they are sometimes reluctant to change to a new drug, even if that new drug promises to be more effective than the older, more familiar one. Trying the new drug requires learning about its properties and side effects. Even if the new drug has received government approvals, its use requires doctors to be willing to "experiment" with the health of their patients. Given these issues, many physicians are unwilling to rapidly adopt new drug therapies. This is one reason that pharmaceutical firms spend so much time and money using their sales forces to educate their physician customers. This kind of education is necessary if a doctor is going to be willing to switch from an old drug to a new one.

Customer-switching costs can even play a role in the grocery store industry. Each grocery store has a particular layout of products. Once customers learn where different products in a particular store are located, they are not likely to change stores because they would then have to relearn the location of products. Many customers want to avoid the time and frustration associated with wandering around a new store looking for some obscure product. Indeed, the cost of switching stores may be large enough to enable some grocery stores to charge higher prices than would be the case without customer-switching costs.

First-Mover Disadvantages

Of course, the advantages of first moving in emerging industries must be balanced against the risks associated with exploiting this opportunity. Emerging industries are characterized by a great deal of uncertainty. When first-moving firms are making critical strategic decisions, it may not be at all clear what the right decisions are. In such highly uncertain settings, a reasonable strategic alternative to first moving may be retaining flexibility. Where first-moving firms attempt to resolve the uncertainty they face by making decisions early and then trying to influence the evolution of an emerging industry, they use flexibility to resolve this uncertainty by delaying decisions until the economically correct path is clear and then moving quickly to take advantage of that path.

Opportunities in Mature Industries: Product Refinement, Service, and Process Innovation

Emerging industries are often formed by the creation of new products or technologies that radically alter the rules of the game in an industry. However, over time, as these new ways of doing business become widely understood, as technologies diffuse through competitors, and as the rate of innovation in new products and technologies drops, an industry begins to enter the mature phase of its development. As described in the Strategy in the Emerging Enterprise feature, this change in the nature of a firm's industry can be difficult to recognize and can create both strategic and operational problems for a firm.

Common characteristics of **mature industries** include (1) slowing growth in total industry demand, (2) the development of experienced repeat customers, (3) a slowdown in increases in production capacity, (4) a slowdown in the introduction of new products or services, (5) an increase in the amount of international competition, and (6) an overall reduction in the profitability of firms in the industry.[43]

The fast-food industry in the United States has matured over the last several years. In the 1960s, the United States had only three large national fast-food chains: McDonald's, Burger King, and Dairy Queen. Through the 1980s, all three of these chains grew rapidly, although the rate of growth at McDonald's outstripped the growth rate of the other two firms. During this time period, however, other fast-food chains also entered the market. These included some national chains, such as Kentucky Fried Chicken, Wendy's, and Taco Bell, and some strong regional chains, such as Jack in the Box and In and Out Burger. By the early 1990s, growth in this industry had slowed considerably. McDonald's announced that it was having difficulty finding locations for new McDonald's that did not impinge on the sales of already existing McDonald's. Except for non–U.S. operations, where competition in the fast-food industry is not as mature, the profitability of most U.S. fast-food companies did not grow as much in the 1990s as it did in the 1960s through the 1980s. Indeed, by 2002, all the major fast-food chains were either not making very much money or, like McDonald's, actually losing money.[44]

Opportunities for firms in mature industries typically shift from the development of new technologies and products in an emerging industry to a greater emphasis on refining a firm's current products, an emphasis on increasing the quality of service, and a focus on reducing manufacturing costs and increased quality through process innovations.

Refining Current Products

In mature industries, such as home detergents, motor oil, and kitchen appliances, few, if any, major technological breakthroughs are likely. However, this does not mean that innovation is not occurring in these industries. Innovation in these industries focuses on extending and improving current products and technologies. In home detergents, innovation recently has focused on changes in packaging and on selling more highly concentrated detergents. In motor oil, packaging changes (from fiber foil cans to plastic containers), additives that keep oil cleaner longer, and oil formulated to operate in four-cylinder engines are recent examples of this kind of innovation. In kitchen appliances, recent improvements include the availability of refrigerators with crushed ice and water through the door, commercial-grade stoves for home use, and dishwashers that automatically adjust the cleaning cycle depending on how dirty the dishes are.[45] In fast foods, firms like McDonald's and Wendy's have introduced healthy, more adult-oriented food to complement their kid-friendly hamburger-heavy menus. This movement has helped restore the profitability of these firms.

Emphasis on Service

When firms in an industry have only limited ability to invest in radical new technologies and products, efforts to differentiate products often turn toward the quality of customer service. A firm that is able to develop a reputation for high-quality customer service may be able to obtain superior performance even though its products are not highly differentiated.

This emphasis on service has become very important in a wide variety of industries. For example, in the convenience food industry, one of the major reasons for slower growth in the fast-food segment has been growth in the so-called "casual dining" segment. This segment includes restaurants such as Chili's and Applebee's. The food sold at fast-food restaurants and casual dining restaurants overlaps—they both sell burgers, soft drinks, salads, chicken, desserts, and so forth—although many consumers believe that the quality of food is superior in the casual dining restaurants. In addition to any perceived differences in the food, however, the level of service in the two kinds of establishments varies significantly. At fast-food restaurants, food is handed to consumers on a tray; in casual dining restaurants, waitstaff actually bring food to consumers on a plate. This level of service is one reason that casual dining is growing in popularity.[46]

On the other hand, the fastest-growing segment of the U.S. restaurant industry is the "fast casual" segment—Panera Bread, Café Rio (a regional Mexican restaurant), and Chipotle. These restaurants deliver high-quality food but avoid the delays often associated with full-service restaurants.

Process Innovation

A firm's **processes** are the activities it engages in to design, produce, and sell its products or services. **Process innovation**, then, is a firm's effort to refine and

Strategy in the Emerging Enterprise

It began with a 5,000-word e-mail sent by Steve Balmer, CEO of Microsoft, to all 57,000 employees. Whereas previous e-mails from Microsoft founder Bill Gates—including one in 1995 calling on the firm to learn how to "ride the wave of the Internet"—inspired the firm to move on to conquer more technological challenges, Balmer's e-mail focused on Microsoft's current state and called on the firm to become more focused and efficient. Balmer also announced that Microsoft would cut its costs by $1 billion during the next fiscal year. One observer described it as the kind of e-mail you would expect to read at Procter & Gamble, not at Microsoft.

Then the other shoe dropped. In a surprise move, Balmer announced that Microsoft would distribute a large portion of its $56 billion cash reserve in the form of a special dividend to stockholders. In what is believed to be the largest such cash dispersion ever, Microsoft distributed $32 billion to its stockholders and used an additional $30 billion to buy back stock. Bill Gates received a $3.2 billion cash dividend. These changes meant that Microsoft's capital structure was more similar to, say, Procter & Gamble's than to an entrepreneurial, high-flying software company.

What happened at Microsoft? Did Microsoft's management conclude that the PC software industry

Microsoft Grows Up

was no longer emerging, but had matured to the point that Microsoft would have to alter some of its traditional strategies? Most observers believe that Balmer's e-mail, and the decision to reduce its cash reserves, signaled that Microsoft had come to this conclusion. In fact, although most of Microsoft's core businesses—its Windows operating systems, its PC applications software, and its server software—are still growing at the rate of about $3 billion a year, if they were growing at historical rates these businesses would be generating $7 billion in new revenues each year. Moreover, Microsoft's new businesses—video games, Internet services, business software, and software for phones and handheld computers—are adding less than $1 billion in new revenues each year. That is, growth in Microsoft's new businesses is not offsetting slower growth in its traditional businesses.

Other indicators of the growing maturity of the PC software industry, and Microsoft's strategic changes, also exist. For example, during 2003 and 2004, Microsoft resolved most of the outstanding antitrust litigation it was facing, abandoned its employee stock option plan in favor of a stock-based compensation scheme popular with slower-growth firms, improved its systems for receiving and acting on feedback from customers, and improved the quality of its relationships with some of its major rivals, including Sun Microsystems, Inc. These are all the actions of a firm that recognizes that the rapid growth opportunities that existed in the software industry when Microsoft was a new company do not exist anymore.

At this point, Microsoft has to choose whether it is going to jump-start its growth through a series of large acquisitions or accept the lower growth rates in its core markets. It has tried to jump-start its growth through acquisitions, a strong indicator that Microsoft, while acknowledging slower growth in its core, has not completely abandoned the idea of growing quickly in some parts of its business.

Sources: J. Greene (2004). "Microsoft's midlife crisis." *BusinessWeek*, April 19, 2004, pp. 88+; R. Guth and S. Thurm (2004). "Microsoft to dole out its cash hoard." *The Wall Street Journal*, Wednesday, July 21, 2004, pp. A1+; S. Hamm (2004). "Microsoft's worst enemy: Success." *BusinessWeek*, July 19, 2004, p. 33; Accessed July 12, 2006.

improve its current processes. Several authors have studied the relationship between process innovation, product innovation, and the maturity of an industry.[47] This work suggests that, in the early stages of industry development, product innovation is very important. However, over time product innovation becomes less important, and process innovations designed to reduce manufacturing costs, increase product quality, and streamline management become more important.

In mature industries, firms can often gain an advantage by manufacturing the same product as competitors, but at a lower cost. Alternatively, firms can manufacture a product that is perceived to be of higher quality and do so at a competitive cost. Process innovations facilitate both the reduction of costs and the increase in quality.

The role of process innovation in more mature industries is perhaps best exemplified by the improvement in quality in U.S. automobiles. In the 1980s, Japanese firms such as Nissan, Toyota, and Honda sold cars that were of significantly higher quality than those produced by U.S. firms General Motors, Ford, and Chrysler. In the face of that competitive disadvantage, the U.S. firms engaged in numerous process reforms to improve the quality of their cars. In the 1980s, U.S. manufacturers were cited for car body panels that did not fit well, bumpers that were hung crookedly on cars, and the wrong engines being placed in cars. Today, the differences in quality between newly manufactured U.S. and Japanese automobiles are very small. Indeed, one well-known judge of initial manufacturing quality—J. D. Powers—now focuses on items such as the quality of a car's cup holders and the maximum distance at which a car's keyless entry system still works to establish quality rankings. The really significant quality issues of the 1980s are virtually gone.[48]

Opportunities in Declining Industries: Leadership, Niche, Harvest, and Divestment

A **declining industry** is an industry that has experienced an absolute decline in unit sales over a sustained period of time.[49] Obviously, firms in a declining industry face more threats than opportunities. Rivalry in a declining industry is likely to be very high, as is the threat of buyers, suppliers, and substitutes. However, even though threats are significant, firms do have opportunities they can exploit. The major strategic opportunities that firms in this kind of industry face are leadership, niche, harvest, and divestment.

Market Leadership

An industry in decline is often characterized by overcapacity in manufacturing, distribution, and so forth. Reduced demand often means that firms in a declining industry will have to endure a significant **shakeout period** until overcapacity is reduced and capacity is brought in line with demand. After the shakeout, a smaller number of lean and focused firms may enjoy a relatively benign environment with few threats and several opportunities. If the industry structure that is likely to exist after a shakeout is quite attractive, firms in an industry before the shakeout may have an incentive to weather the storm of decline—to survive until the situation improves to the point that they can begin to earn higher profits.

If a firm has decided to wait out the storm of decline in hopes of better environmental conditions in the future, it should consider various steps to increase its chances of survival. Most important of these is that a firm must establish itself as a **market leader** in the pre-shakeout industry, most typically by becoming the firm with the largest market share in that industry. The purpose of becoming a market leader is *not* to facilitate tacit collusion (see Chapter 9) or to obtain lower costs from economies of scale (see Chapter 6). Rather, in a declining industry the leader's objective should be to try to facilitate the exit of firms that are not likely to survive a shakeout, thereby obtaining a more favorable competitive environment as quickly as possible.

Market leaders in declining industries can facilitate exit in a variety of ways, including purchasing and then deemphasizing competitors' product lines, purchasing and retiring competitors' manufacturing capacity, manufacturing spare parts for competitors' product lines, and sending unambiguous signals of their intention to stay in an industry and remain a dominant firm. For example, overcapacity problems in the European petrochemical industry were partially resolved when Imperial Chemical Industries (ICI) traded its polyethylene plants to British Petroleum for BP's polyvinylchloride (PVC) plants. In this case, both firms were able to close some excess capacity in specific markets (polyethylene and PVC), while sending clear signals of their intention to remain in these markets.[50]

Market Niche

A firm in a declining industry following a leadership strategy attempts to facilitate exit by other firms, but a firm following a **niche strategy** in a declining industry reduces its scope of operations and focuses on narrow segments of the declining industry. If only a few firms choose a particular niche, then these firms may have a favorable competitive setting, even though the industry as a whole is facing shrinking demand.

Two firms that used the niche approach in a declining market are GTE Sylvania and General Electric (GE) in the vacuum tube industry. Yes, vacuum tubes! The invention of the transistor followed by the semiconductor just about destroyed demand for vacuum tubes in new products. GTE Sylvania and GE rapidly recognized that new product sales in vacuum tubes were drying up. In response, these firms began specializing in supplying *replacement* vacuum tubes to the consumer and military markets. To earn high profits, these firms had to refocus their sales efforts and scale down their sales and manufacturing staffs. Over time, as fewer and fewer firms manufactured vacuum tubes, GTE Sylvania and GE were able to charge very high prices for replacement parts.[51]

Harvest

Leadership and niche strategies, though differing along several dimensions, have one attribute in common: Firms that implement these strategies intend to remain in the industry despite its decline. Firms pursuing a **harvest strategy** in a declining industry do not expect to remain in the industry over the long term. Instead, they engage in a long, systematic, phased withdrawal, extracting as much value as possible during the withdrawal period.

The extraction of value during the implementation of a harvest strategy presumes that there is some value to harvest. Thus, firms that implement this strategy must ordinarily have enjoyed at least some profits at some time in their history, before the industry began declining. Firms can implement a harvest strategy by reducing the range of products they sell, reducing their distribution network, eliminating less profitable customers, reducing product quality, reducing service quality, deferring maintenance and equipment repair, and so forth. In the end, after a period of harvesting in a declining industry, firms can either sell their operations (to a market leader) or simply cease operations.

In principle, the harvest opportunity sounds simple, but in practice it presents some significant management challenges. The movement toward a harvest strategy often means that some of the characteristics of a business that have long been a source of pride to managers may have to be abandoned. Thus, where prior to harvest a firm may have specialized in high-quality service, quality products, and excellent customer value, during the harvest period service quality may fall, product quality may deteriorate, and prices may rise. These changes may be difficult for managers to accept, and higher turnover may be the result. It is also difficult to hire quality managers into a harvesting business because such individuals are likely to seek greater opportunities elsewhere.

For these reasons, few firms explicitly announce a harvest strategy. However, examples can be found. GE seems to be following a harvest strategy in the electric turbine business. Also, United States Steel and the International Steel Group seem to be following this strategy in certain segments of the steel market.[52]

Divestment

The final opportunity facing firms in a declining industry is divestment. Like a harvest strategy, the objective of **divestment** is to extract a firm from a declining industry. However, unlike harvest, divestment occurs quickly, often soon after a pattern of decline has been established. Firms without established competitive advantages may find divestment a superior option to harvest because they have few competitive advantages they can exploit through harvesting.

In the 1980s, GE used this rapid divestment approach to virtually abandon the consumer electronics business. Total demand in this business was more or less stable during the 1980s, but competition (mainly from Asian manufacturers) increased substantially. Rather than remain in this business, GE sold most of its consumer electronics operations and used the capital to enter into the medical imaging industry, where this firm has found an environment more conducive to superior performance.[53]

In the defense business, divestment is the stated strategy of General Dynamics, at least in some of its business segments. General Dynamics' managers recognized early on that the changing defense industry could not support all the incumbent firms. When General Dynamics concluded that it could not remain a leader in some of its businesses, it decided to divest those and concentrate on a few remaining businesses. Since 1991, General Dynamics has sold businesses worth more than $2.83 billion, including its missile systems business, its Cessna aircraft division, and its tactical aircraft division (maker of the very successful F-16 aircraft and partner in the development of the next generation of fighter aircraft, the F-22). These divestitures have left General Dynamics in just three businesses: armored tanks, nuclear submarines, and space launch vehicles. During this time, the market price of General Dynamics stock has returned almost $4.5 billion to its investors, has seen its stock go from $25 per share to a high of $110 per share and has provided a total return to stockholders of 555 percent.[54]

Of course, not all divestments are caused by industry decline. Sometimes firms divest certain operations to focus their efforts on remaining operations, sometimes they divest to raise capital, and sometimes they divest to simplify operations. These types of divestments reflect a firm's diversification strategy and are explored in detail in Chapter 11.

Summary

The strategic management process requires that a firm engage in an analysis of threats and opportunities in its competitive environment before a strategic choice can be made. This analysis begins with an understanding of the firm's general environment. This general environment has six components: technological change, demographic trends, cultural trends, economic climate, legal and political conditions, and specific international events. Although some of these components of the general environment can affect a firm directly, more frequently they affect a firm through their impact on its local environment.

The S-C-P model can be used to develop tools for analyzing threats in a firm's competitive environment. The most influential of these tools focuses on five environmental threats to the profitability of firms in an industry. The five threats are: threat from new competitors, threat from existing direct competitors, threat from superior or low cost substitutes, threat of supplier leverage, and the threat from buyers' influence. The threat of new competition depends on the existence and "height" of barriers to entry. Common barriers to entry include economies of scale, product differentiation, cost advantages independent of scale, and government regulation. The threat of current direct competitors depends on the number and competitiveness of firms in an industry. This threat is high in an industry when there are large numbers of competing firms, competing firms are roughly the same size and have the same influence, growth in an industry is slow, there is no product differentiation, and productive capacity is added in large increments. The threat of superior substitutes depends on how close substitute products and services are—in performance and cost—to products and services in an industry. Whereas direct competitors meet the same customer needs in approximately the same way, substitutes meet the same customer needs, but do so in very different ways. The threat of supplier leverage in an industry depends on the number and distinctiveness of the products suppliers provide to an industry. The threat of supplier leverage increases when a supplier's industry is dominated by a few firms, when suppliers sell unique or highly differentiated products, when suppliers are not threatened by substitutes, when suppliers threaten forward vertical integration, and when firms are not important customers for suppliers. Finally, the threat of buyers' influence depends on the number and size of an industry's customers. The threat of buyers' influence is greater when the number of buyers is small, products sold to buyers are undifferentiated and standard, products sold to buyers are a significant percentage of a buyer's final costs, buyers are not earning significant profits, and buyers threaten backward vertical integration. Taken together, the level of these threats in an industry can be used to determine the expected average performance of firms in an industry.

One additional force in a firm's environment is complementors. Where competitors compete with a firm to divide profits in a market, complementors increase the total size of the market. If you are a CEO of a firm, you know that another firm is a complementor when the value of your products to your customers is higher in combination with this other firm's products than when customers use your products alone. Where firms have strong incentives to reduce the entry of competitors, they can sometimes have strong incentives to increase the entry of complementors.

The S-C-P model can also be used to develop tools for analyzing strategic opportunities in an industry. This is done by identifying generic industry structures and the strategic opportunities available in these different kinds of industries. Four common industry structures are fragmented industries, emerging industries, mature industries, and declining industries. The primary opportunity in fragmented industries is consolidation. In emerging industries, the most important opportunity is first-mover advantages from technological leadership, preemption of strategically valuable assets, or creation of customer-switching costs. In mature industries, the primary opportunities are product refinement, service, and process innovation. In declining industries, opportunities include market leadership, niche, harvest, and divestment.

MyManagementLab®

Go to **mymanagementlab.com** to complete the problems marked with this icon ✪.

Challenge Questions

2.1. Suppose you have to evaluate microfinance ventures. One of the proposals is for opening a hairdresser's shop in Guatemala City. The proposal argues that there must be significant demand for hairdressing and other cosmetic services because the city has lots of such shops already and several new ones open each month. It predicts that the demand for such services will continue to increase, given the increasing number of convenience stores in Guatemala that sell hair coloring dyes and hair straightening solutions. What are the risks involved in this proposal? Would you advise investing in this venture?

✪ **2.2.** One potential threat in an industry is buyers' influence. Yet unless buyers are satisfied, they are likely to look for satisfaction elsewhere. Can the fact that buyers can be threats be reconciled with the need to satisfy buyers?

2.3. Government policies can have a significant impact on the average profitability of firms in an industry. Government, however, is not included as a potential threat. Why should the model be expanded to include government? Why or why not?

2.4. In particular, if an industry has large numbers of complementors, does that make it more attractive or less attractive or does it have no impact on the industry's attractiveness? Justify your answer.

✪ **2.5.** Opportunities analysis seems to suggest that strategic opportunities are available in almost any industry, including declining ones. If that is true, is it fair to say that there is really no such thing as an unattractive industry?

2.6. If there is really no such thing as an unattractive industry, what implications does this have for the applicability of environmental threat analysis?

2.7. Describe an industry that has opportunities for niche and product refinement.

2.8. Describe when the evolution of industry structure from an emerging industry to a mature industry to a declining industry is inevitable.

Problem Set

2.9. Perform an analysis of the profit potential on the following two industries:

The Pharmaceutical Industry

The pharmaceutical industry consists of firms that develop, patent, and distribute drugs. Although this industry does not have significant production economies, it does have important economies in research and development. Product differentiation exists as well because firms often sell branded products. Firms compete in research and development. However, once a product is developed and patented, competition is significantly reduced. Recently, the increased availability of generic, nonbranded drugs has threatened the profitability of some drug lines. Once an effective drug is developed, few, if any, alternatives to that drug usually are available. Drugs are manufactured from commodity chemicals that are available from numerous suppliers. Major customers include doctors and patients. Recently, increased costs have led the federal government and insurance companies to pressure drug companies to reduce their prices.

The Textile Industry

The textile industry consists of firms that manufacture and distribute fabrics for use in clothing, furniture, carpeting, and so forth. Several firms have invested heavily in sophisticated manufacturing technology, and many lower-cost firms located in Asia have begun fabric production. Textiles are not branded products. Recently, tariffs on some imported textiles have been implemented. The industry has numerous firms; the largest have less than 10 percent market share. Traditional fabric materials (such as cotton and wool) have recently been threatened by the development of alternative chemical-based materials (such as nylon and rayon), although many textile companies have begun manufacturing with these new materials as well. Most raw materials are widely available, although some synthetic products periodically may be in short supply. There are numerous textile customers, but textile costs are usually a large percentage of their final product's total costs. Many users shop around the world for the lowest textile prices.

2.10. Perform an opportunities analysis on the following industries:

(a) The fast-food industry in Mexico
(b) Wired telecommunication industry in Nigeria
(c) Computer manufacturing industry in China
(d) The worldwide LED manufacturing industry
(e) The worldwide small-package overnight delivery industry

2.11. Identify two rivals and two complementors for each of the following companies. Rivals could include incumbent competitors, substitutes or potential new entrants.

(a) Toyota
(b) Microsoft
(c) Lenovo
(d) HSBC Bank
(e) Apple

MyManagementLab®

Go to **mymanagementlab.com** for the following Assisted-graded writing questions:

✪ **2.12.** Describe a case when a single firm can be both a competitor and a complementor to the same firm.

✪ **2.13.** Under what constraints can firms also gain first-mover advantages in an emerging industry?

End Notes

1. See (2003). *The big book of business quotations.* New York: Basic Books, p. 209.
2. See Weintraub, A. (2004). "Repairing the engines of life." *BusinessWeek*, May 24, 2004, pp. 99+ for a discussion of recent developments in biotechnology research and the business challenges they have created.
3. See Grow, B. (2004). "Hispanic nation." *BusinessWeek*, March 15, 2004, pp. 59+.
4. Ibid.
5. Barnes, B. (2004). "The WB grows up." *The Wall Street Journal*, July 19, 2004, pp. B1+; money.cnn.com/2006/01/24/news/companies/cbs_warner. Accessed February 2007.
6. These and other cultural differences are described in Rugman, A., and R. Hodgetts (1995). *International business.* New York: McGraw-Hill. A discussion of the dimensions along which country cultures can vary is presented in a later chapter.
7. Early contributors to the structure-conduct-performance model include Mason, E. S. (1939). "Price and production policies of large scale enterprises." *American Economic Review*, 29, pp. 61–74; and Bain, J. S. (1956). *Barriers to new competition.* Cambridge, MA: Harvard

University Press. The major developments in this framework are summarized in Bain, J. S. (1968). *Industrial organization.* New York: John Wiley & Sons, Inc.; and Scherer, F. M. (1980). *Industrial market structure and economic performance.* Boston: Houghton Mifflin. The links between this framework and work in strategic management are discussed by Porter, M. E. (1981a). "The contribution of industrial organization to strategic management." *Academy of Management Review*, 6, pp. 609–620; and Barney, J. B. (1986c). "Types of competition and the theory of strategy: Toward an integrative framework." *Academy of Management Review*, 1, pp. 791–800.
8. See, for example, Porter, M. E. (1979). "How competitive forces shape strategy." *Harvard Business Review*, March–April, pp. 137–156; and Porter, M. E. (1980). *Competitive strategy.* New York: Free Press.
9. Sharma, A., and M. Fatterman. (2013). "Fox, latest underdog, takes on ESPN." *The Wall Street Journal*, Friday, July 26, pp. B1+.
10. These barriers were originally proposed by Bain, J. S. (1968). *Industrial organization.* New York: John Wiley & Sons, Inc. It is actually possible to estimate the "height" of barriers to entry in an industry by comparing the cost of entry into an industry with

barriers and the cost of entry into that industry if barriers did not exist. The difference between these costs is the "height" of the barriers to entry.

11. Another alternative would be for a firm to own and operate more than one plant. If there are economies of scope in this industry, a firm might be able to enter and earn above-normal profits. An economy of scope exists when the value of operating in two businesses simultaneously is greater than the value of operating in these two businesses separately. The concept of economy of scope is explored in more detail in Part 3 of this book.

12. See Ghemawat, P., and H. J. Stander III. (1992). "Nucor at a crossroads." Harvard Business School Case No. 9-793-039.

13. See Montgomery, C. A., and B. Wernerfelt. (1991). "Sources of superior performance: Market share versus industry effects in the U.S. brewing industry." *Management Science*, 37, pp. 954–959.

14. Sorkin, A. R., and M. Merced. (2008). "Brewer bids $46 billion for Anheuser-Busch." *New York Times*, June 12. http://www.nytimes.com/2008/06/12/business/worldbusiness/12beer.html?_r=0

15. Stecklow, S. (1999). "Gallo woos French, but don't expect Bordeaux by the jug." *The Wall Street Journal*, March 26, pp. A1+.

16. Wingfield, N. (2013). "Intertrust sues Apple over patent violations." Bcts.blogs. NYTimes.com, March 20; Swisler, K. (2012). "Yahoo sues Facebook for patent infringement." Allthings.com, March 12; Fingas, J. (2013). "Google countersues BT." www.engadget.com, February 13; "Boston University sues Apple for patent infringement." (2013). www.macworld.com, July 3; "Nokia taking HTC to court over patent violations." (2013). www.mobilemg.com, May 25;Dobie, A. (2013). "Apple looks to add Sony Galaxy S4 to patent infringement suit."www.androidcentral.com, May 14; "Bad Apple." (2013). www.catholic.org, June 5.

17. www.patstats.org. Accessed July 3, 2013.

18. See Kogut, B., and U. Zander. (1992). "Knowledge of the firm, combinative capabilities, and the replication of technology." *Organization Science*, 3, pp. 383–397; and Dierickx, I., and K. Cool. (1989). "Asset stock accumulation and sustainability of competitive advantage." *Management Science*, 35, pp. 1504–1511. Both emphasize the importance of know-how as a barrier to entry into an industry. More generally, intangible resources are seen as particularly important sources of sustained competitive advantage. This will be discussed in more detail in Chapter 5.

19. See Polanyi, M. (1962). *Personal knowledge: Towards a post-critical philosophy*. London: Routledge & Kegan Paul; and Itami, H. (1987). *Mobilizing invisible assets*. Cambridge, MA: Harvard University Press.

20. See Henderson, R., and I. Cockburn. (1994). "Measuring competence: Exploring firm effects in pharmaceutical research." *Strategic Management Journal*, 15, pp. 361–374.

21. See Scherer, F. M. (1980). *Industrial market structure and economic performance*. Boston: Houghton Mifflin.

22. See Saporito, B. (1992). "Why the price wars never end." *Fortune*, March 23, pp. 68–78; and Allen, M., and M. Siconolfi. (1993). "Dell Computer drops planned share offering." *The Wall Street Journal*, February 25, p. A3.

23. Chartier, John. (2002). "Burger battles." CNN/Money, http://money.cnn.com, December 11.

24. See Ghemawat, P., and A. McGahan. (1995). "The U.S. airline industry in 1995." Harvard Business School Case No. 9-795-113.

25. Labich, K. (1992). "Airbus takes off." *Fortune*, June 1, pp. 102–108.

26. See Pollock, E. J. (1993). "Mediation firms alter the legal landscape." *The Wall Street Journal*, March 22, p. B1; Cox, M. (1993). "Electronic campus: Technology threatens to shatter the world of college textbooks." *The Wall Street Journal*, June 1, p. A1; Reilly, P. M. (1993). "At a crossroads: The instant-new age leaves *Time* magazine searching for a mission." *The Wall Street Journal*, May 12, p. A1; Rohwedder, C. (1993). "Europe's smaller food shops face finis." *The Wall Street Journal*, May 12, p. B1; Fatsis, S. (1995). "Major leagues keep minors at a distance." *The Wall Street Journal*, November 8, pp. B1+; Norton, E., and G. Stem. (1995). "Steel and aluminum vie over every ounce in a car's construction." *The Wall Street Journal*, May 9, pp. A1+; Paré, T. P. (1995). "Why the banks lined up against Gates." *Fortune*, May 29, p. 18; "Hitting the mail on the head." *The Economist*, April 30, 1994, pp. 69–70; Pacelle,

M. (1996). "'Big Boxes' by discounters are booming." *The Wall Street Journal*, January 17, p. A2; and Pope, K., and L. Cauley. (1998). "In battle for TV ads, cable is now the enemy." *The Wall Street Journal*, May 6, pp. B1+.

27. Tully, S. (1992). "How to cut those #$%* legal costs." *Fortune*, September 21, pp. 119–124.

28. See DeWitt, W. (1997). "Crown Cork & Seal/Carnaud Metalbox." Harvard Business School Case No. 9-296-019.

29. Perry, N. J. (1993). "What's next for the defense industry." *Fortune*, February 22, pp. 94–100.

30. See "Crown Cork and Seal in 1989." Harvard Business School Case No. 5-395-224.

31. See Brandenburger, A., and B. Nalebuff. (1996). *Co-opetition*. New York: Doubleday.

32. This approach to studying opportunities was also first suggested in Porter, M. E. (1980). *Competitive strategy*. New York: Free Press.

33. Jacob, R. (1992). "Service Corp. International: Acquisitions done the right way." *Fortune*, November 16, p. 96.

34. Porter, M. E. (1980). *Competitive strategy*. New York: Free Press.

35. For the definitive discussion of first-mover advantages, see Lieberman, M., and C. Montgomery. (1988). "First-mover advantages." *Strategic Management Journal*, 9, pp. 41–58.

36. See Ghemawat, P. (1991). *Commitment*. New York: Free Press.

37. See Gilbert, R. J., and D. M. Newbery. (1982). "Preemptive patenting and the persistence of monopoly." *American Economic Review*, 72(3), pp. 514–526.

38. See Bresnahan, T. F. (1985). "Post-entry competition in the plain paper copier market." *American Economic Review*, 85, pp. 15–19, for a discussion of Xerox's patents; and Bright, A. A. (1949). *The electric lamp industry*. New York: Macmillan, for a discussion of General Electric's patents.

39. See Mansfield, E., M. Schwartz, and S. Wagner. (1981). "Imitation costs and patents: An empirical study." *Economic Journal*, 91, pp. 907–918.

40. See Main, O. W. (1955). *The Canadian nickel industry*. Toronto: University of Toronto Press, for a discussion of asset preemption in the oil and gas industry; Ghemawat, P. (1986). "Wal-Mart store's discount operations." Harvard Business School Case No. 9-387-018, for Wal-Mart's preemption strategy; Schmalensee, R. (1978). "Entry deterrence in the ready-to-eat breakfast cereal industry." *Bell Journal of Economics*, 9(2), pp. 305–327; and Robinson, W. T., and C. Fornell. (1985). "Sources of market pioneer advantages in consumer goods industries." *Journal of Marketing Research*, 22(3), pp. 305–307, for a discussion of preemption in the breakfast cereal industry. In this latter case, the preempted valuable asset is shelf space in grocery stores.

41. Klemperer, P. (1986). "Markets with consumer switching costs." Doctoral thesis, Graduate School of Business, Stanford University; and Wernerfelt, B. (1986). "A special case of dynamic pricing policy." *Management Science*, 32, pp. 1562–1566.

42. See Gross, N. (1995). "The technology paradox." *BusinessWeek*, March 6, pp. 691–719; Bond, R. S., and D. F. Lean. (1977). *Sales, promotion, and product differentiation in two prescription drug markets*. Washington, D.C.: U.S. Federal Trade Commission; Montgomery, D. B. (1975). "New product distribution: An analysis of supermarket buyer decision." *Journal of Marketing Research*, 12, pp. 255–264; Ries, A., and J. Trout. (1986). *Marketing warfare*. New York: McGraw-Hill; and Davidson, J. H. (1976). "Why most new consumer brands fail." *Harvard Business Review*, 54, March–April, pp. 117–122, for a discussion of switching costs in these industries.

43. Porter, M. E. (1980). *Competitive strategy*. New York: Free Press.

44. Gibson, R. (1991). "McDonald's insiders increase their sales of company's stock." *The Wall Street Journal*, June 14, p. A1; and Chartier, J. (2002). "Burger battles." CNN/Money, http://money.cnn.com, December 11. McDonald's lost money for only one quarter. It has since repositioned itself with nice upscale fast foods and has returned to profitability.

45. Descriptions of these product refinements can be found in Demetrakakes, P. (1994). "Household-chemical makers concentrate on downsizing." *Packaging*, 39(1), p. 41; Reda, S. (1995). "Motor oil: Hands-on approach." *Stores*, 77(5), pp. 48–49; and Quinn, J. (1995). "KitchenAid." *Incentive*, 169(5), pp. 46–47.

46. Chartier, J. (2002). "Burger battles." CNN/Money, http://money.cnn.com, December 11.

47. See Hayes, R. H., and S. G. Wheelwright. (1979). "The dynamics of process-product life cycles." *Harvard Business Review*, March–April, p. 127.

48. See www.jdpowers.com.

49. See Porter, M. E. (1980). *Competitive strategy.* New York: Free Press; and Harrigan, K. R. (1980). *Strategies for declining businesses.* Lexington, MA: Lexington Books.

50. See Aguilar, F. J., J. L. Bower, and B. Gomes-Casseres. (1985). "Restructuring European petrochemicals: Imperial Chemical Industries, P.L.C." Harvard Business School Case No. 9-385-203.

51. See Harrigan, K. R. (1980). *Strategies for declining businesses.* Lexington, MA: Lexington Books.

52. See Klebnikov, P. (1991). "The powerhouse." *Forbes*, September 2, pp. 46–52; and Rosenbloom, R. S., and C. Christensen. (1990). "Continuous casting investments at USX corporation." Harvard Business School Case No. 9-391-121.

53. Finn, E. A. (1987). "General Eclectic." *Forbes*, March 23, pp. 74–80.

54. See Smith, L. (1993). "Can defense pain be turned to gain?" *Fortune*, February 8, pp. 84–96; Perry, N. J. (1993). "What's next for the defense industry?" *Fortune*, February 22, pp. 94–100; and Dial, J., and K. J. Murphy. (1995). "Incentive, downsizing, and value creation at General Dynamics." *Journal of Financial Economics*, 37, pp. 261–314.

3 Evaluating a Firm's Internal Capabilities

LEARNING OBJECTIVES *After reading this chapter, you should be able to:*

1. Describe the critical assumptions of the resource-based view.

2. Describe four types of resources and capabilities.

3. Apply the VRIO framework to identify the competitive implications of a firm's resources and capabilities.

4. Apply value chain analysis to identify a firm's valuable resources and capabilities.

5. Describe the kinds of resources and capabilities that are likely to be costly to imitate.

6. Describe how a firm uses its structure, formal and informal control processes, and compensation policy to exploit its resources.

7. Discuss how the decision of whether to imitate a firm with a competitive advantage affects the competitive dynamics in an industry.

MyManagementLab®

⭐ **Improve Your Grade!**

Over 10 million students improved their results using the Pearson MyLabs.
Visit **mymanagementlab.com** for simulations, tutorials, and end-of-chapter problems.

When a Noun Becomes a Verb

Google wasn't the first Internet search engine. At least 19 search engines existed—including Lycos, Alta Vista, Excite, Yahoo!, and Ask Jeeves—before Google was introduced in 1998. Nor is Google the only Internet search engine currently operating. Currently, at least 32 Internet search engines exist, including Ask.com, Bing, Baidu, and DuckDuckGo.

However, despite what appears to be an incredibly competitive industry, Google reigns supreme, with a U.S. and worldwide market share in excess of 60 percent of all Internet searches.

Indeed, Google has been so successful that it has been "verbicized." Now, to "google" something means to look something up on the Internet. This is the case even if you don't use Google to search the Web.

Many have wondered what has made Google so successful and whether it will be able to maintain—and even extend—its success. Three attributes of Google have been most widely cited.

First, Google is technically very competent. In the mid-1990s, all other search engines counted key words on Web pages and then reported which Web sites had the most key words. Google conceptualized the search process differently and used the relationship among pages as a way to guide users to those Web sites that were most helpful to them. Most people agree that Google's approach to Internet search was superior.

This technical competence has enabled Google to buy the technologies of several firms—including Keyhole and Global IP Solutions—and then to leverage those technologies

into successful Google products—including Google Earth and Google Hangout.

Second, Google has been unusually successful in monetizing its software—that is, finding ways to make the software it gives to customers for free generate revenues for Google. Perhaps the best example of this is Google's AdWords program—a system that uses demand for Google advertising to precisely price the value of clicking onto a Web site. In 2012, Google advertising generated $10.42 billion in revenue.

Finally, Google's founders—Larry Page and Sergey Brin—are convinced that Google's unique organizational culture is central to their success. Google has a playful yet demanding culture. Developers are held to the highest standards of performance but are also encouraged to spend at least 20 percent of their time working on their own personal projects—many of which have turned into great products for Google. Google expects to meet its product announcement dates, but when it issued some new shares in 2005, it sold 14,159,265 shares, exactly. Why? Because those are the first eight numbers after the decimal point in pi (3.14159265). Google's unofficial slogan—a not-very-subtle dig on Microsoft—is "Don't Do Evil." So, Google doesn't develop proprietary software that it then attempts to sell to users for high prices. Instead, Google trusts its users, follows their lead in developing new products, and adopts an open approach to developing software.

© FocusDigital/Alamy

Whether or not these three attributes of Google are sources of sustained competitive advantage is still up for debate. On the one hand, Google has used all three to develop an open source smart phone operating system—Android—that has emerged as a serious competitor for Apple's operating system. Moreover, Google seems to have figured out how to begin to monetize the success of one of its best-known acquisitions, YouTube.

On the other hand, Google's acquisition of Motorola Mobile for $12.5 billion seems to have created new challenges for the firm. Justified based on the mobile phone patents owned by Motorola, Google must nevertheless find a way to make money manufacturing cell phones. Motorola failed in this effort the last few years it owned Motorola Mobile. And Google has never before owned a business that actually made tangible products, like phones.

There are, of course, lots of different opinions about Google, and it's easy to find them— just "google" Google on the Web, and in less than half a second, you will see more than 2 billion Web sites that are related to Google.

Sources: www.Google.com; D. Vise and M. Malseed (2005). *The Google Story*. NY: Bantam //Wikipedia/history-of-internet-search-engines. Accessed July 5, 2013.

G oogle has been extremely successful, first in the Internet search engine market and later in related markets. What, if anything, about Google's resources and capabilities make it likely that this firm will be able to continue its success? The ideas presented in this chapter help answer this question.

The Resource-Based View of the Firm

In Chapter 2, we saw that it was possible to take some theoretical models developed in economics—specifically the structure-conduct-performance (S-C-P) model—and apply them to develop tools for analyzing a firm's external threats and opportunities. The same is true for analyzing a firm's internal strengths and weaknesses. However, whereas the tools described in Chapter 2 were based on the S-C-P model, the tools described in this chapter are based on the **resource-based view (RBV)** of the firm. The RBV is a model of firm performance that focuses on the resources and capabilities controlled by a firm as sources of competitive advantage.[1]

What Are Resources and Capabilities?

Resources in the RBV are defined as the tangible and intangible assets that a firm controls that it can use to conceive and implement its strategies. Examples of resources include a firm's factories (a tangible asset), its products (a tangible asset), its reputation among customers (an intangible asset), and teamwork among its managers (an intangible asset). eBay's tangible assets include its Web site and associated software. Its intangible assets include its brand name in the auction business.

Capabilities are a subset of a firm's resources and are defined as the tangible and intangible assets that enable a firm to take full advantage of the other resources it controls. That is, capabilities alone do not enable a firm to conceive and implement its strategies, but they enable a firm to use other resources to conceive and implement such strategies. Examples of capabilities might include a firm's marketing skills and teamwork and cooperation among its managers. At eBay, the cooperation among software developers and marketing people that made it possible for eBay to dominate the online action market is an example of a capability.

A firm's resources and capabilities can be classified into four broad categories: financial resources, physical resources, individual resources, and organizational resources. **Financial resources** include all the money, from whatever source, that firms use to conceive and implement strategies. These financial resources include cash from entrepreneurs, equity holders, bondholders, and banks. **Retained earnings**, or the profit that a firm made earlier in its history and invests in itself, are also an important type of financial resource.

Physical resources include all the physical technology used in a firm. This includes a firm's plant and equipment, its geographic location, and its access to raw materials. Specific examples of plant and equipment that are part of a firm's physical resources are a firm's computer hardware and software technology, robots used in manufacturing, and automated warehouses. Geographic location, as a type of physical resource, is important for firms as diverse as Wal-Mart (with its operations in rural markets generating, on average, higher returns than its operations in more competitive urban markets) and L. L. Bean (a catalogue retail firm that believes that its rural Maine location helps its employees identify with the outdoor lifestyle of many of its customers).[2]

Human resources include the training, experience, judgment, intelligence, relationships, and insight of *individual* managers and workers in a firm.[3] The importance of the human resources of well-known entrepreneurs such as Bill Gates (Microsoft) and Steve Jobs (formerly at Apple) is broadly understood. However, valuable human resources are not limited to just entrepreneurs or senior managers. Each employee at a firm like Southwest Airlines is seen as essential for the overall success of the firm. Whether it is the willingness of the gate agent to joke with the harried traveler, or a baggage handler hustling to get a passenger's bag into a plane, or even a pilot's decision to fly in a way that saves fuel—all of these human resources are part of the resource base that has enabled Southwest to gain competitive advantages in the very competitive U.S. airline industry.[4]

Whereas human resources are an attribute of single individuals, **organizational resources** are an attribute of groups of individuals. Organizational resources include a firm's formal reporting structure; its formal and informal planning, controlling, and coordinating systems; its culture and reputation; and informal relations among groups within a firm and between a firm and those in its environment. At Southwest Airlines, relationships among individual resources are an important organizational resource. For example, it is not unusual to see the pilots at Southwest helping to load the bags on an airplane to ensure that the plane leaves on time. This kind of cooperation and dedication shows up in an intense loyalty between Southwest employees and the firm—a loyalty that manifests itself in low employee turnover and high employee productivity, even though more than 80 percent of Southwest's workforce is unionized.

Critical Assumptions of the Resource-Based View

The RBV rests on two fundamental assumptions about the resources and capabilities that firms may control. First, different firms may possess different bundles of resources and capabilities, even if they are competing in the same industry. This is the assumption of firm **resource heterogeneity**. Resource heterogeneity implies that for a given business activity, some firms may be more skilled in accomplishing this activity than other firms. In manufacturing, for example, Toyota continues to be more skilled than, say, General Motors. In product design, Apple continues to be more skilled than, say, IBM. In motorcycles, Harley Davidson's reputation for big, bad, and loud rides separates it from its competitors.

Second, some of these resource and capability differences among firms may be long lasting because it may be very costly for firms without certain resources and capabilities to develop or acquire them. This is the assumption of **resource immobility**. For example, Toyota has had its advantage in manufacturing for at least 30 years. Apple has had product design advantages over IBM since Apple was founded in the 1980s. And eBay has been able to retain its brand reputation since the beginning of the online auction industry. It is not that GM, IBM, and eBay's competitors are unaware of their disadvantages. Indeed, some of these firms—notably GM and IBM—have made progress in addressing their disadvantages. However, despite these efforts, Toyota, Apple, and, to a lesser extent, eBay continue to enjoy advantages over their competition.

Taken together, these two assumptions make it possible to explain why some firms outperform other firms, even if these firms are all competing in the same industry. If a firm possesses valuable resources and capabilities that few other firms possess and if these other firms find it too costly to imitate these resources and capabilities, the firm that possesses these tangible and intangible assets can gain a sustained competitive advantage. The economic logic that underlies the RBV is described in more detail in the Strategy in Depth feature.

Strategy in Depth

The theoretical roots of the resource-based view can be traced to research done by David Ricardo in 1817. Interestingly, Ricardo was not even studying the profitability of firms; he was interested in the economic consequences of owning more or less fertile farm land.

Unlike many other inputs into the production process, the total supply of land is relatively fixed and cannot be significantly increased in response to higher demand and prices. Such inputs are said to be **inelastic in supply** because their quantity of supply is fixed and does not respond to price increases. In these settings, it is possible for those who own higher-quality inputs to gain competitive advantages.

Ricardo's argument concerning land as a productive input is summarized in Figure 3.1. Imagine that there are many parcels of land suitable for growing wheat. Also, suppose that the fertility of these different parcels varies from high fertility (low costs of production) to low fertility (high costs of production). It seems obvious that when the market price for wheat is low, it will only pay farmers with the most fertile land to grow wheat. Only these farmers will have costs low enough to make money when the market price

Ricardian Economics and the Resource-Based View

for wheat is low. As the market price for wheat increases, then farmers with progressively less fertile land will be able to use it to grow wheat. These observations lead to the market supply curve in panel A of Figure 3.1: As prices (P) go up, supply (S) also goes up. At some point on this supply curve, supply will equal demand (D). This point determines the market price for wheat, given supply and demand. This price is called P^* in the figure.

Now consider the situation facing two different kinds of farmers. Ricardo assumed that both these farmers follow traditional economic logic by producing a quantity (q) such that their marginal cost (MC) equals their marginal revenue

(MR); that is, they produce enough wheat so that the cost of producing the last bushel of wheat equals the revenue they will get from selling that last bushel. However, this decision for the farm with less fertile land (in panel B of the figure) generates revenues that exactly equal the average total cost (ATC) of the only capital this farmer is assumed to employ, the cost of his land. In contrast, the farmer with more fertile land (in panel C of the figure) has an average total cost (ATC) less than the market-determined price and thus is able to earn an above-normal economic profit. This is because at the market-determined price, P^*, MC equals ATC for the farmer with less fertile land, whereas MC is greater than ATC for the farmer with more fertile land.

In traditional economic analysis, the profit earned by the farmer with more fertile land should lead other farmers to enter into this market, that is, to obtain some land and produce wheat. However, all the land that can be used to produce wheat in a way that generates at least a normal return given the market price P^* is already in production. In particular, no more very fertile land is available, and fertile land (by assumption) cannot be created. This is what is

The VRIO Framework

Armed with the RBV, it is possible to develop a set of tools for analyzing all the different resources and capabilities a firm might possess and the potential of each of these to generate competitive advantages. In this way, it will be possible to identify a firm's internal strengths and its internal weaknesses. The primary tool for accomplishing this internal analysis is called the VRIO framework.[5] The acronym, *VRIO*, in **VRIO framework** stands for four questions one must ask about a resource or capability to determine its competitive potential: the question of **V**alue, the question of **R**arity, the question of **I**mitability, and the question of **O**rganization. These four questions are summarized in Table 3.1.

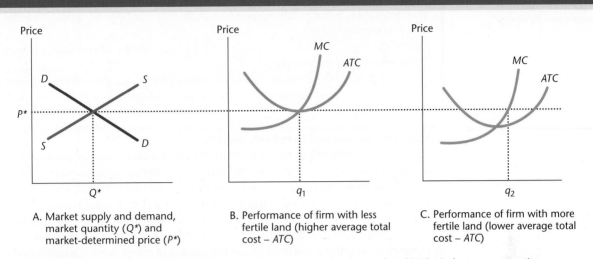

MC = marginal costs, ATC = average total costs, Q = aggregate quantity produced in the industry, q = quantity produced by each firm in the industry

Figure 3.1
The Economics of Land with Different Levels of Fertility

meant by land being inelastic in supply. Thus, the farmer with more fertile land and lower production costs has a sustained competitive advantage over those farmers with less fertile land and higher production costs. Therefore, the farmer with the more fertile land is able to earn an above-normal economic profit.

Of course, at least two events can threaten this sustained competitive advantage. First, market demand may shift down and to the left. This would force farmers with less fertile land to

cease production and would also reduce the profit of those with more fertile land. If demand shifted far enough, this profit might disappear altogether.

Second, farmers with less fertile land may discover low-cost ways of increasing their land's fertility, thereby reducing the competitive advantage of farmers with more fertile land. For example, farmers with less fertile land may be able to use inexpensive fertilizers to increase their land's fertility. The existence of such low-cost fertilizers suggests that, although *land* may be

in fixed supply, *fertility* may not be. If enough farmers can increase the fertility of their land, then the profits originally earned by the farmers with the more fertile land will disappear.

Of course, what the RBV does is recognize that land is not the only productive input that is inelastic in supply and that farmers are not the only firms that benefit from having such resources at their disposal.

Source: D. Ricardo (1817). *Principles of political economy and taxation.* London: J. Murray.

The Question of Value

The **question of value** is: "Do resources and capabilities enable a firm to exploit an external opportunity or neutralize an external threat?" If a firm answers this question with a "yes," then its resources and capabilities are valuable and can be considered *strengths.* If a firm answers this question with a "no," its resources and capabilities are *weaknesses.* There is nothing inherently valuable about a firm's resources and capabilities. Rather, they are only valuable to the extent that they enable a firm to enhance its competitive position. Sometimes, the same resources and capabilities can be strengths in one market and weaknesses in another.

TABLE 3.1 Questions Needed to Conduct a Resource-Based Analysis of a Firm's Internal Strengths and Weaknesses

1. *The Question of Value.* Does a resource enable a firm to exploit an environmental opportunity and/or neutralize an environmental threat?
2. *The Question of Rarity.* Is a resource currently controlled by only a small number of competing firms?
3. *The Question of Imitability.* Do firms without a resource face a cost disadvantage in obtaining or developing it?
4. *The Question of Organization.* Are a firm's other policies and procedures organized to support the exploitation of its valuable, rare, and costly-to-imitate resources?

Valuable Resources and Firm Performance

Sometimes it is difficult to know for sure whether a firm's resources and capabilities really enable it to exploit its external opportunities or neutralize its external threats. Sometimes this requires detailed operational information that may not be readily available. Other times, the full impact of a firm's resources and capabilities on its external opportunities and threats may not be known for some time.

One way to track the impact of a firm's resources and capabilities on its opportunities and threats is to examine the impact of using these resources and capabilities on a firm's revenues and costs. In general, firms that use their resources and capabilities to exploit opportunities or neutralize threats will see an increase in their net revenues, or a decrease in their net costs, or both, compared to the situation in which they were not using these resources and capabilities to exploit opportunities or neutralize threats. That is, the value of these resources and capabilities will generally manifest itself in either higher revenues or lower costs or both, once a firm starts using them to exploit opportunities or neutralize threats.

Applying the Question of Value

For many firms, the answer to the question of value has been "yes." That is, many firms have resources and capabilities that are used to exploit opportunities and neutralize threats, and the use of these resources and capabilities enables these firms to increase their net revenues or decrease their net costs. For example, historically Sony had a great deal of experience in designing, manufacturing, and selling miniaturized electronic technology. Sony used these resources and capabilities to exploit opportunities, including video games, digital cameras, computers and peripherals, handheld computers, home video and audio, portable audio, and car audio. 3M has used its resources and capabilities in substrates, coatings, and adhesives, along with an organizational culture that rewards risk-taking and creativity, to exploit opportunities in office products, including invisible tape and Post-It notes. Sony's and 3M's resources and capabilities—including their specific technological skills and their creative organizational cultures—have made it possible for these firms to respond to, and even create, new opportunities.[6]

Unfortunately, for other firms the answer to the question of value appears to be "no." The merger of AOL and Time Warner was supposed to create a new kind of entertainment and media company; it is now widely recognized that Time Warner has been unable to marshal the resources necessary to create economic value. Time Warner wrote off $90 billion in value in 2002; its stock price has been at record lows, and there have been rumors that it will be broken up. Ironically, many of the segments of this diverse media conglomerate continue to create value. However, the company as a whole has not realized the synergies that it was expected to generate when it was created. Put differently, these synergies—as resources and capabilities—are apparently not valuable.[7]

Strategy in the Emerging Enterprise

Entrepreneurial firms, like all other firms, must be able to answer "yes" to the question of value. That is, decisions by entrepreneurs to organize a firm to exploit an opportunity must increase revenues or reduce costs beyond what would be the case if they did not choose to organize a firm to exploit an opportunity.

However, entrepreneurs often find it difficult to answer the question of value before they actually organize a firm and try to exploit an opportunity. This is because the impact of exploiting an opportunity on a firm's revenues and costs often cannot be known, with certainty, before that opportunity is exploited.

Despite these challenges, entrepreneurs often are required to not only estimate the value of any opportunities they are thinking about exploiting, but to do so in some detail and in a written form. Projections about how organizing a firm to exploit an opportunity will affect a firm's revenues and costs are often the centerpiece of an entrepreneur's **business plan**—a document that summarizes how an entrepreneur will organize a firm to exploit an opportunity, along with the economic implications of exploiting that opportunity.

Two schools of thought exist as to the value of entrepreneurs writing business plans. On the one hand, some authors argue that writing a business plan is likely to be helpful for entrepreneurs because

Are Business Plans Good for Entrepreneurs?

it forces them to be explicit about their assumptions, exposes those assumptions to others for critique and analysis, and helps entrepreneurs focus their efforts on building a new organization and exploiting an opportunity. On the other hand, other authors argue that writing a business plan may actually hurt an entrepreneur's performance because writing such a plan may divert an entrepreneur's attention from more important activities, may give entrepreneurs the illusion that they have more control of their business than they actually do, and may lead to decision-making errors.

Research supports both points of view. Scott Shane and Frederic Delmar have shown that writing a business plan significantly enhances the probability that an entrepreneurial firm will survive. In contrast, Amar Bhide shows that most entrepreneurs go through many different business plans

before they land on one that describes a business opportunity that they actually support. For Bhide, writing the business plan is, at best, a means of helping to create a new opportunity. Because most business plans are abandoned soon after they are written, writing business plans has limited value.

One way to resolve the conflicts among these scholars is to accept that writing a business plan may be very useful in some settings and not so useful in others. In particular, when it is possible for entrepreneurs to collect sufficient information about a potential market opportunity so as to be able to describe the probability of different outcomes associated with exploiting that opportunity—a setting described as *risky* in the entrepreneurship literature—business planning can be very helpful. However, when such information cannot be collected—a setting described as *uncertain* in the entrepreneurship literature—then writing a business plan would be of only limited value, and its disadvantages might outweigh any advantages it might create.

Sources: S. Shane and F. Delmar (2004). "Planning for the market: Business planning before marketing and the continuation of organizing efforts." *Journal of Business Venturing,* 19, pp. 767–785; A. Bhide (2000). *The origin and evolution of new businesses.* New York: Oxford; F. H. Knight (1921). *Risk, uncertainty, and profit.* Chicago: University of Chicago Press; S. Alvarez and J. Barney (2006). "Discovery and creation: Alternative theories in the field of entrepreneurship." *Strategic Entrepreneurship Journal,* 1(1), pp. 11–26.

Using Value Chain Analysis to Identify Potentially Valuable Resources and Capabilities

One way to identify potentially valuable resources and capabilities controlled by a firm is to study that firm's value chain. A firm's **value chain** is the set of business activities in which it engages to develop, produce, and market its products or services. Each step in a firm's value chain requires the application and integration of different resources and capabilities. Because different firms may make different choices about which value chain activities they will engage in, they can end up developing different sets of resources and capabilities. This can be the case even if these firms are all operating in the same industry. These choices can have implications for a firm's strategies, and, as described in the Ethics and Strategy feature, they can also have implications for society more generally.

Consider, for example, the oil industry. Figure 3.2 provides a simplified list of all the business activities that must be completed if crude oil is to be turned into consumer products, such as gasoline. These activities include exploring for crude oil, drilling for crude oil, pumping crude oil, shipping crude oil, buying crude oil, refining crude oil, selling refined products to distributors, shipping refined products, and selling refined products to final customers.

Different firms may make different choices about which of these stages in the oil industry they want to operate. Thus, the firms in the oil industry may have very different resources and capabilities. For example, exploring for crude oil is very expensive and requires substantial financial resources. It also requires access to land (a physical resource), the application of substantial scientific and technical knowledge (individual resources), and an organizational commitment to risk-taking and exploration (organizational resources). Firms that operate in this stage of the oil business are likely to have very different resources and capabilities than those that, for example, sell refined oil products to final customers. To be successful in the retail stage of this industry, a firm needs retail outlets (such as stores and gas stations), which are costly to build and require both financial and physical resources. These outlets, in turn, need to be staffed by salespeople—individual resources—and marketing these products to customers through advertisements and other means can require a commitment to creativity—an organizational resource.

However, even firms that operate in the same set of value chain activities in an industry may approach these activities very differently and therefore may

Figure 3.2 A Simplified Value Chain of Activities of Oil-Based Refined Products such as Gasoline and Motor Oil

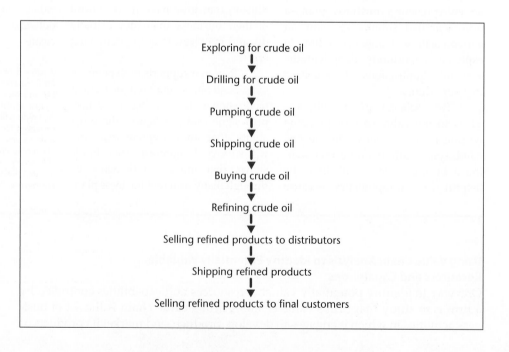

Ethics and Strategy

Strategic management adopts the perspective of a firm's owners in discussing how to gain and sustain competitive advantages. Even when adopting a stakeholder perspective (see the Ethics and Strategy feature in Chapter 1), how a firm can improve its performance and increase the wealth of its owners still takes center stage.

However, an exclusive focus on the performance of a firm and the wealth of its owners can sometimes have broader effects—on society and on the environment—that are not fully recognized. Economists call these broader effects "externalities" because they are external to the core issue in economics and strategic management of how firms can maximize their performance. They are external to this issue because firms generally do not bear the full costs of the externalities their profit-maximizing behavior creates.

Externalities can take many forms. The most obvious of these has to do with pollution and the environment. If, for example, in the process of maximizing its performance a firm engages in activities that pollute the environment, the impact of that pollution is an externality. Such pollution reduces our quality of life and hurts the environment, but the firm creating this pollution often does not bear the full costs of doing so.

Other externalities have to do with a firm's impact on the public's health. For example, when tobacco companies maximize their profits by selling tobacco to children, they are also creating a public health externality. Getting children hooked on tobacco

Externalities and the Broader Consequences of Profit Maximization

early on might be good for the bottom line of a tobacco company, but it increases the chances of these children developing lung cancer, emphysema, heart disease, and the other ailments associated with tobacco. Obviously, these individuals absorb most of the adverse consequences of these diseases, but society suffers as well from the high health care costs that are engendered.

Put differently, while adopting a simple profit-maximizing perspective in choosing and implementing strategies can have positive impacts for a firm, its owners, and its stakeholders, it can also have negative consequences for society as a whole. Two broad solutions to this problem of externalities have been proposed. First, governments can take on the responsibility of directly monitoring and regulating the behavior of firms in areas where these kinds of externalities are likely to develop. Second, governments can use lawsuits and regulations to ensure that firms directly bear more

of the costs of any externalities their behavior might generate. Once these externalities are "internalized," it is then a matter of self-interest for firms not to engage in activities that generate negative externalities.

Consumers can sometimes also help internalize the externalities generated by a firm's behavior by adjusting their consumption patterns to buy products or services only from companies that do not generate negative externalities. Consumers can even be more proactive and let firms know which of their strategies are particularly troubling. For example, many consumers united to boycott firms with operations in South Africa when South Africa was still implementing a policy of apartheid. Ultimately, this pressure not only changed the strategies of many firms; it also helped change South Africa's domestic policies. More recently, consumer pressures on pharmaceutical companies forced these firms to make their AIDS drugs more accessible in less developed countries in Africa; similar pressures forced Nike to adjust the wages and working conditions of the individuals who manufacture Nike's shoes. To the extent that sufficient demand for "socially responsible firms" exists in the marketplace, it may make profit-maximizing sense for a firm to engage in socially responsible behavior by reducing the extent to which its actions generate negative externalities.

Sources: "AIDS in Africa." *British Medical Journal*, June 1, p. 456; J. S. Friedman (2003). "Paying for apartheid." *Nation*, June 6, pp. 7+; L. Lee (2000). "Can Nike still do it?" *BusinessWeek*, February 21, pp. 121+.

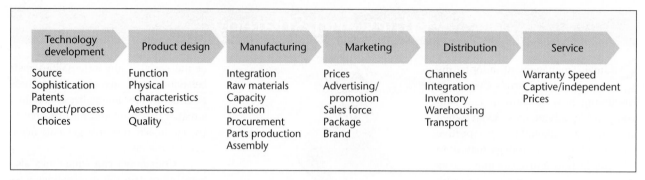

Figure 3.3
The Generic Value Chain Developed by McKinsey and Company

develop very different resources and capabilities associated with these activities. For example, two firms may sell refined oil products to final customers. However, one of these firms may sell only through retail outlets it owns, whereas the second may sell only through retail outlets it does not own. The first firm's financial and physical resources are likely to be very different from the second firm's, although these two firms may have similar individual and organizational resources.

Studying a firm's value chain forces us to think about firm resources and capabilities in a disaggregated way. Although it is possible to characterize a firm's resources and capabilities more broadly, it is usually more helpful to think about how each of the activities a firm engages in affects its financial, physical, individual, and organizational resources. With this understanding, it is possible to begin to recognize potential sources of competitive advantage for a firm in a much more detailed way.

Because this type of analysis can be so helpful in identifying the financial, physical, individual, and organizational resources and capabilities controlled by a firm, several generic value chains for identifying them have been developed. One of these, proposed by the management-consulting firm McKinsey and Company, is presented in Figure 3.3.[8] This relatively simple model suggests that the creation of value almost always involves six distinct activities: technology development, product design, manufacturing, marketing, distribution, and service. Firms can develop distinctive capabilities in any one or any combination of these activities.

The Question of Rarity

Understanding the value of a firm's resources and capabilities is an important first consideration in understanding a firm's internal strengths and weaknesses. However, if a particular resource or capability is controlled by numerous competing firms, then that resource is unlikely to be a source of competitive advantage for any one of them. Instead, valuable but common (i.e., not rare) resources and capabilities are sources of competitive parity. Only when a resource is not controlled by numerous other firms is it likely to be a source of competitive advantage. These observations lead to the **question of rarity**: "How many competing firms already possess particular valuable resources and capabilities?"

Consider, for example, competition among television sports channels. All the major networks broadcast sports. In addition, several sports-only cable channels are available, including the best-known all-sports channel, ESPN. Several years ago, ESPN began televising what were then called alternative sports—skateboarding, snowboarding, mountain biking, and so forth. The surprising popularity of these programs led ESPN to package them into an annual competition called the "X-Games." "X" stands for "extreme," and ESPN has definitely gone to the extreme in including sports in the X-Games. The X-Games have included sports such as sky-surfing, competitive high diving, competitive bungee cord jumping, and so forth. ESPN broadcasts both a summer X-Games and a winter X-Games. No other sports outlet has yet made such a commitment to so-called extreme sports, and it has paid handsome dividends for ESPN—extreme sports have very low-cost broadcast rights and draw a fairly large audience. This commitment to extreme sports—as an example of a valuable and rare capability—has been a source of at least a temporary competitive advantage for ESPN.

Of course, not all of a firm's resources and capabilities have to be valuable and rare. Indeed, most firms have a resource base that is composed primarily of valuable but common resources and capabilities. These resources cannot be sources of even temporary competitive advantage, but are essential if a firm is to gain competitive parity. Under conditions of competitive parity, although no one firm gains a competitive advantage, firms do increase their probability of survival.

Consider, for example, a telephone system as a resource or capability. Because telephone systems are widely available and because virtually all organizations have access to telephone systems, these systems are not rare and thus are not a source of competitive advantage. However, firms that do not possess a telephone system are likely to give their competitors an important advantage and place themselves at a competitive disadvantage.

How rare a valuable resource or capability must be in order to have the potential for generating a competitive advantage varies from situation to situation. It is not difficult to see that, if a firm's valuable resources and capabilities are absolutely unique among a set of current and potential competitors, they can generate a competitive advantage. However, it may be possible for a small number of firms in an industry to possess a particular valuable resource or capability and still obtain a competitive advantage. In general, as long as the number of firms that possess a particular valuable resource or capability is less than the number of firms needed to generate perfect competition dynamics in an industry, that resource or capability can be considered rare and a potential source of competitive advantage.

The Question of Imitability

Firms with valuable and rare resources are often strategic innovators because they are able to conceive and engage in strategies that other firms cannot because they lack the relevant resources and capabilities. These firms may gain the first-mover advantages discussed in Chapter 2.

Valuable and rare organizational resources, however, can be sources of sustained competitive advantage only if firms that do not possess them face a cost disadvantage in obtaining or developing them, compared to firms that already possess them. These kinds of resources are **imperfectly imitable**.[9] These observations lead to the **question of imitability**: "Do firms without a resource or capability face a cost disadvantage in obtaining or developing it compared to firms that already possess it?"

Imagine an industry with five essentially identical firms. Each of these firms manufactures the same products, uses the same raw materials, and sells the products to the same customers through the same distribution channels. It is not hard to see that firms in this kind of industry will have normal economic performance. Now, suppose that one of these firms, for whatever reason, discovers or develops a heretofore unrecognized valuable resource and uses that resource either to exploit an external opportunity or to neutralize an external threat. Obviously, this firm will gain a competitive advantage over the others.

This firm's competitors can respond to this competitive advantage in at least two ways. First, they can ignore the success of this one firm and continue as before. This action, of course, will put them at a competitive disadvantage. Second, these firms can attempt to understand why this one firm is able to be successful and then duplicate its resources to implement a similar strategy. If competitors have no cost disadvantages in acquiring or developing the needed resources, then this imitative approach will generate competitive parity in the industry.

Sometimes, however, for reasons that will be discussed later, competing firms may face an important cost disadvantage in duplicating a successful firm's valuable resources. If this is the case, this one innovative firm may gain a sustained competitive advantage—an advantage that is not competed away through strategic imitation. Firms that possess and exploit costly-to-imitate, rare, and valuable resources in choosing and implementing their strategies may enjoy a period of sustained competitive advantage.[10]

For example, other sports networks have observed the success of ESPN's X-Games and are beginning to broadcast similar competitions. NBC, for example, developed its own version of the X-Games, called the "Gravity Games," and even the Olympics now include sports that were previously perceived as being "too extreme" for this mainline sports competition. Several Fox sports channels broadcast programs that feature extreme sports, and at least one new cable channel (Fuel) broadcasts only extreme sports. Fuel was recently acquired by Fox to provide another outlet for extreme sports on a Fox channel. Whether these efforts will be able to attract the competitors that the X-Games attract, whether winners at these other competitions will gain as much status in their sports as do winners of the X-Games, and whether these other competitions and programs will gain the reputation among viewers enjoyed by ESPN will go a long way to determining whether ESPN's competitive advantage in extreme sports is temporary or sustained.[11]

Forms of Imitation: Direct Duplication and Substitution

In general, imitation occurs in one of two ways: **direct duplication** or **substitution**. Imitating firms can attempt to directly duplicate the resources possessed by the firm with a competitive advantage. Thus, NBC sponsoring an alternative extreme games competition can be thought of as an effort to directly duplicate the resources that enabled ESPN's X-Games to be successful. If the cost of this direct duplication is too high, then a firm with these resources and capabilities may obtain a sustained competitive advantage. If this cost is not too high, then any competitive advantages in this setting will be temporary.

Imitating firms can also attempt to substitute other resources for a costly-to-imitate resource possessed by a firm with a competitive advantage. Extreme sports shows and an extreme sports cable channel are potential substitutes for ESPN's X-Games strategy. These shows appeal to much the same audience as the X-Games, but they do not require the same resources as an X-Games strategy requires (i.e., because they are not competitions, they do not require the network to bring together a large number of athletes all at once). If substitute resources exist and if imitating firms do not face a cost disadvantage in obtaining them, then the competitive advantage of other firms will be temporary. However, if these resources have no substitutes or if the cost of acquiring these substitutes is greater than the cost of obtaining the original resources, then competitive advantages can be sustained.

Why Might It Be Costly to Imitate Another Firm's Resources or Capabilities?

A number of authors have studied why it might be costly for one firm to imitate the resources and capabilities of another. Four sources of costly imitation have been noted.[12] They are summarized in Table 3.2 and discussed in the following text.

Unique Historical Conditions. It may be the case that a firm was able to acquire or develop its resources and capabilities in a low-cost manner because of its unique historical conditions. The ability of firms to acquire, develop, and use resources often depends on their place in time and space. Once time and history pass, firms that do not have space-and-time-dependent resources face a significant cost disadvantage in obtaining and developing them because doing so would require them to re-create history.[13]

ESPN's early commitment to extreme sports is an example of these unique historical conditions. The status and reputation of the X-Games were created because ESPN happened to be the first major sports outlet that took these competitions seriously. The X-Games became the most important competition in many of these extreme sports. Indeed, for snowboarders, winning a gold medal in the X-Games is almost as important as—if not more important than—winning a gold medal in the Winter Olympics. Other sports outlets that hope to be able to compete with the X-Games will have to overcome both the status of ESPN as "the worldwide leader in sports" and its historical advantage in extreme sports. Overcoming these advantages is likely to be costly, making competitive threats from direct duplication, at least, less significant.

Of course, firms can also act to increase the costliness of imitating the resources and capabilities they control. ESPN is doing this by expanding its

TABLE 3.2 Sources of Costly Imitation

Unique Historical Conditions. When a firm gains low-cost access to resources because of its place in time and space, other firms may find these resources to be costly to imitate. Both first-mover advantages and path dependence can create unique historical conditions.

Causal Ambiguity. When competitors cannot tell, for sure, what enables a firm to gain an advantage, that advantage may be costly to imitate. Sources of causal ambiguity include when competitive advantages are based on "taken-for-granted" resources and capabilities, when multiple non-testable hypotheses exist about why a firm has a competitive advantage, and when a firm's advantages are based on complex sets of interrelated capabilities.

Social Complexity. When the resources and capabilities a firm uses to gain a competitive advantage involve interpersonal relationships, trust, culture, and other social resources that are costly to imitate in the short term.

Patents. Only a source of sustained competitive advantage in a few industries, including pharmaceuticals and specialty chemicals.

coverage of extreme sports and by engaging in a "grassroots" marketing campaign that engages young "extreme athletes" in local competitions. The purpose of these efforts is clear: to keep ESPN's status as the most important source of extreme sports competitions intact.[14]

Unique historical circumstances can give a firm a sustained competitive advantage in at least two ways. First, it may be that a particular firm was the first in an industry to recognize and exploit an opportunity, and being first gave the firm one or more of the first-mover advantages discussed in Chapter 2. Thus, although in principle other firms in an industry could have exploited an opportunity, that only one firm did so makes it more costly for other firms to imitate the original firm.

A second way that history can have an impact on a firm builds on the concept of **path dependence**.[15] A process is said to be path dependent when events early in the evolution of a process have significant effects on subsequent events. In the evolution of competitive advantage, path dependence suggests that a firm may gain a competitive advantage in the current period based on the acquisition and development of resources in earlier periods. In these earlier periods, it is often not clear what the full future value of particular resources will be. Because of this uncertainty, firms are able to acquire or develop these resources for less than what will turn out to be their full value. However, once the full value of these resources is revealed, other firms seeking to acquire or develop these resources will need to pay their full known value, which (in general) will be greater than the costs incurred by the firm that acquired or developed these resources in some earlier period. The cost of acquiring both duplicate and substitute resources would rise once their full value became known.

Consider, for example, a firm that purchased land for ranching some time ago and discovered a rich supply of oil on this land in the current period. The difference between the value of this land as a supplier of oil (high) and the value of this land for ranching (low) is a source of competitive advantage for this firm. Moreover, other firms attempting to acquire this or adjacent land will now have to pay for the full value of the land in its use as a supply of oil (high) and thus will be at a cost disadvantage compared to the firm that acquired it some time ago for ranching.

Causal Ambiguity.   A second reason why a firm's resources and capabilities may be costly to imitate is that imitating firms may not understand the relationship between the resources and capabilities controlled by a firm and that firm's competitive advantage. In other words, the relationship between firm resources and capabilities and competitive advantage may be **causally ambiguous**.

At first, it seems unlikely that causal ambiguity about the sources of competitive advantage for a firm would ever exist. Managers in a firm seem likely to understand the sources of their own competitive advantage. If managers in one firm understand the relationship between resources and competitive advantage, then it seems likely that managers in other firms would also be able to discover these relationships and thus would have a clear understanding of which resources and capabilities they should duplicate or seek substitutes for. If there are no other sources of cost disadvantage for imitating firms, imitation should lead to competitive parity and normal economic performance.[16]

However, it is not always the case that managers in a particular firm will fully understand the relationship between the resources and capabilities they control and competitive advantage. This lack of understanding could occur for at least three reasons. First, it may be that the resources and capabilities that generate competitive advantage are so taken for granted, so much a part of the day-to-day experience of managers in a firm, that these managers are unaware of them.[17] Organizational resources and capabilities such as teamwork among top managers, organizational culture, relationships among other employees, and relationships with customers and suppliers may be almost "invisible" to managers in a firm.[18] If managers in firms that have such capabilities do not understand their relationship to competitive advantage, managers in other firms face significant challenges in understanding which resources they should imitate.

Second, managers may have multiple hypotheses about which resources and capabilities enable their firm to gain a competitive advantage, but they may be unable to evaluate which of these resources and capabilities, alone or in combination, actually create the competitive advantage. For example, if one asks successful entrepreneurs what enabled them to be successful, they are likely to reply with several hypotheses, such as "hard work, willingness to take risks, and a high-quality top management team." However, if one asks what happened to unsuccessful entrepreneurs, they, too, are likely to suggest that their firms were characterized by "hard work, willingness to take risks, and a high-quality top management team." It may be the case that "hard work, willingness to take risks, and a high-quality top management team" are important resources and capabilities for entrepreneurial firm success, but other factors may also play a role. Without rigorous experiments, it is difficult to establish which of these resources have a causal relationship with competitive advantage and which do not.

Finally, it may be that not just a few resources and capabilities enable a firm to gain a competitive advantage, but that literally thousands of these organizational attributes, bundled together, generate these advantages. When the resources and capabilities that generate competitive advantage are complex networks of relationships between individuals, groups, and technology, imitation can be costly.

Whenever the sources of competitive advantage are widely diffused across people, locations, and processes in a firm, those sources will be costly to imitate. Perhaps the best example of such a resource is knowledge itself. To the extent that valuable knowledge about a firm's products, processes, customers, and so on is widely diffused throughout an organization, competitors will have difficulty imitating that knowledge, and it can be a source of sustained competitive advantage.[19]

Social Complexity.   A third reason that a firm's resources and capabilities may be costly to imitate is that they may be socially complex phenomena, beyond the ability of firms to systematically manage and influence. When competitive advantages are based on such complex social phenomena, the ability of other firms to imitate these resources and capabilities, either through direct duplication or substitution, is significantly constrained. Efforts to influence these kinds of phenomena are likely to be much more costly than they would be if these phenomena developed in a natural way over time in a firm.[20]

A wide variety of firm resources and capabilities may be **socially complex**. Examples include the interpersonal relations among managers in a firm, a firm's culture, and a firm's reputation among suppliers and customers.[21] Notice that in most of these cases it is possible to specify how these socially complex resources add value to a firm. Thus, there is little or no causal ambiguity surrounding the link between these firm resources and capabilities and competitive advantage. However, understanding that an organizational culture with certain attributes or quality relations among managers can improve a firm's efficiency and effectiveness does not necessarily imply that firms lacking these attributes can engage in systematic efforts to create them or that low-cost substitutes for them exist. For the time being, such social engineering may be beyond the abilities of most firms. At the very least, such social engineering is likely to be much more costly than it would be if socially complex resources evolved naturally within a firm.[22]

It is interesting to note that firms seeking to imitate complex physical technology often do not face the cost disadvantages of imitating complex social phenomena. A great deal of physical technology (machine tools, robots, and so forth) can be purchased in supply markets. Even when a firm develops its own unique physical technology, reverse engineering tends to diffuse this technology among competing firms in a low-cost manner. Indeed, the costs of imitating a successful physical technology are often lower than the costs of developing a new technology.[23]

Although physical technology is usually not costly to imitate, the application of this technology in a firm is likely to call for a wide variety of socially complex organizational resources and capabilities. These organizational resources may be costly to imitate, and if they are valuable and rare, the combination of physical and socially complex resources may be a source of sustained competitive advantage. The importance of socially complex resources and capabilities for firm performance has been studied in detail in the field of strategic human resource management, as described in the Research Made Relevant feature.

Patents.   At first glance, it might appear that a firm's patents would make it very costly for competitors to imitate its products.[24] Patents do have this effect in some industries. For example, patents in the pharmaceutical and specialty chemical industry effectively foreclose other firms from marketing the same products until a firm's patents expire. As suggested in Chapter 2, patents can raise the cost of imitation in a variety of other industries as well.

However, from another point of view a firm's patents may decrease, rather than increase, the costs of imitation. When a firm files for patent protection, it is forced to reveal a significant amount of information about its product. Governments require this information to ensure that the technology in question is patentable. By obtaining a patent, a firm may provide important information to competitors about how to imitate its technology.

Moreover, most technological developments in an industry are diffused throughout firms in that industry in a relatively brief period of time, even if the technology in question is patented, because patented technology is not immune from low-cost imitation. Patents may restrict direct duplication for a time, but they may actually increase the chances of substitution by functionally equivalent technologies.[25]

The Question of Organization

A firm's potential for competitive advantage depends on the value, rarity, and imitability of its resources and capabilities. However, to fully realize this potential, a firm must be organized to exploit its resources and capabilities. These observations lead to the **question of organization**: "Is a firm organized to exploit the full competitive potential of its resources and capabilities?"

Numerous components of a firm's organization are relevant to the question of organization, including its formal reporting structure, its formal and informal management control systems, and its compensation policies. A firm's **formal reporting**

Research Made Relevant

Most empirical tests of the RBV have focused on the extent to which history, causal ambiguity, and social complexity have an impact on the ability of firms to gain and sustain competitive advantages. Among the most important of these tests has been research that examines the extent to which human resource practices that are likely to generate socially complex resources and capabilities are related to firm performance. This area of research is known as *strategic human resources management.*

The first of these tests was conducted as part of a larger study of efficient low-cost manufacturing in the worldwide automobile industry. A group of researchers from Massachusetts Institute of Technology developed rigorous measures of the cost and quality of more than 70 manufacturing plants that assembled mid-size sedans around the world. They discovered that at the time of their study only six of these plants had simultaneous low costs and high-quality manufacturing—a position that obviously would give these plants a competitive advantage in the marketplace.

Strategic Human Resource Management Research

In trying to understand what distinguished these six plants from the others in the sample, the researchers found that, not surprisingly, these six plants had the most modern and up-to-date manufacturing technology. However, so did many of the less effective plants. What distinguished these effective plants was not their manufacturing technology, per se, but their human resource (HR) practices. These six plants all implemented a bundle of such practices that included participative decision making, quality circles, and an emphasis on team production. One of the results of these efforts—and

another distinguishing feature of these six plants—was a high level of employee loyalty and commitment to a plant, as well as the belief that plant managers would treat employees fairly. These socially complex resources and capabilities are the types of resources that the RBV suggests should be sources of sustained competitive advantage.

Later work has followed up on this approach and has examined the impact of HR practices on firm performance outside the manufacturing arena. Using a variety of measures of firm performance and several different measures of HR practices, the results of this research continue to be very consistent with RBV logic. That is, firms that are able to use HR practices to develop socially complex human and organizational resources are able to gain competitive advantages over firms that do not engage in such practices.

Sources: J. P. Womack, D. I. Jones, and D. Roos (1990). *The machine that changed the world.* New York: Rawson; M. Huselid (1995). "The impact of human resource management practices on turnover, productivity, and corporate financial performance." *Academy of Management Journal,* 38, pp. 635–672; J. B. Barney and P. Wright (1998). "On becoming a strategic partner." *Human Resource Management,* 37, pp. 31–46.

structure is a description of whom in the organization reports to whom; it is often embodied in a firm's **organizational chart**. **Management control systems** include a range of formal and informal mechanisms to ensure that managers are behaving in ways consistent with a firm's strategies. **Formal management controls** include a firm's budgeting and reporting activities that keep people higher up in a firm's organizational chart informed about the actions taken by people lower down in a firm's organizational chart. **Informal management controls** might include a firm's culture and the willingness of employees to monitor each other's behavior. **Compensation policies** are the ways that firms pay employees. Such policies create incentives for employees to behave in certain ways.

These components of a firm's organization are often called **complementary resources and capabilities** because they have limited ability to generate competitive advantage in isolation. However, in combination with other resources and capabilities they can enable a firm to realize its full potential for competitive advantage.[26]

For example, it has already been suggested that ESPN may have a sustained competitive advantage in the extreme sports segment of the sports broadcasting industry. However, if ESPN's management had not taken advantage of its opportunities in extreme sports by expanding coverage, ensuring that the best competitors come to ESPN competitions, adding additional competitions, and changing up older competitions, then its potential for competitive advantage would not have been fully realized. Of course, the reason that ESPN has done all these things is because it has an appropriate organizational structure, management controls, and employee compensation policies. By themselves, these attributes of ESPN's organization could not be a source of competitive advantage; however, they were essential for ESPN to realize its full competitive advantage potential.

Having an appropriate organization in place has enabled ESPN to realize the full competitive advantage potential of its other resources and capabilities. Having an inappropriate organization in place prevented Sony from exploiting its valuable, rare, and costly-to-imitate resources and capabilities.

Earlier in this chapter, it was suggested that Sony had unusual experience in designing and building a wide variety of consumer electronics products. In the process of building this giant consumer electronics company, managers at Sony developed and acquired two substantial businesses: Sony Consumer Electronics and Sony Records.

Among the many products developed by the Consumer Electronics business was an early MP3 player (i.e., a portable device that played music and other digital media from a hard drive). The key to MP3 technology was compression—taking analog signals and storing them in a way that they did not take up disproportionate space on the hard drive. Without compression, you could only store a few songs on an MP3 player; with compression, you can store thousands. Sony was a leader in compression technology.

Of course, to be effective, MP3 players must have content to play. Here, the Sony Records Division should have been very helpful to the Consumer Electronics Division: Records had recording contracts with many famous artists, and Consumer Products had the MP3 player (along with compression technology) to play that music.

So, why does Apple—with iPods, iTunes, iPhones, and iPads—dominate the portable music listening market? Apple had no advantages. It was late to the MP3 market (although it did introduce an MP3 player with a particularly elegant interface), it did not own any content, and it had a limited online presence.

One explanation of Apple's success is Sony's failure—despite having the potential to dominate this market, despite its history of dominating similar markets in the past (e.g., the Sony Walkman portable tape player), Sony could not find a way for its two divisions—Consumer Electronics and Music—to cooperate. Put differently, Sony's failure was a failure in organization. The engineers in the Consumer Electronics business could never find a way to work with the artists in the music business.

Of course, Apple had to do a great deal more to take advantage of the opportunity that Sony's organization failure had created for them. Nevertheless, despite its potential, Sony failed to gain or sustain any significant competitive advantages in this lucrative MP3 market.[27]

Applying the VRIO Framework

The questions of value, rarity, imitability, and organization can be brought together into a single framework to understand the return potential associated with exploiting any of a firm's resources or capabilities. This is done in Table 3.3. The relationship of the VRIO framework to strengths and weaknesses is presented in Table 3.4.

If a resource or capability controlled by a firm is not valuable, it will not enable a firm to choose or implement strategies that exploit environmental opportunities or neutralize environmental threats. Organizing to exploit this resource will increase a firm's costs or decrease its revenues. These types of resources are weaknesses. Firms will either have to fix these weaknesses or avoid using them when choosing and implementing strategies. If firms do exploit these kinds of resources and capabilities, they can expect to put themselves at a competitive disadvantage compared to those that either do not possess these nonvaluable resources or do not use them in conceiving and implementing strategies.

If a resource or capability is valuable but not rare, exploitation of this resource in conceiving and implementing strategies will generate competitive parity. Exploiting these types of resources will generally not create competitive advantages, but failure to exploit them can put a firm at a competitive disadvantage. In this sense, valuable-but-not-rare resources can be thought of as organizational strengths.

If a resource or capability is valuable and rare but not costly to imitate, exploiting this resource will generate a temporary competitive advantage for a firm. A firm that exploits this kind of resource is, in an important sense, gaining a first-mover advantage because it is the first firm that is able to exploit a particular resource. However, once competing firms observe this competitive advantage, they will be able to acquire or develop the resources needed to implement this strategy through direct duplication or substitution at no cost disadvantage, compared to the first-moving firm. Over time, any competitive advantage that the first mover obtained would be competed away as other firms imitate the resources needed to compete. Consequently, this type of resource or capability can be thought of as an organizational strength and as a **distinctive competence**.

If a resource or capability is valuable, rare, and costly to imitate, exploiting it will generate a sustained competitive advantage. In this case, competing firms

TABLE 3.3 The VRIO Framework

Is a resource or capability:				
Valuable?	**Rare?**	**Costly to imitate?**	**Exploited by organization?**	**Competitive implications**
No	—	—	No	Competitive disadvantage
Yes	No	—	↑	Competitive parity
Yes	Yes	No		Temporary competitive advantage
Yes	Yes	Yes	↓ Yes	Sustained competitive advantage

TABLE 3.4 The Relationship Between the VRIO Framework and Organizational Strengths and Weaknesses

Is a resource or capability:

Valuable?	Rare?	Costly to imitate?	Exploited by organization?	Strength or weakness
No	—	—	No	Weakness
Yes	No	—	↑	Strength
Yes	Yes	No		Strength and distinctive competence
Yes	Yes	Yes	Yes	Strength and sustainable distinctive competence

face a significant cost disadvantage in imitating a successful firm's resources and capabilities. As suggested earlier, this competitive advantage may reflect the unique history of the successful firm, causal ambiguity about which resources to imitate, the socially complex nature of these resources and capabilities, or any patent advantages a firm might possess. In any case, attempts to compete away the advantages of firms that exploit these resources will not generate competitive advantage, or even competitive parity, for imitating firms. Even if these firms are able to acquire or develop the resources or capabilities in question, the very high costs of doing so would put them at a competitive disadvantage. These kinds of resources and capabilities are organizational strengths and **sustainable distinctive competencies**.

The question of organization operates as an adjustment factor in the VRIO framework. For example, if a firm has a valuable, rare, and costly-to-imitate resource and capability but fails to organize itself to take full advantage of this resource, some of its potential competitive advantage could be lost (this is the Sony example). Extremely poor organization, in this case, could actually lead a firm that has the potential for competitive advantage to gain only competitive parity or competitive disadvantages.

Applying the VRIO Framework to Southwest Airlines

To examine how the VRIO framework can be applied in analyzing real strategic situations, consider the competitive position of Southwest Airlines. Southwest Airlines has been the only consistently profitable airline in the United States over the past 30 years. While many U.S. airlines have gone in and out of bankruptcy, Southwest has remained profitable. How has it been able to gain this competitive advantage?

Potential sources of this competitive advantage fall into two big categories: operational choices Southwest has made and Southwest's approach to managing its people. On the operational side, Southwest has chosen to fly only a single type of aircraft (Boeing 737), only flies into smaller airports, has avoided complicated hub-and-spoke route systems, and, instead, flies a point-to-point system. On the people-management side, despite being highly unionized, Southwest has been able to develop a sense of commitment and loyalty among its employees. It is not unusual to see Southwest employees go well beyond their narrowly defined job responsibilities, helping out in whatever way is necessary to get a plane off the ground safely and on time. Which of these—operational choices or Southwest's approach to managing its people—is more likely to be a source of sustained competitive advantage?

Southwest's Operational Choices and Competitive Advantage

Consider first Southwest's operational choices. First, do these operational choices reduce Southwest's costs or increase the willingness of its customers to pay—that is, are these operational choices valuable? It can be shown that most of Southwest's operational choices have the effect of reducing its costs. For example, by flying only one type of airliner, Southwest is able to reduce the cost of training its maintenance staff, reduce its spare parts inventory, and reduce the time its planes are being repaired. By flying into smaller airports, Southwest reduces the fees it would otherwise have to pay to land at larger airports. Its point-to-point system of routes avoids the costs associated with establishing large hub-and-spoke systems. Overall, these operational choices are valuable.

Second, are these operational choices rare? For most of its history, Southwest's operational choices have been rare. Only recently have large incumbent airlines and smaller new entrants begun to implement similar operational choices.

Third, are these operational choices costly to imitate? Several incumbent airline firms have set up subsidiaries designed to emulate most of Southwest's operational choices. For example, Continental created the Continental Lite division, United created the Ted division, and Delta created the Song division. All of these divisions chose a single type of airplane to fly, flew into smaller airports, adopted a point-to-point route structure, and so forth.

In addition to these incumbent airlines, many new entrants into the airline industry—both in the United States and elsewhere—have adopted similar operational choices as Southwest. In the United States, these new entrants include AirTran Airlines (recently purchased by Southwest), Allegiant Airlines, JetBlue, Skybus Airlines (now bankrupt), Spirit Airlines, and Virgin American Airlines.

Thus, while Southwest's operational choices are valuable and have been rare, they are apparently not costly to imitate. This is not surprising because these operational choices have few of the attributes of resources or capabilities that are costly to imitate. They do not derive from a firm's unique history, they are not path dependent, they are not causally ambiguous, and they are not socially complex.

Finally, is Southwest organized to fully exploit its operational choices? Most observers agree that Southwest's structure, management controls, and compensation policies are consistent with its operational choices.

Taken together, this analysis of Southwest's operational choices suggests that they are valuable, have been rare, but are not costly to imitate. While Southwest is organized to exploit these opportunities, they are likely to be only a source of temporary competitive advantage for Southwest.

Southwest's People-Management and Competitive Advantage

A similar VRIO analysis can be conducted for Southwest's approach to people management. First, is this approach valuable; that is, does it reduce Southwest's costs or increase the willingness of its customers to pay?

Employee commitment and loyalty at Southwest is one explanation of why Southwest is able to get higher levels of employee productivity than most other U.S. airlines. This increased productivity shows up in numerous ways. For example, the average turnaround time for Southwest flights is around 18 minutes. The average turnaround time for the average U.S. airline is 45 minutes. Southwest Airline employees are simply more effective in unloading and loading luggage, fueling, and catering their airplanes than employees in other airlines. This means that Southwest Airlines airplanes are on the ground for less time and in the air more time than its competitors. Of course, an airplane is only making money if it is in the air. This seemingly simple idea is worth hundreds of millions of dollars in lower costs to Southwest.

Have such loyalty and teamwork been rare in the U.S. airline industry? Over the past 15 years, the U.S. airline industry has been wracked by employment strife. Many airlines have had to cut employment, reduce wages, and in other ways strain their relationship with their employees. Overall, in comparison to incumbent airlines, the relationship that Southwest enjoys with its employees has been rare.

Is this relationship costly to imitate? Certainly, relationships between an airline and its employees have many of the attributes that should make them costly to imitate. They emerge over time; they are path dependent, causally ambiguous, and socially complex. It is reasonable to expect that incumbent airlines, airlines that already have strained relationships with their employees, would have difficulty imitating the relationship Southwest enjoys with its employees. Thus, in comparison to incumbent airlines, Southwest's approach to managing its people is probably valuable, rare, and costly to imitate. Assuming it is organized appropriately (and this seems to be the case), this would mean that—relative to incumbent airlines—Southwest has a sustained competitive advantage.

The situation may be somewhat different for new entrants into the U.S. airline industry. These airlines may not have a history of strained employee relationships. As new firms, they may be able to develop more valuable employee relationships from the very beginning. This suggests that, relative to new entrants, Southwest's approach to people management may be valuable and rare, but not costly to imitate. Again, assuming Southwest is organized appropriately, relative to new entrants into the U.S. airline industry, Southwest's people-management capabilities may be a source of only a temporary competitive advantage.

Imitation and Competitive Dynamics in an Industry

Suppose a firm in an industry has conducted an analysis of its resources and capabilities, concludes that it possesses some valuable, rare, and costly-to-imitate resources and capabilities, and uses these to choose a strategy that it implements with the appropriate organizational structure, formal and informal management controls, and compensation policies. The RBV suggests that this firm will gain a competitive advantage even if it is operating in what an environmental threat analysis (see Chapter 2) would suggest is a very unattractive industry. Examples of firms that have competitive advantages in unattractive industries include Southwest Airlines, Nucor Steel, and Wal-Mart, to name a few.

Given that a particular firm in an industry has a competitive advantage, how should other firms respond? Decisions made by other firms given the strategic choices of a particular firm define the nature of the **competitive dynamics** that exist in an industry. In general, other firms in an industry can respond to the advantages of a competitor in one of three ways. First, they can choose to limit their response. For example, when Wal-Mart entered the discount grocery market with the creation of Super Walmarts, some competitors (e.g., Safeway) ignored Wal-Mart's moves and continued on as before. Other competitors (e.g., Kroger) modified some of their tactics, including, for example, selling more prepared foods and more specialty foods than before. Finally, other firms fundamentally altered their strategies (e.g., Target began building stores that also sold discount groceries).

Not Responding to Another Firm's Competitive Advantage

A firm might not respond to another firm's competitive advantage for at least three reasons. First, this firm might have its own competitive advantage. By responding to another firm's competitive advantage, it might destroy, or at least compromise, its own sources of competitive advantage. For example, digital time-keeping has made accurate watches available to most consumers at reasonable prices. A firm such as Casio has a competitive advantage in this market because of its miniaturization and electronic capabilities. Indeed, Casio's market share and performance in the watch business continue to climb although demand for watches, overall, has gone down. How should Rolex—a manufacturer of very expensive, non-electronic watches—respond to Casio? Rolex's decision has been: *Not at all.* Rolex appeals to a very different market segment than Casio. Should Rolex change its strategies—even if it replaced its mechanical self-winding design with the technologically superior digital design—it could easily compromise its competitive advantage in its own niche market.[28] In general, when a firm already possesses its own sources of competitive advantage, it will not respond to different sources of competitive advantage controlled by another firm.

Second, a firm may not respond to another firm's competitive advantage because it does not have the resources and capabilities to do so. A firm with insufficient or inappropriate resources and capabilities—be they physical, financial, human, or organizational—typically will not be able to imitate a successful firm's resources either through direct duplication or substitution. This may very well be the case with US Airways and Southwest Airlines. It may simply be beyond the ability of US Airways to imitate Southwest's managerial resources and capabilities. In this setting, US Airways is likely to find itself at a sustained competitive disadvantage.[29]

Finally, a firm may not respond to the advantages of a competitor because it is trying to reduce the level of rivalry in an industry. Any actions a firm takes that have the effect of reducing the level of rivalry in an industry and that also do not require firms in an industry to directly communicate or negotiate with each other can be thought of as **tacit cooperation**. Explicit cooperation, where firms do directly communicate and negotiate with each other, is discussed in detail in Chapter 9's analysis of strategic alliances.

Reducing the level of rivalry in an industry can benefit all firms operating in that industry. This decision can have the effect of reducing the quantity of goods and services provided in an industry to below the competitive level, actions that will have the effect of increasing the prices of these goods or services. When tacit cooperation has the effect of reducing supply and increasing prices, it is known as **tacit collusion**. Tacit collusion can be illegal in some settings. However, firms can also tacitly cooperate along other dimensions besides quantity and price. These actions can also benefit all the firms in an industry and typically are not illegal.[30]

For example, it may be that firms can tacitly agree not to invest in certain kinds of research and development. Some forms of research and development are very expensive, and although these investments might end up generating products or services that could benefit customers, firms might still prefer to avoid the expense and risk. Firms can also tacitly agree not to market their products in certain ways. For example, before regulations compelled them to do so, most tobacco companies had already decided not to put cigarette vending machines in locations usually frequented by children, even though these machines could have generated significant revenues. Also, firms can tacitly cooperate by agreeing not

TABLE 3.5 Attributes of Industry Structure That Facilitate the Development of Tacit Cooperation

1. Small number of competing firms
2. Homogeneous products and costs
3. Market-share leader
4. High barriers to entry

to engage in certain manufacturing practices, such as outsourcing to developing countries and engaging in environmentally unsound practices.

All of these actions can have the effect of reducing the level of rivalry in an industry. And reducing the level of rivalry can have the effect of increasing the average level of performance for a firm in an industry. However, tacit cooperative relationships among firms are sometimes difficult to maintain. Typically, in order for tacit cooperation to work, an industry must have the structural attributes described in Table 3.5. First, the industry must have relatively few firms. Informally communicating and coordinating strategies among a few firms is difficult enough; it is even more difficult when the industry has a large number of firms. For this reason, tacit cooperation is a viable strategy only when an industry is an oligopoly (see Chapter 2).

Second, firms in this industry must be homogeneous with respect to the products they sell and their cost structure. Having heterogeneous products makes it too easy for a firm to "cheat" on its tacitly cooperative agreements by modifying its products, and heterogeneous cost means that the optimal level of output for a particular firm may be very different from the level agreed to through tacit cooperation. In this setting, a firm might have a strong incentive to increase its output and upset cooperative agreements.

Third, an industry typically has to have at least one strong market-share leader if firms are going to tacitly cooperate. This would be a relatively large firm that has established an example of the kind of behavior that will be mutually beneficial in the industry, and other firms in the industry sometimes fall into line with this example. Indeed, it is often the market-share leader that will choose not to respond to the competitive actions of another firm in the industry in order to maintain cooperative relations.

Finally, the maintenance of tacit cooperation in an industry almost always requires the existence of high barriers to entry. If tacit cooperation is successful, the average performance of firms in an industry will improve. However, this higher level of performance can induce other firms to enter into this industry (see Chapter 2). Such entry will increase the number of firms in an industry and make it very difficult to maintain tacitly cooperative relationships. Thus, it must be very costly for new firms to enter into an industry for those in that industry to maintain their tacit cooperation. The higher these costs, the higher the barriers to entry.

Changing Tactics in Response to Another Firm's Competitive Advantage

Tactics are the specific actions a firm takes to implement its strategies. Examples of tactics include decisions firms make about various attributes of their products—including size, shape, color, and price—specific advertising approaches adopted by a firm, and specific sales and marketing efforts. Generally, firms change their tactics much more frequently than they change their strategies.[31]

When competing firms are pursuing approximately the same strategies, the competitive advantages that any one firm might enjoy at a given point in time are most likely due to the tactics that that firm is pursuing. In this setting, it is not unusual for competing firms to change their tactics by imitating the tactics of the firm with an advantage in order to reduce that firm's advantage. Although changing one's tactics in this manner will only generate competitive parity, this is usually better than the competitive disadvantage these firms were experiencing.

Several industries provide excellent examples of these kinds of tactical interactions. In consumer goods, for example, if one company increases its sales by adding a "lemon scent" to laundry detergent, then lemon scents start showing up in everyone's laundry detergent. If Coke starts selling a soft drink with half the sugar and half the carbs of regular Coke, can Pepsi's low-sugar/low-carb product be far behind? And when Delta Airlines cuts it airfares, can American and United be far behind? Not surprisingly, these kinds of tactical changes, because they initially may be valuable and rare, are seldom costly to imitate and thus are typically only sources of temporary competitive advantage.

Sometimes, rather than simply imitating the tactics of a firm with a competitive advantage, a firm at a disadvantage may "leapfrog" its competitors by developing an entirely new set of tactics. Procter & Gamble engaged in this strategy when it introduced its laundry detergent, Tide, in a new, concentrated formula. This new formulation required new manufacturing and packaging equipment—the smaller box could not be filled in the current manufacturing lines in the industry—which meant that Tide's competitors had to take more time in imitating the concentrated laundry detergent tactic than other tactics pursued in this industry. Nevertheless, within just a few weeks other firms in this market were introducing their own versions of concentrated laundry detergent.

Indeed, some firms can become so skilled at innovating new products and other tactics that this innovative capability can be a source of sustained competitive advantage. Consider, for example, Sony during its heydays. Most observers agree that Sony possessed some special management and innovation skills that enabled it to conceive, design, and manufacture high-quality miniaturized consumer electronics. However, virtually every time Sony brought out a new miniaturized product several of its competitors quickly duplicated that product through reverse engineering, thereby reducing Sony's technological advantage. In what way can Sony's socially complex miniaturization resources and capabilities be a source of sustained competitive advantage when most of Sony's products were quickly imitated through direct duplication?

After Sony introduced each new product, it experienced a rapid increase in profits attributable to the new product's unique features. This increase, however, leads other firms to reverse-engineer the Sony product and introduce their own versions. Increased competition resulted in a reduction in the profits associated with a new product. Thus, at the level of individual products, Sony apparently enjoys only temporary competitive advantages. However, looking at the total returns earned by Sony across all of its new products over time makes clear the source of Sony's sustained competitive advantage: By exploiting its resources and capabilities in miniaturization, Sony was able to constantly introduce new and exciting personal electronics products. No single product generated a sustained competitive advantage, but, over time, across several such product introductions, Sony's resource and capability advantages led to sustained competitive advantages.[32]

Changing Strategies in Response to Another Firm's Competitive Advantage

Finally, firms sometimes respond to another firm's competitive advantage by changing their strategies. Obviously, this does not occur very often, and it typically only occurs when another firm's strategies usurp a firm's competitive advantage. In this setting, a firm will not be able to gain even competitive parity if it maintains its strategy, even if it implements that strategy very effectively.

Changes in consumer tastes, in population demographics, and in the laws that govern a business can all have the effect of rendering what once was a valuable strategy as valueless. However, the most frequent impact is changes in technology. For example, no matter how well made a mechanical calculator is, it is simply inferior to an electronic calculator. No matter how efficient the telegraph was in its day, it is an inferior technology to the telephone. And no matter how quickly one's fingers can move the beads on an abacus, an electronic cash register is a better way of keeping track of sales and making change in a store.

When firms change their strategies, they must proceed through the entire strategic management process, as described in Chapter 1. However, these firms will often have difficulty abandoning their traditional strategies. For most firms, their strategy helps define what they do and who they are. Changing its strategy often requires a firm to change its identity and its purposes. These are difficult changes to make, and many firms wait to change their strategy until absolutely forced to do so by disastrous financial results. By then, these firms not only have to change their strategy—with all that implies—they have to do so in the face of significant financial pressures.

The ability of virtually all strategies to generate competitive advantages typically expires, sooner or later. In general, it is much better for a firm to change its strategy before that strategy is no longer viable. In this way, a firm can make a planned move to a new strategy that maintains whatever resources and capabilities it still possesses while it develops the new resources and capabilities it will need to compete in the future.

Implications of the Resource-Based View

The RBV and the VRIO framework can be applied to individual firms to understand whether these firms will gain competitive advantages, how sustainable these competitive advantages are likely to be, and what the sources of these competitive advantages are. In this way, the RBV and the VRIO framework can be understood as important complements to the threats and opportunities analyses described in Chapter 2.

However, beyond what these frameworks can say about the competitive performance of a particular firm, the RBV has some broader implications for managers seeking to gain competitive advantages. Some of these broader implications are listed in Table 3.6 and discussed in the following section.

Where Does the Responsibility for Competitive Advantage in a Firm Reside?

First, the RBV suggests that competitive advantages can be found in several of the different resources and capabilities controlled by the firm. These resources and capabilities are not limited to those that are controlled directly by a firm's

1. The responsibility for competitive advantage in a firm:
   Competitive advantage is every employee's responsibility.
2. Competitive parity and competitive advantage:
   If all a firm does is what its competition does, it can gain only competitive parity. In gaining competitive advantage, it is better for a firm to exploit its own valuable, rare, and costly-to-imitate resources than to imitate the valuable and rare resources of a competitor.
3. Difficult to implement strategies:
   As long as the cost of strategy implementation is less than the value of strategy implementation, the relative cost of implementing a strategy is more important for competitive advantage than the absolute cost of implementing a strategy.
   Firms can systematically overestimate and underestimate their uniqueness.
4. Socially complex resources:
   Not only can employee empowerment, organizational culture, and teamwork be valuable, they can also be sources of sustained competitive advantage.
5. The role of the organization:
   Organization should support the use of valuable, rare, and costly-to-imitate resources. If conflicts between these attributes of a firm arise, change the organization.

TABLE 3.6 Broader Implications of the Resource-Based View

senior managers. Thus, the responsibility for creating, nurturing, and exploiting valuable, rare, and costly-to-imitate resources and capabilities for competitive advantage is not restricted to senior managers, but falls on every employee in a firm. Therefore, employees should go beyond defining their jobs in functional terms and instead define their jobs in competitive and economic terms.

Consider a simple example. In a recent visit to a very successful automobile manufacturing plant, the plant manager was asked to describe his job responsibilities. He said, "My job is to manage this plant in order to help the firm make and sell the best cars in the world." In response to a similar question, the person in charge of the manufacturing line said, "My job is to manage this manufacturing line in order to help the firm make and sell the best cars in the world." A janitor was also asked to describe his job responsibilities. Although he had not been present in the two earlier interviews, the janitor responded, "My job is to keep this facility clean in order to help the firm make and sell the best cars in the world."

Which of these three employees is most likely to be a source of sustained competitive advantage for this firm? Certainly, the plant manager and the manufacturing line manager *should* define their jobs in terms of helping the firm make and sell the best cars in the world. However, it is unlikely that their responses to this question would be any different than the responses of other senior managers at other manufacturing plants around the world. Put differently, although the definition of these two managers' jobs in terms of enabling the firm to make and sell the best cars in the world is valuable, it is unlikely to be rare, and thus it is likely to be a source of competitive parity, not competitive advantage. However, a janitor who defines her job as helping the firm make and sell the best cars in the world instead of simply to clean the facility is, most would agree, quite unusual. Because it is rare, it might be a source of at least a temporary competitive advantage.[33]

The value created by one janitor defining her job in competitive terms rather than functional terms is not huge, but suppose that all the employees in this plant defined their jobs in these terms. Suddenly, the value that might be created could be substantial. Moreover, the organizational culture and tradition in a firm that would lead employees to define their jobs in this way are likely to be costly for other firms to imitate. Thus, if this approach to defining job responsibilities is broadly diffused in a particular plant, it seems likely to be valuable, rare, and costly to imitate and thus a source of sustained competitive advantage, assuming the firm is organized to take advantage of this unusual resource.

In the end, it is clear that competitive advantage is too important to remain the sole property of senior management. To the extent that employees throughout an organization are empowered to develop and exploit valuable, rare, and costly-to-imitate resources and capabilities in the accomplishment of their job responsibilities, a firm may actually be able to gain sustained competitive advantages.

Competitive Parity and Competitive Advantage

Second, the RBV suggests that, if all a firm does is create value in the same way as its competitors, the best performance it can ever expect to gain is competitive parity. To do better than competitive parity, firms must engage in valuable and rare activities. They must do things to create economic value that other firms have not even thought of, let alone implemented.

This is especially critical for firms that find themselves at a competitive disadvantage. Such a firm certainly should examine its more successful competition, understand what has made this competition so successful, and, where imitation is very low cost, imitate the successful actions of its competitors. In this sense, benchmarking a firm's performance against the performance of its competitors can be extremely important.

However, if this is all that a firm does, it can only expect to gain competitive parity. Gaining competitive advantage depends on a firm discovering its own unique resources and capabilities and how they can be used in choosing and implementing strategies. For a firm seeking competitive advantage, it is better to be excellent in how it develops and exploits its own unique resources and capabilities than it is to be excellent in how it imitates the resources and capabilities of other firms.

This does not imply that firms must always be first movers to gain competitive advantages. Some firms develop valuable, rare, and costly-to-imitate resources and capabilities in being efficient second movers—that is, in rapidly imitating and improving on the product and technological innovations of other firms. Rather than suggesting that firms must always be first movers, the RBV suggests that, in order to gain competitive advantages, firms must implement strategies that rely on valuable, rare, and costly-to-imitate resources and capabilities, whatever those strategies or resources might be.

Difficult-to-Implement Strategies

Third, as firms contemplate different strategic options, they often ask how difficult and costly it will be to implement different strategies. As long as the cost of implementing a strategy is less than the value that a strategy creates, the RBV suggests that the critical question facing firms is not "Is a strategy easy to implement or not?" but rather "Is this strategy easier for us to implement than it is for our competitors to implement?" Firms that already possess the valuable, rare, and costly-to-imitate resources needed to implement a strategy will, in general, find it easier (i.e., less costly) to implement a strategy than firms that first have to develop the required resources and then implement the proposed strategy. For firms that already possess a resource, strategy implementation can be natural and swift.

In understanding the relative costs of implementing a strategy, firms can make two errors. First, they can overestimate the uniqueness of the resources they control. Although every firm's history is unique and no two management teams are exactly the same, this does not always mean that a firm's resources and capabilities will be rare. Firms with similar histories operating in similar industries will often develop similar capabilities. If a firm overestimates the rarity of its resources and capabilities, it can overestimate its ability to generate competitive advantages.

For example, when asked what their most critical sources of competitive advantage are, many firms will cite the quality of their top management team, the quality of their technology, and their commitment to excellence in all that they do. When pushed about their competitors, these same firms will admit that they too have high-quality top management teams, high-quality technology, and a commitment to excellence in all that they do. Although these three attributes can be sources of competitive parity, they cannot be sources of competitive advantage.

Second, firms can sometimes underestimate their uniqueness and thus underestimate the extent to which the strategies they pursue can be sources of sustained competitive advantage. When firms possess valuable, rare, and costly-to-imitate resources, strategy implementation can be relatively easy. In this context, it seems reasonable to expect that other firms will be able to quickly imitate this "easy-to-implement" strategy. Of course, this is not the case if these resources controlled by a firm are, in fact, rare and costly to imitate.

In general, firms must take great care not to overestimate or underestimate their uniqueness. An accurate assessment of the value, rarity, and imitability of a firm's resources is necessary to develop an accurate understanding of the relative costs of implementing a firm's strategies and, thus, the ability of those strategies to generate competitive advantages. Often, firms must employ outside assistance in helping them describe the rarity and imitability of their resources, even though managers in firms will generally be much more familiar with the resources controlled by a firm than outsiders. However, outsiders can provide a measure of objectivity in evaluating the uniqueness of a firm.

Socially Complex Resources

Over the past several decades, much has been written about the importance of employee empowerment, organizational culture, and teamwork for firm performance. Most of this work suggests that firms that empower employees, that have an enabling culture, and that encourage teamwork will, on average, make better strategic choices and implement them more efficiently than firms without these organizational attributes. Using the language of the RBV, most of this work has suggested that employee empowerment, organizational culture, and teamwork, at least in some settings, are economically valuable.[34]

Resource-based logic acknowledges the importance of the value of these organizational attributes. However, it also suggests that these socially complex resources and capabilities can be rare and costly to imitate—and it is these attributes that make it possible for socially complex resources and capabilities to be sources of sustained competitive advantage. Put differently, the RBV actually extends and broadens traditional analyses of the socially complex attributes of firms. Not only can these attributes be valuable, but they can also be rare and costly to imitate and, thus, sources of sustained competitive advantage.

The Role of Organization

Finally, resource-based logic suggests that an organization's structure, control systems, and compensation policies should support and enable a firm's efforts to fully exploit the valuable, rare, and costly-to-imitate resources and capabilities it controls. These attributes of organization, by themselves, are usually not sources of sustained competitive advantage.

These observations suggest that if there is a conflict between the resources a firm controls and that firm's organization, the organization should be changed. However, it is often the case that once a firm's structure, control systems, and compensation policies are put in place they tend to remain, regardless of whether they are consistent with a firm's underlying resources and capabilities. In such settings, a firm will not be able to realize the full competitive potential of its underlying resource base. To the extent that a firm's resources and capabilities are continuously evolving, its organizational structure, control systems, and compensation policies must also evolve. For these attributes of organization to evolve, managers must be aware of their link with a firm's resources and capabilities and of organizational alternatives.

Summary

The RBV is an economic theory that suggests that firm performance is a function of the types of resources and capabilities controlled by firms. Resources are the tangible and intangible assets a firm uses to conceive and implement its strategies. Capabilities are a subset of resources that enable a firm to take advantage of its other resources. Resources and capabilities can be categorized into financial, physical, human, and organizational resources categories.

The RBV makes two assumptions about resources and capabilities: the assumption of resource heterogeneity (that some resources and capabilities may be heterogeneously distributed across competing firms) and the assumption of resource immobility (that this heterogeneity may be long lasting). These two assumptions can be used to describe conditions under which firms will gain competitive advantages by exploiting their resources.

A tool for analyzing a firm's internal strengths and weaknesses can be derived from the RBV. Called the VRIO framework, this tool asks four questions about a firm's resources and capabilities in order to evaluate their competitive potential. These questions are the question of value, the question of rarity, the question of imitability, and the question of organization.

A firm's resources and capabilities are valuable when they enable it to exploit external opportunities or neutralize external threats. Such valuable resources and capabilities are a firm's strengths. Resources and capabilities that are not valuable are a firm's weaknesses. Using valuable resources to exploit external opportunities or neutralize external threats will have the effect of increasing a firm's net revenues or decreasing its net costs.

One way to identify a firm's valuable resources and capabilities is by examining its value chain. A firm's value chain is the list of business activities it engages in to develop, produce, and sell its products or services. Different stages in this value chain require different resources and capabilities, and differences in value chain choices across firms can lead to important differences among the resources and capabilities controlled by different companies. A generic value chain has been developed by McKinsey and Company.

Valuable and common (i.e., not rare) resources and capabilities can be a source of competitive parity. Failure to invest in such resources can create a competitive disadvantage for a firm. Valuable and rare resources can be a source of at least a temporary competitive advantage. There are fewer firms able to control such a resource and still exploit it as a source of at least temporary competitive advantage than there are firms that will generate perfect competition dynamics in an industry.

Valuable, rare, and costly-to-imitate resources and capabilities can be a source of sustained competitive advantage. Imitation can occur through direct duplication or through substitution. A firm's resources and capabilities may be costly to imitate for at least four reasons: unique historical circumstances, causal ambiguity, socially complex resources and capabilities, and patents.

To take full advantage of the potential of its resources and capabilities, a firm must be appropriately organized. A firm's organization consists of its formal reporting structure, its formal and informal control processes, and its compensation policy. These are complementary resources in that they are rarely sources of competitive advantage on their own.

The VRIO framework can be used to identify the competitive implications of a firm's resources and capabilities—whether they are a source of competitive disadvantage, competitive parity, temporary competitive advantage, or sustained competitive advantage—and the extent to which these resources and capabilities are strengths or weaknesses.

When a firm faces a competitor that has a sustained competitive advantage, the firm's options are to not respond, to change its tactics, or to change its strategies. A firm may choose not to respond in this setting for at least three reasons. First, a response might weaken its own sources of sustained competitive advantage. Second, a firm may not have the resources required to respond. Third, a firm may be trying to create or maintain tacit cooperation within an industry.

The RBV has a series of broader managerial implications as well. For example, resource-based logic suggests that competitive advantage is every employee's responsibility. It also suggests that if all a firm does is what its competition does, it can gain only competitive parity, and that in gaining competitive advantage it is better for a firm to exploit its own valuable, rare, and costly-to-imitate resources than to imitate the valuable and rare resources of a competitor. Also, resource-based logic implies that as long as the cost of strategy implementation is less than the value of strategy implementation, the relative cost of implementing a strategy is more important for competitive advantage than the absolute cost of implementing a strategy. It also implies that firms can systematically overestimate and underestimate their uniqueness. With regard to a firm's resources and capabilities, resource-based logic suggests that not only can employee empowerment, organizational culture, and teamwork be valuable; they can also be sources of sustained competitive advantage. Also, if conflicts arise between a firm's valuable, rare, and costly-to-imitate resources and its organization, the organization should be changed.

MyManagementLab®

Go to **mymanagementlab.com** to complete the problems marked with this icon ✪.

Challenge Questions

3.1. Explain which of the following approaches to strategy formulation is more likely to generate economic profits: (a) evaluating external opportunities and threats and then developing resources and capabilities to exploit these opportunities and neutralize these threats or (b) evaluating internal resources and capabilities and then searching for industries where they can be exploited?

3.2. Resource immobility is a key assumption of the resource-based view (RBV) of strategy and hence, the VRIO tool. However, many companies with decades of competitive advantage have started to lose ground to new competitors. Is resource immobility fleeting? How can the RBV and VRIO tools explain such changes in advantage?

3.3. The latest blockbuster drug of a pharmaceutical company or its HR practices, which have evolved to generate a culture of high performance and innovation: which is more important for the company to maintain a sustained competitive advantage?

✪ 3.4. Why would a firm currently experiencing competitive parity be able to gain sustained competitive advantages by studying another firm that is currently experiencing sustained competitive advantages?

3.5. Your former college roommate calls you and asks to borrow $10,000 so that he can open a pizza restaurant in his hometown. He acknowledges that there is a high degree of direct competition in this market, that the cost of entry is low, and that there are numerous substitutes for pizza, but he believes that his pizza restaurant will have some sustained competitive advantages. For example, he is going to have sawdust on his floor, a variety of imported beers, and a late-night delivery service. What are the risks in lending him the money?

3.6. In the text, it is suggested that Boeing did not respond to Airbus's announcement of the development of a super-jumbo aircraft. Assuming this aircraft will give Airbus a competitive advantage in the segment of the airliner business that supplies airplanes

for long international flights, why did Boeing not respond?

3.7. Boeing did not respond to Airbus's announcement of the development of a super-jumbo aircraft. Does it have its own competitive advantage that it does not want to abandon? Explain.

3.8. Boeing did not respond to Airbus's announcement of the development of a super-jumbo aircraft. Does it not have the resources and capabilities needed to respond? Explain.

3.9. List some of the indicators of a firm engaging in an international strategy to develop new resources and capabilities.

✪ 3.10. Between the following two firms, which one is more likely to be successful in exploiting its sources of sustained competitive advantage in its home market than in a highly competitive, nondomestic market: (a) a firm from a less competitive home country or (b) a firm from a more competitive home country? Why?

Problem Set

3.11. Apply the VRIO framework in the following settings. Will the actions described be a source of competitive disadvantage, parity, temporary advantage, or sustained competitive advantage? Explain your answers.

(a) The Japanese automaker Suzuki announces a recall of a 100,000 vehicles in India, where its subsidiary enjoys leading market share.

(b) SAP, the enterprise resource planning software giant, announces the acquisition of Fieldglass, the leading technology provider for procuring and managing temporary workforces for clients.

(c) US Bancorp, one of the top five banks in the US, with over 3000 branches, announced the acquisition of local rival BankEast, which has 10 branches.

(d) Caterpillar, construction equipment manufacturer, patents a new muffler for its machines' exhaust systems.

(e) GlaxoSmithKline, the pharmaceutical company, patents a new, potentially "blockbuster" drug for Alzheimer's disease.

(f) Computer maker Lenovo plans to sponsor a Formula 1 car racing team.

(g) Mobil announces a 5 cent drop in petrol prices across its network of petrol stations in New Zealand.

(h) Accenture deploys a new skills inventory and training system that seeks to develop and deploy consulting resources to relevant client projects.

(i) Deloitte announces a new incentive plan that allows not only partners but also all consultants to share in the profits of the firm.

(j) Red Bull, the energy drink company, launches a new, larger size packaging for its original product.

3.12. Identify three firms you might want to work for. Using the VRIO framework, evaluate the extent to which the resources and capabilities of these firms give them the potential to realize competitive disadvantages, parity, temporary advantages, or sustained advantages. What implications, if any, does this analysis have for the company you might want to work for?

3.13. You have been assigned to estimate the present value of a potential construction project for your company. How would you use the VRIO framework to construct the cash-flow analysis that is a part of any present-value calculation?

MyManagementLab®

Go to **mymanagementlab.com** for the following Assisted-graded writing questions:

✪ **3.14.** Give an example of how you would apply value chain analysis to identify a firm's valuable resources and capabilities.

✪ **3.15.** What is required for a firm to gain a sustained competitive advantage from a resource considered rare?

End Notes

1. The term *the resource-based view* was coined by Wernerfelt, B. (1984). "A resource-based view of the firm." *Strategic Management Journal*, 5, pp. 171–180. Some important early contributors to this theory include Rumelt, R. P. (1984). "Toward a strategic theory of the firm." In R. Lamb (ed.), *Competitive strategic management* (pp. 556–570). Upper Saddle River, NJ: Prentice Hall; and Barney, J. B. (1986). "Strategic factor markets: Expectations, luck and business strategy." *Management Science*, 32, pp. 1512–1514. A second wave of important early resource-based theoretical work includes Barney, J. B. (1991). "Firm resources and sustained competitive advantage." *Journal of Management*, 7, pp. 49–64; Dierickx, I., and K. Cool (1989). "Asset stock accumulation and sustainability of competitive advantage." *Management Science*, 35, pp. 1504–1511; Conner, K. R. (1991). "A historical comparison of resource-based theory and five schools of thought within industrial organization economics: Do we have a new theory of the firm?" *Journal of Management*, 17(1), pp. 121–154; and Peteraf, M. A. (1993). "The cornerstones of competitive advantage: A resource-based view." *Strategic Management Journal*, 14, pp. 179–191. A review of much of this early theoretical literature can be found in Mahoney, J. T., and J. R. Pandian. (1992). "The resource-based view within the conversation of strategic management." *Strategic Management Journal*, 13, pp. 363–380. The theoretical perspective has also spawned a growing body of empirical work, including Brush, T. H., and K. W. Artz. (1999). "Toward a contingent resource-based theory." *Strategic Management Journal*, 20, pp. 223–250; Marcus, A., and D. Geffen. (1998). "The dialectics of competency acquisition." *Strategic Management Journal*, 19, pp. 1145–1168; Brush, T. H., P. Bromiley, and M. Hendrickx. (1999). "The relative influence of industry and corporation on business segment performance." *Strategic Management Journal*, 20, pp. 519–547; Yeoh, P.-L., and K. Roth.

(1999). "An empirical analysis of sustained advantage in the U.S. pharmaceutical industry." *Strategic Management Journal*, 20, pp. 637–653; Roberts, P. (1999). "Product innovation, product-market competition and persistent profitability in the U.S. pharmaceutical industry." *Strategic Management Journal*, 20, pp. 655–670; Gulati, R. (1999). "Network location and learning." *Strategic Management Journal*, 20, pp. 397–420; Lorenzoni, G., and A. Lipparini. (1999). "The leveraging of interfirm relationships as a distinctive organizational capability." *Strategic Management Journal*, 20, pp. 317–338; Majumdar, S. (1998). "On the utilization of resources." *Strategic Management Journal*, 19(9), pp. 809–831; Makadok, R. (1997). "Do inter-firm differences in capabilities affect strategic pricing dynamics?" *Academy of Management Proceedings '97*, pp. 30–34; Silverman, B. S., J. A. Nickerson, and J. Freeman. (1997). "Profitability, transactional alignment, and organizational mortality in the U.S. trucking industry." *Strategic Management Journal*, 18 (Summer special issue), pp. 31–52; Powell, T. C., and A. Dent-Micallef. (1997). "Information technology as competitive advantage." *Strategic Management Journal*, 18(5), pp. 375–405; Miller, D., and J. Shamsie. (1996). "The Resource-based view of the firm in two environments." *Academy of Management Journal*, 39(3), pp. 519–543; and Maijoor, S., and A. Van Witteloostuijn. (1996). "An empirical test of the resource-based theory." *Strategic Management Journal*, 17, pp. 549–569; Barnett, W. P., H. R. Greve, and D. Y. Park. (1994). "An evolutionary model of organizational performance." *Strategic Management Journal*, 15 (Winter special issue), pp. 11–28; Levinthal, D., and J. Myatt. (1994). "Co-evolution of capabilities and industry: The evolution of mutual fund processing." *Strategic Management Journal*, 17, pp. 45–62; Henderson, R., and I. Cockburn. (1994). "Measuring competence? Exploring firm effects in pharmaceutical research." *Strategic Management Journal*, 15, pp. 63–84;

Pisano, G. P. (1994). "Knowledge, integration, and the locus of learning: An empirical analysis of process development." *Strategic Management Journal*, 15, pp. 85–100; and Zajac, E. J., and J. D. Westphal. (1994). "The costs and benefits of managerial incentives and monitoring in large U.S. corporations: When is more not better?" *Strategic Management Journal*, 15, pp. 121–142.

2. Ghemawat, P. (1986). "Wal-Mart stores' discount operations." Harvard Business School Case No. 9-387-018, on Wal-Mart; Kupfer, A. (1991). "The champion of cheap clones." *Fortune*, September 23, pp. 115–120; and Holder, D. (1989). "L. L. Bean, Inc.—1974." Harvard Business School Case No. 9-676-014, on L. L. Bean. Some of Wal-Mart's more recent moves, especially its international acquisitions, are described in Laing, J. R. (1999). "Blimey! Wal-Mart." *Barron's*, 79, p. 14. L. L. Bean's lethargic performance in the 1990s, together with its turnaround plan, is described in Symonds, W. (1998). "Paddling harder at L. L. Bean." *BusinessWeek*, December 7, p. 72.

3. For an early discussion of the importance of human capital in firms, see Becker, G. S. (1964). *Human capital.* New York: Columbia University Press.

4. Heskett, J. L., and R. H. Hallowell. (1993). "Southwest Airlines: 1993 (A)." Harvard Business School Case No. 9-695-023.

5. See Barney, J. (1991). "Firm resources and sustained competitive advantage." *Journal of Management*, 17, pp. 99–120.

6. See Schlender, B. R. (1992). "How Sony keeps the magic going." *Fortune*, February 24, pp. 75–84; and (1999). "The weakling kicks back." *The Economist*, July 3, p. 46, for a discussion of Sony. See Krogh, L., J. Praeger, D. Sorenson, and J. Tomlinson. (1988). "How 3M evaluates its R&D programs." *Research Technology Management*, 31, pp. 10–14.

7. Anders, G. (2002). "AOL's true believers." *Fast Company*, July pp. 96+. In a recent *Wall Street Journal* article, managers of AOL Time Warner admitted they are no longer seeking synergies across their businesses. See Karnitschnig, M. (2006). "That's all, folks: After years of pushing synergy, Time Warner, Inc. says enough." *The Wall Street Journal*, June 2, A1+.

8. See Grant, R. M. (1991). *Contemporary strategy analysis.* Cambridge, MA: Basil Blackwell.

9. Lipman, S., and R. Rumelt. (1982). "Uncertain imitability: An analysis of interfirm differences in efficiency under competition." *Bell Journal of Economics*, 13, pp. 418–438; Barney, J. B. (1986). "Strategic factor markets: Expectations, luck and business strategy." *Management Science*, 32, pp. 1512–1514; and Barney, J. B. (1986). "Organizational culture: Can it be a source of sustained competitive advantage?" *Academy of Management Review*, 11, pp. 656–665.

10. Note that the definition of sustained competitive advantage presented here, though different, is consistent with the definition given in Chapter 1. In particular, a firm that enjoys a competitive advantage for a long period of time (the Chapter 1 definition) does not have its advantage competed away through imitation (the Chapter 3 definition).

11. See Breen, B. (2003). "What's selling in America." *Fast Company*, January, pp. 80+.

12. These explanations of costly imitation were first developed by Dierickx, I., and K. Cool. (1989). "Asset stock accumulation and sustainability of competitive advantage." *Management Science*, 35, pp. 1504–1511; Barney, J. B. (1991). "Firm resources and sustained competitive advantage." *Journal of Management*, 7, pp. 49–64; Mahoney, J. T., and J. R. Pandian. (1992). "The resource-based view within the conversation of strategic management." *Strategic Management Journal*, 13, pp. 363–380; and Peteraf, M. A. (1993). "The cornerstones of competitive advantage: A resource-based view." *Strategic Management Journal*, 14, pp. 179–191.

13. Dierickx, I., and K. Cool. (1989). "Asset stock accumulation and sustainability of competitive advantage." *Management Science*, 35, pp. 1504–1511. In economics, the role of history in determining competitive outcomes was first examined by Arthur, W. B. (1989). "Competing technologies, increasing returns, and lock-in by historical events." *Economic Journal*, 99, pp. 116–131.

14. See Breen, B. (2003). "What's selling in America." *Fast Company*, January, pp. 80+.

15. This term was first suggested by Arthur, W. B. (1989). "Competing technologies, increasing returns, and lock-in by historical events." *Economic Journal*, 99, pp. 116–131. A good example of path dependence is the development of Silicon Valley and the important role that Stanford University and a few early firms played in creating the network of organizations that has since become the center of much of the

electronics business. See Alley, J. (1997). "The heart of Silicon Valley." *Fortune*, July 7, pp. 86+.

16. Reed, R., and R. J. DeFillippi. (1990). "Causal ambiguity, barriers to imitation, and sustainable competitive advantage." *Academy of Management Review*, 15(1), pp. 88–102, suggest that causal ambiguity about the sources of a firm's competitive advantage need only exist among a firm's competitors for it to be a source of sustained competitive advantage. Managers in a firm, they argue, may fully understand the sources of their advantage. However, in a world where employees freely and frequently move from firm to firm, such special insights into the sources of a firm's competitive advantage would not remain proprietary for very long. For this reason, for causal ambiguity to be a source of sustained competitive advantage, both the firm trying to gain such an advantage and those trying to imitate it must face similar levels of causal ambiguity. Indeed, Wal-Mart sued Amazon for trying to steal some of its secrets by hiring employees away from Wal-Mart. See Nelson, E. (1998). "Wal-Mart accuses Amazon.com of stealing its secrets in lawsuit." *The Wall Street Journal*, October 19, p. B10. For a discussion of how difficult it is to maintain secrets, especially in a world of the World Wide Web, see Farnham, A. (1997). "How safe are your secrets?" *Fortune*, September 8, pp. 114+. The international dimensions of the challenges associated with maintaining secrets are discussed in Robinson, E. (1998). "China spies target corporate America." *Fortune*, March 30, pp. 118+.

17. Itami, H. (1987). *Mobilizing invisible assets.* Cambridge, MA: Harvard University Press.

18. See Barney, J. B., and B. Tyler. (1990). "The attributes of top management teams and sustained competitive advantage." In M. Lawless and L. Gomez-Mejia (eds.), *Managing the high technology firm* (pp. 33–48). Greenwich, CT: JAI Press, on teamwork in top management teams; Barney, J. B. (1986). "Organizational culture: Can it be a source of sustained competitive advantage?" *Academy of Management Review*, 11, pp. 656–665, on organizational culture; Henderson, R. M., and I. Cockburn. (1994). "Measuring competence? Exploring firm effects in pharmaceutical research." *Strategic Management Journal*, 15, pp. 63–84, on relationships among employees; and Dyer, J. H., and H. Singh. (1998). "The relational view: Cooperative strategy and sources of interorganizational competitive advantage." *Academy of Management Review*, 23(4), pp. 660–679, on relationships with suppliers and customers.

19. For a discussion of knowledge as a source of competitive advantage in the popular business press, see Stewart, T. (1995). "Getting real about brain power." *Fortune*, November 27, pp. 201+; Stewart, T. (1995). "Mapping corporate knowledge." *Fortune*, October 30, pp. 209+. For the academic version of this same issue, see Simonin, B. L. (1999). "Ambiguity and the process of knowledge transfer in strategic alliances." *Strategic Management Journal*, 20(7), pp. 595–623; Spender, J. C. (1996). "Making knowledge the basis of a dynamic theory of the firm." *Strategic Management Journal*, 17 (Winter special issue), pp. 109–122; Hatfield, D. D., J. P. Liebeskind, and T. C. Opler. (1996). "The effects of corporate restructuring on aggregate industry specialization." *Strategic Management Journal*, 17, pp. 55–72; and Grant, R. M. (1996). "Toward a knowledge-based theory of the firm." *Strategic Management Journal*, 17 (Winter special issue), pp. 109–122.

20. Porras, J., and P. O. Berg. (1978). "The impact of organizational development." *Academy of Management Review*, 3, pp. 249–266, have done one of the few empirical studies on whether systematic efforts to change socially complex resources are effective. They found that such efforts are usually not effective. Although this study is getting older, it is unlikely that current change methods will be any more effective than the methods examined by these authors.

21. See Hambrick, D. (1987). "Top management teams: Key to strategic success." *California Management Review*, 30, pp. 88–108, on top management teams; Barney, J. B. (1986). "Organizational culture: Can it be a source of sustained competitive advantage?" *Academy of Management Review*, 11, pp. 656–665, on culture; Porter, M. E. (1980). *Competitive strategy.* New York: Free Press; and Klein, B., and K. Leffler. (1981). "The role of market forces in assuring contractual performance." *Journal of Political Economy*, 89, pp. 615–641, on relations with customers.

22. See Harris, L. C., and E. Ogbonna. (1999). "Developing a market oriented culture: A critical evaluation." *Journal of Management Studies*, 36(2), pp. 177–196.

23. Lieberman, M. B. (1987). "The learning curve, diffusion, and competitive strategy." *Strategic Management Journal*, 8, pp. 441–452,

has a very good analysis of the cost of imitation in the chemical industry. See also Lieberman, M. B., and D. B. Montgomery. (1988). "First-mover advantages." *Strategic Management Journal*, 9, pp. 41–58.

24. Rumelt, R. P. (1984). "Toward a strategic theory of the firm." In R. Lamb (ed.), *Competitive strategic management* (pp. 556–570). Upper Saddle River, NJ: Prentice Hall, among others, cites patents as a source of costly imitation.

25. Significant debate surrounds the patentability of different kinds of products. For example, although typefaces are not patentable (and cannot be copyrighted), the process for displaying typefaces may be. See Thurm, S. (1998). "Copy this typeface? Court ruling counsels caution." *The Wall Street Journal*, July 15, pp. B1+.

26. For an insightful discussion of these complementary resources, see Amit, R., and P. J. H. Schoemaker. (1993). "Strategic assets and organizational rent." *Strategic Management Journal*, 14(1), pp. 33–45.

27. See H. Tabuchi (2012) How the tech parade passed Sony by. April 15, 2012. *New York Times.* http://www.nytimes.com/2012/04/15/technology/how-sony-fell-behind in the tech parade. Accessed January 27, 2014.

28. (2004). "Casio." *Marketing*, May 6, p. 95; Weisul, K. (2003). "When time is money—and art." *BusinessWeek*, July 21, p. 86.

29. That said, there have been some "cracks" in Southwest's capabilities armor lately. Its CEO suddenly resigned, and its level of profitability dropped precipitously in 2004. Whether these are indicators that Southwest's core strengths are being dissipated or there are short-term problems is not yet known. However, Southwest's stumbling would give US Airways some hope. Trottman, M., S. McCartney, and J. Lublin. (2004). "Southwest's CEO abruptly quits 'draining job.'" *The Wall Street Journal*, July 16, pp. A1+.

30. One should consult a lawyer before getting involved in these forms of tacit cooperation.

31. This aspect of the competitive dynamics in an industry is discussed in Smith, K. G., C. M. Grimm, and M. J. Gannon. (1992). *Dynamics of competitive strategy.* Newberry Park, CA: Sage.

32. Schlender, B. R. (1992). "How Sony keeps the magic going." *Fortune*, February 24, pp. 75–84.

33. Personal communication.

34. See, for example, Peters, T., and R. Waterman. (1982). *In search of excellence.* New York: Harper Collins; Collins, J., and J. Porras. (1994). *Built to last.* New York: Harper Business; Collins, J. (2001). *Good to great.* New York: Harper Collins; and Bennis, W. G., and R. Townsend. (2006). *Reinventing leadership.* New York: Harper Collins.

Case 1–1: You Say You Want a Revolution: SodaStream International*

"Transportation for carbonated drinks in the world utilizes 100 million barrels of oil every year. That is 20 times the BP disaster that hit the Gulf of Mexico."

"I think it is criminal that the industry, led by two big companies, will do anything to protect their antiquated business model. They are generating 35 million bottles and cans every single day in the U.K. alone. World-wide it is one billion bottles and cans, most of which just go to trash, landfill, the oceans or parks. It's insane."

—Daniel Birnbaum, CEO of SodaStream International, in a November 2012 interview with *The Wall Street Journal*.[1]

Anna Claire Butler wet her brush, slicked her hair back, and checked her reflection in the mirror. "My first day on Wall Street!" she thought. Five minutes later, she walked briskly down Broadway Avenue to the 86th Street subway station to catch the downtown 1-2-3 train. After a hot and cramped 20-minute subway ride, Anna Claire stepped into the lobby of the bank that housed the midtown Manhattan offices of Keller & Assoc., her new employer.

Later that day, Anna Claire pushed through the crowd waiting for a table to join her best friend, Beth. After the two friends exchanged hellos, Beth said, "What's wrong with you? You look like you were hit by a bus."

"My feet are killing me. I've got a run in my brand-new stockings, and I'm starving. Worse yet, I have to figure out the soda market and do a presentation to my boss in two days."

"What do you mean, figure out the soda market? You just started. What do you know about it?" asked Beth.

"All I know is that my favorite soda is Diet Coke. Unfortunately, that's not gonna to be enough—not nearly enough—to keep old J. B. Parker happy," said Anna Claire.

"Who's J. B. Parker?" asked Beth.

"Only the man who controls my destiny—the boss-man. He's looking into doing a deal in the carbonated soft drink market. I don't know the details, but I am supposed to do all his legwork in the next 48 hours. He told me to 'show him the money.' By that he meant explain who makes all the money in the industry and how they do it."

"Hmm, that is interesting, very interesting," mused Beth. "You know, SodaStream's stock has been on a roller coaster ride in the past couple of weeks."

"What are you talking about?" asked Anna Claire.

"I'm talking about SodaStream being in play."

"Huh?"

"An Israeli financial newspaper printed a story about Pepsi being in talks to acquire SodaStream in early June.[2] The stock popped almost 8 percent in pre-market trading the day the story came out, but that was before Pepsi nixed the story the same afternoon.[3] I bet that's the deal your boss is working on," Beth said.

"Isn't that the end of it?" Anna Claire asked.

"Apparently not. Pepsi said it wasn't making any large acquisitions, but investors still bid up SodaStream stock in the hopes that Coca-Cola was interested. The stock hit a high of about 78 bucks on takeover rumors, but has now plunged to about $60—well under where it was before the Pepsi rumor hit the press. It didn't help the stock that the *New York Post* ran a story last week that said SodaStream had been shopping itself quietly for the past three months[4]—but no one was interested in buying. I bet your boss is trying to figure out if he should buy the stock on the pullback in the price."

The next morning, Anna Claire arrived at the office at 6:00 and got to work downloading the annual reports for Coca-Cola, PepsiCo, Dr. Pepper Snapple Group, and SodaStream. "Yikes, this is going to be more complicated than I thought. I bet I don't get a wink of sleep for the

---

*This case was prepared by Bonita Austin for the purposes of class discussion. It is reprinted with permission.

next two days," Anna Claire thought ruefully. As Anna Claire clicked on the file containing SodaStream's 10K, her mind was full of questions. "Is SodaStream even in the same market as Coke and Pepsi? Why would investors think Coke or Pepsi might want to buy the company? Is SodaStream a disruptive innovator of the carbonated soft drink market? What do the bottlers have to do with Coke and Pepsi? I guess I'd better figure out what SodaStream does first and then think about the competition."

SodaStream International and the SodaStream System

SodaStream manufactures home soda drinks maker machines, flavor concentrates, and gas cylinders. Founded in 1903 as a subsidiary of W&A Gibley gin distillers, the original SodaStream machines were marketed to British upper-class customers. The machine, dubbed "apparatus for aerating liquids" by inventor Guy Gibley, allowed users to convert ordinary tap water into carbonated water by injecting compressed carbon dioxide gas (CO_2) into a container of water. Marketed to the upper class, the first SodaStream machine was installed at Buckingham Palace.[5] The company introduced flavored syrups in the 1920s

along with commercial machines, followed by the introduction of a home carbonation machine in the 1950s.[6] The modern SodaStream system is pictured below. Consumers purchased a SodaStream machine along with a specially designed, durable plastic bottle, flavor concentrate, and a CO_2 gas cylinder. After filling the bottle with tap water, the user screwed the bottle into the SodaStream machine and depressed a button to add carbonation. The machine injected CO_2 into the water each time the user pushed the button. Once the user had put in the desired amount of carbonation, he added either liquid flavor concentrate to the bottle to his taste or dumped in a pre-measured "cap" of flavor similar to the pre-measured Keurig coffee "caps" made by Green Mountain Coffee Roasters.

U.S. Carbonated Soft Drink Market

According to Beverage Digest, the top 10 carbonated soft drink (CSD) brands held just over 66 percent of the estimated $74 billion market in 2011. All of the top 10 brands belonged to Coca-Cola, PepsiCo, and Dr. Pepper Snapple Group. Table 1 shows the distribution of market shares by company in the United States in 2011 as well as a listing of their brands and place on the top 10 CSD brand list.

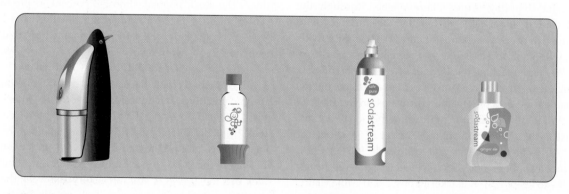

Soda makers: +   **Carbonating bottles:**   +   **CO2 cylinders:**   +   **Flavors:**

- Large variety of designs, price points
- Durable, easy to use

- Reusable
- Hermetically-sealing cap
- BPA-free
- Glass or plastic

- 60 or 130 liters
- Consumers exchange empty cylinders for full ones at retail locations or home delivery via internet/phone

- Full range of regular, diet, "All-Natural," mixers, energy
- 2/3 less sugar and carbs than leading brands; no high-fructose corn syrup

- Over 100 patents

- Carbonation, Design, Functionality, Safety

Source: SodaStream International[7]

Table 1	2011 U.S. Carbonated Soft Drink (CSD) Company Market Shares and Brands	

Company	Market Share	CSD Brands
Coca-Cola Co.	41.9%	Coke (#1), Diet Coke (#2), Sprite (#6), Fanta (#10), Fresca, Mr. Pibb, Barq's
PepsiCo	28.5%	Pepsi (#3), Mountain Dew (#4), Diet Pepsi (#7), Diet Mountain Dew (#8), Sierra Mist
Dr. Pepper Snapple Group	21.1%	Dr Pepper (#5), Diet Dr Pepper (#9), Vernor's, Crush, 7Up, Canada Dry, Stewart's, A&W, Schwepp's, Diet Rite, Squirt, Orangina, RC Cola, Sunkist
Cott Corp.	5.2%	Sam's Choice
National Beverage	2.8%	Faygo, Shasta, Ritz, Big Shot

Source: Business Insider, Dr Pepper Snapple Group 2011 10K, *Stastica, Wall Street Journal*, Beverage-Digest.

The carbonated soft drink market was famous for its market share battles between Coca-Cola and PepsiCo. Notably, PepsiCo aggressively targeted Coke's position with the Pepsi Challenge marketing campaign that ran from 1975 to 1978. The campaign featured blind taste tests by ordinary consumers all over the United States. To their surprise, more than 50 percent of consumers preferred the taste of Pepsi in head-to-head blind taste tests. The innovative campaign allowed Pepsi to build upon market share gains in the early 1970s and challenge Coke's dominant position in the United States for the first time. After 15 consecutive years of market share losses to Pepsi in the United States, Coca-Cola responded with the unsuccessful launch of "New Coke" in 1985. A firestorm of consumer protests resulted in the introduction of the "Coke Classic" line in its signature hourglass plastic bottle a few months later. Interestingly, "New Coke" used a high-fructose corn syrup–sweetened version of the Diet Coke formula (introduced in 1982).

Capitalizing on the strength of the Coke consumer's bond with the brand that became apparent after the launch of "New Coke," Coca-Cola directed much of its efforts from the mid-1980s to 2012 to positioning its flagship brand as a "lifestyle" brand. PepsiCo famously launched a series of marketing campaigns over about a 40-year span featuring popular artists such as Michael Jackson, Ray Charles, Britney Spears, Christina Aguilera, Mariah Carey, Beyonce, and Nicki Minaj. Although advertising expenditures remained high, industry observers in 2010 began to question Pepsi's determination to compete in the category, as Pepsi appeared to "concede" the category to Coke. Diet Coke overtook Pepsi for the first time to become the #2 brand in the CSD industry. Under CEO Indra Nooyi, Pepsi seemed focused on its highly profitable Frito-Lay snack business rather than on the U.S. carbonated soft drink market.

Pepsi responded aggressively to its critics with the 2012 launch of Pepsi Next, a mid-calorie cola. The new product was sweetened with high-fructose corn syrup and three artificial sweeteners. Pepsi's advertising expenditures jumped more than 44 percent—suggesting the fight for market share wasn't over yet (see Table 2). Note that Pepsi boosted advertising on the Pepsi brand by 39 percent and on Mountain Dew by 87 percent in 2012. Moreover, the company stated publicly that it was pouring its research efforts into developing new, natural sweeteners in order to develop healthier alternatives to artificial sweeteners and support its planned new product launches in the future.

Dr Pepper Snapple Group (DPS) stayed on the sidelines of the so-called "cola wars" by staking a claim to the "flavor" segment of the CSD market. The company held two positions on the top 10 brands list in 2011. Its flagship brand, Dr Pepper, held the #5 position in the industry. Diet Dr Pepper was #9 on the list of the largest CSD brands. In 2011, Dr Pepper Snapple group launched a line of reduced-calorie products in 23 flavors accompanied by the slogan "It's Not for Women." Products such as Dr Pepper 10 and

Table 2	U.S. Carbonated Soft Drink Advertising Effectiveness ($ in millions)			

Company	2011	2012	Change	2011 Spending/Share Point
Coca-Cola	$241.4	$253.8	5.1%	$5.76
PepsiCo	$236.7	$341.9	44.4%	$8.31
Dr Pepper Snapple Group	$137.3	$148.1	7.9%	$6.47

Source: Advertising Age: Top 100 Advertisers, author's calculations.

A&W 10 were targeted to young men who are "turned off" by zero-calorie sodas.

Clearly, ad spending signaled that competition was heating up between the major CSD makers in the United States. Industry observers that called the end of the "cola wars" in 2011 may have celebrated Coke's victory prematurely.

Retail Distribution

Sales of carbonated soft drinks to consumers went through two major distribution channels: retail stores and fountain accounts. Sales to retailers accounted for more than 75 percent of total CSD sales in the United States, while fountain drinks generated about 25 percent of industry sales. The largest portion of retail store sales was through supermarkets and discounters. The $1.2 trillion supermarket and discounter industry accounted for 50 percent of all carbonated soft drink sales in the United States in 2011. The top five retailers in the segment—Wal-Mart, Kroger, Target, Costco, and Safeway—generated about 49 percent of all retail sales in the channel. Wal-Mart alone accounted for about 27 percent of retail sales in the supermarket and discounter industry. While figures were not available for individual retailer sales of carbonated soft drinks, PepsiCo stated that Wal-Mart (including Sam's Club) accounted for 11 percent of its sales worldwide in 2011 and 17 percent of its U.S. sales. Although Costco accounted for only about 6 percent of all retail sales in the channel, the company dealt a blow to Coca-Cola in 2012 by switching all of its food courts to Pepsi products. Convenience stores, gas stations, vending machines, and other retailers made up the remainder of CSD industry sales to retail stores.[8]

Sales to restaurants, movie theaters, stadiums, and other fountain drink outlets generated about 25 percent of CSD industry sales. Coca-Cola held an estimated 70 percent of the fountain drink market—dwarfing PepsiCo's estimated 19 percent share and Dr. Pepper's 11 percent share in the channel. McDonalds exclusively sold Coca-Cola products and accounted for half of all food sales in fast-food burger joints in 2011 and so was undoubtedly one of Coca-Cola U.S.'s most important customers. With the estimated 75 percent retail margins on fountain drink sales, McDonald's relationship with Coca-Cola has proven to be a profitable one for the fast-food giant.

Manufacturing and Distribution of Carbonated Soft Drinks

Originally sold by druggists as a healthful tonic, the bubbly potion has been enjoyed by Americans since the early 1800s. The carbonated soft drink itself was a relatively simple concoction consisting of flavoring concentrate, carbonated water, and sweetener. Companies like Coca-Cola, PepsiCo, and Dr Pepper Snapple Group—the concentrate producers—manufactured flavoring concentrate and sold it to licensed bottlers. Bottlers converted concentrate into carbonated beverages by adding carbonated water and packaging the drinks in bottles and cans. The concentrate producers (CPs) added sweeteners such as sucralose or Stevia before selling diet concentrate to the bottlers, while the bottlers added high-fructose corn syrup or cane sugar to full calorie beverages.

For much of the past 25 years, the concentrate producers did not purchase bottles, cans, sugar, or high-fructose corn syrup, as they did not manufacture finished carbonated soda products. They did negotiate supply agreements for their fragmented "bottling systems" in order to increase the buying power of their bottlers systemwide. The concentrate producers created marketing campaigns and promotions for their brands and shared in the considerable marketing costs for their brands with the bottlers. The bottlers were responsible for purchasing raw materials and packaging, manufacturing the finished beverages, distribution and warehousing, and customer service. They paid for promotions and bore some marketing costs, set local prices of the finished beverages, and sold directly to retail stores. Coca-Cola and Pepsi bottlers were prohibited by contractual agreements from making and selling "imitative" products that competed directly with Coca-Cola and PepsiCo beverage brands. For example, a Coca-Cola bottler could not sell Pepsi or Diet Pepsi. In return, the CPs granted the bottlers exclusive distribution rights in geographic areas.

While the independent bottling system was firmly in place in international markets in 2013, both PepsiCo and Coca-Cola had purchased most of their respective bottling systems in the United States in 2010–2011. PepsiCo purchased its two largest bottlers in North America (Pepsi Bottling Group and PepsiAmericas) for a combined value of $7.8 billion in early 2010. The purchase gave Pepsi control of 80 percent of its distributors in North America. Coca-Cola purchased the North American bottling operations of its largest bottler, Coca-Cola Enterprises, in a deal valued at about $12.3 billion in October 2010. Coca-Cola owned 90 percent of its North American bottling system after the CCE deal closed.

The three acquisitions marked a reversal in strategy for both Coca-Cola and PepsiCo. Coca-Cola spun off the bottlers it owned in 1987 as so-called "anchor bottlers." Spinning off the bottlers allowed Coke to push large amounts of capital off of its balance sheet and focus on concentrate production. The capital-intensive bottling business was far less profitable than the lucrative concentrate business. To illustrate, Coca-Cola Enterprises (CCE) had an operating margin of 7.6 percent and a return on average assets of 5 percent in 2009 excluding restructuring charges. Coca-Cola's operating margin was 26.6 percent, and return on average assets was 15.3 percent—more than three times larger than CCE's return on average assets. Pepsi spun off its bottlers in 1999. Pepsi Bottling Group had an operating margin of 7.9 percent and a return on average assets of 4.6 percent in 2009. PepsiCo's operating margin on the North American beverage business was 21.7 percent in 2009.

Coca-Cola and PepsiCo expected the purchase of the majority of their bottling systems in North America to allow both companies to realize significant cost savings and better address the challenges of shifting consumer preferences in the United States. Increasing demand for alternative beverages had strained both companies' bottling systems as bottlers struggled to make investments in equipment and logistics systems that would facilitate a shift away from a manufacturing and inventory management process that was designed for large volume sales of a relatively small number of stock-keeping units. Alternative beverages such as energy drinks and ready-to-drink teas used smaller production runs and had much more complicated and extensive product lines that featured many flavors and sizes of beverages than CSD. These investments were not paying off for the bottlers but were desperately needed by both Coke and Pepsi to remain competitive in the United States.

Investors speculated that both companies would eventually spin off or re-franchise the captive bottlers in the future or separate manufacturing and distribution. Indeed, Coca-Cola announced in April 2013 it had reached an agreement with its major independent bottlers to expand their distribution territories, but not to increase their production capacities. Muhar Kent, chairman and CEO of Coca-Cola, commented, "A strong franchise system had always been the competitive advantage of the Coca-Cola business globally, and today we are accelerating the transformation of our U.S. system in ways that will establish a clear path to achieve our 2020 vision."[9] A few days later, Kent told investors, "In the coming months, we will be collaborating with five of our bottling partners to implement a plan which will include the granting of exclusive territory rights and the sale of distribution assets with cold drink equipment. In the near term, production assets will remain with Coca Cola Refreshments, which will facilitate future implementation of a national product supply system."[10] It appeared that Coca-Cola had begun to transform its traditional manufacturing and distribution model in the United States.

Waning Popularity of Carbonated Soft Drinks

At the turn of the 19th century, there were more than 100 different carbonated soft drink brands (CSD) and 2,763 bottling plants.[11] As the popularity of the beverage increased, the number of bottling plants exploded, peaking at about 6,500 in 1950. Demand for carbonated soft drinks was strong for many years, and the beverage became America's favorite when it surpassed coffee in popularity in 1977. At the peak of its reign as the U.S. consumer's favorite drink in the late 1990s, Americans drank nearly 55 gallons of CSD per year on average, and CSD were 30 percent of all liquid beverage consumption. Beer was the next largest drinks category but only accounted for 12 percent of liquid beverage consumption in the United States.[12] During the 1990s, demand grew at about 3 percent per year on average. Demand for CSD as measured by case volume began to decline in 2005 and fell for seven consecutive years. Nevertheless, Americans still consumed a whopping 42.4 gallons[13] of CSD per capita and the beverage category accounted for about 25 percent of daily beverage consumption. Changes in consumer preferences fueled by health concerns were the largest contributor to the decline in CSD consumption.

Increasingly, U.S. consumers turned to bottled water, energy drinks, ready-to-drink teas, coffee beverages, sports drinks, and juice drinks to quench their thirst. Rising health concerns, especially regarding obesity, and interest in "natural" and "green" products helped fuel demand for alternatives to CSD in the 2000s. Campaigns against CSDs in schools and the 2013 proposed ban on fountain drink serving sizes of more than 16 ounces for full-calorie CSD in New York City highlighted the changes in public opinion about the health effects of CSD consumption. New York Supreme Court Judge Milton Tingling overturned the ban on grounds that the New York Board of Health was established to protect citizens against diseases, not to regulate the city's food supply except when the city faced an imminent threat from disease.[14] Nevertheless, the proposed ban worried beverage makers, as it was an indication the movement to reduce the public's consumption of sugary drinks continued to gain momentum in the United States. Moreover, NYC's attempt to limit CSD consumption was a chilling reminder of the anti-cigarette movement that resulted in the smoking ban in NYC restaurants and bars in 2003.

Bottled water was the largest non-alcoholic alternative drink category to CSD in the U.S. market. Of the estimated 180 gallons of beverages Americans consumed on average per year, bottled water accounted for 29 gallons per person in 2011—up from 18 gallons per capita in 2001. Bottled water sales generated about $11 billion in revenues in 2011, according to a report by Beverage Marketing.[15] Continuing its meteoric rise in popularity, energy drink sales leaped more than 14 percent in 2011 to about $8.9 billion in retail sales. Energy drink leader Monster Inc.'s sales grew more than 16 percent and the company nabbed more than 36 percent of all energy drink sales in 2011. Sports drink sales, pushed up by new low-calorie and no-calorie product introductions, increased almost 9 percent to about $7 billion in 2011. Other alternatives to CSD such as ready-to-drink coffee also experienced strong sales growth in 2011.

Coca-Cola, PepsiCo, and Dr Pepper Snapple Group all acquired significant assets in the non-carbonated soft drink market to satisfy consumer demands for alternative beverages. Investors expected all three companies to continue to explore acquisitions, strategic alliances such as licensing, and homegrown forays into new beverage categories. Coca-Cola was #1 in the non-carbonated soft drink market with a 34 percent share. PepsiCo came in #2 with a 26 percent share, followed by Dr Pepper Snapple Group with an 11 percent share of the non-carbonated soft drink segment in 2012.

Coca-Cola's U.S. brand portfolio included the #2 sports drink brand (Powerade) and #2 bottled water brand (Dasani). The company added Vitamin Water to its line up through the $4.2 billion acquisition of Glaceau—putting Coke in the lead in the fortified water segment. Other key brands included Minute Maid, Fuze, and Glaceau SmartWater. Although it trailed Coca-Cola, PepsiCo had a strong position in non-CSD categories thanks in large part to its $13.4 billion purchase of Quaker Oats in 2001. Quaker's Gatorade brand gave Pepsi an 80 percent share of the fast-growing U.S. sports drink market. While Gatorade's market share had slipped to about 73 percent in 2011, the brand still held a commanding lead in the category.[16] At $3.3 billion in annual sales as of October 2012, Gatorade was one of PepsiCo's most important brands.[17] The company also held the lead in the U.S. bottled water segment with its Aquafina brand. Other key PepsiCo brands included Tropicana, SoBe, Propel, Amp Energy, and licensed brands Lipton Brisk and Starbucks.

Dr Pepper Snapple Group was a distant #3 in the non-carbonated soft drink market but was still a strong competitor in several categories. The company's non-carbonated brands included #1 ready-to-drink tea brand Snapple, along with Hawaiian Punch, Clamato, DejaBlue, Mott's, and Nantucket Nectars.

In addition to consumer concerns over health, demand for CSD proved to be very price elastic. In fact, 160 research studies on the elasticity of demand for food conducted between 1938 and 2007 showed that a 10 percent increase in soft drink prices results in an average –8 percent drop in demand, with an even larger drop for carbonated soft drinks of –9 percent on average for each 1 percent increase in price.[18] CSD manufacturers increased retail prices in 2011 and 2012 to offset higher prices for sweeteners, especially high-fructose corn syrup. Price hikes appeared to be a contributing factor to the decline in consumption of CSD in both years.

SodaStream Business Model

The home drinks system was quite popular in the United Kingdom in the 1970s and 1980s but languished in the 1990s and early 2000s as the company suffered through several changes in ownership. Close to bankruptcy, the firm received a cash infusion from Fortissimo Capital and new management in 2007. Daniel Birnbaum, installed as SodaStream's CEO in 2007, was fresh off of a three-year stint as Nike Israel's general manager and also had established Pillsbury's business in Israel during the late 1990s. Under Birnbaum, the company modified its customer value proposition while retaining its tried-and-true profit model. In order to build the brand, Birnbaum employed three value drivers that took advantage of major societal trends: rising consumer interest in so-called "green" products; increasing consumer concerns over health and wellness, especially obesity; and the apparent change in the zeitgeist away from conspicuous consumption and toward frugality.

As a result, the management team began to position the SodaStream system as an environmentally sound and healthy alternative to prepared carbonated soft drinks. According to SodaStream's corporate Web site, the company seeks to "revolutionize the beverage industry by reducing plastic bottle waste and being an environmentally friendly product…SodaStream's vision is to create a world free from bottles. At SodaStream, we believe it is time to rethink how you make your soda and to understand the positive environmental impact when making soda at home. We are committed to continuously improving as an earth friendly brand and offering eco-friendly products that have a positive impact on our environment." Indeed, the company's Web site prominently features a plastic bottle "counter" at the top of the page that displays management's estimates of the number of plastic bottles that the company's customers "have kept out of landfills" by using the SodaStream refillable system rather than purchasing prepackaged soft drinks. As of July 2013, the count stood at roughly 3.2 billion bottles.

Mindful of consumer concerns over obesity and wellness as well as the broad shift in consumer tastes away from colas to "flavors" over the past few years, SodaStream emphasized that its 100 flavors of syrup allow the consumer to control the amount of concentrate per serving and were available in diet or sugar-free versions. The company's product line included syrups for traditional carbonated soft drinks, energy drinks, fruit drinks, iced teas, and flavored waters.

Along with the boost to its customer value proposition afforded by a major improvement in both machine and concentrate quality, SodaStream stressed consumer cost savings compared to canned or bottled soft drinks. Excluding the upfront costs for the SodaStream machine, SodaStream said consumers spent only $0.25 for 12 ounces of SodaStream soda (the size of a can of Coke or Pepsi) and $0.25 per liter of sparkling water made with a SodaStream machine. The machine ranged in price from $79 for the basic model to $199 for the company's automated model in the United States. Flavorings cost $4.99, $6.99, and $9.99 per bottle. Each bottle of flavoring made between 25 and 33 eight-ounce servings of soda. A refill CO_2 canister (with a returned canister) cost $15 with each canister making about 60 liters of soda.

SodaStream planned to profit from its customer value proposition by sticking with its proven profit model. Like the famous Gillette "blade and razor" model, SodaStream's profit model relied upon follow-up sales of flavor concentrates and gas cylinder refills. SodaStream starter kits accounted for about 43 percent of sales, while consumables (flavor syrups, bottles, and CO_2 refills) generated 57 percent of revenues in 2012. SodaStream machines were profitable but generated gross margins of only an estimated 30 to 32 percent—well below the corporate average gross margin of 54 percent in 2012. In contrast, the consumables business had gross margins of an estimated 72 percent. While the CO_2 refill business produced significantly smaller revenues than sales of flavors and bottles, the refill canisters had astonishingly high gross margins of an estimated 85 to 90 percent.[19] The relatively small plastic bottle segment had the next best gross margins—an estimated 60 to 62 percent. The flavor concentrate business also was a very profitable one with gross margins of an estimated 58 percent.

The company's profit model had several major parts. First, the company was vertically integrated into the manufacturing of gas cylinders, SodaStream machines, and flavor concentrates. The company counted on economies of scale in its Israeli gas cylinder production facility to keep margins high. Its patented fittings on gas cylinders and the SodaStream machines made it difficult for potential competitors to copy this critical element of the SodaStream system. Moreover, regulations on handling and storing hazardous materials—the CO_2 canisters were pressurized—made retailers leery of selling competing cylinders. Second, SodaStream intended to increase both its geographic reach and household penetration of SodaStream machines, which would allow the firm to benefit from the sale of higher-margin consumables to each household with a SodaStream machine in the future. Over time,

management expected the company's already high profit margins to increase as its product mix shifted from low-margin machines to high-margin CO_2 refills and flavor concentrates. As part of its move to increase household penetration and encourage repeat purchases of consumables, SodaStream aggressively pursued licensing partnerships with established beverage brands such as Country Time and Crystal Light. The company also formed a relationship with Samsung to sell a line of refrigerators with built-in SodaStream machines. The refrigerator retailed for $3,900 in 2013. Third, SodaStream pursued relationships with competing home soda machine manufacturers in order to try to establish the SodaStream gas cylinder as the industry standard. As of summer 2013, SodaStream had no significant competitors in the U.S. market.

Financial Results

The company sold its products in 60,000 stores and 45 countries in 2012. A relative newcomer to the U.S. market, SodaStream's U.S. sales were conducted through 15,000 stores, including Williams-Sonoma, Best Buy, Wal-Mart, and Target. As Table 3 shows, the company's 2012 revenues in the Americas were about $158 million—up from about $41 million in 2010. The majority of the company's revenues in the Americas were generated by sales in the U.S. market. Overall revenues had more than doubled from $208 million to $436 million in two years. At the same time, operating profits more than tripled and net income in 2012 skyrocketed to nearly three and a half times net income in 2010. With $62 million in cash and no debt, SodaStream's balance sheet was a strong one. Yet, the company was dwarfed by its larger CSD competitors (see Appendix 1).

SodaStream's Outlook

Despite the company's exceptional financial results, investors worried that the SodaStream system would lose its appeal to consumers as it had in previous decades. With no

Table 3   SodaStream 2010–2012 Revenue

Company	2010	2012	Difference
SodaStream	$41	$158	$117
PepsiCo	$236.7	$341.9	$8.31
Dr Pepper Snapple Group	$137.3	$148.1	$6.47

Source: Business Insider, Dr Pepper Snapple Group 2011 10K, *Stastica, Wall Street Journal,* Beverage-Digest.

buyout in sight, the company had to continue to perform on its own to keep the stock market happy. SodaStream's own research showed that an estimated 5 million consumers worldwide used a SodaStream machine at least once every two weeks. The company sold more than 10 million machines from 2008 to 2012. Still, investors had shown they were willing to bet on companies with far less impressive conversion rates than SodaStream, such as Pandora. SodaStream bulls argued that the company was a "disruptive innovator" that would make canned and bottled soft drinks obsolete. The SodaStream system did not require a capital-intensive bottling system because consumers made the drinks at home with their own CO_2 canisters. SodaStream drinks were inexpensive and relatively healthy. Consumers could customize the product by altering the amount of carbonation and flavor concentrate. The product was environmentally friendly, unlike every other prepackaged beverage on the market. The company's more than 100 soda flavors gave consumers more variety than they could get from the large CSD brands. In addition, the company's money-back satisfaction guarantee was an important signal of quality assurance to the consumer. SodaStream's total marketing expenditures worldwide were substantial at $153 million in 2012.

The company indicated brand building was a top priority by purchasing ad time from the U.S.'s most expensive ad venue: the Super Bowl. However, SodaStream's ad featuring exploding Coke-like and Pepsi-like bottles was banned by CBS from the Super Bowl in the United States. The ad immediately "went viral" on YouTube, according to NewsMax. SodaStream arguably garnered more consumer attention due to the CBS ban and a similar one in the United Kingdom by television industry trade group Clearcast than it would have gotten through the ad.

Still, the system did not yet operate as smoothly as it should because U.S. retailers were unfamiliar with the gas cylinder exchange program and frequently did not know how to give consumers a newly filled but used cylinder for $15 rather than selling them a new cylinder for $25. Information on cylinder exchange often was missing from store shelves, and many flavors frequently were out of stock.

Moreover, SodaStream bears pointed to the lack of significant barriers to entry for a potential SodaStream competitor—should the market become large enough to attract large consumer products companies. A new gas cylinder factory might only cost $100 million to build compared to billions to replicate the Coca-Cola or Pepsi bottling system in the United States alone. SodaStream's product might be a convenient alternative to prepackaged drinks at home, but U.S. consumers were accustomed to being able to purchase a Coke or Pepsi nearly anywhere. The huge popularity of the Coca-Cola "Freestyle" drink-dispensing machine with its 125 different flavor options underlined the company's efforts to respond to consumer demands for flavor variety suggested that SodaStream's flavor variety might have some traction with customers.

As Anna Claire pondered all she had learned about the CSD industry and SodaStream in the past few days, she thought about a quote from Birnbaum, SodaStream's CEO, in response to the CBS Super Bowl ad ban: "Our ad confronts the beverage industry and its arguably outdated business model." He went on to say, "One day we will look back on plastic soda bottles the way we now view cigarettes."[20]

"Perhaps Birnbaum was right," Anna Claire thought.

End Notes

1. Zekaria, S. (2012). "SodaStream fizzes up global market for carbonated and flavored drinks." *The Wall Street Journal*, November 13.
2. Reuters Tel Aviv. (2013). "PepsiCo in talks to buy SodaStream for $2 billion." June 6, www.reuters.com/article/2013/06/06/sodastream-pepsi-idUSL5N0EI0NI20130606.
3. Reuters Tel Aviv. (2013). "PepsiCo denies in talks to buy SodaStream." June 6, www.reuters.com/article/2013/06/06/us-sodastream-pepsi-idUSBRE9550AJ20130606.
4. Kosman, J. (2013). "SodaStream's sale hopes going pffffffft." *New York Post*, July 9, www.nypost.com/p/news/business/sodastream_sale_hopes_going_pffffffft_jFn51VKX0OTiRVKNipLn3J.
5. Stevens, J. (2012). "Remember SodaStream? Now you can just twist 'n sparkle with a clever bottle that even makes your own champagne." *Mail OnLine*, May 11, www.dailymail.co.uk/femail/article-2142925/Remember-SodaStream-Now-just-Twist-n-Sparkle-clever-bottle-makes-Champagne.html.

6. en.wikipedia.org/wiki/Sodastream, July 17, 2013.
7. "SodaStream international presentation: Company overview." July 17, 2013, sodas-tream.investorroom.com/sodastreamoverview.
8. "Breaking down the chain: A guide to the soft drink industry." National Policy and Legal Analysis Network to Prevent Childhood Obesity. Public Health Law and Policy. changelabsolutions.org/publications/breaking-down-chain.
9. (2013). "The Coca-Cola Company commences implementation of 21st Century Beverage Partnership Model in the United States." Coca-Cola press release, April 16, www.coca-colacompany/press-center/press-releases.
10. (2013). "The Coca-Cola Company discusses 1Q 2013 results—earnings call transcript." April 16, seekingalpha.com/article/1344791-the-coca-cola-company-s-ceo-discusses-q1-2013-results-earnings-call-transcript?page=3.
11. Saltzman, H., R. Levy, and J. Hilke. (1999). "Transformation and continuity: The U.S. carbonated soft drink bottling industry and antitrust policy since 1980." *Bureau of Economics Staff Report*. Federal Trade Commission, November.
12. Ibid. Page 5.
13. Esterl, M. (2013). "Fizzy drinks revenue goes from flat to sour." *The Wall Street Journal,* January 18.
14. Adams, B. (2013). "Judge overturns NYC's soda ban." TheBlaze.com, May 11, www.theblaze.com/stories/2013/03/11/report-judge-overturns-nycs-soda-ban/.
15. (2012). "Reinvigorated bottled water bounces back from recessionary years, new report from beverage marketing corporation shows. Press release, May.
16. Edwards, J. (2012). "In Gatorade war, Pepsi seems to have deliberately given up market share to Coke." *Business Insider*, February 1, www.businessinsider.com/why-gatorades-10-point-loss-of-share-to-cokes-powerade-is-not-a-total-disaster-2012-2.
17. (2012). "Apple tops the list of the world's most powerful brands." *Forbes*, October 22, www.forbes.com/sites/kurtbadenhausen/2012/10/02/apple-tops-list-of-the-worlds-most-powerful-brands/.
18. Andreyava, T., M. W. Long, and K. D. Brownell. (2010). "The impact of food prices on consumption: A systematic review of research on the price elasticity of demand for food." *American Journal of Public Health,* 100(2), pp. 216–222.
19. Author's estimates.
20. Elsinger, D. (2013). "SodaStream ad: Banned by CBS from Super Bowl, video goes viral." NewsMax.com, February 4, www.newsmax.com/TheWire/sodastream-ad-super-bowl-cbs/2013/02/04/id/488766.

Other References

1. (2013). "100 leading national advertisers 2013 edition." *Advertising Age,* June 24.
2. (2012). "Special issue: U.S. beverage results for 2012." *Beverage-Digest*, March 20.

APPENDIX A	Selected 2012 Financials—Branded Carbonated Soft Drink Companies ($ in Millions Except EPS and Beta)			
	Coca-Cola	**Dr Pepper Snapple**	**PepsiCo**	**SodaStream**
Sales	$48,017	$5,595	$65,492	$436
Gross Profit	28,964	3,495	34,201	236
Gross Margin	60.3%	62.5%	52.2%	54.0%
Operating Profit	10,779	1,092	9,112	46
Operating Margin	22.4%	19.5%	13.9%	10.4%
Interest Expense	397	125	899	0
Net Income	9,019	629	6,214	44
EPS (fully diluted)	$2.00	$2.96	$3.92	$2.09
Shares Outstanding	4504	2123	1575	2
Cash	$16,551	$366	$6,619	$62
Accounts Receivable	4,759	602	7,041	115
Inventory	3,264	197	3,581	113
Total Assets	86,174	8,929	74,638	412
Accounts Payable	$8,680	$283	$11,903	$86
Total Debt	32,610	2,804	28,359	0
Shareholders Equity	33,168	2,280	22,399	274
Depreciation	1,982	240	2,689	10
Capital Expenditures	2,780	193	2,714	34
Beta (as of 7/18/13)	0.33	−0.04	0.30	1.43
Share Price (7/18/13)	$40.81	$47.91	$86.80	$58.22
North American Sales	41%[a]	100%	57%	36%
International Sales	59%	0%	43%	64%
North American Beverages	41%	100%	33%	36%[b]

[a] U.S. only.

[b] Includes sales of SodaStream machines and gas cylinders.

Case 1–2: True Religion Jeans: Will Going Private Help It Regain Its Congregation?*

True Religion Board Accepts $835 Million Takeover Bid

"It's been more than half a year since the 10-year-old high-end-jeans seller, no longer the must-have brand, put itself up for sale.

True Religion Apparel Inc., the Southern California purveyor of pricey designer denim, may have gotten too small for its britches. More than half a year after putting itself up for sale amid growth struggles and fluctuating stock, the high-end-jeans seller said its board unanimously accepted an $835-million takeover offer from investment firm TowerBrook Capital Partners."

—excerpt from The Los Angeles Times[1]

True Religion Brand Jeans

Founded in 2002 by Jeff Lubell, True Religion had become one of the largest premium denim brands in the United States by 2012. Although True Religion made its debut in upscale department stores and trendy boutiques a decade earlier, the company owned 86 full-price retail stores and 36 outlet stores in the United States as well as 30 stores in international markets by the end of 2012. The company's domestic retail store business accounted for about 60 percent of revenues and 64 percent of operating profit before unallocated corporate expenses in 2012. Just five years earlier, the U.S. retail store segment generated only 17 percent of sales and 25 percent of operating profit before unallocated corporate expenses (see Exhibit 1).

Lubell's vision of the company had come true—at least partly. The company had transformed itself from a jeans designer into an apparel retailer with it own brand à la Buckle and Diesel. At the same time, True Religion had managed to shift its product mix so that sportswear accounted for almost 35 percent of sales in its company-owned stores. Lubell felt these two ingredients were critical to establishing True Religion as a "lifestyle brand."

The ultimate in product differentiation, many companies attempt to create so-called "lifestyle" brands that transcend product category and inspire deep consumer loyalty. Becoming a lifestyle brand was the key to insulating True Religion from the inevitable fluctuations in fashion trends.

Moreover, True Religion's sales had grown at an average annual rate of almost 22 percent from 2007 to 2012 (see Exhibit 2). The company's return on invested capital was an impressive 27 percent, and its return on average assets was 12 percent in 2012. Despite these factors, press articles and analyst reports on True Religion described the company as "the struggling maker of premium denim."[2] A New York Post article titled "Escape from Hell for True Religion" described private equity firm TowerBrook as the company's "savior."[3]

What had gone wrong at True Religion? Was the change in ownership the answer to the company's problems? Could True Religion regain its status as the must-have premium denim brand in the United States? Would the company be forced to pull a "Rock & Republic" and reposition itself as a mid-priced brand? Was premium denim destined to go the way of Flash Dance legwarmers and Crocs as fast fashion from the likes of H&M became more mainstream? Private equity investors had snapped up stakes in both established and up-and-coming premium denim brands in the previous five years. With soon only one publicly traded premium jeans maker (Joe's Jeans) left, should investors stay away from the industry?

A Brief Recap of the Recent History of the U.S. Denim Market

Calvin Klein popularized the concept of premium jeans in the late 1970s. The designer burst onto the jeans scene with shockingly high prices, a skin-tight fit, and a controversial advertising campaign featuring a very young Brooke Shields. As Brooke Shields confided to U.S. consumers that nothing came between her and her "Calvins," the $35-per-pair jeans flew off store shelves. At the time, mainstream Lee and Wrangler blue jeans retailed for about $12 per pair on

*This case was prepared by Bonita Austin for the purposes of class discussion. It is reprinted with permission.

Exhibit 1   True Religion Brand Jeans Operating Segments ($ in thousands)

Net Sales	2007	2008	2009	2010	2011	2012
U.S. Consumer Direct	$29,268	$75,314	$129,030	$189,097	$251,334	$281,583
U.S. Wholesale	111,390	153,235	123,203	104,874	86,268	99,215
International	31,728	40,044	54,479	64,443	78,974	83,824
Core Services[a]	870	1,407	4,289	5,300	3,222	2,663
Total Company Net Sales	$173,256	$270,000	$311,001	$363,714	$419,798	$467,285
Gross Profit						
U.S. Consumer Direct	$22,380	$57,669	$95,276	$136,915	$178,341	$197,328
Gross Margin	76.5%	76.6%	73.8%	72.4%	71.0%	70.1%
U.S. Wholesale	60,007	78,670	65,882	53,362	44,445	50,452
Gross Margin	53.9%	51.3%	53.5%	50.9%	51.5%	50.9%
International	15,498	19,255	30,115	34,402	45,821	49,080
	48.8%	48.1%	55.3%	53.4%	58.0%	58.6%
Other	870	1,407	4,289	5,300	3,222	2,663
Total Company Gross Profit	$98,757	$157,003	$195,564	$229,981	$271,831	$299,525
Total Company Gross Margin	57.0%	58.1%	62.9%	63.2%	64.8%	64.1%

Operating Profit	2007	Restated 2008	Restated 2009	2010	2011	2012
U.S. Consumer Direct	$11,875	$27,810	$44,766	$64,641	$88,453	$93,726
Operating Margin	40.6%	36.9%	34.7%	34.2%	35.2%	33.3%
	$0.252					
U.S. Wholesale	36,405	71,884	60,107	46,265	37,116	44,333
Operating Margin	32.7%	46.9%	48.8%	44.1%	43.0%	44.7%
International	14,718	16,761	25,167	17,487	15,927	7,895
Operating Margin	46.4%	41.9%	46.2%	27.1%	20.2%	9.4%
Core Services[b]	−15,856	−47,579	−52,443	−58,471	−66,885	−67,837
Total Company Operating Profit	$47,143	$68,877	$77,598	$69,923	$74,612	$78,118
Total Company Operating Margin	27.2%	25.5%	25.0%	19.2%	17.8%	16.7%

Assets	2007	2008	2009	2010	2011	2012
U.S. Consumer Direct	$10,167	$36,603	$55,763	$68,418	$78,089	$90,654
U.S. Wholesale	41,248	43,030	31,159	35,001	26,182	27,584
International	6,519	8,362	16,897	24,940	41,700	54,764
Core Services[c]	55,324	78,457	125,987	167,525	214,182	232,714
Total Company Assets	$113,258	$166,452	$229,806	$295,884	$360,153	$405,716

[a] Licensing revenues generated by royalty agreements.
[b] Unallocated corporate expenses.
[c] Unallocated corporate assets.

Source: True Religion Apparel Inc. 10K - 2007, 2008, 2009, 2010, 2011, 2012.

average. Suddenly, jeans were no longer functional wardrobe staples. They were sexy fashion statements. The jeans craze peaked in 1981 when retail sales jumped to a record $6 billion and 520 million pairs.[4] As designer jeans fell out of favor and the prime 14–24-year-old jeans-buying cohort aged, domestic annual jeans sales slid to 416 million pairs by 1985.

Following a protracted decline in the 1980s, the market surpassed its earlier peak and hit annual sales of 511 million pairs in 1995. Denim jeans unit sales grew at a strong 7 to 10 percent per year from 1990 to 1996. Then, in 1997, the denim market experienced a sharp slowdown in growth that lasted until the end of 1999—rising just 3 percent per year on average. For some industry players the slowdown meant disaster. Levi Strauss saw its sales plunge more than 13 percent in 1998, almost 14 percent in 1999, and nearly 10 percent in 2000. U.S. textile giants Cone, Swift, and Burlington cut prices and idled production lines—all victims of a denim glut at retail caused by a shift in fashion trends.

Exhibit 2   True Religion Brand Jeans Selected Financials ($ in thousands except per share amounts)

	2007	2008	2009	2010	2011	2012
Revenues	$173,256	$270,000	$311,001	$363,714	$419,798	$467,285
Cost of Goods Sold	74,429	112,999	115,439	133,735	147,969	167,762
Gross Profit	$98,827	$157,001	$195,562	$229,979	$271,829	$299,523
Gross Margin	57.0%	58.1%	62.9%	63.2%	64.8%	64.1%
Selling, General & Administrative Exp.	51,685	88,125	117,965	160,057	197,218	221,406
Operating Profit	47,142	68,876	77,597	69,922	74,611	78,117
Operating Margin	27.2%	25.5%	25.0%	19.2%	17.8%	16.7%
Other Expense (Income)	−1803	−1065	−169	−403	637	−94
Pretax Profit	48,945	69,941	77,766	70,325	73,974	78,211
Taxes	21,100	25,570	30,434	26,690	28,197	31,513
Tax Rate	43.1%	36.6%	39.1%	38.0%	38.1%	40.3%
Net Income	$27,845	$44,371	$47,332	$43,635	$45,777	$46,698
Redeemable Noncontrolling Interest	0	0	0	139	810	683
Net Income Attributable to True Religion	$27,845	$44,371	$47,332	$43,496	$44,967	$46,015
Net Margin	16.1%	16.4%	15.2%	12.0%	10.7%	9.8%
Earnings Per Share (Diluted)	$1.16	$1.83	$1.92	$1.75	$1.80	$1.82
Average Shares Outstanding (Diluted)	23,949	24,270	24,659	24,852	25,026	25,328
Selected Balance Sheet Figures	**2007**	**2008**	**2009**	**2010**	**2011**	**2012**
Cash & Short-Term Investments	$34,031	$62,095	$110,479	$153,792	$200,366	$186,148
Accounts Receivable	27,898	33,103	27,217	27,856	23,959	31,647
Inventory	20,771	25,828	34,502	41,691	53,320	65,655
Propterty, Plant & Equipment	11,579	28,006	39,693	48,448	53,698	61,565
Total Assets	113,258	166,452	229,806	295,884	360,153	405,716
Accounts Payable	$9,597	$10,633	$11,717	$17,234	$22,872	$30,868
Total Debt	0	0	0	0	0	0
Shareholders' Equity	95,247	142,250	197,854	249,032	299,788	332,935
Total Liabilities & Rquity	229,806	166,452	229,806	295,884	360,153	405,716
Rent Expense	$3,700	$9,300	$16,200	$24,100	$30,600	$37,600
Advertising Expense	1,200	3,900	5,400	8,000	7,900	11,700
Number of Company-Owned Stores	15	42	73	94	109	152

Source: True Religion 10Ks 2007–2012

The introduction of new stretch fabrics and widespread acceptance of "casual Friday" and other office "dress-down" days stimulated demand for khaki, carpenter, and cargo pants and cut into denim demand in the late '90s. Casual wear for work became so socially acceptable during the "dot-com bubble" that even staid Wall Street firms permitted employees to wear "golf casual" rather than formal business attire to work on Fridays in spring and summer. Nevertheless, even as demand for basic five-pocket denim jeans suffered from the shift in consumer preferences in casual wear in the late 1990s, demand for women's fashion jeans grew. Angelo La Grega, president of VF Corporation's Mass Market Denim Division, noted in a 1997 interview with *Women's Wear Daily*, "The business is moving from pure commodity to fashion basics."[5] The primary reason for the resurgence in demand for fashion jeans was the availability of denim jeans in exciting new washes and finishes.

"Distressed" and "dirty" denim hit retail shelves in spring 2000. The new distressed jeans tapped into consumers' taste for vintage denim. Distressed, dirty jeans were already "broken in," wrinkled, and stained and looked as if the owner had worn them for years. The Italian jeans maker Diesel had pushed dirty denim for several seasons before it gained approval from other designers. A few designers like Kenneth Cole also experimented with the new stretch denim, a cotton denim that incorporated 2 percent Lycra spandex to improve wearing comfort.[6]

Against that backdrop, Jerome Dahan and Michael Glasser introduced their 7 For All Mankind premium denim line to a consumer market hungry for fashion innovations. The new denim label would fuel the hottest upscale denim market since the late 1970s and eventually would spark product improvements at every price point in the jeans spectrum. Aspiring as well as established designers would introduce literally hundreds of denim labels in the new decade as they answered the siren call of high growth and high profit margins. Retailers eagerly snapped up new offerings, as their customers demanded the latest hot jeans. The premium denim market, defined as jeans retailing for $100 or more, would jump from a dollar market share of about 1 percent in 2000 to about 10 percent of retail sales in 2012.

U.S. Premium Denim Industry

Many industry observers believed that the estimated $1.7 billion (retail) premium denim market had begun to mature in 2006. Overall U.S. denim jeans ownership peaked at 8.2 pairs of jeans per consumer that year. The appeal of denim was strong, but average jeans ownership had fallen to 6.7 pairs per consumer by the end of 2012.[7] According to a 2012 Cotton Inc. consumer survey, 75 percent of women and 73 percent of men stated they "loved or enjoyed wearing denim." Still, those figures were down 3 percentage points each from the same survey in 2007.[8]

With nearly seven pairs of jeans in the typical American woman's closet and the move away from fashion jeans to basics, it had become increasingly difficult to persuade consumers to buy new pairs of jeans. At the same time, the premium market had shown it was not immune to economic downturns. After years of torrid sales growth, the premium jeans industry experienced its first slowdown in 2007 with sales down about –5 percent. Although the industry seemed to defy economic weakness with sales up an estimated 17 percent in 2008, premium denim revenues slumped an estimated –8 percent in 2009 and fell about –10 percent in 2010.

Industry sales jumped about 11 percent in 2011 and rose an estimated 7 to 8 percent in 2012 to about $1.7 billion at retail as the U.S. economy improved (see Exhibit 3). Nevertheless, the outlook for the market was cloudy. True Religion and Joe's Jeans reported good growth in sales to retail accounts in the first quarter of 2013, but True Religion's company-owned store growth was fueled by sales to outlet stores. 7 For All Mankind brand reported disappointing sales results in the second quarter of 2013 (down –5 percent) due to softness in the upscale department store channel. Moreover, 7's management forecasted implied domestic growth for the brand of only 2 percent per year on average from 2012 to 2017—suggesting tepid

growth for the industry as 7 was one of the largest premium denim brands in the United States.

Many investors were worried about the so-called aspirational shopper. While the core luxury buyer had returned to high-end shopping as the recession ended, aspirational shoppers had largely stayed away. At the same time, enormous improvements in bargain-priced jeans' fabric, fit, and styling encouraged consumers to "trade down" from expensive brands to stalwarts like Levi's, Lee, and Gap jeans. Some analysts estimated that as much as 70 percent of luxury brand sales and 50 percent of the growth in the luxury market was derived from so-called "aspirational" shoppers prior to the recession.[9] Aspirational shoppers—middle-class consumers with luxury tastes—had household incomes between $75,000 and $150,000. Easy credit and rising home prices fueled spending and made the aspirational shopper the target of many brand marketing campaigns in the heady days before the housing bubble burst and unemployment surged to post–Great Depression highs.

Prior to the recession, many premium denim labels defined themselves as "aspirational brands": expensive but not as pricey as couture brands that charged thousands for each piece of clothing. Numerous press articles declared the death of the aspirational shopper and a new "bargain hunting is cool" zeitgeist that would survive after the economy rebounded. A November 2012 consumer survey by Accenture showed nearly two-thirds of American shoppers did not intend to return to pre-recession spending patterns.[10]

While not everyone believed that the aspirational shopper was gone for good, Tiffany's earnings disappointments for holiday 2012 and in the first quarter of 2013 were attributed partly to weakness in aspirational shopper spending on the brand along with increasing product prices. Without the aspirational shopper, new premium denim customers were likely to prove hard to come by in the U.S. market. Still, the Accenture study showed half of the consumers surveyed were likely to make a small luxury purchase in the next six months. Although more consumers were likely to purchase a luxury or gourmet food item, 48 percent of consumers surveyed said they were likely to purchase luxury apparel to mix into a wardrobe of more affordable items.[11]

Investors also were concerned about fashion trends and prices. Embroidered, embellished, and distressed jeans were all the rage from 2002 to 2005. In those days of skyrocketing demand, premium denim designers had many ways to differentiate their products and cash in on current fashion trends. As the U.S. economy began to slow, flashy fashion jeans fell out of favor with consumers whose interest in "basics" increased as their incomes declined. On

Exhibit 3   2012 Selected Financials—Jeans Companies ($ in thousands except per share amounts and betas)

	Buckle	Guess	Joe's	Levi's	Fifth and Pacific[a]	True Religion	VF Corp
Revenues	$1,124,007	$2,658,605	$118,642	$4,610,193	$1,505,094	$467,285	$10,879,855
Gross Profit	499,315	1,067,123	56,170	2,199,331	842,975	299,523	5,061,975
Gross Margin	44.4%	40.1%	47.3%	47.7%	56.0%	64.1%	46.5%
Operating Profit	$258,175	$274,525	$10,717	$333,979	−$34,451	$78,117	$1,465,267
Operating Margin	23.0%	10.3%	9.0%	7.2%	−2.3%	16.7%	13.5%
Interest Expense	$0	$1,640	$376	$134,694	$51,684	$0	$93,605
Net Income	164,305	178,744	5,565	143,850	−74,505	46,015	1,086,138
EPS (fully diluted)	$3.44	$2.05	$0.08	NA	−$0.68	$1.83	$9.70
Shares Outstanding	48,059	86,540	66,849	NA	109,292	25,328	110,205
Cash	$144,022	$335,927	$13,426	$406,134	$59,402	$186,148	$597,461
Accounts Receivable	3,470	324,971	812	500,672	121,591	31,647	1,222,345
Inventory	103,853	369,712	31,318	518,860	220,538	65,655	1,354,158
Total Assets	477,974	1,713,506	86,024	3,170,077	902,523	405,716	9,633,021
Accounts Payable	$34,124	$191,143	$10,893	$225,726	$174,705	$30,868	$562,638
Total Debt	0	1,901	0	1,729,211	406,294	0	1,844,598
Shareholders Equity	289,649	1,100,868	71,739	−101,508	−126,930	332,935	5,125,625
Depreciation	$33,834	$87,197	$1,456	$122,608	$74,411	$13,373	$196,898
Capital Expenditures	30,297	99,591	2,779	83,855	82,792	21,994	251,940
Company Owned Stores	440	1,118	28	511	213[c]	152	65[e]
Licensed/Franchised Stores	0	985	0	1,800	11	0	0
Beta (as of 7/22/13)	1.04	1.71	1.30	NA	2.62	1.08	0.77
Share Price (7/22/13)	$56.42	$31.78	$1.35	NA	$23.17	$31.90	$194.86
Own Brand as % of Sales	34%	100%	100%	100%	100%	100%	100%
U.S. Comparable Store Sales Change	2.1%	−6.6%	10.0%	NA	10.0%[c]	2.7%	NA
U.S. Sales	100%	50.8%	95.8%	50%	95%[d]	82.1%	60%[e]
International Sales	0%	49.2%	4.2%	50%	5%	17.9%	40%

[a] Formerly Liz Claiborne-owns Lucky Jeans.
[b] Guess comparable store sales and sales mix for North America.
[c] Lucky Brand Jeans stores only.
[d] Estimated Lucky Jeans sales only. Does not include other FNP brands.
[e] 7 for All Mankind only.

the plus side, a good pair of dark jeans was considered a "must have" item for women. *Glamour* magazine put jeans at #7 on its list of "10 Wardrobe Items Every Woman Should Own."[12] On the negative side, Topher Gaylord, then-president of 7 For All Mankind, commented in a 2009 interview with the *New York Daily News*, "We really don't believe consumers today understand the value of premium denim."[13] It was hard to differentiate a plain, dark blue pair of expensive jeans from less expensive basic jeans. In an interview with Reuters, industry analyst Eric Beder said, "Premium denim slows down when the trend goes basic. How do you recognize it's premium? How much differentiation is there in that pair of $189 jeans compared to a $79 pair when they are just dark and straight?"[14]

Skinny jeans had played well with consumers over the past five years, but they were as difficult to differentiate as other types of basic jeans. Colored denim and jeggings (denim leggings) had attracted consumers back to the premium market in 2011 and 2012. In general, they did not command super premium prices and so gave consumers a more affordable entry-level price point during the recession. Those offerings continued to drive premium purchases in 2013, but premium jeans designers were scrambling to find the next big thing in jeans. Designers were experimenting with wax and rubber coatings as well as patterned denim. Thus far, nothing had taken off with consumers. Moreover, the dip in denim's overall popularity from 2008 to 2012 had not gone unnoticed by retailers. Retailers cut denim jeans floor space allocation and increased floor space for women's dresses and skirts and men's athletic wear and non-denim pants in 2012–2013 compared with 2010–2011.[15]

Price points continued to be an issue for premium denim designers in 2013. Prior to the recession, consumers had been willing to pay sometimes as much as $600 for a pair of jeans that was "just right." "It was all just a fad," said Jeff Rudes, founder of fast-growing J Brand premium jeans.[16] Even though the economy improved, many consumers remained reluctant to pay up for the "right" pair of jeans. *The Wall Street Journal* and *The New York Times* ran stories about the gulf between premium jeans prices at the cash register and the price the designers paid to make consumers' favorite jeans. A 2011 *Wall Street Journal* article quoted Lubell as saying True Religion's best-selling "Super T" jeans cost only about $50 to make, wholesaled for $152, and retailed at $335 per pair.[17] The press coverage only served to reinforce consumers' doubts about whether the most expensive jeans were "worth it."

Notably, only about 15 percent of 7 For All Mankind's denim jeans were priced at $200 or more in 2013—up from 5 percent in 2009 but down sharply from 25 percent in 2008 and the pre-recession peak of 30 percent.[18] A survey of the Internet shopping sites of the top five premium jeans brands revealed that on average four of the five had prices below $200 on 83 percent of their jeans. True Religion was the outlier with 56 percent of its product line priced at $200 or above. Interestingly, the company had chosen to buck the industry trend and had increased the amount of pricier jeans in its line, up from 45 percent in 2010.

Industry insiders were concerned about a new tariff on U.S. exports of women's jeans to the European Union that became effective on May 1, 2013. The 38 percent tariff was tough on the premium jeans industry as about 75 percent of all premium jeans were manufactured in Los Angeles. Lower-end jeans typically were produced outside of the United States due to the relatively high U.S. labor costs. The tariff was three times larger than the old tariff on women's jeans. "Made in the USA" carried cachet with consumers in the European premium jeans market. Lowering costs by relocating manufacturing to low–labor cost countries was likely to hurt the brand images of expensive jeans as the brands risked losing their authenticity by moving out of the United States. Some premium denim makers were experimenting with less expensive fibers in order to lower costs, but consumers so far had not flocked to the cotton blends.

Premium denim labels had already experienced cost pressures as cotton prices hit a post–Civil War high in 2010. The 68 percent jump in average cotton prices in 2010

was followed by an additional surge of 48 percent in 2011. Denim designers cheered as cotton prices plunged 43 percent in 2012. The price relief continued through March 2013. Drought conditions and lower acreage allotted to cotton production by farmers in the United States along with aggressive cotton stockpiling by the Chinese government pushed cotton prices up in April and May 2013. A cotton price spike was the last thing the premium denim makers needed, given consumers' reluctance to pay up for jeans.

Still, it appeared that Americans' nearly 140-year old love affair with denim was still going strong in 2013. The question for the industry remained was the market still "Rich & Skinny"—like denim guru Glasser's premium brand—or had it become more like Cheap Monday, the Swedish line of mid-priced jeans?

Competitive Landscape

Despite the exodus of weaker brands during the recession, the premium denim market remained crowded. The top four premium jeans brands held an estimated combined 70 percent share of the market in 2012—up from an estimated combined share of 65 to 68 percent in 2007, but down from an estimated 80 percent in 2009. Conventional wisdom held that the underlying slowing industry growth combined with the economic downturn would result in a shakeout that would leave the strongest premium denim makers in control of the market. That had not turned out to be the case. In fact, only three of the top five brands in 2010 remained in the top five in 2012; J Brand and Hudson had replaced Citizens of Humanity and Rock & Republic in the top five. True Religion and 7 For All Mankind were still the top brands in the segment, but both had shown signs of losing some of their grip on the category in the past two years. The remaining 30 percent of the market was split between dozens of denim labels.

A July 2013 Internet survey of the five major U.S. upscale department stores and two prominent denim boutiques revealed that each carried 66 different brands of women's premium jeans on average. The same retailers carried only 28 brands on average in December 2010. However, some retailers sold many more brands. Notably, trendsetting California-based Revolve Clothing offered 86 different brands of premium women's jeans—up from 55 in 2010. Similarly, Nordstrom sold 74 brands of women's premium jeans compared with 45 brands in 2010. The explosion in brands highlighted several features of the premium denim market.

First, it remained relatively easy to launch a new brand and gain retail shelf space. Though this was long a major barrier to entry in consumer products categories, the fickle nature of many premium denim consumers made getting retail distribution much less of a problem for an innovative denim entrée. Fashion consumers were always on the lookout for the latest, most fashionable items. The shift from the fashion jean to the wardrobe staple had not diminished the importance of innovation in style, fit, finish, and fabric to consumers. Brands that missed key fashion trends frequently were discarded in favor of upstarts, and retailers were happy to offer the products as with an average retail mark up of 2.2 times wholesale; their premium denim margins were high.

Second, upscale retailers continued to try to differentiate their stores from their rivals' stores through product offerings and a fashion "point of view". Established large brands had to fend off the advances of upstarts and smaller brands as jeans lines attempted to segment the premium market and carve out their own niches. The high margins and returns of the larger players along with low capital requirements enticed new "jeaners" or denim specialists to enter the segment. As denim designer Mik Serfontaine stated in a 2010 interview for the Sundance Channel documentary *Dirty Denim*, "Make up some samples and take it to the trade show—you're in business."[19] Moreover, established fashion designers such as Donna Karan and Helmut Lang could knock out a few jeans styles and get shelf space on the strength of their broad apparel lines. While these designers might not pose a serious threat to the big premium brands, if industry growth remained low after the economy rebounded, the premium denim labels would have to deal with them as every market share point would be important.

Third, the success of a premium denim line depended heavily upon the market and fashion insights of the head designer. It was notoriously difficult for even the savviest designers to generate hit after hit in the fast-moving fashion world. Once a semiannual event, new style launches had become a monthly event in some market segments such as the popular fast fashion category. Retailers such as H&M, Forever 21, and Zara had begun to transform the fashion industry. H&M wanted to "surprise" its customers and always have something new in stock in order to generate repeat business. Zara could design and produce its own products and get them on the shelf within a month. The biannual fashion cycle had become a year-round fashion cycle.

Premium denim was not immune to the nearly constant pressure to introduce new products to induce consumers to purchase—especially now that the underlying growth of the U.S. premium denim market appeared to have experienced a secular slowdown. With seemingly everyone wearing either premium jeans or less-expensive

jeans with premium features, consumers needed a reason to buy new jeans. In late 2010, Jeff Rudes gave consumers something new to purchase by testing and then launching a line of brightly colored jeans under his J Brand line. So far, nothing had emerged to take the place of the popular colored jeans or the ubiquitous skinny jean, and both were easily copied.

Retailers constantly were on the lookout for the next hot brand as premium denim buyers were fickle. In a recent Cotton Inc. survey of premium denim consumers, 84 percent of those surveyed indicated they were willing to try a new brand.[20] In fact, jeans designers launched new brands even in the depths of the recession and downturn in the market. Current/Elliott is "…the most refreshing denim line to come out of LA's jeans scene in a long, long time," according to a Vogue magazine article. Current/Elliott gained traction in upscale department stores as the new "it-jeans" following its 2008 launch. The brand looked as if it had staying power as upscale department store retailers devoted nearly 70 percent more "e-shelf space" or Internet shelf space to the line as to True Religion in 2013.

Table 1 shows the top 11 women's premium jeans brands by e-shelf space devoted to them by the five major upscale department stores, and two denim boutiques in July 2013, compared with e-space in the same Internet stores in December 2010. Upscale retailers cut physical shelf space devoted to premium jeans in their

Table 1	July 2013 e-Shelf Space Survey Top Premium Denim Brands Selected Upscale Retailer Internet Sites	
	Internet Shelf Space	
Designer (Women's)	**2010**	**2013**
7 For All Mankind	13%	8%
AG Jeans	3%	5%
Citizens of Humanity	11%	5%
Current/Elliott	4%	5%
Genetic Denim	2%	2%
Hudson	3%	4%
J Brand	6%	10%
Joe's	7%	3%
Paige Premium	7%	4%
NYDJ	6%	4%
Rag & Bone	1%	5%
True Religion	6%	3%
All Others	31%	42%

Sources: Internet sites of Bergdorf Goodman, Bloomingdale's Neiman-Marcus, Nordstrom, Revolve Clothing, Saks, and ShopBop.com

brick-and-mortar stores but nearly tripled the amount of premium jeans on their Internet shopping sites between December 2010 and July 2013.

While it was not possible to draw a direct line from e-shelf space to market shares, the Internet survey clearly showed smaller jeans brands had encroached upon the e-shelf space of the larger brands as retailers increased their efforts to satisfy the desires of their customers for hot fashion items and unique looks. J Brand, AG Jeans, and Rag & Bone were the big winners with the retailers surveyed. J Brand, now majority owned by Star Capital, had been an up-and-comer prior to the recession. The three early movers in the premium denim market—7 For All Mankind, True Religion, and Citizens of Humanity—each lost a substantial amount of e-shelf space between 2010 and 2013. Given True Religion's aggressive push into the retail business it is not surprising that the company's major retail accounts would choose to cut back their shelf space allocations. Still, the e-shelf space loss again raised the question of whether the older brands remained relevant a decade or more after their launches into the category. Had J Brand, AG Jeans, and Rag & Bone done a better job in creating fashion trends than the industry stalwarts? If so, would their design teams be able to keep their fingers on the pulse of the fickle fashionista?

Manufacturing Process and Supply Chain

One bale of cotton can be made into 215 pairs of men's jeans or 250 pairs of women's jeans, according to the National Cotton Council.[21] At 480 pounds per bale and a 2012 average world cotton price of about $0.89 per pound, raw cotton accounted for an estimated $1.71 per pair of women's jeans. How did less than $2 per pair of cotton result in jeans that retailed for $100 to $350 per pair?

Premium jeans ranged from traditional 100 percent cotton denim jeans to jeans made from stretch denim—a combination of cotton and spandex—to jeans made from denim fabric composed of cotton and small amounts of polyester. Nevertheless, cotton was the major raw material for premium jeans. The top five cotton-producing nations were China, India, the United States, Pakistan, and Brazil in 2012. The big five accounted for 79 percent of the world's cotton supply, according to the U.S. Department of Agriculture. China alone produced 29 percent of the world supply of cotton. Number-two producer India supplied 22 percent of the world's cotton. At number three in the world, the United States produced 17.3 million

480-pound bales of cotton or 14 percent of the world supply.[22] China was the largest consumer of cotton in the world. The United States was the largest exporter of cotton in the world.

Cotton prices had been in a long-term decline as worldwide production costs fell with farm technology and farming practice improvements. After hitting their lowest levels in more than 30 years in 2001, cotton prices rebounded in 2002 only to slump for another four years. Prices rose slightly over 10 percent in 2007 and about 14 percent in 2008.[23] As a result of the "worst global consumption contraction in 65 years," cotton prices fell 12 percent on average in 2009. Unusually low stockpiles, heavy rains and flooding in China and Pakistan, and export restrictions in India reduced the cotton supply and pushed prices up to a 150-year high in 2010. Calendar year prices were up 68 percent on average to nearly $1.00 per pound. Prices surged an additional 48 percent on average in 2011 to about $1.05 per pound before easing back to $0.89 per pound in 2012.[24] While cotton prices continued to ease in the first quarter of 2013, they picked up again in May and June. Cotton consumers were worried that the combination of aggressive stockpiling by the Chinese government, drought conditions in much of the United States, and less acreage earmarked for U.S. cotton production would push prices back to 2011 levels. At $0.93 per pound, June's cotton prices were well below cotton highs in 2011 but far above historic levels of around $0.66 per pound.

U.S. denim producers dominated worldwide production and exports of the fabric for many years but had been surpassed by China due to favorable production costs. U.S. production had declined for years as manufacturers closed American mills and relocated capacity to lower-cost countries. North Carolina–based Cone Mills, known as the "King of Denim," was the world's largest producer of denim fabric for most of its 120-year existence. While the company remained a major player in the industry, Cone struggled against low-cost international competition and the phaseout of U.S. denim fabric quotas. The company was known for its ability to produce high-quality denim and had been the sole supplier of denim to Levi's for nearly 40 years.

Established in 1891 by the Cone brothers, Cone Denim was a subsidiary of publicly traded International Textile Group in 2013. The division had found a profitable niche in serving premium denim customers. Massive restructuring efforts and a focus on high-valued-added materials allowed the company's denim division to turn a profit in 2009 and remain profitable for the next three years—despite high cotton prices. International Textile Group's bottom-weight woven fabrics division generated $566 million in revenues and $29 million in operating profit in 2012. The division's operating margin improved somewhat as its product mix shifted to more profitable lines. Nevertheless, sales declined slightly in 2012 as the company was forced to pass on the relief in cotton prices to its customers in the form of price cuts. Unfortunately, much of its inventory remained tied to the older, higher cotton costs. Management remained concerned about the outlook for cotton prices as customers were reluctant to accept higher denim costs but demanded lower denim prices as soon as cotton prices eased.

Most domestic premium jeans companies preferred to source denim fabric from U.S. suppliers like Cone's famous White Oak Mill. Their designers felt the fabric was superior in quality and gave their jeans "authenticity" associated with being made in the United States. Premium denim jeans companies all demanded high quality, and many were willing to pay for Cone's special vintage selvage denim made on narrow Draper fly-shuttle looms that went out of production in the 1970s. Highly prized by denim zealots for its durability and beauty, selvage denim was used only in the most expensive jeans. According to Kenneth Kunberger, International Textile Group's chief operating officer, Cone's White Oak Mill was the only mill in the world using the old fly-shuttle looms in 2012.[25] Some premium jeans makers swore by Japanese and Italian denim fabric. At any rate, denim fabric makers like Cone and privately held Swift Denim had low margins and little bargaining power. As it had been for more than a decade, the issue for U.S. denim makers in 2013 was survival in the face of intense competition from foreign competitors.

In jeans made of stretch denim, cotton content typically ranged from 95 to 99 percent with spandex making up the rest of the fiber in the stretch denim fabric. The incorporation of spandex into cotton denim allowed women's jeans to be form fitting but comfortable due to the "give" of the spandex fibers. The use of "stretch" in premium jeans was limited by spandex's inability to withstand harsher finishing treatments like bleaching as well as the lack of rigidity of high spandex content denim and its relative lack of durability. High cotton prices and the 38 percent tariff the European Union imposed on U.S. premium denim exports in 2013 had denim designers experimenting with less expensive alternative fibers such as Tencel. Premium denim consumers still demanded cotton garments and had not yet accepted alternatives.

Each pair of jeans used about 1.5 yards of denim fabric. While basic denim went for $2 to $3 per yard, premium denim typically sold for about $7 per yard but could wholesale for $15 or more per yard. The usual fabric cost per pair was around $11. Most upscale jeans companies did not own their own manufacturing capacity; rather, they used contract manufacturers to cut and sew the fabric into jeans. There were thousands of cut-and-sew operations around the world, but the U.S. premium brands all used U.S. manufacturers. About 75 percent of all premium denim was made in Los Angeles in 2012. The premium denim companies liked the shorter lead times and lower shipping costs as well as high quality control they got by using domestic suppliers. In addition, they felt U.S. consumers wanted and expected their expensive jeans to be "made in America"—the inventor of blue jeans. Manufacturing costs came in at about $10 per pair with another $2 per pair spent on shipping.

Garments went from the factory to denim laundries, which were responsible for the all-important finishing process. Many jeans designers hung their shingles out in Los Angeles due to the prevalence of laundries in the LA area. "Raw" jeans underwent a variety of labor-intensive finishing processes including special washes, sand blasting, painting, bleaching, ripping, tearing, the addition of whiskers, the application of resins, baking, and pocket embroidery. One popular process, stonewashing, literally involved putting jeans in huge washers full of pumice stones in order to break the denim fibers down and make them softer.

One pair of jeans could undergo 15 different treatments before achieving the desired "look." The finishing process added about $12 per pair to the cost of a pair of premium jeans.[21] However, some washes could run to $16 per pair or even much higher. In the Sundance Channel documentary *Dirty Denim*, Chip Foster (co-founder of Chip N Pepper) points out a pair of jeans with a $25 wash made to give the appearance of having been worn extensively.[26] According to the designer, it would take approximately six years of wear to get the same look provided by the expensive wash.

Lubell dissected the manufacturing cost of a pair of $310 (retail) True Religion "Phantom" jeans for *The Wall Street Journal* in 2011.[27] According to Lubell, raw Phantom jeans cost $56 to make. Wash expenses added $6 to $16 per pair to the cost of the jeans for a total manufacturing cost of $62 to $72 for a finished pair. True Religion marked up the jeans 2.2 to 2.5 times to $140 to $160 per pair and sold them to retailers. Retailers then tacked on an additional $150 to $170 per pair to arrive at the cash register price of $310 per pair. The retail markup on a pair of premium jeans averaged 2.2 times. Through this markup process, the designers and their retail partners captured the lion's share of the profits in the industry.

The contract manufacturing model had worked well for denim designers, even though it created an opportunity for jeans cut-and-sew operators to forward vertically integrate into jeans design and marketing. Drawing on its experience in manufacturing denim, Grupo Denim launched Vintage Revolution premium jeans in fall 2010. The Mexican company was vertically integrated into pattern design, manufacturing, and finishing. Grupo Denim hired premium denim veteran Michael Press as CEO. Vintage Revolution debuted in 400 major department and specialty stores in the United States. Vintage Revolution jeans retailed for $118 to $140 per pair as Grupo Denim had a significant cost advantage compared with other premium jeans marketers and chose to pass on some of its savings to consumers. Despite the company's cost advantages, the line tumbled from the premium ranks to the low end of the mid-priced tier of the market—retailing for $35 to $40 per pair at Sears and other mid-priced department stores in 2013.

Outsourcing was the norm in the U.S. premium denim market, but some prominent premium denim designers began to bring key aspects of the manufacturing process in-house from 2010 to 2013. Most notably, 7 For All Mankind started manufacturing operations in its Vernon, California, headquarters by bringing in-house denim cutting, embroidery and finishing. The company added sewing to the internal process in 2011. The company intended to make all of its own jeans without relying on outside contractors. "One [factor] was controlling our destiny, having more control of our process. There was some cost advantage. The other was speed to market. In today's world, we need to be quicker," said Barry Miguel, president of 7 For All Mankind.[28] 7 For All Mankind was unusually well equipped to handle the challenge of backward vertical integration as its parent company, VF Corporation, was the largest apparel company in the world and had been making Lee jeans since 1889 and Wrangler's since the 1940s. VF Corporation hoped to bring its expertise in research and development as well as enormous purchasing power to 7 to hold down cost increases and develop innovative products. VF Corporation CEO Steve Wiseman liked to say the company was the largest zipper buyer in the world.

Retailers' demand for quicker speed to market was a powerful motive for producing domestically. Peter Kim, president of Hudson Jeans, said that in 2010 he could take eight to 12 weeks to produce and ship a new style and between six to eight weeks to fill a reorder. A year later, Kim said he needed to deliver new styles in six to eight weeks and fill reorders in two to six weeks. Hudson's approach was to outsource most production tasks to companies in the LA area—all within a few miles of the firm's headquarters. Bringing all of the production process in-house would reduce the turnaround time on new products even further. However, Hudson's Kim noted that doing the entire manufacturing process in-house "was like running 10 or 12 other businesses."[29]

J Brand's approach was to share its headquarters space with an independent but captive manufacturer. It was this relationship and proximity to the factory that allowed Jeff Rudes to observe the return of colors to the high-fashion runways in Europe in September 2010 and launch a test line of brightly colored denim jeans in Barney's NY five months later. A short time later, J Brand rolled out its line of colored denim nationwide.

While it was possible for the jeans companies to backward vertically integrate into the finishing end of production, very few U.S. designers had opted to do so as it generally fell out of the area of management expertise and required meaningful capital investment. Citizens of Humanity brand was an exception as the line reportedly produced 1,000,000 pairs of jeans per year in its own denim laundry in Los Angeles.[30] Moreover, different laundries had developed distinctive skills with different types of finishes. LA's washhouses were known for their high levels of technical skill and for innovation. As industry growth slowed, more denim companies might opt for ownership of denim laundries despite the barriers to entry. The wash and other finishing treatments had become increasingly important differentiating features of premium denim lines—making keeping the finishing details proprietary critical to success. Washhouses typically did not work exclusively for one premium denim customer. While the designers endeavored to keep details about fit and finish secret, it was extremely difficult to do so given the nature of the denim laundries and their processes. Many denim designers had so far opted to stick with the traditional contract manufacturing model, but the model appeared to be changing in 2013.

Lifestyle Brands and the Diesel Model

As the ultimate in product differentiation, many companies attempt to create so-called "lifestyle" brands that transcend product category and inspire deep consumer loyalty. Three of the top five best-selling premium denim companies were attempting to transform their denim labels into lifestyle brands by emulating the Diesel model. Once thought to be the key to continued high growth, "lifestyle brand status" may have become critical to survival by 2013.

In the 2007 Touchstone movie *Wild Hogs*, the character Dudley Frank (played by William H. Macy) proudly declares; "I got a tat." He pulls down his black leather jacket to reveal a multicolored version of the Apple corporate logo tattooed on his right shoulder.[16] Dudley Frank, a computer programmer, identified so closely with the Apple brand and its core values, he chose to have it etched into his skin.[31]

Only a handful of companies had been able to establish such a strong association with a particular way of living that their brands symbolized the core values embodied in that lifestyle: Ralph Lauren, Harley-Davidson, Nike, Apple, Abercrombie & Fitch, Diesel, and a few others. Examples of failed attempts to transform regular brands into lifestyle brands abounded, such as McDonald's, Starbucks, Microsoft, and Uggs.

The appeal of the lifestyle brand was threefold: potential for sales growth, brand premiums (high margins), and protection from downturns in product cycles. Developing a strong emotional bond with consumers that went beyond product functionality could allow a company to go beyond using mere line extensions to generate growth. Lifestyle brands had the potential to move into a whole host of related product categories. In some cases, a brand could be used as a growth platform even in product categories that were seemingly unrelated to its original market due to the strength of the brand's identity with its associated lifestyle. Harley-Davidson, the motorcycle manufacturer, successfully extended its brand to a wide variety of product categories including clothing, footwear, eyewear, jewelry, Christmas ornaments, trucks, and wine bottle stoppers, among others.

The creation of a strong sense of identity with a brand by consumers also had the potential to let a company charge a premium for its products as relative prices could be less important than the consumer's relationship with the brand. In addition, diversifying into related product categories such as footwear for an apparel label could help protect a brand from downturns related to changes in fashion trends—thus reducing risk in the volatile fashion business. The measure of success in creating a lifestyle brand was the degree to which revenues and profits were diversified away from the original product line.

Within the domestic premium denim market, both of the top premium denim companies were attempting to do just that—create lifestyle brands that would allow them to move outside of the denim business. 7 For All Mankind and True Religion were attempting to emulate the Diesel brand model. Although the brand's roots were in the denim market, only about 35 percent of Diesel's revenues were derived from denim sales by 2010. Sales of products as diverse as wine, cars, fragrances, sunglasses, shoes, and watches as well as non-denim apparel generated the remaining 65 percent of revenues.[32] In addition to product diversification, the company had forward vertically integrated into wholly company-owned and partly owned (with distributor partners) retail stores around the world. It also operated a Web site that both promoted the Diesel lifestyle and sold products. The company's motto, [Diesel] "For Successful Living," and its Web site's invitation to consumers to join "the cult" highlighted the strong linkage between the brand and its customers.

Founded in 1978 by Renzo Rosso and Adriano Goldschmeid, the Italian denim company sold through 5,000 distribution points in 80 countries including 300 Diesel brand stores. With 50 stores in the United States in 2010, *The Wall Street Journal* put the privately held company's worldwide sales at $1.81 billion.[33]

Premium denim juggernaut 7 For All Mankind had taken its company-owned store count from 10 in the United States in 2008 to 65 worldwide by the end of 2012. In addition, there were 60 independently operated 7 For All Mankind partnership stores in international markets. Perhaps more importantly, 7 management recognized that the key to a successful lifestyle brand was its core brand identity. Successful luxury lifestyle brands such as Dior, Gucci, Armani, and Versace all embodied the lifestyle and values of iconic designers. In order to more clearly define its core brand identity to the consumer, 7 hired acclaimed actor and director James Franco in 2012. Franco added his fashion and directing sensibilities to 7's 2012 and 2013 advertising campaigns. Franco directed a series of films, titled "The Beautiful Odyssey," for 7 that appeared on the brand's YouTube channel.

True Religion had increased its U.S. store base from 89 in December 2010 to 86 full-priced stores and 36 outlets. The company owned another 20 full-priced stores and 10 outlets in international markets. As True Religion transformed itself into an apparel retailer, it had been successful in gaining ground in non-denim categories with its most devoted consumers. By the end of 2012, sportswear generated 35 percent of sales in True Religion stores, up from 20 percent in 2008. Nevertheless, the company had been largely unsuccessful at persuading its influential wholesale accounts to take on its non-denim offerings. The company's self-described California hippie–Bohemian chic with influence from the Wild West image appeared to have proven to be difficult to translate into a clear brand identity that could transfer to non-jeans product categories in a way that resonated with retailers and consumers. Somehow True Religion management needed to persuade its less devoted consumers that the Buddha strumming a guitar and the horseshoe stitching on the back pockets of its jeans were timeless symbols of a desirable lifestyle.

In a March 2008 interview with *Women's Wear Daily*, Diesel's Steve Birkhold said; "It will take these brands a long time to get to what Diesel already has, which is the full lifestyle. You can't go from being a flat denim brand with a huge wholesale distribution to being a lifestyle denim brand with a niche retail distribution unless you have the product engine to fuel it. That's where I think Diesel is differentiated."[34]

7 For All Mankind and the Premium Denim Market

The premium denim market was populated with fanciful brand names and was characterized by all the melodrama of the best television soap operas. Rich & Skinny, Citizens of Humanity, Earnest Sewn, True Religion, Joe's Jeans, Rag & Bone, Paige Premium, and Not Your Daughter's Jeans were some of the premium denim labels launched on the heels of 7 For All Mankind's successful debut. "7," as it was affectionately referred to in the fashion press, was the brainchild of LA designer Dahan and salesman Glasser.

Dahan was the head designer for Lucky jeans and a former designer for Guess jeans. Glasser started the sportswear brand Democracy in 1990. The two men approached Peter Koral, owner of California sportswear maker L'Koral, in 2000 with the idea of launching a new jeans line at the nearly unheard of price points of $100 to $160 per pair. In contrast, the average price paid for jeans in the U.S. market was just less than $21. More than half of the jeans sold in the United States that year retailed for less than $20 per pair. "Designer" denim had been all but dead for nearly 20 years. Nevertheless, Koral agreed to provide financial backing to the venture in return for a 50 percent ownership stake in the line.

For the first time in denim's history, designers turned their attention to creating a pair of jeans whose function was to flatter and enhance women's figures rather than to serve as durable casual wear or a skintight spot to paste a designer name for those fortunate enough to both afford it and carry it off. Dahan deconstructed the basic five-pocket jean and reengineered it with an eye toward enhancing and flattering women's bodies. He added a distinctive stitching design to the back pockets of 7s so consumers could easily identify the product and be identified with it. Dahan used a stylish bootcut coupled with a low-rise, slim-fit, high-quality denim and subtle detailing to create a one-of-a-kind silhouette. One 20-something woman commented in a 2003 *Boston Herald* industry article, "I remember when 7 jeans would pay for themselves because when you went out you'd look so good that guys would buy you drinks."[35] As Charles Lessor, the former CFO of competitor True Religion Brand Jeans, noted succinctly in the same article, "It's all about the butt."[36] 7s made a woman's derriere look great, and women rushed to stores to buy them. Celebrity trendsetters like Cameron Diaz were photographed wearing 7s in everyday life. The line's popularity exploded, and it generated an unprecedented $13 million in first-year sales accompanied by $2 million in net profits. Two years later in 2003, the brand did $80 million in sales before jumping to $130 million in revenues in 2004.

The brand's success did not go unnoticed. Los Angeles became the denim capital of the world despite the fact that North Carolina–based mega-brands Lee and Wrangler's operations were far from the glitz of the City of Angels and brand leader Levi's was headquartered in San Francisco. There was a veritable volcanic eruption in the number of premium denim brands between 2001 and 2003. According to STS Market Research, consumers purchased 297 denim brands in 2001. That number jumped to 350 in 2002 and 438 in 2003—a 47 percent increase in two years, accounting for a third of all apparel brands purchased in the United States.[37] The new brands mimicked the 7 model of in-house design, outsourcing production and finishing, using the highest-quality denim, and selling to trendy upscale boutiques and high-end department stores.

Below the surface at 7 For All Mankind, things were not going well between the partners. Dahan and Glasser left 7 and filed a $20 million lawsuit against Peter Koral in 2002. The lawsuit accused Koral of using profits from 7 to prop up his knitwear business and failing to live up to the partners' oral agreement to establish 7 as a separate entity once sales hit $12 million. Koral claimed he plowed all the profits back into the brand. Further, he maintained that his partners gave up their share of the company by leaving to start a competing product line. A judge awarded the two men $55.5 million in September 2004, $50 million for the combined 50 percent share of 7 and $5.5 million in profits from 2001 and 2002.

With $20 million in net profits on $60 million in sales in their second year of business, it is no wonder that Dahan and Glasser immediately applied their expertise to creating another premium denim brand. The two started Citizens of Humanity in 2002 using the same general business model that had served them so well with 7 For All Mankind. Glasser focused his merchandising and marketing efforts on the same accounts he did business with at 7 like Nordstrom, Barney's, and Neiman Marcus. Dahan updated his designs and added new washes and detailing.

Citizens had an even bigger first year than 7 due to soaring demand for high-priced denim. In 2003, the line generated $23 million in sales. Sales leaped to $80 million reportedly accompanied by a whopping $35 million in profits in 2005. The brand sold in 35 countries with about 90 percent of its revenues coming from the sale of women's jeans. Dahan bought out his partner in 2005 and then sold 66 percent of Citizens to the Boston venture capital firm Berkshire Partners in 2006. According to press accounts, the majority stake in the privately held firm fetched $250 million to $300 million or 3.8 to 4.5 times estimated 2006 sales of $100 million. With the backing of Berkshire Partners, Citizens purchased GoldSign jeans from Adriano Goldschmeid along with his denim laundry in 2007 for an undisclosed sum.

In March 2005, Peter Koral sold 50 percent of 7 For All Mankind to the investment bank Bear Sterns. Although specific terms of the deal were not disclosed, Mr. Koral confirmed publicly that Bear Sterns paid $75 million to $100 million for its stake in the firm. The brand had sales of about $200 million in 2004 so the deal was valued at 0.75 times to 1.0 times sales. The buzz on Wall Street was that the line had the potential to morph into a large global lifestyle brand. Denim giant VF Corporation picked up all of 7 For All Mankind in mid-2007 for a cool $775 million. The maker of Lee, Wrangler, and Rustler jeans pegged 2007 sales of the #1 premium denim brand at about $300 million, valuing the brand at nearly 2.6 times sales.

VF Corporation and 7 For All Mankind

VF Corporation was the world's largest apparel company with 2012 revenues of $10.8 billion. The company began in 1899 as a glove and mitten manufacturer but diversified into women's silk lingerie in 1914. The company retained the initials "VF" after dropping the Vanity Fair moniker following the acquisition of Lee jeans in 1969. Lee was one of the oldest apparel brands in the United States, having been established in 1899 (about 25 years after Levi Strauss). VF went on to acquire Wrangler and Rustler as part of its friendly acquisition of Blue Bell in 1986. In 2007, VF Corporation acquired 7 For All Mankind, the leading premium denim brand in the United States.

VF Corporation adopted a new corporate strategy in 2004. Its vision was to "grow by building leading lifestyle brands that excite consumers around the world."[38] In other words, the company wanted to transform itself into a global lifestyle apparel company with 60 percent of revenues being derived from lifestyle brands by 2015. As part of that initiative, it sought to stay on top of the apparel market by combining design and science to create value-added products for consumers. According to company statements, "innovation is about much more than delivering a new product, fabric, or style…Innovation is a holistic process, one that touches every aspect of our enterprise—branding, supply chain management, global expansion, even our corporate citizenship initiatives."[39] Management saw growth in lifestyle brands, an increase

in company-owned stores, and international expansion as keys to longer-term success. In particular, VF Corporation planned to double the number of company-owned stores and increase its product mix to 60 percent lifestyle brands by 2015. By the end of 2012, VF owned 1,129 stores around the world, including 1,049 single-brand stores. Direct-to-consumer sales accounted for 21 percent of global revenues.

VF had massive global operation in which it managed 450 million units across 36 brands in nearly every country in the world in 2012. Unlike many of its competitors, VF used a mix of 29 company-owned-and-operated manufacturing facilities and 1,900 contract manufacturers. As is noted in VF's 2012 10K filing, company-owned facilities in the western hemisphere generally delivered lower-cost product, but contractor-sourced goods offered more flexibility and shorter lead times. As a result, VF balanced the need for lower-cost manufacturing costs with the ability to hold lower inventories resulting from the use of contractors. In addition to global sourcing of raw materials and manufacturing, the company used "best of class" technology to manage its resources. Best of class technology extended to inventory management at the retail level. VF employed a point-of-sale inventory management system that allowed it to gather daily sales information down to the individual store and SKU level (size, style, color detail). The company believed this point-of-sale inventory system gave it an advantage over its less sophisticated competitors. Its five largest customers accounted for 16 percent of 2012 sales and were all located in the United States. The company's single largest customer was Wal-Mart, which accounted for 8 percent of 2012.

The company's brands were organized into "coalitions" including jeanswear, outdoor, imagewear, sportswear, and contemporary. The jeanswear coalition was made up of the so-called "heritage brands" Lee, Wrangler, and Rustler. VF management felt the jeanswear and imagewear (licensed and work apparel) coalitions would likely generate strong profits and cash flow with low-single-digit growth longer term. The outdoor, sportswear, and contemporary coalitions were to be the growth engines of VF in management's view. These lifestyle brand groups were expected to grow at a mid-single-digit to low-double-digit rate in the long term.

7 For All Mankind was placed into the newly created contemporary group in August 2007, which also included the recently acquired lucy[R] brand. When acquired in August 2007, domestic sales accounted for 75 percent of 7's total revenues. By the end of 2012, international revenues had jumped to 37 percent of brand sales. While some of the increase was due to VF Corporation's aggressive

expansion in international markets, the U.S. business had suffered due to the recession and slumping premium denim industry sales. 7 For All Mankind's large share of the premium segment made it difficult for the brand to outperform the category.

Nevertheless, 7 appeared to be struggling to maintain its position in the market as it lost ground to the likes of True Religion and J Brand, and the premium denim category recovered. VF Corporation had taken a nearly $200 million impairment charge to the 7 brand in 2010—indicating that the asset was no longer worth the $775 million that the company paid for it less than three years earlier. At VF's June 2013 Investor Day, management stated that 7's 2012 total revenues came in at $300 million[40]—putting the brand's revenues at about the same level as estimated 2007 revenues.

While management expected an average of 7 to 8 percent annual growth through 2017, first-half 2013 results were discouraging. 7's revenues fell in the second quarter reportedly due to softness in the high-end department store channel. Management revised its 2013 growth forecast to "low single digit growth" from "high single digit growth" as 7's revenues fell 5 percent or more in the quarter.[41] Recent results raised questions about the relevance of 7's brand to premium denim consumers and the likelihood that the brand could make the jump to lifestyle status

A strong competitor in all of its markets, the North Carolina–based VF Corporation spent $575 million on advertising and promotions in 2012. The company possessed a formidable stable of brands including Timberland, North Face, Nautica, Vans, Reef, and Majestic. As of June 2013, the company had $320 million in cash and $1.9 billion in total debt. Shareholder's equity stood at $5.2 billion.

VF Corporation Acquires and Repositions Rock & Republic from Super Premium to Mid-Priced

VF picked up the assets of rival premium denim label Rock & Republic out of bankruptcy in March 2011 for $58.1 million. Notably, VF did not retain the services of the brand's flamboyant founder, Michael Ball.

According to company press, Rock & Republic "transcends the denim world with its luxe yet edgy approach to fashion." Its first collection "mixed an edgy, rebellious style with sophistication," which "inspires music and fashion industries alike." The company paired with Victoria Beckham (Posh Spice) to create signature jeans marketed under the Rock & Republic brand name, but

the relationship soured and was dissolved. Co-founded by Ball and Andrea Bernholtz in 2002, Rock & Republic retailed its premium denim jeans for $186 to $330 per pair. The privately held company had become something of a force in the premium denim market by appealing to the fickle tastes of the most fashion-forward, affluent young consumers. Rock & Republic was all about trendy and fast. Nevertheless, the company moved in sync with the rest of the premium denim segment away from embellished jeans to cleaner and less provocative styling and raised its waistlines in 2007. Company co-founder Bernholtz commented to *Women's Wear Daily*, "It's [the rise is] just not as low as it was before with everything hanging out. It's that quarter of an inch between sexy and slutty."[42]

Rock & Republic reportedly did $2.4 million in sales in 2002 and about $23 million in 2004. Ball claimed the company did more than $100 million in sales in 2006. The outspoken Ball said he had a plan that would allow Rock & Republic to "literally dominate our market in the next fifteen years."[43] Ball's plan revolved around transforming Rock & Republic into a full-line lifestyle brand including shoes, eyewear, and retail store ownership.

While it was easy to dismiss the outspoken Ball as an insignificant player in the denim market, Rock & Republic's success with the fashion-forward consumer had other companies looking over their shoulders. The jeans featured a distinctive, stylized "R" on each back pocket, high-quality denim, and a flattering fit. The brand commanded even higher price points than True Religion, and consumers appeared willing to pay them. As Ball told the *Daily News Record* in a 2006 interview, "If you want Rock, you have to pay top dollar—you have to pay to be in the VIP section."[44] Ball's view of the brand's cache may ultimately have been its downfall as the company was forced to file for bankruptcy in 2010.

VF Corporation quickly moved to reposition the line and take advantage of its appeal to fashion-forward consumers. In April 2011, VF announced that Rock & Republic would be available exclusively in Kohl's department stores. The line launched in Kohl's 1,150 mid-priced family-oriented U.S. stores in spring 2012. According to the company's fact book, 52 percent of the company's $4.2 billion in revenues were derived from exclusive brands like Rock & Republic. The retailer's objective was to "continue to offer exceptional value, quality, and convenience."[45] Rock & Republic women's jeans retailed for $88 on Kohl's Web site but were regularly sale-priced at $49.99 or below. Details on Rock's first year as a mass-market brand were not available, but Kohl's management seemed pleased with the line's performance.

Joe's Jeans

Moroccan-born Joe Dahan (no relation to Jerome Dahan of 7 and Citizens fame) entered the fashion business with a line of men's formal wear and dress shirts in 1986 that rang up $8 million in sales when Joe was just 17 years old.[46] From 1996 to 2001, Dahan was the head designer for Azteca Productions, a private-label manufacturer of sportswear and denim. Dahan entered the premium denim market in 2001 with five styles of fashion jeans under the Joe's Jeans brand. The products retailed for $124 to $155 per pair. In March 2001, Innovo Group purchased the rights to the Joe's Jeans brand from Azteca and moved into the premium denim market. Innovo later changed its name to Joe's Jeans and trades on the NASDAQ market under the JOEZ symbol.

Joe's Jeans emphasized fit rather than the hottest trend. As Dahan said in a 2005 interview, "We've always been about clean, even when the market was embellished. We're not about fast or trendy."[47] Joe's Jeans aficionados sang the praises of the line, claiming the jeans had an "insanely good fit." Dahan's attention to fit paid off with first year sales coming in at $9.1 million. The line retailed at tony department stores like Barney's New York, Nordstrom, Bloomingdale's, and Macy's as well as boutiques catering to affluent shoppers. The company's 10 largest customers accounted for 61 percent of sales in 2012. Nordstrom, Bloomingdale's, and Macy's were Joe's three largest customers. In 2009, the three together accounted for 47 percent of sales. Joe's, like its larger competitors, had moved to open its own retail stores in order to boost margins and reduce its dependence on upscale department store retailers. By the end of 2012, Joe's owned 11 full-priced retail stores and 19 outlet stores in the United States. Total sales rang up at more than $118 million in 2012 with about 95 percent of sales derived from the U.S. market.

Joe's took two major steps to improve its position in the U.S. market in 2012 and 2013. Hedging its bets on premium denim, the company launched an exclusive line else™ sold primarily by Macy's. The new line was priced at $68—putting it squarely in the mid-priced segment of the jeans market. From February to December 2012, else™ generated about $7.5 million in sales. In July 2013, Joe's announced it had reached an agreement to purchase premium denim brand, Hudson for about $98 million. Marc Crossman, president and chief executive officer of Joe's Jeans, stated, "We are extremely excited about joining forces with Hudson Jeans. Once the acquisition is complete, we expect to nearly double the size of our business, meaningfully increase our international and e-commerce penetration, and enhance our overall prospects for growth."[48] Crossman went on to say that he expected to be able to leverage the company's sourcing capabilities to realize cost savings and significantly reduce input costs. With the addition of Hudson, Joe's became a more formidable competitor in the premium denim industry.

True Religion Brand Jeans

Lubell had struck out on two occasions previously in his attempt to shift from textile salesman to independent jeans designer. He and his wife launched two jeans labels in the late 1990s—Bella Dahl and Jeffri Jeans—and lost both after running out of cash. Events turned ugly when Bella Dahl Inc. couldn't keep up with payments to its factory and had to file for bankruptcy in late 2000. Several lawsuits later, Lubell was on his own with no assets or ownership in his jeans creations. In 2002, the Lubells launched a new premium denim line, True Religion Brand Jeans. Lubell registered his new line's trademarks in his name and formed a holding company that he owned and controlled called Guru Denim. Things would turn out differently this time for the 46-year-old Los Angeles resident.

The brand hit store shelves in December 2002 with five styles of women's jeans available in five different "washes" under the True Religion label. (7s were only available in two basic styles at the time.) The corporate logo appeared on every tag and featured a fat, smiling Buddha strumming a guitar. According to a November 2002 WWD article, "True Religion has an "evolutionary" mannish styling." WWD interviewed Lubell for the article and quoted him as saying "there are a lot of women who love to wear their boyfriend's jeans or husband's jeans. This plays off of that." The jeans had one of the lowest rises on the market and some of the highest prices. Lubell created "buzz" for the line by sending celebrity trendsetters free pairs of jeans with the hope they would appear in photos in the popular press wearing jeans with True Religion's signature horseshoe-shaped back pocket stitching. The strategy worked, and the line's sales took off. First-year sales came in at $2.4 million and jumped to $27.7 million in 2004.

The popularity of "distressed," "destroyed," and "embellished" jeans helped drive growth in the premium denim segment for years. The Joey Destroyed model had been one of True Religion's best-selling products. The jeans model featured pre-washed denim that had been artfully aged and ripped so that most of the front of the left thigh was made up of strings rather than solid fabric. The designers added in a ripped left knee and extensive tearing on the front of the right thigh to complete the destroyed look (an extreme version of distressing). Embellished jeans also had been very popular for a number of years in the early part of the product lifecycle. So-called embellishments ranged from elaborate embroidery to the addition of sparkly crystals and metallic threads. True Religion marketed women's jeans with intricate embroidery on the back pockets like the Miss Groovy, Buddha, Fairy Girl, Godiva, and Geisha Girl designs. All of these popular "looks" required a substantial amount of additional labor to produce relative to basic denim looks. They all commanded a significant premium to the more basic models in the True Religion portfolio with prices starting well above $200 per pair. Some True Religion models went for more than $500 per pair at retail.

In 2008, premium denim designers responded to the mood of the times and moved away from elaborate finishing details back to more basic styles as consumers became interested in styles that would stay fashionable for years rather than for a season. True Religion followed suit and emphasized the lower-priced, more basic items in its lineup. Nevertheless, the brand remained one of the highest priced on the market with an average selling point of $196 for women's jeans and $192 for men's jeans in 2009. In company-owned stores, True Religion's price peaked at a staggering $272 per pair in the first quarter of 2009. The company had not been as successful historically in the basic end of the premium market as had 7 and Citizens. Indeed, True Religion's wholesale sales plummeted 20 percent during 2009 and 15 percent in 2010, followed by an 18 percent drop in 2011.

The company relied on Lubell's fashion sense and ability to spot the right trends to sell the "hottest" jean styles. He occupied the unusual position of CEO and "chief merchant" at True Religion. Lubell had an impressive track record, but True Religion's sales to the wholesale off-price channel had become worryingly large by 2009. The company used off-price retailers such as Nordstrom Rack as well as its own outlet stores to sell slow-moving and obsolete inventory. Moreover, the recession and a series of fashion missteps cost True Religion some of its followers. Lubell initially dismissed skinny jeans as a fad and was slow to introduce a True Religion version of the popular pants. Lubell considered True Religion to be a trendsetter rather than a follower. After all, he pioneered the incredibly popular oversized stitching on jeans as well as the ultra-destroyed look among others. According to Diana Katz, an analyst at Lazard Capital, "He thought they'd trend back to bell bottoms and wider bottoms, but it never happened."[49] Similarly, Lubell missed the colored denim trend and refused to lower prices on True Religion products. After a lot of sales pressure, Lubell rolled out a lower-priced line of simpler, cleaner jeans with a small,

unobtrusive logo on the back pocket. True Religion consumers did not respond well to the line as part of the appeal of the brand lay in its garish oversized back-pocket stitching and instantly recognizable logo. Moreover, the jeans were priced at $230 compared with $150 for similar jeans from competing brands. The line was discontinued.

True Religion planned to introduce a new "core denim" assortment in 2013 and increase the differentiation between its women's and men's jeans. While True Religion had struggled in the women's denim segment, the company's men's line held its own from 2009 to 2012. The company made three other key changes in 2013. It shifted some design responsibilities for its European business to Europe from California and began a consumer preference study. The company expected the study to give it insights into consumer purchase behavior that would allow its designers a greater opportunity to spot promising fashion trends. Finally, Lubell stepped down as the company's chief merchant and CEO in March 2013. Lubell would remain a creative consultant to True Religion but would no longer be responsible for its designs and operations. In this way, True Religion's board hoped to avoid the fate of Rock & Republic and reinvigorate the brand.

True Religion's Strategy

The company's initial strategy was to emphasize distribution through upscale department stores and boutiques and outsource every function except design and marketing to third parties. By the end of 2005, True Religion jeans sold in about 600 specialty stores and boutique shops as well as about 200 upscale department stores. Its customer lineup was a "who's who" of upscale retailers including Nordstrom, Neiman Marcus, Saks Fifth Avenue, Barney's, Henri Bendel, Bergdorf Goodman, Bloomingdale's, and Marshall Fields. By late 2006, True Religion's focus had shifted away from selling products wholesale to selling its products through company-owned stores.

True Religion management, under then-President Michael Buckley, had started to vertically integrate into retail for several reasons. First, the company had faced resistance from retailers when it tried to diversify away from denim jeans into adjacent clothing categories such as sportswear. Big retailers viewed True Religion as a denim label—not as an apparel brand. Owning its own stores allowed True Religion to introduce a broader range of apparel to its customers. Management hoped that the sell-through figures from company-owned stores on non-denim items would persuade its retail accounts to carry the full line of True Religion apparel. Diversifying into other apparel categories and related product lines was absolutely critical to achieving management's goal of creating a lifestyle brand.

In its full-priced company-owned stores, sales of non-denim items had increased from 10 percent of sales to 35 percent of sales in six years. However, non-denim items only accounted for an estimated 20 percent of the company's total U.S. sales, as True Religion largely had been unable to persuade its retail accounts to carry its non-denim items. Moreover, the company's licensing revenues were a puny $2.7 million in 2012—down from more than $5 million in 2010. Licensing was critical to establishing a lifestyle brand especially for a relatively small company with specialized management expertise. In order to expand into non-apparel categories, True Religion needed partners—partners that would manufacture and market True Religion–branded fragrances, sunglasses, jewelry, watches, and any other products that fit with True Religion's brand image.

Second, the margins in the company-owned stores were even higher than True Religion's very high denim margins as the company captured the retail markup as well as its traditional wholesale markup. Management estimated that retail store gross margin would come in at 75 percent and "four-wall contribution margin" would be about 40 percent as the company captured the benefits of the typical retail markup on its products as well as existing wholesale margin. Third, company-owned outlet stores gave True Religion a place to sell seconds, irregulars, and slow-moving merchandise. Without these outlet stores, True Religion brand products could surface in any type of discount outlet—potentially damaging the brand's premium positioning. Prior to 2007, True Religion jeans appeared in Filene's Basement, Costco, Century 21, and similar outlets on occasion.

Fourth, retail industry mergers and bankruptcies periodically caused manufacturers to miss sales and earnings forecasts. Using company-owned stores helped reduce the firm's dependence on retailers and reduced the risk of major disruptions in sales. Company-owned stores and e-commerce accounted for 60 percent of revenues in 2012 compared with 17 percent in 2007. In total, True Religion owned 122 stores in the United States and 30 international stores at year-end 2012. Over time, management planned to open 100 stores in the United States. Nordstrom and Nordstrom Rack remained True Religion's most important retail account. While 2012 figures were unavailable, Nordstrom alone accounted for 15.2 percent of the company's net sales in 2009.

As True Religion expanded the number of company-owned stores, its retail business took off—growing 57 percent per year on average for the five years

ended December 2012. Operating profit before unallocated corporate expenses grew at a slower rate but nonetheless averaged 51 percent per year growth over the period. At first glance, it was difficult to understand how the company could have been characterized as "struggling" and in need of a "savior." Investors were focused on four issues: the sharp slowdown in growth in the U.S. direct-to-consumer business (company-owned stores) and the accompanying huge drop in gross profit margin for the segment, the persistent weakness in wholesale sales especially in women's jeans, and the collapse in profits from international markets that occurred despite strong sales growth in those markets.

Some of the slowdown in the direct-to-consumer segment growth in the United States was attributable to the law of large numbers. As the business became larger, it took a greater and greater amount of incremental sales in absolute dollars to generate the same sales growth rate. In 2009, the direct-to-consumer business reported a 71 percent jump in revenues to $129 million or an increase of about $54 million. The same $54 million increase would have resulted in only 21 percent growth in 2012 as the business had nearly doubled to $251 million. Nevertheless, investors were concerned when the high-flying direct-to-consumer business reported a mere 12 percent increase in revenues despite almost a 12 percent increase in the total number of stores owned. The company's same store sales (sales in stores open for 13 months or more) were up 2.7 percent for the year.

At the beginning of the retail store expansion plan, then-company President Buckley estimated that retail store gross margin would come in at 75 percent and "four-wall contribution margin would be about 40 percent as the company captured the benefits of the typical retail markup on its products as well as existing wholesale margin. For the first few years of the expansion, management's prediction turned out to be an accurate one as gross margin for the consumer direct segment (company-owned stores and e-commerce) leaped to a peak of nearly 77 percent in 2008 before dipping to 74 percent in 2009 and ending up at about 70 percent in 2012. Similarly, segment operating profit margin before unallocated corporate expense plunged from a peak of 40.6 percent in 2007 to 33.3 percent in 2012. Some of the dropoff in profit margins was attributable to the costs of rolling out so many stores in a relatively short period of time. However, most of the decline in profitability was a result of two factors: an unfavorable mix shift toward sales in outlet stores and the overall decline in average denim prices paid in the company's stores. Both factors suggested the underlying appeal of the brand was waning among the fashion-forward affluent crowd True

Religion had wooed so assiduously for the past decade. More shoppers looking for True Religion jeans in outlet stores was likely a result of fewer shoppers being willing to pay up for jeans priced above $200 per pair, in line with industry trends toward lower-priced jeans. The fashion missteps that had plagued the company over the past few years had forced True Religion to discount more of its product line to move the product. Exhibit 4 below shows the decline in average prices paid by consumers for True Religion Jeans (excluding sportswear) in company-owned stores from their peak in the first quarter of 2009 through the fourth quarter of 2012.

At the same time, company-store growth appeared to be fueled mainly by store expansion and discounting, True Religion's wholesale business had increasingly shifted away from full-line department stores toward off-price channels. In recent quarters, shoppers had gravitated to the most heavily discounted True Religion items in off-price stores. The combination of all of these factors had investors spooked as concerns about the underlying health of the brand came to the forefront. One bright spot for the brand suggested it had not yet lost its cache. Sales to the specialty boutique channel had increased for 11 straight quarters. Much of the brand's success in its early days was due to the endorsement of specialty boutique owners. Improving sales trends with these savvy buyers could signal that the brand was regaining its momentum in the U.S. market.

True Religion's brand positioning as a "Made in the USA" product based upon a unique combination of a Wild West, cowboy heritage paired with a California-hippie-bohemian image had played well in international markets, especially in Japan during the brand's early days. Affluent Japanese consumers paid top dollar for American icons like vintage Levis. True Religion capitalized on its American origins by purchasing its high-quality denim fabric from Cone Mills and using domestic contract manufacturers and LA washhouses to finish its jeans. Management felt the "authenticity" of an American-made jean was a critical aspect of the brand's image—particularly in international markets. Eric Beder, an analyst with Brean Murray, told the *Los Angeles Times* in 2009, "In the U.S., people care that their jeans are manufactured here. To consumers outside the U.S., it's crucial...In order to be considered a real premium brand, you need to have the Made in the USA label on it."[50] True Religion offshored production of non-denim items such as hoodies and T-shirts, where country of origin was not important to consumers.

An enormous disappointment in Japanese sales in 2006 prompted management to reconsider the distributor model. Full-year sales to Japan plunged 50 percent from about $30 million to about $15 million. True Religion fought accusations from the financial press that it had "stuffed" the Japanese retail trade with product in the back half of 2005 in order to meet aggressive sales forecasts. Management's analysis of the retail distribution for the brand in Japan suggested that the company needed to pull back and eliminate marginal accounts in order to preserve the brand's exclusive image. As a result of the lessons it learned in Japan, management decided to switch from a distributor model to company-owned subsidiaries or joint ventures in order to better control the brand's retail placement and image. While distributors still accounted for a large part of True Religion's international sales in 2012, the company began to transition in 2008 from a wholesale business to a retail business following

Exhibit 4   Average Price/Pair Company-Owned Stores

Sources: True Religion quarterly management comments and author's estimates.

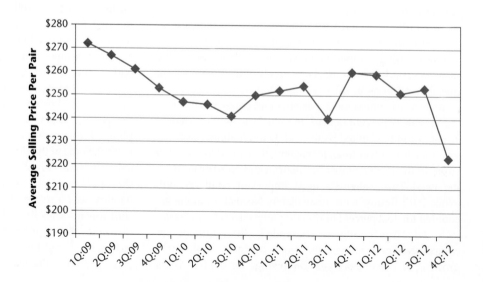

the pattern it used in the U.S. market. True Religion operated 20 full-priced stores and 10 outlets in international markets at the end of 2012.

International sales growth came in at a strong 26 percent average annual rate for the five-year period ended December 2012. Operating profits were about $15 million in 2007 and rose to a peak of about $25 million in 2009. The company's wholesale business struggled even as its retail business (company-owned stores) gained traction in key international markets. International operating profits declined sharply to about $7 million in 2012 as the company rolled out its retail stores and established in-house sales forces in many international markets. Selling, general, and administrative expenses for the international division climbed 121 percent per year on average over the five-year period. SG&A jumped 38 percent in 2012 alone. Management asserted that the increased expenses were needed to establish its retail business in international markets. Investors impatiently awaited improved international profits and margins.

Management Changes and the Future of True Religion

The company named denim industry veteran Buckley to the newly created post of president in April 2006. Buckley was president and CEO of Ben Sherman's North American business from 2001 to 2005. Prior to 2001, Buckley served as a vice president of denim giant Diesel USA for four years. He was to be responsible for day-to-day operations, including retail expansion, licensing, sourcing, and production. Lubell would remain in his post of chairman and CEO but devote more of his time to product design. Lubell commented to *WWD*, "Now I feel like I have a true partner and associate to help build the company and realize my vision of becoming a $1B brand."[51]

In August 2006, the company tapped Levi Strauss Europe designer Ziahaad Wells to be its design director. The following March, True Religion named Peter Collins as CFO. Collins was the former corporate controller for Nordstrom. Collins managed a staff of 100 and was an expert on compliance with Sarbanes-Oxley requirements. In addition, Collins had valuable accounting experience in international operations. He reported to Buckley in his new position at True Religion. In January 2010, True Religion added Lynn Koplin as COO. Koplin was formerly president of Tommy Bahama's women's division.

True Religion's financial performance generally was strong between 2006 and the first quarter of 2009. The company was well on its way to establishing 100 company-owned stores in the United States. The True Religion brand appeared strong at the #2 position in the U.S. market. Then, in May 2010, Buckley abruptly resigned from the company. Two days before his resignation, Buckley sold more than 193,000 shares of stock. The company offered no explanation for Buckley's resignation and promptly replaced him with Mike Egeck about two weeks later. Egeck had served as the CEO of 7 For All Mankind. Four months later, True Religion reported disappointing sales and earnings and lowered its full-year 2010 forecast. The timing of Buckley's departure and the speed at which he was replaced suggested Lubell was aware that Buckley planned to leave—or had forced him out. As chairman and CEO, Lubell had an enormous amount of influence with the company's board of directors. Egeck left True Religion to "pursue other opportunities" in August 2011. Egeck was reportedly "poached" by Hurley to become its CEO. True Religion promoted Koplin to replace Egeck. Koplin now succeeds Lubell as the company's interim CEO.

True Religion's strategy and objectives had been clear under the guidance of Lubell and Buckley. The company stuck to its approach of adding retail stores and transforming itself into an upscale purveyor of its own brand under Egeck and after his departure. Although neither Lubell nor Koplin had publicly commented about the Lubell's long-standing objective of reaching $1 billion in sales, the company's actions demonstrated that it pursued "lifestyle" brand status for the denim label. It was not clear in July 2013 that the company's sale to private equity firm TowerBrook would enhance its position in the premium denim industry. Always a strong cash generator, True Religion had not suffered from a lack of capital to fund its expansion plans. Nevertheless, the sale did afford the company an opportunity to bring in fresh management and design talent while giving Lubell a graceful and profitable exit from the company. Would TowerBrook prove to be more patient than institutional investors? Would new ownership give the team at True Religion more freedom to experiment with design out of the public spotlight? Could True Religion regain its "must have brand" status in the important U.S. premium denim market, or would the brand be forced to reposition itself at lower price points to survive? Lubell's tenure as chairman, CEO, and chief merchant had been an eventful and profitable one. What would Lubell do now with his $25 million golden parachute from the sale of True Religion?

End Notes

1. Hsu, T. (2013). "True Religion board accepts $835 million takeover bid." *Los Angeles Times*, May 10, www.luxurydaily.com/64-pc-us-shoppers-reluctant-to-return-to-old-buying-habits-study. Accessed July 10, 2013.
2. De La Merced, M. J. (2012). "True Religion puts itself up for sale." *New York Times*, October 1, dealbook.nytimes.com/2012/10/10/true-religion-puts-itself-up-for-sale/?ref=truereligionapparelinc&_r=0. Accessed July 26, 2013.
3. Covert, J. (2013). "Escape from hell for True Religion." *New York Post*, May 11, www.nypost.com/p/news/business/escape_from_hell_for_true_religion_irDO7jxZYTFFLz7Jt76DLJ. Accessed July 25, 2013.
4. (1991). "A comfortable fit: Levi Strauss has prospered by combining maverick marketing with gentle style of management (company profile)." *The Economist (U.S.)*. Economist Newspaper Ltd., June 22. Retrieved from High Beam.
5. Ozzard, J. (1997). "Shortening the denim pipeline (inventory management)." *Women's Wear Daily*, May 8.
6. Knight, M. (1999). "Hot new jeans will be down and dirty at MAGIC; for spring 2000, light washes are re-creating that old, friendly, worn blue denim look." *Daily News Record*, May 23.
7. lifestylemonitor.cottoninc.com/how-many-denim-garments-do-men-and-women-own/. Accessed July 25, 2013.
8. lifestylemonitor.cottoninc.com/men-and-women-love-wearing-denim/. Accessed July 25, 2013.
9. Klara, R. (2010). "The 'aspirational' consumer: R.I.P." Brandweek.com, November 7. Accessed December 31, 2010.
10. Carr, T. (2012). "64 pc US shoppers reluctant to return old buying habits: Study." *Luxury Daily*, July 11, www.luxurydaily.com/64-pc-us-shoppers-reluctant-to-return-to-old-buying-habits-study. Accessed July 25, 2013.
11. (2012). "Luxury shopping survey: November 2012." Accenture Management Consulting—Sales 7 Customer Services.
12. Pantin, L. (2012). "10 Wardrobe Essentials Every Woman Should Own." *Glamour*, August 10, www.glamour.com/fashion/2012/08/10-wardrobe-essentials-every-woman-should-own#slide=replay.
13. Hazlett, A. (2009). "The death of $200 + jeans?!" *New York Daily News*, July 31, www.nydailynews.com/2.1353/death-200-jeans-article-1.176339. Accessed July 15, 2013.
14. Sage, A. (2010). "Analysis: Garmentos proclaim the end of denim dominance." *Reuters Business & Financial News*, August 27.
15. Lifestyle Monitor: Cotton Inc. (2013). "Driving demand for denim jeans." July 15. lifestylemonitor.cottoninc.com/driving-demand-for-denim-jeans.
16. Wilson, E. (2009). "Preshrunk prices." *New York Times*, October 28, www.nytimes.com/2009/10/29/fashion/29JEANS.html?pagewanted=all. Accessed July 15, 2013.
17. Binkley, C. (2011). "How can jeans cost $300?" *Wall Street Journal*, July 7, online.wsj.com/article/SB10001424052702303365804576429730284498872.html?mg=id-wsj. Accessed July 25, 2013.
18. Hazlett, A. (2009). "The death of $200 + jeans?!" *New York Daily News*, July 31, www.nydailynews.com/2.1353/death-200-jeans-article-1.176339. Accessed July 15, 2013.
19. Keeve, D. "*Dirty Denim* introduction." Sundance Channel Documentary. www.sundancechannel.com/digital-shorts/#/theme/64930111001/64683988001. Accessed December 30, 2010.
20. Cotton Inc. Press Release. (2005). "Premium denim: Fit to be tried." September 12.
21. World Cotton Supply and Demand. National Cotton Council of America. www.cotton.org/econ/cropinfo/supply-demand.cfm. Accessed December 30, 2010.
22. USDA: Foreign Agricultural Service. (2013). "Table 04: Cotton area, yield and production." July 11, www.fas.usda.gov/psdonline/psdreport.aspx?hidReportRetrievalName=BVS&hidReportRetrievalID=851&hidReportRetrievalTemplateID=1. Accessed July 26, 2013.

23. National Cotton Council. "Monthly prices." www.cotton.org/econ/prices/monthly. cfm. Accessed July 25, 2013.

24. Ibid.

25. (2012). "An old mill, back in fashion." *Bloomberg Business Week*, May 21–27, www.conedenim.com/Bloomberg_May_2012.html. Accessed July 26, 2013.

26. Keeve, D. "*Dirty Denim* Episode 2: The wash." Sundance Channel Documentary. www.sundancechannel.com/digital-shorts/#/theme/64930111001/64571005001. Accessed December 30, 2010.

27. Binkley, C. (2011). "How can jeans cost $300?" *Wall Street Journal*, July 7, online.wsj.com/article/SB10001424052702303365804576429730284498872.html?mg=id-wsj. Accessed July 25, 2013.

28. (2011). "L.A. jeans makers put premium on local production." Khanh T.L. Tran WWD: *Women's Wear Daily*, 202(97), p. 14b-1.

29. Ibid.

30. "AG Jeans exclusive interview." blog.stylesight.com/denim/ag-jeans-exclusive-interview. Accessed July 25, 2013.

31. blog.wired.com/cultofmac/2007/03/William_h_macy.html. Accessed December 2008.

32. Passariello, C. (2010). "Ditching designers to sell clothes." *Wall Street Journal*, March 5.

33. Ibid.

34. Tucker, R. (2013). "Birkhold readies Diesel USA for growth push." *Women's Wear Daily*, March 13.

35. Radsken, J. (2003). "Fashion: Jeans splicing; express knockoffs do a number on Seven's fans." *Boston Herald*, August 14.

36. Ibid.

37. Tuner, D. (2005). "Understanding the EPS/HVI advantage in a world without quota." EPS Conference Presentation (Singapore), April 20.

38. www.vfc.com/about/vision-values. Accessed December 2008.

39. Ibid.

40. Kellogg, S. (2013). "Contemporary brands presentation." VF Corporation, June 11, phx.corporate-ir.net/phoenix.zhtml?c=61559&p=irol-irhome. Accessed July 23, 2013.

41. VF Corporation. "CEO discusses Q2 2013 results—earnings call transcript." seekingalpha.com/article/1558802-vf-corp-vfc-ceo-discusses-q2-2013-results-earnings-call-transcript. Accessed July 26, 2013.

42. McGuiness, D. (2006). "Predicting the denim fallout (trends and forecast)." *Women's Wear Daily*, February 9.

43. (2006). Interview with Michael Ball. *Daily News Record*.

44. Ibid.

45. "Kohl's fact book." www.kohlscorporation.com/InvestorRelations/sec-filings.htm. Accessed July 26, 2013. Harmon, A. (2007)

46. "Blue blood: The Dahan brothers reflect on the highs and lows of developing their denim lines (occupation overview)." *Daily News Record*, October 15.

47. Ibid.

48. (2013). "Joe's Jeans to acquire Hudson Clothing." Joe's Jeans company press release. July 15, phx.corporate-ir.net/phoenix.zhtml?c=84356&p=irol-newsArticle&ID=1837779&highlight=. Accessed July 25, 2013.

49. Morrissey, J. (2012). "Looking for investor faith in True Religion." *Fortune*, November 20, management.fortune.cnn.com/2012/11/20/true-religion-jeffrey-lubell. Accessed July 20, 2013.

50. White, R. (2009). "In L.A. pricey denim jumps off the racks." *Los Angeles Times*, May 27.

51. Tschorn, A. (2006). "True Religion taps Michael Buckley; former head of Ben Sherman's U.S. business appointed president of denim label (True Religion Apparel Inc.)." *Daily News Record*, April 17.

Case 1–3: Walmart Stores, Inc., in 2013

In November of 2013 Doug McMillon had just been named the CEO of Walmart Stores, Inc. effective February 1, 2014. McMillon had unique preparation for the job. He had held senior executive positions in Walmart's domestic operations and had presided over both the company's international operations and Sam's Club, Walmart's discount club chain. McMillon would likely need to draw upon his diverse experiences to successfully lead the company in the face of mounting challenges.

As recently as 1979, Walmart had been a regional retailer little known outside the South with 229 discount stores compared to the industry leader Kmart's 1,891 stores. In less than 25 years, Walmart had risen to become the largest U.S. corporation in sales. With more than $469 billion in revenues (see Exhibits 1 and 2), Walmart had far eclipsed not only Kmart but all retail competitors. Yet another measure of Walmart's dominance was that it accounted for approximately 45 percent of general merchandise, 30 percent of health and beauty aids, and 29 percent of non-food grocery sales[1] in the United States. *Forbes* put Walmart's success into perspective:

> ...all that's left for Walmart is mop-up. It already sells more toys than Toys "R" Us, more clothes than the Gap and Limited combined and more food than Kroger. If it were its own economy, Walmart Stores would rank 30th in the world, right behind Saudi Arabia. Growing at 11 percent a year, Walmart would hit half a trillion dollars in sales by early in the next decade.[2]

Despite its remarkable record of success, though, Walmart was not without challenges. Many observers believed that the company would find it increasingly difficult

Exhibit 1   Walmart Stores, Inc., Income Statement, 2009–2013

In millions of USD (except for per share items)	2013	2012	2011	2010
Revenue	469,162.00	446,950.00	421,849.00	408,085.00
Total Revenue	469,162.00	446,950.00	421,849.00	408,085.00
Cost of Revenue, Total	352,488.00	335,127.00	314,946.00	304,106.00
Gross Profit	116,674.00	111,823.00	106,903.00	103,979.00
Selling/General/Admin. Expenses, Total	88,873.00	85,265.00	81,361.00	79,717.00
Unusual Expense (Income)	—	—	—	260
Total Operating Expense	441,361.00	420,392.00	396,307.00	384,083.00
Operating Income	27,801.00	26,558.00	25,542.00	24,002.00
Income Before Tax	25,737.00	24,398.00	23,538.00	22,118.00
Income After Tax	17,756.00	16,454.00	15,959.00	14,962.00
Minority Interest	−757	−688	−604	−513
Net Income Before Extra Items	16,999.00	15,766.00	15,355.00	14,449.00
Net Income	16,999.00	15,699.00	16,389.00	14,370.00
Income Available to Common Excl. Extra Items	16,999.00	15,766.00	15,355.00	14,449.00
Income Available to Common Incl. Extra Items	16,999.00	15,699.00	16,389.00	14,370.00
Diluted Weighted Average Shares	3,389.00	3,474.00	3,670.00	3,877.00
Diluted EPS Excluding Extraordinary Items	5.02	4.54	4.18	3.73
Dividends per Share—Common Stock Primary Issue	1.59	1.46	1.21	1.09
Diluted Normalized EPS	5.02	4.54	4.18	3.77

Exhibit 2 Walmart Stores, Inc., Balance Sheet

In millions of USD (except for per share items)	2013	2012	2011	2010
Cash and Equivalents	7,066.00	6,003.00	6,891.00	7,907.00
Cash and Short-Term Investments	7,066.00	6,003.00	6,891.00	7,907.00
Accounts Receivable—Trade, Net	6,768.00	5,937.00	5,089.00	4,144.00
Total Receivables, Net	6,768.00	5,937.00	5,089.00	4,144.00
Total Inventory	43,803.00	40,714.00	36,437.00	32,713.00
Prepaid Expenses	1,588.00	1,774.00	2,960.00	3,128.00
Other Current Assets, Total	715	547	635	140
Total Current Assets	59,940.00	54,975.00	52,012.00	48,032.00
Property/Plant/Equipment, Total—Gross	171,724.00	160,938.00	154,489.00	143,517.00
Accumulated Depreciation, Total	−55,043.00	−48,614.00	−46,611.00	−41,210.00
Goodwill, Net	20,497.00	20,651.00	16,763.00	16,126.00
Other Long-Term Assets, Total	5,987.00	5,456.00	4,129.00	3,942.00
Total Assets	203,105.00	193,406.00	180,782.00	170,407.00
Accounts Payable	38,080.00	36,608.00	33,676.00	30,451.00
Accrued Expenses	18,808.00	18,180.00	18,701.00	18,734.00
Notes Payable/Short-Term Debt	6,805.00	4,047.00	1,031.00	523
Current Port. of LT Debt/Capital Leases	5,914.00	2,301.00	4,991.00	4,396.00
Other Current Liabilities, Total	2,211.00	1,164.00	204	1,439.00
Total Current Liabilities	71,818.00	62,300.00	58,603.00	55,543.00
Long-Term Debt	38,394.00	44,070.00	40,692.00	33,231.00
Capital Lease Obligations	3,023.00	3,009.00	3,150.00	3,170.00
Total Long-Term Debt	41,417.00	47,079.00	43,842.00	36,401.00
Total Debt	54,136.00	53,427.00	49,864.00	41,320.00
Deferred Income Tax	7,613.00	7,862.00	6,682.00	5,508.00
Minority Interest	5,914.00	4,850.00	3,113.00	2,487.00
Total Liabilities	126,762.00	122,091.00	112,240.00	99,939.00
Common Stock, Total	332	342	352	378
Additional Paid-In Capital	3,620.00	3,692.00	3,577.00	3,803.00
Retained Earnings (Accumulated Deficit)	72,978.00	68,691.00	63,967.00	66,357.00
Other Equity, Total	−587	−1,410.00	586	−147
Total Equity	76,343.00	71,315.00	68,542.00	70,468.00
Total Liabilities and Shareholders' Equity	203,105.00	193,406.00	180,782.00	170,407.00
Total Common Shares Outstanding	3,314.00	3,418.00	3,516.00	3,786.00

to sustain its remarkable record of growth (see Exhibit 3). Walmart faced a maturing market in its core business that would not likely see the growth rates it had previously enjoyed. Growth in same-store sales had declined in multiple quarters in the previous year. Many investors believed that Walmart had reached a point of saturation with its stores. Supercenters had provided significant growth for Walmart, but it was not clear how long they could deliver the company's customary growth rates. The company added new stores at a prodigious rate, but the new stores often cannibalized sales from nearby Walmart stores. Walmart faced problems in other business areas as

Exhibit 3   Walmart Sales Growth by Segment, 2011–2013 (in millions USD)

	2013			2012			2011	
	Net Sales	**Percent of Total**	**Percent Change**	**Net Sales**	**Percent of Total**	**Percent Change**	**Net Sales**	**Percent of Total**
Walmart U.S.	$274,490	58.9%	3.9%	$264,186	59.5%	1.5%	$260,261	62.1%
Walmart International	$135,201	29.0%	7.4%	$125,873	28.4%	15.2%	$125,873	26.1%
Sam's Club	$56,423	12.1%	4.9%	$3,795	12.1%	8.8%	$53,795	11.8%

well. The Walmart–owned Sam's Club warehouse stores had not measured up to Costco, their leading competitor. International operations were another challenge for Walmart. Faced with slowing growth domestically, it had tried to capitalize on international opportunities. These international efforts, however, had met with only mixed success at best.

Walmart was also a target for critics who attacked its record on social issues.[3] Walmart had been blamed for pushing production from the United States to low-wage overseas producers. Some claimed that Walmart had almost single-handedly depressed wage growth in the U.S. economy. For many, Walmart had become a symbol of capitalism that had run out of control. Indeed, *Time* magazine asked, "Will Walmart Steal Christmas?"[4] Much of the criticism directed at Walmart did not go beyond angry rhetoric. In many cases, however, Walmart had faced stiff community opposition to building new stores.

With such challenges, some investment analysts questioned whether it was even possible for a company like Walmart, with more than $469 billion in sales, to sustain its accustomed high growth rates. To do so, Walmart would have to address a number of challenges such as maturing markets, competition in discount retailing from both traditional competitors and specialty retailers, aggressive efforts by competitors to imitate Walmart's products and processes, international expansion and increasing competition from online retailers. Indeed, some believed that Walmart would need to find new business if it were to continue its historic success.

The Discount Retail Industry

General retailing in the United States evolved dramatically during the 20th century. Before 1950, general retailing most often took the form of Main Street department stores.

These stores typically sold a wide variety of general merchandise. Department stores were also different from other retailers in that they emphasized service and credit. Before World War II, few stores allowed customers to take goods directly from shelves. Instead, sales clerks served customers at store counters. Not until the 1950s did self-help department stores begin to spread. Discount retail stores also began to emerge in the late 1950s. Discount retailers emphasized low prices and generally offered less service, credit, and return privileges. Their growth was spawned by the repeal of fair trade laws in many states. Many states had passed such laws during the Depression to protect local grocers from chains such as the Atlantic & Pacific Company. The laws fixed prices so that local merchants could not be undercut on price. The repeal of these laws freed discounters to offer prices below the manufacturer's suggested retail price.

Among discount retailers, there were both general and specialty chains. General chains carried a wide assortment of hard and soft goods. Specialty retailers, on the other hand, focused on a fairly narrow range of goods such as office products or sporting goods. Specialty discount retailers such as Office Depot, Home Depot, Staples, Best Buy, and Lowe's began to enjoy widespread success in the 1980s. One result of the emergence of both general and specialty discount retailers was the decline of some of the best-known traditional retailers. Moderate-priced general retailers such as Sears and JC Penney had seen their market share decline in response to the rise of discount stores.

A number of factors explained why discount retailers had enjoyed such success at the expense of general old-line retailers. Consumers' greater concern for value, broadly defined, was perhaps most central. Value in the industry was not precisely defined but involved price, service, quality, and convenience. One example of this value orientation was in apparel. Consumers who once shunned the private-label clothing lines found in discount stores as a source of stigma were increasingly buying labels offered by Kmart, Target, and Walmart. According to one estimate, discount stores were enjoying double-digit growth in apparel while clothing sales in department stores had decreased since the 1990s.

Another aspect of consumers' concern for value involved price. Retail consumers were less reliant on established brand names in a wide variety of goods and showed a greater willingness to purchase the private-label brands of firms such as JC Penney, Sears, Kmart, and Walmart. Convenience had also taken on greater importance for customers. As demographics shifted to include more working mothers and longer workweeks, many American workers placed a greater emphasis on fast, efficient shopping trips. More consumers desired "one-stop shopping," where a broad range of goods were available in one store to minimize the time they spent shopping. This trend accelerated in the previous decade with the spread of supercenters. Supercenters, which combined traditional discount retail stores with supermarkets under one roof, grew to more than $100 billion in sales by 2001 and blurred some of the traditional lines in retailing.

Larger firms had an advantage in discount retailing. The proportion of retail sales that went to multi-store chains had risen dramatically since the 1970s. The number of retail business failures had risen markedly. Most of these failures were individual stores and small chains, but some discount chains such as Venture, Bradlee, and Caldor had filed for bankruptcy. Large size enabled firms to spread their overhead costs over more stores. Larger firms were also able to distribute their advertising costs over a broader base. Perhaps the greatest advantage of size, however, was in relationships with suppliers. Increased size led to savings in negotiating price reductions, but it also helped in other important ways. Suppliers were more likely to engage in arrangements with large store chains such as cooperative advertising and electronic data interchange (EDI) links.

The Internet posed an increasing threat to discount retailers as more people became comfortable with shopping online. Internet shopping was appealing because of the convenience and selection available, but perhaps the most attractive aspect was the competitive pricing. Some Internet retailers were able to offer steep discounts because of lower overhead costs. Additionally, customers were able to quickly compare prices between different Internet retailers. Most, if not all, major retailers sold goods via the Internet.

Large discount retailers such as Walmart derived considerable purchasing clout with suppliers because of their immense size. Even many of the company's largest suppliers gained a high proportion of their sales from Walmart (see Exhibit 4). Suppliers with more than $1 billion

Exhibit 4   Proportion of Sales That Suppliers Receive from Walmart

Company	Walmart Share of Sales
Rayovac	26%
Dial	24
Hasbro	17
Procter & Gamble	17
Newell Rubbermaid	15
Gillette	12
Fruit of the Loom	10
H.J. Heinz	10
Kimberly-Clark	10
Kraft	10

Source: Hopkins, J. (2003). "Wal-Mart's influence grows." *USA Today*, Jan. 21.

in sales such as Newell, Fruit of the Loom, Sunbeam, and Fieldcrest Cannon received more than 15 percent of their sales from Walmart. Many of these large manufacturers also sold a substantial proportion of their output to Kmart, Target, and other discount retailers. Walmart's purchasing clout was considerable, though, even compared to other large retailers. For example, Walmart accounted for more than 28 percent of Dial's sales, and it was estimated that it would have to double sales to its next seven largest customers to replace the sales made to Walmart.[5] Frequently, smaller manufacturers were even more reliant on the large discount retailers such as Walmart. For example, Walmart accounted for as much as 50 percent of revenues for many smaller suppliers.

Private-label goods offered by discount stores had become much more important in the recent years and presented new challenges in supplier relationships. Managing private labels required a high level of coordination between designers and manufacturers (who were often foreign). Investment in systems that could track production and inventory was also necessary.

Technology investments in sophisticated inventory management systems, state-of-the-art distribution centers, and other aspects of logistics were seen as critically important for all discount retailers. Discount retailers were spending large sums of money on computer and telecommunications technology in order to lower their costs in these areas. The widespread use of Universal Product Codes (UPC) allowed retailers to more accurately track inventories for shopkeeping units (SKUs) and better match inventory to demand. Discount retailers also used EDI to shorten the distribution cycle. EDI involved the electronic transmission of sales and inventory data from the registers and computers of discounters directly to suppliers' computers. Often, replenishment of inventories was triggered without human intervention. Thus, EDI removed the need for several intermediate steps in procurement such as data entry by the discounter, ordering by purchasers, data entry by the supplier, and even some production scheduling by supplier managers. Walmart was also pushing the adoption of radio frequency identification (RFID), a new technology for tracking and identifying products. RFID promised to eliminate the need for employees to scan UPC codes and would also dramatically reduce shrinkage, another term for shoplifting and employee pilferage. Suppliers anticipated that RFID would be costly to implement, but the benefits for Walmart were estimated to be as high as $8 billion in labor savings and $2 billion in reducing shrinkage. The implementation of RFID had not materialized in the way Walmart had envisioned and, by 2013, was still evolving in ways not forecasted by the company.

Another important aspect of managing inventory was accurate forecasting. Having the right quantity of products in the correct stores was essential to success. Stories of retailers having an abundance of snow sleds in Florida stores while stores in other areas with heavy snowfall had none were common examples of the challenges in managing inventory. Discounters used variables such as past store sales, the presence of competition, variation in seasonal demand, and year-to-year calendar changes to arrive at their forecasts.

Point-of-sale (POS) scanning enabled retailers to gain information for any purchase on the dollar amount of the purchase, category of merchandise, color, vendor, and SKU number. POS scanning, while valuable in managing inventory, was also seen as a potentially significant marketing tool. Databases of such information offered retailers the potential to "micromarket" to their customers. Upscale department stores had used the POS database marketing more extensively than discounters. Walmart, however, had used such information extensively. For example, POS data showed that customers who purchased children's videos typically bought more than one. Based on this finding, Walmart emphasized placing other children's videos near displays of hot-selling videos.

Competitors

Competition in discount retailing came from both general and specialty discount stores. Among the general discount retailers, Walmart was the largest, followed by Target and

Kmart. Kmart had approximately 10 times more sales than the next largest retailers Dollar General and ShopKo. The most formidable specialty discount retailers included office supply chains such as Office Depot with more than $10 billion in sales, Staples with approximately $24 billion, Toys "R" Us with more than $11 billion, and Best Buy in electronics with approximately $45 billion. In warehouse clubs, Costco and Sam's Club dominated. Costco was the leader with more than $99 billion in sales, followed by Sam's Warehouse Club with $56 billion in revenue. BJ's Wholesale Club followed far behind with around 11 billion in sales before being acquired by a private equity firm in 2011.

Once Walmart's largest competitor, Kmart had experienced a long slide in performance. Kmart operated approximately 1,300 stores, about the same number it had had three years previously. Traditionally, Kmart's discount philosophy had differed from Walmart's. Kmart discount centers sought to price close to, but not necessarily lower than, Walmart's everyday low prices (EDLP). More emphasis was placed on sale items at Kmart. Pricing strategy revolved around several key items that were advertised in Kmart's 73 million advertising circulars distributed in newspapers each Sunday. These items were priced sharply lower than competitors' prices. The effective implementation of this strategy had been impeded by Kmart's difficulty in keeping shelves stocked with sale items and by Walmart's willingness to match Kmart's sale prices. An attempt to imitate Walmart's everyday low pricing strategy failed to deliver sales growth; at the same time, it squeezed margins, so Kmart returned to its traditional pricing strategy in 2003.

Kmart sought to follow Walmart's pattern in many of its activities. The company expressed a commitment to building a strong culture that emphasized performance, teamwork, and respect for individuals who, borrowing from Walmart, were referred to as associates. Establishing such a culture was particularly challenging in the midst of workforce reductions that had taken Kmart from 373,000 employees in 1990 to 307,000 at the end of 1995, and then an even more precipitous drop to 158,000 in 2004. Kmart had also adopted Walmart departmental structure within stores. Another area in which Kmart emulated Walmart was in offering larger income potential to store managers. Each store manager's bonus was linked to an index of customer satisfaction. Kmart had also sought to close the gap between it and Walmart in technology and distribution.

Target, Walmart's other large national competitor, was owned by Target Corporation, formerly Dayton Hudson Corporation, based in Minneapolis, Minnesota. In 2013, Target operated 1,763 stores, which was an increase of only 11 stores from three years earlier. This accounted for $65.4 billion in sales and $2.5 billion in profits. Target was considered an "upscale discounter." The median income of Target shoppers, at $64,000, was considerably higher than its two main competitors, and 50 percent of its customers had completed college.[7] Target attracted a more affluent clientele through a more trendy and upscale product mix and through a store ambience that differed from most discounters in aspects such as wider aisles and brighter lighting. The company also emphasized design much more in its products and had partnered with a number of designers to develop products across a broad range of apparel and housewares. Target had also introduced a proprietary credit card, the Target Guest Card, to differentiate it from other discounters. The conventional wisdom in the industry suggested that pricing at Target was generally not as low as Walmart but was lower than middle-market department stores such as JC Penney and Mervyn's. As with Walmart and Kmart, supercenters were also high on Target's list of strategic priorities. The supercenters, named Super Targets, had opened in many cities, and the company planned to aggressively grow in this area. Promotions were an important part of Target's marketing approach. Each week, more than 100 million Target advertising circulars were distributed in Sunday newspapers. Holiday promotions were also emphasized at Target. Like Kmart, Target had traditionally focused much of its effort on metropolitan areas. Early in the decade, more than half of its stores were in 30 metropolitan markets. By 2012, Target estimated that about 10 percent of its stores were in urban areas. Enticed by the growth of large cities relative to suburbs, Target introduced a new downsized format in Chicago in 2012 and planned several other such stores dubbed City for San Francisco, Seattle, and other large cities. Target's philanthropic activities were well known. Each year, the company gave 5 percent of its pre-tax earnings to not-for-profit organizations—St. Jude Children's Research Hospital and local schools were perhaps Target's highest philanthropic priorities.

While Target had been an increasingly formidable competitor, many believed that the greatest competitive threat to Walmart came from a firm with no bricks and mortar stores: Amazon.com. Amazon began in 1994 as an online bookseller. Before long, Amazon offered other media products such as music CDs, movies (VHS and DVD), software, and video games. By 2013, with sales of $61 billion (in contrast, Walmart's online sales were $7.7 billion), Amazon emphasized price, selection, and convenience and sold a wide diversity of products including perhaps anything that could be purchased at a traditional discount retailer along with a seemingly inexhaustible array of products that could be purchased at the most specialized retailers. In the typical Amazon model, customers selected and purchased items online. Through technology, the company then located the product in large warehouses known as fulfillment centers. The product was then processed and sent to the customer via a third party such as UPS or Fedex. Amazon had invested heavily in its fulfillment capability. By 2013, it had about 35 large fulfillment centers spread throughout the U.S. with another 25 in Europe and 13 in Asia. For a flat annual fee of $79, customers could receive free two-day shipping and discounted one-day shipping rates on eligible products. Additionally, the company had made very visible moves into technology with its own line of Kindle readers and tablets. Its Prime Instant Video, with over 38,000 movies and TV episodes, competed against online firms such as Netflix and Hulu in the online distribution of media content.

Amazon also hosted a large number of third-party sellers. Customers could view products sold by these sellers, purchase the product through Amazon and then the seller would ship to the customer. Amazon had begun giving these third-party sellers the option of warehousing their inventory in Amazon's fulfillment network.

Amazon could claim multiple advantages over bricks and mortar retailers. The firm did not have to deal with the extensive overhead involved with traditional stores. Its selection of products was vastly wider than that available in any traditional store. Yet another advantage for Amazon was that customers did not have to pay a state sales tax on many products purchased. For many shoppers, the convenience of shopping online was appealing. Like Walmart, Amazon employed an everyday low pricing strategy. There were some disadvantages to online shopping. Customers typically had to pay shipping costs and wait for products to be shipped. Amazon Prime negated the cost problem and limited the wait time as well. Online sales of consumer products were growing by as much as 20 percent a year. Brick and mortar stores such as Walmart, Best Buy, Macy's and others were trying to close the online gap with Amazon by embracing what some described as omni-channel fulfillment or ship-from-store. In the omni-channel model, retailers would route the fulfillment of online orders through retail stores near the customer. Though promising, the omni-channel model required sophisticated technology to locate products and reliable execution from local stores in fulfilling orders, a capability generally found more in warehouses than retail outlets.

Amazon's performance offered some indication of the rapid growth in the online sale of consumer products. The company went from $24.5 billion in sales in 2009 to

34.2 billion in 2010, to $48 billion in 2011, to $61 billion in 2012. Amazon was renowned for its long-term perspective. It had clearly traded short-term profits in favor of investing in technology and infrastructure intended to help it achieve dominance in online retailing. Walmart had not been blind to the rise and importance of online retailing generally and, more specifically, the threat from Amazon. From the early days of online commerce, it had sought to build a strong position in online commerce yet lagged dramatically behind Amazon in 2013.

Walmart's History

Walmart was started in 1962 by Sam Walton. The discount retail industry was then in its infancy. A couple of regional firms had experimented with discount retailing, but that year three major retail firms joined Walmart in entering the discount industry. Kresge Corporation started Kmart, Dayton Hudson began Target, and the venerable F. W. Woolworth initiated Woolco. Sam Walton had been the most successful franchisee in the Ben Franklin variety store chain, but discount stores threatened the success of his 18 stores. Walton was convinced that discount retailing would have a bright future even though most in the industry were highly skeptical of the concept. Indeed, Walton was quickly rebuffed in his efforts to convince Ben Franklin and others to provide financial backing for his proposed venture into discounting. With no major chains willing to back him, Walton risked his home and all his property to secure financing for the first Walmart in Rogers, Arkansas.

Of the four new ventures in discount retailing started that year, Walmart seemed the least likely to succeed. Most Walmart stores were in northwestern Arkansas and adjacent areas of Oklahoma, Missouri, and Kansas. Walton had started his retailing career with Ben Franklin in small towns because his wife Helen did not want to live in any city with a population of more than 10,000 people. He had chosen northwestern Arkansas as a base because it allowed him to take advantage of the quail-hunting season in four states. Walmart was, in Sam Walton's words, "underfinanced and undercapitalized"[8] in the beginning. Nevertheless, Walton sought to grow Walmart as fast as he could, because he feared new competitors would preempt growth opportunities if Walmart did not open stores in new towns. After five years, Walmart had 19 stores and sales of $9 million. In contrast, Kmart had 250 stores and $800 million in sales.

Walton retained many of the practices regarding customer service and satisfaction that he had learned in the variety stores business. The central focus of Walmart, however, was on price. Walton sought to make Walmart the low-priced provider of any product it sold. As Walton said,

> What we were obsessed with was keeping our prices below everybody else's. Our dedication to that idea was total. Everybody worked like crazy to keep the expenses down. We didn't have systems. We didn't have ordering programs. We didn't have a basic merchandise assortment. We certainly didn't have any sort of computers. In fact, when I look at it today, I realize that so much of what we did in the beginning was really poorly done. But we managed to sell our merchandise as low as we possibly could and that kept us right-side up for the first ten years…. The idea was simple: when customers thought of Walmart, they should think of low prices and satisfaction guaranteed. They could be pretty sure they wouldn't find it any cheaper anywhere else, and if they didn't like it, they could bring it back.[9]

By 1970, Walmart had expanded to 30 stores in the small towns of Arkansas, Missouri, and Oklahoma. Sam Walton, however, was personally several million dollars in debt. For Walmart to expand beyond its small region required an infusion of capital beyond what the Walton family could provide. Walton thus decided to offer Walmart stock publicly. The initial public offering yielded nearly $5 million in capital. By the early 1990s, 100 shares of that initial stock offering would increase in value from $1,650 to more than $3,000,000.

The other problem that plagued Walmart in its early years was finding a way to keep its costs down. Large vendors were reluctant to call on Walmart and, when they did do business with the company, they would dictate the price and quantity of what they sold. Walton described the situation, "I don't mind saying that we were the victims of a good bit of arrogance from a lot of vendors in those days. They didn't need us, and they acted that way."[10] Another problem that contributed to high costs was distribution. Distributors did not service Walmart with the same care that they did its larger competitors. Walton saw that "the only alternative was to build our own warehouse so we could buy in volume at attractive prices and store the merchandise."[11]

Walmart increased from 32 stores in 1970 to 859 stores 15 years later. For much of that time, Walmart retained its small-town focus. More than half its stores were in towns with populations of less than 25,000. Because of its small-town operations, Walmart was not highly visible to many others in the retail industry. By 1985, though, that had changed. Forbes named Sam Walton the richest man in America. Furthermore, Walmart had begun to expand from its small-town base in the South and had established a strong presence in several large cities. By the 1990s, it had spread throughout the United States in both large cities and small towns.

Walmart in 2013

By the beginning of 2013, Walmart's activities had spread beyond its historical roots in domestic discount centers. The number of domestic discount centers had declined to 561 from a high 1,995 in 1996. Many discount centers had been converted to supercenters, which had increased to 3,158 stores. Walmart Supercenters combined full-line supermarkets and discount centers into one store. Walmart also operated 620 Sam's Clubs, which were warehouse membership clubs. In 1999, Walmart opened its first Neighborhood Markets, which were supermarkets, and it expanded to 286 in operation by 2013.

Operations

From its beginning, Walmart had focused on EDLP. EDLP saved on advertising costs and on labor costs because employees did not have to rearrange stock before and after sales. The company changed its traditional slogan, "Always the Lowest Price," in the 1990s to "Always Low Prices. *Always*." In late 2007, Walmart changed its tagline to "Save Money, Live Better." Despite the changes in slogan, however, Walmart continued to price goods lower than its competitors (see Exhibit 5). When faced with a decline in profits in the late 1990s, Walmart considered raising margins.[12] Instead of pricing 7 to 8 percent below competitors, some managers believed that pricing only about 6 percent below would raise gross margins without jeopardizing sales. Some managers and board members, however, were skeptical that price hikes would work at Walmart. They reasoned that Walmart's culture and identity were so closely attached to low prices that broad price increases would clash with the company's bedrock beliefs.

Exhibit 5   Comparison of Prices at Walmart, Kmart, and Target, Nov. 2008

Item	Walmart	Kmart	Target
Oral B Pulsar ProHealth Toothbrush	5.97	6.19	4.74
Crest ProHealth Toothpaste 6 oz.	3.62	3.99	3.79
Pantene Pro V 2-in-1 25.4 oz	5.88	7.79	5.29
Head & Shoulders Classic 14.2 oz	4.72	5.49	4.89
Edge Shave Gel 7 oz	2.27	2.79	1.89
Schick Extreme 3 8 pk	9.97	11.99	9.99
Gillette Mach 3 Disposable 3 pk	6.12	6.99	5.59
1-a-Day Women's Vitamins 100 tab	6.87	8.49	6.89
1-a-Day Energy Vitamins 50 tab	7.87	8.49	6.89
Bausch & Lomb ReNu	6.97	8.29	6.19
Advil Liquigel 40 tablets	6.48	7.29	5.34
Prestone Extended Life Antifreeze 1 gal		14.49	9.04
Penzoil Motor Oil 5W-30 1 qt	3.57	3.49	3.29
Armour All Glass Wipes 25	4.24	4.29	4.24
TopFlite D2 Straight Golf Balls 15	14.95	15.99	14.99
Perfect Pullup		99.99	99.99
Colemand Quickbed Queen	19.88	24.99	24.99
Crayola Colored Pencils 12 ct	1.88	2.59	1.99
Scott Double-Sided Tape	2.97	3.19	2.99

Some prices are sale prices.

Another concern was that competitors might seize any opportunity to narrow the gap with Walmart. While the reason was unclear, it appeared that some narrowing on price was occurring by 2008. One study showed that the price gap between Walmart and Kroger had shrunk to 7.5 percent in 2007 from 15 percent a few years earlier.[13] Some analysts worried that many shoppers would switch to other retailers as the gap narrowed.

Walmart's low prices were at least partly due to its aggressive use of technology. Walmart had pioneered the use of technology in retail operations for many years and still possessed significant advantages over its competitors. It was the leader in forging EDI links with suppliers. Its Retail Link technology gave over 3,200 vendors POS data and authorization to replace inventory for more than 3,000 stores.[14] Competitors had responded to Walmart's advantage in logistics and EDI by forming cooperative exchanges, but despite their efforts, a large gap remained between Walmart and its competitors.[15] As a result, Walmart possessed a substantial advantage in information about supply and demand, which reduced both the number of items that were either overstocked or out of stock.

November 2003 was also notable for another Walmart technological initiative. It announced plans to implement RFID to all products by January 2005, a goal that had still not been realized by 2010. RFID, as its name implies, involves the use of tags that transmit radio signals. It had the potential to track inventory more precisely than traditional methods and to eventually reduce much of the labor involved in activities such as manually scanning bar codes for incoming goods. Some analysts estimated that Walmart's cost savings from RFID could run as high as $8 billion.[16] Some information technology observers suggested that Walmart had only experienced lukewarm results from RFID as many suppliers struggled to comply with the company's demands. Walmart focused its RFID implementation efforts on tagging pallets for Sam's Club stores and promotional displays in Walmarts. Reportedly, some Sam's Club suppliers were warned they would be assessed a stiff fine for every pallet that was not tagged with RFID, but by 2009 the fines had been reduced to just 12 cents a pallett.

Technology was only one area where Walmart exploited advantages through its relationships with suppliers. Walmart's clout was clearly evident in the payment terms it had with its suppliers. Suppliers frequently offered 2 percent discounts to customers who paid their bills within 15 days. Walmart typically paid its bills at close to 30 days from the time of purchase but still usually received a 2 percent discount on the gross amount of an invoice rather than the net amount.[17] Several suppliers

had attributed performance problems to Walmart's actions. Rubbermaid, for example, experienced higher raw materials costs in the 1990s that Walmart did not allow it to pass along in the form of higher prices. At the same time, Walmart gave more shelf space to Rubbermaid's lower-cost competitors. As a result, Rubbermaid's profits dropped by 30 percent and it was forced to cut its workforce by more than 1,000 employees.[18] Besides pushing for low prices, the large discounters also required suppliers to pick up an increasing amount of inventory and merchandising costs. Walmart required large suppliers such as Procter & Gamble to place large contingents of employees at its Bentonville, Arkansas, headquarters in order to service its account.

Although several companies such as Rubbermaid and the pickle vendor Vlasic had experienced dramatic downfalls largely through being squeezed by Walmart, other companies suggested that their relationship with Walmart had made them much more efficient.[19] Some critics suggested, however, that these extreme efficiency pressures had driven many suppliers to move production from the United States to nations such as China that had much lower wages. Walmart set standards for all of its suppliers in areas such as child labor and safety. A 2001 audit, however, revealed that as many as one-third of Walmart's international suppliers were in "serious violation" of the standards.[20] Walmart pursued steps to help suppliers address the violations, but it was unclear how successful these efforts were.

A *Fast Company* article on Walmart interviewed several former suppliers of the company and concluded: "To a person, all those interviewed credit Walmart with a fundamental integrity in its dealings that's unusual in the world of consumer goods, retailing, and groceries. Walmart does not cheat its suppliers, it keeps its word, it pays its bills briskly. 'They are tough people but very honest; they treat you honestly,' says Peter Campanella, a former Corning manager."[21]

At the heart of Walmart's success was its distribution system. To a large extent, it had been born out of the necessity of servicing so many stores in small towns while trying to maintain low prices. Walmart used distribution centers to achieve efficiencies in logistics. Initially, distribution centers were large facilities—the first were 72,000 square feet—that served 80 to 100 Walmart stores within a 250-mile radius. Newer distribution centers were considerably larger than the early ones and in some cases served a wider geographical radius. Walmart had far more distribution centers than any of its competitors. Cross-docking was a particularly important practice of these centers.[22] In cross-docking, goods were delivered to distribution centers and often simply loaded from one dock to another or even from one truck to another without ever sitting in inventory. Cross-docking reduced Walmart's cost of sales by 2 to 3 percent compared to competitors. Cross-docking was receiving a great deal of attention among retailers with most attempting to implement it for a greater proportion of goods. It was extremely difficult to manage, however, because of the close coordination and timing required between the store, manufacturer, and warehouse. As one supplier noted, "Everyone from the forklift driver on up to me, the CEO, knew we had to deliver on time. Not 10 minutes late. And not 45 minutes early, either …. The message came through clearly: You have this 30-second delivery window. Either you're there or you're out."[23] Because of the close coordination needed, cross-docking required an information system that effectively linked stores, warehouses, and manufacturers. Most major retailers were finding it difficult to duplicate Walmart's success at cross-docking.

Walmart's focus on logistics manifested itself in other ways. Before 2006, the company essentially employed two distribution networks, one for general merchandise and one for groceries. The company created High Velocity Distribution Centers in 2006 that distributed both grocery and general merchandise goods that needed more frequent replenishment. Walmart's logistics system also included a fleet of more than 2,000 company-owned trucks. It was able to routinely ship goods from distribution centers to stores within 48 hours of receiving an order. Store shelves were replenished twice a week on average in contrast to the industry average of once every two weeks.[24]

Walmart stores typically included many departments in areas such as soft goods/domestics, hard goods, stationery and candy, pharmaceuticals, records and electronics, sporting goods, toys, shoes, and jewelry. The selection of products varied from one region to another. Department managers and in some cases associates (or employees) had the authority to change prices in response to competitors. This was in stark contrast to the traditional practice of many chains where prices were centrally set at a company's headquarters. Walmart's use of technology was particularly useful in determining the mix of goods in each store. The company used historical selling data and complex models that included many variables such as local demographics to decide what items should be placed in each store.

Unlike many of its competitors, Walmart had no regional offices until 2006. Instead, regional vice presidents maintained their offices at company headquarters in Bentonville, Arkansas. The absence of regional offices was estimated to save Walmart as much as 1 percent of sales. Regional managers visited stores from Monday to Thursday of each week. Each Saturday at 7:30 A.M.,

regional vice presidents and a few hundred other managers and employees met with the firm's top managers to discuss the previous week's results and discuss different directions for the next week. Regional managers then conveyed information from the meeting to managers in the field via the videoconferencing links that were present in each store. In 2006, Walmart shifted this policy by requiring many of its 27 regional managers to live in the areas they supervised.

Aside from Walmart's impact on suppliers, it was frequently criticized for its employment practices, which critics characterized as being low in both wages and benefits. Charles Fishman acknowledged that Walmart saved customers $30 billion on groceries alone and possibly as much as $150 billion overall when its effect on competitor pricing was considered, but he estimated that while Walmart created 125,000 jobs in 2005, it destroyed 127,500.[25] Others agreed that Walmart's employment and supplier practices resulted in negative externalities on employees, communities, and taxpayers. Harvard professor Pankaj Ghemawat responded to Fishman by calculating that—based on Fishman's numbers—Walmart created customer savings ranging from $12 million to $60 million for each job lost.[26] He also argued that, because Walmart operated more heavily in lower-income areas of the poorest one-third of the United States, low-income customers were much more likely to benefit from Walmart's lower prices. Another criticism of Walmart was that it consistently drove small local retailers out of business when it introduced new stores in small towns and that employees in such rural areas were increasingly at the mercy of Walmart, essentially redistributing wealth from these areas to Bentonville. Jack and Suzy Welch defended Walmart by pointing out that employees in these areas were better off after a Walmart opened:

> In most small towns the storeowner drove the best car, lived in the fanciest house, and belonged to the country club. Meanwhile, employees weren't exactly sharing the wealth. They rarely had life insurance or health benefits and certainly did not receive much in the way of training or big salaries. And few of these storeowners had plans for growth or expansion…a killer for employees seeking life-changing careers.[27]

Sam's Club

A notable exception to Walmart's dominance in discount retailing was in the warehouse club segment. Despite significant efforts by Walmart's Sam's Club, Costco was the established leader. Sam's Club had almost exactly the same number of stores as Costco—620 to 622—yet, Costco

Exhibit 6   Costco Versus Sam's Club

	Costco	Sam's Club
Year founded	1983	1983
U.S. revenues	$99.137 billion	$56.4 billion
Number of stores	622	620
Presidents (or equivalents, since founding)	2	12
Membership cardholders	70.2 million	47 million
Members' average salary	$77,000/$74,000/$96,000	N.A.
Annual membership fees	$55	$40
Average sales per square foot	$814 (2009)	$586 (2009)
Average sales per store	$168.8 million	$87.1 million
Starting hourly wage	$11.50	N.A.
Employee turnover per year	17% (2006)	44% (Walmart, 2006)
Private label (as % of sales)	Approximately 20%	Approximately 10%

still reported almost twice the sales—$105 billion versus $54 billion for Sam's. Costco stores averaged considerably more revenue per store than Sam's Club (see Exhibit 6).

To the casual observer, Costco and Sam's Clubs appeared to be very similar. Both charged small membership fees, and both were "warehouse" stores that sold goods from pallets. The goods were often packaged or bundled into larger quantities than typical retailers offered. Beneath these similarities, however, were important differences. Costco focused on more upscale small business owners and consumers while Sam's, following Walmart's pattern, had positioned itself more to the mass middle market. Relative to Costco, Sam's was also concentrated more in smaller cities.

Consistent with its more upscale strategy, Costco stocked more luxury and premium-branded items than Sam's Club had traditionally done. This changed somewhat when Sam's began to stock more high-end merchandise after the 1990s, but some questioned whether or not its typical customers demanded such items. A Costco executive pointed to the differences between Costco and Sam's customers by describing a scene where a Sam's customer responded to a $39 price on a Ralph Lauren Polo shirt by saying, "Can you imagine? Who in their right mind would buy a T-shirt for $39?" Despite the focus on pricier goods, Costco still focused intensely on managing costs and keeping prices down. Costco set a goal of 10 percent margins and capped markups at 14 percent (compared with the usual 40 percent markup by department stores). Managers were discouraged from exceeding the margin goals.

Some analysts claimed that Sam's Club's lackluster performance was a result of a copycat strategy. Costco was the first of the two competitors to sell fresh meat, produce, and gasoline and to introduce a premium private label for many goods. In each case, Sam's followed suit two to four years later.

"By looking at what Costco did and trying to emulate it, Sam's didn't carve out its own unique strategy," says Michael Clayman, editor of the trade newsletter Warehouse Club Focus. And at least one of the "me too" moves made things worse. Soon after Costco and Price Club merged in 1993, Sam's bulked up by purchasing Pace warehouse clubs from Kmart. Many of the 91 stores were marginal operations in marginal locations. Analysts say that Sam's Club management became distracted as it tried to integrate the Pace stores into its system.[28]

To close the gap against Costco, Walmart in 2003 started to integrate the activities of Sam's Club and Walmart more. Buyers for the two coordinated their efforts to get better prices from suppliers.

Culture

Perhaps the most distinctive aspect of Walmart was its culture. To a large extent, Walmart's culture was an extension of Sam Walton's philosophy and was rooted in the early experiences and practices of Walmart. The Walmart culture emphasized values such as thriftiness, hard work, innovation, and continuous improvement. As Walton wrote,

> Because wherever we've been, we've always tried to instill in our folks the idea that we at Walmart have our own way of doing things. It may be different and it may take some folks a while to adjust to it at first. But it's straight and honest and basically pretty simple to figure it out if you want to. And whether or not other folks want to accommodate us, we pretty much stick to what we believe in because it's proven to be very, very successful.[29]

Walmart's thriftiness was consistent with its obsession with controlling costs. One observer joked that "the Walmart folks stay at Mo 3, where they don't even leave the light on for you."[30] This was not, however, far from the truth. Walton told of early buying trips to New York where several Walmart managers shared the same hotel room and walked everywhere they went rather than use taxis. One of the early managers described how these early trips taught managers to work hard and keep costs low:

> From the very beginning, Sam was always trying to instill in us that you just didn't go to New York and roll with the flow. We always walked everywhere. We never took cabs. And Sam had an equation for the trips: expenses should never exceed 1 percent of our purchases, so we would all crowd in these little hotel rooms somewhere down around Madison Square Garden....We never finished up until about twelve-thirty at night, and we'd all go out for a beer except Mr. Walton. He'd say, "I'll meet you at breakfast at six o'clock." And we'd say, "Mr. Walton, there's no reason to meet that early. We can't even get into the buildings that early." And he'd just say, "We'll find something to do."[31]

The roots of Walmart's emphasis on innovation and continuous improvement can also be seen in Walton's example. Walton's drive for achievement was evident early in life. He achieved the rank of Eagle Scout earlier than anyone previously had in the state of Missouri. Later, in high school, he quarterbacked the undefeated state champion football team and played guard on the undefeated state champion basketball team while serving as student body president. This same drive was evident in Walton's early retailing efforts. He studied other retailers by spending time in their stores, asking endless questions, and taking notes about various store practices. Walton was quick to borrow a new idea if he thought it would increase sales and profits. When, in his early days at Ben Franklin, Walton read about two variety stores in Minnesota that were using self-service, he immediately took an all-night bus ride to visit the stores. Upon his return from Minnesota, he converted one of his stores to self-service, which, at the time, was only the third variety store in the United States to do so. Later, he was one of the first to see the potential of discount retailing.

Walton also emphasized always looking for ways to improve. Walmart managers were encouraged to critique their own operations. Managers met regularly to discuss their store operations. Lessons learned in one store were quickly spread to other stores. Walmart managers also carefully analyzed the activities of their competitors and tried to borrow practices that worked well. Walton stressed the importance of observing what other firms did well rather than what they did wrong. Another way in which Walmart had focused on improvement from its earliest days was in information and measurement. Long before Walmart had any computers, Walton would personally enter measures on several variables for each store into a ledger he carried with him. Information technology enabled Walmart to extend this emphasis on information and measurement.

International Operations

Walmart's entry into the international retail arena had been somewhat recent. As late as 1992, Walmart's entire international operations consisted of only 162,535 square feet of retail space in Mexico. By 2013, however, international sales contributed nearly 30 percent of the company's sales. With growth rates of 7.4 percent in sales and 8.3 percent in operating income, Walmart's international growth exceeded that of its domestic operations. Although it was the company's fastest-growing division—going from about $59 billion in sales in 2006 to more than $135 billion in 2013—Walmart's performance in international markets had been mixed, or as *Forbes* put it, "Overseas, Walmart has won some—and lost a lot."[32] Only a few years earlier, more than 80 percent of Walmart's international revenue came from only three countries: Canada, Mexico, and the United Kingdom.

Walmart had tried a variety of approaches and faced a diverse set of challenges in the different countries it entered. Entry into international markets had ranged from greenfield development to franchising, joint ventures, and acquisitions. Each country that Walmart had entered had presented new and unique challenges. In China, Walmart had to deal with a backward supply chain. In Japan, it had to negotiate an environment that was hostile to large chains and protective of its small retailers. Strong foreign competitors were the problem in Brazil and Argentina. Labor unions had plagued Walmart's entry into Germany along with unforeseen difficulties in integrating acquisitions. Mistakes in choosing store locations had hampered the company in South Korea and Hong Kong.

Walmart approached international operations with much the same philosophy it had used in the United States. "We're still very young at this, we're still learning,"[33] stated John Menzer, former chief executive of Walmart International. Menzer's approach was to have country presidents make decisions. His thinking was that it would facilitate the faster implementation of decisions. Each country president made decisions regarding his or her own sourcing, merchandising, and real estate. Menzer concluded, "Over time all you really have is speed. I think that's our most important asset."[34]

In most countries, entrenched competitors responded vigorously to Walmart's entry. For example, Tesco, the United Kingdom's biggest grocer, responded by opening supercenters. In China, Lianhua and Huilan, the two largest retailers, merged in 2003 into one state-owned entity named the Bailan Group. Walmart was also not alone among major international retailers in seeking new growth in South America and Asia. One international competitor, the French retailer Carrefour, was already the leading retailer in Brazil and Argentina. Carrefour expanded into China in the late 1990s with a hypermarket in Shanghai. In Asia, Makro, a Dutch wholesale club retailer, was the regional leader. Both of the European firms were viewed as able, experienced competitors. The Japanese retailer, Yaohan, moved its headquarters from Tokyo to Hong Kong with the aim of becoming the world's largest retailer. Helped by the close relationship between Chairman Kazuo Wada and Mao's successor Deng Xiaoping, Yaohan was the first foreign retail firm to receive a license to operate in China and planned to open more than 1,000 stores there. Like Walmart, these international firms were motivated to expand internationally by slowing down growth in their own domestic markets.

Some analysts feared that the pace of expansion by these major retailers was faster than the rate of growth in the market and could result in a price war. Like Walmart, these competitors had also found difficulty in moving into international markets and adapting to local differences. Both Carrefour and Makro had experienced visible failures in their international efforts. Folkert Schukken, chairman of Makro, noted this challenge: "We have trouble selling the same toilet paper in Belgium and Holland." The chairman of Carrefour, Daniel Bernard, agreed, "If people think that going international is a solution to their problems at home, they will learn by spilling their blood. Global retailing demands a huge investment and gives no guarantee of a return."[35]

Walmart sought aggressive growth in its international operations. The company added 497 units during 2013. Walmart's early activities in a country typically involved acquisitions, but it had emphasized organic growth more in recent years.

Looking Ahead

Walmart CEO Doug McMillon faced the daunting challenge of achieving the company's accustomed growth rates despite its enormous size. A 5 percent organic growth rate would require the firm to add the equivalent of a firm ranking 129th in the *Fortune* 500 each year. To put that into perspective, the company's growth in revenues would need to nearly equal the total sales of Nike and exceed the sales of companies as large as Xerox and Kimberly Clark. What strategic priorities would allow Walmart to achieve that amount of growth? Or would the company need to adjust its aspirations?

End Notes

1. Standard and Poor's Industry Surveys. *Retailing*, February 1998.
2. Upbin, B. "Wall-to-wall Wal-Mart." *Forbes*, April 12, 2004.
3. Nordlinger, J. (2004). "The new colossus: Wal-Mart is America's store, and the world's and its enemies are sadly behind." *National Review*, April 19, 2004.
4. Ibid.
5. Fishman, C. (2003). "The Wal-Mart you don't know." *Fast Company*, December 2003.
6. Berner, R. (2004). "The next Warren Buffett?" *BusinessWeek*, November 22, 2004.
7. Standard and Poor's Industry Surveys. (1998). *Retailing: General*, February 5, 1998.
8. Walton, S. (with J. Huey). (1993). *Sam Walton: Made in America*. New York: Doubleday, p. 63.
9. Ibid., pp. 64–65. 10. Ibid., p. 66.
10. Ibid., p. 66.

11. (1982). *Forbes*, August 16, p. 43.
12. Pulliam, S. (1996). "Wal-Mart considers raising prices, drawing praise from analysts, but concern from board." *Wall Street Journal*, March 8, 1996, p. C2.
13. Bianco, A. (2007). "Wal-Mart's midlife crisis." *BusinessWeek*, April 30, 2007.
14. Standard and Poor 's Industry Surveys. (1998). *Retailing: General*, February 5, 1998.
15. Useem, J. (2003). "America's most admired companies." *Fortune*, February 18, 2003.
16. Boyle, M. (2003). *Fortune*, November 10, 2003, p. 46.
17. Schifrin, M. (1996). "The big squeeze." *Forbes*, March 11, 1996.
18. Ibid.
19. Fishman, C. (2003). "The Wal-Mart you don't know." *Fast Company*, December 2003.
20. Walmart Web site.
21. Fishman, C. (2003). "The Wal-Mart you don't know." *Fast Company*, December 2003, p. 73.
22. Stalk, G., P. Evans, and L. E. Schulman. (1992). "Competing on capabilities: The new rules of corporate strategy." *Harvard Business Review*, March/April 1992, pp. 57–58.
23. Fishman, C. (2003). "The Wal-Mart you don't know." *Fast Company*, December 2003, p. 73.
24. Stalk G., P. Evans, and L. E. Schulman. (1992). "Competing on capabilities: The new rules of corporate strategy." *Harvard Business Review*, March/April 1992, pp. 57–58.
25. Fishman, C. (2006). "Wal-Mart and the decent society: Who knew that shopping was so important." *Academy of Management Perspectives*, August 2006.
26. Ghemawat, P. (2006). "Business, society, and the 'Wal-Mart effect." *Academy of Management Perspectives*, August 2006.
27. Welch, J., and S. Welch. (2006). "What's right about Wal-Mart." *BusinessWeek*, May 1, 2006, p. 112.
28. Helyar, J. (2003). "The only company Wal-Mart fears." *Fortune*, November 24, 2003, p. 158.
29. Walton, S. (with J. Huey). (1993). *Sam Walton: Made in America*. New York: Doubleday, p. 85.
30. Loeb, M. (1994). "Editor's desk: The secret of two successes." *Fortune*, May 2, 1994.
31. Walton, S. (with J. Huey). (1993). *Sam Walton: Made in America*. New York: Doubleday, p. 84.
32. Upbin, B. (2004). "Wall-to-wall Wal-Mart." *Forbes*, April 12, 2004.
33. Ibid.
34. Ibid.
35. Rapoport, C. (1995). "Retailers go global." *Fortune*, February 20, 1995.

Case 1–4: Harlequin Enterprises: The Mira Decision*[1]

IVEY | Publishing

During June 1993, Harlequin management was deciding whether or not to launch MIRA, a new line of single-title women's fiction novels. With the increased popularity of single-title women's fiction, Harlequin's leading position as the world's largest romance publisher was being threatened. While Harlequin was the dominant and very profitable producer of *series* romance novels, research indicated that many customers were reading as many *single-title* romance and women's fiction books as series romances. Facing a steady loss of share in a growing total women's fiction market, Harlequin convened a task force in December 1992 to study the possibility of relaunching a single-title women's fiction program. Donna Hayes, vice-president of direct marketing, stated:

> *Industry trends reveal that demand for single-title women's fiction continues to grow while demand for series romance remains stable. Our strengths lie in series romance ... by any account, launching MIRA (single-title) will still be a challenge for us. How do we successfully launch a single-title women's fiction program?*

Tentatively named "MIRA," Harlequin's proposed single-title program would focus exclusively on women's fiction. Management hoped MIRA's launch would provide the opportunity to continue Harlequin's history of strong revenue growth.

*Ken Mark prepared this case under the supervision of Professors Rod White and Mary Crossan solely to provide material for class discussion. The authors do not intend to illustrate either effective or ineffective handling of a managerial situation. The authors may have disguised certain names and other identifying information to protect confidentiality.

Hayes, leader of the MIRA team, knew this was a significant decision for Harlequin. Several years earlier an attempt at single-title publishing—Worldwide Library—had failed. Before going to her executive group for approval, Hayes thought about the decisions the company faced if it wished to enter single-title women's fiction publishing: What were the growth and profitability implications if Harlequin broadened its scope from series romance to single-title women's fiction? What fundamental changes would have to be made to Harlequin's current business model? Did the company have the necessary resources and capabilities to succeed in this new arena? If the company proceeds, how should it go about launching MIRA?

The Publishing Industry[2]

Apart from educational material, traditional single-title book publishing was typically a high-risk venture. Each book was a new product with all the risks attendant on any new product introduction. The risks varied with the author's reputation, the subject matter, and thus the predictability of the market's response. Among the numerous decisions facing the publisher were selecting manuscripts out of the thousands submitted each year, deciding how many copies to print, and deciding how to promote the book.

Insiders judged one key to success in publishing was the creative genius needed to identify good young authors among the hundreds of would-be writers, and then publish and develop them through their careers. Years ago, Sol Stein of Stein and Day Publishers had commented, "Most successful publishers are creative editors at heart and contribute more than risk capital and marketing expertise to the books they publish. If a publisher does not add value to what he publishes, he's a printer, not a publisher."

Traditional single-title publishers allowed distributors 50 percent margins (from which the retailer's margin would come).[3] Some other typical costs included royalty payments of more than 12 percent, warehouse and handling costs of 4 percent, and selling expenses at 5.5 percent. Advertising generally required 6 percent and printing costs[4] required another 12 percent. The remainder was earnings before indirect overhead. Typically, indirect overhead accounted for two percent of the retail price of a book. Because of author advances, pre-publication, promotion, and fixed costs of printing, break-even volumes were significant. And if the publisher failed to sell enough books, the losses could be substantial. Harlequin's core business, series romance fiction, was significantly different from traditional single-title publishing.

Harlequin Enterprises Limited

The word *romance* and the name Harlequin had become synonymous over the last half-century. Founded in 1949, Harlequin began applying its revolutionary approach to publishing—a packaged, consumer-goods strategy—in 1968 shortly after acquiring the publishing business of U.K.-based Mills & Boon. Each book was part of an identifiable product line, consistently delivering the expected benefit to the consumer. With a growth rate of 25 percent per year during the 1970s, Harlequin became the world's largest publisher of women's series romance fiction. It was during this time that Torstar, a newspaper publisher, acquired all of Harlequin Enterprises Ltd.

Over the years, many book publishers had attempted to enter Harlequin's segment of the industry. All had eventually withdrawn. Only once had Harlequin's dominance in series romance fiction been seriously challenged. The "romance wars" began in 1980 when Harlequin took over U.S. distribution of its series products from Simon & Schuster (S&S), a large single-title publisher with established paperback distribution. Subsequently, S&S began publishing series romance fiction under the Silhouette imprint. After several years, a truce was negotiated between Harlequin and S&S. Harlequin acquired Silhouette, S&S's series romance business, and S&S got a 20-year deal as Harlequin's sole U.S. distributor for series fiction.

During the late 1980s and early 1990s, growth in the series market slowed. Harlequin was able to maintain revenues by publishing longer and more expensive series products and generally raising prices. However, as shown in Table 1, global unit volume was no longer growing.

Harlequin's Target Market and Products

Harlequin books were sold in more than 100 international markets in more than 23 languages around the world. Along with romance fiction, Harlequin participated in the series mystery and male action-adventure markets under its Worldwide Library and Gold Eagle imprints. Harlequin had an estimated 20 million readers in North America and 50 million readers around the world.

With a median age of 41, the Harlequin's romance series reader was likely to be married, well educated, and working outside the home. More than half of Harlequin readers spent at least three hours reading per week. Harlequin series readers were brand loyal; a survey indicated four out of five readers would continue to buy Harlequin books in the next year. Larry Heisey, Harlequin's former chief executive officer and chairman, expanded on the value of Harlequin's products: "I think our books are so popular because they provide relaxation and escape…. We get many letters from people who tell us how much these books mean to them."

While Harlequin had advertised its series product on television, current marketing efforts centered on print media. Harlequin advertised in leading women's magazines such as *Cosmopolitan, Glamour, Redbook,* and *Good Housekeeping*, and general interest magazines such as *People*. The print advertisement usually featured one of Harlequin's series products and also promoted the company's brands.

Romance Series Product: Well Defined and Consistent

Under the Harlequin and Silhouette brands, Harlequin published 13 different series with 64 titles each month. Each series was distinctly positioned, featuring a particular genre (e.g., historical romances) or level of explicitness. Isabel Swift, editorial director of Silhouette, described the different types of series books published by Harlequin:

> *Our different lines deliver different promises to our readers. For example, Harlequin Temptation's tagline is sassy, sexy, and seductive, promising that each*

Table 1   Total Unit Sales (in $000s)

Year	1988	1989	1990	1991	1992	1993
Operating Revenue	344,574	326,539	348,358	357,013	417,884	443,825
Operating Profit	48,142	56,217	57,769	52,385	61,842	62,589
Total Unit Sales	202	191	196	193	205	199

Exhibit 1 Harlequin/ Silhouette
Series Positioning Scales

Source: Company files.

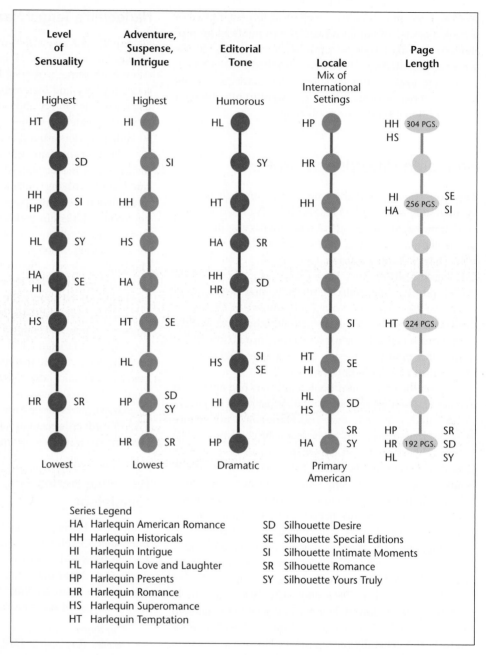

		Series Legend		
	HA	Harlequin American Romance	SD	Silhouette Desire
	HH	Harlequin Historicals	SE	Silhouette Special Editions
	HI	Harlequin Intrigue	SI	Silhouette Intimate Moments
	HL	Harlequin Love and Laughter	SR	Silhouette Romance
	HP	Harlequin Presents	SY	Silhouette Yours Truly
	HR	Harlequin Romance		
	HS	Harlequin Superomance		
	HT	Harlequin Temptation		

*story will deliver a sexy, fun, contemporary romance
between one man and one woman, whereas the Silhouette Romance title, in comparison, is a tender read
within a framework of more traditional values.*

Overall, the product portfolio offered a wide variety
of stories to capture readers' interests. For the positioning
of Harlequin's series, see Exhibit 1. Sold in more than a
dozen countries. Harlequin had the ability to publish series
books worldwide. The average retail price of a Harlequin
series novel was $4.40,[5] significantly less than the $7 retail

price for the typical single-title paperback novel, and much
less than the $15 to $25 for longer, hardcover titles by best-
selling authors.

Harlequin's series romance product was fundamentally different from that of traditional single-title publishers: content, length, artwork size, basic formats, and print
were all well defined to ensure a consistent product. Each
book was not a new product, but rather an addition to
a clearly defined product line. Unlike single-title books,
Harlequin's series products had a common format. They

$3.99 U.S./$4.50 CAN.

Exhibit 2   Typical Harlequin Series Romance Products

Source: Company files.

measured 105 millimeters by 168 millimeters and fit neatly into specially designed racks located primarily in supermarkets and drugstores. Most product lines were 192 to 256 pages in length; some were up to 304 pages in length. Cover designs differed slightly by product line and country, but the look and feel was similar (see Exhibit 2).

Harlequin provided prospective series romance authors with plot, style, and book length guidelines. However, crafting the stories still demanded skill and work. As David Galloway, chief executive officer of Torstar, Harlequin's parent company, and the former head of Harlequin observed:

> The books are quite simply good stories. If they weren't, we wouldn't be getting the repeat purchases we do. A lot of writers think they can dash off a Harlequin, but they can't. We've had submissions from Ph.D.'s in English who can certainly write but they can't tell a story.

To ensure a consistent product emerged, Harlequin's editors assessed many elements, including plot, story line, main character(s), setting, percentage of romance in the plot, level of realism, level of fantasy, sensuality, social and/or individual problems, happy ending, and reading impact. Even though many different authors contributed to series romance, Harlequin's editors ensured a consistent finished product, satisfying the needs of their loyal series romance readers. The consequences of this uniformity were significant. The reader was buying a Harlequin novel, and advertising promoted the Harlequin brands rather than a particular book or author.

Bookstores were not the primary channel for series romance novels. Most retail purchases were made at supermarkets or drugstores and increasingly mass merchandisers like Wal-Mart. But many avid Harlequin readers got the product delivered to their home every month through Harlequin's direct mail service. The standardized size and format made warehousing and distribution more efficient. In addition, the product's consistency enabled standing order distribution to retail. As Pam Laycock, director of new product development, explained:

> *A major contributor to our success as a series publisher is our standing order distribution. Each series is distributed to a retail location in a predetermined configuration—for example in a series where we publish four titles per month, a retailer may take six copies per title and this level of distribution is generally agreed upon and maintained for the entire year. This approach enables us to more accurately predict monthly print quantities and achieve significant print cost effectiveness.*

Orders (and sales) for conventional single-title books were not as predictable. Another significant difference was that series romance books were part of Harlequin's standing order distribution plan. And more like magazines, they were displayed on retail shelves for four weeks. Harlequin's distributors then removed and returned any unsold books, and replaced them with the next month's offerings. By comparison, single-title books were typically displayed at retail from 6 to 12 months or more.

Harlequin's series romance business did not generate or even encourage best-sellers. "Best-sellers (in series romance) would ruin our system," a Harlequin insider stated. "Our objective is consistency in volume. We have no winners and no losers." Unsold books could be returned to the publisher for credit. A consequence of Harlequin's even and predictable sales was that order regulation and returns could be more easily optimized to maximize the contribution to profits.

A comparison of Harlequin's series business model and the operations of traditional "one-off" publishers is presented in Exhibit 3.

With a consistent quality product, standing orders, predictable retail traffic patterns, and the ability to produce and deliver books at low costs, Harlequin had achieved great success. Harlequin's series romance business had consistently earned a return on sales of 15 percent. As shown in Exhibit 4, this figure compared favorably with larger traditional publishers.

Loriana Sacilotto, director of retail marketing, explained why Harlequin outperformed other traditional single-title publishers:

> *There are a variety of reasons why other publishers do not achieve the same margins we enjoy. The main reason is that they are broad in their publishing focus whereas we focus on women's fiction. They don't have the same reader recognition, trust and relationships. We invest in it.*

Harlequin Business System

The Global Author–Editor Team.   Harlequin had established a strong level of reader trust and brand equity by consistently delivering quality content. Editors in three acquisition centers in Toronto, New York, and London were responsible for working closely with 1,300-plus authors to develop and publish more than 1,000 new titles annually. In

Exhibit 3   Comparing Harlequin's Series Business Model and a Traditional Publisher's

	Harlequin Series	**Single-Title Publisher**
Editorial	Emphasizes consistency within established guidelines	Requires separate judgment on potential consumer demand for each manuscript
Rights	Uses standardized contract	Can be a complex process, involving subrights, hard/soft deals, advances, and tying up authors for future books
Author Management	Less dependent on specific authors	Vulnerable to key authors changing publisher
Production	Uses consistent format with focus on efficiency	Emphasizes package, size, and format—cost control secondary
Marketing	Builds the imprint/series	Builds each title/author
Distribution	Supermarkets, drugstores, mass merchandisers, big-box bookstores. Large direct mail	Bookstores (all types) Book clubs and mass merchandisers
Selling	Emphasizes servicing, rack placement, and order regulation	Cover, in-store placement, critical reviews, special promotional tactics (e.g., author signings)
Order Regulation/ Information Systems	Utilizes very sophisticated shipping and returns handling procedures	Historically has not received much attention, and hence, is not as sophisticated

Exhibit 4   Comparison of Harlequin's Performance with Traditional Publishers—1993 (in millions of dollars)

	Harlequin[a]	Simon and Schuster[b]	Harper/Avon[c]
Sales Revenue	417.8	1,929.0	1,210.4
Operating Profit	61.8	218.4	160.8
Identifiable Assets	319.2	2,875.8	2,528.0
R.O.S.	14.8%	11.3%	13.2%
R.O.I.A.	19.4%	7.6%	6.4%

[a] Canadian dollars   [b] U.S. dollars (Cdn$1.20 = US$1)   [c] Australian dollars (Cdn$0.80 = AUD$1)

addition to the work of its regular writers, Harlequin received approximately 30,000 unsolicited manuscripts per year. Typically, about 100 of these were accepted in any given year.

Series authors received royalties of 13 percent of retail book price. Harlequin's typical series authors had more than 100,000 of each of their books distributed worldwide.

Harlequin's series romance product focused solely on front-list sales. In the publishing world, *front-list* sales refers to the first print runs of a book supporting its initial market launch. *Back-list* refers to books reprinted and reissued years after the book's initial run (often to support an author's subsequent books). Harlequin's series romance novels—unlike a traditional publisher's single-title books—were not available on back-list. However, Harlequin retained these rights.

Printing was a highly competitive business and Harlequin subcontracted its requirements. Costs per series book were typically $0.44 per book compared to the competitors' average costs of $0.88 per single-title soft cover book.

Distribution, Selling, and Promotion.   With its standing orders, Harlequin's distribution costs per book were $0.18, with selling expenses at an average of $0.09 per book. Because it was the dominant player in series romance, Harlequin had relatively low advertising and promotion costs—about $0.22 per book.

In Canada, Harlequin had its own distribution. Elsewhere in the world, independent distributors were employed. In the United States, Pocketbooks, the sales division of Simon & Schuster, a large traditional publisher, handled Harlequin's series romance books. Supermarkets, drugstores, discount department stores, and mass merchandisers accounted for 70 percent of North American retail sales. Specialty big-box bookstores like Barnes and Noble and other chains and independent bookstores accounted for the remainder of retail sales. Globally, Harlequin's products were in over 250,000 retail outlets. Eighty thousand of these outlets were in North America;

almost 50,000 of these were supermarkets and drugstores. Harlequin's series products were in 70 percent of supermarkets, but only 55 percent of bookstores. In Europe, kiosks and tobacconists accounted for the largest proportion of retail outlets.

The direct channel handled direct-to-reader book sales. Harlequin's "Reader Service" book club was an important source of sales and profits. Investing in advertising to acquire readers, this direct mail operation offered frequent Harlequin readers the possibility of purchasing every book the company published, delivered right to their doorstep. In the United States, six books were sold through the book club for every 10 sold at retail. Furthermore, a book sold through the book club yielded Harlequin the full cover price, whereas a book sold at retail netted the company approximately half the retail price, and required advertising, distribution costs, and the acceptance of returns from retailers.

Rise of Single-Title Romance

The proliferation of titles and authors during the "Romance Wars" had resulted in the emergence of single-titles as a significant factor in the women's romance fiction market. Exhibit 5 provides the sales breakdown for romance novels.

In an attempt to capitalize on readers' growing appetite for single-titles, Harlequin launched Worldwide Library in 1986, its first single-title publishing program. This move also gave Harlequin's more accomplished series authors another outlet. Laycock commented:

> *Several authors who began their writing careers with Harlequin writing series romance wanted broader opportunities—opportunities that they saw in the single-title women's fiction publishing arena. Prior to the launch of Worldwide Library, Harlequin didn't have publishing opportunities to meet the desires of these authors. As a result, authors would seek out competitive publishers to support their single-title works.*

Exhibit 5   Romance Novel Sales in North America (millions of units)

	1985	1986	1987	1988	1989	1990
Harlequin series romance	77	79	80	82	83	85
Other romance series publishers	12	12	13	13	14	14
Single-title romance books by other publishers	72	79	86	94	102	112
Total romance books	**161**	**170**	**179**	**189**	**199**	**211**

Exhibit 6   Range of Worldwide Titles (1987)

Book Title	Type/Genre	Unit Sales Data	Harlequin Series Author?
Longest Pleasure	Romance	304,000	Yes
Quarantine	Horror	62,000	No
Eve of Regression	Psychological Thriller	55,000	No
War Moon	Suspense	72,000	No
Illusion	Psychological Suspense	35,000	No
Dream Escape	Romance	297,000	Yes
Alien Planet	Science Fiction	71,000	No

Exhibit 7   Monthly Single-Title Romance Output Analysis North American Market

Single-Title Romance by Category	1985	1989	1991
Contemporary	2	6	12
Historical	22	37	43
Regency	6	8	17
Total	**30**	**51**	**72**
By Publisher			
Zebra (Kensington Publishing)	5	15	21
Bantam/Dell	2	2	8
Diamond	0	0	4
Harper Paperbacks	0	0	3
Avon	4	5	6
Jove	2	2	4
Leisure Books	3	3	5
NAL/Signet	6	7	8
Pocket Books (Simon and Schuster)	1	6	3
Ballantine/Fawcett, Onyx, SMP	4	7	7
Warner Books/Popular Library	3	4	3
Total	**30**	**51**	**72**

Source: Company files.

By 1988, Worldwide was shut down as a result of several problems. "Worldwide could never decide if it was a romance program, a women's fiction program, or a general fiction program," a Harlequin insider commented. Exhibit 6 illustrates a list of typical titles published at Worldwide.

With the shutdown of Worldwide Library, popular authors moved to other publishers. As shown in Exhibit 7, other publishers continued to exploit the popularity of single-title romance novels.

Eager to find ways to grow its publishing business, Harlequin's management reexamined the publishing market. A broader analysis revealed that although Harlequin's series romance had captured well over 80 percent of the North American series romance market by 1990, Harlequin's estimated share of the North American *women's fiction* market was only about 5 percent. Table 2 provides a breakdown of the women's fiction market.

There was substantial overlap in the readership of series romance fiction and other fiction. Mark Mailman, vice president of market research and analysis, added:

> One compelling reason to get into single-title publishing is that when we look at our research on customers, they're reading 20 Harlequin books and 20 single-title books from other publishers. We have an opportunity to take a greater share of that market.

Table 2   North American Women's Fiction Market Size Estimate, 1993 (as a percentage of overall segment sizes in US$ millions)

	General Fiction	Romance	Mystery	Sci-Fi	Total Fiction
Total Segment Size	2,222	1,220	353	476	4,271
Estimated Women's Fiction Share of Segment	60%	100%	60%	38%	69%

Harlequin's Single-Title Task Force

Faced with slow or no growth in series romance, a Harlequin task force convened in 1992 to study the feasibility of launching a new women's fiction single-title program. To begin, they examined why Worldwide had failed and concluded that overall lack of success was attributable to: editorial parameters that were too broad; less than optimal North American retail distribution; very few Worldwide titles distributed through the direct-to-reader channel; global support for the program was not timely and universal; and the selection of authors and titles was unsuccessful. The task force report stated:

> In the past few years, sell-through efficiencies in the supermarket channels are not as great as the sell-through efficiencies in both mass merchandisers and bookstores. The more efficient retailer knew that the consumer was spending her discretionary reading dollar to buy a diversity of romantic reads, including those that had previously been thought of as mainstream.
>
> Since a single-title strategy requires a single-title solicitation from the sales force and more expensive single-title packaging, two of Harlequin's strategic lynchpins of our earlier decades have to be re-thought (for single-title): standing order program and same format production. However, Harlequin can still capitalize on its global base and its ability to distribute widely to points of purchase that women visit on a regular basis.

MIRA Launch Decision

The task force was preparing its recommendation for MIRA, Harlequin's proposed women's fiction single-title program. The addition of single titles would make a welcome contribution to overhead costs. Currently, indirect overhead costs per series novel were $0.09 per book. Because infrastructure was already in place, it was estimated that MIRA novels would not incur additional indirect overhead costs. Printing costs for single-titles were expected to be $0.71 per book (350 pages on average). Estimated advertising and promotional costs for new single-titles were 6 percent of (the higher) retail price.

Author Management

In the single-title market, authors were categorized into three groups, based on their sales potential: brand new, mid-list, and best-seller (see Exhibit 8). Depending on the author group royalties, sales, and promotional support varied. Best-selling authors were expected to sell more than a million books. Publishers were known to sign established authors for up to a five-book contract with large multimillion dollar advances. It had not been determined whether MIRA should follow suit. In addition to author advances, typical royalties per MIRA-type book were estimated to be 13 percent of the $6.75 retail price.

Exhibit 8   General Industry Contract Terms for Fiction Category by Author Group

	Brand-New Author	Mid-List Author	Best-Selling Author
Advance	$10,000 to $30,000	$80,000 to $200,000	$1 million to $5 million
Royalties	5% to 13%	8% to 15%	10% to 17%
Overseas Publishing Schedule	Within 18 months	Within 12 months	Simultaneous
Overseas Publishing Markets	Major markets	All markets	All markets
Minimum Distribution	30,000 to 80,000	100,000 to 400,000	>1 million
Promotional Support per book	Possibly some support (up to $50,000)	Support ($100,000)	Very strong support (more than $300,000)

Sources: Industry sources and casewriter estimates.

A Different Format

Women's fiction books were expected to have many differences from well-defined series romance books. Unlike series romance, topics would cover a broader range of segments including general fiction, science fiction, and mystery. Women's fiction books would be longer in length: 100,000 to 400,000 words compared with a series romance book length of 75,000 words. Naturally, book sizes would be bigger in terms of page length: from 250 to 400 pages versus a norm of 192 to 304 pages for series romance.

Distribution

Harlequin had a strong distribution network for its series romances through supermarkets, drugstores, and discount department stores. Single-title women's fiction novels required more mainstream distribution focusing on retail bookstores. In addition, standing order distribution, a hallmark of Harlequin's series romance business model, would have to be abandoned in favor of relying on orders generated by the distributor's sales force for single-titles.

Success in the United States would be key for MIRA, and in this market, Harlequin relied upon Simon and Schuster's sales force. Since S&S was a major single-title publisher, Harlequin did not know how much support MIRA would be afforded. Harlequin was considering offering better margins to the distributors than those it offered for series romance distribution. Expenses for single-title distribution were expected to be $0.27 per book.

MIRA books would rely more heavily upon distribution through bookstores when distributed through the same channels as the series product. Retailers would be encouraged to shelve MIRA books separately from the series offering. The more intensive selling effort for single titles would require 4 percent of the single title retail price. The new single-title program planned to offer $3.38 in margin to the distribution channel for single-title books (50 percent of the typical retail price of $6.75) versus $2.42 for series books (45 percent of the $4.40 suggested retail price).

Acquiring Single-Title Rights

Harlequin subsidiaries in some countries were already buying rights to publish single titles. By launching MIRA Harlequin could negotiate better global-author deals. The task force report added: "By acquiring mainstream titles through a central acquiring office, the collective clout of Harlequin could create the likelihood of better-selling mainstream titles marketed by all countries in the global enterprise."

Harlequin's author and editor relationships remained strong, so much so that many series authors were enthusiastic about maintaining a long-term relationship with a trusted editor as they pursued their break-out mainstream book. With MIRA, these authors could remain loyal to Harlequin.

How Best to Proceed

There were many issues to be resolved prior to any launch of MIRA. Most pressing was the question of whether Harlequin had the resources and capabilities to succeed in its new women's fiction segment. Certainly there were elements of its series business model that could be transferred to the broader women's fiction market. But what were the gaps? What else did Harlequin need?

Hayes had several options if MIRA was launched. Several established best-selling authors had begun their writing careers with Harlequin and had moved on to writing single-title books. These authors had established reputations. Harlequin could approach one or more of these authors to sign with MIRA/Harlequin. Such an arrangement would involve a multi-book contract and substantial advances. While risky, this approach would ensure that MIRA's launch attracted attention.

A different, seemingly less risky alternative was to tap into Harlequin's extensive back-list collection and reissue a selection of novels by current best-selling authors currently signed with rival single-title publishers. The physical size of the book and page length could be extended to 250 pages from 192 by adjusting format. In addition, a new, MIRA-branded cover could be produced to repackage the books. Coincident with the launch of this back-list, Harlequin's editors would cultivate and develop existing series authors, encouraging them to write single-title books for MIRA.

Returning to the strategic dilemma that Harlequin faced, Swift commented on the challenge of successfully launching MIRA:

> Our biggest challenge is the requirement to publish on a title-by-title basis. Every new book will have to stand on its own, with its own cover, a new marketing plan and possibly even an author tour. Can we as a company develop the flexibility to remain nimble? How patient should we be in waiting for success? Given Worldwide's poor results, how should we approach this challenge?

End Notes

1. To protect confidentiality, all financial information within this case study has been disguised.
2. This section is adapted from the Richard Ivey School of Business case # 9A87M002. Harlequin Enterprises Limited—1979, Peter Killing.
3. All amounts are a percentage of the suggested retail price.
4. Numbers are for the typical paperback. Hardcover books cost more to produce, but as a percentage of its higher retail price, printing costs were roughly the same proportion.
5. All amounts in Canadian dollars unless otherwise specified.

2 BUSINESS-LEVEL STRATEGIES

4 Cost Leadership

LEARNING OBJECTIVES *After reading this chapter, you should be able to:*

1. Define cost leadership.

2. Identify six reasons firms can differ in their costs.

3. Identify four reasons economies of scale can exist and four reasons diseconomies of scale can exist.

4. Explain the relationship between cost advantages due to learning-curve economies and a firm's market share, as well as the limitations of this logic.

5. Identify how cost leadership helps neutralize each of the major threats in an industry.

6. Identify the bases of cost leadership that are more likely to be rare and costly to imitate.

7. Explain how firms use a functional organizational structure to implement business-level strategies, such as cost leadership.

8. Describe the formal and informal management controls and compensation policies firms use to implement cost leadership strategies.

MyManagementLab®

✪ **Improve Your Grade!**
Over 10 million students improved their results using the Pearson MyLabs.
Visit **mymanagementlab.com** for simulations, tutorials, and end-of-chapter problems.

The World's Lowest-Cost Airline

Everyone's heard of low-cost airlines—Southwest, EasyJet, and JetBlue, for example. But have you heard of the world's lowest-cost airline? This airline currently gives 25 percent of its seats away for free. Its goal is to double that within a couple of years. And yet, in 2013, this airline announced record annual profits of €569 million, up 13 percent; an increase in passenger traffic of 5 percent (from €75.8 million to €79.3 million); and an increase in revenues of 13 percent (from €4325 million to €4884 million). And this in spite of continued increases in jet fuel prices during this same time period!

The name of this airline is Ryanair. Headquartered in Dublin, Ireland, Ryanair flies short flights throughout Western Europe. In 1985, Ryanair's founders started a small airline to fly between Ireland and England. For six years, this airline barely broke even. Then, in 1991, Michael O'Leary—current CEO at Ryanair—was brought on board. O'Leary traveled to the United States and studied the most successful low-cost airline in the world at that time: Southwest Airlines. O'Leary became convinced that, once European airspace was deregulated, an airline that adopted Southwest's model of quick turnarounds, no frills, no business class, flying into smaller regional airports, and using only a single kind of aircraft could be extremely successful. Prices in the European air market were fully deregulated in 1997.

Since then, Ryanair has become an even lower-cost airline than Southwest. Indeed, it calls itself the only "ultra-low cost carrier."

For example, like Southwest, Ryanair only flies a single type of aircraft—a Boeing 737–800. However, to save on the cost of its airplanes, Ryanair orders them without window shades and with

seats that do not recline. This saves several hundred thousand dollars per plane and also reduces ongoing maintenance costs. Both Southwest and Ryanair try to make it easy for consumers to order tickets online, thereby avoiding the costs of call centers and travel agents. However, just 59 percent of Southwest's tickets are sold online; 98 percent of Ryanair's tickets are sold online.

This focus on low costs allows Ryanair to have the lowest prices possible for a seat on its airplanes. The average fare on Southwest is $92; the average fare on Ryanair is $53. But, even at those low prices, Ryanair is still able to earn comfortable margins.

However, those net margins don't come just from Ryanair's low costs. They also reflect the fact that the fare you pay Ryanair

includes only the seat and virtually no other services. If you want any other services, you have to pay extra for them. For example, you want to check bags? It will cost $9.95 per bag. You want a snack on the airplane? It will cost you $5.50. For that, you get a not-very-tasty hot dog. You want a bottle of water? It will cost you $3.50. You want a blanket or pillow—they cost $2.50 each.

In addition, flight attendants will sell you all sorts of extras to keep you occupied during your flight. These include scratch-card games, perfume, digital cameras ($137.50), and MP3 players ($165). During 2007, Ryanair began offering in-flight mobile telephone service. Not only did this enable passengers to call their friends and family, Ryanair also used this service to introduce mobile gambling on its planes. Now, on your way from London to Paris, you can play blackjack, poker, and slot machines.

Finally, to further increase revenues, Ryanair sells space on its planes to advertisers. When your seat tray is up, you may see an ad for a cell phone from Vodaphone. When the tray is down, you may see an ad from Hertz.

All of these actions enable Ryanair to keep its profits up while keeping its fares as low as possible. And the results of this strategy have been impressive—from near bankruptcy in 1991, Ryanair is now among the largest international airlines in the world.

Of course, this success did not happen without some controversy. For example, in October 2006, Ryanair was chosen as the most disliked European airline in a poll of some 4,000 readers of TripAdvisor, a British Web site for frequent travelers. Ryanair's response: These frequent travelers usually have their companies pay for their travel. If they had to pay for their own tickets, they would prefer Ryanair. Also, Ryanair's strong anti-union stance has caused it political problems in many of the union-dominated countries where it flies. Finally, Ryanair has been criticized for some of its lax security and safety procedures, for how it treats disabled passengers, and for the cleanliness of its planes.

However, if you want to fly from London to Barcelona for $49 round trip, it's hard to beat Ryanair.

Source: K. Capell (2006). "Wal-Mart with wings." *BusinessWeek,* November 27, pp. 44–46; www//en.wikipedia.org/wiki/Ryanair; and Peter Arnold, Inc. www.Ryanair.com

Ryanair has been profitable in an industry—the airline industry—that has historically been populated by bankrupt firms. It does this by implementing an aggressive low-cost strategy.

What Is Business-Level Strategy?

Part 1 of this book introduced the basic tools required to conduct a strategic analysis: tools for analyzing external threats and opportunities (in Chapter 2) and tools for analyzing internal strengths and weaknesses (in Chapter 3). Once these two analyses have been completed, it is possible to begin making strategic choices. As explained in Chapter 1, strategic choices fall into two large categories: business strategies and corporate strategies. **Business-level strategies** are actions firms take to gain competitive advantages in a single market or industry. **Corporate-level strategies** are actions firms take to gain competitive advantages by operating in multiple markets or industries simultaneously.

The two business-level strategies discussed in this book are cost leadership (this chapter) and product differentiation (Chapter 5). The importance of these two business-level strategies is so widely recognized that they are often called **generic business strategies**.

What Is Cost Leadership?

A firm that chooses a **cost leadership business strategy** focuses on gaining advantages by reducing its costs to below those of all its competitors. This does not mean that this firm abandons other business or corporate strategies. Indeed, a single-minded focus on *just* reducing costs can lead a firm to make low-cost products that no one wants to buy. However, a firm pursuing a cost leadership strategy focuses much of its effort on keeping its costs low.

Numerous firms have pursued cost leadership strategies. Ryanair clearly follows this strategy in the airline industry, Timex and Casio in the watch industry, and BIC in the disposable pen and razor market. All these firms advertise their products. However, these advertisements tend to emphasize reliability and low prices—the kinds of product attributes that are usually emphasized by firms pursuing cost leadership strategies.

In automobiles, Fiat has implemented a cost leadership strategy with its emphasis on low-priced cars for basic transportation. Like Ryanair, Timex, Casio, and BIC, Fiat spends a significant amount of money advertising its products, but its advertisements tend to emphasize its sporty sexy styling and low price. Fiat has positioned its cars as fun and inexpensive, not a high-performance sports car or a luxurious status symbol. Fiat's ability to sell these fun and inexpensive automobiles depends on its design choices (keep it simple) and its low manufacturing costs.[1]

Sources of Cost Advantages

An individual firm may have a cost advantage over its competitors for a number of reasons. Cost advantages are possible even when competing firms produce similar products. Some of the most important of these sources of cost advantage are listed in Table 4.1 and discussed in this section.

1. Size differences and economies of scale
2. Size differences and diseconomies of scale
3. Experience differences and learning-curve economies
4. Differential low-cost access to productive inputs
5. Technological advantages independent of scale
6. Policy choices

TABLE 4.1 Important Sources of Cost Advantages for Firms

Size Differences and Economies of Scale

One of the most widely cited sources of cost advantages for a firm is its size. When there are significant economies of scale in manufacturing, marketing, distribution, service, or other functions of a business, larger firms (up to some point) have a cost advantage over smaller firms. The concept of economies of scale was first defined in Chapter 2. **Economies of scale** are said to exist when the increase in firm size (measured in terms of volume of production) is associated with lower costs (measured in terms of average costs per unit of production), as depicted in Figure 4.1. As the volume of production in a firm increases, the average cost per unit decreases until some optimal volume of production (point X) is reached, after which the average costs per unit of production begins to rise because of **diseconomies of scale** (a concept discussed in more detail later in this chapter).

If the relationship between volume of production and average costs per unit of production depicted in Figure 4.1 holds, and if a firm in an industry has the largest volume of production (but not greater than the optimal level, X), then that firm will have a cost advantage in that industry. Increasing the volume of production can reduce a firm's costs for several reasons. Some of the most important of these reasons are summarized in Table 4.2 and discussed in the following text.

Volume of Production and Specialized Machines.   When a firm has high levels of production, it is often able to purchase and use specialized manufacturing tools that cannot be kept in operation in small firms. Manufacturing managers at BIC

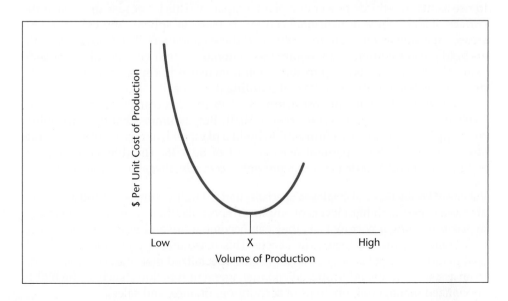

Figure 4.1   Economies of Scale

TABLE 4.2 Why Higher Volumes of Production in a Firm Can Lead to Lower Costs

> With higher production volume . . .
>
> 1. firms can use specialized machines . . .
> 2. firms can build larger plants . . .
> 3. firms can increase employee specialization . . .
> 4. firms can spread overhead costs across more units produced . . .
>
> . . . which can lower per-unit production costs.

Corporation, for example, have emphasized this important advantage of high volumes of production. A former director of manufacturing at BIC once observed:

> *We are in the automation business. Because of our large volume, one tenth of 1 cent in savings turns out to be enormous. . . . One advantage of the high-volume business is that you can get the best equipment and amortize it entirely over a short period of time (4 to 5 months). I'm always looking for new equipment. If I see a cost-savings machine, I can buy it. I'm not constrained by money.*[2]

Only firms with BIC's level of production in the pen industry have the ability to reduce their costs in this manner.

Volume of Production and the Cost of Plant and Equipment.   High volumes of production may also enable a firm to build larger manufacturing operations. In some industries, the cost of building these manufacturing operations per unit of production is lower than the cost of building smaller manufacturing operations per unit of production. Thus, large-volume firms, other factors being equal, will be able to build lower-per-unit-cost manufacturing operations and will have lower average costs of production.

The link between volume of production and the cost of building manufacturing operations is particularly important in industries characterized by **process manufacturing**—chemical, oil refining, paper and pulp manufacturing, and so forth. Because of the physical geometry of process manufacturing facilities, the costs of constructing a processing plant with increased capacity can be expected to rise as the two-thirds power of a plant's capacity. This is because the area of the surface of some three-dimensional containers (such as spheres and cylinders) increases at a slower rate than the volume of these containers. Thus, larger containers hold greater volumes and require less material per unit volume for the outside skins of these containers. Up to some point, increases in capacity come at a less-than-proportionate rise in the cost of building this capacity.[3]

For example, it might cost a firm $100 to build a plant with a capacity of 1,000 units, for a per-unit average cost of $0.01. But, assuming that the "two-thirds rule" applies, it might cost a firm $465 to build a plant with a capacity of 10,000 units ($465 = 10,000^{2/3}$), for a per-unit average cost of $0.0046. The difference between $0.01 per unit and $0.0046 per unit represents a cost advantage for a large firm.

Volume of Production and Employee Specialization.   High volumes of production are also associated with high levels of employee specialization. As workers specialize in accomplishing a narrow task, they can become more and more efficient at this task, thereby reducing their firm's costs. This reasoning applies both in specialized manufacturing tasks (such as the highly specialized manufacturing functions in an assembly line) and in specialized management functions (such as the highly specialized managerial functions of accounting, finance, and sales).

Smaller firms often do not possess the volume of production needed to justify this level of employee specialization. With smaller volumes of production, highly specialized employees may not have enough work to keep them busy an entire workday. This low volume of production is one reason why smaller firms often have employees that perform multiple business functions and often use outside contract employees and part-time workers to accomplish highly specialized functions, such as accounting, taxes, and human resource management.

Volume of Production and Overhead Costs.   A firm with high volumes of production has the luxury of spreading its overhead costs over more units and thereby reducing the overhead costs per unit. Suppose, in a particular industry, that the operation of a variety of accounting, control, and research and development functions, regardless of a firm's size, is $100,000. Clearly, a firm that manufactures 1,000 units is imposing a cost of $100 per unit to cover overhead expenses. However, a firm that manufactures 10,000 units is imposing a cost of $10 per unit to cover overhead. Again, the larger-volume firm's average per-unit costs are lower than the small-volume firm's average per-unit cost.

Size Differences and Diseconomies of Scale

Just as economies of scale can generate cost advantages for larger firms, important diseconomies of scale can actually increase costs if firms grow too large. As Figure 4.1 shows, if the volume of production rises beyond some optimal point (point X in the figure), this can actually lead to an increase in per-unit costs. If other firms in an industry have grown beyond the optimal firm size, a smaller firm (with a level of production closer to the optimal) may obtain a cost advantage even when all firms in the industry are producing very similar products. Some important sources of diseconomies of scale for a firm are listed in Table 4.3 and discussed in this section.

Physical Limits to Efficient Size.   Applying the two-thirds rule to the construction of manufacturing facilities seems to imply, for some industries at least, that larger is always better. However, there are some important physical limitations to the size of some manufacturing processes. Engineers have found, for example, that cement kilns develop unstable internal aerodynamics at capacities of above 7 million barrels per year. Others have suggested that scaling up nuclear reactors from small installations to huge facilities generates forces and physical processes that, though undetectable in smaller facilities, can become significant in larger operations. These physical limitations on manufacturing processes reflect the underlying physics and engineering in a manufacturing process and suggest when the cost curve in Figure 4.1 will begin to rise.[4]

Managerial Diseconomies.   Although the underlying physics and engineering in a manufacturing process have an important impact on a firm's costs, managerial diseconomies are perhaps an even more important cause of these cost increases.

TABLE 4.3 Major Sources of Diseconomies of Scale

When the volume of production gets too large . . .

1. physical limits to efficient size . . .
2. managerial diseconomies . . .
3. worker de-motivation . . .
4. distance to markets and suppliers . . .

. . . can increase per-unit costs.

As a firm increases in size, it often increases in complexity, and the ability of managers to control and operate it efficiently becomes limited.

One well-known example of a manufacturing plant that grew too large and thus became inefficient is Crown, Cork and Seal's can-manufacturing plant in Philadelphia. Through the early part of this century, this Philadelphia facility handled as many as 75 different can-manufacturing lines. The most efficient plants in the industry, however, were running from 10 to 15 lines simultaneously. The huge Philadelphia facility was simply too large to operate efficiently and was characterized by large numbers of breakdowns, a high percentage of idle lines, and poor-quality products.[5]

Worker De-Motivation.   A third source of diseconomies of scale depends on the relationship between firm size, employee specialization, and employee motivation. It has already been suggested that one of the advantages of increased volumes of production is that it allows workers to specialize in smaller and more narrowly defined production tasks. With specialization, workers become more and more efficient at the particular task facing them.

However, a significant stream of research suggests that these types of very specialized jobs can be unmotivating for employees. Based on motivational theories taken from social psychology, this work suggests that as workers are removed further from the complete product that is the end result of a manufacturing process, the role that a worker's job plays in the overall manufacturing process becomes more and more obscure. As workers become mere "cogs in a manufacturing machine," worker motivation wanes, and productivity and quality can both suffer.[6]

Distance to Markets and Suppliers.   A final source of diseconomies of scale can be the distance between a large manufacturing facility and where the goods in question are to be sold or where essential raw materials are purchased. Any reductions in cost attributable to the exploitation of economies of scale in manufacturing may be more than offset by large transportation costs associated with moving supplies and products to and from the manufacturing facility. Firms that build highly efficient plants without recognizing these significant transportation costs may put themselves at a competitive disadvantage compared to firms with slightly less efficient plants that are located closer to suppliers and key markets.

Experience Differences and Learning-Curve Economies

A third possible source of cost advantages for firms in a particular business depends on their different cumulative levels of production. In some circumstances, firms with the greatest experience in manufacturing a product or service will have the lowest costs in an industry and thus will have a cost-based advantage. The link between cumulative volumes of production and cost has been formalized in the concept of the **learning curve**. The relationship between cumulative volumes of production and per-unit costs is graphically represented in Figure 4.2.

The Learning Curve and Economies of Scale.   As depicted in Figure 4.2, the learning curve is very similar to the concept of economies of scale. However, there are two important differences. First, whereas economies of scale focus on the relationship between the volume of production at a given point in time and average unit costs, the learning curve focuses on the relationship between the *cumulative* volume of production—that is, how much a firm has produced over time—and average unit costs. Second, where diseconomies of scale are presumed to exist if a firm gets too

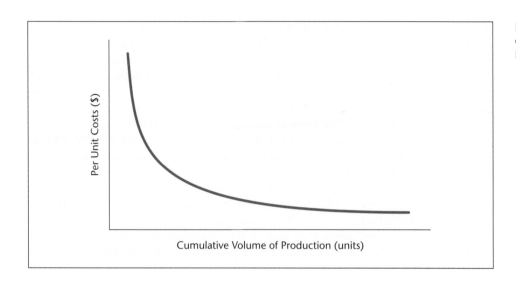

Figure 4.2   The Learning
Curve and the Cost of
Production

Per Unit Costs ($)

Cumulative Volume of Production (units)

large, there is no corresponding increase in costs in the learning-curve model as the cumulative volume of production grows. Rather, costs continue to fall until they approach the lowest technologically possible cost.

The Learning Curve and Cost Advantages.   The learning-curve model is based on the empirical observation that the costs of producing a unit of output fall as the cumulative volume of output increases. This relationship was first observed in the construction of aircraft before World War II. Research showed that the labor costs per aircraft fell by 20 percent each time the cumulative volume of production doubled.[7] A similar pattern has been observed in numerous industries, including the manufacture of ships, computers, spacecraft, and semiconductors. In all these cases, increases in cumulative production have been associated with detailed learning about how to make production as efficient as possible.

However, learning-curve cost advantages are not restricted to manufacturing. Learning can be associated with any business function, from purchasing raw materials to distribution and service. Service industries can also experience important learning effects. The learning curve applies whenever the cost of accomplishing a business activity falls as a function of the cumulative number of times a firm has engaged in that activity.[8]

The Learning Curve and Competitive Advantage.   The learning-curve model summarized in Figure 4.2 has been used to develop a model of cost-based competitive advantage that links learning with market share and average production costs.[9]

The logic behind this application of the learning-curve model is straightforward: The first firm that successfully moves down the learning curve will obtain a cost advantage over rivals. To move a production process down the learning curve, a firm needs to have higher levels of cumulative volume of production. Of course, firms successful at producing high volumes of output need to sell that output to customers. In selling this output, firms are increasing their market share. Thus, to drive down the learning curve and obtain a cost advantage, firms must aggressively acquire market share.

This application of learning-curve logic has been criticized by a wide variety of authors.[10] Two criticisms are particularly salient. First, although the acquisition of market share is likely to allow a firm to reduce its production costs, the acquisition of share itself is expensive. Indeed, as described in the Research Made Relevant feature, sometimes the cost of acquiring share may rise to equal its value.

The second major criticism of this application of the learning-curve model is that there is, in this logic, no room for any other business or corporate strategies. In other words, this application of the learning curve implicitly assumes that firms can compete only on the basis of their low costs and that other strategies are not possible. Most industries, however, are characterized by opportunities for at least some of these other strategies, and thus this strict application of the learning-curve model can be misleading.[11]

These criticisms aside, it is still the case that in many industries firms with larger cumulative levels of production, other things being equal, will have lower average production costs. Thus, experience in all the facets of production can be a source of cost advantage even if the single-minded pursuit of market share to obtain these cost reductions may not give a firm above normal economic returns.

Differential Low-Cost Access to Productive Inputs

Besides economies of scale, diseconomies of scale, and learning-curve cost advantages, differential low-cost access to productive inputs may create cost differences among firms producing similar products in an industry. **Productive inputs** are any supplies used by a firm in conducting its business activities; they include, among other things, labor, capital, land, and raw materials. A firm that has differential low-cost access to one or more of these factors is likely to have lower economic costs compared to rivals.

Consider, for example, an oil company with fields in Saudi Arabia compared to an oil company with fields in the North Sea. The cost of obtaining crude oil for the first firm is considerably less than the cost of obtaining crude oil for the second. North Sea drilling involves the construction of giant offshore drilling platforms, housing workers on floating cities, and transporting oil across an often-stormy sea. Drilling in Saudi Arabia requires only the simplest drilling technologies because the oil is found relatively close to the surface.

Of course, in order to create a cost advantage, the cost of acquiring low-cost productive inputs must be less than the cost savings generated by these factors. For example, even though it may be much less costly to drill for oil in Saudi Arabia than in the North Sea, if it is very expensive to purchase the rights to drill in Saudi Arabia compared to the costs of the rights to drill in the North Sea, the potential cost advantages of drilling in Saudi Arabia can be lost. As with all sources of cost advantages, firms must be careful to weigh the cost of acquiring that advantage against the value of that advantage for the firm.

Differential access to raw materials such as oil, coal, and copper ore can be important determinants of a cost advantage. However, differential access to other productive inputs can be just as important. For example, it may be easier (i.e., less costly) to recruit highly trained electronics engineers for firms located near where these engineers receive their schooling than for firms located some distance away. This lower cost of recruiting is a partial explanation of the development of geographic technology centers such as Silicon Valley in California, Route 128 in Massachusetts, and the Research Triangle in North Carolina. In all three cases, firms are located physically close to several universities that train the engineers that are the lifeblood of high-technology companies. The search for low-cost labor can create ethical dilemmas, as described in the Ethics and Strategy feature.

Research Made Relevant

Research on the relationship between market share and firm performance has continued over many decades. Early work identified market share as the primary determinant of firm performance. Indeed, one particularly influential article identified market share as being *the key* to firm profitability.

This initial conclusion about the relationship between market share and firm performance was based on the observed positive correlation between these two variables. That is, firms with large market share tend to be highly profitable; firms with low market share tend to be less profitable. The logical conclusion of this empirical finding seems to be that if a firm wants to increase its profitability, it should increase its market share.

Not so fast. It turns out that the relationship between market share and firm profits is not that simple. Consider the following scenario: Suppose that 10 companies all conclude that the key to their profitability is gaining market share. To acquire share from each other, each firm will probably increase its advertising and other marketing expenses as well as reduce its prices. This has the effect of putting a price on the market share that a firm seeks to acquire—that is, these competing firms are creating what might be called a "market-for-market share." And because there

How Valuable Is Market Share—Really?

are 10 firms competing for share in this market, this market is likely to be highly competitive. Returns to acquiring share in such competitive markets for market share should fall to a normal economic level.

All this analysis suggests that although there may be a cross-sectional positive correlation between market share and firm performance—that is, at a given point in time, market share and firm performance may be positively correlated—this correlation may not be positive over time, as firms seek to increase their market share. Several papers have examined this hypothesis. Two of the most influential of these papers—by Dick Rumelt and Robin Wensley and by Cynthia Montgomery and Birger Wernerfelt—have shown

that markets for market share often do emerge in industries, that these markets are often very competitive, and that acquiring market share in these competitive markets does not improve a firm's economic performance. Indeed, in their study of the consolidation of the beer industry Montgomery and Wernerfelt showed that firms such as Anheuser-Busch and Miller paid so much for the market share they acquired that it actually reduced their profitability.

The general consensus in the literature now seems to be that large market share is an outcome of a competitive process within an industry, not an appropriate objective of firm managers, per se. Thus, firms with particularly valuable strategies will naturally attract more customers, which, in turn, suggests that they will often have higher market share. That is, a firm's valuable strategies generate both high levels of firm performance and large market share. This, in turn, explains the positive correlation between market share and firm performance.

Sources: R. D. Buzzell, B. T. Gale, and R. M. Sultan (1975). "Market share—the key to profitability." *Harvard Business Review,* 53, pp. 97–106; R. Rumelt and R. Wensley (1981). "In search of the market share effect." *Proceedings of the Academy of Management Meetings, 1981,* pp. 2–6; C. Montgomery and B. Wernerfelt (1991). "Sources of superior performance: Market share versus industry effects in the U.S. brewing industry." *Management Science,* 37, pp. 954–959.

Technological Advantages Independent of Scale
Another possible source of cost advantage in an industry may be the different technologies that firms employ to manage their business. It has already been suggested that larger firms may have technology-based cost advantages that reflect their ability to exploit economies of scale (e.g., the two-thirds rule).

Traditionally, discussion of technology-based cost advantages has focused on the machines, computers, and other physical tools that firms use to manage their business. Clearly, in some industries, these physical technology differences between firms can create important cost differences—even when the firms in question are approximately the same size in terms of volume of production. In the steel industry, for example, technological advances can substantially reduce the cost of producing steel. Firms with the latest steel-manufacturing technology will typically enjoy some cost advantage compared to similar-sized firms that do not have the latest technology. The same applies in the manufacturing of semiconductors, automobiles, consumer electronics, and a wide variety of other products.[12]

These physical technology cost advantages apply in service firms as well as in manufacturing firms. For example, early in its history Charles Schwab, a leading discount brokerage, purchased a computer system that enabled it to complete customer transactions more rapidly and at a lower cost than its rivals.[13] Kaiser-Permanente, the largest HMO in the United States, has invested in information technology that doctors can use to avoid incorrect diagnoses and procedures that can adversely affect a patient's health. By avoiding these medical mistakes, Kaiser-Permanente can substantially reduce its costs of providing medical service.[14]

However, the concept of technology can be easily broadened to include not just the physical tools that firms use to manage their business, but any processes within a firm used in this way. This concept of firm technology includes not only the **technological hardware** of companies—the machines and robots—but also the **technological software** of firms—things such as the quality of relations between labor and management, an organization's culture, and the quality of managerial controls. All these characteristics of a firm can have an impact on a firm's economic costs.[15]

Policy Choices

Thus far, this discussion has focused on reasons why a firm can gain a cost advantage despite producing products that are similar to competing firms' products. When firms produce essentially the same outputs, differences in economies of scale, learning-curve advantages, differential access to productive inputs, and differences in technology can all create cost advantages (and disadvantages) for them. However, firms can also make choices about the kinds of products and services they will sell—choices that have an impact on their relative cost position. These choices are called **policy choices**.

In general, firms that are attempting to implement a cost leadership strategy will choose to produce relatively simple standardized products that sell for relatively low prices compared to the products and prices firms pursuing other business or corporate strategies choose. These kinds of products often tend to have high volumes of sales, which (if significant economies of scale exist) tend to reduce costs even further.

These kinds of choices in product and pricing tend to have a very broad impact on a cost leader's operations. In these firms, the task of reducing costs is not delegated to a single function or a special task force within the firm, but is the responsibility of every manager and employee. Cost reduction sometimes becomes the central objective of the firm. Indeed, in this setting management must be constantly alert to cost-cutting efforts that reduce the ability of the firm to meet customers' needs. This kind of cost-cutting culture is central to Ryanair's ability to implement its cost leadership strategy.

Ethics and Strategy

One of the most important productive inputs in almost all companies is labor. Getting differential low-cost access to labor can give a firm a cost advantage.

This search for low labor costs has led some firms to engage in an international "race to the bottom." It is well known that the wage rates of most U.S. and Western European workers are much higher than the wage rates of workers in other, less developed parts of the world. While a firm might have to pay its employees $20 per hour (in wages and benefits) to make sneakers and basketball shoes in the United States, that same firm may only have to pay an employee in the Philippines or Malaysia or China $1.00 per day to make the same sneakers and basketball shoes—shoes the firm might be able to sell for $250 a pair in the United States and Europe. Thus, many firms look to overseas manufacturing as a way to keep their labor cost low.

But this search for low labor cost has some important unintended consequences. First, the location of the lowest cost labor rates in the world changes over time. It used to be that Mexico had the lowest labor rates, then Korea and the Philippines, then Malaysia, then China, now Vietnam. As the infrastructures of each of these countries evolve to the point that they

The Race to the Bottom

can support worldwide manufacturing, firms abandon their relationships with firms in prior countries in search of still lower costs in new countries. The only way former "low-cost centers" can compete is to drive their costs even lower.

This sometimes leads to a second unintended consequence of the "race to the bottom": horrendous working conditions and low wages in these low-cost manufacturing settings. Employees earning $1 for working a 10-hour day, six days a week may look good on the corporate bottom line, but many observers are deeply concerned about the moral and ethical issues associated with this strategy. Indeed, several companies—including Nike and Kmart—have been forced to increase the wages and improve the

working conditions of many of their overseas employees.

An even more horrific result of this "race to the bottom" has been the reemergence of what amounts to slavery in some Western European countries and some parts of the United States. In search of the promise of a better life, illegal immigrants are sometimes brought to Western European countries or the United States and forced to work in illegal, underground factories. These illegal immigrants are sometimes forced to work as many as 20 hours a day, for little or no pay—supposedly to "pay off" the price of bringing them out of their less developed countries. And because of their illegal status and language barriers, they often do not feel empowered to go to the local authorities.

Of course, the people who create and manage these facilities are criminals and deserve contempt. But what about the companies that purchase the services of these illegal and immoral manufacturing operations? Aren't they also culpable, both legally and morally?

Sources: R. DeGeorge (2000). "Ethics in international business—A contradiction in terms?" *Business Credit*, 102, pp. 50+; G. Edmondson, K. Carlisle, I. Resch, K. Nickel Anhalt, and H. Dawley (2000). "Workers in bondage." *BusinessWeek*, November 27, pp. 146+; D. Winter (2000). "Facing globalization." *Ward's Auto World*, 36, pp. 7+.

The Value of Cost Leadership

There is little doubt that cost differences can exist among firms, even when those firms are selling very similar products. Policy choices about the kinds of products firms in an industry choose to produce can also create important cost differences. But under what conditions will these kinds of cost advantages actually create value for a firm?

Cost Leadership and Environmental Threats

It was suggested in Chapter 3 that one way to tell if a resource or capability—such as the ability of a firm to have a cost advantage—actually creates value for a firm is by whether that resource or capability enables a firm to neutralize its external threats or exploit its external opportunities. The ability of a cost leadership position to neutralize external threats will be examined here. The ability of such a position to enable a firm to exploit opportunities will be left as an exercise. The specific economic consequences of cost leadership are discussed in the Strategy in Depth feature.

A cost leadership competitive strategy helps reduce the threat of new entrants by creating cost-based barriers to entry. Recall that many of the barriers to entry cited in Chapter 2, including economies of scale and cost advantages independent of scale, assume that incumbent firms have lower costs than potential entrants. If an incumbent firm is a cost leader, for any of the reasons just listed, then new entrants may have to invest heavily to reduce their costs prior to entry. Often, new entrants will enter using another business strategy (e.g., product differentiation) rather than attempting to compete on costs.

Firms with a low-cost position also reduce the threat of rivalry. The threat of rivalry is reduced through pricing strategies that low-cost firms can engage in and through their relative impact on the performance of a low-cost firm and its higher-cost rivals.

As suggested in Chapter 2, substitutes become a threat to a firm when their cost and performance, relative to a firm's current products or services, become more attractive to customers. Thus, when the price of crude oil goes up, substitutes for crude oil become more attractive. When the cost and performance of electronic calculators improve, demand for mechanical adding machines disappears.

In this situation, cost leaders have the ability to keep their products and services attractive relative to substitutes. While high-cost firms may have to charge high prices to cover their costs, thus making substitutes more attractive, cost leaders can keep their prices low and still earn normal or above-normal economic profits.

Suppliers can become a threat to a firm by charging higher prices for the goods or services they supply or by reducing the quality of those goods or services. However, when a supplier sells to a cost leader, that firm has greater flexibility in absorbing higher-cost supplies than does a high-cost firm. Higher supply costs may destroy any above-normal profits for high-cost firms but still allow a cost leader firm to earn an above-normal profit.

Cost leadership based on large volumes of production and economies of scale can also reduce the threat of suppliers. Large volumes of production imply large purchases of raw materials and other supplies. Suppliers are not likely to jeopardize these sales by threatening their customers. Indeed, as was suggested earlier, buyers are often able to use their purchasing volume to extract volume discounts from suppliers.

Cost leadership can also reduce the threat of buyers. Powerful buyers are a threat to firms when they insist on low prices or higher quality and service from their suppliers. Lower prices threaten firm revenues; higher quality can increase a firm's costs. Cost leaders can have their revenues reduced by buyer threats and still have normal or above-normal performance. These firms can also absorb the greater costs of increased quality or service and still have a cost advantage over their competition.

Strategy in Depth

Another way to demonstrate that cost leadership can be a source of economic value is to directly examine the economic profits generated by a firm with a cost advantage operating in an otherwise very competitive industry. This is done in Figure 4.3.

The firms depicted in this figure are **price takers**—that is, the price of the products or services they sell is determined by market conditions and not by individual decisions of firms. This implies that there is effectively no product differentiation in this market and that no one firm's sales constitute a large percentage of this market.

The price of goods or services in this type of market (P^*) is determined by aggregate industry supply and demand. This industry price determines the demand facing an individual firm in this market. Because these firms are price takers, the demand facing an individual firm is horizontal—that is, firm decisions about levels of output have a negligible impact on overall industry supply and thus a negligible impact on the market-determined price. A firm in this setting maximizes its economic performance by

The Economics of Cost Leadership

producing a quantity of output (Q) so that marginal revenue equals marginal cost (MC). The ability of firms to earn economic profits in this setting depends upon the relationship between the market-determined price (P^*) and the average total cost (ATC) of a firm at the quantity it chooses to produce.

Firms in the market depicted in Figure 4.3 fall into two categories. All but one firm have the average-total-cost curve ATC_2 and marginal-cost curve MC_2. However, one firm in this industry has the average-total-cost

curve ATC_1 and marginal-cost curve MC_1. Notice that ATC_1 is less than ATC_2 at the performance-maximizing quantities produced by these two kinds of firms (Q_1 and Q_2, respectively). In this particular example, firms with common average-total-cost curves are earning zero economic profits, while the low-cost firm is earning an economic profit (equal to the shaded area in the figure). A variety of other examples could also be constructed: The cost leader firm could be earning zero economic profits, while other firms in the market are incurring economic losses; the cost leader firm could be earning substantial economic profits, while other firms are earning smaller economic profits; the cost leader firm could be incurring small economic losses, while the other firms are incurring substantial economic losses; and so forth. However, in all these examples the cost leader's economic performance is greater than the economic performance of other firms in the industry. Thus, cost leadership can have an important impact on a firm's economic performance.

Figure 4.3   Cost Leadership and Economic Performance

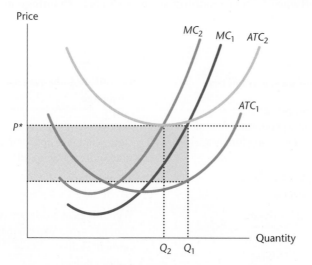

Buyers can also be a threat through backward vertical integration. Being a cost leader deters backward vertical integration by buyers because a buyer that vertically integrates backward will often not have costs as low as an incumbent cost leader. Rather than vertically integrating backward and increasing its cost of supplies, powerful buyers usually prefer to continue purchasing from their low-cost suppliers.

Finally, if cost leadership is based on large volumes of production, then the threat of buyers may be reduced because buyers may depend on just a few firms for the goods or services they purchase. This dependence reduces the willingness of buyers to threaten a selling firm.

Cost Leadership and Sustained Competitive Advantage

Given that cost leadership can be valuable, an important question becomes "Under what conditions will firms implementing this business strategy be able to maintain that leadership to obtain a sustained competitive advantage?" If cost leadership strategies can be implemented by numerous firms in an industry or if no firms face a cost disadvantage in imitating a cost leadership strategy, then being a cost leader will not generate a sustained competitive advantage for a firm. As suggested in Chapter 3, the ability of a valuable cost leadership competitive strategy to generate a sustained competitive advantage depends on that strategy being rare and costly to imitate, either through direct duplication or substitution. As suggested in Tables 4.4 and 4.5, the rarity and imitability of a cost leadership strategy depend, at least in part, on the sources of that cost advantage.

The Rarity of Sources of Cost Advantage

Some of the sources of cost advantage listed in Table 4.4 are likely to be rare among a set of competing firms; others are less likely to be rare. Sources of cost advantage that are likely to be rare include learning-curve economies (at least in emerging industries), differential low-cost access to productive inputs, and technological "software." The remaining sources of cost advantage are less likely to be rare.

TABLE 4.4 The Rarity of Sources of Cost Advantage

Likely-to-be-rare sources of cost advantage	Less-likely-to-be-rare sources of cost advantage
Learning-curve economies of scale (especially in emerging businesses)	Economies of scale (except when efficient plant size approximately equals total industry demand)
Differential low-cost access to productive inputs	Diseconomies of scale
Technological "software"	Technological hardware (unless a firm has proprietary hardware development skills)
	Policy choices

Rare Sources of Cost Advantage

Early in the evolution of an industry, substantial differences in the cumulative volume of production of different firms are not unusual. Indeed, this was one of the major benefits associated with first-mover advantages, discussed in Chapter 2. These differences in cumulative volume of production, in combination with substantial learning-curve economies, suggest that, in some settings, learning-curve advantages may be rare and thus a source of at least temporary competitive advantage.

The definition of differential access to productive inputs implies that this access is often rare. Certainly, if large numbers of competing firms have this same access, then it cannot be a source of competitive advantage.

Technological software is also likely to be rare among a set of competing firms. These software attributes represent each firm's path through history. If these histories are unique, then the technological software they create may also be rare. Of course, if several competing firms experience similar paths through history, the technological software in these firms is less likely to be rare.

Less Rare Sources of Cost Advantage

When the efficient size of a firm or plant is significantly smaller than the total size of an industry, there will usually be numerous efficient firms or plants in that industry, and a cost leadership strategy based on economies of scale will not be rare. For example, if the efficient firm or plant size in an industry is 500 units, and the total size of the industry (measured in units produced) is 500,000 units, then there are likely to be numerous efficient firms or plants in this industry, and economies of scale are not likely to give any one firm a cost-based competitive advantage.

Cost advantages based on diseconomies of scale are also not likely to be rare. It is unusual for numerous firms to adopt levels of production in excess of optimal levels. If only a few firms are too large in this sense, then several competing firms in an industry that are *not* too large will have cost advantages over the firms that are too large. However, because several firms will enjoy these cost advantages, they are not rare.

One important exception to this generalization may be when changes in technology significantly reduce the most efficient scale of an operation. Given such changes in technology, several firms may be inefficiently large. If a small number of firms happen to be sized appropriately, then the cost advantages these firms obtain in this way may be rare. Such changes in technology have made large integrated steel producers "too big" relative to smaller mini-mills. Thus, mini-mills have a cost advantage over larger integrated steel firms.

Technological hardware is also not likely to be rare, especially if it is developed by suppliers and sold on the open market. However, if a firm has proprietary technology development skills, it may possess rare technological hardware that creates cost advantages.

Finally, policy choices by themselves are not likely to be a rare source of cost advantage, particularly if the product or service attributes in question are easy to observe and describe.

The Imitability of Sources of Cost Advantage

Even when a particular source of cost advantage is rare, it must be costly to imitate in order to be a source of sustained competitive advantage. Both direct duplication and substitution, as forms of imitation, are important. Again, the imitability of a cost advantage depends, at least in part, on the source of that advantage.

TABLE 4.5 Direct Duplication of Cost Leadership

		Basis for costly duplication		
	Source of Cost Advantage	History	Uncertainty	Social Complexity
Low-cost duplication possible	1. Economies of scale	—	—	—
	2. Diseconomies of scale	—	—	—
May be costly to duplicate	3. Learning-curve economies	*	—	—
	4. Technological "hardware"	—	*	*
	5. Policy choices	*	—	—
Usually costly to duplicate	6. Differential low-cost access to productive inputs	***	—	**
	7. Technological "software"	***	**	***

— = not a source of costly imitation, * = somewhat likely to be a source of costly imitation, ** = likely to be a source of costly imitation, *** = very likely to be a source of costly imitation

Easy-to-Duplicate Sources of Cost Advantage

In general, economies of scale and diseconomies of scale are relatively easy-to-duplicate bases of cost leadership. As can be seen in Table 4.5, these sources of cost advantage do not build on history, uncertainty, or socially complex resources and capabilities and thus are not protected from duplication for these reasons.

For example, if a small number of firms obtain a cost advantage based on economies of scale and if the relationship between production scale and costs is widely understood among competing firms, then firms at a cost disadvantage will rapidly adjust their production to exploit these economies of scale. This can be done by either growing a firm's current operations to the point that the firm exploits economies or by combining previously separate operations to obtain these economies. Both actions enable a firm at a cost disadvantage to begin using specialized machines, reduce the cost of plant and equipment, increase employee specialization, and spread overhead costs more effectively.

Indeed, perhaps the only time economies of scale are not subject to low-cost duplication is when the efficient size of operations is a significant percentage of total demand in an industry. Of course, this is the situation described in Chapter 2's discussion of economies of scale as a barrier to entry. For example, as suggested earlier, BIC Corporation, with its dominant market share in the disposable pen market, has apparently been able to gain and retain an important cost advantage in that market based on economies of scale. BIC's ability to retain this advantage reflects the fact that the optimal plant size in the disposable pen market is a significant percentage of the pen market, and thus economies of scale act as a barrier to entry in that market.

Like economies of scale, in many settings diseconomies of scale will not be a source of sustained competitive advantage for firms that have *not* grown too large. In the short run, firms experiencing significant diseconomies can shrink the size of their operations to become more efficient. In the long run, firms that fail to adjust their size will earn below-normal economic performance and cease operations.

Although in many ways reducing the size of operations to improve efficiency seems like a simple problem for managers in firms or plants, in practice it is often a difficult change to implement. Because of uncertainty, managers in a firm or plant that is too large may not understand that diseconomies of scale have increased their costs. Sometimes, managers conclude that the problem is that employees are not working hard enough, that problems in production can be fixed, and so forth. These firms or plants may continue their inefficient operations for some time, despite costs that are higher than the industry average.[16]

Other psychological processes can also delay the abandonment of operations that are too large. One of these phenomena is known as **escalation of commitment**: Sometimes, managers committed to an incorrect (cost-increasing or revenue-reducing) course of action *increase* their commitment to this action as its limitations become manifest. For example, a manager who believes that the optimal firm size in an industry is larger than the actual optimal size may remain committed to large operations despite costs that are higher than the industry average.[17]

For all these reasons, firms suffering from diseconomies of scale must often turn to outside managers to assist in reducing costs. Outsiders bring a fresh view to the organization's problems and are not committed to the practices that generated the problems in the first place.[18]

Bases of Cost Leadership That May Be Costly to Duplicate

Although cost advantages based on learning-curve economies are rare (especially in emerging industries), they are usually not costly to duplicate. As suggested in Chapter 2, for learning-curve cost advantages to be a source of sustained competitive advantage the learning obtained by a firm must be proprietary. Most recent empirical work suggests that in most industries learning is not proprietary and thus can be rapidly duplicated as competing firms move down the learning curve by increasing their cumulative volume of production.[19]

However, the fact that learning is not costly to duplicate in *most* industries does not mean it is never costly to duplicate. In some industries, the ability of firms to learn from their production experience may vary significantly. For example, some firms treat production errors as failures and systematically punish employees who make those errors. These firms effectively reduce risk-taking among their production employees and thus reduce the chances of learning how to improve their production process. Alternatively, other firms treat production errors as opportunities to learn how to improve their production process. These firms are likely to move rapidly down the learning curve and retain cost advantages, despite the cumulative volume of production of competing firms. These different responses to production errors reflect the organizational cultures of these different firms. Because organizational cultures are socially complex, they can be very costly to duplicate.[20]

Because technological hardware can usually be purchased across supply markets, it is also not likely to be difficult to duplicate. Sometimes, however, technological hardware can be proprietary or closely bundled with other unique, costly-to-duplicate resources controlled by a firm. In this case, technological hardware *can* be costly to duplicate.

It is unusual, but not impossible, for policy choices, per se, to be a source of sustained competitive cost advantages for a firm. As suggested earlier, if the policies in question focus on easy to observe and easy to describe product characteristics, then duplication is likely, and cost advantages based on policy choices will be temporary. However, if policy choices reflect complex decision processes within a firm, teamwork among different parts of the design and manufacturing process, or any of the software commitments discussed previously, then policy choices can be a source of sustained competitive advantage, as long as only a few firms have the ability to make these choices.

Indeed, most of the successful firms that operate in unattractive industries make policy choices that are costly to imitate because they reflect historical, causally ambiguous, and socially complex firm processes. Thus, for example, Wal-Mart's supply chain management strategy—a policy with clear low-cost implications—actually reflects Wal-Mart's unique history, its socially complex relations with suppliers, and its unique organizational culture. And Ryanair's low-price pricing strategy—a strategy that reflects its low-cost position—is possible because of the kind of airplane fleet Ryanair has built over time, the commitment of its employees to Ryanair's success, a charismatic founder, and its unique organizational culture. Because these policies reflect costly-to-imitate attributes of these firms, they can be sources of sustained competitive advantage.

However, for these and other firms, it is not these policy choices, per se, that create sustainable cost leadership advantages. Rather, it is how these policies flow from the historical, causally ambiguous, and socially complex processes within a firm that makes them costly to duplicate. This has been the case for the Oakland A's baseball team, as described in the Strategy in the Emerging Enterprise feature.

Costly-to-Duplicate Sources of Cost Advantage

Differential access to low-cost productive inputs and technological software is usually a costly-to-duplicate basis of cost leadership. This is because these inputs often build on historical, uncertain, and socially complex resources and capabilities. As suggested earlier, differential access to productive inputs often depends on the location of a firm. Moreover, to be a source of economic profits, this valuable location must be obtained before its full value is widely understood. Both these attributes of differential access to productive inputs suggest that if, in fact, it is rare, it will often be costly to duplicate. First, some locations are unique and cannot be duplicated. For example, most private golf clubs would like to own courses with the spectacular beauty of Pebble Beach in Monterey, California, but there is only one Pebble Beach—a course that runs parallel to some of the most beautiful oceanfront scenery in the world. Although "scenery" is an important factor of production in running and managing a golf course, the re-creation of Pebble Beach's scenery at some other location is simply beyond our technology.

Second, even if a location is not unique, once its value is revealed, acquisition of that location is not likely to generate economic profits. Thus, for example, although being located in Silicon Valley provides access to some important low-cost productive inputs for electronics firms, firms that moved to this location after its value was revealed have substantially higher costs than firms that moved there before its full value was revealed. These higher costs effectively reduce the economic profit that otherwise could have been generated. Referring to the discussion in Chapter 3, these arguments suggest that gaining differential access to productive inputs in a way that generates economic profits may reflect a firm's unique path through history.

Technological software is also likely to be difficult to duplicate and often can be a source of sustained competitive advantage. As suggested in Chapter 3, the values, beliefs, culture, and teamwork that constitute this software are socially complex and may be immune from competitive duplication. Firms with cost advantages rooted in these socially complex resources incorporate cost savings in every aspect of their organization; they constantly focus on improving the quality and cost of their operations, and they have employees who are firmly committed to, and understand, what it takes to be a cost leader. Other firms may talk about low costs; these firms live cost leadership. Ryanair, Dell, Wal-Mart, and Southwest are all examples of such firms. If there are few firms in an industry with these kinds of beliefs and commitments, then they can gain a sustained competitive advantage from their cost advantage.

Substitutes for Sources of Cost Advantage

In an important sense, all of the sources of cost advantage listed in this chapter are at least partial substitutes for each other. Thus, for example, one firm may reduce its cost through exploiting economies of scale in large-scale production, and a competing firm may reduce its costs through exploiting learning-curve economies and large cumulative volume of production. If these different activities have similar effects on a firm's cost position and if they are equally costly to implement, then they are strategic substitutes for each other.

Because of the substitute effects of different sources of cost advantage, it is not unusual for firms pursuing cost leadership to simultaneously pursue *all* the cost-reduction activities discussed in this chapter. Implemention of this *bundle* of cost-reducing activities may have few substitutes. If duplicating this bundle of activities is also rare and difficult, then a firm may be able to gain a sustained competitive advantage from doing so.

Several of the other strategies discussed in later chapters can also have the effect of reducing a firm's costs and thus may be substitutes for the sources of cost reduction discussed in this chapter. For example, one common motivation for firms implementing strategic alliance strategies is to exploit economies of scale in combination with other firms. Thus, a strategic alliance that reduces a firm's costs may be a substitute for a firm exploiting economies of scale on its own to reduce its costs. As is discussed in more detail in Chapter 8, many of the strategic alliances among aluminum mining and smelting companies are motivated by realizing economies of scale and cost reduction. Also, corporate diversification strategies often enable firms to exploit economies of scale across different businesses within which they operate. In this setting, each of these businesses—treated separately—may have scale disadvantages, but collectively their scale creates the same low-cost position as that of an individual firm that fully exploits economies of scale to reduce costs in a single business (see Chapter 9).

Organizing to Implement Cost Leadership

As with all strategies, firms seeking to implement cost leadership strategies must adopt an organizational structure, management controls, and compensation policies that reinforce this strategy. Some key issues associated with using these organizing tools to implement cost leadership are summarized in Table 4.6.

Baseball in the United States has a problem. Most observers agree that it is better for fans if there is competitive balance in the league—that is, if, at the beginning of the year, the fans of several teams believe that their team has a chance to go to the World Series and win it all. However, the economic reality of competition in baseball is that only a small number of financially successful teams in large cities—the New York Yankees, the Los Angeles Dodgers, the Chicago Cubs, the Los Angeles Angels—have the resources necessary to compete for a spot in the World Series year after year. So-called "small-market teams," such as the Pittsburgh Pirates or the Milwaukee Brewers, may be able to compete every once in a while, but these exceptions prove the general rule—teams from large markets usually win the World Series.

And then there is Oakland and the Oakland A's. Oakland (with a population of just over 400,000) is the smallest— and least glamorous—of the three cities in the San Francisco Bay Area, the other two being San Francisco and San Jose. The A's play in an outdated stadium to an average crowd of 25,586 fans—ranking twenty-fourth among the 30 major league baseball teams in the United States. In 2013, the A's player payroll was $65 million, about one-fifth of the Yankees' player payroll.

Despite these liabilities, from 1999 to 2012, the A's either won their division or placed second in all but four years. This compares favorably to any major league team during this time period, including teams with much higher payrolls. And the team made money!

What is the "secret" to the A's success? Their general manager, William Lamar Beane, says that it has to do with three factors: how players are evaluated, making sure that every personnel decision in the organization is consistent with this approach to evaluation, and

The Oakland A's: Inventing a New Way to Play Competitive Baseball

ensuring that all personnel decisions are thought of as business decisions.

The criteria used by the A's to evaluate players are easy enough to state. For batters, the A's focus on on-base percentage (i.e., how often a batter reaches base) and total bases (a measure of the ability of a batter to hit for power); that is, they focus on the ability of players to get on base and score. For pitchers, the A's focus on the percentage of first pitches that are strikes and the quality of a pitcher's fast ball. First-pitch strikes and throwing a good fast ball are correlated with keeping runners off base. Thus, not surprisingly, the A's criteria for evaluating pitchers are the reverse of their criteria for evaluating hitters.

Although these evaluation criteria are easy to state, getting the entire organization to apply them consistently in scouting, choosing, developing, and managing players is much more difficult. Almost every baseball player and fan has his or her own favorite way to evaluate players. However, if you want to work in the A's organization, you must be willing to let go of your personal favorite and evaluate players the A's way. The result is that players that come through the A's farm system— the minor leagues where younger players are developed until they are ready to play in the major leagues—learn a single way of playing baseball instead of learning a new approach to the game

every time they change managers or coaches. One of the implications of this consistency has been that the A's farm system has been among the most productive in baseball.

This consistent farm system enables the A's to treat personnel decisions—including decisions about whether they should re-sign a star player or let him go to another team—as business decisions. The A's simply do not have the resources necessary to play the personnel game the same way as the Los Angeles Dodgers or the New York Yankees. When these teams need a particular kind of player, they go and sign one. Oakland has to rely more on its farm system. But because its farm system performs so well, the A's can let so-called "superstars" go to other teams, knowing that they are likely to have a younger— and cheaper—player in the minor leagues, just waiting for the chance to play in "the show"—the players' nickname for the major leagues. This allows the A's to keep their payroll costs down and remain profitable, despite relatively small crowds, while still fielding a team that competes virtually every year for the right to play in the World Series.

Of course, an important question becomes: How sustainable is the A's competitive advantage? The evaluation criteria themselves are not a source of sustained competitive advantage. However, the socially complex nature of how these criteria are consistently applied throughout the A's organization may be a source of sustained competitive advantage in enabling the A's to gain the differential access to low-cost productive inputs—in this case, baseball players.

Sources: K. Hammonds (2003). "How to play Beane ball." *Fast Company,* May, pp. 84+; M. Lewis (2003). *Moneyball.* New York: Norton; A. McGahan, J. F. McGuire, and J. Kou (1997). "The baseball strike." Harvard Business School Case No. 9-796-059; www.cbssports.com/mlb/story/21989238/baseball-payrolls-list. Accessed August 21, 2013; espn.go.com/mlb/attendance/-/sort/Allavg. Accessed August 21, 2013.

TABLE 4.6 Organizing to Realize the Full Potential of Cost Leadership Strategies

Organization structure: Functional structure with

1. Few layers in the reporting structure
2. Simple reporting relationships
3. Small corporate staff
4. Focus on narrow range of business functions

Management control systems

1. Tight cost control systems
2. Quantitative cost goals
3. Close supervision of labor, raw material, inventory, and other costs
4. A cost leadership philosophy

Compensation policies

1. Reward for cost reduction
2. Incentives for all employees to be involved in cost reduction

Organizational Structure in Implementing Cost Leadership

As suggested in Table 4.6, firms implementing cost leadership strategies will generally adopt what is known as a **functional organizational structure**.[21] An example of a functional organization structure is presented in Figure 4.4. Indeed, this functional organizational structure is the structure used to implement all business-level strategies a firm might pursue, although this structure is modified when used to implement these different strategies.

In a functional structure, each of the major business functions is managed by a **functional manager**. For example, if manufacturing, marketing, finance, accounting, and sales are all included within a functional organization, then a manufacturing manager leads that function, a marketing manager leads that function, a finance manager leads that function, and so forth. In a functional organizational structure, all these functional managers report to one person. This person has many different titles—including *president, CEO, chair,* or *founder.* However, for purposes of this discussion, this person will be called the **chief executive officer (CEO)**.

The CEO in a functional organization has a unique status. Everyone else in this company is a functional specialist. The manufacturing people manufacture, the marketing people market, the finance people finance, and so forth. Indeed, only one person in the functional organization has to have a multifunctional perspective: the CEO. This role is so important that sometimes the functional organization is called a **U-form structure**, where the "U" stands for "unitary"— because there is only one person in this organization that has a broad, multifunctional corporate perspective.

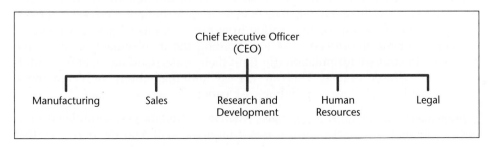

Figure 4.4 An Example of the U-form Organizational Structure

When used to implement a cost leadership strategy, this U-form structure is kept as simple as possible. As suggested in Table 4.6, firms implementing cost leadership strategies will have relatively few layers in their reporting structure. Complicated reporting structures, including **matrix structures** where one employee reports to two or more people, are usually avoided.[22] Corporate staff in these organizations is kept small. Such firms do not operate in a wide range of business functions, but instead operate only in those few business functions where they have valuable, rare, and costly-to-imitate resources and capabilities.

One excellent example of a firm pursuing a cost leadership strategy is Nucor Steel. A leader in the mini-mill industry, Nucor has only five layers in its reporting structure, compared to 12 to 15 in its major higher-cost competitors. Most operating decisions at Nucor are delegated to plant managers, who have full profit-and-loss responsibility for their operations. Corporate staff at Nucor is small and focuses its efforts on accounting for revenues and costs and on exploring new manufacturing processes to further reduce Nucor's operating expenses and expand its business opportunities. Nucor's former president Ken Iverson believed that Nucor does only two things well: build plants efficiently and run them effectively. Thus, Nucor focuses its efforts in these areas and subcontracts many of its other business functions, including the purchase of its raw materials, to outside vendors.[23]

Responsibilities of the CEO in a Functional Organization

The CEO in a U-form organization has two basic responsibilities: (1) to formulate the strategy of the firm and (2) to coordinate the activities of the functional specialists in the firm to facilitate the implementation of this strategy. In the special case of a cost leadership strategy, the CEO must decide on which bases such a strategy should be founded—including any of those listed in Table 4.1—and then coordinate functions within a firm to make sure that the economic potential of this strategy is fully realized.

Strategy Formulation. The CEO in a U-form organization engages in strategy formulation by applying the strategic management process described in Chapter 1. A CEO establishes the firm's mission and associated objectives, evaluates environmental threats and opportunities, understands the firm's strengths and weaknesses, and then chooses one or more of the business and corporate strategies discussed in this book. In the case of a cost leadership strategy, the application of the strategic management process must lead a CEO to conclude that the best chance for achieving a firm's mission is for that firm to adopt a cost leadership business-level strategy.

Although the responsibility for strategy formulation in a U-form organization ultimately rests with the CEO, this individual needs to draw on the insights, analysis, and involvement of functional managers throughout the firm. CEOs who fail to involve functional managers in strategy formulation run several risks. First, strategic choices made in isolation from functional managers may be made without complete information. Second, limiting the involvement of functional managers in strategy formulation can limit their understanding of, and commitment to, the chosen strategy. This can severely limit their ability, and willingness, to implement any strategy—including cost leadership—that is chosen.[24]

Coordinating Functions for Strategy Implementation. Even the best-formulated strategy is competitively irrelevant if it is not implemented. And the only way that strategies can be effectively implemented is if all the functions within a firm are aligned in a way consistent with this strategy.

For example, compare two firms pursuing a cost leadership strategy. All but one of the first firm's functions—marketing—are aligned with this cost leadership strategy. All of the second firm's functions—including marketing—are aligned with this cost leadership strategy. Because marketing is not aligned with the first firm's cost leadership strategy, this firm is likely to advertise products that it does not sell. That is, this might advertise its products on the basis of their style and performance, but sell products that are reliable (but not stylish) and inexpensive (but not high performers). A firm that markets products it does not actually sell is likely to disappoint its customers. In contrast, the second firm that has all of its functions—including marketing—aligned with its chosen strategy is more likely to advertise products it actually sells and thus is less likely to disappoint its customers. In the long run, it seems reasonable to expect this second firm to outperform the first, at least with respect to implementing a cost leadership strategy.

Of course, alignment is required of all of a firm's functional areas, not just marketing. Also, misalignment can emerge in any of a firm's functional areas. Some common misalignments between a firm's cost leadership strategy and its functional activities are listed in Table 4.7.

Management Controls in Implementing Cost Leadership

As suggested in Table 4.6, cost leadership firms are typically characterized by very tight cost-control systems; frequent and detailed cost-control reports; an emphasis on quantitative cost goals and targets; and close supervision of labor, raw materials, inventory, and other costs. Again, Nucor Steel is an example of a cost leadership firm that has implemented these kinds of control systems. At Nucor, groups of employees are given weekly cost and productivity improvement goals. Groups that meet or exceed these goals receive extra compensation. Plant managers are held responsible for cost and profit performance. A plant manager who does not meet corporate performance expectations cannot expect a long career

TABLE 4.7 Common Misalignments Between Business Functions and a Cost Leadership Strategy

	When Function Is *Aligned* with Cost Leadership Strategies	When Function Is *Misaligned* with Cost Leadership Strategies
Manufacturing	Lean, low cost, good quality	Inefficient, high cost, poor quality
Marketing	Emphasize value, reliability, and price	Emphasize style and performance
Research and Development	Focus on product extensions and process improvements	Focus on radical new technologies and products
Finance	Focus on low cost and stable financial structure	Focus on nontraditional financial instruments
Accounting	Collect cost data and adopt conservative accounting principles	Collect no-cost data and adopt very aggressive accounting principles
Sales	Focus on value, reliability, and low price	Focus on style and performance and high price

at Nucor. Similar group-oriented cost-reduction systems are in place at some of Nucor's major competitors, including Chaparral Steel.[25]

Less formal management control systems also drive a cost-reduction philosophy at cost leadership firms. For example, although Wal-Mart is one of the most successful retail operations in the world, its Arkansas headquarters is plain and simple. Indeed, some have suggested that Wal-Mart's headquarters looks like a warehouse. Its style of interior decoration was once described as "early bus station." Wal-Mart even involves its customers in reducing costs by asking them to "help keep your costs low" by returning shopping carts to the designated areas in Wal-Mart's parking lots.[26]

Compensation Policies and Implementing Cost Leadership Strategies

As suggested in Table 4.6, compensation in cost leadership firms is usually tied directly to cost-reducing efforts. Such firms often provide incentives for employees to work together to reduce costs and increase or maintain quality, and they expect *every* employee to take responsibility for both costs and quality. For example, an important expense for retail stores like Wal-Mart is "shrinkage"—a nice way of saying people steal stuff. About half the shrinkage in most stores comes from employees stealing their own companies' products.

Wal-Mart used to have a serious problem with shrinkage. Among other solutions (including hiring "greeters" whose real job is to discourage shoplifters), Wal-Mart developed a compensation scheme that took half the cost savings created by reduced shrinkage and shared it with employees in the form of a bonus. With this incentive in place, Wal-Mart's shrinkage problems dropped significantly.

Summary

Firms producing essentially the same products can have different costs for several reasons. Some of the most important of these are: (1) size differences and economies of scale, (2) size differences and diseconomies of scale, (3) experience differences and learning-curve economies, (4) differential access to productive inputs, and (5) technological advantages independent of scale. In addition, firms competing in the same industry can make policy choices about the kinds of products and services to sell that can have an important impact on their relative cost position. Cost leadership in an industry can be valuable by assisting a firm in reducing the threat of each of the five environmental threats in an industry outlined in Chapter 2.

Each of the sources of cost advantage discussed in this chapter can be a source of sustained competitive advantage if it is rare and costly to imitate. Overall, learning-curve economies, differential access to productive inputs, and technological "software" are more likely to be rare than other sources of cost advantage. Differential access to productive inputs and technological "software" is more likely to be costly to imitate—either through direct duplication or through substitution—than the other sources of cost advantage. Thus, differential access to productive inputs and technological "software" will often be more likely to be a source of sustained competitive advantage than cost advantages based on other sources.

Of course, to realize the full potential of these competitive advantages, a firm must be organized appropriately. Organizing to implement a strategy always involves a firm's organizational structure, its management control systems, and its compensation policies. The organizational structure used to implement cost leadership—and other business strategies—is called a *functional,* or *U-form,* structure. The CEO is the only person in this structure who has a corporate perspective. The CEO has two responsibilities: to formulate a firm's strategy and to implement it by coordinating functions within a firm. Ensuring that a firm's functions are aligned with its strategy is essential to successful strategy implementation.

When used to implement a cost leadership strategy, the U-form structure generally has few layers, simple reporting relationships, and a small corporate staff. It focuses on a narrow range of business functions. The management control systems used to implement these strategies generally include tight cost controls; quantitative cost goals; close supervision of labor, raw materials, inventory, and other costs; and a cost leadership culture and mentality. Finally, compensation policies in these firms typically reward cost reduction and provide incentives for everyone in the organization to be part of the cost-reduction effort.

MyManagementLab®

Go to **mymanagementlab.com** to complete the problems marked with this icon ⭐.

Challenge Questions

4.1. Ryanair, Wal-Mart, Timex, Casio, and Hyundai are all cited as examples of firms pursuing cost leadership strategies, but these firms make substantial investments in advertising, which seems more likely to be associated with a product differentiation strategy. Are these firms really pursuing a cost leadership strategy, or are they pursuing a product differentiation strategy by emphasizing their lower costs?

⭐ **4.2.** When economies of scale exist, firms with large volumes of production will have lower costs than those with smaller volumes of production. The realization of these economies of scale, however, is far from automatic. What actions can firms take to ensure that they realize whatever economies of scale are created by their volume of production?

4.3. A firm may choose a strategy of cost leadership in an industry where customers are very price insensitive, e.g., in luxury goods. Given that most competitors will focus on differentiating their products in such an industry, is cost leadership a poor choice? What can a cost leadership strategy hope to achieve in such an industry?

⭐ **4.4.** When firms do engage in "forward pricing" what risks, if any, do they face?

4.5. One way of thinking about organizing to implement cost leadership strategies is that firms pursuing this strategy should be highly centralized, have high levels of direct supervision, and keep employee wages to an absolute minimum. Another approach is to decentralize decision-making authority—to ensure that individuals

who know the most about reducing costs make decisions about how to reduce costs. This, in turn, would imply less direct supervision and somewhat higher levels of employee wages. Why is this?

4.6. Economies of scale and differential low-cost access to productive inputs are two drivers of cost leadership. Are these two factors related?

4.7. Often, the first step in determining if cost leadership is a feasible strategy for a company is to analyze the costs of key activities (e.g., using the value chain tool) relative to competitors. However, many companies increasingly outsource some of their value added activities to temporary workforces. How would you modify the value chain approach to support this cost analysis?

Problem Set

4.8. The economies of scale curve in Figure 4.1 can be represented algebraically in the following equation:

$$\text{Average costs} = a + bQ + cQ^2$$

where Q is the quantity produced by a firm and a, b, and c are coefficients that are estimated from industry data. For example, it has been shown that the economies of scale curve for U.S. savings and loans is:

$$\text{Average costs} = 2.38 - .615A + .54A^2$$

where A is a savings and loan's total assets. Using this equation, what is the optimal size of a savings and loan? (Hint: Plug in different values of A and calculate average costs. The lowest possible average cost is the optimal size for a savings and loan.)

4.9. The learning curve depicted in Figure 4.2 can be represented algebraically by the following equation:

$$\text{Average time to produce } x \text{ units} = ax^{-\beta}$$

where x is the total number of units produced by a firm in its history, a is the amount of time it took a firm to produce its first unit, and β is a coefficient that describes the rate of learning in a firm.

Suppose it takes a team of workers 45 hours to assemble its first product ($a = 45$) and 40.5 hours to assemble the second. When a firm doubles its production (in this case, from one to two units) and cuts its production time (in this case, from 45 hours to 40.5 hours), learning is said to have occurred (in this case, a 40.5/45, or 90 percent, learning curve). The β for a 90 percent learning curve is 0.3219. Thus, this firm's learning curve is:

$$\text{Average time to produce } x \text{ units} = 45x^{-0.3219}$$

What is the average amount of time it will take this firm to produce six products? (Hint: Simply plug "6" in for x in the equation and solve.) What is the total time it took this firm to produce these six products? (Hint: Simply multiply the number of units produced, 6, by the average time it will take to produce these six products.) What is the average time it will take this firm to produce five products? What is the total time it will take this firm to produce five products? So, what is the total time it will take this firm to produce its sixth product? (Hint: Subtract the total time needed to produce five products from the total time needed to produce six products.)

Suppose a new firm is going to start producing these same products. Assuming this new firm does not learn anything from established firms, what will its cost disadvantage be when it assembles its first product? (Hint: Compare the costs of the experienced firm's sixth product with the cost of the new firm's first product.)

MyManagementLab®

Go to **mymanagementlab.com** for the following Assisted-graded writing questions:

⭐ **4.10.** What are the implications and considerations for a small business that chooses a cost leadership business strategy?

⭐ **4.11.** Discuss the impact of a cost leadership strategy on environmental threats.

End Notes

1. Kiley, D. (2011). "Fiat headed back to U.S. after 27 years." http://autos.aol.com/article/fiat-500-coming-to-america/ Accessed Aug 21, 2013.
2. Christensen, C. R., N. A. Berg, and M. S. Salter. (1980). *Policy formulation and administration: A casebook of senior management problems in business*, 8th ed. Homewood, IL: Irwin, p. 163.
3. Scherer, F. M. (1980). *Industrial market structure and economic performance*. Boston: Houghton Mifflin; Moore, F. T. (1959). "Economies of scale: Some statistical evidence." *Quarterly Journal of Economics*, 73, pp. 232–245; and Lau, L. J., and S. Tamura. (1972). "Economies of scale, technical progress, and the nonhomothetic leontief production function." *Journal of Political Economy*, 80, pp. 1167–1187.
4. Scherer, F. M. (1980). *Industrial market structure and economic performance*. Boston: Houghton Mifflin; and Perrow, C. (1984). *Normal accidents: Living with high-risk technologies*. New York: Basic Books.
5. Hamermesh, R. G., and R. S. Rosenbloom. (1989). "Crown Cork and Seal Co., Inc." Harvard Business School Case No. 9-388-096.
6. See Hackman, J. R., and G. R. Oldham. (1980). *Work redesign*. Reading, MA: Addison-Wesley.
7. This relationship was first noticed in 1925 by the commander of Wright-Patterson Air Force Base in Dayton, Ohio.
8. Learning curves have been estimated for numerous industries. Boston Consulting Group. (1970). "Perspectives on experience." Boston: BCG, presents learning curves for over 20 industries while Lieberman, M. (1984). "The learning curve and pricing in the chemical processing industries." *Rand Journal of Economics*, 15, pp. 213–228, estimates learning curves for 37 chemical products.
9. See Henderson, B. (1974). *The experience curve reviewed III—How does it work?* Boston: Boston Consulting Group; and Boston Consulting Group. (1970). "Perspectives on experience." Boston: BCG.
10. Hall, G., and S. Howell. (1985). "The experience curve from the economist's perspective." *Strategic Management Journal*, 6, pp. 197–212.
11. Hill, C. W. L. (1988). "Differentiation versus low-cost or differentiation and low-cost: A contingency framework." *Academy of Management Review*, 13(3), pp. 401–412.
12. See Ghemawat, P., and H. J. Stander III. (1992). "Nucor at a crossroads." Harvard Business School Case No. 9-793-039 on technology in steel manufacturing and cost advantages; Shaffer, R. A. (1995). "Intel as conquistador." *Forbes*, February 27, p. 130 on technology in semiconductor manufacturing and cost advantages; Monteverde, K., and D. Teece. (1982). "Supplier switching costs and vertical integration in the automobile industry." *Rand Journal of Economics*, 13(1), pp. 206–213; and McCormick, J., and N. Stone. (1990). "From national champion to global competitor: An interview with Thomson's Alain Gomez." *Harvard Business Review*, May/June, pp. 126–135 on technology in consumer electronic manufacturing and cost advantages.
13. Schultz, E. (1989). "Climbing high with discount brokers." *Fortune*, Fall (special issue), pp. 219–223.
14. Schonfeld, E. (1998). "Can computers cure health care?" *Fortune*, March 30, pp. 111+.
15. Ibid.
16. See Meyer, M. W., and L. B. Zucker. (1989). *Permanently failing organizations*. Newbury Park, CA: Sage.
17. Staw, B. M. (1981). "The escalation of commitment to a course of action." *Academy of Management Review*, 6, pp. 577–587.
18. Hesterly, W. S. (1989). *Top management succession as a determinant of firm performance and de-escalation: An agency problem*. Unpublished doctoral dissertation, University of California, Los Angeles.
19. Barney, J. B. (1986). "Organizational culture: Can it be a source of sustained competitive advantage?" *Academy of Management Review*, 11, pp. 656–665.
20. See Spence, A. M. (1981). "The learning curve and competition." *Bell Journal of Economics*, 12, pp. 49–70, on why learning needs to be proprietary; Mansfield, E. (1985). "How rapidly does new industrial technology leak out?" *Journal of Industrial Economics*, 34(2), pp. 217–223; Lieberman, M. B. (1982). *The learning-curve, pricing and market structure in the chemical processing industries*. Unpublished doctoral dissertation, Harvard University; Lieberman, M. B. (1987). "The learning curve, diffusion, and competitive strategy." *Strategic Management Journal*, 8, pp. 441–452, on why it usually is not proprietary.
21. Williamson, O. (1975). *Markets and hierarchies*. New York: Free Press.
22. Davis, S. M., and P. R. Lawrence. (1977). *Matrix*. Reading, MA: Addison-Wesley.
23. See Ghemawat, P., and H. J. Stander III. (1992). "Nucor at a crossroads." Harvard Business School Case No. 9-793-039.
24. See Floyd, S. W., and B. Woldridge. (1992). "Middle management involvement in strategy and its association with strategic type: A research note." *Strategic Management Journal*, 13, pp. 153–167.
25. Ibid.
26. Walton, S. (1992). *Sam Walton, Made in America: My story*. New York: Doubleday.

5 Product Differentiation

LEARNING OBJECTIVES *After reading this chapter, you should be able to:*

1. Define product differentiation.

2. Describe 11 bases of product differentiation and how they can be grouped into three categories.

3. Describe how product differentiation is ultimately limited only by managerial creativity.

4. Describe how product differentiation can be used to neutralize environmental threats and exploit environmental opportunities.

5. Describe those bases of product differentiation that are not likely to be costly to duplicate, those that may be

costly to duplicate, and those that will often be costly to duplicate.

6. Describe the main substitutes for product differentiation strategies.

7. Describe how organizational structure, control processes, and compensation policies can be used to implement product differentiation strategies.

8. Discuss whether it is possible for a firm to implement cost leadership and product differentiation strategies simultaneously.

MyManagementLab®

⭐ **Improve Your Grade!**
More than 10 million students improved their results using the Pearson MyLabs.
Visit **mymanagementlab.com** for simulations, tutorials, and end-of-chapter problems.

Who Is Victoria, and What Is Her Secret?

Sexy. Glamorous. Mysterious. Victoria's Secret is the world's leading specialty retailer of lingerie and beauty products. With 2012 sales of $6.12 billion and operating income of $1 billion, Victoria's Secret sells its mix of sexy lingerie, prestige fragrances, and fashion-inspired collections through more than 1,000 retail stores and the almost 400 million catalogues it distributes each year.

But all this glamour and success leaves the two central questions about this firm unanswered: "Who is Victoria?" and "What is her secret?"

It turns out that Victoria is a retired fashion model who lives in an up-and-coming fashionable district in London. She has a committed relationship and is thinking about starting a family. However, these maternal instincts are balanced by Victoria's adventurous and sexy side. She loves good food, classical music, and great wine. She travels frequently and is as much at home in New York, Paris, and Los Angeles as she is in London. Her fashion tastes are edgy enough to never be boring, but practical enough to never be extreme. Her lingerie is an essential part of her wardrobe. Sexy and alluring, but never cheap, trashy, or vulgar, Victoria's lingerie is the perfect complement to her overall lifestyle. Most important, while Victoria knows she is beautiful and sexy, she also knows that it is her brains, not her looks, that have enabled her to succeed in life.

This is who Victoria is. This is the woman that Victoria's Secret's designers design for, the woman Victoria's Secret marketers create advertising for, and the woman to whom all Victoria's Secret sales associates are trained to sell.

And this is her secret—Victoria doesn't really exist. Or, more precisely, the number of real women in the entire world who are like Victoria is very small—no more than a handful. So why would a company like Victoria's Secret organize all of its design, marketing, and sales efforts around meeting the lingerie needs of a woman who, for all practical purposes, doesn't really exist?

Victoria's Secret knows how few of its actual customers are like Victoria. However, it is convinced that many of its customers would like to be treated as if they were Victoria, if only for a time, when they come into a Victoria's Secret store. Victoria's Secret is not just selling lingerie; it is selling an

Image Source/Getty

opportunity, almost a fantasy, to be like Victoria—to live in an exciting and sexy city, to travel the world, to have refined, yet edgy, tastes. To buy and wear Victoria's Secret lingerie is—if only for a moment or two—an opportunity to experience life as Victoria experiences it.

Practically speaking, building an entire company around meeting the needs of a customer who does not actually exist creates some interesting problems. You can't just call Victoria on the phone and ask her about trends in her lifestyle; you can't form a focus group of people like Victoria and ask them to evaluate new lines of lingerie. In a sense, not only has Victoria's Secret invented Victoria; it also had to invent Victoria's lifestyle—and the lingerie, fragrances, and accessories that go along with that lifestyle. And as long as the lifestyle that it invents for Victoria is desirable to, but just beyond the reach of, its actual customers, Victoria's Secret will continue to be able to sell a romantic fantasy—along with its bras and panties.

Sources: www.limitedbrands.com accessed August 24, 2013; www.victoriassecret.com accessed August 24, 2013.

Victoria's Secret uses the fictional character "Victoria" to help implement its product differentiation strategy. As successful as this effort is, however, this is only one of many ways that firms can try to differentiate their products.

What Is Product Differentiation?

Whereas RyanAir exemplifies a firm pursuing a cost leadership strategy, Victoria's Secret exemplifies a firm pursuing a product differentiation strategy. **Product differentiation** is a business strategy where firms attempt to gain a competitive advantage by increasing the perceived value of their products or services relative to the perceived value of other firms' products or services. These other firms can be rivals or firms that provide substitute products or services. By increasing the perceived value of its products or services, a firm will be able to charge a higher price than it would otherwise. This higher price can increase a firm's revenues and generate competitive advantages.

A firm's attempts to create differences in the relative perceived value of its products or services often are made by altering the objective properties of those products or services. Rolex attempts to differentiate its watches from Timex and Casio watches by manufacturing them with solid gold cases. Mercedes attempts to differentiate its cars from Fiat's cars through sophisticated engineering and high performance. Victoria's Secret attempts to differentiate its shopping experience from Wal-Mart, and other retailers, through the merchandise it sells and the way it sells it.

Although firms often alter the objective properties of their products or services in order to implement a product differentiation strategy, the existence of product differentiation, in the end, is *always* a matter of customer perception. Products sold by two different firms may be very similar, but if customers believe the first is more valuable than the second, then the first product has a differentiation advantage.

In the world of "craft" or "microbrewery" beers, for example, the consumers' image of how a beer is brewed may be very different from how it is actually brewed. Boston Beer Company, for example, sells Samuel Adams Beer. Customers can tour the Boston Beer Company, where they will see a small row of fermenting tanks and two 10-barrel kettles being tended by a brewmaster wearing rubber boots. However, Samuel Adams Beer was not actually brewed in this small factory. Instead, it was, for much of its history, brewed—in 200-barrel steel tanks—in Cincinnati, Ohio, by the Hudepohl-Schoenling Brewing Company, a contract brewing firm that also manufactured Hudy Bold Beer and Little Kings Cream Ale. Maui Beer Company's Aloha Lager brand was brewed in Portland, Oregon, and Pete's Wicked Ale (a craft beer that claims it is brewed "one batch at a time. Carefully.") was brewed in batches of 400 barrels each by Stroh Brewery Company, makers of Old Milwaukee Beer. However, the more consumers believe there are important differences between these "craft" beers and more traditional brews—despite many of their common manufacturing methods—the more willing they will be to pay more for a craft beer. This willingness to pay more suggests that an important "perceptual" basis of product differentiation exists for these craft beers.[1] If products or services are *perceived* as being different in a way that is valued by consumers, then product differentiation exists.

Just as perceptions can create product differentiation between products that are essentially identical, the lack of perceived differences between products with very different characteristics can prevent product differentiation. For example, consumers with an untrained palate may not be able to distinguish between two different wines, even though expert wine tasters would be very much aware of their differences. Those who are not aware of these differences, even if they exist, will not be willing to pay more for one wine over the other. In this sense, for these consumers at least, these two wines, though different, are not differentiated.

Product differentiation is always a matter of customer perceptions, but firms can take a variety of actions to influence these perceptions. These actions can be thought of as different bases of product differentiation.

Bases of Product Differentiation

A large number of authors, drawing on both theory and empirical research, have developed lists of ways firms can differentiate their products or services.[2] Some of these are listed in Table 5.1. Although the purpose of all these bases of product differentiation is to create the perception that a firm's products or services are unusually valuable, different bases of product differentiation attempt to accomplish this objective in different ways. For example, the first four bases of product differentiation listed in Table 5.1 attempt to create this perception by focusing directly on the attributes of the products or services a firm sells. The second three attempt to create this perception by developing a relationship between a firm and its customers. The last five attempt to create this perception through linkages within and between firms. Of course, these bases of product differentiation are not mutually exclusive. Indeed, firms will often attempt to differentiate their products or services along multiple dimensions simultaneously. An empirical method for identifying ways that firms have differentiated their products is discussed in the Research Made Relevant feature.

Focusing on the Attributes of a Firm's Products or Services
The first group of bases of product differentiation identified in Table 5.1 focuses on the attributes of a firm's products or services.

TABLE 5.1 Ways Firms Can Differentiate Their Products

To differentiate its products, a firm can focus directly on the attributes of its products or services:

1. Product features
2. Product complexity
3. Timing of product introduction
4. Location

or on relationships between itself and its customers:
5. Product customization
6. Consumer marketing
7. Product reputation

or on linkages within or between firms:
8. Linkages among functions within a firm
9. Linkages with other firms
10. Product mix
11. Distribution channels
12. Service and support

Sources: M. E. Porter (1980). *Competitive strategy*. New York: Free Press; R. E. Caves and P. Williamson (1985). "What is product differentiation, really?" *Journal of Industrial Economics*, 34, pp. 113–132.

Product Features.   The most obvious way that firms can try to differentiate their products is by altering the features of the products they sell. One industry in which firms are constantly modifying product features to attempt to differentiate their products is the automobile industry. Chrysler, for example, introduced the "cab forward" design to try to give its cars a distinctive look, whereas Audi went with a more radical flowing and curved design to differentiate its cars. For emergency situations, General Motors (GM) introduced the "On Star" system, which instantly connects drivers to GM operators 24 hours a day, while Mercedes-Benz continued to develop its "crumple zone" system to ensure passenger safety in a crash. In body construction, General Motors continues to develop its "uni-body" construction system where different parts of a car are welded to each other rather than built on a single frame—while Jaguar introduced a 100 percent aluminum body to help differentiate its top-of-the-line model from other luxury cars. Mazda continues to tinker with the motor and suspension of its sporty Miata, while Nissan introduced the 370Z—a continuation of the famous 240Z line—and Porsche changed from air-cooled to water-cooled engines in its 911 series of sports cars. All these—and many more—changes in the attributes of automobiles are examples of firms trying to differentiate their products by altering product features.

Product Complexity.   Product complexity can be thought of as a special case of altering a product's features to create product differentiation. In a given industry, product complexity can vary significantly. The BIC "crystal pen," for example, has only a handful of parts, whereas a Cross or a Mont Blanc pen has many more parts. To the extent that these differences in product complexity convince consumers that the products of some firms are more valuable than the products of other firms, product complexity can be a basis of product differentiation.

Timing of Product Introduction.   Introducing a product at the right time can also help create product differentiation. As suggested in Chapter 2, in some industry settings (e.g., in emerging industries) *the* critical issue is to be a first mover—to introduce a new product before all other firms. Being first in emerging industries can enable a firm to set important technological standards, preempt strategically valuable assets, and develop customer-switching costs. These first-mover advantages can create a perception among customers that the products or services of the first-moving firm are somehow more valuable than the products or services of other firms.[3]

Timing-based product differentiation, however, does not depend only on being a first mover. Sometimes, a firm can be a later mover in an industry but introduce products or services at just the right time and thereby gain a competitive advantage. This can happen when the ultimate success of a product or service depends on the availability of complementary products or technologies. For example, the domination of Microsoft's MS-DOS operating system, and thus ultimately the domination of Windows, was only possible because IBM introduced its version of the personal computer. Without the IBM PC, it would have been difficult for any operating system—including MS-DOS—to have such a large market presence.[4]

Location.   The physical location of a firm can also be a source of product differentiation.[5] Consider, for example, Disney's operations in Orlando, Florida. Beginning with The Magic Kingdom and EPCOT Center, Disney built a world-class destination resort in Orlando. Over the years, Disney has added numerous attractions to its core entertainment activities, including Disney Studios, more than 11,000 Disney-owned hotel rooms, a $100 million sports center, an automobile racing track, an after-hours entertainment district, and, most recently, a $1 billion theme park called

Research Made Relevant

Of all the possible bases of product differentiation that might exist in a particular market, how does one pinpoint those that have actually been used? Research in strategic management and marketing has shown that the bases of product differentiation can be identified using multiple regression analysis to estimate what are called **hedonic prices**. A hedonic price is that part of the price of a product or service that is attributable to a particular characteristic of that product or service.

The logic behind hedonic prices is straightforward. If customers are willing to spend more for a product with a particular attribute than they are willing to spend for that same product without that attribute, then that attribute differentiates the first product from the second. That is, this attribute is a basis of product differentiation in this market.

Consider, for example, the price of used cars. The market price of a used car can be determined through the use of a variety of used car buying guides. These guides typically establish the base price of a used car. This base price typically includes product features that are common to almost all cars—a radio, a standard engine, a heater/defroster. Because these

Discovering the Bases of Product Differentiation

product attributes are common to virtually all cars, they are not a basis for product differentiation.

However, in addition to these common features, the base price of an automobile is adjusted based on some less common features—a high-end stereo system, a larger engine, air-conditioning. How much the base price of the car is adjusted when these features are added—$300 for a high-end stereo, $500 for a larger engine, $200 for air-conditioning—are the hedonic prices of these product attributes. These product attributes differentiate well-equipped cars from less-well-equipped cars and, because consumers are willing to pay more for

well-equipped cars, can be thought of as bases of product differentiation in this market.

Multiple regression techniques are used to estimate these hedonic prices in the following way. For our simple car example, the following regression equation is estimated:

$$Price = a_1 + b_1(Stereo) + b_2(Engine) + b_3(AC)$$

where *Price* is the retail price of cars, *Stereo* is a variable describing whether a car has a high-end stereo, *Engine* is a variable describing whether a car has a large engine, and *AC* is a variable describing whether a car has air-conditioning. If the hedonic prices for these features are those suggested earlier, the results of running this regression analysis would be:

$$Price = \$7{,}800 + \$300(Stereo) + \$500(Engine) + \$200(AC)$$

where $7,800 is the base price of this type of used car.

Sources: D. Hay and D. Morris (1979). *Industrial economics: Theory and evidence*. Oxford: Oxford University Press; K. Cowling and J. Cubbin (1971). "Price, quality, and advertising competition." *Economica*, 38, pp. 378–394.

"The Animal Kingdom"—all in and around Orlando. Now, families can travel from around the world to Orlando, knowing that in a single location they can enjoy a full range of Disney adventures.[6]

Focusing on the Relationship Between a Firm and Its Customers

The second group of bases of product differentiation identified in Table 5.1 focuses on relationships between a firm and its customers.

Product Customization.   Products can also be differentiated by the extent to which they are customized for particular customer applications. Product customization is an important basis for product differentiation in a wide variety of industries, from enterprise software to bicycles.

Enterprise software is software that is designed to support all of a firm's critical business functions, including human resources, payroll, customer service, sales, quality control, and so forth. Major competitors in this industry include Oracle and SAP. However, although these firms sell basic software packages, most firms find it necessary to customize these basic packages to meet their specific business needs. The ability to build complex software packages that can also be customized to meet the specific needs of a particular customer is an important basis of product differentiation in this marketplace.

In the bicycle industry, consumers can spend as little as $50 on a bicycle, and as much as—well, almost as much as they want on a bicycle, easily in excess of $10,000. High-end bicycles use, of course, the very best components, such as brakes and gears. But what really distinguishes these bicycles is their feel when they are ridden. Once a serious rider becomes accustomed to a particular bicycle, it is very difficult for that rider to switch to alternative suppliers.

Consumer Marketing.   Differential emphasis on consumer marketing has been a basis for product differentiation in a wide variety of industries. Through advertising and other consumer marketing efforts, firms attempt to alter the perceptions of current and potential customers, whether or not specific attributes of a firm's products or services are actually altered.

For example, in the soft drink industry, Mountain Dew—a product of PepsiCo—was originally marketed as a fruity, lightly carbonated drink that tasted "as light as a morning dew in the mountains." However, beginning in the late 1990s Mountain Dew's marketing efforts changed dramatically. "As light as a morning dew in the mountains" became "Do the Dew," and Mountain Dew focused its marketing efforts on young, mostly male, extreme-sports–oriented consumers. Young men riding snowboards, roller blades, mountain bikes, and skateboards—mostly upside down—became central to most Mountain Dew commercials. Mountain Dew became a sponsor of a wide variety of extreme sports contests and an important sponsor of the X Games on ESPN. Note that this radical repositioning of Mountain Dew depended entirely on changes in consumer marketing. The features of the underlying product were not changed.

Reputation.   Perhaps the most important relationship between a firm and its customers depends on a firm's reputation in its marketplace. Indeed, a firm's **reputation** is really no more than a socially complex relationship between a firm and its customers. Once developed, a firm's reputation can last a long time, even if the basis for that reputation no longer exists.[7]

A firm that has tried to exploit its reputation for cutting-edge entertainment is MTV, a division of Viacom, Inc. Although several well-known video artists—including Madonna—have had their videos banned from MTV, it has still been able to develop a reputation for risk-taking on television. MTV believes that its viewers have come to expect the unexpected in MTV programming. One of the first efforts to exploit, and reinforce, this reputation for risk-taking was *Beavis and Butthead*, an animated series starring two teenage boys with serious social and emotional development problems. More recently, MTV exploited its reputation by inventing an entirely new genre of television—"reality TV"—through its *Real World* and *Road Rules* programs. Not only are these shows cheap to produce, they build on the reputation that MTV has for providing entertainment that is a little risky, a little sexy, and a little controversial. Indeed, MTV has been so successful in providing this kind of entertainment that it had to form an entirely new cable station—MTV 2—to actually show music videos.[8]

Focusing on Links Within and Between Firms

The third group of bases of product differentiation identified in Table 5.1 focuses on links within and between firms.

Linkages Between Functions. A less obvious but still important way in which a firm can attempt to differentiate its products is through linking different functions within the firm. For example, research in the pharmaceutical industry suggests that firms vary in the extent to which they are able to integrate different scientific specialties—such as genetics, biology, chemistry, and pharmacology—to develop new drugs. Firms that are able to form effective multidisciplinary teams to explore new drug categories have what some have called an **architectural competence,** that is, the ability to use organizational structure to facilitate coordination among scientific disciplines to conduct research. Firms that have this competence are able to more effectively pursue product differentiation strategies—by introducing new and powerful drugs—than those that do not have this competence. And in the pharmaceutical industry, where firms that introduce such drugs can experience very large positive returns, the ability to coordinate across functions is an important source of competitive advantage.[9]

Links with Other Firms. Another basis of product differentiation is linkages with other firms. Here, instead of differentiating products or services on the basis of linkages between functions within a single firm or linkages between different products, differentiation is based on explicit linkages between one firm's products and the products or services of other firms.

This form of product differentiation has increased in popularity over the past several years. For example, with the growth in popularity of stock car racing in the United States, more and more corporations are looking to link their products or services with famous names and cars in NASCAR. Firms such as Burger King, McDonald's Target, Taco Bell, GEICO, Farmers Insurance, Lowe's, FedEx, 5-Hour Energy, and Miller Lite have all been major sponsors of NASCAR teams. In one year, the Coca-Cola Corporation filled orders for more than 200,000 NASCAR-themed vending machines. Visa struggled to keep up with demand for its NASCAR affinity cards, and more than 1 million NASCAR Barbies were sold by Mattel—generating revenues of about $50 million. Notice that none of these firms, except GEICO and Farmers, sells products for automobiles. Rather, these firms seek to associate themselves with NASCAR because of the sport's popularity.[10]

In general, linkages between firms that differentiate their products are examples of cooperative strategic alliance strategies. The conditions under which cooperative strategic alliances create value and are sources of sustained competitive advantage are discussed in detail in Chapter 9.

Product Mix. One of the outcomes of links among functions within a firm and links between firms can be changes in the mix of products a firm brings to the market. This mix of products or services can be a source of product differentiation, especially when (1) those products or services are technologically linked or (2) when a single set of customers purchases several of a firm's products or services.

For example, technological interconnectivity is an extremely important selling point in the information technology business and, thus, an important basis of potential product differentiation. However, seamless interconnectivity—where Company A's computers talk to Company B's computers across Company C's data line merging a database created by Company D's software with a database created by Company E's software to be used in a calling center that operates with

Company F's technology—has been extremely difficult to realize. For this reason, some information technology firms try to realize the goal of interconnectivity by adjusting their product mix, that is, by selling a bundle of products whose interconnectivity they can control and guarantee to customers. This goal of selling a bundle of interconnected technologies can influence a firm's research and development, strategic alliance, and merger and acquisition strategies because all these activities can influence the set of products a firm brings to market.

Shopping malls are an example of the second kind of linkage among a mix of products—where products have a common set of customers. Many customers prefer to go to one location, to shop at several stores at once, rather than travel to a series of locations to shop. This one-stop shopping reduces travel time and helps turn shopping into a social experience. Mall development companies have recognized that the value of several stores brought together in a particular location is greater than the value of those stores if they were isolated, and they have invested to help create this mix of retail shopping opportunities.[11]

Distribution Channels. Linkages within and between firms can also have an impact on how a firm chooses to distribute its products, and distribution channels can be a basis of product differentiation. For example, in the soft drink industry, Coca-Cola, PepsiCo, and 7-Up all distribute their drinks through a network of independent and company-owned bottlers. These firms manufacture key ingredients for their soft drinks and ship these ingredients to local bottlers, who add carbonated water, package the drinks in bottles or cans, and distribute the final product to soft drink outlets in a given geographic area. Each local bottler has exclusive rights to distribute a particular brand in a geographic location.

Canada Dry has adopted a completely different distribution network. Instead of relying on local bottlers, Canada Dry packages its soft drinks in several locations and then ships them directly to wholesale grocers, who distribute the product to local grocery stores, convenience stores, and other retail outlets.

One of the consequences of these alternative distribution strategies is that Canada Dry has a relatively strong presence in grocery stores but a relatively small presence in soft drink vending machines. The vending machine market is dominated by Coca-Cola and PepsiCo. These two firms have local distributors that maintain and stock vending machines. Canada Dry has no local distributors and is able to get its products into vending machines only when they are purchased by local Coca-Cola or Pepsi distributors. These local distributors are likely to purchase and stock Canada Dry products such as Canada Dry ginger ale, but they are contractually prohibited from purchasing Canada Dry's various cola products.[12]

Service and Support. Finally, products have been differentiated by the level of service and support associated with them. For example, some personal computer firms have very low levels of service provided by independent service dealers. Others have outsourced service and support functions to overseas companies, often in India. On the other hand, some firms continue to staff support centers with highly qualified individuals, thereby providing a high level of support.[13]

Product Differentiation and Creativity

The bases of product differentiation listed in Table 5.1 indicate a broad range of ways in which firms can differentiate their products and services. In the end, however, any effort to list all possible ways to differentiate products and services is doomed to failure. Product differentiation is ultimately an expression of the creativity of individuals and groups within firms. It is limited only by the opportunities that exist, or that can be created, in a particular industry and by the willingness and ability of firms to creatively explore ways to take advantage of those opportunities. It is not unreasonable to expect that the day some academic researcher claims to have developed the definitive list of bases of product differentiation, some creative engineer, marketing specialist, or manager will think of yet another way to differentiate his or her product.

The Value of Product Differentiation

V R I O

In order to have the potential for generating competitive advantages, the bases of product differentiation upon which a firm competes must be valuable. The market conditions under which product differentiation can be valuable are discussed in the Strategy in Depth feature. More generally, in order to be valuable, bases of product differentiation must enable a firm to neutralize its threats and/or exploit its opportunities.

Product Differentiation and Environmental Threats

Successful product differentiation helps a firm respond to each of the environmental threats identified. For example, product differentiation helps reduce the threat of new entry by forcing potential entrants to an industry to absorb not only the standard costs of beginning business, but also the additional costs associated with overcoming incumbent firms' product differentiation advantages. The relationship between product differentiation and new entry has already been discussed in Chapter 2.

Product differentiation reduces the threat of rivalry because each firm in an industry attempts to carve out its own unique product niche. Rivalry is not reduced to zero because these products still compete with one another for a common set of customers, but it is somewhat attenuated because the customers each firm seeks are different. For example, both a Rolls-Royce and a Fiat satisfy the same basic consumer need—transportation—but it is unlikely that potential customers of Rolls-Royce will also be interested in purchasing a Fiat or vice versa.

Product differentiation also helps firms reduce the threat of substitutes by making a firm's current products appear more attractive than substitute products. For example, fresh food can be thought of as a substitute for frozen processed foods. In order to make its frozen processed foods more attractive than fresh foods, products such as Stouffer's and Swanson are marketed heavily through television advertisements, newspaper ads, point-of-purchase displays, and coupons.

Product differentiation can also reduce the threat of powerful suppliers. Powerful suppliers can raise the prices of the products or services they provide. Often, these increased supply costs must be passed on to a firm's customers in the form of higher prices if a firm's profit margin is not to deteriorate. A firm without a highly differentiated product may find it difficult to pass its increased costs on to customers because these customers will have numerous other ways to purchase similar products or services from a firm's competitors. However, a firm with a highly differentiated product may have loyal customers or customers who

Strategy in Depth

The two classic treatments of the relationship between product differentiation and firm value, developed independently and published at approximately the same time, are by Edward Chamberlin and Joan Robinson.

Both Chamberlin and Robinson examine product differentiation and firm performance relative to perfect competition. As explained in Chapter 2, under perfect competition, it is assumed that there are numerous firms in an industry, each controlling a small proportion of the market, and the products or services sold by these firms are assumed to be identical. Under these conditions, firms face a horizontal demand curve (because they have no control over the price of the products they sell), and they maximize their economic performance by producing and selling output such that marginal revenue equals marginal costs. The maximum economic performance a firm in a perfectly competitive market can obtain, assuming no cost differences across firms, is normal economic performance.

When firms sell differentiated products, they gain some ability to adjust their prices. A firm can sell its output at very high prices and produce relatively smaller amounts of output, or it can sell its output at very low prices and produce relatively greater amounts of output. These

The Economics of Product Differentiation

trade-offs between price and quantity produced suggest that firms selling differentiated products face a downward-sloping demand curve, rather than the horizontal demand curve for firms in a perfectly competitive market. Firms selling differentiated products and facing a downward-sloping demand curve are in an industry structure described by Chamberlin as **monopolistic competition.** It is as if, within the market niche defined by a firm's differentiated product, a firm possesses a monopoly.

Firms in monopolistically competitive markets still maximize their economic profit by producing and selling a quantity of products such that marginal revenue equals

marginal cost. The price that firms can charge at this optimal point depends on the demand they face for their differentiated product. If demand is large, then the price that can be charged is greater; if demand is low, then the price that can be charged is lower. However, if a firm's average total cost is below the price it can charge (i.e., if average total cost is less than the demand-determined price), then a firm selling a differentiated product can earn an above-normal economic profit.

Consider the example presented in Figure 5.1. Several curves are relevant in this figure. First, note that a firm in this industry faces downward-sloping demand (D). This means that the industry is not perfectly competitive and that a firm has some control over the prices it will charge for its products. Also, the marginal-revenue curve (MR) is downward sloping and everywhere lower than the demand curve. Marginal revenue is downward sloping because in order to sell additional levels of output of a single product, a firm must be willing to lower its price. The marginal-revenue curve is lower than the demand curve because this lower price applies to all the products sold by a firm, not just to any additional products the firm

are unable to purchase similar products or services from other firms. These types of customers are more likely to accept increased prices. Thus, a powerful supplier may be able to raise its prices, but, up to some point, these increases will not reduce the profitability of a firm selling a highly differentiated product.

Finally, product differentiation can reduce the threat of powerful buyers. When a firm sells a highly differentiated product, it enjoys a "quasi-monopoly" in that segment of the market. Buyers interested in purchasing this particular product must buy it from a particular firm. Any potential buyer power is reduced by the ability of a firm to withhold highly valued products or services from a buyer.

sells. The marginal-cost curve (MC) is upward sloping, indicating that in order to produce additional outputs a firm must accept additional costs. The average-total-cost curve (ATC) can have a variety of shapes, depending on the economies of scale, the cost of productive inputs, and other cost phenomena described in Chapter 4.

These four curves (demand, marginal revenue, marginal cost, and average total cost) can be used to determine the level of economic profit for a firm under monopolistic competition. To maximize profit, the firm produces an amount (Q_e) such that marginal costs equal marginal revenues. To determine the price of a firm's output at this level of production, a vertical line is drawn from the point where marginal costs equal marginal revenues. This line will intersect with the demand curve. Where this vertical line intersects demand, a horizontal line is drawn to the vertical (price) axis to determine the price a firm can

charge. In the figure, this price is P_e. At the point P_e, average total cost is less than the price. The total revenue obtained by the firm in this situation (price × quantity) is indicated by the shaded area in the figure. The economic profit portion of this total revenue is indicated by the crosshatched section of the shaded portion of the figure. Because this crosshatched section is above average total costs in the figure, it represents a competitive advantage. If this section was below average total costs, it would represent a competitive disadvantage.

Chamberlin and Robinson go on to discuss the impact of entry into the market niche defined by a firm's differentiated product. As discussed

in Chapter 2, a basic assumption of S-C-P models is that the existence of above-normal economic performance motivates entry into an industry or into a market niche within an industry. In monopolistically competitive industries, such entry means that the demand curve facing incumbent firms shifts downward and to the left. This implies that an incumbent firm's customers will buy less of its output if it maintains its prices or (equivalently) that a firm will have to lower its prices to maintain its current volume of sales. In the long run, entry into this market niche can lead to a situation where the price of goods or services sold when a firm produces output such that marginal cost equals marginal revenue is exactly equal to that firm's average total cost. At this point, a firm earns zero economic profits even if it still sells a differentiated product.

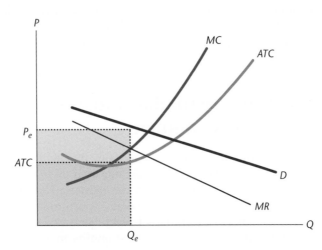

Sources: E. H. Chamberlin (1933). *The economics of monopolistic competition.* Cambridge, MA: MIT Press; J. Robinson (1934). "What is perfect competition?" *Quarterly Journal of Economics,* 49, pp. 104–120.

Figure 5.1   Product Differentiation and Firm Performance: The Analysis of Monopolistic Competition

Product Differentiation and Environmental Opportunities

Product differentiation can also help a firm take advantage of environmental opportunities. For example, in fragmented industries firms can use product differentiation strategies to help consolidate a market. In the office-paper industry, Xerox has used its brand name to become the leading seller of paper for office copy machines and printers. Arguing that its paper is specially manufactured to avoid jamming in its own copy machines, Xerox was able to brand what had been a commodity product and facilitate the consolidation of what had been a very fragmented industry.[14]

The role of product differentiation in emerging industries was discussed in Chapter 2. By being a first mover in these industries, firms can gain product differentiation advantages based on perceived technological leadership, preemption of strategically valuable assets, and buyer loyalty due to high switching costs.

In mature industries, product differentiation efforts often switch from attempts to introduce radically new technologies to product refinement as a basis of product differentiation. For example, in the mature retail gasoline market firms attempt to differentiate their products by selling slightly modified gasoline (cleaner-burning gasoline, gasoline that cleans fuel injectors, and so forth) and by altering the product mix (linking gasoline sales with convenience stores). In mature markets, it is sometimes difficult to find ways to actually refine a product or service. In such settings, firms can sometimes be tempted to exaggerate the extent to which they have refined and improved their products or services. The implications of these exaggerations are discussed in the Ethics and Strategy feature.

Product differentiation can also be an important strategic option in a declining industry. Product-differentiating firms may be able to become leaders in this kind of industry (based on their reputation, unique product attributes, or some other product differentiation basis). Alternatively, highly differentiated firms may be able to discover a viable market niche that will enable them to survive despite the overall decline in the market.

Finally, the decision to implement a product differentiation strategy can have a significant impact on how a firm acts in a global industry. For example, several firms in the retail clothing industry with important product differentiation advantages in their home markets are beginning to enter into the U.S. retail clothing market. These firms include Sweden's H & M Hennes & Mauritz AB, with its emphasis on "cheap chic"; the Dutch firm Mexx; the Spanish company Zara; and the French sportswear company Lacoste.[15]

 # Product Differentiation and Sustained Competitive Advantage

Product differentiation strategies add value by enabling firms to charge prices for their products or services that are greater than their average total cost. Firms that implement this strategy successfully can reduce a variety of environmental threats and exploit a variety of environmental opportunities. However, as discussed in Chapter 3, the ability of a strategy to add value to a firm must be linked with rare and costly-to-imitate organizational strengths in order to generate a sustained competitive advantage. Each of the bases of product differentiation listed earlier in this chapter varies with respect to how likely it is to be rare and costly to imitate.

Rare Bases for Product Differentiation

The concept of product differentiation generally assumes that the number of firms that have been able to differentiate their products in a particular way is, at some point in time, smaller than the number of firms needed to generate perfect competition dynamics. Indeed, the reason that highly differentiated firms can charge a price for their product that is greater than average total cost is because these firms are using a basis for product differentiation that few competing firms are also using.

Ultimately, the rarity of a product differentiation strategy depends on the ability of individual firms to be creative in finding new ways to differentiate their

Ethics and Strategy

One of the most common ways to try to differentiate a product is to make claims about that product's performance. In general, high-performance products command a price premium over low-performance products. However, the potential price advantages enjoyed by high-performance products can sometimes lead firms to make claims about their products that, at the least, strain credibility and, at the most, simply lie about what their products can do.

Some of these claims are easily dismissed as harmless exaggerations. Few people actually believe that using a particular type of whitening toothpaste is going to make your in-laws like you or that not wearing a particular type of deodorant is going to cause patrons in a bar to collapse when you lift your arms in victory after a foosball game. These exaggerations are harmless and present few ethical challenges.

However, in the field of health care, exaggerated product performance claims can have serious consequences. This can happen when a patient takes a medication with exaggerated performance claims instead of a medication with more modest, although accurate, performance claims. A history of false medical performance claims in the United States led to the formation of the Food and Drug Administration (FDA), a federal regulatory agency charged with evaluating the efficacy of drugs before they are marketed. Historically, the

Product Claims and the Ethical Dilemmas in Health Care

FDA has adopted the "gold standard" of drug approval—not only must a drug demonstrate that it does what it claims, it must also demonstrate that it does not do any significant harm to the patient. Patients can be confident that drugs that pass the FDA approval process meet the highest standards in the world.

However, this "gold standard" of approval creates important ethical dilemmas—mostly stemming from the time it takes a drug to pass the FDA approval process. This process can take between five and seven years. During FDA trials, patients who might otherwise benefit from a drug are not allowed to use it because it has not yet received FDA approval. Thus, although the FDA approval process may work very well for people who may need a drug sometime in the future, it works less well for those who need a drug right now.

A growing suspicion among some consumers that the FDA process may prevent effective drugs from being marketed has helped feed the growth of alternative treatments—usually based on some herbal or more natural formula. Such treatments are careful to note that their claims—everything from regrowing hair to losing weight to enhancing athletic performance to quitting smoking—have not been tested by the FDA. And yet these claims are still made.

Some of these performance claims seem at least reasonable. For example, it is now widely accepted that ephedra does behave as an amphetamine and thus is likely to enhance strength and athletic performance. Others—including those that claim that a mixture of herbs can actually increase the size of male genitals—seem far-fetched, at best. Indeed, a recent analysis of herbal treatments making this claim found no ingredients that could have this effect, but did find an unacceptably high concentration of bacteria from animal feces that can cause serious stomach disorders. Firms that sell products on the basis of exaggerated and unsubstantiated claims face their own ethical dilemmas. And, without the FDA to ensure product safety and efficacy, the adage *caveat emptor*—let the buyer beware—seems like good advice.

Sources: J. Angwin (2003). "Some 'enlargement pills' pack impurities." *The Wall Street Journal*, April 8, p. B1; G. Pisano (1991). "Nucleon, Inc." Harvard Business School Case No. 9-692-041.

products. As suggested earlier, highly creative firms will be able to discover or create new ways to do this. These kinds of firms will always be one step ahead of the competition because rival firms will often be trying to imitate these firms' last product differentiation moves while creative firms are working on their next one.

The Imitability of Product Differentiation

Valuable and rare bases of product differentiation must be costly to imitate if they are to be sources of sustained competitive advantage. Both direct duplication and substitution, as approaches to imitation, are important in understanding the ability of product differentiation to generate competitive advantages.

Direct Duplication of Product Differentiation

As discussed in Chapter 4, firms that successfully implement a cost leadership strategy can choose whether they want to reveal this strategic choice to their competition by adjusting their prices. If they keep their prices high—despite their cost advantages—the existence of those cost advantages may not be revealed to competitors. Of course, other firms—such as Wal-Mart—that are confident that their cost advantages cannot be duplicated at low cost are willing to reveal their cost advantage through charging lower prices for their products or services.

Firms pursuing product differentiation strategies usually do not have this option. More often than not, the act of selling a highly differentiated product or service reveals the basis upon which a firm is trying to differentiate its products. In fact, most firms go to great lengths to let their customers know how they are differentiating their products, and in the process of informing potential customers they also inform their competitors. Indeed, if competitors are not sure how a firm is differentiating its product, all they need to do is purchase that product themselves. Their own experience with the product—its features and other attributes—will tell them all they need to know about this firm's product differentiation strategy.

Knowing how a firm is differentiating its products, however, does not necessarily mean that competitors will be able to duplicate the strategy at low cost. The ability to duplicate a valuable and rare product differentiation strategy depends on the basis upon which a firm is differentiating its products. As suggested in Table 5.2, some bases of product differentiation—including the use of product features—are almost always easy to duplicate. Others—including product mix, links with other firms, product customization, product complexity, and consumer marketing—can sometimes be costly to duplicate. Finally, still other bases of product differentiation—including links between functions, timing, location, reputation, distribution channels, and service and support—are usually costly to duplicate.

How costly it is to duplicate a particular basis of product differentiation depends on the kinds of resources and capabilities that basis uses. When those resources and capabilities are acquired in unique historical settings, when there is some uncertainty about how to build these resources and capabilities, or when these resources and capabilities are socially complex in nature, then product differentiation strategies that exploit these kinds of resources and capabilities will be costly to imitate. These strategies can be a source of sustained competitive advantage for a firm. However, when a product differentiation strategy exploits resources and capabilities that do not possess these attributes, then those strategies are likely to be less costly to duplicate and, even if they are valuable and rare, will only be sources of temporary competitive advantage.

Bases of Product Differentiation That Are Easy to Duplicate.   The one basis of product differentiation in Table 5.2 that is identified as almost always being easy to duplicate is product features. The irony is that product features are by far the most popular way for firms to try to differentiate their products. Rarely do product

	History	Uncertainty	Social Complexity
Low-cost duplication usually possible			
1. Product features	—	—	—
May be costly to duplicate			
2. Product mix	*	*	*
3. Links with other firms	*	—	**
4. Product customization	*	—	**
5. Product complexity	*	—	*
6. Consumer marketing	—	**	—
Usually costly to duplicate			
7. Links between functions	*	*	**
8. Timing	***	*	—
9. Location	***	—	—
10. Reputation	***	**	***
11. Distribution channels	**	*	**
12. Service and support	*	*	**

TABLE 5.2 Bases of Product Differentiation and the Cost of Duplication

— = Not likely to be a source of costly duplication,   * = Somewhat likely to be a source of costly duplication,
** = Likely to be a source of costly duplication,   *** = Very likely to be a source of costly duplication

features, by themselves, enable a firm to gain sustained competitive advantages from a product differentiation strategy.

For example, virtually every one of the product features used in the automobile industry to differentiate the products of different automobile companies has been duplicated. Chrysler's "cab forward" design has been incorporated into the design of many manufacturers. The curved, sporty styling of the Audi has surfaced in cars manufactured by Lexus and General Motors. GM's "On Star" system has been duplicated by Mercedes. Mercedes' crumple-zone technology has become the industry standard, as has GM's uni-body construction method. Indeed, only the Mazda Miata, Nissan 370Z, and Porsche 911 have remained unduplicated—and this has little to do with the product features of these cars and much more to do with their reputation.

The only time product features, per se, can be a source of sustained competitive advantage for a firm is when those features are protected by patents. However, as was discussed in Chapters 2 and 3, even patents provide only limited protection from direct duplication, except in very unusual settings.

Although product features, by themselves, are usually not a source of sustained competitive advantage, they can be a source of a temporary competitive advantage. During the period of time when a firm has a temporary competitive advantage from implementing a product differentiation strategy based on product features, it may be able to attract new customers. Once these customers try the product, they may discover other features of a firm's products that make them attractive. If these other features are costly to duplicate, then they can be a source of sustained competitive advantage, even though the features that originally attracted a customer to a firm's products will often be rapidly duplicated by competitors.

Bases of Product Differentiation That May Be Costly to Duplicate.   Some bases of product differentiation may be costly to duplicate, at least in some circumstances. The first of these, listed in Table 5.2, is product mix.

Duplicating the features of another firm's products is usually not difficult. However, if that firm brings a series of products to market, if each of these products has unique features, and most important, if the products are highly integrated with each other, then this mix of products may be costly to duplicate. Certainly, the technological integration of the mix of information technology products sold by IBM and other firms has been relatively difficult to duplicate for firms that do not manufacture all these products themselves.

However, when this basis of a product mix advantage is a common customer, then duplication is often less difficult. Thus, although having a mall that brings several stores together in a single place is a source of competitive advantage over stand-alone stores, it is not a competitive advantage over other malls that provide the same service. Because there continue to be opportunities to build such malls, the fact that malls make it easier for a common set of customers to shop does not give any one mall a sustained competitive advantage.

Links with other firms may also be costly to duplicate, especially when those links depend on socially complex relationships. The extent to which interfirm links can provide sources of sustained competitive advantage is discussed in more detail in Chapter 9.

In the same way, product customization and product complexity are often easy-to-duplicate bases of product differentiation. However, sometimes the ability of a firm to customize its products for one of its customers depends on the close relationships it has developed with those customers. Product customization of this sort depends on the willingness of a firm to share often-proprietary details about its operations, products, research and development, or other characteristics with a supplying firm. Willingness to share this kind of information, in turn, depends on the ability of each firm to trust and rely on the other. The firm opening its operations to a supplier must trust that that supplier will not make this information broadly available to competing firms. The firm supplying customized products must trust that its customer will not take unfair advantage of it. If two firms have developed these kinds of socially complex relationships, and few other firms have them, then links with other firms will be costly to duplicate and a source of sustained competitive advantage.

The product customization seen in both enterprise software and in high-end customized bicycles has these socially complex features. In a real sense, when these products are purchased, a relationship with a supplier is being established— a relationship that is likely to last a long period of time. Once this relationship is established, partners are likely to be unwilling to abandon it, unless, of course, a party to the exchange tries to take unfair advantage of another party to that exchange. This possibility is discussed in detail in Chapter 9.

Finally, consumer marketing, though a very common form of product differentiation, is often easy to duplicate. Thus, whereas Mountain Dew has established itself as the "extreme games" drink, other drinks, including Gatorade, have also begun to tap into this market segment. Of course, every once in a while an advertising campaign or slogan, a point-of-purchase display, or some other attribute of a consumer marketing campaign will unexpectedly catch on and create greater-than-expected product awareness. In beer, marketing campaigns such as "Tastes great, less filling," "Why ask why?," the "Budweiser Frogs," and "What's Up?" have had these unusual effects. If a firm, in relation with its various consumer marketing agencies, is systematically able to develop these superior consumer marketing campaigns, then it may be able to obtain a sustained competitive advantage. However, if such campaigns are unpredictable and largely a matter of a firm's good luck, they cannot be expected to be a source of sustained competitive advantage.

Bases of Product Differentiation That Are Usually Costly to Duplicate.   The remaining bases of product differentiation listed in Table 5.2 are usually costly to duplicate. Firms that differentiate their products on these bases may be able to obtain sustained competitive advantages.

Linkages across functions within a single firm are usually a costly-to-duplicate basis of product differentiation. Whereas linkages with other firms can be either easy or costly to duplicate, depending on the nature of the relationship that exists between firms, linkages across functions within a single firm usually require socially complex, trusting relations. There are numerous built-in conflicts between functions and divisions within a single firm. Organizations that have a history and culture that support cooperative relations among conflicting divisions may be able to set aside functional and divisional conflicts to cooperate in delivering a differentiated product to the market. However, firms with a history of conflict across functional and divisional boundaries face a significant, and costly, challenge in altering these socially complex, historical patterns.

Indeed, the research on architectural competence in pharmaceutical firms suggests that not only do some firms possess this competence, but that other firms do not. Moreover, despite the significant advantages that accrue to firms with this competence, firms without this competence have, on average, been unable to develop it. All this suggests that such a competence, if it is also rare, is likely to be costly to duplicate and thus a source of sustained competitive advantage.

Timing is also a difficult-to-duplicate basis of product differentiation. As suggested in Chapter 3, it is difficult (if not impossible) to re-create a firm's unique history. If that history endows a firm with special resources and capabilities it can use to differentiate its products, this product differentiation strategy can be a source of sustained competitive advantage. Rivals of a firm with such a timing-based product differentiation advantage may need to seek alternative ways to differentiate their products. Thus, it is not surprising that universities that compete with the oldest universities in the country find alternative ways to differentiate themselves—through their size, the quality of their extramural sports, their diversity—rather than relying on their age.

Location is often a difficult-to-duplicate basis of product differentiation. This is especially the case when a firm's location is unique. For example, research on the hotel preferences of business travelers suggests that location is a major determinant of the decision to stay in a hotel. Hotels that are convenient to both major transportation and commercial centers in a city are preferred, other things being equal, to hotels in other types of locations. Indeed, location has been shown to be a more important decision criterion for business travelers than price. If only a few hotels in a city have these prime locations and if no further hotel development is possible, then hotels with these locations can gain sustained competitive advantages.

Of all the bases of product differentiation listed in this chapter, perhaps none is more difficult to duplicate than a firm's reputation. As suggested earlier, a firm's reputation is actually a socially complex relationship between a firm and its customers, based on years of experience, commitment, and trust. Reputations are not built quickly, nor can they be bought and sold. Rather, they can only be developed over time by consistent investment in the relationship between a firm and its customers. A firm with a positive reputation can enjoy a significant competitive advantage, whereas a firm with a negative reputation, or no reputation, may have to invest significant amounts over long periods of time to match the differentiated firm.

Distribution channels can also be a costly-to-duplicate basis of product differentiation, for at least two reasons. First, relations between a firm and its distribution channels are often socially complex and thus costly to duplicate. Second, the supply of distribution channels may be limited. Firms that already have access to these channels may be able to use them, but firms that do not have such access may be forced to create their own or develop new channels. Creating new channels or developing entirely new means of distribution can be difficult and costly undertakings.[16] These costs are one of the primary motivations underlying many international joint ventures (see Chapter 9).

Finally, level of service and support can be a costly-to-duplicate basis of product differentiation. In most industries, it is usually not too costly to provide a minimum level of service and support. In home electronics, this minimum level of service can be provided by a network of independent electronic repair shops. In automobiles, this level of service can be provided by service facilities associated with dealerships. In fast foods, this level of service can be provided by a minimum level of employee training.

However, moving beyond this minimum level of service and support can be difficult for at least two reasons. First, increasing the quality of service and support may involve substantial amounts of costly training. McDonald's has created a sophisticated training facility (Hamburger University) to maintain its unusually high level of service in fast foods. General Electric has invested heavily in training for service and support over the past several years. Many Japanese automakers spent millions on training employees to help support auto dealerships before they opened U.S. manufacturing facilities.[17]

More important than the direct costs of the training needed to provide high-quality service and support, these bases of product differentiation often reflect the attitude of a firm and its employees toward customers. In many firms throughout the world, the customer has become "the bad guy." This is, in many ways, understandable. Employees tend to interact with their customers less frequently than they interact with other employees. When they do interact with customers, they are often the recipients of complaints directed at the firm. In these settings, hostility toward the customer can develop. Such hostility is, of course, inconsistent with a product differentiation strategy based on customer service and support.

In the end, high levels of customer service and support are based on socially complex relations between firms and customers. Firms that have conflicts with their customers may face some difficulty duplicating the high levels of service and support provided by competing firms.

Substitutes for Product Differentiation

The bases of product differentiation outlined in this chapter vary in how rare they are likely to be and in how difficult they are to duplicate. However, the ability of the bases of product differentiation to generate a sustained competitive advantage also depends on whether low-cost substitutes exist.

Substitutes for bases of product differentiation can take two forms. First, many of the bases of product differentiation listed in Table 5.1 can be partial substitutes for each other. For example, product features, product customization, and product complexity are all very similar bases of product differentiation and thus can act as substitutes for each other. A particular firm may try to develop a competitive advantage by differentiating its products on the basis of product customization only to find that its customization advantages are reduced as another firm alters the features of its products. In a similar way, linkages between functions, linkages between firms, and product mix, as bases of product differentiation, can also be substitutes for each other. IBM links its sales, service, and consulting functions to differentiate itself in the computer market. Other computer firms, however, may develop close relationships with computer service companies and consulting firms to close this product differentiation advantage. Given that different bases of product differentiation are often partial substitutes for each other, it is not surprising that firms pursue these multiple bases of product differentiation simultaneously.

Second, other strategies discussed throughout this book can be substitutes for many of the bases of product differentiation listed in Table 5.1. One firm may try to gain a competitive advantage through adjusting its product mix, and another firm may substitute strategic alliances to create the same type of product differentiation. For example, Southwest Airlines' continued emphasis on friendly, on-time, low-cost service and United Airlines' emphasis on its links to Lufthansa and other worldwide airlines through the Star Alliance can both be seen as product differentiation efforts that are at least partial substitutes.[18]

In contrast, some of the other bases of product differentiation discussed in this chapter have few obvious close substitutes. These include timing, location, distribution channels, and service and support. To the extent that these bases of product differentiation are also valuable, rare, and difficult to duplicate, they may be sources of sustained competitive advantage.

Organizing to Implement Product Differentiation

V R I O

As was suggested in Chapter 3, the ability to implement a strategy depends on the adjustment of a firm's structure, its management controls, and its compensation policies to be consistent with that strategy. Whereas strategy implementation for firms adopting a cost leadership strategy focuses on reducing a firm's costs and increasing its efficiency, strategy implementation for a firm adopting a product differentiation strategy must focus on innovation, creativity, and product performance. Whereas cost-leading firms are all about customer value, product-differentiating firms are all about style. How the need for style is reflected in a firm's structure, controls, and compensation policies is summarized in Table 5.3.

TABLE 5.3 Organizing to Implement Product Differentiation Strategies

Organizational Structure:
1. Cross-divisional/cross-functional product development teams
2. Complex matrix structures
3. Isolated pockets of intense creative efforts: Skunk works

Management Control Systems:
1. Broad decision-making guidelines
2. Managerial freedom within guidelines
3. A policy of experimentation

Compensation Policies:
1. Rewards for risk-taking, not punishment for failures
2. Rewards for creative flair
3. Multidimensional performance measurement

Organizational Structure and Implementing Product Differentiation

Both cost leadership and product differentiation strategies are implemented through the use of a functional, or U-form, organizational structure. However, whereas the U-form structure used to implement a cost leadership strategy has few layers, simple reporting relationships, a small corporate staff, and a focus on only a few business functions, the U-form structure for a firm implementing a product differentiation strategy can be somewhat more complex. For example, these firms often use temporary cross-divisional *and* cross-functional teams to manage the development and implementation of new, innovative, and highly differentiated products. These teams bring individuals from different businesses and different functional areas together to cooperate on a particular new product or service.

One firm that has used these cross-divisional and cross-functional teams effectively is the British advertising agency WPP. WPP owns several very large advertising agencies, several public relations firms, several market research companies, and so forth. Each of these businesses operates relatively independently in most areas. However, the corporation has identified a few markets where cross-divisional and cross-functional collaboration is important. One of these is the health care market. To exploit opportunities in the health care market, WPP, the corporation, forms teams of advertising specialists, market research specialists, public relations specialists, and so on, drawn from each of the businesses it owns. The resulting cross-divisional teams are given the responsibility of developing new and highly differentiated approaches to developing marketing strategies for their clients in the health care industry.[19]

The creation of cross-divisional or cross-functional teams often implies that a firm has implemented some form of matrix structure. As suggested in Chapter 4, a **matrix structure** exists when individuals in a firm have two or more "bosses" simultaneously. Thus, for example, if a person from one of WPP's advertising agencies is assigned temporarily to a cross-divisional team, that person has two bosses: the head of the temporary team and the boss back in the advertising agency. Managing two bosses simultaneously can be very challenging, especially when they have conflicting interests. And as we will see in Chapter 8, the interests of these multiple bosses *will* often conflict.

A particularly important form of the cross-divisional or cross-functional team exists when this team is relieved of all other responsibilities in the firm and focuses all its attention on developing a new innovative product or service. The best-known example of this approach to developing a differentiated product occurred at the Lockheed Corporation during the 1950s and 1960s when small groups of engineers were put on very focused teams to develop sophisticated and top-secret military aircraft. These teams would have a section of the Lockheed facility dedicated to their efforts and designated as off-limits to almost all other employees. The joke was that these intensive creative efforts were so engaging that members of these teams actually would forget to shower—hence the name **"skunk works."** Skunk works have been used by numerous firms to focus the creative energy required to develop and introduce highly differentiated products.[20]

Management Controls and Implementing Product Differentiation

The first two management controls helpful for implementing product differentiation listed in Table 5.3—broad decision-making guidelines and managerial freedom within those guidelines—often go together. How some firms have used

Strategy in the Emerging Enterprise

So much innovation in both small and large organizations focuses on repositioning a firm's products along established bases of competition—a more fuel-efficient car, a better-cleaning shampoo, a less expensive insurance policy. While these efforts can, for a time, be a source of product differentiation, for reasons discussed in Chapter 3, they are usually not sustainable.

For this reason, two scholars—W. Chan Kim and Renee Mauborgne—began studying firms that did not just reposition their products in well-established competitive markets but, instead, transcended their competition to identify entirely new markets. They called these markets "blue oceans" because they are not crowded with competitors seeking to improve their positions but instead are empty of competitors and give firms the opportunity to grow quickly. For these authors, blue oceans emerge when managers discover that the only way to beat the competition is to stop *trying* to beat the competition.

Examples of companies that have created blue oceans include Cirque du Soleil—a firm that redefined what a circus was to become an international entertainment sensation—and Casella Wines—a firm whose [yellow tail] brand made drinking wine a simple alternative to drinking beer. Both

Going in Search of Blue Oceans

these companies did not try to compete with established firms; they created a new competitive space where these firms were irrelevant.

So, how can a firm create a blue ocean? Kim and Mauborgne suggest that firms begin by understanding the bases of competition that exist within an industry already. In the U.S. wine industry, for example, Casella identified seven bases of competition: price, an elite image in packaging, consumer marketing, aging quality of wine, vineyard prestige, taste complexity, and a diverse range of wines. With these bases of product differentiation identified, firms should then ask four questions about competition in their industry:

1. Which factors that the industry currently competes on should be *eliminated*?

2. Which factors that the industry currently competes on should be *reduced well below* the industry's standard?
3. Which factors should be *raised well above* the industry's standard?
4. Which factors should be *created* that the industry has never offered?

By applying these four questions to the bases of competition identified by Casella, this firm decided that elite packaging, aging quality wine, vineyard prestige, and taste complexity all complicated the wine drinking experience and could be eliminated. They also created new bases for competition: easy drinking, ease of selection, and fun and adventure. The result was a wine brand—[yellow tail]—that has grown faster than any other wine over the past 10 years.

Some firms have found it difficult to apply these principles to develop blue oceans for their businesses. Nevertheless, by systematically seeking ways to redefine the bases of competition in an industry, some firms have been able to create entirely new markets where competition does not exist.

Source: W. Chan Kim and Renee Mauborgne (2005). *Blue ocean strategy*. Cambridge: Harvard Business School Press.

these kinds of controls to build entirely new markets is described in the Strategy in the Emerging Enterprise feature.

Broad decision-making guidelines help bring order to what otherwise might be a chaotic decision-making process. When managers have no constraints in their decision making, they can make decisions that are disconnected from each other and inconsistent with a firm's overall mission and objectives. This results in decisions that are either not implemented or not implemented well.

However, if these decision-making guidelines become too narrow, they can stifle creativity within a firm. As was suggested earlier, a firm's ability to differentiate its products is limited only by its creativity. Thus, decision guidelines must be narrow enough to ensure that the decisions made are consistent with a firm's mission and objectives. Yet these guidelines also must be broad enough so that managerial creativity is not destroyed. In well-managed firms implementing product differentiation strategies, as long as managerial decisions fall within the broad decision-making guidelines in a firm, managers have the right—in fact, are expected—to make creative decisions.

A firm that has worked hard to reach this balance between chaos and control is 3M. In an effort to provide guiding principles that define the range of acceptable decisions at 3M, its senior managers have developed a set of innovating principles. These are presented in Table 5.4 and define the boundaries of innovative chaos at 3M. Within these boundaries, managers and engineers are expected to be creative and innovative in developing highly differentiated products and services.[21]

Another firm that has managed this tension well is British Airways (BA). BA has extensive training programs to teach its flight attendants how to provide world-class service, especially for its business-class customers. This training constitutes standard operating procedures that give purpose and structure to BA's efforts to provide a differentiated service in the highly competitive airline industry. Interestingly, however, BA also trains its flight attendants in when to violate these standard policies and procedures. By recognizing that no set of management controls can ever anticipate all the special situations that can occur when providing service to customers, BA empowers its employees to meet specific customer needs. This enables BA to have both a clearly defined product differentiation strategy and the flexibility to adjust this strategy as the situation dictates.[22]

Firms can also facilitate the implementation of a product differentiation strategy by adopting a **policy of experimentation.** Such a policy exists when firms are committed to engaging in several related product differentiation efforts simultaneously. That these product differentiation efforts are related suggests that a firm has some vision about how a particular market is likely to unfold over time. However, that there are several of these product differentiation efforts occurring simultaneously suggests that a firm is not overly committed to a particular narrow vision about how a market is going to evolve. Rather, several different experiments facilitate the exploration of different futures in a marketplace. Indeed, successful experiments can actually help define the future evolution of a marketplace.

Consider, for example, Charles Schwab, the innovative discount broker. In the face of increased competition from full-service and Internet-based brokerage firms, Schwab engaged in a series of experiments to discover the next generation of products it could offer to its customers and the different ways it could differentiate those products. Schwab investigated software for simplifying online mutual fund selection, online futures trading, and online company research. It also formed an exploratory alliance with Goldman Sachs to evaluate the possibility of enabling Schwab customers to trade in initial public offerings. Not all of Schwab's experiments led to the introduction of highly differentiated products. For example, based on some experimental investments, Schwab decided not to enter the credit card market. However, by experimenting with a range of possible product differentiation moves, it was able to develop a range of new products for the fast-changing financial services industry.[23]

TABLE 5.4 Guiding Innovative Principles at 3M*

1. **Vision.** Declare the importance of innovation; make it part of the company's self-image.

   "Our efforts to encourage and support innovation are proof that we really do intend to achieve our vision of ourselves ... that we intend to become what we want to be ... as a business and as creative individuals."

2. **Foresight.** Find out where technologies and markets are going. Identify articulated and unarticulated needs of customers.

   "If you are working on a next-generation medical imaging device, you'll probably talk to radiologists, but you might also sit down with people who enhance images from interplanetary space probes."

3. **Stretch goals.** Set goals that will make you and the organization stretch to make quantum improvements. Although many projects are pursued, place your biggest bets on those that change the basis of competition and redefine the industry.

   "We have a number of stretch goals at 3M. The first states that we will drive 30 percent of all sales from products introduced in the past 4 years.... To establish a sense of urgency, we've recently added another goal, which is that we want 10 percent of our sales to come from products that have been in the market for just 1 year.... Innovation is time sensitive ... you need to move quickly."

4. **Empowerment.** Hire good people and trust them, delegate responsibilities, provide slack resources, and get out of the way. Be tolerant of initiative and the mistakes that occur because of that initiative.

   "William McKnight [a former chairman of 3M] came up with one way to institutionalize a tolerance of individual effort. He said that all technical employees could devote 15 percent of their time to a project of their own invention. In other words, they could manage themselves for 15 percent of the time.... The number is not so important as the message, which is this: The system has some slack in it. If you have a good idea, and the commitment to squirrel away time to work on it and the raw nerve to skirt your lab manager's expressed desires, then go for it.

   "Put another way, we want to institutionalize a bit of rebellion in our labs. We can't have all our people off totally on their own ... we do believe in discipline ... but at the same time 3M management encourages a healthy disrespect for 3M management. This is not the sort of thing we publicize in our annual report, but the stories we tell—with relish—are frequently about 3Mers who have circumvented their supervisors and succeeded.

   "We also recognize that when you let people follow their own lead ... everyone doesn't wind up at the same place. You can't ask people to have unique visions and march in lockstep. Some people are very precise, detail-oriented people ... and others are fuzzy thinkers and visionaries ... and this is exactly what we want."

5. **Communications.** Open, extensive exchanges according to ground rules in forums that are present for sharing ideas and where networking is each individual's responsibility. Multiple methods for sharing information are necessary.

   "When innovators communicate with each other, you can leverage their discoveries. This is critically important because it allows companies to get the maximum return on their substantial investments in new technologies. It also acts as a stimulus to further innovation. Indeed, we believe that the ability to combine and transfer technologies is as important as the original discovery of a technology."

6. **Rewards and recognition.** Emphasize individual recognition more than monetary rewards through peer recognition and by choice of managerial or technical promotion routes. "Innovation is an intensely human activity."

   "I've laid out six elements of 3M's corporate culture that contribute to a tradition of innovation: vision, foresight, stretch goals, empowerment, communication, and recognition.... The list is ... too orderly. Innovation at 3M is anything but orderly. It is sensible, in that our efforts are directed at reaching our goals, but the organization ... and the process ... and sometimes the people can be chaotic. We are managing in chaos, and this is the right way to manage if you want innovation. It's been said that the competition never knows what we are going to come up with next. The fact is, neither do we."

*As expressed by W. Coyne (1996). *Building a tradition of innovation.* The Fifth U.K. Innovation Lecture, Department of Trade and Industry, London. Cited in Van de Ven et al. (1999), pp. 198–200.

Compensation Policies and Implementing Product Differentiation Strategies

The compensation policies used to implement product differentiation listed in Table 5.3 very much complement the organizational structure and managerial controls listed in that table. For example, a policy of experimentation has little impact on the ability of a firm to implement product differentiation strategies if every time an innovative experiment fails individuals are punished for taking risks. Thus, compensation policies that reward risk-taking and celebrate a creative flair help to enable a firm to implement its product differentiation strategy.

Consider, for example, Nordstrom. Nordstrom is a department store that celebrates the risk-taking and creative flair of its associates as they try to satisfy their customers' needs. The story is often told of a Nordstrom sales associate who allowed a customer to return a set of tires to the store because she wasn't satisfied with them. What makes this story interesting—whether or not it is true—is that Nordstrom doesn't sell tires. But this sales associate felt empowered to make what was obviously a risky decision, and this decision is celebrated within Nordstrom as an example of the kind of service that Nordstrom's customers should expect.

The last compensation policy listed in Table 5.3 is multidimensional performance measurement. In implementing a cost leadership strategy, compensation should focus on providing appropriate incentives for managers and employees to reduce costs. Various forms of cash payments, stock, and stock options can all be tied to the attainment of specific cost goals and thus can be used to create incentives for realizing cost advantages. Similar techniques can be used to create incentives for helping a firm implement its product differentiation advantage. However, because the implementation of a product differentiation strategy generally involves the integration of multiple business functions, often through the use of product development teams, compensation schemes designed to help implement this strategy must generally recognize its multifunctional character.

Thus, rather than focusing only on a single dimension of performance, these firms often examine employee performance along multiple dimensions simultaneously. Examples of such dimensions include not only a product's sales and profitability, but customer satisfaction, an employee's willingness to cooperate with other businesses and functions within a firm, an employee's ability to effectively facilitate cross-divisional and cross-functional teams, and an employee's ability to engage in creative decision making.

Can Firms Implement Product Differentiation and Cost Leadership Simultaneously?

The arguments developed in Chapter 4 and in this chapter suggest that cost leadership and product differentiation business strategies, under certain conditions, can both create sustained competitive advantages. Given the beneficial impact of both strategies on a firm's competitive position, an important question becomes: Can a single firm simultaneously implement both strategies? After all, if each separately can improve a firm's performance, wouldn't it be better for a firm to implement both?

No: These Strategies Cannot Be Implemented Simultaneously

A quick comparison of the organizational requirements for the successful implementation of cost leadership strategies and product differentiation strategies presented in Table 5.5 summarizes one perspective on the question of whether these strategies can be implemented simultaneously. In this view, the organizational requirements of these strategies are essentially contradictory. Cost leadership requires simple reporting relationships, whereas product differentiation requires cross-divisional/cross-functional linkages. Cost leadership requires intense labor supervision, whereas product differentiation requires less intense supervision of creative employees. Cost leadership requires rewards for cost reduction, whereas product differentiation requires rewards for creative flair. It is reasonable to ask "Can a single firm combine these multiple contradictory skills and abilities?"

Some have argued that firms attempting to implement both strategies will end up doing neither well. This logic suggests that there are often only two ways to earn superior economic performance within a single industry: (1) by selling high-priced products and gaining small market share (product differentiation) or (2) by selling low-priced products and gaining large market share (cost leadership). Firms that do not make this choice of strategies (medium price, medium market share) or that attempt to implement both strategies will fail. These firms are said to be "stuck in the middle."[24]

TABLE 5.5 The Organizational Requirements for Implementing Cost Leadership and Product Differentiation Strategies

Cost leadership	Organizational structure
Product differentiation	**Organizational structure**
1. Few layers in the reporting structure	1. Cross-divisional/cross-functional product development teams
2. Simple reporting relationships	2. Willingness to explore new structures to exploit new opportunities
3. Small corporate staff	3. Isolated pockets of intense creative efforts
4. Focus on narrow range of business functions	
Management control systems	**Management control systems**
1. Tight cost-control systems	1. Broad decision-making guidelines
2. Quantitative cost goals	2. Managerial freedom within guidelines
3. Close supervision of labor, raw material, inventory, and other costs	3. Policy of experimentation
4. A cost leadership philosophy	
Compensation policies	**Compensation policies**
1. Reward for cost reduction	1. Rewards for risk-taking, not punishment for failures
2. Incentives for all employees to be involved in cost reduction	2. Rewards for creative flair
	3. Multidimensional performance measurement

Yes: These Strategies Can Be Implemented Simultaneously

More recent work contradicts assertions about being "stuck in the middle." This work suggests that firms that are successful in both cost leadership and product differentiation can often expect to gain a sustained competitive advantage. This advantage reflects at least two processes.

Differentiation, Market Share, and Low-Cost Leadership

Firms able to successfully differentiate their products and services are likely to see an increase in their volume of sales. This is especially the case if the basis of product differentiation is attractive to a large number of potential customers. Thus, product differentiation can lead to increased volumes of sales. It has already been established (in Chapter 4) that an increased volume of sales can lead to economies of scale, learning, and other forms of cost reduction. So, successful product differentiation can, in turn, lead to cost reductions and a cost leadership position.[25]

This is the situation that best describes McDonald's. McDonald's has traditionally followed a product differentiation strategy, emphasizing cleanliness, consistency, and fun in its fast-food outlets. Over time, McDonald's has used its differentiated product to become the market share leader in the fast-food industry. This market position has enabled it to reduce its costs, so that it is now the cost leader in fast foods as well. Thus, McDonald's level of profitability depends both on its product differentiation strategy and its low-cost strategy. Either one of these two strategies by itself would be difficult to overcome; together they give McDonald's a very costly-to-imitate competitive advantage.[26]

Managing Organizational Contradictions

Product differentiation can lead to high market share and low costs. It may also be the case that some firms develop special skills in managing the contradictions that are part of simultaneously implementing low-cost and product differentiation strategies. Some recent research on automobile manufacturing helps describe these special skills.[27] Traditional thinking in automotive manufacturing was that plants could either reduce manufacturing costs by speeding up the assembly line or increase the quality of the cars they made by slowing the line, emphasizing team-based production, and so forth. In general, it was thought that plants could not simultaneously build low-cost/high-quality (i.e., low-cost *and* highly differentiated) automobiles.

Several researchers have examined this traditional wisdom. They began by developing rigorous measures of the cost and quality performance of automobile plants and then applied these measures to more than 70 auto plants throughout the world that assembled mid-size sedans. What they discovered was six plants in the entire world that had, at the time this research was done, very low costs *and* very high quality.[28]

In examining what made these six plants different from other auto plants, the researchers focused on a broad range of manufacturing policies, management practices, and cultural variables. Three important findings emerged. First, these six plants had the best manufacturing technology hardware available—robots, laser-guided paint machines, and so forth. However, because many of the plants in the study had these same technologies, manufacturing technology by itself was not enough to make these six plants special. In addition, policies and procedures at these plants implemented a range of highly participative, group-oriented management techniques, including participative management, team production, and total quality management. As important, employees in these plants had a sense of loyalty and commitment toward the plant they worked for—a belief that they would be treated fairly by their plant managers.

What this research shows is that firms *can* simultaneously implement cost leadership and product differentiation strategies if they learn how to manage the contradictions inherent in these two strategies. The management of these contradictions, in turn, depends on socially complex relations among employees, between employees and the technology they use, and between employees and the firm for which they work. These relations are not only valuable (because they enable a firm to implement cost leadership and differentiation strategies) but also socially complex and thus likely to be costly to imitate and a source of sustained competitive advantage.

Recently, many scholars have backed away from the original "stuck in the middle" arguments and now suggest that low-cost firms must have competitive levels of product differentiation to survive and that product differentiation firms must have competitive levels of cost to survive.[29] For example, the fashion design company Versace—the ultimate product differentiating firm—has hired a new CEO and controller to help control its costs.[30]

Summary

Product differentiation exists when customers perceive a particular firm's products to be more valuable than other firms' products. Although differentiation can have several bases, it is, in the end, always a matter of customer perception. Bases of product differentiation include: (1) attributes of the products or services a firm sells (including product features, product complexity, the timing of product introduction, and location); (2) relations between a firm and its customers (including product customization, consumer marketing, and reputation); and (3) links within and between firms (including links between functions, links with other firms, a firm's product mix, its distribution system, and its level of service and support). However, in the end, product differentiation is limited only by the creativity of a firm's managers.

Product differentiation is valuable to the extent that it enables a firm to set its prices higher than what it would otherwise be able to. Each of the bases of product differentiation identified can be used to neutralize environmental threats and exploit environmental opportunities. The rarity and imitability of bases of product differentiation vary. Highly imitable bases of product differentiation include product features. Somewhat imitable bases include product mix, links with other firms, product customization, and consumer marketing. Costly-to-imitate bases of product differentiation include linking business functions, timing, location, reputation, and service and support.

The implementation of a product differentiation strategy involves management of organizational structure, management controls, and compensation policies. Structurally, it is not unusual for firms implementing product differentiation strategies to use cross-divisional and cross-functional teams, together with teams that are focused exclusively on a particular product differentiation effort, so-called "skunk works." Managerial controls that provide free managerial decision making within broad decision-making guidelines can be helpful in implementing product differentiation strategies, as is a policy of experimentation. Finally, compensation policies that tolerate risk-taking and a creative flair and that measure employee performance along multiple dimensions simultaneously can also be helpful in implementing product differentiation strategies.

A variety of organizational attributes is required to successfully implement a product differentiation strategy. Some have argued that contradictions between these organizational characteristics and those required to implement a cost leadership strategy mean that firms that attempt to do both will perform poorly. More recent research has noted the relationship between product differentiation, market share, and low costs and has observed that some firms have learned to manage the contradictions between cost leadership and product differentiation.

MyManagementLab®

Go to **mymanagementlab.com** to complete the problems marked with this icon ⭐.

Challenge Questions

5.1. Should a firm pursue differentiation strategy in an industry where customers are very price sensitive? As low prices are often supported by low costs, in such a market, what can a differentiation strategy hope to achieve?

⭐ **5.2.** Product features are often the focus of product differentiation efforts. Yet product features are among the easiest-to-imitate bases of product differentiation and thus among the least likely bases of product differentiation to be a source of sustained competitive advantage. This appears

paradoxical. How can you resolve this paradox?

5.3. What are the strengths and weaknesses of using regression analysis and hedonic prices to describe the bases of product differentiation?

5.4. Some researchers believe that a firm pursuing differentiation can sustain its advantage, despite the threat of imitation, by constant upgrades to product/service features. With the help of examples, discuss

the feasibility of deterring imitation using this approach.

⭐ **5.5.** Implementing a product differentiation strategy seems to require just the right mix of control and creativity. How do you know if a firm has the right mix?

5.6. Is it possible to evaluate the mix of control and creativity when implementing a product differentiation strategy before problems associated with being out of balance manifest themselves? If yes, how? If no, why not?

5.7. Think of two examples of a company that pursued a differentiation strategy and whose sustainability was threatened by substitutes (not imitators). How should the companies respond? What are the implications for sustaining differentiation advantage, in general?

Problem Set

5-8. In what ways do the following products pursue a strategy of differentiation?

(a) Louis Vuitton bags
(b) Samsung smartphones
(c) BBC television series
(d) Marlboro cigarettes
(e) Tencent
(f) Apple iPod

5-9. Which, if any, of the bases of product differentiation in the previous question are likely to be sources of sustained competitive advantage? Why?

5-10. Suppose you obtained the following regression results, where the starred (*) coefficients are statistically significant. What could you say about the bases of product differentiation in this market? (Hint: A regression coefficient is statistically significant when it is so large that its effect is very unlikely to have emerged by chance.)

$$
\begin{aligned}
\text{House Price} = {} & 125{,}000^* + 15{,}000^*(\text{More than three bedrooms}) \\
& + \$18{,}000^*(\text{More than 3,500 square feet}) \\
& + \$150(\text{Has plumbing}) + \$180(\text{Has lawn}) \\
& + 17{,}000^*(\text{Lot larger than 1/2 acre})
\end{aligned}
$$

How much would you expect to pay for a four-bedroom, 3,800-square-foot house on a one-acre lot? How much for a four-bedroom, 2,700-square-foot house on a quarter-acre lot? Do these results say anything about the sustainability of competitive advantages in this market?

5-11. Which of the following management controls and compensation policies is consistent with implementing cost leadership? With product differentiation? With both cost leadership and product differentiation? With neither cost leadership nor product differentiation?

(a) Firm-wide stock options
(b) Compensation that rewards each function separately for meeting its own objectives
(c) A detailed financial budget plan
(d) A document that describes, in detail, how the innovation process will unfold in a firm
(e) A policy that reduces the compensation of a manager who introduces a product that fails in the market
(f) A policy that reduces the compensation of a manager who introduces several products that fail in the market
(g) The creation of a purchasing council to discuss how different business units can reduce their costs

5-12. Identify three industries or markets where it is unlikely that firms will be able to simultaneously implement cost leadership and product differentiation. Which firms in this industry are implementing cost leadership strategies? Which are implementing product differentiation strategies? Are any firms "stuck in the middle"? If yes, which ones? If no, why not? Are any firms implementing both cost leadership and product differentiation strategies? If yes, which ones? If no, why not?

MyManagementLab®

Go to **mymanagementlab.com** for the following Assisted-graded writing questions:

✪ **5.13.** How can product differentiation be used to neutralize environmental threats and exploit environmental opportunities?

✪ **5.14.** How can organizational structure be used to implement product differentiation strategies?

End Notes

1. See Ono, Y. (1996). "Who really makes that cute little beer? You'd be surprised." *The Wall Street Journal*, April 15, pp. A1+. Since this 1996 article, some of these craft beer companies have changed the way they manufacture the beers to be more consistent with the image they are trying to project.
2. See Porter, M. E. (1980). *Competitive strategy.* New York: Free Press; and Caves, R. E., and P. Williamson. (1985). "What is product differentiation, really?" *Journal of Industrial Organization Economics*, 34, pp. 113–132.
3. Lieberman, M. B., and D. B. Montgomery. (1988). "First-mover advantages." *Strategic Management Journal*, 9, pp. 41–58.
4. Carroll, P. (1993). *Big blues: The unmaking of IBM.* New York: Crown Publishers.
5. These ideas were first developed in Hotelling, H. (1929). "Stability in competition." *Economic Journal*, 39, pp. 41–57; and Ricardo, D. (1817). *Principles of political economy and taxation.* London: J. Murray.
6. See Gunther, M. (1998). "Disney's call of the wild." *Fortune*, April 13, pp. 120–124.
7. The idea of reputation is explained in Klein, B., and K. Leffler. (1981). "The role of market forces in assuring contractual performance." *Journal of Political Economy*, 89, pp. 615–641.
8. See Robichaux M. (1995). "It's a book! A T-shirt! A toy! No, just MTV trying to be Disney." *The Wall Street Journal*, February 8, pp. A1+.
9. See Henderson, R., and I. Cockburn. (1994). "Measuring competence? Exploring firm effects in pharmaceutical research." *Strategic Management Journal*, 15, pp. 63–84.
10. See Johnson, R. (1999). "Speed sells." *Fortune*, April 12, pp. 56–70. In the last few years, NASCAR's popularity has begun to wane. For example, NASCAR television ratings have been consistently down since 2005. www.jayski.com/news/pages/story/NASCAR-television-ratings
11. Kotler, P. (1986). *Principles of marketing.* Upper Saddle River, NJ: Prentice Hall.
12. Porter, M. E., and R. Wayland. (1991). "Coca-Cola vs. Pepsi-Cola and the soft drink industry." Harvard Business School Case No. 9-391-179.
13. Ghemawat, P. (1993). "Sears, Roebuck and Company: The merchandise group." Harvard Business School Case No. 9-794-039.
14. Welsh, J. (1998). "Office-paper firms pursue elusive goal: Brand loyalty." *The Wall Street Journal*, September 21, p. B6.
15. See White, E., and K. Palmer. (2003). "U.S. retailing 101." *The Wall Street Journal*, August 12, pp. B1+.
16. See Hennart, J. F. (1988). "A transaction cost theory of equity joint ventures." *Strategic Management Journal*, 9, pp. 361–374.
17. Deutsch, C. H. (1991). "How is it done? For a small fee…" *New York Times*, October 27, p. 25; and Armstrong, L. (1991). "Services: The customer as 'Honored Guest.'" *BusinessWeek*, October 25, p. 104.
18. See Yoffie, D. (1994). "Swissair's alliances (A)." Harvard Business School Case No. 9-794-152.
19. "WPP—Integrating icons." Harvard Business School Case No. 9-396-249.
20. Orosz, J. J. (2002). "Big funds need a 'Skunk Works' to stir ideas." *Chronicle of Philanthropy*, June 27, p. 47.
21. Van de Ven, A., D. Polley, R. Garud, and S. Venkatraman. (1999). *The innovation journey.* New York: Oxford, pp. 198–200.
22. Prokesch, S. (1995). "Competing on customer service: An interview with British Airways' Sir Colin Marshall." *Harvard Business Review*, November–December, p. 101. Now if they wouldn't lose our luggage at Heathrow, they would be a great airline.
23. Position, L. L. (1999). "David S. Pottruck." *BusinessWeek*, September 27, EB 51.
24. Porter, M. E. (1980). *Competitive strategy.* New York: Free Press.
25. Hill, C. W. L. (1988). "Differentiation versus low cost or differentiation and low cost: A contingency framework." *Academy of Management Review*, 13(3), pp. 401–412.
26. Gibson, R. (1995). "Food: At McDonald's, new recipes for buns, eggs." *The Wall Street Journal*, June 13, p. B1.
27. Originally discussed in the Research Made Relevant feature in Chapter 3.
28. Womack, J. P., D. I. Jones, and D. Roos. (1990). *The machine that changed the world.* New York: Rawson.
29. Porter, M. E. (1985). *Competitive advantage.* New York: Free Press.
30. Agins, T., and A. Galloni. (2003). "Facing a squeeze, Versace struggles to trim the fat." *The Wall Street Journal*, September 30, pp. A1+.

PART 2 CASES

Case 2–1: Airasia X: Can the Low Cost Model go Long Haul?

IVEY | Publishing

Ben Forrey, Professor Andreas Schotter, Professor Jonathan Doh and Professor Thomas Lawton wrote this case solely to provide material for class discussion. The authors do not intend to illustrate either effective or ineffective handling of a managerial situation. The authors may have disguised certain names and other identifying information to protect confidentiality.

On March 11, 2011, after a busy week in Kuala Lumpur at AirAsia X's global headquarters, Darren Wright, head of commercial operations, sat in seat 44C on a late night flight back home to Australia. Wright, who had only recently been appointed to this position, was responsible for managing the airline's direct revenue generating activities including ticket sales, ancillary onboard sales, and all global marketing and advertising activities. In addition, he served as the company's country manager for Australia. While Wright observed the cabin crew selling duty-free merchandise to passengers, he reflected on five of his most pressing challenges: First, how best to leverage the extensive network of the regional sister company AirAsia in selecting new and profitable destinations for AirAsia X, the long haul[1] venture of the group? Second, how to increase revenues without raising ticket prices? Third, how best to globally position the airline's brand in non-Asian markets? Fourth, how to shift his marketing team's mentality away from a start-up mindset? And finally, how to prepare for a global initial public offering within the next 12 months?

The Beginning: Airasia and the Budget Model

In 2001, just a few days prior to the World Trade Center terrorist attacks in the United States, former music executive and entrepreneur Tony Fernandes launched AirAsia. Fernandes'

idea was to bring a low cost airline model to Malaysia similar to what Ryanair in Europe and Southwest Airlines in the U.S. offered. From the outset, Fernandes contemplated adapting a global, long haul element to the typically regional budget airline model. He believed he could provide affordable long distance intercontinental air travel for the rapidly growing new middle class throughout Asia, something that had not been done in that region and had been attempted with only mixed success in other geographic regions. AirAsia's initial business plan included a route between Fernandes' current home in Kuala Lumpur and his boyhood home in London, England.

However, several of Fernandes' closest advisors convinced him to initially focus on building a strong intra-Asian flight network instead of dealing with the difficulties of getting passengers to Europe. They argued a low cost network in Asia would one day attract European tourists and budget conscious business travellers, which would then support the launch of an ultra-competitive intercontinental airline. Consequently, Fernandes put his plans to fly to non-Asian destinations on hold. Within the following six years, starting with only two planes, he grew the airline into Southeast Asia's largest and most comprehensive flight network. In 2007, AirAsia operated nearly 30 aircraft and several regional subsidiary companies including Malaysia AirAsia, Thai AirAsia, Indonesia AirAsia, Vietnam AirAsia and AirAsia X[2] (from now on referred to as X). The corporate slogan of AirAsia became: "Now Everyone Can Fly!"

To prove the point, AirAsia routinely offered one-way fares as low as US$3.00. In 2008 and 2009, AirAsia won the prestigious Skytrax[3] "World's Best Low Cost Airline Award."

The Launch of X

In early 2007, Fernandes finally felt the timing and the existing infrastructure of AirAsia's route network provided the right conditions for entering the intercontinental air travel market. Despite constant claims from industry insiders that low cost, long haul flights would never be profitable,[4] Fernandes pushed forward with the expansion. After a few months of strategizing, he realized, due to the substantial differences between long haul and short haul airline operations, the new business had to be—at least legally— separated from the regional AirAsia entity. Different levels of financial risk, legal issues with landing rights, and the substantial complexities in operating across very different time zones and cultural arenas all played a factor. However, establishing a new airline was much more complicated than starting any other type of business. The process of getting the necessary approvals and certifications could take years. Coincidentally during this time, Malaysian Airlines expressed interest in taking over the routes of a small local Malaysian commuter airline Fernandes and a group of Malaysian investors also owned. He swiftly transferred the routes to Malaysian Airlines and used these freed up airline certifications to launch the new long haul carrier.

Fernandes wanted an appropriate name addition to AirAsia that would, on the one hand, take advantage of the strong brand and, on the other, reflect the new, expanded services. Without much thought, he called the new airline AirAsia X. At the same time, Fernandes recruited a young CEO from outside the airline industry to launch the new airline (see Exhibit 1). Both, the selection of then 36-year old Azran Osman-Rani along with the unconventional new

Azran Osman-Rani, CEO

Azran Osman-Rani was the son of two university educators. As a young child, both of Azran's parents had foreign teaching assignments outside of Malaysia, and several years of Azran's youth were spent in the United States and the Philippines. When he reached university age, Azran attended Stanford University in the United States and received a bachelor's degree in electrical engineering and graduate degree in economics. Upon graduation, Azran became a consultant and spent time at Booz Allen Hamilton and then at McKinsey & Company in Asia, and held posts in Thailand, Indonesia, Singapore and South Korea. Azran was asked to return to Malaysia to help the Kuala Lumpur Stock Exchange automate its trading activities and transform it from a private into a publicly traded entity. Happy being back home in Malaysia, Azran joined Astro all Asia Networks, Malaysia's top cable TV provider as Director of Business Development. It was while in this capacity that Azran was approached by AirAsia founder Tony Fernandes and asked to become the CEO of X. He accepted after Fernandes told him that: "…everyone is saying it can't be done." Osman-Rani became the CEO of X at only 36 years of age.

Darren Wright, Head of Commercial Operations and Australia Country Manager

Darren Wright, a native of Australia, had been with X since its first flight in November 2007. A lifelong surfer, Darren spent his summers during university as a surf guide in Bali, Indonesia. After graduating, Darren joined a local government department focused on agribusiness marketing. Seizing an opportunity to expand his management skills, he joined Australia's largest travel agency, Flight Centre, where he oversaw the sales of all airline tickets around the world. After five years of building the Flight Centre brand, Darren joined the start-up Australian airline Virgin Blue as the Director of Marketing in 2002. Seeking a new challenge, Darren was introduced to X in 2007 by a mutual friend of X's CEO, Azran Osman-Rani, and he accepted the opportunity to become the country manager for Australia. Darren assumed responsibility for all operational and marketing activities for three destinations within Australia. Happy in his role as country manager, Darren was asked to serve as the Head of Commercial Operations for the airline in June 2010 with direct responsibility for all activities that generated revenue including marketing and public relations, ticket sales, onboard sales, revenue management and all fee programs. His intimate knowledge of surfing had helped the airline achieve a leading brand position among the surf community in Australia and worldwide. Darren relocated to Kuala Lumpur in 2011 after spending six months splitting his time between headquarters and Australia.

Exhibit 1   Key Management BIOS

Source: Company files

airline name were typical of Fernandes—the polar opposite of how most traditional airline industry executives would proceed. In an interview, Osman-Rani stated:

> *People always ask us what the significance of the X in AirAsia X is, and I just have to tell them that it has no special story behind it. It is just what we called the airline at the beginning in order to get the business started. It then kind of stuck. Now we believe that the name fits us really well. We like to think that we are the 'X-factor' to the success of the AirAsia Group.*

From an operating standpoint, long haul required a larger type of airplane compared to the model AirAsia was currently flying. In keeping with AirAsia's low cost approach, the aircraft choice fell ultimately on Airbus Industry's A330 type aircraft. AirAsia not only had a large fleet of Airbus airplanes already, but also knew Airbus would provide more favorable financing terms than its main competitor, Boeing. The AirAsia group became one of the world's largest operators of Airbus aircraft.

While legally a separate corporate entity, X was launched as a franchise of AirAsia, allowing it to leverage some existing infrastructure resources. For example, initially some of AirAsia's pilots, engineers, and cabin crews were cross-trained to operate both aircraft types and all ticket sales were integrated into a single website and booking system. All maintenance, training, customer service, and back office activities were performed jointly, including all marketing and administrative functions. The ability of AirAsia to financially and operationally support X during its start-up period proved key to the successful launch.

Australia's Gold Coast became X's first destination. X's inaugural flight to Australia took place on November 2, 2007. Three years later, in the summer of 2010, X received its eleventh aircraft and flew to 15 destinations on three continents. The substantial differences between long haul and short haul operating requirements became more and more apparent, so management decided to formally separate X from AirAsia. With this separation, 100 per cent of all maintenance, administration, flight operations and marketing activities were now managed by X independently with its own resources. The decision to separate the two companies was also made in preparation for a global IPO anticipated in late 2011 or early 2012.

The Airasia X Business Model: Differentiating Around Low Cost

While the AirAsia model closely followed what Southwest Airlines and Ryanair practiced in Europe and the United States—albeit with some unique and distinctive features—the long haul budget airline model developed by X was considered an innovation. Conventional aviation wisdom assumed an airline could not sustain profitable operations by charging low fares for long haul flights.[5] The basic operating costs per flight were deemed too high and average flight bookings were either too low or too seasonal to make money. It appeared the cost leadership model based on scale simply might not work for long haul flights.

Historically, long haul operations targeted either business travelers or affluent individual travelers, competing on service differentiation and route network integration. Most, if not all, airline executives around the globe believed passengers would never choose to fly long distances if amenities such as checked baggage, food and beverages, and onboard entertainment were not included in the ticket price. Furthermore, the assumption that a premium class cabin was a necessity[6] was unquestionable. In fact, many of the leading global long haul airlines operated business class only flights between, for example, Singapore and Los Angeles or London and New York City. Fernandes did not agree. He was certain his largely Asian clientele would embrace the opportunity to travel to distant locations if the price was right, despite the fact that some of the comfort features associated with other airlines would be lacking. Fernandes, together with Osman-Rani, built upon the belief that many of their Asian clients would jump at the chance to fly farther if it were more affordable.

While X maintained its laser-like focus on low cost, it also built on AirAsia's experience in using low costs to attract new customer segments in new ways. In this sense, AirAsia was effectively differentiating around low cost, and building that distinct approach into its branding and customer engagement.

Targeting the Base

Instead of focusing on the upper levels of the wealth pyramid, X targeted a much larger potential passenger pool that would not ordinarily consider flying to intercontinental destinations, but was characterized by substantially lower but rapidly growing disposable income. In order to attract these new customers, X's published fares included the seat and all departure/landing taxes but explicitly excluded all frills. The inclusion of the taxes and fees in the advertised ticket price made the calculation of out of pocket costs very simple to understand. Optional items such as seat assignments, checked baggage, onboard food and beverages, inflight entertainment, flight transfers or changes, pillows and blankets, and the like were all available for purchase separately based on a fixed price list.

This clarity reduced the hurdle for the lower income clientele to decide on a flight compared to the confusion and hassle traditional carriers create with their hidden fees and brokerage-like variation in real out of pocket costs. It was not uncommon for established international carriers to add up to 30 per cent in surcharges to the posted ticket price.

Similar to most airlines around the world, X's operations focused strongly on flight safety. However, this was where operating similarities ended. As a point of reference, the average U.S. budget airline's cost per seat mile in 2009 was approximately US$0.09 per mile. X's cost per seat mile was just over US$0.02 per mile in 2009, less than one quarter of the cost of the traditional low budget airlines. Given the drastic disparity between X's operating costs and those of other airlines, many experts wondered how this was achieved, especially considering a significant portion of the operating costs of the airline (e.g. fuel and aircraft pricing) was driven by global forces out of individual carriers' control.

The reason was surprisingly simple. From the beginning, X operated as an ultra-lean company, with the bare minimum number of staff hired to achieve safety and effectively complete only the basic transportation tasks. Additionally, labor costs in Malaysia, and the absence of unionization, helped keep human resource costs low. Until it reached the necessary scale, X shared resources with AirAsia, focused on avoiding duplicate processes. X did not invest in terminal or other non-airplane related infrastructure that would increase fixed asset overheads.

Many factors contributed to the development of an extreme low cost seeking culture within every activity of the company. These factors included the company's emerging market heritage, the struggles to overcome the depressed economic environment during AirAsia's launch, the negative effects of 9/11 on the airline industry and diligent benchmarking against the successful models Ryanair and Southwest Airlines operated. Osman-Rani made it his mission to create an airline that would withstand any kind of major external environmental shocks, including pandemic disease, terrorist attacks, natural disasters, economic crises, or oil price spikes. Consequently, X survived and expanded when other regional competitors such as Hong Kong-based Oasis and Zoom Airlines ceased operations at the height of the global financial crisis. Wright stated:

> It sometimes surprises passengers that when they land in Kuala Lumpur, they get off the airplane directly onto the airport tarmac and not into a gate area at a terminal. Why should we build gates, or pay expensive gate lease fees if it will only add costs to the ticket price? When people wonder 'what are we going to do' when they land and it is raining outside, we just smile and hand them an umbrella.

Besides being the low cost leader, other significant aspects of X's business model included aircraft selection, higher utilization of space by maximizing seating capacity, aircraft utilization, customer focused paid a la carte inflight experience, including premium seats, operational simplicity and other unique intangibles.

Aircraft Selection and Seat Configuration

By flying Airbus A330s and later adding four engine A340 aircraft to the fleet, X was able to leverage the strong relationship with Airbus Industries previously initiated by AirAsia. A large pool of Airbus trained mechanics was available to meet the maintenance needs of both airlines at the Kuala Lumpur home base. Tremendous time and cost savings were achieved by utilizing cross training initiatives. The young age of X's fleet also helped the airline achieve the highest possible fuel efficiencies. The airline was one of the first to order the yet to be built A350 model which some heralded as the most fuel-efficient airliner ever.

As of February 2011, X operated a fleet of eleven aircraft; nine Airbus A330s with 377 total seats (12 premium and 365 economy) and two Airbus A340s with 327 seats (18 premium and 309 economy). A comparison of its competitors operating the same A330 indicated that X generally had approximately 20 per cent higher seating capacity on the same airplane than most other carriers (see Exhibit 2). This 20 per cent higher capacity allowed for X to charge

Exhibit 2   Comparison of Typical A330 Aircraft Seating Versus X'S Seating

Airline	A330 Premium Seats	A330 Economy Seats	Total Seats
Delta Airlines	34	264	298
Cathay Pacific Airlines	44	267	311
Jetstar Airlines	38	265	303
AirAsia X Airlines	**12**	**365**	**377**

Source: Company files

up to 20 per cent lower fees and earn the same revenue as its competitors without even considering the lower labor costs, terminal costs and general operating expenses.

To achieve the extra capacity, X used a 3-3-3 seating configuration throughout the airplane in one large single economy class. This seating configuration was not favored by other airlines because of the perceived inconvenience to the passengers seated by the windows. They had to get by two other passengers in order to access or exit their seats. The most common configuration was 2-4-2, which allowed for only eight seats per row. To address passenger comfort despite the higher than typical capacity, X reduced the width of the seats but provided more legroom instead. According to an internal company survey, this was what long haul travelers really preferred. The company also designed an innovative new headrest better suited for sleeping during longer flights.

Luxury for the Masses: Flat Bed Seats

Another unique option on X's flights was introduced in 2010—a limited number of premium seats in a small section of the airplane (between three and five per cent of available seats only). These seats reclined to a fully flat position for sleeping, a first in the world of budget airlines. On a traditional full service airline, these seats would be the business class or first class seats (see Exhibit 3). However, on X, these seats did not automatically come with all the premium complimentary amenity offerings. These additional offerings had to be paid for just like standard seats. Wright commented:

We realized the most sought after premium feature when flying long distance is the ability to lie flat and sleep, so it was an easy decision. In fact, these seats are so popular almost every one is sold on every flight. We are currently looking at what it will mean to double the number of flat bed seats available on our flights. The decision to introduce the world's most affordable flat bed seat was one of the best decisions we ever made, and I believe it really sets us apart from anyone else. It provides extreme value for money.

Aircraft Utilization

Since the X model focused on achieving scale instead of a differentiated mix between premium and economy, a higher than typical aircraft utilization was required to break even.[7] In 2010, on average, each of X's aircraft was in the air for 16 hours every day versus the industry average of 11 hours per day.[8] In order to achieve this kind of utilization, the airline had to deviate from fixed flight departure and arrival times. These times changed from day to day—an absolute novelty in the industry. For example, if on Mondays the departure time for a specific destination was 2:00 p.m. it could be 11:00 a.m. on Tuesdays and then 9:00 p.m. on Wednesdays. While this was considered contrary to industry norms, there was evidence many passengers only cared about their individual flight timings, and not a regular daily schedule. X's model proved if the price was low enough, even very early morning or late night departures would be popular with passengers.

This utilization model also helped X reduce its operating and capital costs. In airline finance, interest payments are allocated on a per flight basis and with more flights per

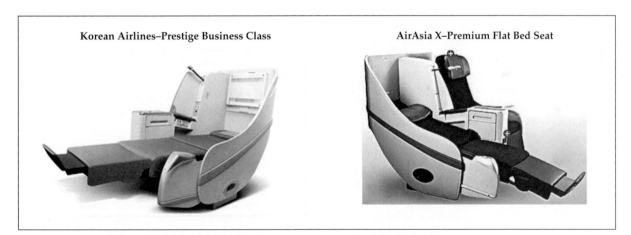

Korean Airlines–Prestige Business Class   **AirAsia X–Premium Flat Bed Seat**

Exhibit 3   Typical Business Class Seat Versus Airasia X Premium Seat

Source: Company files

day for the same aircraft than its competitors would fly, X was able to decrease the overall interest and financing period. Debt was deferred or spread out over more flights, which significantly reduced the fixed operating costs of X.

A La Carte In-Flight Experience

"Try ordering more than one meal the next time you fly Singapore Airlines. You can't," explained Wright. "On any AirAsia X flight you can eat as much as you want—that is until we have nothing left to sell to you." To lower costs while generating additional revenue from onboard services, X's management decided all food and beverages were to be booked separately from the ticket. A reduced price pre-booking option was implemented to encourage sales. However, nearly 50 per cent of all food was purchased inflight despite the pre-booking option.

Additionally, a large selection of AirAsia branded merchandise and duty free goods were carried on board for sale. Traditionally on most budget airlines, inflight entertainment was not offered. X decided to offer individual inflight entertainment for a fee in all seat backs on all flights. The seatback option later evolved into a portable media player offered on selected flights. Cabin crews doubled as product sales people, and despite having significantly fewer flight attendants per flight compared to full service carriers, surveys showed X's cabin crews provided some of the swiftest and friendliest service in the industry. X put special emphasis on training flight crews to be client focused and skilled in selling services and products.

Keep it Simple, Stupid

Initially, the only ticket option available on X was a one-way point-to-point fare. The goal was reduced purchasing complexity. Passengers always knew they would either reach their final destination directly or that they had to handle connections to other flights independently. In December 2010, X launched a limited flight transfer option between a handful of selected X and AirAsia destinations at its hub in Kuala Lumpur. The selection of the routes was strategic and based on a combination of passenger demand and connecting times no greater than six hours.

Another early decision was to postpone the implementation of a reward program in order to keep the booking process and pricing model simple and transparent to the clients. X never charged any online, telephone or personal booking fees. X did not provide refunds after tickets were purchased except under very exceptional circumstances. It was not until December 2010 that "BIG," a low frills frequent flyer program, was launched. In January 2011, the AirAsia Group launched a new option to accept flight bookings up to just four hours prior to departure.

Company Culture

From the very beginning, X aimed to avoid the emergence of corporate hierarchy based on rank, age, gender, or seniority. At the airline's headquarters, all senior executives and department heads worked in one large open office space without any partition walls or closed meeting rooms. This created the same unpretentious and casual atmosphere one could experience when flying on one of X's aircrafts. Everybody was addressed by first name, even the CEO. All employees were referred to officially as "All Stars."

Azran Osman-Rani explained: "We are probably the only airline in the world where the chief pilot sits right next to the chief engineer, and the head of marketing." It was Osman-Rani's vision to foster a corporate culture where any member of the company could openly see and approach any colleague. He also instilled a healthy "work hard—play harder" mentality that appeared to encourage each employee to show up extremely dedicated every day. "For us at X, culture eats strategy for lunch," stated Osman-Rani. These approaches were previously unheard of in Malaysia, a country where the business culture is based on old traditions.

Early Success: Why X Survived When Others Failed

The global financial crisis of 2008 caused a real shakeout in the airline industry generally, including among low cost carriers. But throughout this period, X thrived relative to the industry. X enjoyed a significant advantage over other low cost long haul carriers because it could draw on the resources of its parent company, AirAsia. Senthil Balan, director of route and network planning at X, explained:

> Our website was up and running from day one. Right from the beginning we had cockpit, cabin, and maintenance crews with considerable budget airline experience in place. Operationally, we could go to the well and draw upon resources to provide catering, fuel, and legal advice without the usual inefficiencies that start-ups have to battle with. When I first joined, there was already a team of people doing what I was going to be doing, so it made things easier during the first few months.

Maintaining Low Costs at KL

At its home base in Kuala Lumpur, AirAsia faced a dilemma. Kuala Lumpur International Airport (KLIA) had one of the most modern and beautiful terminals in the world, but it also had high gate fees compared to other regional airports. AirAsia, with strong local political support, was allowed to construct AirAsia's own low cost carrier terminal (LCCT). The building housed the group's headquarters and handled all of its flight operations.[9] The LCCT was designed to handle 10 million passengers a year. However, for 2011, the projections were an estimated 18 million passengers, more than the entire yearly airport traffic of Honolulu, Hawaii, United States, Auckland, New Zealand or Vienna, Austria.[10]

Leveraging the Feeder Network and Scaling the Model

X benefitted from the connectivity and passenger feed of the AirAsia network to fill its larger aircraft. Unlike its Hong Kong based low cost competitor Oasis, which only served the Hong Kong to London and Hong Kong to Vancouver routes, X had access to hundreds of feeder flights to and from 78 destinations. Due to the global financial crisis, Oasis ceased operations in April 2008.[11]

AirAsia targeted a customer demographic overlooked by traditional airlines and even by other budget carriers. Competitors, including MaxJet and EOS Airlines from the United States and Oasis from Hong Kong, fought for budget travelers from the middle and upper middle class. X deliberately targeted new travelers with less disposable income from the economic base of the pyramid instead. Those new customers previously either chose other means of transportation, including busses and trains, or they did not travel at all. Osman-Rani commented: "Obviously flying is still a luxury for many people, but our mission is bringing down the fares so low, that hopefully more people than ever before can experience the freedom of long distance travel."

Training and Development

AirAsia was very focused on the low cost model and to differentiate itself from the traditional airline model it established its own training academy for new pilots, engineers and cabin crews. The goal was to develop a specific AirAsia mindset. Although many pilots joined the company with thousands of hours of flight experience accumulated at other airlines, most members of the cabin crews were new to the airline industry. X benefited from the existing infrastructure and the operating model alignment already put in place by AirAsia.

Sales Outlets

Together with AirAsia, X sold its tickets primarily through its website, AirAsia.com. To reduce costs, X strived for 100 per cent online sales. However, the operating regions with the most promising potential had low but steadily growing Internet penetrations. The company was also exploring the sales of tickets by cell phone. Despite the additional costs, AirAsia Group operated ticket offices, ticket kiosk machines, and sales counters at each airport. The group also operated several call centers throughout the world. Additionally, particularly in countries such as Australia, where travel agents were still the preferred choice for ticketing, X had agreements with many local travel agencies.

Traditional and Nontraditional Marketing

Most global companies used social media to varying degrees and for different purposes. AirAsia was so committed to social media that, in June, 2010, they acquired KoolRed, their own social networking platform. KoolRed[12] was essentially the Asian equivalent of Facebook but with a greater focus on travel related content. Other airlines mainly used social media sites as customer feedback tools and disgruntled passengers overly frequented these sites. Often these sites were heavily moderated, creating an even more hostile reaction. This was no exception for AirAsia. However, AirAsia allowed all content, no matter its viewpoint. As a result, within the global airline industry, only U.S. based Southwest Airlines had more *friends* following an airline. With the exception of Australia, all social media activities were managed centrally from Malaysia. In late 2010, the company decided the U.K., France, India, South Korea, Japan and New Zealand would begin managing social media platforms locally in order to achieve closer and more effective customer communication. X India for example was working to penetrate the massive mobile phone messaging platform.

AirAsia.com had approximately one million individual visitors every day. In addition, management was well aware of the growing e-commerce acceptance rate among Asian consumers. In 2011, AirAsia.com had evolved into a huge portal for online business in Asia. In addition to airline tickets, AirAsia sold concert tickets, travel insurance, hotel rooms, vacation packages, and even everyday merchandise such as shoes and handbags. Osman-Rani hoped X would be able to capture the trickle down effect and increase ancillary sales. One important tactic in achieving these goals was the localization of the website. AirAsia.com was designed for 24 countries in nine languages although X served only 10 different countries at the time. In comparison, the website for the world's largest airline, U.S. based United Airlines, was designed for 30 countries utilizing 11 different languages.

Traditional and Non-traditional marketing

Even though Internet penetration and e-commerce were growing rapidly throughout Asia, print media were still important for raising brand awareness and for communicating deals in all of X's markets. Hence, X spent approximately 30 per cent of its communication budget on ads in prominent daily and weekly newspapers. In addition, X organized dozens of free journalist familiarization trips every year. The goal of these trips was to generate favorable reviews from the participants to be published in specific travel journals for budget backpackers, students, surfers, outdoor and shopping enthusiasts.

Full Service Airlines do it Differently = Yield Factor Versus Load Factor

Budget airlines typically used revenue management differently than full service airlines. A full service airline would seek to create a proprietary mix of profit margin per seat (yield factor) in combination with a utilization factor following the numbers of seats sold (load factor) that would be calculated based on complicated algorithms and real time ticket price adjustments for each individual flight. Prices for the different seating categories would vary based on the targeted passenger mix per destination and the current demand. For example, Singapore Airlines offered a traditional three-tier service consisting of a mix of first, business, and economy class on a single airplane. Singapore Airlines over the years had developed strong capabilities around the full service concept, which resulted in consistent rankings among the top airlines in this category in the world. The airline also structured all its activities and resources around this differentiation model. Singapore Airlines developed even more differentiated offerings including a business class only service to Los Angeles. This passenger segment was underserved on this particular route and provided

extremely high yield factors and lower load factor break-even points. Full service airlines relied on higher yields rather than higher load factors to generate profits.[13]

Budget airlines, however, did not typically emphasize profit margins per seat (yield factor), instead they concentrated on seats sold (load factor). The conventional assumption in the airline industry was that the only way to generate higher loads would be to sell seats at a lower price point. A strong strategic focus was put on cost savings. In order to avoid the cost trap, full service airlines would compete based on differentiation along yield factor generating value added activities. This naturally put the focus on the more affluent customer segments. The challenge for budget airlines, however, was that direct costs were largely dependent on external factors including fuel prices, maintenance costs, airport landing and terminal fees. These direct costs were extremely difficult to influence and created a much higher vulnerability for budget airlines since those additional costs could often not easily be transferred to customers. If ticket prices were too high, leisure travelers would simply not fly or migrate to full service airlines since price gaps would be lower during these periods.

Similar to other budget airlines, X modeled the break-even point for each flight on a combined *fixed cost-direct cost* mix and then established the relevant break-even fare. During the active sales process, a dynamic model was used following a complicated demand estimation model. This dynamic model was critical especially considering the low margins approach. Budget airlines often cut prices just to fill seats believing some revenue was better than no revenue. This tactic was also at the core of X's sales strategy. Using this approach since its inception, X experienced some months when routes had high load factors, but created in less than the budgeted revenues due to low yields.

Since X flew long distances competing head to head with full service airlines, the adoption of the pure low cost model was considered insufficient. Sensing this alignment issue, Wright, as the manager for revenue management, convinced Osman-Rani to recruit a seasoned executive with extensive airline industry revenue management experience in order to close this expertise gap. The newly established revenue management team began operating in December 2010. Wright requested a thorough analysis of X's revenue model, passenger profile and passenger needs as the team's first deliverable.

X's Passenger Profile

At the end of 2010, approximately 60 per cent of X's passengers were Malaysian nationals. The remaining 40 per cent were a combination of customers either originating from an X destination or transferring to or from an AirAsia or other airline's flight in Kuala Lumpur. One of the initial motivations behind launching X was to provide an extremely affordable intercontinental air travel alternative for less affluent Malaysian residents. As X grew, it became increasingly more important to cater to a broader passenger segment across different needs categories. The challenge was to make these adjustments without negatively affecting the less affluent Malaysian passenger base. The special attention paid to the latter passenger base continued to drive operational initiatives such as food menus, merchandise offerings and the marketing and sales tools, including the way technology was utilized.

A Big Sale = Website Crash and Hours on Hold

X was known for launching new routes at very low fares. For example, the Kuala Lumpur to Delhi route was launched for only US$53, London, U.K. to Kuala Lumpur for US$157, and Tokyo to Kuala Lumpur for US$58. These were all-inclusive fares, a hallmark of X. These low fares resulted in huge sales during the initial 24 to 72 hours of ticketing. When AirAsia or X had a massive fare sale, it was always designed to surprise consumers and influence them to purchase the low priced fares immediately. However, AirAsia.com did not have the bandwidth and server infrastructure to handle the sudden spike in web traffic on promotional sales days. Peak website traffic could easily top one million visitors per hour and the online booking system occasionally crashed. This led customers to then contact an AirAsia callcenter, which was equally overloaded.

While X believed the massive web traffic generated by AirAsia's sales was great for the company, it did prevent significant numbers of customers booking tickets from receiving services for already booked flights. Once, during a massive sales period for AirAsia, an already ticketed X passenger in Australia calling to confirm some unrelated travel details sat on hold, at the expense of X, for nearly seven hours before he could reach a customer service representative. The risk was more affluent travelers in particular, or those who could also fly on full service airlines, would eventually not return for future travels because of the hassle. To help mitigate the problem, X established its own dedicated call centre in August of 2010. This new X call centre could handle Korean, Japanese and French language inquiries, something AirAsia's other call center could not handle. However, X still had to rely on the current capabilities and limitations of the general AirAsia.com website. In November 2010, when tickets to Paris went on sale, AirAsia.com had issues processing credit cards from the EU for the first six hours, although over 30,000 tickets were sold within the first 36 hours.

No-shows lead to onboard wastage

When fares were at their lowest, X's customers—particularly those in Malaysia—would purchase a ticket for travel even when the trip was several months away. They would then work harder and save on other expenditures to earn enough money to cover the other trip related expenses. The frenzy to secure cheap tickets temporarily made some travelers ignore the realities of foreign travel. The biggest problem was securing a visa for the destination country. Especially for Malaysian nationals, it can be difficult or very costly to obtain a visa for countries in Europe, North America or even Japan. When Malaysian passengers could not secure a visa by the date of departure, they could not fly. Unaware of this, X would purchase and upload meals and merchandise for sale to these passengers. Additionally, the weight and balance of the airplane and loading calculations of the cargo could be altered when a significant number of passengers were not seated as planned. X was successfully fulfilling its mission statement—to allow "everyone to fly." Unfortunately X also experienced challenges when serving passengers who had never flown before. Wright explained:

> We have seen it most when a passenger arrives at check-in a few hours prior to departure and they don't have a visa to enter the country they are flying to. We serve passengers from countries where passport penetration can be very low, and sometimes they are not aware of the existence of visas. We try our best to educate our passengers the best we can before they purchase their tickets, but it can be difficult, and we are in no way involved with issuing visas for any country. Our policy is clearly stated that we do not provide refunds, but unfortunately some of our passengers expect that and this has become one of the challenges of serving a historically underserved market.

Where is AirAsia X . . . . in Asia!

During one of the first meetings of X managers in 2007, a map of the world was placed on a table. A circle that represented the operationally optimal flying time of eight hours from Kuala Lumpur was drawn on the map, and it became clear X would only be limited by the number of planes in its fleet, and not by a lack of attractive and viable destinations.

After 2008, with much of the developed world dealing with the global financial crisis, most of Asia was enjoying strong economic growth. The middle classes of highly populated countries such as China, India, Indonesia, Vietnam, the Philippines and Thailand were now more and more able to afford air travel. In addition, traveling to foreign countries was one of the most desired items on the wish list of these demographics. The explosive growth of the entire AirAsia Group could be partly attributed to the fact that Kuala Lumpur was in a very central location in relation to the world's most populated and fastest developing economies. Malaysia was a very popular tourist destination for travelers from Iran, Saudi Arabia and much of the Middle East due to a shared Islamic heritage and the lack of visa requirements for travelers from these countries.

Constraints of Expansion

For X, network expansion was no small task. Two essential elements were required to serve new destinations—first, an airplane, and second, bi-lateral landing and operating rights. The list price for a new Airbus A330 aircraft was US$200 million. By leveraging the successful track record of AirAsia, and finding investors who believed in the potential of the low cost long haul model, X was able to steadily expand its fleet of wide body aircraft from only one in 2007 to 11 in 2011. In addition to the capital expenditure, overcoming the regulatory hurdles for bilateral landing rights was even more difficult. All local governments would try to protect their own home country airlines first, before allowing outside competition, and Malaysia was no exception. X's expansion, however, was limited at times primarily by the Malaysian government, which was reluctant to approve routes that would provide stiff competition to the state owned Malaysian Airlines.

Viability of New Destinations

To fit the competitive model of high load factors, it was critically important for X to select the destinations providing the highest probability of sustained success. Director of route and network planning Senthil Balan explained:

> There are a hundred different things we look at, however, there are four basic criteria that must be satisfied; first, is the destination appealing both from a Malaysian traveler perspective as well as from the entire AirAsia network perspective; second, what are the historical passenger numbers between the two areas as well as the traffic breakdown by direction of travel? Either must be large enough fro us to enter the market. Third, the propensity to travel, both on the route in question as well as the overall propensity to travel by the local population at either end of the flight;

> and fourth, what is the commitment of support, both economic incentives and marketing contribution, that will be provided by the destination's tourism organization and airport authority?

Wright added: "For example in less than one week, X sold over 80,000 seats between Kuala Lumpur and Seoul—all this for a route that was only anticipated to generate 100,000 seats annually."

X also pursued alternative opportunities. For example, in November 2010, X dedicated one of its planes to a charter operation used to ferry religious pilgrims from different Asian countries and the Middle East to and from Saudi Arabia before, during and after the annual pilgrimage to Mecca. While this charter evolved into an excellent and unplanned source of revenue, it was only temporary. On the other hand, it also served as an excellent exploratory trial for some new routes. In November 2010, X's eleventh aircraft—a brand new Airbus A330—was to be delivered to help launch the upcoming Seoul, South Korea and Tokyo, Japan routes scheduled for a December 2010 launch. Balan knew after the charter ended and all of the routine yearly maintenance checks were completed, he would have essentially one spare aircraft available to launch a new route. Balan and his staff analyzed numerous destinations including Saudi Arabia, Nepal, Japan, Australia, and Europe against the four factors previously outlined. Due to the lack of approval by the Malaysian government, none of these destinations could be realized. At this point, facing a deadline to launch the new route in order to avoid aircraft underutilization, Balan began to explore more deeply a hunch he had been having for some time.

Growing up in New Zealand, Balan was very familiar with the many tourist attractions New Zealand could offer to Asian travelers. He was keenly aware of the recent success Singapore Airlines enjoyed by flying non-stop from nearby Singapore to both Auckland on the north island, and Christchurch on the south Island.

Balan approached Wright and floated the idea of launching a service to Christchurch. Wright suspected the route would do well given the allure of the south island's natural beauty, and the fact Singapore Airlines sold out most of its flights between Singapore and Christchurch at a price close to two to three times what X would charge. Wright offered to make a few phone calls to his tourism contacts in New Zealand, and scheduled a meeting in Kuala Lumpur with the Christchurch Airport Authority. Balan easily matched Kuala Lumpur and Christchurch against all of his criteria, while his team found ways to make the break-even fare and the utilization of the aircraft fit into the overall route network.

Balan and his team had to then convince X's majority shareholder—Tony Fernandes—Christchurch was the best next destination. During the following two weeks, Balan met periodically with Fernandes to keep him briefed while the Christchurch Airport Authority officials traveled to Kuala Lumpur and offered their plan to ensure sustainable success of the route. The airport partnered with local and national tourism and economic development entities to present a package of incentives, commitments, and contributions for an initial five-year period to demonstrate their faith in the viability of the route.[14]

Fernandes gave Balan approval. The Kuala Lumpur to Christchurch flight was approximately 11 hours in duration and the initial launch fare was set at NZ$99 (US$75). The route was announced on December 1, 2010, with the typical X splashy advertising burst (see Exhibit 4), and the first flight was scheduled for April 1, 2011. On December 8, 2010, one week after tickets went on sale, Wright excitedly stated, "Within six hours 17,000 tickets had been sold for Christchurch, and nearly 44,000 within the first three days. That is the equivalent of every seat on every flight for more than seven months. It feels great when everything comes together like this."

Growing Revenue, Maintaining Low Ticket Price

The challenge for X and other low cost airlines was increasing revenues while still maintaining a lower priced ticket than its competitors. Unlike full service airlines such as American Airlines or Lufthansa Airlines, with packaged service offerings included in their ticket prices, AirAsia X did not believe the best or only time to generate revenue from a passenger was at the time of booking. X built its revenue model on the notion that passengers were willing to spend money throughout the entire travel experience. Onboard food and beverages, cabin amenities such as pillows and blankets, and digital media players with music, games and movies were marketed aggressively. Cabin crews were trained in customer service and incentivized to push sales. In addition to the usual duty-free items like alcohol, tobacco, chocolate and fashion products, X also sold travel related merchandise such as travel adapters, train and bus tickets, prepaid phone cards, scarves and hats and scale models of their aircraft. X's onboard sales per passenger were more than three times the amount Singapore Airlines generated.

Fees and Meals

A survey of the global airline industry in early 2011 pointed to the widespread adoption of fees for checked baggage. X was no exception to the trend. In 2010, approximately 8 per cent of overall revenue came from checked baggage fees. X provided a discount for prepaid baggage compared to at check-in fees. Approximately 95 per cent of all checked bags were pre-paid.

Passengers had the option of pre-booking a hot meal that came with a small bottle of mineral water. The only other pre-booked option was a comfort kit, which included an inflatable travel pillow, an eye mask and a blanket. In September 2010, X began to manage the flight cabin more strategically as a retail space and started to analyze onboard product offerings. Wright stated:

> If we are going to pay a cost to procure and upload items to sell on each flight, we need to make sure we are only loading those items that really do sell and sell well. Unlike full service airlines where there is one meal item for each passenger on board, we need to be very conscious of our wastage and unsold inventory. We think the retail mindset of viewing the cabin more like shelf space, and what sells best and where and when do we place it applies to us. We have to break away from the traditional industry norms. Ideally we are aiming to strike a better balance between offering more pre-booked options and drilling down to what really sells best onboard to maximize our ancillary revenue.

Exhibit 4   Airasia X Advertisements

Source: Company files

Game Changers

When X introduced the world's first flat bed seat on a budget airline in 2009, the conventional airline industry was bewildered.[15] Wright explained:

> Our competitors use the exact same seat in business class as we use, and it costs us a fraction of their costs to fill it and fly it. The concept behind the bold move is actually quite basic. All we are doing is going back to giving long haul travelers what they really want and that is a place to lie down and sleep comfortably without the caviar and champagne. We are always looking to be the first to do things. We consider ourselves game changers. At the beginning, this was strictly prudence and driven by survival instincts. Today it is this spirit driving our strategy. Whether it be to provide entertainment on USB thumb drives to passengers for a fraction of the current costs, or to simply rent them a long lasting battery source to use for their own laptop and media devices, it just makes great business sense to stretch the boundaries.

Flight Transfers

Until December 2010, all X flights were sold as point to point only, and all passengers had to collect their bags, clear customs, and self connect to other flights independently, even within the AirAsia Group's network. This worked well for vacationers, yet it frustrated some travelers accustomed to automatic baggage transfers from their first departure point to their final destination.

With a network that could support several transfer choices in December 2010, X began to sell the option of booking tickets to destinations beyond just their point-to-point hub in Kuala Lumpur. The flight transfer option was priced at the nominal fee of US$3. However the added value of convenience attracted more and more flyers to book tickets on X flights. Wright explained:

> This change was really the first step to add to our original value proposition externally. As our network continues to grow, we envision the day when all passenger segments from backpackers, to families on vacation, to business executives will seek out ways to connect through Kuala Lumpur because of the affordable fares and high frequency of flights offered on our network every day.

The new connecting option was particularly popular on the highly traveled segments between the UK and Australia. While the connecting concept was originally intended to be between different X flights only, AirAsia quickly realized the powerful marketing potential of the idea. In January 2011, the entire AirAsia group network rolled out flight transfers—marketed as "Fly-Thru"—but only on select routes.

Building the Global Brand

In a far-sighted move to improve brand recognition, X chose high profile sport sponsoring as a marketing tool. Osman-Rani stated:

> X's sponsorship of Manchester United started years before the brand flew to and from the UK. It drip-fed into peoples' consciousness to such a degree that when the inaugural service came to London in March 2009 the first plane-load was made up of 28 per cent British citizens, 18 per cent from other EU countries and 7 per cent from Australia. Normally, more than 70 per cent of passengers on a maiden flight are from an airline's home country.[16] Look at the United States. We currently have no tangible plans to launch a flight, but it is definitely one of our long-term target destinations. This was the reason behind the decision to establish a sponsoring agreement with the Oakland Raiders National Football League team in 2009. The idea is that by the time we start a service we have already established solid brand awareness. You've got to think ahead and not follow the crowd.

X also currently sponsored the Lotus Formula One Racing Team as well as the Asian Basketball League.

When X prepared to launch, the decision was made to emphasize a single brand identity among all AirAsia Group companies despite the differing customer demographics for short haul versus long haul flights. This decision created a singular AirAsia brand that was very recognizable and strong in Malaysia and throughout Southeast Asia, but only marginally known in other parts of the world. All but one of X's aircraft were painted with the large AirAsia.com logo.

To the casual observer, it was difficult to distinguish AirAsia from X with the exception of X's much larger airplanes. The decision to create a public perception as one seamless airline brought both its share of advantages and challenges to X,[17] The AirAsia brand was positioned as fun, hip and affordable, and considered to be one of the most recognizable brands in Southeast Asia. The distinctive celebrity personalities of both AirAsia CEO Tony Fernandes and X CEO Azran Osman-Rani added significant value to each brand.

For passengers outside of Southeast Asia, however, it could be confusing to visit AirAsia.com and to see the many promotional ads for cheap flights from Kuala Lumpur to Phuket, while trying to find their own departure airports. On the other hand, some passengers that specifically sought out the ultra low fares for intra-Asia flights were surprised to learn that X flew to destinations outside of Asia.

A pointed example of the complexities that exist in maintaining one singular brand, but two different operational models was the shared e-mail database of each company's best customers. Open for anyone to join, a large database of tens of thousands of e-mail addresses was shared between AirAsia and X to publicize new items and special fare sales. Since the sister company AirAsia relied on filling as many seats as possible on a much shorter turnaround basis, they routinely—as often as three times a week—sent blast e-mails with new fare promotions.

X employees observed their friends telling others: "Don't worry, they are always going to have a sale, so there is no rush to buy." From the X point of view, this constant barrage of 'buy now' e-mails diluted the urgency of the promotional long haul fares and actually worked to gradually alienate the existing X customer base. In the two-month period of September through October 2010, the rate at which these e-mails were even opened by recipients dropped from 25 per cent to 15 per cent.

Distinctive Advertising

Similar to AirAsia, X's advertising was very explicit and often sarcastic or humorous in nature[18]. Wright commented:

We were brainstorming how best to market our flat bed seats in Australia, where sarcastic ads are just part of the culture when one of our team members came up with "Our Premium seats are a Flat – Out – Lie. Trust Us." I instantly loved it. It's true, but also slightly edgy— just enough for the message to stick. For us, attracting attention is usually best accomplished by doing what everyone else won't. There are so many professional surf tours now around the globe, so we decided to do the exact opposite. We came up with the "No-Pro Tour." Now any amateur surfers can post videos of themselves to our site and if the video is voted most popular by the website audience, they'll win flights on X to some of the world's best surf destinations. This has been a great way to get a viral response to a customer segment that fits perfectly with our business model.

Wright continued:

Most companies only joke about some of the things that we seriously consider and often times do. When we were planning the launch party for our Christchurch route, we considered releasing 99 New Zealand sheep, painted red and with an X logo shaved into the wool into the city square to powerfully signify the NZ$99 fare. We began making plans for our founder, Tony Fernandes, to travel to Antarctica and plant an X flag at the pole. With so many old and boring airline messages out there today, we have to find more and more creative ways to get our message around. Not every message is fun and games,

but there is a lot of that in all we do. We recently made three television commercials for CNN targeting seasoned business travelers. Our most effective spot showcased a guy drenched by his water bottle because he forgot he was seated in one of our flat bed seats when he sat back.

Long Haul versus Short Haul and the Challenge of a Single Brand

With only a handful of exceptions, all of the world's low cost airlines flew what was known as short haul routes no longer than five hours in duration. Five hours, however, is long enough to travel between Los Angeles and New York City, London to Tel Aviv, Sydney to Perth, or Lima to São Paulo. X's position as a long haul carrier meant all its flights were at least five hours in duration with the longest non-stop routes being more than 13 hours. On the surface, one might assume simply doubling the distance of a flight would not alter passenger psychographics or demographics, however, that was not the case.

Traditionally, airlines focused on elevating their brand by providing a super premium level of comfort, more amenities and better service on their longest flights. Over the decades, long haul travelers had come to expect this when flying longer distances. At its inception, X's long haul flying experience did not include a first or business class cabin, complimentary inflight entertainment, or complimentary food and beverage, or even reclining seats. Reclining seats were added later mainly for health and minimal comfort related reasons and with no impact on loads. However, X also tried to target the more comfort-seeking passengers as well. According to Wright:

Unfortunately, there are business travelers out there that could potentially fly with us on our international trunk routes and book our flat bed seats, but they only know us as AirAsia. They don't understand that X is a separate airline, and they don't know that we offer a more comfortable flying experience. Our unified marketing approach does not really help us in this regard.

For shorter flights, seasoned fliers were more willing to do without amenities if the price was right, but the same customer demographic expected a different comfort level on long haul flights. Income disparity between passengers was not as much a factor on short haul as on long haul. Osman-Rani stated:

When Southwest in the United States flies between Houston and Dallas for US$49, you will have young and old, rich and poor on every flight. Not so with the longer flights. And that is where we fit into the marketplace, we are the brand that is literally turning dreams into reality for so many people and opening up the skies to everyone.

In addition to the differences in perceived in-flight comfort, X deviated from the short haul models because it was not as easy to capture the last minute passenger. Particularly due to the Internet and social media, last minute fares had become an extremely viable tool to fill airline seats. According to Wright:

> The reality is that the decision process to buy a one-hour long domestic flight and the decision process to buy an eight-hour intercontinental flight requiring passports and visas are drastically different. Most people sitting in our seats have been thinking about and planning their trip for weeks if not months in advance. I think eventually, the strength of the X brand needs to be more about our network and frequency and value for money, than it needs to be about the occasional ridiculously low promotional fare.

Can a Glocal Focus Work: Being Global and Malaysian

X was a company of just over 1,000 employees, 99 per cent of which were Malaysian nationals. CEO Azran Osman-Rani and his upper management team all had foreign education, work, or living experiences. However, much of the rest of the team had never been exposed to international business practices. In early 2011, 60 per cent of X's passengers were Malaysians, though this ratio was about to shift with the addition of new routes. Balan commented: "We have never really had people with an outsider's viewpoint, and I think that will be a huge asset for us as we become more diverse and grow." Supporting this position, Osman-Rani stated:

> We expect to have to make alterations to our business model as we expand to serve new and different markets, and that includes our workforce. At the same time, it is critical to remain disciplined in keeping our costs low, so we can adapt and change. We can't afford to hire seasoned highly paid airline executives. It will disturb our culture.

Looking Ahead: A Global IPO and Other Priorities

As of early 2011, all advertising and media purchases were placed through local media service agencies located in the target markets. X headquarters staff coordinated the advertising activities for 12 countries and 15 cities, while remote teams in Australia and the United Kingdom managed their respective country's advertising independently. The problem was Wright did not have one consolidated report outlining

the global marketing expenditures. He commented: "We are great at being nimble and addressing each local market's needs, but we can do a much better job if we integrate our adverting activities globally. We could be more cost-effective and reduce the potential risk of misalignments."

Revenue Management: Plan Versus React

One of the greatest challenges for X was matching their advertising activities to their revenue management activities. Wright explained:

> There have been times in our history that the day the advertisement came out the fare advertised had already been sold out. While that's not perfect, it's much better than where we find ourselves often, and that is to always be reacting to this week's unsold ticket numbers. We are reaching a scale now that to sell off any seat at a ridiculous fare just to fill it will not enhance our brand value in the long term. We need to start leveraging our brand a little more than our fares.

In November 2010, while profitable for the year and with 85 per cent of all remaining seats already sold, X was 50 million Malaysian ringgit or US$15 million short of its projected revenue for the year. Wright met with his revenue management team to devise a strategy to meet the year-end target. Meeting the target was extremely important to Osman-Rani as well; he wanted to confidently stand in front of the board of directors and demonstrate the airline was ready for an IPO. "Without proving we can meet our budgets, it will become difficult to convince investors we know what we are doing and that we are a promising investment," explained Wright. X met their 2010 budgeted revenues.

From its inception, all major items acquired by the company were expensed. At the time of the operational split from AirAsia in August, 2010, Osman-Rani recruited a new CFO and gave her authority to overhaul anything and everything to get set for the future IPO.[19] One of the first initiatives she undertook was to establish an inventory system that utilized amortization and depreciation in order to improve financial ratios. At the same time, Osman-Rani decided that quality control of in-flight meals and merchandise could best be managed by taking the procurement duties away from AirAsia and external suppliers. He created an in-house position dedicated to quality management. From a technology perspective, X began to investigate a new handheld inventory tracking system to be used in flight by cabin crews. The new tool would allow X to be more like a retailer and digitally track inventories and wastage real time. They could also find merchandise more easily across different carts on one aircraft. This system helped to stock up on merchandise at the airport more quickly and effectively.

Making Nice: Balancing Domestic Political Relationships

Shortly after the inception of AirAsia X, the Malaysian Transport Ministry was forced into a love-hate relationship with the airline. The success of X helped the Malaysian economy, but some within the government believed this happened at the expense of the national airline—Malaysian Airlines (MAS). The relationship struggles between X and the Malaysian government could be best illustrated by the clash over the rights to fly between Kuala Lumpur and Sydney, Australia. Although the Australian government indicated it would allow X to fly to Sydney, the Malaysian government steadfastly defended state owned Malaysian Airlines' monopoly on the route and did not grant X permission to fly. X pushed back publicly in September 2010 by painting one of their airplanes with a message asking to open up the skies to Sydney. In October 2010, sister company AirAsia overtook Malaysian Airlines' market capitalization for the first time and became the country's largest airline. Within a week, X's management was summoned to meet with the Ministry of Transport and flatly told X would not be flying to Sydney in the foreseeable future.

For X, potentially the single most limiting factor to growth of their business was the Malaysian government's protectionist stance in favor of Malaysian Airlines. While X was granted permission to launch many new routes from Kuala Lumpur, Malaysian Airlines did not serve any of those routes. In early 2011, the Ministry of Transport worked with X to establish the twenty most vital air routes for the Malaysian economy, and once that list was finalized, hopefully a plan to share equal rights along with Malaysian Airlines to serve those routes could be established.

There was a significant amount of public and government pressure to list X on the Kuala Lumpur Stock Exchange (KLSE) for its upcoming IPO. However, from X's perspective there were concerns the company could be caught in a no-win situation if they listed on the KLSE. There was fear that the success of the IPO could be greatly reduced due to the little value it possessed for those Malaysian investors already holding shares of AirAsia. If X chose to list in Hong Kong or New York instead, the Malaysian government could further slow down some of X's expansion plans, including continuing to prohibit X from getting the approvals to fly to certain foreign destinations. X's IPO was scheduled for late 2011 or early 2012.

Conclusions

With more than 1,000 employees of its own, a core challenge for X was to maintain its entrepreneurial and flexible culture that had attracted some of Malaysia's best and brightest. Since its inception, X deliberately maintained a bold culture, using adjectives that began with X such as "Xcited, Xcellence, X-Rated, Xtc." Compared with AirAsia, X was a more relaxed and open environment, and enjoyed a much lower employee attrition rate. There were concerns that, with the planned growth and internationalization of the organization, this culture could get lost. In a corporate video made for new hires, Osman-Rani invited all of his team members to focus on maintaining the "X-factor" as their top priority in whatever they did while the company moved towards the IPO. This emphasis on culture might prove a key differentiator as the market became more crowded. Projected growth figures of 56 per cent by 2014 for air travel in the wider Asian market were stimulating fleet and route expansion across the region.[20] Challenges to both AirAsia and AirAsia X were multiplying, both from rival low cost operators such as the Philippines' Cebu Pacific and Indonesia's Lion Air, as well as from established full service carriers like Thai Airways and Japan's All Nippon Airlines (ANA).

In May 2011, X's IPO plans appeared to receive a boost when Singapore Airlines announced their intention to launch a long haul budget carrier. This move by one of the industry's preeminent players gave credibility to X's business model and growth targets. As X's CEO Azran Osman-Rani commented, "The plans will definitely help us with our IPO and give us credibility—there is a market for running a long haul low cost airline."[21]

Even so, challenges and questions remained in the run up to an IPO and beyond. Despite Osman-Rani's upbeat assessment, the market entry of an operationally efficient, globally respected airline like Singapore Airlines put increased pressure on X to list quickly and expand rapidly. Would X's first move advantage suffice in the next phase of competition? Could X make money, particularly as the market became more contested? Would their brand and customer value proposition succeed beyond Southeast Asia? In the long term, how viable was a long haul, global cost leadership strategy in the airline industry?

These questions played on the mind of Wright as he eased into his seat and tried to get some sleep on his red eye flight to Australia. The answers would not come easily but they needed to come swiftly if he was to prepare for a successful IPO and build on X's head start in the global long haul, low cost market.

End Notes

1. Within the airline industry flights greater than five hours in duration are referred to as "long haul" flying.
2. www.airasia.com/my/en/flightinfo/routemap.page?, accessed July 10, 2011.
3. www.skytraxresearch.com/General/ranking.htm, accessed July 10, 2011.
4. www.centreforaviation.com/news/2009/11/18/lcc-challenges-hybridisation-long-haul-low-cost-being-stuck-in-the-middle-and-consolidation/page1, accessed July 10, 2011.
5. www.flightglobal.com/articles/2010/04/21/340855/interview-air-arabia-chief-executive-adel-ali.html, accessed May 13, 2011.
6. http://boardingarea.com/blogs/onemileatatime/2010/12/27/a-note-about-premium-cabins-and-becoming-jaded/, accessed July 15, 2011.
7. http://web.mit.edu/airlinedata/www/Res_Glossary.html, accessed July 10, 2011.
8. Jens Flottau, "Airline Profits Will Get Pinched In 2011," *Aviation Week*, December 17, 2010.
9. http://lcct.klia.com.my/, accessed July 10, 2011.
10. Airport Council International rankings 2009, accessed July 10, 2011.
11. www.oasishongkong.com/, accessed May 31, 2011.
12. www.koolred.com/, accessed July 10, 2011.
13. www.airlearn.net/images/UVa-Pricing-Jan09.pdf, accessed July 10, 2011.
14. www.travelio.net/airasia-x-deal.html.
15. www.centreforaviation.com/news/2010/06/24/airasia-x-becomes-first-lcc-offer-low-cost-flatbed-seats-as-expansion-rolls-on/page1, accessed July 10, 2011.
16. Pip Brooking, "AirAsia X: Using Sponsorship to Build a Brand/Interview/M&M," *M&M Global-International Media & Marketing News & Analysis*, October 11, 2010, www.mandmglobal.com/global-accounts/activity/11-10-10/airasia-x-using-sponsorship-to-build-a-brand.aspx, accessed January 20, 2011.
17. http://blog.airasia.com/index.php/surfing, accessed July 10, 2011.
18. http://adsoftheworld.com/media/print/air_asia_x_phuket_ill_go?size=_original, accessed July 10, 2011.
19. www.businessweek.com/ap/financialnews/D9G6V0QG0.htm, accessed July 10, 2011.
20. Eric Bellman, "Competition takes off in Asia's budget airline market," *The Wall Street Journal*, July 22, 2011.
21. Cited in Jeeva Arulampalam, "AirAsia X IPO gets a boost," *The Star Online*, May 30, 2011.

Case 2-2: Ryanair—The Low Fares Airline: Whither Now?*

"There is only one thing in the world worse than being talked about, and that is not being talked about," declared Lord Charles in Oscar Wilde's novel, *The Picture of Dorian Gray*. This could have been the mantra of budget airline Ryanair, Europe's largest carrier by passenger numbers and market capitalization in 2010. The airline was given to making controversial news, whether it was annoying the Queen of Spain by using her picture without permission in marketing material or announcing plans to charge passengers to use toilets on its flights or engaging in high-profile battles with the European Commission. Ryanair also made news with its achievements, such as winning international awards, like Best Managed Airline, or receiving a 2009 FT-ArcelorMittal Boldness in Business Award in the Drivers of Change category. This award announcement said that Ryanair had "changed the airline business outside North America—driving the way the industry operates through its pricing, the destinations it flies to and the passenger numbers it carries."[1] Ryanair had been the budget airline pioneer in Europe, rigorously following a low-cost strategy. It had enjoyed remarkable growth and in the five years to 2009, was the most profitable airline in the world, according to *Air Transport* magazine.

Despite this apparent success, Ryanair faced issues. The most pressing, shared by all airlines, was an industry that was "structurally sick" and "in intensive care,"[2] with plunging demand in the global economic recession and uncertainty about oil prices. What strategy should Ryanair use to weather this storm? Would the crisis produce a long-term change in industry structure? Could Ryanair take advantage of the situation as it had in the past, by growing when others were cutting back? A predicament of its own making was Ryanair's 29.8 percent shareholding in Aer Lingus, the Irish national carrier, following an abortive takeover attempt. Aer Lingus's flagging share price had necessitated drastic write-downs, which had dragged Ryanair's results into losses in 2009, the first since its flotation 12 years earlier.

Overview of Ryanair

In 2010, Ryanair had 44 bases and 1,200-plus routes across 27 countries, connecting 160 destinations. It operated a fleet of 256 new Boeing 737-800 aircraft with firm orders for a further 64 aircraft to be delivered over the following two years. It employed 8,100-plus people and had carried almost 67 million passengers in 2010, expecting to carry approximately 73.5 million passengers for fiscal 2011.

Ryanair was founded in 1985 by the Tony Ryan family to provide scheduled passenger services between Ireland and the United Kingdom, as an alternative to then-state monopoly airline Aer Lingus. Initially, Ryanair was a full-service conventional airline, with two classes of seating, leasing three different types of aircraft. Despite growth in passenger volumes, by the end of 1990, the company had flown through much turbulence, disposing of five chief executives and accumulating losses of IR£20 million. Its fight to survive in the early 1990s saw the airline transform itself to become Europe's first low-fare, no-frills carrier, built on the model of Southwest Airlines, the successful Texas-based operator. A new management team, led by Michael O'Leary, then a reluctant recruit, was appointed. Ryanair, floated on the Dublin Stock Exchange in 1997, is quoted on the Dublin and London Stock exchanges and on NASDAQ, where it was admitted to the NASDAQ-100 in 2002.

Mixed Fortunes

Mixed Results

Ryanair designated itself as the "World's Favourite Airline" on the basis that, in 2010, IATA ranked it as the world's largest international airline by passenger numbers—despite the fact that it had already been calling itself the world's favorite airline for a number of years. It was now the eighth-largest airline in the world (when the large U.S. carriers' domestic traffic is included). Over the following five years, Ryanair intended to grow to become the second-largest airline in the world, ranked only behind its mentor Southwest.

Releasing Ryanair's 2010 results in June 2010, O'Leary announced, "We can be proud of delivering a 200 percent increase in profits and traffic growth during a global recession when many of our competitors have announced losses or cutbacks, while more have gone bankrupt." Revenues had risen 2 percent to €2,988 million, as fares fell 13 percent to €34.95. Unit costs fell 19 percent due to lower fuel costs and rigorous cost control. Fuel costs declined 29 percent as oil prices fell from $104 to $62 per barrel. Fuel hedging was extended to 90 percent for full year 2011, 50 percent for quarter 1 and 20 percent of quarter 2 of 2012. Airport and handling costs declined by 9 percent, despite price increases at Dublin and Stansted, two of Ryanair's busiest bases. Ancillary sales grew 11 percent to €664 million, slightly lower than traffic growth and constituting 22 percent of total revenues. The balance sheet had strengthened with a cash rise of €535 million to €2.8 billion. According to the airline, currency hedging had locked in the cost of aircraft purchases in 2010–2011.

The full-year 2010 improvement in profit had followed a particularly miserable 2009, when Ryanair plunged to a €180 million loss, as its €144 million operating profit was eradicated by a €222 million write-down of its Aer Lingus shares and an accelerated €51.6 million depreciation charge. Excluding these exceptional charges, underlying profits fell 78 percent from €480.9 million to €105 million. This was due largely to a surge in fuel prices in the first half of fiscal 2009, as Ryanair failed to hedge when oil prices rose to $147 a barrel in July 2008. Then, bowing to shareholder pressure to cover against rocketing prices, it locked in fuel costs at $124 a barrel for 80 percent of its consumption during the third quarter—just as oil prices crashed to a low of $33 a barrel during that period. Passenger numbers rose 15 percent from 50.9 million to 58.5 million. Average fares fell 8 percent to €40. (Ryanair's financial data are given in Exhibits 1a and 1b, and operating data are given in Exhibit 1c.)

Exhibit 1a   Ryanair Consolidated Income Statement

	Year end March 31, 2010	Year end March 31, 2009	Year end March 31, 2008
	€M	€M	€000
Operating revenues			
Scheduled revenues	2,324.5	2,343.9	2,225.7
Ancillary revenues	663.6	598.1	488.1
Total operating revenues—continuing operations	2,988.1	2,942.0	2,713.8
Operating expenses			
Staff costs	(335.0)	(309.3)	(285.3)
Depreciation	(235.4)	(256.1)	(176.0)
Fuel and oil	(893.9)	(1,257.1)	(791.3)
Maintenance, materials, and repairs	(86.0)	(66.8)	(56.7)
Marketing and distribution costs	(144.8)	(12.8)	(17.2)
Aircraft rentals	(95.5)	(78.2)	(72.7)
Route charges	(336.3)	(286.6)	(259.3)
Airport and handling charges	(459.1)	(443.4)	(396.3)
Other	—*	(139.1)	(122.0)
Total operating expenses	**(2,586.0)**	**(2,849.3)**	**(2,176.8)**
Operating profit—continuing operations	402.1	92.6	537.1
Other income / (expenses)			
Finance income	23.5	75.5	83.9
Finance expense	(72.1)	(130.5)	(97.1)
Foreign exchange gain / (losses)	(1.0)	4.4	(5.6)
Loss on impairment of available-for-sale financial asset	(13.5)	(222.5)	(91.6)
Gain on disposal of property, plant and equipment	2.0	—	12.2
Total other income / (expenses)	**(61.1)**	**(273.1)**	**(98.2)**
Profit / (Loss) / before tax	341.0	(180.5)	438.9
Tax on profit / (loss) on ordinary activities	(35.7)	11.3	(48.2)
Profit / (Loss) for the year — all attributable to equity holders of parent	**305.3**	**(169.2)**	**390.7**
Basic earnings per ordinary share (eurocents)	20.68	(11.44)	25.84
Diluted earnings per ordinary share (eurocents)	20.60	(11.44)	25.62
Number of ordinary shares (in 000s)	1,476.4	1,478.5	1,512.0
Number of diluted shares (in 000s)	1,481.7	1,478.5	1,524.9

*Consolidated with Marketing & Distribution in 2010

Source: Ryanair Annual Report 2010.

Exhibit 1b   Ryanair Consolidated Balance Sheet

	March 31, 2010	March 31, 2009
	€M	€M
Non-current assets		
Property, plant, and equipment	4,314.2	3,644.8
Intangible assets	46.8	46.8
Available for sale financial assets	116.2	93.2
Derivative financial instruments	22.8	60.0
Total non-current assets	4,500.0	3,844.8
Current assets		
Inventories	2.5	2.1
Other assets	80.6	91.0
Current tax	—	—
Trade receivables	44.3	41.8
Derivative financial instruments	122.6	130.0
Restricted cash	67.8	291.6
Financial assets: cash > 3 months	1,267.7	403.4
Cash and cash equivalents	1,477.9	1,583.2
Total current assets	3,063.4	2,543.1
Total assets	7,563.4	6,387.9
Current liabilities		
Trade payables	154.0	132.7
Accrued expenses and other liabilities	1,088.2	905.8
Current maturities of debt	265.5	202.9
Current tax	0.9	0.4
Derivative financial instruments	41.0	137.4
Total current liabilities	1,549.6	1,379.2
Non-current liabilities		
Provisions	102.9	72.0
Derivative financial instruments	35.4	54.1
Deferred tax	199.6	155.5
Other creditors	136.6	106.5
Non-current maturities of debt	2,690.7	2,195.5
Total non-current liabilities	3,165.2	2,583.6
Shareholders' equity		
Issued share capital	9.4	9.4
Share premium account	631.9	617.4
Capital redemption reserve	0.5	0.5
Retained earnings	2,083.5	1,777.7
Other reserves	123.3	20.1
Shareholders' equity	2,848.6	2,425.1
Total liabilities and shareholders' equity	7,563.4	6,387.9

Source: Ryanair Annual Report 2010.

Ancillary Revenues

Ryanair provides various ancillary services connected with its airline service, including in-flight beverage, food, and merchandise sales and Internet-related services. Ryanair also distributes accommodation, travel insurance, and car rentals through its Web site. Providing these services through the Internet enables Ryanair to increase sales while reducing unit costs. In 2010, Ryanair's Web site ranked 12th by number of visits for e-tailers in the United Kingdom (behind EasyJet, which ranked 10th). Ancillary

Exhibit 1c Ryanair Selected Operating Data

	2010	2009	2008	2007
Average Yield per Revenue Passenger Mile ("RPM") (€)	0.052	0.060	0.065	0.070
Average Yield per Available Seat Miles ("ASM") (€)	0.043	0.050	0.054	0.059
Average Fuel Cost per U.S. Gallon (€)	1.515	2.351	1.674	1.826
Cost per ASM (CASM) (€)	0.047	0.058	0.051	0.054
Breakeven Load Factor	73%	79%	79%	77%
Operating Margin	13%	5%	20%	21%
Average Booked Passenger Fare (€)	34.95	40.02	43.70	44.10
Ancillary Revenue per Booked Passenger (€)	9.98	10.21	9.58	8.52

Other Data

	2010	2009	2008	2007
Revenue Passengers Booked	66,503,999	58,565,663	50,931,723	42,509,112
Revenue Passenger Miles	44,841	39,202	34,452	26,943
Available Seat Miles	53,470	47,102	41,342	32,043
Booked Passenger Load Factor	82%	81%	82%	82%
Average Length of Passenger Haul (miles)	661	654	662	621
Sectors Flown	427,900	380,915	330,598	272,889
Number of Airports Served	153	143	147	123
Average Daily Flight Hour Utilization (hours)	8.89	9.59	9.87	9.77
Employees at Period End	7,168	6,616	5,920	4,462
Employees per Aircraft	31	36	36	34
Booked Passengers per Employee	9,253	8,852	8,603	9,527

Source: Ryanair Annual Report 2010

services accounted for 22 percent of Ryanair's total operating revenues, compared with 20.3 percent in 2009. However, it might be that ancillary revenue generation could have its limits, as they had, in fact, dropped from €10.20 in 2009 to €9.98 per passenger in 2010.

Ancillary revenue initiatives were constantly being introduced by Ryanair, such as onboard and online gambling and a trial in-flight mobile phone service in 2009. A poll of *Financial Times'* readers had produced a 72 percent negative response to the question, "Should mobile phones be allowed on aircraft?" Among the comments was "Just another reason not to fly Ryanair."[5] However, O'Leary

declared, "If you want a quiet flight, use another airline. Ryanair is noisy, full, and we are always trying to sell you something."[6] In March 2010, despite a promising trial on 50 aircraft, Ryanair announced the suspension of its onboard telephone service due to a failure to reach an agreement with the Swiss provider, OnAir, on a plan to roll out the service to Ryanair's entire fleet.

Ryanair was the first airline to introduce charges for check-in luggage. Virtually all budget airlines have followed suit, as they have with other Ryanair initiatives. It has continued to find ways of charging passengers for services once considered intrinsic to an airline ticket.

Passengers were charged extra for checking in at the airport rather than online (which also incurs a charge), although those with hold luggage did not have the option of checking in online. While avoiding pre-assigned seats, an extra charge procures "priority boarding." Interestingly, Aer Lingus took up a similar idea by enabling passengers to book seats online for a charge of €5.

Some of Ryanair's revenue-generating ideas have provoked controversy—and publicity. One of the most talked about was its intention to charge passengers a £1 charge to use the lavatory by installing a coin slot on its aircraft. While it has not implemented this concept, (it may contravene security rules), the idea generated much publicity. Another idea mooted by Ryanair was a "fat tax" for overweight passengers. (In fact, several U.S. airlines already require obese passengers who spill over into neighboring seats to buy a second seat.) In an online poll of more than 30,000 respondents, the fat tax idea was approved by one in three. However, the airline later announced that it would not implement the surcharge because it could not collect it without disrupting its 25-minute turnarounds and online check-in process. The same online poll, supposedly to generate ideas for additional revenue, also gained 25 percent approval for a €1 levy to use onboard toilet paper with O'Leary's face on it.

Investor Perspectives

Since its flotation in 1996, Ryanair had never declared or paid dividends on its shares. Instead, Ryanair retained its earnings to fund its business operations, including the acquisition of additional aircraft required for entry into new markets, expansion of its existing services, and routine replacements of its fleet. However, thanks to a healthy balance sheet and the suspension of its aircraft-buying program when negotiations with Boeing broke down, the no-dividend policy changed in 2010. The company declared a special €500 million dividend with the possibility of a further similar dividend in 2013. Previously, its healthy cash position had caused the company to seek alternative ways of improving the liquidity and marketability of its stock through a series of share buy-backs of the equivalent of about 1.2 percent of the issued share capital between 2006 and 2009. Ryanair shares reached a high of €6.30 in April 2007 and plummeted to €1.97 in October 2008 as global equity markets were reeling. By mid-2009, the shares were trading in the €3.20 to €3.40 range, with an expected medium term target of €4.20, based on expected earnings and a PE ratio of 13. In mid-2009, its rival EasyJet shares had a PE ratio of 29. Ryanair had often underperformed other budget airline peers on its PE ratio. However, this offered an upside potential for capital gains, according to Davy, the company's stockbrokers.

Ryanair's Operations

O'Leary said, "Any fool can sell low airfares and lose money. The difficult bit is to sell the lowest airfares and make profits. If you don't make profits, you can't lower your airfares or reward your people or invest in new aircraft or take on the really big airlines like BA (British Airways) and Lufthansa."[7] Certainly, Ryanair had stuck closely to the low-cost/low-fares model. Ever-decreasing costs was its theme, as it constantly adapted its model to the European arena and changing conditions. In this respect, Ryanair differed in its application of the Southwest Airlines budget airline prototype and its main European rival, EasyJet, as they were not as frill-cutting. One observer described the difference between EasyJet and Ryanair: "EasyJet, you understand is classy cheap, rather than just plain cheap."[8]

The Ryanair Fleet

Ryanair continued its fleet commonality policy, using Boeing 737 planes, to maintain staff training and aircraft maintenance costs as low as possible. Over the years, it purchased new, more environmentally friendly aircraft, reducing the average age of its aircraft to 3.3 years, among the youngest fleets in Europe. The newer aircraft produced 50 percent less emissions, 45 percent less fuel burn, and 45 percent lower noise emissions per seat. Winglet modification provided better performance and a 2 percent reduction in fleet fuel consumption, a saving the company believed could be improved. Despite larger seat capacity, new aircraft did not require more crew. In 2009, in aircraft buying mode, Ryanair sought to repeat its 2002 coup when it placed aircraft orders at the bottom of the market. However, in late 2009, talks with Boeing for the purchase of 200 aircraft between 2013 and 2015 broke down. Notwithstanding strict adherence to Boeing 737 planes, in an attempt to extract ever greater discounts from Boeing, Ryanair invited Airbus, the European aircraft manufacturer, to enter into preliminary bidding for a multimillion-dollar order for 200-plus short-haul aircraft. However, Airbus rebuffed the Ryanair invitation, declaring this sales campaign would be too expensive and time consuming. Yet Ryanair hinted that it had an interest in Airbus's new generation of fuel-efficient aircraft and, moreover, that it had the economies of scale to run a mixed fleet between Boeing and Airbus models.

Staff Costs and Productivity

Ryanair refuses to recognize trade unions and negotiates with Employee Representative Committees (ERCs). Its 2010 employee count of 7,032 people, composed of more than 25 different nationalities, had doubled over the previous three years. This was accounted for almost entirely by flight and cabin crew to service expansion. Ryanair's employees earned productivity-based incentive payments, consisting of 39 percent and 37 percent of total pay for cabin crew and pilots respectively. By tailoring rosters, the carrier maximized productivity and time off for crew members, complying with EU regulations that impose a ceiling on pilot flying hours to prevent dangerous fatigue. Its passenger-per-employee ratio of 9,457 was the highest in the industry. After a series of pay increases for cabin staff and pilots, in late 2009, staff agreed to a one-year pay freeze.

Passenger Service Costs

Ryanair pioneered cost-cutting/yield-enhancing measures for passenger check-in and luggage handling. One was priority boarding and Web-based check-in. More than half of its passengers availed of this, thus saving on check-in staff, airport facilities, and time. Charging for check-in bags encouraged passengers to travel with fewer and, if possible, zero check-in luggage, thus saving on costs and enhancing speed. Before Ryanair began to charge for checked-in bags, 80 percent of passengers were traveling with checked-in luggage; two years later this had fallen to 30 percent of passengers. From October 2009, it adopted a 100 percent Web check-in policy, enabling a reduction in staff numbers, calculated to save €50 million per year. Ryanair claims that "passengers love Web checkin. Never again will they have to arrive early at an airport to waste time in a useless check-in queue. As more passengers travel with carry-on luggage only, they are delighted to discover that they will never again waste valuable time at arrival baggage carousels either. These measures allow Ryanair to save our passengers valuable time, as well as lots of."[9] A natural next step announced by Ryanair was a move to 100 percent carry-on luggage. Additional bags would be brought by passengers to the boarding gate, where they would be placed it in the hold and returned as passengers deplane on arrival. These efficiencies would allow more efficient airport terminals to be developed without expensive check-in desks, baggage halls, or computerized baggage systems "and enable Ryanair to make flying even cheaper, easier and much more fun again," claimed the company.[10] The feasibility of the proposals to require passengers to carry hold baggage through security to the aircraft was yet to be tested.

Airport Charges and Route Policy

Consistent with the budget airline model, Ryanair's routes were point-to-point only. This reduced airport charges by avoiding congested main airports, choosing secondary and regional destinations, eager to increase passenger throughput. Usually these airports were significantly further from the city centers they served than the main airports, "from nowhere to nowhere" in the words of Sir Stelios Haji-Ioannou, founder of EasyJet, Ryanair's biggest competitor.[11] Ryanair uses Frankfurt Hahn, 123 kilometers from Frankfurt; Torp, 100 kilometers from Oslo; and Charleroi, 60 kilometers from Brussels. In December 2003, the Advertising Standards Authority rebuked Ryanair and upheld a misleading advertising complaint against it for attaching "Lyon" to its advertisements for flights to St Etienne. A passenger had turned up at Lyon Airport, only to discover that her flight was leaving from St Etienne, 75 kilometers away.

Ryanair continued to protest at charges and conditions at some airports, especially Stansted and Dublin, two of its main hubs. The airline was "deeply concerned by continued understaffing of security at Stansted which led to repeated passenger and flight delays...management of Stansted security is inept, and BAA has again proven that it is incapable of providing adequate or appropriate security services at Stansted. This shambles again highlights that BAA is an inefficient, incompetent airport monopoly."[12] When BAA appealed its break-up, ordered by the UK Competition Commission in 2009, Ryanair secured the right to intervene in the appeal in support of the Commission and later applauded the loss of the appeal by BAA. Meanwhile, Ryanair bemoaned a €10 tourist tax being levied in Ireland, along with a 40 percent price increase at Dublin Airport, largely to pay for a second terminal costing €1.2 billion, initially commissioned in the heyday of the Irish Celtic Tiger and derided by Ryanair as a white elephant. Ryanair acted against Dublin and various UK airports by cutting its capacity and shifting its aircraft to countries, such as Spain, with cheaper airports and lower or nonexistent passenger taxes.

Marketing Strategy

Following the introduction of its Internet-based reservations and ticketing service, enabling passengers to make reservations and purchase tickets directly through the Web site, Ryanair's reliance on travel agents had been eliminated. It had promoted its Web site heavily through newspaper, radio, and television advertising. As a result, Internet bookings accounted for 99 percent of all reservations.

Ryanair minimized its marketing and advertising costs, relying on free publicity, by its own admission, "through controversial and topical advertising, press conferences and publicity stunts." Other marketing activities include distribution of advertising and promotional material and cooperative advertising campaigns with other travel-related entities and local tourist boards.

As referred to earlier, one of Ryanair's publicity stunts was its unauthorized use of a photograph of Spanish Queen Sofia after she took a £13 flight from Santander Northern Spain to London. When it incurred the Queen's displeasure, Ryanair apologized and promised to donate €5000 to a charity of her choice. In another instance of controversy over using pictures of the rich and famous, in 2008, Ryanair was forced to pay a fine of €60,000 to President Sarkozy of France and his Italian bride, Carla Bruni, for using their images with the slogan, "With Ryanair, all my family can come to my wedding." It also used the face of Spanish Prime Minister Zapatero in an advertisement depicting him supposedly musing over its offers.

So, What About Aer Lingus?

According to a commentator in the *Financial Times*, "Ryanair's bid for Aer Lingus was a *folie de grandeur*."[13] Even O'Leary admitted it was "a stupid investment. At the time, it was the right strategy to go for one combined airline but it has now proven to be a disaster."[14] During 2007, in a shock bid, Ryanair had acquired a 25.2 percent stake in Aer Lingus, only a week after the flotation of the national carrier. It subsequently increased its interest to 29.8 percent, at a total aggregate cost of €407.2 million. By July 2009, the investment had been written down to €79.7 million. At the time of the initial bid, Ryanair declared its intention to retain the Aer Lingus brand and "up-grade their dated long-haul product, and reduce their short-haul fares by 2.5 percent per year for a minimum of 4 years...one strong Irish airline group will be rewarding for consumers and will enable both to vigorously compete with the mega carriers in Europe...there are significant opportunities, by combining the purchasing power of Ryanair and Aer Lingus, to substantially reduce its operating costs, increase efficiencies, and pass these savings on in the form of lower fares to Aer Lingus' consumers."[15]

It had been an achievement for the Irish government finally to have floated Aer Lingus after several false starts over a number of years. Once they recovered their collective breaths, Aer Lingus and its board firmly rejected the Ryanair approach, stating that it had acted in "a hostile, anticompetitive manner designed to eliminate a rival at a derisory price." A combined Ryanair–Aer Lingus operation would account for 80 percent of all flights between Ireland and other European countries. Affirming that his company was fundamentally opposed to a merger with Ryanair, even if it raised its price, then-Aer Lingus Chief Executive Dermot Mannion stated, "I cannot conceive of the circumstances where the Aer Lingus management and Ryanair would be able to work harmoniously together...this is simply a reflection of the fact that these organisations have been competing head to head, without fear or favour, for 20 years. It would be like merging Manchester United and Liverpool football clubs."[16]

In fact, the bid was opposed by a loose alliance representing almost 47 percent of Aer Lingus shares. This included the Irish government, which still retained a 25.4 percent holding, two investment funds operated on behalf of Aer Lingus pilots accounting for about 4 percent of shares, and Irish telecom tycoon Denis O'Brien, who bought 2.1 percent of shares explicitly to complicate Ryanair's move. A critical 12.6 percent of the shareholding was controlled by the Aer Lingus employee share ownership trust (ESOT), which had the right to appoint two directors and a stake in future profits. Its members rejected the Ryanair offer by a 97 percent majority vote, dismissing Ryanair's claim that each ESOT member stood to receive an average of €60,000 from the transaction. They asserted that its members would receive only €32,000 after borrowing costs.

Having abandoned this bid due to the shareholder opposition and a blocking decision by the European Commission on competition grounds, Ryanair came back in December 2008 with an offer of €1.40 per share, a premium of approximately 25 percent over the closing price. It proposed to keep Aer Lingus as a separate company, maintaining the Aer Lingus brand, to double Aer Lingus' short-haul fleet from 33 to 66 aircraft, and to create 1,000 associated new jobs over a five-year period. It claimed that if the offer was accepted, the Irish government would receive more than €180 million and the ESOT members and other employees who owned 18 percent of Aer Lingus would receive more than €137 million in cash. However, in January 2009, when the offer was rejected by Aer Lingus management and by the ESOT and other parties, Ryanair decided to withdraw it.

Aer Lingus' fortunes continued to deteriorate, with the company announcing losses for 2008 and projecting even worse for 2009. In July of that year, its shares were trading at less than €0.50. In April, its CEO, Dermot Mannion, resigned after controversy over a potential secret payoff deal in the event of a hostile takeover. While Ryanair did not have a seat on the board, it continued to denigrate Aer Lingus, forecasting "a bleak future as a loss making, subscale, regional airline, which has a high cost base and declining traffic numbers."[17] Meanwhile, the two airlines continued to compete vigorously, especially within the Irish market.

In July 2009, Aer Lingus appointed a CEO to replace Dermot Mannion. This was Christoph Mueller, known as "axe man," former CEO of Sabena Airlines before it went bust in 2001. Mueller had already crossed swords with Ryanair when it compared its own fares to those of Sabena in advertisements that were alleged to be misleading, offensive, and defamatory. When Ryanair lost a court case over the matter and was ordered to publish an apology in Belgian newspapers and on its Web site, it used the apology to continue its publicity about its relatively lower fares.

In July 2010, the European General Court upheld the European Commission's decision, as well as a verdict in a case brought by Aer Lingus, to block the takeover of Aer Lingus by Ryanair. However, it did not go as far as forcing Ryanair to sell its stake in Aer Lingus, an action that Aer Lingus wanted the Court to impose. Upon hearing the Court decision, O'Leary declared that he had not ruled out making a third bid for Aer Lingus at some future date. Despite the European level judgment, later in 2010, the UK Office of Fair Trade (OFT) announced that it would conduct a preliminary competition investigation into Ryanair's 29.8 percent holding in Aer Lingus. Ryanair, of course, rejected the investigation, arguing that the UK OFT had no jurisdiction in the matter and a four-month time limit after the European ruling for the case to be brought had elapsed.

Risks and Challenges

Apart from its foray into Aer Lingus, Ryanair faced various challenges in 2009, some specific to itself and some general to the aviation industry.

Sharp Economic Downturn

The global recession commencing in 2008 created unfavorable economic conditions such as high unemployment rates and constrained credit markets, with reduced spending by leisure and business passengers alike. This constrained Ryanair's scope to raise fares, putting downward pressure on yields. Continued recession could restrict the company's passenger volume growth.

Input Costs

Fuel. Perhaps the greatest concern in input costs is fuel. Jet fuel prices are subject to wide fluctuations, increases in demand, and disruptions in supply, factors that Ryanair can neither predict nor control. In such unpredictable circumstances, even hedging is only palliative. The situation is compounded by exchange rate uncertainties, although declines of the U.S. dollar against the euro and sterling worked in Ryanair's favor, as fuel prices are denominated in dollars. Ryanair's declaration of "no fuel surcharges ever" and its reliance on low fares limit its capacity to pass on increased fuel costs.

Airport Charges and Government Taxes. Ryanair is especially sensitive to airports that raise charges, like Stansted and Dublin. Indirectly, it is also vulnerable to extra taxes and charges, such as a €10 tourist tax imposed by the Irish government.

Passenger Compensation. On February 17, 2005, a new EU regulation (EU 261) came into effect, providing for standardized and immediate assistance for air passengers at EU airports for delays, cancellations, and denied boarding. It was initially expected that the compensation costs would amount to a sector-wide bill of €200 million annually.

Passengers affected by cancellations must be offered a refund or rerouting and free care and assistance while waiting for their rerouted flight—specifically, meals, refreshments, and hotel accommodation where an overnight stay is necessary. Financial compensation is payable, unless the airline can prove unavoidable exceptional circumstances, like political instability, weather conditions, security and safety risks, or strikes. For Ryanair, the typical compensation cost would likely fall into the €250 category, based on the average distance of its flights. Passengers subject to long delays would also be entitled to similar assistance. Until April 2010, the new regulation was largely ignored and had no material impact on Ryanair, despite the emergence of online "advisors" to help passengers make claims against airlines when their flights have been canceled or delayed.

Volcanic Ash Repercussions and Further Threats

However, the situation with respect to compensation was highlighted dramatically with the eruption of Iceland's Eyjafjallajokull volcano, causing volcanic ash that closed airspace in Europe for six days in April 2010, with further sporadic disruptions in May. The losses to Europe's air sector resulting from flight cancellations and compensation were estimated at €2.5 billion. These closures resulted in the cancellation of 9,490 Ryanair flights for 1.5 million passengers. Many airlines were demanding government aid to make up for lost revenue and the cost of feeding and lodging stranded passengers. The airlines contended that flawed computer models used by member states were partly to blame for grounding planes even after it was safe to resume services. The EU Commission noted that fiscal conditions prevented cash-strapped governments from offering aid to airlines, even if the rules could be bent to allow such aid. Ryanair argued strongly against offering aid to airlines, as did EasyJet, on grounds that it could be used as a back door to prop up ailing airlines, especially national carriers.

Initially Ryanair declared that it would not compensate passengers for food and accommodation expenses incurred as a result of canceled flights, although it would offer refunds. It argued strenuously about how ludicrous it was that passengers could charge airlines unlimited sums to cover their expenses, no matter how cheap had been the cost of their ticket. Furthermore, Ryanair claimed that the compensation regulations were discriminatory because competitor ferry, coach, and train operators were obliged to reimburse passengers only to a maximum of the ticket price paid. Such a situation was not sustainable for the airlines, especially because the disruption to air traffic from ash cloud from the erupting volcano could continue sporadically and indefinitely, depending on the strength of the volcano and weather conditions. However, several days into the crisis, Ryanair did an about-turn, saying it would comply with the EU compensation regulation, but it would continue to work alongside other low-fare airlines to alter the regulation to put a reasonable limit on compensation. O'Leary said that Ryanair would reimburse "reasonable costs" to passengers caught up in the chaos in April. Asked if Ryanair would make it difficult to make claims, O'Leary responded, "Perish the thought."[18] Ryanair expected to refund these monies and reimburse passengers reasonable expenses, although it would take a substantial period of time to complete this and management estimated that the approximate costs of this and the non-recoverable fiscal costs incurred during the cancellations would be in the order of €50 million.

At the end of May 2010, it was announced that the Eyjafjallajokull volcano had subsided and was unlikely to cause any further problems in the short to medium term. However, later in 2010, Ryanair was obliged to cancel flights to and from Spain during wildcat strikes by Spanish air traffic controllers in August and then in December when unusually severe winter weather forced the closure of a number of airports for several days. Again, this entailed not only lost revenue but issues of compensation.

Growth and Reducing Yields

Growth plans by Ryanair entailed investment in new aircraft and routes. If growth in passenger traffic did not keep pace with its planned fleet expansion, overcapacity could result. Related pressures were additional marketing costs and reduced yields from lower fares to promote added routes, especially to airports new to the Ryanair system. In its drive for growth, Ryanair was likely to encounter increased competition, putting even more downward pressure on yields, as airlines struggled to fill vacant seats to cover fixed costs.

Industrial Relations

In light of the recession and financial losses, Ryanair negotiated with all employee groups and secured a pay freeze for fiscal 2009 and 2010. It also planned to make 250 people redundant at Dublin Airport.

Ryanair came under fire for refusing to recognize unions and allegedly providing poor working conditions (for example, staff are banned from charging their own mobile phones at work to reduce the company's electricity bill). It conducted collective bargaining with employees on pay, work practices, and conditions of employment through internal elected Employee Representation Committees. However, the British Airline Pilots Association (BALPA) was constantly attempting to organize Ryanair pilots in the United Kingdom and legal action was pending in this regard in 2011.

In July 2006, the Irish High Court ruled that Ryanair had bullied pilots to accept new contracts, where pilots would have to pay €15,000 for retraining on new aircraft if they left the airline or if the company were forced to negotiate with unions during the following five years. Some Ryanair managers were judged to have given false evidence in court. Meanwhile, Ryanair was contesting the claims of some pilots for victimization under the new contracts. By 2009, only 11 of the 64 pilots who had lodged the claim remained with the company and still had claims.

Ryanair was ordered to pay "well in excess" of €1 million in legal costs after a court refused the airline access to the names and addresses of pilots who posted critical comments about the company, on a site hosted by the British and Irish pilots' unions. O'Leary claimed anonymous pilots were using a Web site to intimidate and harass foreign-based pilots to dissuade them from working for the company. The pilots involved used code names such as "ihateryanair" and "cant-fly-wontfly." Nonetheless, in effect, Ryanair appeared to have no problems recruiting cabin staff, including pilots, to meet its needs.

Environmental Concerns

Aviation fuel had been exempt from carbon taxes, but the EU had established an Emissions Trading Scheme to encompass the aviation industry commencing in 2012. Ryanair was predicted to be the fourth-most adversely affected airline in the world with a shortfall of 2.8 tonnes in CO_2 allowances, equivalent to €40 million in extra costs. This is despite its young fleet of fuel-efficient, minimal pollution aircraft. Therefore, Ryanair has contended that any environmental taxation scheme should be to the benefit of more efficient carriers, so airlines with low load factors that generate high fuel consumption and emissions per passenger and those offering connecting rather than point-to-point flights should be penalized.

Sundry Legal Actions

Ryanair has been in litigation with the EU about alleged receipt of state aid at certain airports. An EU ruling in 2004 held that Ryanair had received illegal state aid from publicly owned Charleroi Airport, its Brussels base. Ryanair was ordered to repay €4 million. The Belgian authorities were claiming back a further €2.3 million in the Irish courts for the reimbursement to Ryanair of startup costs at Charleroi. On appeal, the original EU decision was overturned in December 2008, Ryanair was refunded its €4 million, and the Belgian authorities withdrew their claim. Nonetheless, the EU launched further investigations into allegations of illegal aid, purportedly subsidizing Ryanair at publicly owned airports, such as Lubeck and Frankfurt Hahn in Germany and Shannon in Ireland. Other legal challenges were launched against Ryanair by competitors. On another front Ryanair was vigorously opposing French government attempts to protect Air France-KLM by forcing EasyJet and Ryanair to move their French-based staff from British employment contracts to more expensive French ones.

Often, Ryanair took the initiative on alleged illegal aid to rivals. For example, it filed a complaint with the EU Commission accusing Air France-KLM of attempting to block competition after the French airline filed a case, alleging that Marseille was acting illegally by offering discount airlines cut-price fees at its second, no-frills terminal. That complaint came a month after Ryanair called on the Commission to investigate allegations that Air France had received almost €1 billion in illegal state aid, benefiting unfairly from up to 50 percent discounted landing and passenger charges on flights within France. Adverse rulings on these airport cases could curtail Ryanair's growth, if it was prevented from striking advantageous deals with publicly owned airports and confined to the fewer privately owned airports across Europe.

On another front, Ryanair was being sued by three airport authorities over alleged delays in paying airport charges. After the company applied for the judge hearing the case to withdraw on grounds of bias toward Ryanair in previous proceedings, the judge did indeed withdraw, not because he admitted Ryanair's charges but to avoid delay in the case. However, when pulling out, Justice Peter Kelly of the Irish High Court stood by his previous comments that "Ryanair told untruths to and about the court and...that the airline and the truth made uncomfortable bedfellows."[19]

In 2009, Ryanair took a successful legal action against TUI, a screen scraper, to prevent it from selling Ryanair flights on grounds that it had no agreement to do so and accusing it of charging a fictitious £40 "fuel surcharge" and falsely inflating airfares to consumers buying Ryanair tickets. (Screen scrapers are Web sites that compare costs from different airlines and can also book flights.) Having secured its legal victory for "Ryanair and consumers," the carrier declared its intention to "pursue unlawful and misleading tickettouts in the courts in the interest of our passengers."[20]

Customer Services and Perceptions

In 2003, Ryanair published a Passenger Charter, which includes doctrines on low fares, redress, and punctuality. Its annual report offers figures to show its superiority over competitors with respect to punctuality, completed flights, and fewest bags lost per thousand passengers.

However, its Skytrax two-star rating is among the worst for budget airlines. In Europe, only bmibaby and Wizzair achieve as low a rating. There have been suggestions that Ryanair's "obsessive focus on the bottom line may have dented its public image. In an infamous incident, it charged a disabled man £18 (€25) to use a wheelchair."[21] In response to protests over the charge, Ryanair imposed a 50-cent wheelchair levy on every passenger ticket. Campaigners for the disabled accused Ryanair of profiteering, declaring that the levy should be no more than 3 cents. It was the only major airline in Europe to impose such wheelchair charges.

There was growing attention to extra charges continually being imposed by Ryanair on passengers, many on unavoidable services such as check-in. In some instances, these extra charges made Ryanair more expensive than BA.[22] Examples were a family of four traveling to Ibiza from London with three bags for a two-week holiday costing £1157 with Ryanair versus £913 with BA and £634 with

EasyJet. A single passenger traveling to Venice from London for a week at Christmas with one bag would pay a total £139 on Ryanair compared to £89 on BA and £121 on EasyJet.

Ryanair features on many consumer complaint interactive Web sites and some blogs have been established specifically to disparage the airline. In a blog titled "20 reasons never to fly Ryanair," extra charges for booking fees, baggage overweight and low weight limits, premium rate helplines, and the fact that "you are always being flogged stuff" were enumerated.[23] Claiming that the service is provided by a third party, Ryanair even charges passengers a €10 service fee to collect lost property. When the *Irish Times* put Ryanair customers' gripes on the Pricewatch blog to its head of communications, Stephen McNamara, his response was to dismiss them as "subjective and inaccurate rubbish" and even implied Pricewatch had made them up to further some class of anti-Ryanair agenda.[24] Among the complaints were, "Customers want to be treated like a human being, to get to their desired destination (not 50/60 miles away)…to be allowed to bring luggage without persecution…a complete and utter lack of communication when flights run late…I'm sick of that miserable booking charge/service charge/admin charge system."

So, why are so many people willing to put up with an airline that, in the words of *The Economist*, "has become a byword for appalling customer service, misleading advertising claims and jeering rudeness?"[25] Ryanair has responded to such comments, declaring that, in effect, customers vote with their feet by choosing Ryanair for its four tenets of customer service: low fares, a good on-time record, few cancellations, and few lost bags. "If you want anything more—go away," admonishes O'Leary.[26] The *Financial Times* aerospace correspondent observed that Ryanair still offered relative value compared with rail alternatives, at least on a journey from London to Scotland, even when Ryanair extras are factored in.

Other Risks and Challenges

As listed in its own report, Ryanair faced other risks, some particular to itself and some generic to the industry:

- risks associated with growth in uncertain highly competitive markets, such as downward pressure on fares and margins;
- prices and availability of new aircraft;
- potential impairments from Ryanair's 29.8 percent stake in Aer Lingus;
- threats of terrorist attacks;
- potential outbreak of airborne diseases, such as swine flu;
- dependence on key personnel (especially O'Leary);
- dependence on external service providers;
- dependence on its Web site; and
- the continued acceptance of budget carriers with respect to safety. Tied in with the latter are potential rises in insurance costs.

Ryanair's Competitive Space

Globally, airlines were hit hard during the economic downturn with a $9.9 billion loss in 2009 and $16 billion in 2008, but in 2010 it was believed that the cyclical movement of the airline industry had begun to improve as the International Air Transport Association (IATA) had actually predicted a $2.5 billion airline industry profit forecast for 2010. However, European carriers were still expected to generate losses of $2.8 billion, aggravated by the disruption from the volcanic ash in April and May. In 2009, of the mainstream European carriers, only Lufthansa made a net profit. BA, Air France-KLM, and Scandinavian Air Systems (SAS) all made severe losses, due to declining traffic from long-haul business-class passengers. The woes of these legacy carriers were compounded by huge pension fund deficits.

Some industry analysts considered the possibility that the economic recession could offer an opportunity for budget carriers, as passengers who continued to travel were expected to trade down. By mid-2009, budget airlines accounted for more than 35 percent of scheduled intra-European traffic. Ryanair was the clear market share leader, with EasyJet another dominant force. (Exhibit 2). The two were often compared and contrasted because both operated mainly out of the United Kingdom and served the same markets. However, it was a matter for debate as to whether EasyJet's use of primary airports would be better than Ryanair's at capturing the traffic trading down from network carriers.

Other budget carriers of diverse size and growth ambitions, trajectories, and regional emphases varied in different levels of services to passengers and use of main versus secondary airports. The comparison with the U.S. budget airline market in Exhibit 2 indicates that penetration in Europe is less than in the United States, which suggests scope for growth in the sector in Europe. It also raises the question as to whether the extent of dominance enjoyed by Southwest offers a model for Ryanair to assert itself further. Another possible development trajectory for Ryanair was to follow up on its announcement in 2007 to offer €10 transatlantic flights, an idea that had not yet taken off and appeared to have been shelved as of 2009.

Exhibit 2 Budget Airlines Sundry Data: Europe and United States (2008–09)

European Market Position				U.S. Market Position	
Airline	Pax (m)>	Rating*	Airports#	Airline	Pax (m)<
Aigle Azur	1.46		26	AirTran	24.6
Air Berlin	28.6	4	126	Allegiant Air	3.9
Belle Air	0.46		24	American Trans Air (ATA)	0.4
Bmibaby	3.87	2	32	Frontier Airlines	10.1
Brussels Airlines	5.4	3	62	GoJet Airlines	1.5
Clickair^	6.3	3	40	Horizon Airlines (Alaska Air)	6.5
EasyJet	44.6	3	110	Island Air Hawaii	0.5
FlyBe	7.5	3	65	JetBlue Airways	20.5
Germanwings	7.6	3	70	Midwest Airline Inc.	3.0
Jet2.com	3.5	3	51	Shuttle America Corp.	3.5
Meridiana	1.9	3	30	Southwest Airlines	101.9
Monarch Airlines	3.9		21	Spirit Airlines	5.5
Myair.com^	1.5		27	Sun County Airlines	1.3
Niki Airline	2.1	3	33	USA 3000 Airlines	0.8
Norwegian	9.1	3	85	Virgin America	2.5
Ryanair	57.7	2	140		
Sky Europe^	3.6	3	30		
Sterling^	3.8		39		
Sverigeflyg	0.5		15		
transavia.com	5.5	3	88		
TUIfly	10.5		75		
Vueling Airlines	5.9	3	45		
Windjet	2.7		28		
Wizz Air	5.9	3	58		

> Sources: European Low Fares Airlines Association (ELFAA), company reports.

< Sources: CIA, Bureau of Transportation Statistics.

* Skytrax star rating from 1 to 5 (not all airlines rated)

Number of airports served; Sources: European Low Fares Airlines Association (ELFAA), company reports.

^ These airlines have ceased operations.

Total Passengers (Pax)

| European Budget Airlines | 223.9 | Total Pax U.S. Budget Airlines |
| 186.4 | | |

Ryanair as % of Total: 26%   *Southwest as % of Total: 55%*

Key Population Data   **Key Population Data**
Population EU 27 (m) 500   Population U.S. (m) 307

Key Population Ratios   **Key Population Ratios**
Budget ratio to EU 27 population 0.45   Budget ratio to U.S. population 0.61

Competitors and Comparators

The following section describes Ryanair's budget airline competitors and some selected other carriers. Exhibits 3 and 4 show comparative fare levels and punctuality statistics, as well as airport distances for Ryanair versus other airlines. This is in addition to the Skytrax star ratings in Exhibit 2, based on the perception of delivered front-line product and service quality for Ryanair and other budget airlines. There are no externally verified published data on customer complaints, lost baggage, and flight cancellations, so it is not possible to check out the veracity of Ryanair's claims to superiority on these factors. See Exhibits 5 and 6 for financial and operational comparisons with competitors and benchmark airline operators, including Southwest Airlines.

EasyJet

EasyJet, the second-largest budget airline in Europe, was Ryanair's greatest rival. As of the end of 2009, EasyJet served 114 airports in 27 countries on 422 routes with

Exhibit 3   Comparative Fare Levels
(same booking dates and approximate departure times, includes one piece of luggage)

Route: Dublin–London: Weekend Return (2 Nights)

Airline	From	To	Total Price €
Aer Lingus	Dublin	Heathrow	108.98
Bmi British Midland	Dublin	Heathrow	103.59
Ryanair	Dublin	Gatwick	166.00
Ryanair	Dublin	Stansted	74.98
Ryanair	Dublin	Luton	81.98

Route: Dublin–London: Weekday Return (3 Nights)

Airline	From	To	Total Price €
Aer Lingus	Dublin	Heathrow	97.99
Bmi British Midland	Dublin	Heathrow	85.59
Ryanair	Dublin	Gatwick	113.35
Ryanair	Dublin	Stansted	69.98
Ryanair	Dublin	Luton	67.98

Route: Rome–London: Weekend Return (2 Nights)

Airline	From	To	Total Price €
Alitalia	Rome (Fiumicino)	Heathrow	200.15
British Airways	Rome (Fiumicino)	Gatwick	275.61
British Airways	Rome (Fiumicino)	Heathrow	308.04
Easyjet	Rome (Fiumicino)	Gatwick	220.15
Ryanair	Rome (Ciampino)	Stansted	187.88

Route: Rome–London: Weekday Return (3 Nights)

Airline	From	To	Total Price €
Alitalia	Rome (Fiumicino)	Heathrow	244.68
British Airways	Rome (Fiumicino)	Gatwick	571.16
British Airways	Rome (Fiumicino)	Heathrow	542.04
Easyjet	Rome (Fiumicino)	Gatwick	396.15
Ryanair	Rome (Ciampino)	Stansted	218.78

Route: Berlin–London: Weekend Return (2 Nights)

Airline	From	To	Total Price €
Air Berlin	Berlin (Tegel)	Stansted	285.00
British Airways	Berlin (Tegel)	Heathrow	152.62
Easyjet	Berlin (Schonefeld)	Gatwick	123.15
Easyjet	Berlin (Schonefeld)	Luton	154.69
Lufthansa	Berlin Tegel	Heathrow	218.00
Ryanair	Berlin (Schonefeld)	Stansted	113.67

Route: Berlin–London: Weekday Return (3 Nights)

Airline	From	To	Total Price €
Air Berlin	Berlin (Tegel)	Stansted	193.00
British Airways	Berlin (Tegel)	Heathrow	126.62
Easyjet	Berlin (Schonefeld)	Gatwick	150.15
Easyjet	Berlin (Schonefeld)	Luton	146.69
Lufthansa	Berlin (Tegel)	Heathrow	261.00
Ryanair	Berlin (Schonefeld)	Stansted	149.19

Route: London–Oslo: Weekend Return (2 Nights)

Airline	From	To	Total Price €
British Airways	Heathrow	Oslo Gardermoen	279.00
Bmi British Midland	Heathrow	Oslo Gardermoen	316.00
Norwegian	Gatwick	Oslo Gardermoen	304.20
Ryanair	Stansted	Rygge	166.00
Ryanair	Stansted	Torp	74.98
Sas	Heathrow	Oslo Gardermoen	262.73

(continued)

Exhibit 3 **Comparative Fare Levels** (*continued*)

Route: London–Oslo: Weekday Return (3 Nights)

Airline	From	To	Total Price €
British Airways	Heathrow	Oslo Gardermoen	309.40
Bmi British Midland	Heathrow	Oslo Gardermoen	320.00
Norwegian	Gatwick	Oslo Gardermoen	196.00
Ryanair	Stansted	Rygge	110.00
Ryanair	Stansted	Torp	121.50
Sas	Heathrow	Oslo Gardermoen	324.36

Airports Distance To City Center (point 0)

Airports	Distance (kms):
Stansted	61
Heathrow	25
Luton	55
Gatwick	45
Dublin	12
Rome (Fiumicino)	32
Rome (Ciampino)	15
Berlin (Tegel)	8
Berlin (Schonefeld)	18
Oslo Gardermoen	47
Rygge (Oslo)	66
Stockholm Arlanda	40
Stockholm Skvasta	100
Stockholm Vasteras	87
Torp (Oslo)	110

Airbus aircraft. Ryanair and EasyJet frequently attacked each other as part of their "public relations." When accused by EasyJet of introducing stealth charges, Ryanair retaliated by pointing out that, even with taxes included, its average fare was well below EasyJet's. Ryanair said that EasyJet had charged each passenger £14 (€20) more per ticket than Ryanair, thereby overcharging their passengers by £413 (€600) million in a year. In fact, eventually, EasyJet had followed many of Ryanair's extra charge initiatives, such as a fee for check-in baggage.

Based at London Luton Airport, EasyJet was founded by Greek Cypriot EasyGroup entrepreneur Sir Stelios Haji-Ioannou in 1995. Although it was listed on the London Stock Exchange, members of the Haji-Ioannou family still owned almost 40 percent of the company in 2010. The business model of EasyJet is somewhat different to Ryanair in that it uses more centrally located airports, thus incurring higher airport charges, but more actively courts the business traveler. For example, Schiphol in Amsterdam and Orly Airport in Paris are hubs, while the airline also uses Charles de Gaulle Airport in the French capital. In 2009, EasyJet grew the number of business passengers in spite of an overall decline in the business travel market. EasyJet won a number of industry awards in 2009, including Best European Budget Airline (World Traveler Awards), Best Airline Website (Travolution), and the Condé Nast Traveler Best Low Cost Airline award (for the sixth consecutive year).

In March 2008, EasyJet purchased GB Airways, a franchise of British Airways, headquartered at London Gatwick, in a deal worth £103.5 million. The takeover was used to expand EasyJet operations at Gatwick and start operations at Manchester. While all GB aircraft (fortuitously Airbus) were transferred to EasyJet, slots used by GB Airways at London Heathrow Airport were not included in the sale.

Compared with Ryanair, EasyJet traditionally struggled on the profit front, as it strove to bring down its costs. However, from the mid-2000s, its results moved into profit. In contrast to airline industry peers, the airline traded resiliently in 2009 during the recession, as it was one of the few airlines globally to make a profit, with an underlying pretax profit of £43.7 million. Revenue grew by 12.9 percent to £2,666.8 million, partially offsetting the £86.1 million increase in unit fuel costs (equivalent to £1.63 per seat). The carrier claimed to have given itself a platform

Exhibit 4   Punctuality Statistics
(a) Comparative Punctuality on Selected Routes for 2009

London -> Dublin

Rank	Airline	Operating from London Airports					Avg. Delay (mins)	OTP Within 15	1 hr+ late (%)	3 hrs+ late (%)	Total Flights
		LHR	LGW	LCY	STN	LTN					
1	British Airways *		✓				6.86	87.88	1.81	0.54	553
2	City Jet			✓			7.5	86.62	2.56	0.34	2,967
3	bmi British Midland	✓					9.27	82.21	3	0.23	4,402
4	BA CityFlyer **			✓			11.22	82.69	6.73	0.48	208
5	Aer Lingus	✓	✓				12.32	76.98	4.22	0.42	11,146
6	Ryanair		✓		✓		12.71	76.43	3.38	0.64	11,839
	AVERAGE ALL 6 AIRLINES > > >						**11.47**	**78.66**	**3.54**	**0.47**	**31,115**

* - British Airways discontinued LGW-DUB during March 2009
** - BA CityFlyer discontinued LCY-DUB during March 2009

London -> Rome

Data relate to flights to and from Fiumicino and Ciampino airports.

Rank	Airline	Operating from London Airports					Avg. Delay (mins)	OTP Within 15	1 hr+ late (%)	3 hrs+ late (%)	Total Flights
		LHR	LGW	LCY	STN	LTN					
1	British Airways	✓	✓				11.1	78.88	3.64	0.46	5,408
2	Ryanair				✓		14.44	75.07	3.61	0.95	2,411
3	Alitalia	✓					18.29	63.61	6.63	0.56	3,226
4	EasyJet		✓				21.2	57.61	7.77	0.76	1,840
	AVERAGE ALL 4 AIRLINES > > >						**14.97**	**71.31**	**4.97**	**0.62**	**12,885**

London -> Dusseldorf

Data relate to flights to and from Dusseldorf and Niederrhein airports.

Rank	Airline	Operating from London Airports					Avg. Delay (mins)	OTP Within 15	1 hr+ late (%)	3 hrs+ late (%)	Total Flights
		LHR	LGW	LCY	STN	LTN					
1	Eurowings *			✓			3.53	94.71	1.76	0.25	397
2	Lufthansa City Line ^			✓			6.51	86.97	2.08	0	913
3	Lufthansa	✓					7.01	86.49	2.31	0.1	2,858
4	British Airways	✓					7.37	85.64	2.59	0.19	3,704
5	Air Berlin			✓			11.34	81.54	3.59	1.09	2,199
6	Ryanair **		✓		✓		11.98	81.75	3.91	0.98	1,737
7	Flybe ^^		✓				15.68	71.65	4.43	0.44	903
	AVERAGE ALL 7 AIRLINES> > >						**9.02**	**83.97**	**2.95**	**0.44**	**12,711**

^ - Lufthansa City Line commenced LCY DUS during May 2009
^^ - Flybe commenced LGW DUS during June 2009
* - Eurowings discontinued LCY DUS during April 2009
** - Ryanair discontinued LGW NRN during March 2009

(continued)

Exhibit 4   Punctuality Statistics

(a) Comparative Punctuality on Selected Routes for 2009 (*continued*)

London -> Barcelona

Data relate to flights to and from Barcelona, Gerona and Reus airports.

Rank	Airline	Operating from London Airports					Avg. Delay (mins)	OTP Within 15	1 hr+ late (%)	3 hrs+ late (%)	Total Flights
		LHR	LGW	LCY	STN	LTN					
1	Ryanair		✓		✓	✓	9.7	82.73	2.39	0.5	3,979
2	British Airways *	✓	✓				12.32	76.27	4.14	0.44	4,542
3	EasyJet		✓		✓	✓	14.27	73.88	5.18	0.42	4,981
4	Iberia **	✓					15.75	69.35	5.76	0.65	2,013
5	BA CityFlyer ***			✓			25.22	54.59	11.91	0.25	403
	AVERAGE ALL 5 AIRLINES> > >						**13.04**	**75.71**	**4.43**	**0.47**	**15,918**

* - British Airways discontinued LGW BCN during October 2009

** - Iberia discontinued LHR BCN during October 2009

*** - BA CityFlyer discontinued LCY BCN during October 2009

London -> Oslo

Data relate to flights to and from Gardermoen and Torp airports.

Rank	Airline	Operating from London Airports					Avg. Delay (mins)	OTP Within 15	1 hr+ late (%)	3 hrs+ late (%)	Total Flights
		LHR	LGW	LCY	STN	LTN					
1	Scandinavian SAS	✓					7.36	86.84	2.19	0.32	3,420
2	British Airways	✓					8.28	85.59	2.79	0.28	2,831
3	Ryanair				✓		8.38	83.81	2.19	0.18	2,742
4	Transwede Airlines*			✓			14.57	74.34	3.98	0.88	226
5	Norwegian Air Shuttle**		✓		✓		14.93	71.01	5.11	0.35	1,721
	AVERAGE ALL 5 AIRLINES > > >						**9.19**	**83.01**	**2.84**	**0.29**	**10,940**

* - Transwede Airlines discontinued LCY-OSL during March 2009

** - Norwegian Air Shuttle discontinued STN-OSL during March 2009

for profitable growth in the medium term from which to achieve a 15 percent return on equity through improvements in network quality by taking advantage of capacity cuts by other carriers to advance its position, gaining share in important markets such as Milan, Paris, Madrid, and London Gatwick, and increasing its slot portfolio at congested airports by more than 10 percent. Other measures taken to improve performance were lower-cost deals with key suppliers and enhancements to its Web site. The board agreed to a fleet plan that would deliver about a 7.5 percent growth per annum in seats flown over the next five years, enabling EasyJet to grow its share of the European short-haul market from about 7 percent to 10 percent.

However, all was not well in the EasyJet boardroom. In May 2010, Sir Stelios and another nonexecutive board member he had nominated, Robert Rothenberg, declared open warfare on EasyJet by resigning from its board to become "shareholder activists" against its expansion plans. Sir Stelios was continuing his campaign started in 2008, objecting to "the management's strategy of relentless growth in aircraft numbers and lack of focus on profit margin increase," notwithstanding that the dispute had earlier appeared to be resolved with a compromise that would see the airline keep expanding by 7.5 percent a year.

The resignation of Sir Stelios came just three days after he delivered a blast at departing chief executive Andy Harrison, declaring he was "over-rated and had increased nothing but the size of his bonus since joining the airline in late 2005." These comments were seen as a parting shot at the chief executive after a 2008 boardroom row over EasyJet's growth strategy that preceded the announced departures of Harrison and the airline's finance director and chairman.[27] EasyJet's incoming chief executive was to be Carolyn McCall, the head of the Guardian Media Group. Sir Stelios added that he "feels sorry for the outgoing chief executive's new employers," Whitbread, owner of Premier Inn and Costa Coffee. Sir Stelios continued, "Over the past five years Andy Harrison developed a love affair with

Exhibit 4(b)   Punctuality Performance of Scheduled Airlines

	Average Delay (mins.)			Within 15 mins (%)		> 1 hour late (%)	
	2009 Rank	2008	2009	2008	2009	2008	2009
bmi regional	1st	5.6	4.8	89.9	93.3	1.8	2.0
KLM	2nd	11.4	5.8	78.6	90.6	3.6	1.6
VLM Airlines	3rd	12.5	6.0	75.7	90.5	3.6	2.2
City Jet / Scot Airways	4th	13.4	7.0	71.8	88.4	4.0	2.4
Brussels Airlines	5th	10.2	7.7	79.3	85.7	2.6	2.0
Eastern Airways	6th	6.6	7.9	88.8	88.9	2.0	3.0
Scandinavian SAS	7th	15.0	8.1	70.2	86.0	4.9	2.6
Swiss Airlines	8th	13.3	8.7	72.0	83.1	3.4	2.5
Air Berlin	9th	8.8	9.0	83.0	85.7	2.2	3.5
Loganair	10th	8.7	9.0	86.9	87.9	3.5	3.6
bmi British Midland	11th	15.3	9.3	69.8	83.4	5.5	3.2
Aer Arann	12th	11.2	9.4	83.8	87.5	5.2	3.9
TAP Air Portugal	13th	17.0	9.7	65.6	81.8	5.8	3.5
Lufthansa	14th	12.3	10.0	75.4	80.9	3.8	3.2
Air France	15th	15.4	10.5	66.5	79.5	4.4	3.2
British Airways	16th	17.6	11.0	66.8	81.1	6.3	3.6
BA Cityflyer	17th	20.3	11.0	62.3	80.5	9.5	4.3
bmi baby	18th	15.8	11.0	76.8	83.4	7.4	4.3
Ryanair	19th	12.3	11.0	76.4	79.9	2.9	2.9
Flybe	20th	13.0	11.2	79.0	83.3	5.4	4.5
Air Southwest	21st	10.2	11.6	80.7	82.0	3.8	5.2
Aer Lingus	22nd	17.8	12.0	65.0	79.2	6.7	4.4
United Airlines	23rd	18.6	13.0	68.3	80.1	7.7	5.0
EasyJet	24th	16.1	13.7	71.2	77.0	6.1	5.2
Alitalia	25th	16.2	13.9	66.7	73.6	5.8	5.2
American Airlines	26th	18.1	15.1	68.7	74.2	7.1	5.8
Monarch Scheduled	27th	18.4	15.8	72.8	78.0	7.2	5.8
Wizz Air	28th	22.4	16.7	66.1	73.1	7.5	5.6
Iberia	29th	20.1	17.2	62.6	68.9	8.2	6.3
Emirates	30th	22.1	17.6	53.7	61.9	7.1	4.3
Air Canada	31st	21.2	17.6	66.1	72.1	7.2	6.0
Continental Airlines	32nd	23.0	18.9	65.4	71.7	10.4	7.9
Virgin Atlantic	33rd	27.9	19.4	56.8	68.4	12.3	8.2
Jet2	34th	16.4	21.5	73.3	65.7	6.5	7.6
flyglobespan	35th	16.1	25.0	76.3	69.6	6.8	7.8

2009 Ranking by January–December average delay (ascending). Analysis includes arrivals and departures at UK reporting airports.

Source: www.flightontime.info

Exhibit 5   Comparative Airline Financial Statistics

	Air Berlin 2009 (€ millions)	Aer Lingus 2009 (€ millions)	Norwegian 2009 (NOK millions)	British Airways 2009 (£GBP millions)	EasyJet 2009 (£GBP millions)	Lufthansa 2005 (€ millions)	Southwest 2009 ($USD millions)
Total Revenue	3,282.79	1,205.70	7,309.00	8,992.00	2,666.80	22,283.00	10,350.00
Operating Costs:							
Employee Costs	440.70	312.20	1,303.00	2,193.00	342.90	5,996.00	3,468.00
Sales/MarketingDistribution	71.90	45.50	149.00	369.00	83.50	748.00	
Airport Charges	697.10	252.00	1,038.00	603.00	481.50	3,762.00	718.00
Ground Handling		101.70	723.00	1,021.00	255.90		
Fuel	715.40	331.70	1,423.00	2,969.00	807.20	3,645.00	3,044.00
Maintenance	187.30	70.50	660.00	510.00	161.60	717.00	719.00
Lease Charges	366.00	55.80	620.00	73.00	116.20	338.00	186.00
Depreciation	109.10	82.70	149.00	694.00	55.40	1,475.00	616.00
Operating Profit (Loss)	28.50	(81.02)	571.90	(220.00)	60.10	271.00	262.00
Net Profit (Loss)	(9.50)	(130.08)	623.00	(358.00)	71.20	(112.00)	99.00
Operating Margin (%)	0.86	(6.70)	7.80	(2.40)	2.30	1.20	2.50
Net Margin (%)	(0.29)	(10.80)	8.50	(3.90)	2.70	0.50	0.96

Sources: Annual Reports for Air Berlin (2010), Aer Lingus (2010), Norwegian (2010), British Airways (2010), EasyJet (2010), Lufthansa (2006), Southwest Airlines (2010)

Exhibit 6 Comparative Airline Operational Statistics

	Aer Lingus 2009 €[a]	British Airways 2009 £GBP	EasyJet 2009 £GBP	Lufthansa 2005 €	Southwest 2009 $USD	Wizz 2009	Air Berlin 2009 €	Norwegian 2009 NOK
Fleet	35	245	181	722	445	26	152	46
Average Daily Aircraft Hours	10.2	10.68	11		11.7			10.3
Capacity (billions)[b]	13.22	148.5	58.2	206.3	98	7.8	50.7	13.5
Passengers (millions)	9.31	33.1	45.2	76.5	86.3		27.9	10.8
Revenue Passenger Distance Units (millions)[c]	9.97	114.3	50.6	160.6	74.5		39.2	10.6
Average Length of Haul	1048 km	644 km	1101km	1177.9	775 miles		1402 km	
Revenue per Passenger	€77.10		42.43		93.68		106.28	
Revenue per Revenue Passenger Distance Unit	7.4 cent	.0685/RPK			.1329/RPM		7.57 cent.	
Cost per Revenue Passenger Unit	5.41 cent	.0528/ASK	4.58 pence					
Revenue per Capacity Unit			4.51 pence		.1056/ASM		5.86 cent.	0.49
Operating Cost per Capacity Unit					.1029/ASM			
Load Factor (%)	75.4	72	85.5	77.9	76	83	77.3	78
Average Staff	3844	41473	6478	112320	31,729	945	8278	1684
Destinations	73	150	114	120[d]	68	50	134	93

[a] short haul except for staff, = total for company
[b] available seat kilometres (ASK) except Southwest available seat miles (ASM)
[c] revenue per kilometer (RPK) except for Southwest revenue per mile (RPM)
[d] short haul

Sources: Annual reports. Wizz Air (2010).

Airbus, squandered £2.4 billion, doubling the size of the fleet, while he paid no dividends and the share price has gone sideways."[28]

People close to the airline said they believed the move was related to a separate brand licence dispute between the airline and Sir Stelios, whose private EasyGroup owns the "Easy" brand and licenses it to EasyJet. The dispute was settled out of court in October 2010, whereby a previous annual payment of £1 by EasyJet to use the "Easy" name was turned into a minimum £4 million per year in a 50-year agreement.

The altercations occurred as EasyJet was forced to cut its 2010 full-year profit guidance by £50 million because of the volcanic ash disruption from the eruption of Iceland's Eyjafjallajokull volcano that had closed airspace in Europe for six days, obliging EasyJet to cancel 6,512 flights in April 2010. This disruption was followed by a summer of delayed flights and canceled services, resulting in the dismissal of EasyJet's director of operations by new CEO McCall, who appeared to be placating Stelios when she announced a maiden dividend, slower growth plans, and tougher negotiations for new aircraft, involving both Airbus and Boeing.

The fierce rivalry between Ryanair and EasyJet was highlighted in a libel action brought by Stelios against Ryanair over a Ryanair advertisement depicting Stelios as Pinocchio (whose nose grew ever longer as he told more fibs), tagging him as "Mr. Late Again" on the basis of EasyJet's refusal to publish its punctuality statistics. Initially, when Stelios objected to the advertisements as personal and libelous, O'Leary refused to apologize and suggested that the dispute should be settled by a sumo wrestling contest or a race around Trafalgar Square. However, O'Leary ended up apologizing unreservedly to Stelios, as Ryanair agreed to pay a £50,000 penalty and published a half- page apology in a national newspaper. Stelios promised to donate the money to charity, saying, "I would like to dedicate this little victory to all those members of the travelling public who have suffered verbal abuse and hidden extras at the hands of O'Leary."[29]

Air Berlin

Originally a charter airline that started operations from Berlin in 1979, Air Berlin expanded into scheduled services and styled itself as a low-cost airline. However, it did not operate with a pure low-cost carrier model. Most notably, instead of only point-topoint service, Air Berlin offered guaranteed connections via its hubs. The airline also offered free services including in-flight meals and drinks, newspapers, and assigned seating. On flights operated on the Airbus A330-200, a dedicated business class section was offered. Air Berlin also ran a frequent flyer program, "topbonus," in collaboration with hotel and car rental partners as well as sundry marginal airlines. Air Berlin had won numerous awards every year, including being designated as the best low-cost carrier in Europe from Skytrax and, in 2010, a best business travel award for short-haul airlines.

The airline first floated on the stock exchange in May 2006, with its initial share-price range reduced from €15.0 to €17.5 before finally opening at €12 due to rising fuel costs and other market pressures at that time. As a result of the IPO, the company claimed to have more than €400 million in the bank to be used to fund further expansion, including aircraft purchases. Since its announcement as a low cost airline in the mid-2000s, it had only made a profit once, in 2006.

From 2009 onward, Air Berlin announced measures to strengthen its efficiency and profitability, through a "Jump" performance program. The aim was a significant improvement of turnover, income per available seat kilometer (ASK), and revenue per passenger kilometer (RPK). Operations were to be subjected to continuous and strict cost control, and any opportunities for performance improvement on the ground and in the air would be consistently explored and implemented. In this context, the introduction of the Q400 turboprop aircraft, first used in 2008 and featuring significantly lower fuel consumption, was of great importance. In addition to the improvement of operational performance, Air Berlin's priority was in strengthening its balance sheet, reducing indebtedness in a targeted manner, by selling strategically unnecessary assets or activities.

In 2009, revenue per available seat kilometer (ASK) increased to 5.75 eurocents, for a 7 percent increase over the previous year (2008: 5.38 eurocents). The company declared that opportunities for growth would continue to be exploited, provided that corresponding income prospects were present. This applied particularly to the expansion of attractive routes and feeder networks, together with strategic partners, and increased targeting of select clients, such as business passengers. The "Jump" performance improvement program led to a marked improvement in operating income, with losses in 2009 of €9.5 million, down from €83.5 million. Also the balance sheet had been significantly improved with a capital increase of 64 percent and a debt decrease of 25 percent, despite the terrible trading conditions brought on by the global financial crisis. However, these were due in large part to a drop in jet fuel prices rather than to measures taken by the company. Despite improvements in cost containment and expansion, 2010 was not very promising profit-wise.

The carrier had been very active in acquiring shares in and integrating with other airlines. This included former Formula One racing driver Niki Lauda's airline Niki, acquired in 2004. The two airlines considered their cooperation a "low fares alliance." Air Berlin held 24 percent of Lauda's enterprise, operating a mixed fleet of Boeing 737s and Airbus A320s. In 2006, Air Berlin acquired dba, formerly Deutsch British Airways, a budget airline based in Munich.

In March 2007, Air Berlin took over German leisure airline LTU, thereby gaining access to the long-haul market and becoming the fourth-largest airline group in Europe in terms of passenger traffic. This deal led to the introduction of Airbus A321 and Airbus A330 aircraft into the Air Berlin fleet. With the merger of the LTU operations, aircraft, and crew, the LTU brand was shut down. Later in 2007, Air Berlin acquired a 49 percent shareholding in Swiss charter airline Belair, otherwise owned by tour operator Hotelplan. A month later, in September 2007, Air Berlin announced an acquisition of its direct competitor Condor in a deal that saw Condor's owner, the Thomas Cook Group, taking a 30 percent stake in Air Berlin. However, the deal was scrapped in July 2008, owing to a variety of considerations, including the rapidly increasing price of jet fuel.

In 2009, a strategic partnership agreement with TUI Travel was signed, based on a cross-ownership of Air Berlin and its direct competitor TUIfly of 19.9 percent in each other's shares. Thereby, Air Berlin took over all German domestic TUIfly routes, as well as those to Italy, Croatia, and Austria. All of TUIfly's Boeing 737-700 aircraft were merged into Air Berlin's fleet, leaving TUI to focus on serving the charter market with the 21 aircraft of its remaining fleet. Also in 2009, Air Berlin announced a cooperation with Pegasus Airlines, thus allowing its customers access to a broader range of destinations and flights to and within Turkey on a codeshare-like basis.

Norwegian Airlines

Norwegian was founded in 1993 as a regional airline taking over routes in western Norway after the bankruptcy of Busy Bee. Until 2002, it operated Fokker 50 aircraft on wet lease for Braathens. Following the 2002 merger of the two domestic incumbents Braathens and Scandinavian Airlines, Norwegian established a domestic low-cost carrier. It had since expanded quickly. By 2010, it was the second-largest airline in Scandinavia and the fourth-largest low-cost carrier in Europe. In 2009, it transported 10.8 million people on 150 routes to 85 destinations across Europe into North Africa and the Middle East. As of the end of 2009, Norwegian operated 46 Boeing 737 aircraft.

Norwegian's main hub was Oslo Airport, Gardermoen, with secondary hub operations at Bergen, Trondheim, Stavanger, Moss, Copenhagen, Stockholm, and Warsaw. It offered a high-frequency domestic flight schedule within Scandinavia, combined with a lowfrequency service to international destinations from its focus cities. Despite the economic downturn, Norwegian Air reported significant passenger growth for 2009 with an 18 percent rise from the previous year, as it expanded rapidly with new routes. In 2010, the airline was set to grow further with the addition of 70 Boeing 737-800 aircraft over the next five years. Norwegian charged passengers for checked-in luggage (€6 each way per bag) as well as onboard snacks and meals and seat selection.

In January 2009, Air Transport World (ATW) named Norwegian "Market Leader of the Year." The award recognized Norwegian for several accomplishments: successful adaptation of the low-cost model to the Scandinavian air travel market; its strategy to combine low fares with high tech alongside a strong emphasis on customer-focused information technology; swift market response in 2008 to the collapse of Sterling, a Danish budget carrier; and the ability to stay profitable in challenging times.

In February 2010, Norwegian was upgraded to "buy" from "neutral" by Goldman Sachs, which cited its compelling valuation and benefits from a route network with little significant competition, in particular from large low-cost carriers such as Ryanair or EasyJet; a resilient Norwegian economy; and strong growth in ancillary revenues.

Wizz Air

Wizz Air is a Hungary-based carrier operating budget scheduled services linking Poland, Hungary, Bulgaria, Croatia, Romania, and Slovenia with points in the Mediterranean, United Kingdom, Ireland, Germany, France, Italy and Scandinavia. The airline, which operates 22 Airbus A320s from 10 bases spread across mainland Europe, was founded in Katowice, Poland, in 2003 as a privately owned budget carrier by Jozsef Varadi, former CEO of Malév, the Hungarian flag carrier. Having considered the Ryanair versus the EasyJet model, the founders of Wizz Air decided to adopt the Ryanair model: to be as lowcost and no frills as possible.

An investor group led by Indigo Partners LLC, founders of Singapore-based low-cost carrier Tiger Airways, became the largest shareholder in December 2004. Budapest became the second operating base in June 2005. Despite the economic climate Wizz continued to expand and set up bases around its core Central and Eastern European markets, with 72 aircraft due to be delivered over the following five years from 2009.

As a private company Wizz Air did not publish any detailed financial information. However, it appeared that the carrier had yet to make a profit and faced massive challenges in terms of financing and effectively deploying aircraft. Its further expansion required substantial investment and cash reserves, which may not have been readily available from Indigo when it was stretched with other investments, including Tiger Airways. Nonetheless, the challenging economic climate faced by Wizz Air could have been viewed as an opportunity with many existing carriers in their target countries reducing capacity and in danger of shutdown (Malev, Aerosvit, LOT-Centralwings).

Wizz Air had assiduously adopted the Ryanair model, so the two airlines consequently shared many similarities, such as the same sort of unflattering comments about them on blog Web sites. However, Wizz merited a three-star Skytrax rating compared with two stars for Ryanair. Both carriers operated to secondary airports, but Wizz operated longer average stage lengths, which resulted in high aircraft utilization of 13 hours daily.

It had even been suggested it would make strategic sense for the two airlines to merge, given the similarity of their cost-cutting cultures.[30] So far, there was little overlap between the route systems of the two carriers, so there could have been complementarity in combining their routes. However, Ryanair operated Boeing 737s, while Wizz Air operated A320s. Such a "merger" would hardly have been a merger, but more a takeover by Ryanair, and it could have met with opposition from EU competition authorities.

Aer Lingus

Ryanair continues to hold a 29.8 percent share of Aer Lingus. The carrier, operating short- and long-haul services, was the national state-owned airline of Ireland until it was floated in October 2006. The events of 9/11 were particularly traumatic for Aer Lingus, as the airline teetered on the verge of bankruptcy. It put in place a plan for a flotation, which had already been postponed several times. In late 2001, the choice was to change, be taken over, or be liquidated. Led by a determined and focused chief executive, Willie Walsh (who was to become the CEO of British Airways in 2005), and his senior management team, the company set about cutting costs. One ingredient of its cost reduction was a severance program, costing more than €100 million, whereby 2,000 of its 6,000 employees left the group. By the end of 2002, Aer Lingus had turned a 2001 €125 million loss into a €33 million profit, and it continued to improve still further, posting a net profit of €88.9 million in 2005.

In essence, Aer Lingus maintained that it had transformed itself into a low-fares airline and that it matched Ryanair fares or was only very slightly higher on most routes. The airline's chief operating officer said that "Aer Lingus no longer offers a gold-plated service to customers, but offers a more practical and appropriate service…it clearly differentiates itself from no-frills carriers. We fly to main airports and not 50 miles away. We assign seats for passengers, we beat low fares competitors on punctuality, even though we fly to more congested airports, and we always fulfil our commitment to customers—unlike no frills carriers."[31]

In its defense document against the Ryanair takeover bid in October 2006, the airline proclaimed a strong track record of growth, with a return on capital and operating margin second only to Ryanair in the European airline industry, leading the Irish market in terms of technological innovation and value-added service innovations such as self-check-in, advance seat selection, Web check-in, and a dynamic and easy-to-use online booking service. Its customer proposition was "Low Fares, Way Better," flying to more convenient airports and posting leading punctuality statistics at Heathrow. A survey conducted by the airline found that customers considered Aer Lingus a better value for the money than Ryanair, even at slightly higher fares. Aer Lingus achieved more than three times as much short-haul passenger growth as Ryanair from Dublin in 2005, with substantial opportunities to grow ancillary revenues. Staff productivity improved from 3,475 to 6,108 passengers per employee between 2001 and 2005.

However, from 2008, Aer Lingus' fortunes began to deteriorate in the face of the gathering recession, rising fuel costs, and fierce competition on all its routes, resulting in losses for the years 2008 and 2009. Christophe Mueller joined the company as CEO in September 2009 and set about trying to staunch losses suffered by the airline as it expanded during a recession that hit its three main markets of Ireland, the United Kingdom, and the United States. Mueller outlined a plan to achieve cost savings of €97 million a year by the end of 2011, in part by cutting staff numbers by nearly a fifth and removing several senior pilots who were among the airline's most expensive employees. The airline was also targeting higher yields rather than simply pursuing market share. Gross cash balances had increased by €90.4 million since December 31, 2009 to €918.9 million. The cost reduction program, involving staff and pay cuts, alongside work increases had been approved in a 74 percent positive staff ballot. The network had been enhanced through an extended code-share agreement with United Airlines and the launch of an Aer Lingus Regional franchise. The company was on target to achieve pretax profits of €31 million in 2010 and €74 million in 2011, driven by a 12.5 percent increase in revenue per passenger.

Investors seemed optimistic about the new strategy. The airline had burned through €400 million cash in 2009, but still had a strong balance sheet with gross cash and deposits of €825 million, of which €770 million was unencumbered. Mueller declared that in a worst-case scenario, Aer Lingus could run for at least four and half years without running out of cash. Mueller had also declared that the large Ryanair holding remained a deterrent to other airlines that might wish to take a stake in Aer Lingus.

Revamping the strategic approach and culture of the airline was a priority in Mueller's ambition to improve revenue. Thus, the airline rebranded itself as "Ireland's civilised airline" as it unveiled a plan to position itself midway between Ryanair and high-end carriers such as British Airways, which some analysts compared with the positioning of EasyJet. The airline's "civilised" tag was seen as a dig at Ryanair.[32] While Aer Lingus hoped to lure business travelers with faster check-in times, pre-paid meals, and conveniently located airports, rather than the secondary ones for which Ryanair was known, it would not focus on the quality lounges and free food and drinks associated with full-service airlines.

Southwest Airlines

Ryanair was the first European airline to model itself on the successful formula of Southwest Airlines in Texas by offering itself as a low-fare, no-frills carrier, serving short-haul city pairs and providing single-class air transportation. As of 2010, Southwest operated more than 3,200 flights a day coast to coast, making it the largest U.S. carrier based on domestic passengers carried.

Southwest, founded in 1967, was the perceived underdog in the ferocious price wars launched by the established airlines when the new carrier entered their markets after deregulation. Southwest is the only airline to have survived the shakeout of new entrants in the sharply competitive U.S. environment. This survival served to inspire Southwest, so that it styled itself more as a freedom fighter rather than a mere corporation, listing "five symbols of freedom" in its annual report: its people, its low fares, its customers, its operations, and its advertising/promotions/marketing:

- *People*: Southwest had an acknowledged unique culture, largely attributable to its staff members and their commitment to the company and its customers. The creation of a "fun" environment was one of the ways in which the airline differentiated itself. The corporate culture of the company, referred to by Herb Kelleher, its iconic founder and chairman until 2008, as "a patina of spirituality" was ingrained in its people. A family loyalty feeling was further inculcated by staff development processes such as team training, 80 percent internal promotion, and recognition events and practices. Staff turnover was well below the industry average. Overall compensation included profit-sharing schemes. The workforce was almost entirely unionized. Southwest had consistently been ranked as one of the best companies to work for in the United States.

- *Low fares*: Southwest claimed to have the lowest fares with the simplest fare structure in the U.S. domestic airline industry. More than 80 percent of customers bought travel on a ticketless basis and approximately 80 percent of Southwest customers checked in online or at a kiosk in 2010.

- *Customers*: Southwest claims to give people the freedom to fly, first and foremost with its low fares, but also with its streamlined service to provide for short-haul customers needs—frequent departures to meet customer demands for schedule frequency and flexibility, nonstop services, and conveniently located airports near city centers. The carrier also targeted business travelers who constituted a substantial proportion of its passengers. Southwest had a frequent flyer program, Rapid Rewards, whereby a free round trip was given to a customer who had purchased eight round trips on the same route. The carrier had declined to join competitors in charging for the first and second checked bags. However, passengers could incur extra charges for *Business Select* fares offering priority seating, security lane access, a premium beverage coupon, and flight credits. Other services liable for extra charges were Pets Onboard, Unaccompanied Minor service, and Early Bird Check-in.

- *Operations*: To maintain low fares, Southwest contained its costs on many fronts. Its point-to-point route system with frequent daily departures from the same airport was cheaper than most of its competitors' hub-and-spoke systems. However, while three-fourths of its passengers flew point to point, connecting traffic grew with corresponding revenues of tens of millions of dollars in 2009. The carrier flew into less congested airports of small cities or the smaller airports of large cities. This saved time as well as money in landing charges. The airline did not engage in interline baggage transfer and served only drinks and simple snacks on board for free, while charging for alcoholic beverages. These operations resulted in shorter time to turn around an aircraft, claimed by the company to be less than half the industry standard. This meant greater utilization of aircraft and lower unit costs.

The airline used only one aircraft type, the Boeing 737, in an all-coach configuration. This substantially reduced costs due to simplified operations, training, scheduling, and maintenance. Cost containment was aided at Southwest by a cost- and time-conscious workforce, constantly on the look-out for money-saving ideas. Despite heavy unionization, there was virtually no job demarcation, as staff performed tasks allocated to other people if it saved time and money.

From its inception, Southwest had received many awards and recognitions. It has been recognized as received Best Low Cost/No Frills Airline, finalist for Best Airline based in North America, Favorite Domestic Airline and ranked #1 in Best Customer Service, Best Airfare Prices, Best On-Time Service, Best Baggage Service, and Best Value Frequent Flier program, and Best Low Cost Carrier.

In March 2009, Southwest Airlines was ranked number one in the category for airlines in *Institutional Investor's* magazine poll of America's Most Shareholder Friendly Companies, an award it had received many times previously. Southwest Airlines was named the seventh-most admired Company in *Fortune* magazine's ranking of the 50 Most Admired Companies in the World in 2009, the only U.S. airline to make the list and the 13th consecutive year that Southwest had been named to the Most Admired List. Moreover, its renowned founder and CEO, Kelleher, was also lauded with awards, culminating in his enshrinement in the National Aviation Hall of Fame upon his retirement as chairman in 2008, to be replaced by Gary Kelly, who had already replaced Kelleher as CEO in 2004. Kelly, a CPA, had been CFO and originally joined Southwest in 1986 as controller. Like his predecessor, Kelly has been the recipient of numerous awards, including one of the best CEOs in America for 2008, 2009, and 2010 by *Institutional Investor* magazine.

In 2009, notwithstanding the recession and turmoil in the airline industry, Southwest remained profitable, producing its 37th consecutive year of profitability, although net income dropped to $99 million from $178 million the year before. Staying in the black was due to various measures:

- an aggressive advertising campaign to affirm that Bags Fly Free only on Southwest, resulting in increased market share worth $1 billion and record load factors;
- rationalizing unpopular and unprofitable routes and redeploying capacity to developing markets;
- picking up market share from defunct carriers, like Frontier Airlines;
- other revenue intiatives, such as new products like onboard wireless Internet access, enhancements to southwest.com, and continued development of Rapid Rewards; and
- containing costs and maximizing productivity.

Southwest also concentrated on maintaining financial strength, with total liquidity of $3 billion expected to rise

in 2010. The balance sheet was investment-grade strong and also expected to improve even more in 2010. However, prompted by slowing growth and rising costs, in 2010, Southwest acquired AirTran, a rival U.S. budget carrier, in one of the world's biggest no-frills airline tie-ups. Would this takeover deal by Southwest serve as yet another role model for other budget carriers around the world?

Leading Ryanair into the Future

"It is good to have someone like Michael O'Leary around. He scares people to death." This praise of Ryanair's CEO came from none other than his fellow Irishman, Willie Walsh, CEO of BA.[33] O'Leary had been described as "at turns, arrogant and rude, then charming, affable and humorous, has terrorised rivals and regulators for more than a decade. And so far, they have waited in vain for him to trip up or his enthusiasm to wane."[34] In fact, O'Leary had been pronouncing his intention to depart from the airline "in two years' time" since 2005. He had declared that he would sever all links with the airline, refusing to "move upstairs" as chairman. "You don't need a doddery old bastard hanging around the place," he proclaimed.[35]

O'Leary bred racehorses at his Gigginstown Stud 50 miles (80 kilometers) from Dublin. In 2006, his horse, War of Attrition won the Cheltenham Gold Cup, one of the most prestigious races in steeplechasing, while another, Hear the Echo, won the Irish Grand National in 2008. He stayed in budget hotels and always flew Ryanair, startling fellow passengers by taking their boarding passes at the gate and by boarding the plane last where he invariably got a middle seat. He did not sit in an executive lounge, had no BlackBerry, and did not use email.

In 2010, O'Leary held just under 4 percent of Ryanair's share capital, having sold 5 million shares at €3.90. Although O'Leary consistently praised the contributions and achievements of his management team, Ryanair was inextricably identified with him. He was credited with singlehandedly transforming European air transport. In 2001, O'Leary received the European Businessman of the Year Award from *Fortune* magazine; in 2004, *The Financial Times* named him as one of 25 European "business stars" who have made a difference. The newspaper described him as personifying "the brash new Irish business elite" and possessing "a head for numbers, a shrewd marketing brain and a ruthless competitive streak."[36]

Present and former staff have praised O'Leary's leadership style. "Michael's genius is his ability to motivate and energise people...There is an incredible energy in that place. People work incredibly hard and get a lot out of it. They operate a very lean operation…It is without peer," said Tim Jeans, a former sales and marketing director of Ryanair, currently CEO of a small low-cost rival, MyTravelLite.[37]

O'Leary's publicity-seeking antics are legendary. These included his "declaration of war" on EasyJet when, wearing an army uniform, he drove a tank to EasyJet's headquarters at Luton Airport. In another stunt, when Ryanair opened its hub at Milan Bergamo, he flew there aboard a jet bearing the slogan "Arrividerci Alitalia." He had also dressed up as St. Patrick and as the Pope to promote ticket offers. Another provocative idea enunciated by O'Leary was the recommendation that co-pilots could be done away with on flights, so aircraft could fly with just one pilot, because "the computer does most of the flying now" and "a flight attendant could do the job of a co-pilot, if needed."[38] In fact, he even went so far as to suggest that under present arrangements, "maybe the second pilot could be doing some of the in-flight service."[39]

O'Leary's outspokenness has made him a figure of public debate. "He is called everything from 'arrogant pig' to 'messiah.'"[40] His avowed enemies included trade unions, politicians who imposed airport taxes (calling former UK Prime Minister Gordon Brown a "twit" and a "Scottish miser"[41]), environmentalists, bloggers who ranted about poor service, travel agents, reporters who expected free seats, regulators and the EU Commission, and airport owners like BAA, whom he once called "overcharging rapists."[42] An EU Commissioner, Philippe Busquin, denounced O'Leary as "irritating…and insists he is not the only Commissioner who is allergic to the mere mention of the name of Ryanair's arrogant chief."[43]

Irish Times columnist John McManus suggested that "maybe it's time for Ryanair to jettison O'Leary," asserting that O'Leary had become a caricature of himself, fulfilling all 15 warning signs of an executive about to fail.[44] Professor Sydney Finklestein of the Tuck Business School at Dartmouth U.S. identified the 15 signs under five headings: ignoring change, the wrong vision, getting too close, arrogant attitudes, and old formulae. But having demonstrated the extent that O'Leary met the Finklestein criteria, McManus concluded: "So, is it time for Ryanair to dump O'Leary? Depends whether you prefer the track record of one of the most successful businessmen in modern aviation or the theories of a U.S. academic from an Ivy League school."

Perhaps the last words should go to O'Leary himself: "We could make a mistake and I could get hung," he said. He reiterated a point he had often made before: "It is okay doing the cheeky chappie, running around Europe, thumbing your nose, but I am not Herb Kelleher (the legendary founder of the original budget airline, Southwest Airlines). He was a genius and I am not."[45]

So, how do these comments and his hands-on management style fit with O'Leary's declaration to part company with Ryanair? Would he really go, and if so, what would happen to Ryanair and its ambitions? No one really knew the answer to these questions, but it would certainly lie in O'Leary's propensity to surprise his admirers and detractors alike.

End Notes

1. (2009). "The FT ArcelorMittal Boldness in Business Awards." *Financial Times* supplement, March 20, p.25.
2. Done, K. (2009). "Airline industry in intensive care." *Financial Times*, March 25, p.22.
3. Done, K. (2009). "Ryanair sees opportunities in rivals' distress." *Financial Times*, July 28, p.15.
4. Done, K. (2009). Ibid. Aldi and Lidl are German discount hypermarkets, renowned for their low prices and spreading quickly across Europe.
5. *Financial Times*, 2006. September 9, p. 16.
6. Done, K., and T. Braithwaite. (2006). "Ryanair to allow mobile phone calls next year." *Financial Times*, August 31, p.1.
7. Ryanair annual report. (2001).
8. Guthrie, J. (2009). "Sir Stelios beknighted as suits prove bolder risk takers." *Financial Times*, July 30, p. 16.
9. Ryanair annual report. (2009).
10. Ibid.
11. Lyall, S. (2009). "No apologies from the boss of a no-frills airline." *The New York Times*, August 1 (*The Saturday Profile*).

12. Ryanair 2007 half yearly results.
13. LEX. (2009). "Ryanair." *Financial Times*, June 3, p. 16.
14. Noonan, L. (2009). "O'Leary admits stake in Aer Lingus was stupid disaster." *Irish Independent*, March 6.
15. (2006). Statement from Ryanair's half yearly results presentation, November 6.
16. Pogatchnik, S. (2006). "Aer Lingus rejects Ryanair takeover offer." *Business Week* on-line, November 3. Manchester United and Liverpool have a longstanding legendary rivalry in English football.
17. Ryanair full year results. (2009).
18. (2010). Guardian newspaper blog, www.guardian.co.uk/world/blog/2010/apr/22/iceland-volcanocompensation. Accessed May 19, 2010.
19. Carolan, M. (2010). "Judge pulls out of Ryanair case without altering previous findings or comments." *Irish Times*, June 22.
20. (2009). Ryanair press release, May 29.
21. Milmo, D. (2006). "Ryanair—The World's Least Favorite Airline." *The Guardian*. October 26.
22. Waite, R., and S. Swinford. (2009). "Ryanair more expensive than BA on some flights." *Sunday Times*, August 9.
23. Money Central. (2009). "WBLG: Twenty reasons never to fly Ryanair." *Times Online*, March 20.
24. Pope, C. (2009). "Pricewatch daily." *Irish Times*, August 14, p. 11.
25. Lyall, S. (2009). "No apologies from the boss of a no-frills airline." *The New York Times*, August 1 *(The Saturday Profile)*.
26. Ibid.
27. Clark, P. (2010). "EasyJet founder quits board." *Financial Times*, May 15, p. 12.
28. Clark, P. (2010). "EasyJet founder savages Harrison." *Financial Times*, May 12, p. 22.
29. (2010). "Ryanair and O'Leary apologise to EasyJet founder of Pinocchio ads." *Irish Times*, July 6.
30. Centre for Asia Pacific Aviation. (2009). "Ryanair meets Wizz Air: Does a merger make sense?" July 8. http://www.centreforaviation.com/news/2009/07/08/ryanair-meets-wizz-air-does-amerger-make-sense. Accessed May 2010.
31. Creaton, S. (2003). "Aer Lingus's new model airline takes off." *Irish Times*, August 8, p. 52.
32. Clark, P. (2010). "Aer Lingus brands itself 'civilised' airline." *Financial Times*, January 27, p. 18.
33. Done, K. (2008). "O'Leary shows it is not yet the end for budget air travel." *Financial Times*, August 2, p. 11.
34. The FT ArcelorMittal Boldness in Business Awards. (2009). *Financial Times* supplement, March 20, p. 21.
35. Dalby, D. (2005). "I'm going for good, O'Leary tells Ryanair." *Sunday Times*, November 20, News, p. 3.
36. Groom, B. (2004). "Leaders of the new Europe: Business stars chart a course for the profits of the future." *Financial Times*, April 20.
37. Bowley, G. (2003). "How low can you go?" *Financial Times Magazine*, 9, June 21.
38. Clark, P. (2010). "Ryanair's latest no-frills idea: sack the boss." *Financial Times*, September 14.
39. Hancock, C. (2010.). "The Friday interview: Michael O'Leary, Ryanair chief executive." *Irish Times*, Business This Week, September 24.
40. Ibid. Bowley, 2003.
41. Lyall, S. (2009). "No apologies from the boss of a no-frills airline." *The New York Times*, August 1 *(The Saturday Profile)*.
42. Ibid.
43. Creaton, S. (2004). "Turbulent times for Ryanair's high-flier." *Irish Times*, January 31.
44. McManus, J. (2003). "Maybe it's time for Ryanair to jettison O'Leary." *Irish Times*, August 11.
45. Bowley, G. (2003). "How low can you go?" *Financial Times Magazine*, 9, June 21.

Case 2-3: The Levi's Personal Pair Proposal

WISCONSIN
SCHOOL OF BUSINESS

The Levi's Personal Pair Proposal[1]

"I'll have my recommendation to you by the end of the week." Heidi Green hung up the phone and surveyed her calendar for appointments that could be pushed into the next week. It was a rainy afternoon in December 1994, and she had yet to recover from the pre-holiday rush to get product out to retailers.

She had three days to prepare a presentation for the Executive Committee on a new concept called Personal Pair. Custom Clothing Technology Corporation (CCTC) had approached Levi Strauss with the joint venture proposal that would marry Levi's core products with the emerging technologies of mass customization. Jeans could be customized in style and fit to meet each customer's unique needs and taste. If CCTC was correct, this would reach the higher end of the jeans market, yielding stronger profit margins due to both the price premium and the streamlined production process involved.

On the other hand, the technology was new to Levi Strauss and the idea could turn out to be an expensive and time-consuming proposal that would come back later to haunt her, as she would have to manage the venture. The initial market studies seemed supportive, but there was no way to know how customers would respond to the program because there was nothing quite like it out there. She also was unsure whether the program would work as smoothly in practice as the plan suggested.

Company Background and History

Levi Strauss and Co. is a privately held company owned by the family of its founder, Levi Strauss. The Bavarian immigrant was the creator of durable work pants from cloth used for ships' sails, which were reinforced with his patented rivets. The now-famous "waist-overalls," were originally created more than 130 years ago for use by California gold rush workers. These were later seen as utilitarian farm- or factory-wear. By the 1950's, Levi's jeans had acquired a Hollywood cachet, as the likes of Marilyn Monroe, James Dean, Marlon Brando, Elvis, and Bob Dylan proudly wore them, giving off an air of rebellious hipness. The jeans would become a political statement and an American icon, as all jeans soon became known generically as "Levi's." The baby boomer generation next adopted the jeans as a fashion statement, and from 1964–1975, the company's annual sales grew tenfold, from $100 million to $1 billion.[2] By the late 70's, Levi's had become synonymous with the terms "authentic," "genuine," "original," and "real," and wearing them allowed the wearer to make a statement. According to some who recognize the brand's recognition even over that of Coke, Marlboro, Nike or Microsoft, "Levi Strauss has been, and remains, both the largest brand-apparel company in the world and the number one purveyor of blue jeans in the world."

While blue jeans remained the company's mainstay, the San Francisco-based company also sold pants made of corduroy, twill, and various other fabrics, as well as shorts, skirts, jackets, and outerwear. The company, with its highly recognizable brand name, held a top position in many of its markets and was sold in more than 80 countries. More than half of the company's revenue was from its U.S. sales; nevertheless, Europe and Asia were highly profitable markets. Latin America and Canada were secondary markets, with smaller contributions to overall profits. As the graphic (below) shows, apparel imports were increasing faster than exports during this period.

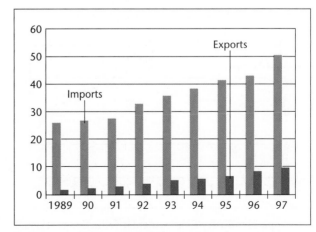

Import and Exports of Apparel (in billions of dollars)

Source: U.S. Department of Commerce.

The company's non-denim brand, Dockers, was introduced in 1986 and was sold in the United States, Canada, Mexico, and Europe. While it was composed of both women's and men's clothing, the men's line of khaki pants occupied the leading position in U.S. sales of khaki trousers and sold well with baby boomers. Sales of Dockers had steadily increased with the rise in casual workplaces, and this line of non-denim products had helped in allowing Levi's to be less reliant on the denim industry.

Competition and the Denim Industry

Denim was "one of the fastest-growing apparel fabrics," and sales have been increasing approximately 10% per year. According to some surveys, an average American consumer owns 17 denim items, which includes 6–7 pairs of jeans.[3] Levi Strauss and Company held the largest market share in 1990, at 31%, followed by VF Corporation's Lee and Wrangler (17.9%), designer labels (6%), The Gap (3%), and department store private labels (3.2%). By 1995, women's jeans had grown to a $2 billion market, of which Levi's held first place.

However, at the same time, many jeans producers were starting to move production to low-cost overseas facilities, which allowed for cost (especially labor) advantages. As the graph (below) shows, this trend was represented throughout the apparel industry and is clearly visible in employment statistics. Indeed, JC Penney, one of Levi's long-time partners, had become a competitor by introducing a cheaper alternative, the Arizona label. They and other rivals had realized that by sourcing all production in cheap overseas facilities they could enter the business with a cost advantage over Levi Strauss.

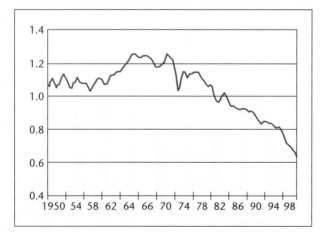

U.S. Apparel Industry Employment (production workers, in millions)

Source: Bureau of Labor Statistics.

Levi's as a private company, which viewed itself as having a strong "social conscience," wanted to avoid being seen as exploiting disadvantaged workers. Accordingly, they preferred to have their jeans "U.S.-made," and Levi Strauss was a leader in providing generous salary and benefits packages to its employees.

Accordingly, it did not relish the notion of entering into price-based competition with rivals committed to overseas production. Their delayed response led to some significant incursions by rivals into Levi's core product arenas.

Levi's also wanted to avoid price-based competition because they had a history of brand recognition and brand loyalty. They were accustomed to the Levi's brand carrying enough clout to justify a reasonable price premium. However, over the years, the brand name carried less cachet, and as hundreds of competitors with similar products dotted the landscape, it became necessary to create valued features that would help to differentiate the product in the eyes of consumers.

Levi Strauss' financial performance is summarized in Exhibit 1 for the period from 1990–1994. While the company was profitable throughout the period, revenue growth had clearly slowed and income growth was quite uneven. This is especially apparent for 1994, the current year, where net income dropped by 35% due to fierce competition for market share and narrowing margins.

Cost Structure

Exhibit 2 provides an estimate of the cost and margins on an average pair of jeans sold through Levi's two outlets. Much of their product is sold through wholesale channels, to be distributed by competing retailers. However, Levi's maintains a chain of Original Levi's Stores (OLS) primarily to help keep them closer to the customer. The profit per pair of jeans is about 30% lower in the wholesale channel ($2 as opposed to $3). This is driven by the 30% margin that accrues to the channel, and which is somewhat balanced by the higher costs of operating the OLS outlets (especially the additional SG&A costs for operating the stores).

Exhibit 2 also indicates the ongoing investment per pair of jeans. Once this is considered, the wholesale outlets are nearly twice as profitable—the pre-tax return on invested capital is 15%, as opposed to 8%. Here, the OLS outlets require additional investment in inventory ($8/pair), which is normally borne by the retailer, and the capital tied up in the retail stores ($20/pair).

Exhibit 1 Levi Strauss Financial Performance					
	1994	**1993**	**1992**	**1991**	**1990**
Income Statement					
Net Sales	$6,074,321	$5,892,479	$5,570,290	$4,902,882	$4,247,150
Cost of Goods	$3,632,406	$3,638,152	$3,431,469	$3,024,330	$2,651,338
Gross Profit	$2,441,915	$2,254,327	$2,138,821	$1,878,552	$1,595,812
Selling G&A Exp	$1,472,786	$1,394,170	$1,309,352	$1,147,465	$922,785
Non Operating Income	−$18,410	$8,300	−$142,045	$31,650	−$36,403
Interest Exp	$19,824	$37,144	$53,303	$71,384	$82,956
Income Before Taxes	$930,895	$831,313	$634,121	$691,353	$553,668
Taxes	$373,402	$338,902	$271,673	$324,812	$288,753
Net Inc Before Ext Items	$557,493	$492,411	$362,448	$366,541	$264,915
Ext Items	−$236,517	$0	−$1,611	−$9,875	−$13,746
Net Income	$320,976	$492,411	$360,837	$356,666	$251,169
Growth					
Sales Growth	3.1%	5.8%	13.6%	15.4%	
Net Income Growth	−34.8%	36.5%	1.2%	42.0%	
Key Financial Ratios					
Quick Ratio	1.57	1.03	0.76	0.87	0.73
SG&A/Sales	24.25	23.66	23.51	23.4	21.73
Receivables Turnover	6.68	6.87	7.67	7.31	6.88
Inventories Turnover	7.76	7.44	7.64	7.5	7.29
Total Debt/Equity	2.57	10.57	34.39	71.82	22.21
Net Inc/Sales	5.28	8.36	6.48	7.27	5.91
Net Inc/Total assets	8.18	15.84	12.53	13.54	10.51

Mass Customization

Mass customization uses emerging communication and computer technologies to bypass the limitations of traditional mass production methods. From a strategic standpoint, the concept is based on the idea that "the ultimate niche is a market of one."[4] Previously, it was thought that highly-customized products were necessarily expensive to produce; however, with the advent of various information technologies, meeting the customer's needs for flexibility and greater choice in the marketplace is becoming more and more economical.

> "A silent revolution is stirring in the way things are made and services are delivered. Companies with millions of customers are starting to build products designed just for you. You can, of course, buy a Dell computer assembled to your exact specifications… But you can also buy pills with the exact blend of vitamins, minerals, and herbs that you like, glasses molded to fit your face precisely, CD's with music tracks that you choose, cosmetics mixed to match your skin tone, textbooks whose chapters are picked out by your professor, a loan structured to meet your financial profile, or a night at a hotel where everyone knows your favorite wine. And if your child does not like any of Mattel's 125 different Barbie dolls, she will soon be able to design her own."[5]

There is, of course, a delicate balance between providing consumers enough flexibility to meet their needs without so much that the decision-making process becomes perplexing and the company's costs spiral out of control trying to meet the customers' phantom needs.

In the early 90's, Levi Strauss found itself facing a dual set of competitors. There were the low-cost, high-volume producers with a distinct advantage over Levi's, and there were also the higher-cost producers of jeans that targeted the affluent end of the denim-buying public. As a high-volume producer with a cost disadvantage, Levi's increasingly found itself at a disadvantage in both the upper and lower ends of the apparel market.

Personal Pair Proposal

Proponents of the Personal Pair project envisioned a niche that would allow Levi's to avoid competing against the low-cost high-volume producers. Market research revealed that only a quarter of women were truly happy with the fit of their jeans, and the company hoped to attract higher-income customers who would be willing to pay a little extra for a perfect fit.

Exhibit 2   Profitability Analysis of Women's Jeans

	Wholesale Channel	Original Levi's Store Channel	Personal Pair?	Notes
Operations, per pair				
Gross Revenue	$35	$50		$50 retail price with a 30% channel margin.
Less Markdowns	(3)	(5)		Avg. channel markdowns of $5; 60% born by mfg.
Net Revenue	32	45		
Costs				
Cotton	5	5		
Mfg. Conversion	7	7		High labor content since all jeans hand-sewn. Wholly-owned distribution network for OLS channel. Add $2 for warehouse to store.
Distribution	9	11		
Total	21	23		
COGS				
Gross Margin	11	22		
SG&A	9[1]	19[2]		
Profit Before	$2	$3		
Tax				
Investment, per pair				
Inventory	$4	$12		77 days for Levi's wholesale channel & 240 days for OLS stores to include retail inventory.
Less A/P	(1)	(1)		Reflects 27 days of Accounts Payable.
Accounts	4	0		51-day collection period for wholesale. Retail customers pay immediately.
Receivable				
Net Working Capital	7	11		
Factory PP&E	5	5		Reflects a sales to fixed asset turnover of 5.33.
Distribution PP&E	1	2		Doubled for OLS channel due to additional retail distribution investment (estimate).
Retail Store	0	20		$2.4M/OLS store for 120,000 pairs sold/yr (est.).
Total Investment	$13	$38		
Pre-tax return on invested capital	15%	8%		

[1] At $9, a little higher than Levi's overall 25% SG&A due to supply chain problems with women's jeans.
[2] The additional $10 reflects an average 22% store expense for retail clothiers (Compact Disclosure database).

Source: Adapted from Carr, 1998.

In addition, a mass customization model could lower costs as well as provide the differentiation advantage since the re-engineered process is often more efficient once new technologies are applied. For example, the mass customization model, which operates on the "pull-driven" approach of having the customer drive the production process, would lower distribution costs and inventories of unsold products.

Personal Pair was a jeans customization program made possible through a joint venture with Custom Clothing Technology Corporation (CCTC), in Newton, Massachusetts. CCTC approached Levi Strauss, described the potential of its technology and suggested that, together, the two companies could enter the mass customization arena.

The Personal Pair proposal reflected a form of collaborative customization. This approach helps customers who find the array of choices in the marketplace overwhelming, to narrow down their specific needs. The company enters into a dialogue with customers to help them understand what they need, and is then able to provide specialized products that meet that specific need. Collaborative customizers are able to keep inventories of finished products at a minimum, which brings new products to market faster. That is, they manufacture products in a "just-in-time" fashion to respond to specific customer requests.

How It Would Work.   Original Levi's Stores (OLS) would be equipped with networked PC's and Personal Pair kiosks. Trained sales clerks would measure customers' waist, hips, rise, and inseam, resulting in one of 4,224 possible size combinations—a dramatic increase over the 40 combinations

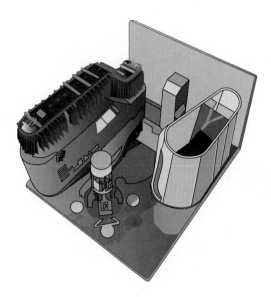

normally available to customers. The computer would then generate a code number that corresponded to one of 400 prototype pairs of jeans kept in the kiosk. Within three tries, more measurements would be taken and a perfect fit would be obtained; the customer would then pay for the jeans and opt for Federal Express delivery ($5 extra) or store pickup, with a full money-back guarantee on every pair.

The order was then sent to CCTC in Boston via a Lotus Notes computer program. This program would "translate" the order and match it with a pre-existing pattern at the Tennessee manufacturing facility. The correct pattern would be pulled, "read," and transferred to the cut station, where each pair was cut individually. A sewing line composed of eight flexible team members would process the order, it would be sent to be laundered, and would be inspected and packed for shipping. A bar code would be sewn into each pair to simplify reordering details, and the customer would have a custom-fit pair within three weeks.

Once the program was underway, the proposal suggested that about half of the orders would be from existing customers. Reordering would be simplified and encouraged by the bar code sewn into each pair. In addition, reorders could be handled through a web-based interface.

Pricing.   There was some question about how much of a price premium the new product would command. The proposal called for a $15 premium (over the standard $50/pair off the rack) and focus groups suggested that women, in particular, would consider this a fair price to pay for superior fit. However, other's argued that this price point was a bit optimistic, suggesting that $5 or $10 might be more realistic given the lower-priced alternatives.

Planned Scope.   The initial proposal was to equip four Original Levi's Stores (OLS) with Personal Pair kiosks and specialized PC's. Once the systems were worked out, this would be expanded to more than 60 kiosks across the U.S. and Canada. In addition, they envisioned opening kiosks in London where they estimated that the product would command a premium of £19 over the original £46 price for standard jeans. The jeans would still be produced in Tennessee and shipped via Federal Express.

Cost Impact.   Although the new process would require some investments in technology and process changes, many other costs were projected to drop. These are illustrated by the complex supply chain for the OLS channel (Exhibit 3) and the relatively simple supply chain for the proposed Personal Pair program (Exhibit 4).

■ The most obvious ongoing cost savings would be in distribution. Here, the order is transmitted electronically and the final product is shipped directly to the customer at his/her expense. These costs would be nearly eliminated in the proposed program.

■ Manufacturing and raw materials would not change much since all jeans are hand sewn and would use the same materials for the traditional and mass-customized processes.

■ The portion of SG&A expenses attributable to retail operations ($10/pair in Exhibit 2) would be reduced if 50% of the sales are reorders that do not incur incremental costs in the retail stores ($5/pair savings). However, CCTC would incur its own SG&A costs that would have to be considered (about $3/pair).

■ Finally, no price adjustments would be needed in such a tight channel since there would be no inventory of finished product. In the retail channel, about $1/3$ of jeans are sold at a discount to clear out aging stock (the discounts average 30%).[6]

Investment Impact.   While the factory PP&E was not projected to change much (they would continue to use the same facilities), a number of other factors would impact the invested capital tied up in a pair of jeans (both positively and negatively) under the proposed program:

Increases in invested capital:

■ First, there would be an initial $3 million required to integrate the systems of CCTC with Levi's existing systems. This was relatively small since it was a matter of integrating existing systems in the two companies.

■ CCTC would also require additional IT investments estimated at $10/pair to maintain the system and upgrade it regularly as scale requirements increased.

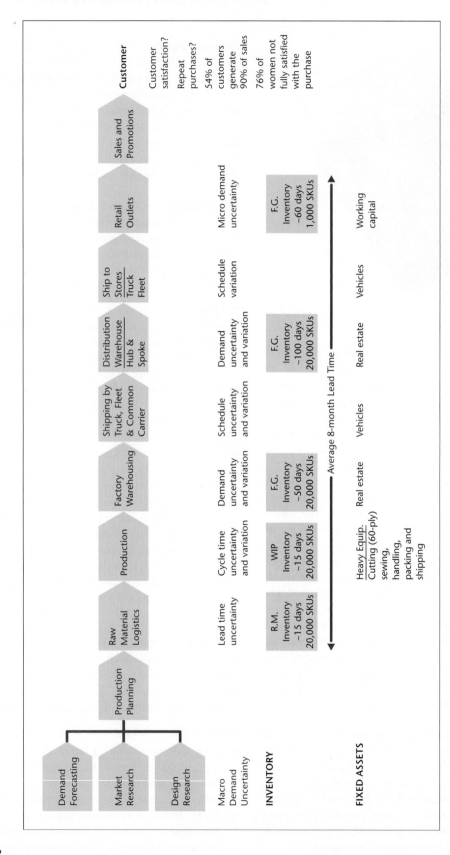

Exhibit 3 Traditional Original Levi's Store Supply Chain

Source: Adapted from Carr, 1998.

Exhibit 4   Personal Pair Value Chain

*Although this approach changes cutting from 60-ply to one, it does not otherwise change manufacturing since jeans were, and are, sewn one pair at a time.

| Personal Pair kiosk in retail store | EDI link to manufacturing via CCTC | Raw material logistics | Manufacturing the one pair of jeans* | Pack pair for daily pickup at factory by FedEx | FedEx directly to customer |

- In addition, the kiosks would take up about $\frac{1}{3}$ of the space in the OLS retail stores (about \$7/pair for retail space).

Decreases in invested capital:

- The required inventory was significantly lower under the proposed program. Recent estimates calculated Levi's average inventory at about 8 months.[7] In contrast, the Personal Pair program called for no inventory of finished product and only a small inventory of raw materials (about \$1/pair).

- Finally, the proposal suggested that accounts receivable would lead to a net gain of about \$2/pair since customers would have paid about 3 weeks prior to receiving the product (similar to the Amazon.com model).

Integrating Elements of Mass Customization at Levi Strauss.   In order for a company to transform an existing product into one that is cost-efficient to mass produce, certain product modifications must be made. The Personal Pair proposal incorporated several of the key elements suggested as helpful for implementing successful mass-customization programs.[8]

First, it is important to introduce the differentiating component of the product (that which must be customized) as late in the production process as possible. For example, paint is not mixed by the manufacturer, but at the point of sale, after being demanded by individual customers. Unfortunately, the making of personalized jeans would not lend itself to a differentiating component late in the production process. Therefore, in this case, the customizing would have to take place at the beginning of the process.

Then, it is helpful if either the product or the process of manufacturing can be easily separated into production modules. Steps in the process can then be reassembled in a different order. For example, a sweater manufacturer might wait until the last possible moment to dye its products in different colors for each season, instead of dying the wool first and knitting the sweaters. This allows for much more flexibility and helps the manufacturer to keep up with fast moving fashion trends. The Personal Pair proposal suggested that the manufacturing process would be modified to allow for better flow—specifically teams would be used to allow for more flexibility and handling of custom products. Unfortunately, since elements in the jean manufacturing process do not always come together in the same way, it would be important that employees accumulate a large range of skills to accommodate idiosyncratic problems that cannot be anticipated.

Finally, it is helpful if either the products or the sub-processes in the manufacturing chain are standardized. This allows for more efficient production and inventory management, whether it be for different types of domestic uses or different markets (for example, international as well as domestic markets were served by a printer manufacturer that allowed all its printers to be adjusted for both 110/220-volt usage). Here, the Personal Pair proposal called for a complex computer program with computerized patterns that were then beamed directly to the cutting floor. This would help them to integrate some technology-enhanced sub-processes with existing standard labor-intensive manufacturing methods.

It also goes without saying that all the parts of the new mass customization process need to come together in an "instantaneous, costless, seamless and frictionless manner."[9]

The Decision

As Heidi leaned back and gazed outside at the rain-soaked plaza, she considered the pros and cons to the proposal. The proposal carried several risks that she could not fully quantify. First, there was the ability of Levi Strauss to implement new technologies. Second, the cost savings in the proposal were based on CCTC's estimates in their proposal for the program. Would the program still be successful if the costs turned out to be very different? Third, market research indicated that women were not satisfied about fit. How much would they be willing to pay for a better fit?

On another level, she wondered about the competition. If the program were successful, would their low-cost rivals dive into this market as well? Did Levi's have any advantage here? What if they did not move forward with the proposal? Would one of their rivals partner with CCTC?

Bibliography

1. Aron, Laurie Joan, From Push to Pull: The Supply Chain Management Shifts, *Apparel Industry Magazine*, June 1998, Volume 59, Issue 6, p. 58–59.
2. *Apparel Industry Magazine*, Jeanswear Gets Squeezed: Plants Close at Levi's, VF, March 1999, Volume 60, Issue 3, p. 10.
3. Billington, Jim, How to Customize for the Real World, *Harvard Management Update*, Reprint #U9704A, 1997.
4. Bounds, Wendy, Inside Levi's Race to Restore a Tarnished Brand, *Wall Street Journal*, August 4, 1998, p. B1.
5. Carr, Lawrence, William Lawler, and John Shank, Levi's Personal Pair Cases A, B, and Teaching Note, F.W. Olin Graduate School of Business, Babson College, December 1998, #BAB020, BAB021, and BAB520.
6. Chaplin, Heather, The Truth Hurts, *American Demographics*, April 1999, Volume 21, Issue 4, p. 68–9.
7. Charlet, Jean-Claude, and Erik Brynjolfsson, BroadVision, *Stanford University Graduate School of Business Case* #OIT–21, March 1998.
8. Church, Elizabeth, Personal Pair Didn't Fit into Levi Strauss's Plans, *The Globe and Mail*, May 27, 1999, p. B13.
9. Collett, Stacy, Levi Shuts Plants, Misses Trends, *Computerworld*, March 1, 1999, p. 16.
10. *Economist, The*, Keeping the Customer Satisfied, July 14, 2001, p. 9–10.
11. *Economist, The*, Special Report, Mass Customization: A Long March, July 14, 2001, p. 63–65.
12. Ellison, Sarah, Levi's is Ironing Some Wrinkles out of its Sales, *Wall Street Journal*, February 12, 2001, p. B9.
13. Espen, Hal, Levi's Blues, *The New York Times Magazine*, March 21, 1999, p. 6.
14. Esquivel, Josephine R. and Huong Chu Belpedio, Textile and Apparel Suppliers Industry Overview, Morgan Stanley Dean Witter, March 14, 2001, p. 1–72.
15. Feitzinger, Edward and Hau L. Lee, Mass Customization at Hewlett-Packard: The Power of Postponement, *Harvard Business Review*, January–February 1997, Reprint #97101, p. 116–121.
16. FITCH Company Reports, Levi Strauss and Co., February 15, 2001, www.fitchratings.com.
17. FITCH Company Reports, Levi Strauss and Co., October 31, 2000, www.fitchratings.com.
18. FITCH Company Reports, Levi Strauss and Co., March 18, 1999, www.fitchratings.com.
11. Gilbert, Charles, Did Modules Fail Levi's or Did Levi's Fail Modules?, *Apparel Industry Magazine*, September 1998, Volume 59, Issue 9, p. 88–92.
12. Gilmore, James H., The Four Faces of Mass Customization, *Harvard Business Review*, January–February 1997, Reprint #97103, p. 91–101.
13. Ginsberg, Steve, Ripped Levi's: Blunders, Bad Luck Take Toll, *San Francisco Business Times*, December 11–17, 1998, Vol. 13, Issue 18.
12. Hill, Suzette, Levi Strauss and Co.: Icon in Revolution, *Apparel Industry Magazine*, January 1999, Volume 60, Issue 1, p. 66–69.
13. Hill, Suzette, Levi Strauss Puts a New Spin on Brand Management, *Apparel Industry Magazine*, November 1998, p. 46–7.
14. Hofman, Mike, Searching for the Mountain of Youth, *Inc*, December 1999, Volume 21, Issue 18, p. 33–36.
15. Homer, Eric, Levi's Zips Up First Ever Private Deal, *Private Placement Letter*, July 23, 2001.
16. Hunt, Bryan C. and Mark O. Doehla, Denim Industry, FirstUnion Industry Report, February 23, 1999.
17. Jastrow, David, Saying No to Web Sales, *Computer Reseller News*, November 29, 1999, Issue 871, p. 73.

18. Johnson, Greg, Jeans War: Survival of the Fittest, *The Los Angeles Times*, December 3, 1998, p. C1.
19. King, Ralph T., Jr., Jeans Therapy: Levi's Factory Workers are Assigned to Teams, and Morale Takes a Hit, *Wall Street Journal*, May 20, 1998, p. A1.
20. Laberis, Bill, Levi's Shows IT May Not Be Driver it Pretends To Be, *Computerworld*, April 12, 1999, Vol. 33, Issue 15, p. 36.
21. Lee, Julian, Can Levi's Ever Be Cool Again?, *Marketing*, April 15, 1999, p. 28–9.
22. Lee, Louise, Can Levi's Be Cool Again?, *Business Week*, March 13, 2000, p. 144–148.
23. Levi Strauss and Company Promotional Materials.
24. Levine, Bettijane, Fashion Fallout from the Levi Strauss Layoffs, *The Los Angeles Times*, March 1, 1999, p. 1.
25. Magretta, Joan, The Power of Virtual Integration: An Interview with Dell Computer's Michael Dell, *Harvard Business Review*, March–April 1998, Reprint #98208, p. 73–84.
26. Meadows, Shawn, Levi Shifts On-Line Strategy, *Bobbin*, January 2000, Vol. 41, Issue 5, p. 8.
27. Merrill Lynch Company Report, Levi Strauss and Co., Global Securities Research and Economics Group, March 23, 2001.
28. Merrill Lynch Company Report, Levi Strauss and Co., Global Securities Research and Economics Group, January 11, 2001.
29. Merrill Lynch Company Report, Levi Strauss and Co., Global Securities Research and Economics Group, September 20, 2000.
30. Munk, Nina, How Levi's Trashed a Great American Brand, *Fortune*, April 12, 1999, Vol. 139, Issue 7, p. 82–90.
31. *New York Times*, The View from Outside: Levi's Needs More Than a Patch," February 28, 1999, p. 4.
32. Pine, B. Joseph II, Serve Each Customer Efficiently and Uniquely, *Network Transformation*, BCR, January 1996, p. 2–5.
33. Pine, B. Joseph II, Bart Victor, and Andrew C. Boynton, Making Mass Customization Work, *Harvard Business Review*, September–October 1993, Reprint #93509, p. 108–116.
34. Pressler, Margaret Webb, Mending Time at Levi's: Jeans Maker Struggles to Recapture Youth Market, Reshape its Culture, *The Washington Post*, April 12, 1998, p. HO1.
35. Reidy, Chris, In Marketplace, They're No Longer Such a Great Fit, *Boston Globe*, February 23, 1999, p. A1.
36. Reda, Susan, Internet Channel Conflicts, *Stores*, December 1999, Vol. 81, Issue 12, p. 24–28.
37. Robson, Douglas, Levi Showing New Signs of Fraying in San Francisco, *San Francisco Business Times*, October 15, 1999, Volume 14, Issue 10, p. 1.
38. Rosenbush, Steve, Personalizing Service on Web, *USAToday*, November 16, 1998, p. 15E.
39. Schoenberger, Karl, Tough Jeans, A Soft Heart and Frayed Earnings, *New York Times*, June 25, 2000, p. 3.
40. Schonfeld, Erick, The Customized, Digitized, Have-it-Your-Way Economy, *Fortune*, September 28, 1998.
41. Stoughton, Stephanie, Jeans Market Now a Tight Fit for Levi's; Denim Leader Missed Marketing Opportunities, Failed to Spot Trends, *The Washington Post*, February 23, 1999, p. E1.
42. Trebay, Guy, What's Stonewashed, Ripped, Mended and $2,222?, *New York Times*, April 17, 2001, p. 10, col. 1.
43. Voight, Joan, Red, White, and Blue: An American Icon Fades Away, *Adweek*, April 26, 1999, Vol. 40, Issue 17, p. 28–35.
44. Watson, Richard T., Sigmund Akselsen, and Leyland F. Pitt, Attractors: Building Mountains in the Flat Landscape of the World Wide Web, *California Management Review*, Volume 40, Number 2, Winter 1998, p. 36–54.
45. Zito, Kelly, Levi Reveals Rare Look at Inner Secrets, *San Francisco Chronicle*, May 6, 2000, p. B1.

End Notes

1. This case was prepared by Farah Mihoubi under the supervision of Associate Professor Russell Coff of the Goizueta Business School, as the basis for class discussion, rather than to illustrate either effective or ineffective management. Information assembled from published sources and interviews with company sources. Copyright 2013, by the Wisconsin School of Business, All rights reserved.
2. Espen, 1999.
3. Levine, 1999.
4. Schonfeld, 1998.
5. Schonfeld, 1998.
6. Carr, 1998.
7. Carr, 1998.
8. Billington, 1997.
9. Pine, Victor, and Boynton, 1993, p. 112.

Case 2–4: Papa John's International, Inc.*

Papa John's International was a classic American success story. Founder John Schnatter had started selling pizza out of a makeshift kitchen in a small lounge in Indiana and in a little more than a decade had built a business that included more than 4,000 locations. After a slowdown in growth following the 2008 economic crisis, Papa John's had returned to its pre-crisis pattern of opening more than 200 stores per year. Such ambition was not without challenges. The U.S. economy had changed over the two decades that Papa John's had been in business due to an aging population and to the severe economic crisis that faced the nation starting in 2008. The economy had been particularly challenging for firms serving food and drinks. Though clearly profitable (see Exhibit 1), Papa John's had enjoyed relatively incremental growth in the new century. Despite the challenges, the leadership at Papa John's believed that the company had developed some important advantages that could be leveraged for high growth in either the United States or international markets or perhaps even in activities that went beyond pizza. The question facing Papa John's executives was which path would produce rapid but profitable growth.

Firm History and Background

Papa John's founder Schnatter realized as a young person that he loved pizza more than most people, and this love was reflected in his early jobs. He started working for Rocky's Sub Pub in Jeffersonville, Indiana, as a 15-year-old high school student. While attending college, he worked for Greek's Pizzeria. Upon graduating from college in 1983, he returned home to Jeffersonville, Indiana, and began working for his father at Mick's Lounge. In 1984, Schnatter sold his prized 1972 Z28 Camaro and bought out the co-owner of Mick's Lounge. He knew that Mick's was not doing well financially, but believed that after getting Mick's to run at a profit, he might try selling pizza. Something was missing from national pizza chains, he had concluded—a superior-quality traditional pizza. After converting a broom closet in the back of Mick's Lounge to a kitchen with $1,600 worth of used restaurant equipment, Schnatter began selling pizza to the tavern's customers.[1]

By using fresh dough and superior-quality ingredients, Schnatter believed that he could make a better pizza than others. The tavern's patrons would be brutally honest about the quality of his pizzas and provided rapid and candid feedback. Through trial and error, he created a pizza that the tavern customers loved. Once pizzas were selling well, Schnatter leased space next to Mick's Lounge and opened the first Papa John's restaurant in 1985. This was the beginning of Papa John's Pizza. Schnatter credited his father and grandfather with instilling in him the sense of pride in one's work, the importance of a strong work ethic, and the belief that a person should focus on what he or she does best and do it better than anyone else.[2]

When Schnatter opened his first Papa John's, his expectations were not very high. When asked about his strategy and plans for his business when he started his first Papa John's, he stated, "I never thought we'd get this big. It still baffles my mind. My original goal was to make $50,000 a year. In 1984, I dreamed of possibly owning 100 stores. I never imagined having the success we now have."[3] The first Papa John's was a sit-down restaurant. Schnatter learned that he wasn't very good at the sit-down restaurant when he tried to serve too many different items. He paid careful attention to what customers liked and did not like and adjusted his menu accordingly. Schnatter concluded "the Papa John's you know today is a function of what the customer told us they wanted. We simply listened to the customer. The customer wanted the pizza delivered. They did not want a sit-down pizza shop that served fifty other things."[4]

The company grew rapidly, opening eight stores during its first year of operation. Papa John's generated revenues of $500,000 in its first year.[5] In January 1986, Papa John's sold its first franchise. The company remained private until the initial public stock offering on June 8, 1993, under the symbol PZZA. Papa John's total revenues for the year ending in December 1992 were close to $50 million, having roughly doubled in size every year since 1986. After going public, the company experienced an accelerated domestic growth in the number of restaurants and opened its first international restaurant in 1998. International growth was aided by the 205-unit acquisition of "Perfect Pizza," the quality leader for pizzas in the United Kingdom.

This domestic and international growth continued unabated until 2001, when it decreased dramatically leading to a 1 percent contraction in domestic growth in 2003.

*This case is adapted from a report prepared by Rebekah Meier, Wade Okelberry, Odie Washington, Chad Witcher, and J. C. Woelich.

In millions of USD (except for per share items)

	2012	2011	2010	2009
Income Statement				
Revenue	1,342.65	1,217.88	1,126.40	1,078.55
Other Revenue, Total	—	—	—	—
Total Revenue	1,342.65	1,217.88	1,126.40	1,078.55
Cost of Revenue, Total	970.71	892.1	817.29	774.31
Gross Profit	371.94	325.78	309.1	304.24
Selling/General/Admin. Expenses, Total	186.5	160.92	157.13	170.69
Research and Development	—	—	—	—
Depreciation/Amortization	32.8	32.68	32.41	31.45
Interest Expense (Income)—Net Operating	—	—	—	—
Unusual Expense (Income)	0.36	1.75	−5.63	−17.23
Other Operating Expenses, Total	52.48	43.42	38.46	24.12
Total Operating Expense	1,242.85	1,130.87	1,039.65	983.33
Operating Income	99.81	87.02	86.74	95.22
Income Before Tax	98.39	84.79	83.31	84.19
Income After Tax	66	58.47	56.06	57.48
Minority Interest	−4.34	−3.73	−3.48	−3.76
Net Income Before Extra Items	61.66	54.73	52.58	53.73
Net Income	61.66	54.73	52.58	53.73
Income Available to Common Excl. Extra Items	61.66	54.73	52.58	53.73
Income Available to Common Incl. Extra Items	61.66	54.73	52.58	53.73
Dilution Adjustment	0	0	0	0.14
Diluted Weighted Average Shares	23.91	25.31	26.47	27.91
Diluted EPS Excluding Extraordinary Items	2.58	2.16	1.99	1.93
Diluted Normalized EPS	2.59	2.21	1.84	1.51
Balance Sheet				
Cash and Equivalents	16.4	18.94	47.83	25.46
Cash and Short-Term Investments	16.4	18.94	47.83	25.46
Accounts Receivable—Trade, Net	44.65	28.17	25.36	22.12
Total Receivables, Net	49.22	32.39	30.09	22.12
Total Inventory	22.18	20.09	17.4	15.58
Prepaid Expenses	12.78	10.21	10.01	8.7
Other Current Assets, Total	18.05	13.19	14.14	12.16
Total Current Assets	118.63	94.82	119.47	84
Property/Plant/Equipment, Total—Gross	487.96	445.71	424.69	402.06
Accumulated Depreciation, Total	−291.3	−263.81	−239.32	−214.09
Goodwill, Net	78.96	75.08	74.7	75.07
Long-Term Investments	—	—	—	—
Other Long Term Assets, Total	31.63	27.06	25.34	28.95
Total Assets	438.41	390.38	417.49	393.73
Accounts Payable	32.62	32.97	31.57	26.99
Accrued Expenses	60.53	44.2	42.83	54.24
Notes Payable/Short-Term Debt	0	0	0	0
Other Current liabilities, Total	10.43	3.97	1.79	5.85
Total Current Liabilities	103.58	81.13	76.18	87.08
Long-Term Debt	88.26	51.49	99.02	99.05
Total Long-Term Debt	88.26	51.49	99.02	99.05
Total Debt	88.26	51.49	99.02	99.05
Deferred Income Tax	10.67	6.69	0	0
Minority Interest	18.22	15.03	13.48	8.17
Other Liabilities, Total	36.17	30.39	33.2	22.55
Total Liabilities	256.89	184.74	221.88	216.86
Common Stock, Total	0.37	0.37	0.36	0.36
Additional Paid-In Capital	280.9	262.46	245.38	231.72
Retained Earnings (Accumulated Deficit)	356.46	294.8	240.07	191.21
Treasury Stock—Common	−458.05	−353.83	−291.05	−245.34
Other Equity, Total	1.82	1.85	1.01	1.48
Total Equity	181.51	205.65	195.61	176.87
Total Liabilities and Shareholders' Equity	438.41	390.38	417.49	393.73
Total Common Shares Outstanding	22.24	24.02	25.44	26.93

Exhibit 1 Papa Johns, Inc., Income Statement and Balance Sheet, 2009–2012

Exhibit 2   Papa John's Restaurant Growth with Projections to 2017

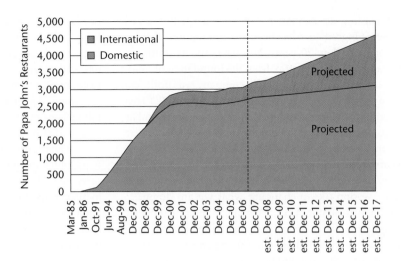

Since 2003, growth has been positive and relatively stable, and Papa John's executives believed that there was significant opportunity for domestic unit growth. Papa John's was among the highest return on invested capital (ROIC) in the restaurant category. While domestic growth was anticipated to be stable, international opportunities were significantly large and promising. Papa John's had 350 domestic restaurants and 1,100 international restaurants that were contractually scheduled to open over the following 10 years.[6] Exhibit 2 shows the historical growth of Papa John's restaurants including projected growth through 2017.

Business Structure

Papa John's had five major reportable segments of its business: domestic restaurants, domestic commissaries, domestic franchises, international operations, and variable interest entities. Domestic restaurants were restaurants that were wholly owned by Papa John's in the contiguous 48 states. Domestic franchises were restaurants in which Papa John's had licensed to franchisees for a franchise fee. These franchisee restaurants, as well as company-owned restaurants, were supported by domestic commissaries that supplied pizza dough, food products, paper products, small wares, and cleaning supplies twice weekly to each restaurant. There were 10 regional commissaries that supported domestic restaurants and franchises.

An important part of Papa John's strategy revolved around the central commissary. It allowed Papa John's to exercise control over the quality and consistency of its products. When asked about the central commissary,

Schnatter stated, "The commissary was added out of necessity. It did not start as a strategic decision to ensure quality. It started out of financial need. We simply did not have the money to put a mixer in every store. We had stores in Jeffersonville, Clarksville, and New Albany, so we just put a mixer in the middle store and made all the dough there. I can remember in 1987, we had a commissary, but we were doing it all by hand. We just grew into the commissary system. I wish I could say that it was a part of a grand plan that I envisioned from the time I started in the broom closet of Mick's Lounge, but it was not."[7]

The commissary system was frequently cited by industry analysts and company officials as a key factor in the success of Papa John's. The system not only reduced labor costs and reduced waste because the dough was premeasured, but it maintained control over the consistency of the product. The centralized production facility supplied all of the Papa John's stores with the same high-quality ingredients for their pizza. One of the most important aspects of this system is that it allowed Papa John's to start up more stores because it did not require the purchase of additional expensive equipment for each store. Part of the company's strategy was to expand into new markets only after a commissary had been built that could support the growth and geographical expansion of restaurants.[8]

Schnatter stated, "Papa John's Mission Statement and Values represent the basic beliefs and purpose of the company. They are not just words printed on a piece of paper. They are truly what we believe and live here at Papa John's."[9]

According to Schnatter, "making a quality pizza using better Ingredients has been the foundation of Papa John's for more than 20 years. You have my commitment that Papa John's will not stray from the foundation of quality and superiority upon which the company was built. We will always strive to be your Better Pizza Company."[10] This unwavering focus enabled Papa John's to be rated number one in customer satisfaction among all pizza chains in the American Customer Satisfaction Index for nine consecutive years from 1999 to 2008. As Schnatter had remarked in a 1997 interview, "We keep it simple, consistent, and focused. We don't keep changing what we are doing."[11] Papa John's president, USA, William Van Epps, echoed this emphasis, "While other national pizza chains have recently focused their national marketing efforts on deeply discounted or reduced-ingredients pizzas and other offerings such as pasta, I am proud of our system for remaining focused on delivering a superior-quality pizza."[12]

Papa John's core strategy was to sell a high-quality pizza for takeout or delivery. Its focus on using the highest-quality ingredients to produce a high-quality pizza was communicated in its motto: "Better Ingredients. Better Pizza." Schnatter considered it a sign of success when Pizza Hut sued Papa John's over the assertion that it had better ingredients and, therefore, a better pizza. Papa John's was ultimately successful in proving it used fresher ingredients and was, therefore, able to continue using its slogan. Papa John's stated goal was to build the strongest brand loyalty of all pizzerias internationally. Early on, Schnatter also introduced a signature bonus that served to signal the quality of the product: Each pizza was accompanied by a container of the company's special garlic sauce and two pepperoncinis.

Technology, Menu Enhancements, and Company Growth

Papa John's had long strived to be on the cutting edge of the use of technology. The company made ordering pizza even more convenient with the introduction of online ordering in 2001. It was the first pizza company to offer online ordering. Papa John's online sales grew exponentially in the first decade of the 21st century with growth rates of more than 50 percent a year not unusual. In November 2007, Papa John's led the way, once again, by offering text message ordering.[13] More than 20 percent of all Papa John's sales came online or via text. Papa John's was also using both the Internet and mobile technologies to make potential customers aware of current promotions and to allow them to easily order a pizza from virtually anywhere.

In October 2006, Papa John's introduced online ordering in Spanish in an attempt to meet growing customer needs and expectations. According to Javier Souto, Papa John's regional marketing director, "Papa John's has proven to be a technology leader in the pizza industry as the only national pizza chain to offer online ordering for all of its restaurants and now we are pleased to offer that service to our many Spanish-speaking customers."[14] In 2012, Papa John's became the first pizza chain to offer online ordering in Canada.

Papa John's also extended its menu. In January 2006, Papa John's announced that it was adding dessert pizzas to its carryout and delivery menus. "We created Papa's Sweetreats in direct response to consumer demand," said Catherine Hull, Papa John's vice president of strategy and brand marketing.[15] In July 2008, Papa John's introduced another permanent addition to its menu: Chocolate Pastry Delight.

Menu additions and new ways to order did not signal a change in strategy, according to company executives. Nigel Travis, president and CEO of Papa John's, stated in the company annual report 2007, "our stated strategy from a year ago remains unchanged. We will continue to focus on quality, growing the brand globally, and competing aggressively. It has proven the right course in a challenging economic time and has the opportunity to be even more successful as the economy rebounds." Papa John's targeted restaurants in the international arena as the company's primary source of long-term growth. Papa John's saw its use of innovative marketing, product offerings, and industry-leading technology as a major advantage over its competitors.[16]

Papa John's outlined its company strategy in one annual report as follows: "Our goal is to build the strongest brand loyalty of all pizzerias internationally. The key elements of our strategy include the following":

High-Quality Menu Offerings. Domestic Papa John's restaurants offer a menu of high-quality pizza along with side items, including breadsticks, cheesesticks, chicken poppers and wings, dessert items and canned or bottled beverages. Papa John's traditional crust pizza is prepared using fresh dough (never frozen). Papa John's pizzas are made from a proprietary blend of wheat flour, cheese made from 100% real mozzarella, fresh-packed pizza sauce made from vine-ripened tomatoes (not from concentrate) and a proprietary mix of savory spices, and a choice of high-quality meat (100% beef, pork and chicken with no fillers) and vegetable toppings. Domestically, all ingredients and toppings can be purchased from our Quality Control Center ("QC Center") system, which delivers to individual restaurants twice weekly. To ensure consistent food quality, each domestic franchisee is required to purchase dough and tomato sauce from our QC Centers and to purchase all other supplies *from our QC Centers or other approved suppliers. Internationally, the menu may be more diverse than in our domestic operations to meet local tastes and customs. QC Centers outside the U.S. may be operated by franchisees pursuant to license agreements or by other third parties. We provide significant assistance to licensed international QC Centers in sourcing approved quality suppliers.*

In addition to our fresh dough traditional crust pizza, we offer a thin crust pizza, which is a par-baked product produced by a third-party vendor. Our traditional crust pizza offers a container of our special garlic sauce and a pepperoncini pepper. Each thin crust pizza is served with a packet of special seasonings and a pepperoncini pepper.

We continue to test new product offerings both domestically and internationally. The new products can become a part of the permanent menu if they meet certain established guidelines.

Efficient Operating System. *We believe our operating and distribution systems, restaurant layout and designated delivery areas result in lower restaurant operating costs and improved food quality and promote superior customer service. Our QC Center system takes advantage of volume purchasing of food and supplies and provides consistency and efficiencies of scale in fresh dough production. This eliminates the need for each restaurant to order food from multiple vendors and commit substantial labor and other resources to dough preparation.*

Commitment to Team Member Training and Development. *We are committed to the development and motivation of our team members through training programs, incentive and recognition programs and opportunities for advancement. Team member training programs are conducted for corporate team members and offered to our franchisees electronically and at training locations across the United States and internationally. We offer performance-based financial incentives to corporate and restaurant team members at various levels.*

Marketing. *Our marketing strategy consists of both national and local components. Our domestic national strategy includes national advertising via television, print, direct mail, digital and social media channels. Our online and digital marketing activities have increased significantly over the past several years in response to increasing consumer use of online and mobile web technology.*

Our local restaurant-level marketing programs target consumers within the delivery area of each restaurant through the use of local TV, radio, print materials, targeted direct mail, store-to-door flyers, digital display advertising, email marketing, text messages and local social media. Local marketing efforts also *include a variety of community-oriented activities within schools, sports venues and other organizations supported with some of the same advertising vehicles mentioned above.*

In international markets, we target customers who live or work within a small radius of a Papa John's restaurant. Certain markets can effectively use television and radio as part of their marketing strategies. The majority of the marketing efforts include using print materials such as flyers, newspaper inserts, in-store marketing materials, and to a growing extent, digital marketing such as display, search engine marketing, email, and SMS text. Local marketing efforts, such as sponsoring or participating in community events, sporting events and school programs, are also used to build customer awareness.

Strong Franchise System. *We are committed to developing and maintaining a strong franchise system by attracting experienced operators, supporting them to expand and grow their business and monitoring their compliance with our high standards. We seek to attract franchisees with experience in restaurant or retail operations and with the financial resources and management capability to open single or multiple locations. We devote significant resources to provide Papa John's franchisees with assistance in restaurant operations, management training, team member training, marketing, site selection and restaurant design. (Annual Report, 2012)*

Cost Management and Operational Support Systems

Papa John's subleased retail locations to franchise owners. Papa John's had lowered the number of corporate-owned stores by about 5 percent in recent years in an effort to lower its lease payments. Leasing building space gave Papa John's the flexibility to move locations quickly with minimal cost, should a profitable location turn bad.

Papa John's also leased the trailers used to distribute ingredients from the commissary centers to the retail locations, typically on an eight-year lease agreement. By leasing the trailers, Papa John's was able to manage its shipping logistics and costs in a structured manner while not being required to maintain the trailers as they aged.

As Papa John's Pizza started to grow, Schnatter recognized the importance of sharing his passion for pizza with others in his company. The Operation Support Service and Training (OSST) Center was created and was actively engaged in the training and development of "team" members. In order to instill his passion into his new franchisees and corporate employees, Schnatter had them complete a management training program at the OSST Center when they started with the company. The aim of this training was to help franchise owners be successful and to instill in them a firm understanding of the Papa John's culture. Making franchisees feel like they were in a partnership with Papa John's facilitated a level of buy-in that the company believed was seldom found in restaurant chains.

Throughout Papa John's tremendous growth during its first 10 years of operation, its marketing programs targeted the delivery area of each restaurant, primarily through direct mailings and direct store-to-door couponing. In an effort to improve the marketing campaign, Schnatter realized that he needed to find a printing company that could offer consistent high-quality service at a reasonable price. In the mid-1990s, Schnatter found a printer that met his expectations better than most. The decision to vertically integrate into the business of printing was made. The franchise owners were not required to use the in-house printing service. The in-house printing operation was required to earn the business of each franchisee. In an effort to keep costs low within the printing division, Papa John's regularly accepted outside print jobs. It was not uncommon to print a flyer for a real estate company between jobs for a Papa John's franchise. In additional efforts to keep costs low, the printing presses were operated 24 hours a day.

From its beginning, Papa John's had been active in community affairs, from supporting local sports teams with fundraising opportunities to offering college scholarships. Papa John's had awarded more than $5 million in college scholarships. Papa John's actively supported the National FFA, Cerebral Palsy K.I.D.S. Center, and Children's Miracle Network, to name only a few. Papa John's executives believed that giving back to the community was good business.

Papa John's had entered into numerous marketing partnerships over the years. For example, Papa John's aligned with Coca-Cola to offer only Coke products in its stores. When Papa John's added a pan pizza to its menu, it enlisted the aid of former Miami Dolphins quarterback Dan Marino. At the time, this was the most intensive new product launch ever undertaken by Papa John's. Another combined effort for Papa John's involved coordinating with eBay for a limited edition Superman pan pizza box. In Kentucky, Papa John's and Blockbuster video combined efforts in a "take dinner and a movie online" in which the customer would receive a free 30-day trial of Blockbuster online with an online pizza purchase at papajohns.com.

By using a combination of internal and external resources, Papa John's was determined to not compete with its competition on price. Focusing on a quality product, active participation in the local communities in which it

operated, and product branding enabled Papa John's to hold its own with the other pizza chains. Papa John's had worked to create a product branded in such a way that customers came to expect the very best pizza; and they were willing to pay a premium price. Papa John's was committed to holding firm on the quality and prices of its pizzas.

The Restaurant Industry and Pizza Segment

The restaurant industry had historically been very attractive to entrepreneurs. Most of these new entrants opened single locations. The relatively low capital requirements made the restaurant business very attractive to small-scale entrepreneurs. Some of these businesses succeeded, but there was an intense amount of competition. There were relatively high fixed costs associated with entering into the restaurant business. These factors caused many of the new businesses to fail. However, for the businesses that succeeded, the payback on the investment could be quite high. After sales reached the break-even point, a relatively high percentage of incremental revenues became profit.

Restaurant analysts were generally amazed at how successfully Schnatter built Papa John's. Michael Fineman, a restaurant analyst with Raymond James in St. Petersburg, Florida, stated, "Here's an industry that appears to be mature and saturated, and here comes John Schnatter with his company Papa John's. He has proven to be a fantastic visionary."[17]

Large restaurant chains, like Papa John's, were able to realize economies of scale that made competition extremely difficult for small operators. Some of these advantages included purchasing power in negotiating food and packaging supply contracts, as well as real estate purchasing, location selection, menu development, and marketing.

Papa John's operated in the highly competitive pizza restaurant market, where the cost of entry was relatively low and product differentiation was difficult. Other pizza chains tried to compete in ways other than Papa John's emphasis. Some chains focused on being less expensive or having a broad menu. According to the one analyst, "the pizza chain segment struggled to find the right balance of promotions and pricing to keep both customers and profits. The pizza category is also suffering from a longer-term trend, in which the growth of take-out food capabilities at full service restaurants and the creation of more diversified menus at fast-food competitors have given consumers other options. In response, competition among pizza chains has recently centered on new product offerings, such as pasta and desserts. The segment has also pulled back on heavily price-based promotions that have dominated the marketing messages in recent years." (S&P Industry Surveys [2007]) The meal options available for consumers were increasing both for convenience dining and at-home consumption. The quality of frozen pizza available at grocery stores had improved significantly in recent years. A broader trend was that restaurant and quick-service restaurant dinner occasions were declining, which was significant for pizza restaurants such as Papa John's, which gained 70 percent of its sales from dinner orders. Declining restaurant and quick-service restaurant dining was attributed to an increase in at-home dinner preparation, linked to a decline in the percentage of women in the workforce.[18]

The large number of restaurant types throughout North America made it unlikely that any firm would gain a competitive advantage by offering one style or type of cuisine. The one principle that made Papa John's rare in the restaurant industry was its ongoing passion to offer the perfect pizza. Many companies claimed to place quality at the forefront of their business, but often the commitment to quality went no deeper than public relations and was not a core value.

Papa John's commitment to the highest-quality ingredients created challenges in managing the supply of the foods that went into its pizza. The volatility in the price of cheese had been a major problem for Papa John's. Cheese material costs contribute approximately 35 to 40 percent of Papa John's restaurants' food costs. In order to reduce the cheese price volatility, Papa John's partnered with a third-party entity formed by franchisees, BIBP Commodities, Inc., whose sole purpose was to reduce cheese price volatility to domestic system-wide restaurants. This allowed Papa John's to purchase cheese from BIBP at a fixed quarterly price. Profits and losses from BIBP were then passed on to Papa John's.[19]

Rising costs challenged pizza restaurants in multiple areas. Labor costs, as well as food commodity costs, were rising in the industry. "Although restaurants are experiencing cost increases for labor, utilities, and transportation, perhaps no other factor has prompted restaurants to increase their prices in 2008 more than food commodity cost inflation." (S&P Industry Surveys [2008]) Rising energy costs had a dual impact on Papa John's and its competitors. Food prices of products related to corn were increasing even more rapidly because of corn's use as an alternative fuel. Fluctuating in-store utility costs and delivery driver fuel costs were an ongoing source of concern. In 2007–08, such costs had risen dramatically. Another potential threat of rising costs stemmed from legislation at the federal level as well as many states that mandated a higher minimum wage.

Many companies, including Papa John's, engaged in forward pricing to stabilize food costs. "Forward pricing is a hedging strategy whereby a company negotiates with a supplier to purchase a certain amount of a product at a given price. Some supply contracts, signed by larger chains, can lock in less volatile food products for an entire year. Some of the products subject to the greatest variability, especially dairy products, can be locked in only for shorter periods."[20]

The *S&P Industry Survey* referred to 2007 and 2008 as a "perfect storm" of events in the industry. "Based on recent corporate actions taken in response to current weak industry conditions, we have a sense of growing crisis within the industry."[21] According to the survey, it was clear that there had been "deterioration from last fall, when we noted that the high price of gasoline and concerns about the U.S. housing market had forced many consumers to scale back the portion of the household budget allocated toward dining out. In addition to these still-serious issues, we must add an increasingly challenging outlook for restaurants' food and labor costs to the mix." Some analysts forecasted that 2009 would be the "most challenging environment ever faced by the modern restaurant industry."[22] Analysts expected the weakest sales performances by the domestic restaurant industry in nearly four decades.

Another important factor that was affecting the restaurant industry was a decline in travel. In mid-2008, economists expected further declines in travel. With less travel, fewer people dined out while on vacation or on business trips.

Of the $200 -plus- billion restaurant market, the pizza segment currently held 6.7 percent of the market. Pizza Hut, a division of Yum! Brands, Inc., was the leader, followed by Domino's Pizza, Inc., Papa John's International, Inc., and Little Caesars (a division of Ilitch Holdings, Inc.). Each was a large, nationally known pizza provider. These four accounted for 88 percent of the aggregate sales in the pizza chain restaurant segment; each was significantly larger than the #5 chain Chuck E. Cheese's (operated by CEC Entertainment, Inc.).

Economic trends played an important role in the number of consumers that dined out. When asked about the tough economic times the country faced in late 2008 and the effect they would have on Papa John's, Schnatter stated, "it is a tough time for our country. In the 90s we were seeing really good growth in this industry; however, the industry has softened and it has gotten very competitive. I foresee some pizza casualties in the future and it may be hard for some to survive. I think if the trend continues that we have seen over the last eighteen months, it is going to be tough on everybody. I think there are going to be a lot of people out there closing up shop." Schnatter continued by saying, "I think it's going to be a real test for all the operators in our category to see who is up to the task and who is not. We are going to separate the men from the boys, really quickly."[23]

Papa John's Looking Forward

In May 2007, Schnatter stepped down as the executive chairman of Papa John's to serve just as the head of the board of directors. In this new role, he planned to remain as spokesman for the company with no cash compensation, just stock options. Schnatter stated, "with Nigel Travis having led the company for the last two years as president and CEO, and the strength of our Board and the management team supporting him, the time is right for me to pull back a bit from the day-to-day operation of the company. I'm fine working for stock options alone—that way, I get compensated only if the rest of the shareholders win through a stock price increase."[24]

Schnatter was optimistic about the future of Papa John's. He wanted to see Papa John's get back on the path of opening 200 to 300 stores per year. Over the following five years, he wanted to see Papa John's reach the 4,000-store mark and, long term, he aspired to see 6,000 to 7,000 stores worldwide.[25] Papa John's also sought to reduce the number of company-run stores by turning them into franchising opportunities. At the end of 2012, Papa John's operated 3,204 stores in North America and another 959 internationally. Papa John's owned 20 percent of the North American stores but only 5 percent of the international stores, which were all in China. Franchising more of its current company-run stores offered Papa John's some important benefits. Franchise royalties were based on a percentage of sales and not on a percentage of profits, which allowed Papa John's to ensure a steady stream of revenue even in a difficult operating environment.

Papa John's had several options at its disposal. Among them were international market expansion, increased domestic market penetration, and related diversification (primarily via strategic acquisitions). The case for international expansion was based on the conclusion that the U.S. pizza industry (and quick-serve restaurant industry in general) had matured and that the most significant growth opportunities were beyond U.S. borders.

Pizza Hut benefited from a first-mover advantage in several, if not most, attractive international markets. With over 1,000 stores, Pizza Hut operated more stores in China than Papa John's throughout the world. It operated more than 5,200 stores, more than five times the number of Papa John's. Historically, Papa John's international efforts centered in Mexico, Canada, the United Kingdom, the Middle East, and Asia. Some believed that Asian markets would generally favor quality-centered business models due to higher preferences for quality. Another favorable trend in these markets was a growing income base for the local population.

In building its international infrastructure, the company would need to cultivate new relationships and develop new skills. One critical element was the company's ability to continue to partner with local producers in order to maintain tight quality control and keep ingredients fresh. In terms of new skills, Papa John's needed to develop the ability to modify its standard smaller carry-out restaurant blueprint. Looking at the success of firms such as McDonald's or Yum! Brands, Inc.'s Kentucky Fried Chicken, there was persuasive evidence that international customers tended to view their eating-out experience as more of a formal dining event. Thus, the standard Papa John's takeout restaurant model would need to be expanded to accommodate a sit-down dining area for patrons.

In addition to expanding internationally, Papa John's sought to grow and maintain its domestic market share. Traditionally, restaurants did this by adding new menu items or introducing a value selection such as McDonald's dollar menu or Little Caesars' Hot-N-Ready $5 pizza offering. For Papa John's, these strategies presented the risk of overextending its menu and, consequently, reducing its overall brand quality or ability to charge premium prices.

Extending the company's co-branding efforts was another possible avenue for domestic growth. For example, Papa John's partnered with firms such as Nestlé to provide some of its dessert menu offerings. There were a vast number of co-branding opportunities that were, in theory at least, possible.

A third alternative for Papa John's involved diversifying from pizza. For example, Papa John's could develop or acquire an additional restaurant chain under a different brand. Such an approach would allow Papa John's to compete in another restaurant category without fear of diluting its quality brand. Other competitors in the industry had operated chains in multiple categories. McDonald's, for example, had invested in Chipotle Mexican Grill and

Boston Market before disposing of its investments in 2006 and 2007, respectively. Yum! Brands, Inc., operated Pizza Hut, Taco Bell, Kentucky Fried Chicken, and A&W. With the growing influence of the Hispanic population and culture in the United States, some believed that a Hispanic/Mexican-themed restaurant would allow the company to benefit from this trend without impairing the Papa John's franchise.

End Notes

1. Interview with John Schnatter, October 2008.
2. Ibid.
3. Ibid.
4. Ibid.
5. (2008) Hoover's Profiles. Papa John's International, Inc.
6. UBS London investor meeting on August 22, 2008.
7. Interview with John Schnatter, October 2008.
8. Hoover's Profiles. Papa John's International, Inc.
9. Interview with John Schnatter, October 2008.
10. Ibid.
11. Walkup, C. (1997). "John Schnatter." *Food Industry*, January.
12. Papa John's press release, May 20, 2008.
13. (2007). *Pizza Today*, November 19.
14. (2006). *Pizza Today*, October 16.
15. (2006). *Pizza Today*, January 17.
16. Papa John's International, Inc., annual report 2007.
17. Walkup, C. (1997). "John Schnatter." *Food Industry*, January.
18. UBS London investor meeting on August 22, 2008.
19. Ibid.
20. *Standard & Poor's Industry Surveys,* September 4, 2008.
21. Ibid.
22. Ibid.
23. Interview with John Schnatter, October 2008.
24. Papa John's press release, May 14, 2007.
25. Interview with John Schnatter, October 2008.

3 CORPORATE STRATEGIES

6 Vertical Integration

LEARNING OBJECTIVES   *After reading this chapter, you should be able to:*

1. Define vertical integration, forward vertical integration, and backward vertical integration.

2. Discuss how vertical integration can create value by reducing the threat of opportunism.

3. Discuss how vertical integration can create value by enabling a firm to exploit its valuable, rare, and costly-to-imitate resources and capabilities.

4. Discuss how vertical integration can create value by enabling a firm to retain its flexibility.

5. Describe conditions under which vertical integration may be rare and costly to imitate.

6. Describe how the functional organization structure, management controls, and compensation policies are used to implement vertical integration.

Outsourcing Research

First it was simple manufacturing—toys, dog food, and the like—that was outsourced to Asia. This was OK because even though manufacturing could be outsourced to China and India, the real value driver of the Western economy—services—could never be outsourced. Or at least that was what we thought.

And then firms started outsourcing call centers and tax preparation and travel planning and a host of other services to India and the Philippines. Anything that could be done on a phone or online, it seemed, could be done cheaper in Asia. Sometimes, the quality of the service was compromised, but with training and additional technological development, maybe even these problems could be addressed. And this was OK because the real value driver of the Western economy—research and intellectual property—could never be outsourced. Or at least that was what we thought.

Now, it turns out that some leading Western pharmaceutical firms—including Merck, Eli Lilly, and Johnson & Johnson—have begun outsourcing some critical aspects of the pharmaceutical research and development process to pharmaceutical firms in India. This seemed impossible just a few years ago.

In the 1970s, India announced that it would not honor international pharmaceutical patents. This policy decision had at least two important implications for the pharmaceutical industry in India. First, it led to the founding of thousands of generic drug manufacturers there—firms that reverse engineered patented drugs produced by U.S. and Western European pharmaceutical companies and then sold them on world markets for a fraction of their original price. Second, virtually no pharmaceutical research and development took place in India. After all, why spend

all the time and money needed to develop a new drug when generic drug firms would instantly reverse engineer your technology and undercut your ability to make a profit?

All this changed in 2003 when the Indian government reversed its policies and began honoring global pharmaceutical patents. Now, for the first time in more than two decades, Indian firms could tap into their pool of highly educated scientists and engineers and begin engaging in original research. But developing the skills needed to do world-class pharmaceutical research on your own is difficult and time-consuming. So, Indian firms began searching for potential partners in the West.

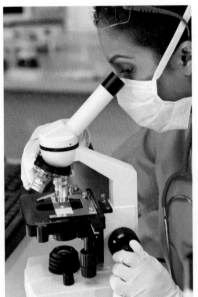

Darren Baker/Shutterstock

In the beginning, Western pharmaceutical companies outsourced only very routine lab work to their new Indian partners. But many of these firms found that their Indian partners were well-managed, with potentially significant technical capability, and willing to do more research-oriented kinds of work. Since 2007, a surprisingly large number of Western pharmaceutical firms have begun outsourcing progressively more important parts of the research and development process to their Indian partners.

And what do the Western firms get out of this outsourcing? Not surprisingly—low costs. It costs about $250,000 per year to employ a Ph.D. chemist in the West. That same $250,000 buys five such scientists in India. Five times as many scientists means that pharmaceutical firms can develop and test more compounds faster by working with their Indian partners than they could do on their own. The mantra in R&D—"fail fast and cheap"—is more easily realized when much of the early testing of potential drugs is done in India and not the West.

Of course, testing compounds developed by Western firms is not exactly doing basic research in pharmaceuticals. Early results indicate that Indian R&D efforts in pharmaceuticals have met with only limited success. For example, an alliance between Eli Lilly and its Indian partner, Zydus, was called off in early 2012. Disappointing results have also emerged in alliances between Merck and Novartis and their Indian partners. Also, recently the Indian government has begun to not recognize global pharmaceutical patents and is contemplating putting price limits on some drugs sold in India. All this will probably make it more difficult for true drug R&D to emerge in India. However, if Indian firms can develop R&D capabilities, their lower costs may make them attractive outsourcing parties for international pharmaceutical firms.

Sources: M. Kripalani and P. Engardio (2003). "The rise of India." *BusinessWeek*, December 8, pp. 66+; K. J. Delaney (2003). "Outsourcing jobs—and workers—to India." *The Wall Street Journal*, October 13, pp. B1+; B. Eihhorn (2006). "A dragon in R&D." *BusinessWeek*, November 6, pp. 44+; P. Engardio and A. Weintraub (2008). "Outsourcing the drug industry." *BusinessWeek*, September 5, 2008, pp. 48–52; Peter Arnold, Inc. (2012). "Zydus, Eli Lilly drug discovery deal off." *The Economic Times*, January 2; J. Lamattina (2012). "It's time to stop outsourcing Pharma R&D to India." www.forbes.com/sites/Johnlamattina/2012/10/11/its-time-to-stop-outsourcing-pharma-RD-to-India. Accessed August 20, 2013.

Themdecision to hire an offshore company to accomplish a specific business function is an example of a decision that determines the level of a firm's vertical integration. This is the case whether the company that is hired to perform these services is located in the United States or India.

What Is Corporate Strategy?

Vertical integration is the first corporate strategy examined in detail in this book. As suggested in Chapter 1, **business strategy** is a firm's theory of how to gain competitive advantage in a single business or industry. The two business strategies discussed in this book are cost leadership and product differentiation. **Corporate strategy** is a firm's theory of how to gain competitive advantage by operating in several businesses simultaneously. Decisions about whether to vertically integrate often determine whether a firm is operating in a single business or industry or in multiple businesses or industries. Other corporate strategies discussed in this book include strategic alliances, diversification, and mergers and acquisitions.

What Is Vertical Integration?

The concept of a firm's value chain was first introduced in Chapter 3. As a reminder, a **value chain** is that set of activities that must be accomplished to bring a product or service from raw materials to the point that it can be sold to a final customer. A simplified value chain of the oil and gas industry, originally presented in Figure 3.2, is reproduced in Figure 6.1.

A firm's level of **vertical integration** is simply the number of steps in this value chain that a firm accomplishes within its boundaries. Firms that are more vertically integrated accomplish more stages of the value chain within their boundaries than firms that are less vertically integrated. A more sophisticated approach to measuring the degree of a firm's vertical integration is presented in the Strategy in Depth feature.

A firm engages in **backward vertical integration** when it incorporates more stages of the value chain within its boundaries and those stages bring it closer to the beginning of the value chain, that is, closer to gaining access to raw materials. When computer companies developed all their own software, they were engaging in backward vertical integration because these actions are close to the beginning of the value chain. When they began using independent companies operating in India to develop this software, they were less vertically integrated backward.

A firm engages in **forward vertical integration** when it incorporates more stages of the value chain within its boundaries and those stages bring it closer to the end of the value chain; that is, closer to interacting directly with final customers. When companies staffed and operated their own call centers in the United States, they were engaging in forward vertical integration because these activities brought them closer to the ultimate customer. When they started using independent companies in India to staff and operate these centers, they were less vertically integrated forward.

Of course, in choosing how to organize its value chain, a firm has more choices than whether to vertically integrate or not vertically integrate. Indeed, between these two extremes a wide range of somewhat vertically integrated options exists. These alternatives include various types of strategic alliances and joint ventures, the primary topic of Chapter 9.

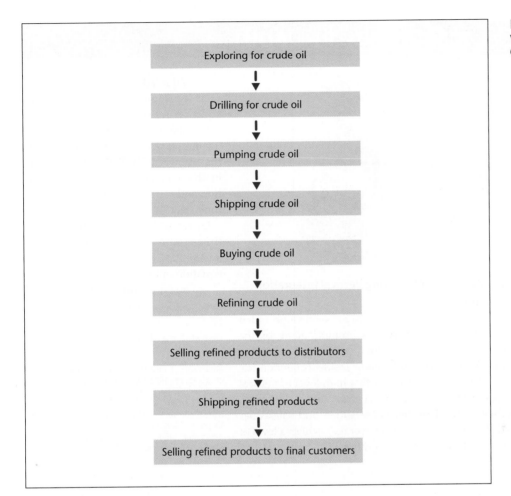

Figure 6.1 A Simplified Value Chain of Activities in the Oil and Gas Industry

The Value of Vertical Integration

The question of vertical integration—which stages of the value chain should be included within a firm's boundaries and why—has been studied by many scholars for almost 100 years. The reason this question has been of such interest was first articulated by Nobel Prize–winning economist Ronald Coase. In a famous article originally published in 1937, Coase asked a simple question: Given how efficiently markets can be used to organize economic exchanges among thousands, even hundreds of thousands, of separate individuals, why would markets, as a method for managing economic exchanges, ever be replaced by firms? In markets, almost as if by magic, Adam Smith's "invisible hand" coordinates the quantity and quality of goods and services produced with the quantity and quality of goods and services demanded through the adjustment of prices—all without a centralized controlling authority. However, in firms, centralized bureaucrats monitor and control subordinates who, in turn, battle each other for "turf" and control of inefficient internal "fiefdoms." Why would the "beauty" of the invisible hand ever be replaced by the clumsy "visible hand" of the modern corporation?[1]

Strategy in Depth

It is sometimes possible to observe which stages of the value chain a firm is engaging in and, thus, the level of that firm's vertical integration. Sometimes, however, it is more difficult to directly observe a firm's level of vertical integration. This is especially true when a firm believes that its level of vertical integration is a potential source of competitive advantage. In this case, the firm would not likely reveal this information freely to competitors.

In this situation, it is possible to get a sense of the degree of a firm's vertical integration—though not a complete list of the steps in the value chain integrated by the firm—from a close examination of the firm's **value added as a percentage of sales.** Valued added as a percentage of sales measures that percentage of a firm's sales that is generated by activities done within the boundaries of a firm. A firm

Measuring Vertical Integration

with a high ratio between value added and sales has brought many of the value-creating activities associated with its business inside its boundaries, consistent with a high level of vertical integration. A firm with a low ratio between value added and sales does not have, on average, as high a level of vertical integration.

Value added as a percentage of sales is computed using the following equation in Exhibit 1.

The sum of net income and income taxes is subtracted in both the numerator and the denominator in this equation to control for inflation and changes in the tax code over time. Net income, income taxes, and sales can all be taken directly from a firm's profit and loss statement. Value added can be calculated using the equation in Exhibit 2.

Again, most of the numbers needed to calculate value added can be found either in a firm's profit and loss statement or in its balance sheet.

Sources: A. Laffer (1969). "Vertical integration by corporations: 1929–1965." *Review of Economics and Statistics,* 51, pp. 91–93; I. Tucker and R. P. Wilder (1977). "Trends in vertical integration in the U.S. manufacturing sector." *Journal of Industrial Economics,* 26, pp. 81–94; K. Harrigan (1986). "Matching vertical integration strategies to competitive conditions." *Strategic Management Journal,* 7, pp. 535–555.

Exhibit 1

$$\text{vertical integration}_i = \frac{\text{value added}_i - (\text{net income}_i + \text{income taxes}_i)}{\text{sales}_i - (\text{net income}_i + \text{income taxes}_i)}$$

where,

$$\text{vertical integration}_i = \text{the level of vertical integration for firm}_i$$
$$\text{value added}_i = \text{the level of value added for firm}_i$$
$$\text{net inform}_i = \text{the level of net income for firm}_i$$
$$\text{income taxes}_i = \text{firm}_i\text{'s income taxes}$$
$$\text{sales}_i = \text{firm}_i\text{'s sales}$$

Exhibit 2

$$\text{value added} = \text{depreciation} + \text{amortization} + \text{fixed charges} + \text{interest expense}$$
$$+ \text{labor and related expenses} + \text{pension and retirement}$$
$$\text{expenses} + \text{income taxes} + \text{net income (after taxes)}$$
$$+ \text{rental expense}$$

Coase began to answer his own question when he observed that sometimes the cost of using a market to manage an economic exchange must be higher than the cost of using vertical integration and bringing an exchange within the boundary of a firm. Over the years, efforts have focused on identifying the conditions under which this would be the case. The resulting work has described several different situations where vertical integration can either increase a firm's revenues or decrease its costs compared with not vertically integrating, that is, several situations where vertical integration can be valuable. The following sections present three of the most influential of these explanations of when vertical integration can create value for a firm.

Vertical Integration and the Threat of Opportunism

One of the best-known explanations of when vertical integration can be valuable focuses on using vertical integration to reduce the threat of opportunism.[2] **Opportunism** exists when a firm is unfairly exploited in an exchange. Examples of opportunism include when a party to an exchange expects a high level of quality in a product it is purchasing, only to discover it has received a lower level of quality than it expected; when a party to an exchange expects to receive a service by a particular point in time and that service is delivered late (or early); and when a party to an exchange expects to pay a price to complete this exchange and its exchange partner demands a higher price than what was previously agreed.

Obviously, when one of its exchange partners behaves opportunistically, this reduces the economic value of a firm. One way to reduce the threat of opportunism is to bring an exchange within the boundary of a firm, that is, to vertically integrate into this exchange. This way, managers in a firm can monitor and control this exchange instead of relying on the market to manage it. If the exchange that is brought within the boundary of a firm brings a firm closer to its ultimate suppliers, it is an example of backward vertical integration. If the exchange that is brought within the boundary of a firm brings a firm closer to its ultimate customer, it is an example of forward vertical integration.

Of course, firms should only bring market exchanges within their boundaries when the cost of vertical integration is less than the cost of opportunism. If the cost of vertical integration is greater than the cost of opportunism, then firms should not vertically integrate into an exchange. This is the case for both backward and forward vertical integration decisions.

So, when will the threat of opportunism be large enough to warrant vertical integration? Research has shown that the threat of opportunism is greatest when a party to an exchange has made transaction-specific investments. A **transaction-specific investment** is any investment in an exchange that has significantly more value in the current exchange than it does in alternative exchanges. Perhaps the easiest way to understand the concept of a transaction-specific investment is through an example.

Consider the economic exchange between an oil refining company and an oil pipeline building company, which is depicted in Figure 6.2. As can be seen in the figure, this oil refinery is built on the edge of a deep-water bay. Because of this, the refinery has been receiving supplies of crude oil from large tanker ships. However, an oil field exists several miles distant from the refinery, but the only way to transport crude oil from the oil field to the refinery is with trucks—a very expensive way to move crude oil, especially compared to large tankers. But if the oil refining company could find a way to get crude oil from this field cheaply, it would probably make this refinery even more valuable.

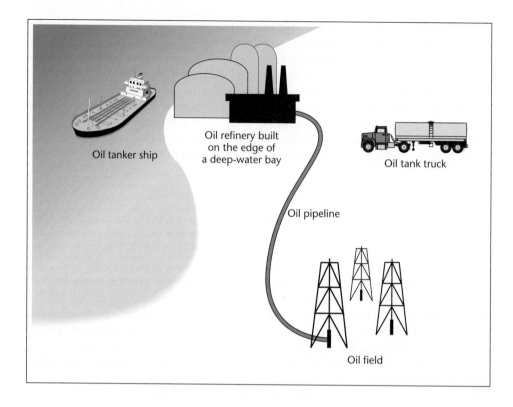

Oil tanker ship

Oil refinery built on the edge of a deep-water bay

Oil tank truck

Oil pipeline

Oil field

Enter the pipeline company. Suppose this pipeline company approaches the refinery and offers to build a pipeline from the oil field to the refinery. In return, all the pipeline company expects is for the refinery to promise to buy a certain number of barrels of crude at an agreed-to price for some period of time, say, five years, through the pipeline. If reasonable prices can be negotiated, the oil refinery is likely to find this offer attractive, for the cost of crude oil carried by the pipeline is likely to be lower than the cost of crude oil delivered by ship or by truck. Based on this analysis, the refinery and the oil pipeline company are likely to cooperate and the pipeline is likely to be built.

Now, five years go by, and it is time to renegotiate the contract. Which of these two firms has made the largest transaction-specific investments? Remember that a transaction-specific investment is any investment in an exchange that is more valuable in that particular exchange than in alternative exchanges.

What specific investments has the refinery made? Well, how much is this refinery worth if this exchange with the pipeline company is not renewed? Its value would probably drop some because oil through the pipeline is probably cheaper than oil through ships or trucks. So, if the refinery doesn't use the pipeline any longer, it will have to use these alternative supplies. This will reduce its value some—say, from $1 million to $900,000. This $100,000 difference is the size of the transaction-specific investment made by the refining company.

However, the transaction-specific investment made by the pipeline firm is probably much larger. Suppose the pipeline is worth $750,000 as long as it is pumping oil to the refinery. But if it is not pumping oil, how much is it worth? Not very much. An oil pipeline that is not pumping oil has limited alternative uses. It has value either as scrap or (perhaps) as the world's largest enclosed water slide. If the value of the pipeline is only $10,000 if it is not pumping oil to the refinery, then the level of transaction-specific investment made by the pipeline firm is substantially larger than that made by the firm that owns the refinery: $750,000 − $10,000, or $740,000, for the pipeline company versus $100,000 for the refining company.

So, which company is at greater risk of opportunism when the contract is renegotiated—the refinery or the pipeline company? Obviously, the pipeline company has more to lose. If it cannot come to an agreement with the oil refining company, it will lose $740,000. If the refinery cannot come to an agreement with the pipeline company, it will lose $100,000. Knowing this, the refining company can squeeze the pipeline company during the renegotiation by insisting on lower prices or more timely deliveries of higher-quality crude oil, and the pipeline company really cannot do much about it.

Of course, managers in the pipeline firm are not stupid. They know that after the first five years of their exchange with the refining company they will be in a very difficult bargaining position. So, in anticipation, they will insist on much higher prices for building the oil pipeline in the first place than would otherwise be the case. This will drive up the cost of building the pipeline, perhaps to the point that it is no longer cheaper than getting crude oil from ships. If this is the case, then the pipeline will not be built, even though if it could be built and the threat of opportunism eliminated, both the refining company and the pipeline company would be better off.

One way to solve this problem is for the oil refining company to buy the oil pipeline company—that is, for the oil refinery to backward vertically integrate.[3] When this happens, the incentive for the oil refinery to exploit the vulnerability of the pipeline company will be reduced. After all, if the refinery business tries to rip off the pipeline business, it only hurts itself because it owns the pipeline business.

This, then, is the essence of opportunism-based explanations of when vertical integration creates value: Transaction-specific investments make parties to an exchange vulnerable to opportunism, and vertical integration solves this vulnerability problem. Using language developed in Chapter 3, this approach suggests that vertical integration is valuable when it reduces threats from a firm's powerful suppliers or powerful buyers due to any transaction-specific investments a firm has made.

This logic explains part of the vertical integration decisions made by U.S. pharmaceutical firms discussed in the opening case of this chapter. As the risks of opportunism associated with outsourcing to Indian partners fell, U.S. pharmaceutical companies felt more comfortable gaining access to the low costs of Indian firms, and outsourcing increased.

Vertical Integration and Firm Capabilities

A second approach to vertical integration decisions focuses on a firm's capabilities and its ability to generate sustained competitive advantages.[4] This approach has two broad implications. First, it suggests that firms should vertically integrate into those business activities where they possess valuable, rare, and costly-to-imitate resources and capabilities. This way, firms can appropriate at least some of the profits that using these capabilities to exploit environmental opportunities will create. Second, this approach also suggests that firms should not vertically integrate into business activities where they do not possess the resources necessary to gain competitive advantages. Such vertical integration decisions would not be a source of profits to a firm, because it does not possess any of the valuable, rare, or costly-to-imitate resources needed to gain competitive advantages in these business activities. Indeed, to the extent that some other firms have competitive advantages in these business activities, vertically integrating into them could put a firm at a competitive disadvantage.

This, then, is the essence of the capabilities approach to vertical integration: If a firm possesses valuable, rare, and costly-to-imitate resources in a business activity, it should vertically integrate into that activity; otherwise, no vertical integration. This perspective can sometimes lead to vertical integration decisions that conflict with decisions derived from opportunism-based explanations of vertical integration.

Consider, for example, firms acting as suppliers to Wal-Mart. Wal-Mart has a huge competitive advantage in the discount retail industry. In principle, firms that sell to Wal-Mart could vertically integrate forward into the discount retail market to sell their own products. That is, these firms could begin to compete against Wal-Mart. However, such efforts are not likely to be a source of competitive advantage for these firms. Wal-Mart's resources and capabilities are just too extensive and costly to imitate for most of these suppliers. So, instead of forward vertical integration, most of these firms sell their products through Wal-Mart.

Of course, the problem is that by relying so much on Wal-Mart, these firms are making significant transaction-specific investments. If they stop selling to Wal-Mart, they may go out of business. However, this decision will have a limited impact on Wal-Mart. Wal-Mart can go to any number of suppliers around the world that are willing to replace this failed firm. So, Wal-Mart's suppliers are at risk of opportunism in this exchange, and indeed, it is well-known that Wal-Mart can squeeze its suppliers, in terms of the quality of the products it purchases, the price at which it purchases them, and the way in which these products are delivered.

So the tension between these two approaches to vertical integration becomes clear. Concerns about opportunism suggest that Wal-Mart's suppliers should vertically integrate forward. Concerns about having a competitive disadvantage if they do vertically integrate forward suggest that Wal-Mart's suppliers should not vertically integrate. So, should they or shouldn't they vertically integrate?

Not many of Wal-Mart's suppliers have been able to resolve this difficult problem. Most do not vertically integrate into the discount retail industry. However, they try to reduce the level of transaction-specific investment they make with Wal-Mart by supplying other discount retailers, both in the United States and abroad. They also try to use their special capabilities to differentiate their products so much that Wal-Mart's customers insist on Wal-Mart selling these products. And these firms constantly search for cheaper ways to make and distribute higher-quality products.

This capabilities analysis explains why outsourcing all of U.S. pharmaceutical research to low-cost Indian companies—discussed in the opening case of this chapter—has not occurred. It turns out that those basic R&D capabilities are very difficult to develop, and while Indian firms can engage in less sophisticated compound testing, they are not yet sufficiently skilled to engage in basic R&D. The result—U.S. pharmaceutical firms are very tentative about outsourcing their basic R&D.

Vertical Integration and Flexibility

A third perspective on vertical integration focuses on the impact of this decision on a firm's flexibility. **Flexibility** refers to how costly it is for a firm to alter its strategic and organizational decisions. Flexibility is high when the cost of changing strategic choices is low; flexibility is low when the cost of changing strategic choices is high.

So, which is less flexible—vertical integration or no vertical integration? Research suggests that, in general, vertically integrating is less flexible than not vertically integrating.[5] This is because once a firm has vertically integrated, it has committed its organizational structure, its management controls, and its compensation policies to a particular vertically integrated way of doing business. Undoing this decision often means changing these aspects of an organization.

Suppose, for example, that a vertically integrated firm decides to get out of a particular business. To do so, the firm will have to sell or close its factories (actions that can adversely affect both the employees it has to lay off and those that remain), alter its supply relationships, hurt customers that have come to rely on it as a partner, and change its internal reporting structure. In contrast, if a non-vertically integrated firm decides to get out of a business, it simply stops. It cancels whatever contracts it might have had in place and ceases operations in that business. The cost of exiting a non-vertically integrated business is generally much lower than the cost of exiting a vertically integrated business.

Of course, flexibility is not always valuable. In fact, flexibility is only valuable when the decision-making setting a firm is facing is uncertain. A decision-making setting is **uncertain** when the future value of an exchange cannot be known when investments in that exchange are being made. In such settings, less vertical integration is better than more vertical integration. This is because vertically integrating into an exchange is less flexible than not vertically integrating into an exchange. If an exchange turns out not to be valuable, it is usually more costly for firms that have vertically integrated into an exchange to exit that exchange compared with those that have not vertically integrated.

Consider, for example, a pharmaceutical firm making investments in biotechnology. The outcome of biotechnology research is very uncertain. If a pharmaceutical company vertically integrates into a particular type of biotechnology research by hiring particular types of scientists, building an expensive laboratory, and developing the other skills necessary to do this particular type of biotechnology research, it has made a very large investment. Now suppose that this research turns out not to be profitable. This firm has made huge investments that now have little value. As important, it has failed to make investments in other areas of biotechnology that could turn out to be valuable.

A flexibility-based approach to vertical integration suggests that rather than vertically integrating into a business activity whose value is highly uncertain, firms should not vertically integrate but should instead form a strategic alliance to manage this exchange. A strategic alliance is more flexible than vertical integration but still gives a firm enough information about an exchange to estimate its value over time.

An alliance has a second advantage in this setting. The downside risks associated with investing in a strategic alliance are known and fixed. They equal the cost of creating and maintaining the alliance. If an uncertain investment turns out not to be valuable, parties to this alliance know the maximum amount they can lose—an amount equal to the cost of creating and maintaining the alliance. On the other hand, if this exchange turns out to be very valuable, then maintaining an alliance can give a firm access to this huge upside potential. This partially explains why, to the extent that U.S. pharmaceutical firms outsource basic R&D to Indian partners, they do so through joint ventures. These aspects of strategic alliances will be discussed in more detail in Chapter 9.

Each of these explanations of vertical integration has received significant empirical attention in the academic literature. Some of these studies are described in the Research Made Relevant feature.

Applying the Theories to the Management of Call Centers

One of the most common business functions to be outsourced, and even off-shored, is a firm's call center activities. So, what do these three theories say about how call centers should be managed: When should they be brought within the boundaries of a firm, and when should they be outsourced? Each of these theories will be discussed in turn.

Transaction-Specific Investments and Managing Call Centers

When applying opportunism-based explanations of vertical integration, start by looking for actual or potential transaction-specific investments that would need to be made in order to complete an exchange. High levels of such investments suggest the need for vertical integration; low levels of such investments suggest that vertically integrating this exchange is not necessary.

When the call-center approach to providing customer service was first developed in the 1980s, it required substantial levels of transaction-specific investment. First, a great deal of special-purpose equipment had to be purchased. And although this equipment could be used for any call center, it had little value except within a call center. Thus, this equipment was an example of a somewhat specific investment.

More important, in order to provide service in call centers, call-center employees would have to be fully aware of all the problems likely to emerge

Research Made Relevant

Of the three explanations of vertical integration discussed here, opportunism-based explanations are the oldest and thus have received the greatest empirical support. One review of this empirical work, by Professor Joe Mahoney of the University of Illinois, observes that the core assertion of this approach—that high levels of transaction-specific investment lead to higher levels of vertical integration—receives consistent empirical support.

More recent work has begun to examine the trade-offs among these three explanations of vertical integration by examining their effects on vertical integration simultaneously. For example, Professor Tim Folta of Purdue University examined the opportunism and flexibility approaches to vertical integration simultaneously. His results show that the basic assertion of the opportunism approach still holds. However, when he incorporates uncertainty into his empirical analysis,

Empirical Tests of Theories of Vertical Integration

he finds that firms engage in less vertical integration than predicted by opportunism by itself. In other words, firms apparently worry not only about transaction-specific investments when they make vertical integration choices; they also worry about how costly it is to reverse those investments in the face of high uncertainty.

An even more recent study by Michael Leiblein from The Ohio State University and Doug Miller from the University of Illinois examines all three of these explanations of vertical integration simultaneously. These authors studied vertical integration decisions in the semiconductor manufacturing industry and found that all three explanations hold. That is, firms in this industry worry about transaction-specific investment, the capabilities they possess, the capabilities they would like to possess, and the uncertainty of the markets within which they operate when they make vertical integration choices.

Sources: J. Mahoney (1992). "The choice of organizational form: Vertical financial ownership versus other methods of vertical integration." *Strategic Management Journal*, 13, pp. 559–584; T. Folta (1998). "Governance and uncertainty: The trade-off between administrative control and commitment." *Strategic Management Journal*, 19, pp. 1007–1028; M. Leiblein and D. Miller (2003). "An empirical examination of transaction- and firm-level influences on the vertical boundaries of the firm." *Strategic Management Journal*, 24(9), pp. 839–859.

with the use of a firm's products. This requires a firm to study its products very closely and then to train call-center employees to be able to respond to any problems customers might have. This training was sometimes very complex and time-consuming and represented substantial transaction-specific investments on the part of call-center employees. Only employees that worked full time for a large corporation—where job security was usually high for productive workers—would be willing to make these kinds of specific investments. Thus, vertical integration into call-center management made a great deal of sense.

However, as information technology improved, firms found it was possible to train call-center employees much faster. Now, all call-center employees had to do was follow scripts that were prewritten and preloaded onto their computers. By asking a few scripted questions, call-center employees could diagnose most problems. In addition, solutions to those problems were also included on an employee's computer. Only really unusual problems could not be handled by employees working off these computer scripts. Because the level of specific investment required to use these scripts was much lower, employees were willing to work for companies without the job security usually associated with large firms. Indeed, call centers became good part-time and temporary employment opportunities. Because the level of specific investment required to work in these call centers was much lower, not vertically integrating into call-center management made a great deal of sense.

Capabilities and Managing Call Centers

In opportunism-based explanations of vertical integration, you start by looking for transaction-specific investments and then make vertical integration decisions based on these investments. In capability-based approaches, you start by looking for valuable, rare, and costly-to-imitate resources and capabilities and then make vertical integration decisions appropriately.

In the early days of call-center management, how well a firm operated its call centers could actually be a source of competitive advantage. During this time period, the technology was new, and the training required to answer a customer's questions was extensive. Firms that developed special capabilities in managing these processes could gain competitive advantages and thus would vertically integrate into call-center management.

However, over time, as more and more call-center management suppliers were created and as the technology and training required to staff a call center became more widely available, the ability of a call center to be a source of competitive advantage for a firm dropped. That is, the ability to manage a call center was still valuable, but it was no longer rare or costly to imitate. In this setting, it is not surprising to see firms getting out of the call-center management business, outsourcing this business to low-cost specialist firms, and focusing on those business functions where they might be able to gain a sustained competitive advantage.

Flexibility and Managing Call Centers

Opportunism logic suggests starting with a search for transaction-specific investments; capabilities logic suggests starting with a search for valuable, rare, and costly-to-imitate resources and capabilities. Flexibility logic suggests starting by looking for sources of uncertainty in an exchange.

One of the biggest uncertainties in providing customer service through call centers is the question of whether the people staffing the phones actually help a firm's customers. This is a particularly troubling concern for firms that are selling complex products that can have numerous types of problems. A variety of technological solutions have been developed to try to address this uncertainty. But, if a firm vertically integrates into the call-center management business, it is committing to a particular technological solution. This solution may not work, or it may not work as well as some other solutions.

In the face of this uncertainty, maintaining relationships with several different call-center management companies—each of whom have adopted different technological solutions to the problem of how to use call-center employees to assist customers who are using very complex products—gives a firm technological flexibility that it would not otherwise have. Once a superior solution is identified, then a firm no longer needs this flexibility and may choose to vertically integrate into call-center management or not, depending on opportunism and capabilities considerations.

Integrating Different Theories of Vertical Integration

At first glance, having three different explanations about how vertical integration can create value seems troubling. After all, won't these explanations sometimes contradict each other?

The answer to this question is yes. We have already seen such a contradiction in the case of opportunism and capabilities explanations of whether Wal-Mart suppliers should forward vertically integrate into the discount retail industry.

However, more often than not, these three explanations are complementary in nature. That is, each approach generally leads to the same conclusion about how a firm should vertically integrate. Moreover, sometimes it is simply easier to apply one of these approaches to evaluate a firm's vertical integration choices than the other two. Having a "tool kit" that includes three explanations of vertical integration enables the analyst to choose the approach that is most likely to be a source of insight in a particular situation.

Even when these explanations make contradictory assertions about vertical integration, having multiple approaches can be helpful. In this context, having multiple explanations can highlight the trade-offs that a firm is making when choosing its vertical integration strategy. Thus, for example, if opportunism-based explanations suggest that vertical integration is necessary because of high transaction-specific investments, capabilities-based explanations caution about the cost of developing the resources and capabilities necessary to vertically integrate and flexibility concerns caution about the risks that committing to vertical integration imply, and the costs and benefits of whatever vertical integration decision is ultimately made can be understood very clearly.

Overall, having three explanations of vertical integration has several advantages for those looking to analyze the vertical integration choices of real firms. Of course, applying these explanations can create important ethical dilemmas for a firm, especially when it becomes clear that a firm needs to become less vertically integrated than it has historically been. Some of these dilemmas are discussed in the Ethics and Strategy feature.

Vertical Integration and Sustained Competitive Advantage

Of course, in order for vertical integration to be a source of sustained competitive advantage, not only must it be valuable (because it responds to threats of opportunism; enables a firm to exploit its own or other firms' valuable, rare, and costly-to-imitate resources; or gives a firm flexibility), it must also be rare and costly to imitate, and a firm must be organized to implement it correctly.

The Rarity of Vertical Integration

A firm's vertical integration strategy is rare when few competing firms are able to create value by vertically integrating in the same way. A firm's vertical integration strategy can be rare because it is one of a small number of competing firms that is able to vertically integrate efficiently or because it is one of a small number of firms that is able to adopt a non-vertically integrated approach to managing an exchange.

Rare Vertical Integration

A firm may be able to create value through vertical integration, when most of its competitors are not able to, for at least three reasons. Not surprisingly, these reasons parallel the three explanations of vertical integration presented in this chapter.

Ethics and Strategy

Imagine a firm that has successfully operated in a vertically integrated manner for decades. Employees come to work, they know their jobs, they know how to work together effectively, they know where to park. The job is not just the economic center of their lives; it has become the social center as well. Most of their friends work in the same company, in the same function, as they do. The future appears to be much as the past—stable employment and effective work, all aiming toward a comfortable and well-planned retirement. And then the firm adopts a new outsourcing strategy. It changes its vertical integration strategy by becoming less vertically integrated and purchasing services from outside suppliers that it used to obtain internally.

The economics of outsourcing can be compelling. Outsourcing can help firms reduce costs and focus their efforts on those business functions that are central to their competitive advantage. When done well, outsourcing creates value—value that firms can share with their owners, their stockholders.

Indeed, outsourcing is becoming a trend in business. Some observers

The Ethics of Outsourcing

predict that by 2015, an additional 3.3 million jobs in the United States will be outsourced, many to operations overseas.

But what of the employees whose jobs are taken away? What of their lifetime of commitment, their steady and reliable work? What of their stable and secure retirement? Outsourcing often devastates lives, even as it creates economic value. Of course, some firms go out of their way to soften the impact of outsourcing on their employees. Those that are near retirement age are often

given an opportunity to retire early. Others receive severance payments in recognition of their years of service. Other firms hire "outplacement" companies—firms that specialize in placing suddenly unemployed people in new jobs and new careers.

But all these efforts to soften the blow do not make the blow go away. Many employees assume that they have an implicit contract with the firms they work for. That contract is: "As long as I do my job well, I will have a job." That contract is being replaced with: "As long as a firm wants to employ me, I will have a job." In such a world, it is not surprising that many employees now look first to maintain their employability in their current job—by receiving additional training and experiences that might be valuable at numerous other employers—and are concerned less with what they can do to improve the performance of the firm they work for.

Sources: S. Steele-Carlin (2003). "Outsourcing poised for growth in 2002." *FreelanceJobsNews.com*, October 20; (2003). "Who wins in off-shoring?" *McKinseyQuarterly.com*, October 20.

Rare Transaction-Specific Investment and Vertical Integration.   First, a firm may have developed a new technology or a new approach to doing business that requires its business partners to make substantial transaction-specific investments. Firms that engage in these activities will find it in their self-interest to vertically integrate, whereas firms that have not engaged in these activities will not find it in their self-interest to vertically integrate. If these activities are rare and costly to imitate, they can be a source of competitive advantage for a vertically integrating firm.

For example, many firms in the computer industry are offshoring some of their key business functions. However, one firm—Dell—brought one of these functions—its technical call center for business customers—back from India and re-vertically integrated it into its business function.[6] The problems faced by corporate customers are typically much more complicated than those faced by individual consumers. Thus, it is much more difficult to provide call-center employees with the training they need to address corporate problems. Moreover, because corporate technologies change more rapidly than many consumer technologies, keeping call-center employees up to date on how to service corporate customers is also more complicated than having call-center employees provide services to its noncorporate customers. Because Dell needs the people staffing its corporate call centers to make substantial specific investments in its technology and in understanding its customers, it has found it necessary to bring these individuals within the boundaries of the firm and to re-vertically integrate the operation of this particular type of service center.

If Dell, through this vertical integration decision, is able to satisfy its customers more effectively than its competitors and if the cost of managing this call center is not too high, then this vertical integration decision is both valuable and rare and thus a source of at least a temporary competitive advantage for Dell.

Rare Capabilities and Vertical Integration.   A firm such as Dell might also conclude that it has unusual skills, either in operating a call center or in providing the training that is needed to staff certain kinds of call centers. If those capabilities are valuable and rare, then vertically integrating into businesses that exploit these capabilities can enable a firm to gain at least a temporary competitive advantage. Indeed, the belief that a firm possesses valuable and rare capabilities is often a justification for rare vertical integration decisions in an industry.

Rare Uncertainty and Vertical Integration.   Finally, a firm may be able to gain an advantage from vertically integrating when it resolves some uncertainty it faces sooner than its competition. Suppose, for example, that several firms in an industry all begin investing in a very uncertain technology. Flexibility logic suggests that, to the extent possible, these firms will prefer to not vertically integrate into the manufacturing of this technology until its designs and features stabilize and market demand for this technology is well established.

However, imagine that one of these firms is able to resolve these uncertainties before any other firm. This firm no longer needs to retain the flexibility that is so valuable under conditions of uncertainty. Instead, this firm might be able to, say, design special-purpose machines that can efficiently manufacture this technology. Such machines are not flexible, but they can be very efficient.

Of course, outside vendors would have to make substantial transaction-specific investments to use these machines. Outside vendors may be reluctant to make these investments. In this setting, this firm may find it necessary to vertically integrate to be able to use its machines to produce this technology. Thus, this firm, by resolving uncertainty faster than its competitors, is able to gain some of the advantages of vertical integration sooner than its competitors. Whereas the competition is still focusing on flexibility in the face of uncertainty, this firm gets to focus on production efficiency in meeting customers' product demands. This can obviously be a source of competitive advantage.

Rare Vertical Dis-Integration

Each of the examples of vertical integration and competitive advantage described so far has focused on a firm's ability to vertically integrate to create competitive advantage. However, firms can also gain competitive advantages through their decisions to vertically dis-integrate, that is, through the decision to outsource an activity that used to be within the boundaries of the firm. Whenever a firm is among the first in its industry to conclude that the level of specific investment required to manage an economic exchange is no longer high, or that a particular exchange is no longer rare or costly to imitate, or that the level of uncertainty about the value of an exchange has increased, it may be among the first in its industry to vertically dis-integrate this exchange. Such activities, to the extent they are valuable, will be rare and, thus, a source of at least a temporary competitive advantage.

The Imitability of Vertical Integration

The extent to which these rare vertical integration decisions can be sources of sustained competitive advantage depends, as always, on the imitability of the rare resources that give a firm at least a temporary competitive advantage. Both direct duplication and substitution can be used to imitate another firm's valuable and rare vertical integration choices.

Direct Duplication of Vertical Integration

Direct duplication occurs when competitors develop or obtain the resources and capabilities that enable another firm to implement a valuable and rare vertical integration strategy. To the extent that these resources and capabilities are path dependent, socially complex, or causally ambiguous, they may be immune from direct duplication and, thus, a source of sustained competitive advantage.

With respect to offshoring business functions, it seems that the very popularity of this strategy suggests that it is highly imitable. Indeed, this strategy is becoming so common that firms that move in the other direction by vertically integrating a call center and managing it in the United States (like Dell) make news.

But the fact that many firms are implementing this strategy does not mean that they are all equally successful in doing so. These differences in performance may reflect some subtle and complex capabilities that some of these outsourcing firms possess but others do not. These are the kinds of resources and capabilities that may be sources of sustained competitive advantage.

Some of the resources that might enable a firm to implement a valuable and rare vertical integration strategy may not be susceptible to direct duplication. These might include a firm's ability to analyze the attributes of its economic exchanges and its ability to conceive and implement vertical integration strategies. Both of these capabilities may be socially complex and path dependent—built up over years of experience.

Substitutes for Vertical Integration

The major substitute for vertical integration—strategic alliances—is the major topic of Chapter 9. An analysis of how strategic alliances can substitute for vertical integration will be delayed until then.

V R I O   Organizing to Implement Vertical Integration

Organizing to implement vertical integration involves the same organizing tools as implementing any business or corporate strategy: organizational structure, management controls, and compensation policies.

Organizational Structure and Implementing Vertical Integration

The organizational structure that is used to implement a cost leadership and product differentiation strategy—the functional, or U-form, structure—is also used to implement a vertical integration strategy. Indeed, each of the exchanges included within the boundaries of a firm as a result of vertical integration decisions are incorporated into one of the functions in a functional organizational structure. Decisions about which manufacturing activities to vertically integrate into determine the range and responsibilities of the manufacturing function within a functionally organized firm; decisions about which marketing activities to vertically integrate into determine the range and responsibilities of the marketing function within a functionally organized firm; and so forth. Thus, in an important sense, vertical integration decisions made by a firm determine the structure of a functionally organized firm.

The chief executive officer (CEO) in this vertically integrated, functionally organized firm has the same two responsibilities that were first identified in Chapter 4: strategy formulation and strategy implementation. However, these two responsibilities take on added dimensions when implementing vertical integration decisions. In particular, although the CEO must take the lead in making decisions about whether each individual function should be vertically integrated into a firm, this person must also work to resolve conflicts that naturally arise between vertically integrated functions. The particular roles of the CEO in smaller entrepreneurial firms are described in the Strategy in the Emerging Enterprise feature.

Resolving Functional Conflicts in a Vertically Integrated Firm

From a CEO's perspective, coordinating functional specialists to implement a vertical integration strategy almost always involves conflict resolution. Conflicts among functional managers in a U-form organization are both expected and normal. Indeed, if there is no conflict among certain functional managers in a U-form organization, then some of these managers probably are not doing their jobs. The task facing the CEO is not to pretend this conflict does not exist or to ignore it, but to manage it in a way that facilitates strategy implementation.

Consider, for example, the relationship between manufacturing and sales managers. Typically, manufacturing managers prefer to manufacture a single product with long production runs. Sales managers, however, generally prefer to sell numerous customized products. Manufacturing managers generally do not like large inventories of finished products; sales managers generally prefer large inventories of finished products that facilitate rapid deliveries to customers. If these various interests of manufacturing and sales managers do not, at least sometimes, come into conflict in a vertically integrated U-form organization, then the manufacturing manager is not focusing enough on cost reduction and quality improvement in manufacturing or the sales manager is not focusing enough on meeting customer needs in a timely way or both.

Numerous other conflicts arise among functional managers in a vertically integrated U-form organization. Accountants often focus on maximizing managerial accountability and close analysis of costs; research and development managers may fear that such accounting practices will interfere with innovation and creativity. Finance managers often focus on the relationship between a firm and its external capital markets; human resource managers are more concerned with the relationship between a firm and external labor markets.

In this context, the CEO's job is to help resolve conflicts in ways that facilitate the implementation of the firm's strategy. Functional managers do not have to "like" one another. However, if a firm's vertical integration strategy is correct, the reason that a function has been included within the boundaries of a firm is that this decision creates value for the firm. Allowing functional conflicts to get in the way of taking advantage of each of the functions within a firm's boundaries can destroy this potential value.

Strategy in the Emerging Enterprise

With a net worth of more than $2.8 billion, Oprah Winfrey heads one of the most successful multimedia organizations in the United States. One of the businesses she owns—Harpo Productions—produced one of the most successful daytime television shows ever (with revenues of more than $300 million a year); launched one of the most successful magazines ever (with 2.5 million paid subscribers it is larger than *Vogue* and *Fortune*); and a movie production unit. One investment banker estimates that if Harpo, Inc., was a publicly traded firm, it would be valued at $575 million. Other properties Oprah owns—including investments, real estate, a stake in the cable television channel Oxygen, and stock options in Viacom—generate another $468 million in revenues per year.

And Oprah Winfrey does not consider herself to be a CEO.

She heads a multimedia conglomerate that employs more than 12,000 people. Her film studio has produced more than 25 movies and more than a dozen television productions. The introduction of her magazine was once described as the most successful magazine product launch ever. She formed a joint venture with the Discovery Channel to introduce a new cable channel. And in 1985, she was nominated for an Academy Award. But Oprah Winfrey does not think of herself as a CEO.

Oprah, Inc.

Certainly, her decision-making style is not typical of most CEOs. She has been quoted as describing her business decision making as "leaps of faith" and "If I called a strategic planning meeting, there would be dead silence, and then people would fall out of their chairs laughing."

However, she has made other decisions that put her firmly in control of her empire. For example, in 1987, she hired a tough Chicago entertainment attorney—Jeff Jacobs—as president of her business empire, Harpo, Inc. Whereas Oprah's business decisions are made from her gut and from her heart, Jacobs makes sure that the numbers add up to more revenues and profits for Harpo. She has also been unwilling to license her name to other firms, unlike Martha Stewart, who licensed her name to Kmart. Oprah has made strategic alliances with King

World (to distribute her TV show), with ABC (to broadcast her movies), with Hearst (to distribute her magazine), with Oxygen (to distribute some other television programs), and with the Discovery Channel. But she has never given up control of her business. And she has not taken her firm public. She currently owns 90 percent of Harpo's stock. She was once quoted as saying, "If I lost control of my business, I'd lose myself—or at least the ability to be myself."

To help control this growing business, Oprah and Jacobs hired a chief operating officer (COO), Tim Bennett, who then created several functional departments, including accounting, legal, and human resources, to help manage the firm. With thousands of employees, offices in Chicago and Los Angeles, and a real organization, Harpo is a real company, and Oprah is a real CEO—albeit a CEO with a slightly different approach to making business decisions.

That said, when Oprah's television network, OWN, started losing money, Oprah quickly took over as CEO and chief creative officer. Such decisive action makes Oprah seem more CEO-like all the time.

Sources: P. Sellers (2002). "The business of being Oprah." *Fortune*, April 1, pp. 50+; Oprah.com accessed August 30, 2013; Hoovers.com/Harpo Inc.; accessed August 30, 2013.

Management Controls and Implementing Vertical Integration

Although having the correct organizational structure is important for firms implementing their vertical integration strategies, that structure must be supported by a variety of management control processes. Among the most important of these processes are the budgeting process and the management committee oversight process, which can also help CEOs resolve the functional conflicts that are common within vertically integrated firms.

The Budgeting Process

Budgeting is one of the most important control mechanisms available to CEOs in vertically integrated U-form organizations. Indeed, in most U-form companies enormous management effort goes into the creation of budgets and the evaluation of performance relative to budgets. Budgets are developed for costs, revenues, and a variety of other activities performed by a firm's functional managers. Often, managerial compensation and promotion opportunities depend on the ability of a manager to meet budget expectations.

Although budgets are an important control tool, they can also have unintended negative consequences. For example, the use of budgets can lead functional managers to overemphasize short-term behavior that is easy to measure and underemphasize longer-term behavior that is more difficult to measure. Thus, for example, the strategically correct thing for a functional manager to do might be to increase expenditures for maintenance and management training, thereby ensuring that the function will have both the technology and the skilled people needed to do the job in the future. An overemphasis on meeting current budget requirements, however, might lead this manager to delay maintenance and training expenditures. By meeting short-term budgetary demands, this manager may be sacrificing the long-term viability of this function, compromising the long-term viability of the firm.

CEOs can do a variety of things to counter the "short-termism" effects of the budgeting process. For example, research suggests that evaluating a functional manager's performance relative to budgets can be an effective control device when (1) the process used in developing budgets is open and participative, (2) the process reflects the economic reality facing functional managers and the firm, and (3) quantitative evaluations of a functional manager's performance are augmented by qualitative evaluations of that performance. Adopting an open and participative process for setting budgets helps ensure that budget targets are realistic and that functional managers understand and accept them. Including qualitative criteria for evaluation reduces the chances that functional managers will engage in behaviors that are very harmful in the long run but enable them to make budget in the short run.[7]

The Management Committee Oversight Process

In addition to budgets, vertically integrated U-form organizations can use various internal management committees as management control devices. Two particularly common internal management committees are the **executive committee** and the **operations committee** (although these committees have many different names in different organizations).

The executive committee in a U-form organization typically consists of the CEO and two or three key functional senior managers. It normally meets weekly and reviews the performance of the firm on a short-term basis. Functions represented on this committee generally include accounting, legal, and other functions (such as manufacturing or sales) that are most central to the firm's short-term business success. The fundamental purpose of the executive committee is to track the short-term performance of the firm, to note and correct any budget variances for functional managers, and to respond to any crises that might emerge. Obviously, the executive committee can help avoid many functional conflicts in a vertically integrated firm before they arise.

In addition to the executive committee, another group of managers meets regularly to help control the operations of the firm. Often called the *operations committee,* this committee typically meets monthly and usually consists of the CEO and each of the heads of the functional areas included in the firm. The executive committee is a subset of the operations committee.

The primary objective of the operations committee is to track firm performance over time intervals slightly longer than the weekly interval of primary interest to the executive committee and to monitor longer-term strategic investments and activities. Such investments might include plant expansions, the introduction of new products, and the implementation of cost-reduction or quality improvement programs. The operations committee provides a forum in which senior functional managers can come together to share concerns and opportunities and to coordinate efforts to implement strategies. Obviously, the operations committee can help resolve functional conflicts in a vertically integrated firm after they arise.

In addition to these two standing committees, various other committees and task forces can be organized within the U-form organization to manage specific projects and tasks. These additional groups are typically chaired by a member of the executive or operations committee and report to one or both of these standing committees, as warranted.

Compensation in Implementing Vertical Integration Strategies

Organizational structure and management control systems can have an important impact on the ability of a firm to implement its vertical integration strategy. However, a firm's compensation policies can be important as well.

We have already seen how compensation can play a role in implementing cost leadership and product differentiation and how compensation can be tied to budgets to help implement vertical integration. However, the three explanations of vertical integration presented in this chapter have important compensation implications as well. We will first discuss the compensation challenges these three explanations suggest and then discuss ways these challenges can be addressed.

Opportunism-Based Vertical Integration and Compensation Policy

Opportunism-based approaches to vertical integration suggest that employees who make firm-specific investments in their jobs will often be able to create more value for a firm than employees who do not. Firm-specific investments are a type of transaction-specific investment. Whereas transaction-specific investments are investments that have more value in a particular exchange than in alternative exchanges, **firm-specific investments** are investments made by employees that have more value in a particular firm than in alternative firms.[8]

Examples of firm-specific investments include an employee's understanding of a particular firm's culture, his or her personal relationships with others in the firm, and an employee's knowledge about a firm's unique business processes. All this knowledge can be used by an employee to create a great deal of value in a firm. However, this knowledge has almost no value in other firms. The effort to create this knowledge is thus a firm-specific investment.

Despite the value that an employee's firm-specific investments can create, opportunism-based explanations of vertical integration suggest that employees will often be reluctant to make these investments because, once they do, they become vulnerable in their exchange with this firm. For example, an employee who has made very significant firm-specific investments may not be able to quit and go to work for another company, even if he or she is passed over for promotion, does not receive a raise, or is even actively discriminated against. This is because by quitting this firm, this employee loses all the investment he or she made in this particular firm. Because this employee has few employment options other than his or her current firm, this firm can treat this employee badly and the employee can do little about it. This is why employees are often reluctant to make firm-specific investments.

But the firm needs its employees to make such investments if it is to realize its full economic potential. Thus, one of the tasks of compensation policy is to create incentives for employees whose firm-specific investments could create great value to actually make those investments.

Capabilities and Compensation

Capability explanations of vertical integration also acknowledge the importance of firm-specific investments in creating value for a firm. Indeed, many of the valuable, rare, and costly-to-imitate resources and capabilities that can exist in a firm are a manifestation of firm-specific investments made by a firm's employees. However, whereas opportunism explanations of vertical integration tend to focus on firm-specific investments made by individual employees, capabilities explanations tend to focus on firm-specific investments made by groups of employees.[9]

In Chapter 3, it was suggested that one of the reasons that a firm's valuable and rare resources may be costly to imitate is that these resources are socially complex in nature. Socially complex resources reflect the teamwork, cooperation, and culture that have evolved within a firm—capabilities that can increase the value of a firm significantly, but capabilities that other firms will often find costly to imitate, at least in the short to medium term. Moreover, these are capabilities that exist because several employees—not just a single employee—have made specific investments in a firm.

From the point of view of designing a compensation policy, capabilities analysis suggests that not only should a firm's compensation policy encourage employees whose firm-specific investments could create value to actually make those investments; it also recognizes that these investments will often be collective in nature—that, for example, until all the members of a critical management team make firm-specific commitments to that team, that team's ability to create and sustain competitive advantages will be significantly limited.

Flexibility and Compensation

Flexibility explanations of vertical integration also have some important implications for compensation. In particular, because the creation of flexibility in a firm depends on employees being willing to engage in activities that have fixed and known downside risks and significant upside potential, it follows that compensation that has fixed and known downside risks and significant upside potential would encourage employees to choose and implement flexible vertical integration strategies.

Compensation Alternatives

Table 6.1 lists several compensation alternatives and how they are related to each of the three explanations of vertical integration discussed in this chapter. Not

Opportunism explanations	Salary
	Cash bonuses for individual performance
	Stock grants for individual performance
Capabilities explanations	Cash bonuses for corporate or group performance
	Stock grants for corporate or group performance
Flexibility explanations	Stock options for individual, corporate, or group performance

TABLE 6.1 Types of Compensation and Approaches to Making Vertical Integration Decisions

surprisingly, opportunism-based explanations suggest that compensation that focuses on individual employees and how they can make firm-specific investments will be important for firms implementing their vertical integration strategies. Such individual compensation includes an employee's salary, cash bonuses based on individual performance, and **stock grants**—or payments to employees in a firm's stock—based on individual performance.

Capabilities explanations of vertical integration suggest that compensation that focuses on groups of employees making firm-specific investments in valuable, rare, and costly-to-imitate resources and capabilities will be particularly important for firms implementing vertical integration strategies. Such collective compensation includes cash bonuses based on a firm's overall performance and stock grants based on a firm's overall performance.

Finally, flexibility logic suggests that compensation that has a fixed and known downside risk and significant upside potential is important for firms implementing vertical integration strategies. **Stock options,** whereby employees are given the right, but not the obligation, to purchase stock at predetermined prices, are a form of compensation that has these characteristics. Stock options can be granted based on an individual employee's performance or the performance of the firm as a whole.

The task facing CEOs looking to implement a vertical integration strategy through compensation policy is to determine what kinds of employee behavior they need to have for this strategy to create sustained competitive advantages and then to use the appropriate compensation policy. Not surprisingly, most CEOs find that all three explanations of vertical integration are important in their decision making. Thus, not surprisingly, many firms adopt compensation policies that feature a mix of the compensation policies listed in Table 6.1. Most firms use both individual and corporate-wide compensation schemes along with salaries, cash bonuses, stock grants, and stock options for employees who have the greatest impact on a firm's overall performance.

Summary

Vertical integration is defined as the number of stages in an industry's value chain that a firm has brought within its boundaries. Forward vertical integration brings a firm closer to its ultimate customer; backward vertical integration brings a firm closer to the sources of its raw materials. In making vertical integration decisions for a particular business activity, firms can choose to be not vertically integrated, somewhat vertically integrated, or vertically integrated.

Vertical integration can create value in three different ways: First, it can reduce opportunistic threats from a firm's buyers and suppliers due to transaction-specific investments the firm may have made. A transaction-specific investment is an investment that has more value in a particular exchange than in any alternative exchanges. Second, vertical integration can create value by enabling a firm to exploit its valuable, rare, and costly-to-imitate resources and capabilities. Firms should vertically integrate into activities in which they enjoy such advantages and should not vertically integrate into other activities. Third, vertical integration typically only creates value under conditions of low uncertainty. Under high uncertainty, vertical integration can commit a firm to a costly-to-reverse course of action and the flexibility of a non-vertically integrated approach may be preferred.

Often, all three approaches to vertical integration will generate similar conclusions. However, even when they suggest different vertical integration strategies, they can still be helpful to management.

The ability of valuable vertical integration strategies to generate a sustained competitive advantage depends on how rare and costly to imitate the strategies are. Vertical integration strategies can be rare in two ways: (1) when a firm is vertically integrated while most competing firms are not vertically integrated and (2) when a firm is not vertically integrated while most competing firms are. These rare vertical integration strategies are possible when firms vary in the extent to which the strategies they pursue require transaction-specific investments; they vary in the resources and capabilities they control; or they vary in the level of uncertainty they face.

The ability to directly duplicate a firm's vertical integration strategies depends on how costly it is to directly duplicate the resources and capabilities that enable a firm to pursue these strategies. The closest substitute for vertical integration—strategic alliances—is discussed in more detail in Chapter 9.

Organizing to implement vertical integration depends on a firm's organizational structure, its management controls, and its compensation policies. The organizational structure most commonly used to implement vertical integration is the functional, or U-form, organization, which involves cost leadership and product differentiation strategies. In a vertically integrated U-form organization, the CEO must focus not only on deciding which functions to vertically integrate into, but also on how to resolve conflicts that inevitably arise in a functionally organized vertically integrated firm. Two management controls that can be used to help implement vertical integration strategies and resolve these functional conflicts are the budgeting process and management oversight committees.

Each of the three explanations of vertical integration suggests different kinds of compensation policies that a firm looking to implement vertical integration should pursue. Opportunism-based explanations suggest individual-based compensation—including salaries and cash bonus and stock grants based on individual performance; capabilities-based explanations suggest group-based compensation—including cash bonuses and stock grants based on corporate or group performance; and flexibility-based explanations suggest flexible compensation—including stock options based on individual, group, or corporate performance. Because all three approaches to vertical integration are often operating in a firm, it is not surprising that many firms employ all these devices in compensating employees whose actions are likely to have a significant impact on firm performance.

MyManagementLab®

Go to **mymanagementlab.com** to complete the problems marked with this icon ⊛.

Challenge Questions

6.1. Some firms have engaged in backward vertical integration strategies in order to appropriate the economic profits that would have been earned by suppliers selling to them. How is this motivation for backward vertical integration related to the opportunism logic for vertical integration described in this chapter? (Hint: Compare the competitive conditions under which firms may earn economic profits to the competitive conditions under which firms will be motivated to avoid opportunism through vertical integration.)

6.2. Can you think of examples when firms vertically integrate to reduce high uncertainty? Explain lack of consistency with the flexibility logic.

6.3. You are about to purchase a used car. What can you do to protect yourself from the threats in this situation?

6.4. How is buying a car like and unlike vertical integration decisions?

✪ **6.5.** What are the competitive implications for firms if they assume that all potential exchange partners cannot be trusted?

6.6. Common conflicts between sales and manufacturing are mentioned in the text. What conflicts might exist between other functional areas? Consider the following pairings: research and development and manufacturing; finance and manufacturing; marketing and sales; and accounting and everyone else?

✪ **6.7.** What could a CEO do to help resolve the conflicts found between functional areas of the organization?

6.8. Under what conditions would you accept a lower-paying job over a higher-paying one?

6.9. What implications does your accepting a lower-paying job over a higher-paying one have for your potential employer's compensation policy?

Problem Set

6.10. In each of the pairs given below, which firm is more vertically integrated? Visit the company Web sites to gather supporting information.

(a) Vodafone and Airtel
(b) Adolph Coors Brewing and Heineken
(c) BMW and Lotus
(d) L'Oreal and Avon Cosmetics

6.11. What is the level of transaction specific investment for each player in the following transactions? Which player is at greater risk of being taken advantage of?

(a) A small, independent aluminum can plant just opened up near a large energy drinks manufacturer. The energy drinks company has 2 captive canning facilities on site and a plastics bottler within 50 kilometers. There is no other beverage company within a 200 km radius.

(b) A large and diversified law firm in Israel has outsourced its intellectual property research work to a specialist Indian firm. The Israeli contract constitutes 80% of the revenue for the Indian firm, while the outsourced work represents a cost saving of 10% for the Israeli firm. The Indian firm has invested in software and ongoing training that is customized to the Israeli context. They were one of 9 firms that had responded to the Israeli firm's request for proposals.

(c) A number of computer manufacturers rely on Intel to provide them with logic chips (CPUs), which are the "brains" of a computer. The computer manufacturers adapt their assembly processes, components and even some of the software, to the latest chips from Intel. Intel supplies to several dozen such manufacturers, and has very few competitors.

(d) There are only a few nuclear-powered aircraft carriers in the world today, most operated by the US Navy. Each of these very complex "super carriers" have been built by a single builder – Ingalls Shipbuilding, as promulgated by the US Department of Defense.

6.12. In each of the following situations, would you recommend vertical integration or no vertical integration? Explain.

(a) Firm A needs a new and unique technology for its product line. No substitute technologies are available. Should Firm A make this technology or buy it?

(b) Firm I has been selling its products through a distributor for some time. It has become the market share leader. Unfortunately, this distributor has not been able to keep up with the evolving technology and customers are complaining. No alternative distributors are available. Should Firm I keep its current distributor, or should it begin distribution on its own?

(c) Firm Alpha has manufactured its own products for years. Recently, however, one of these products has become more and more like a commodity. Several firms are now able to manufacture this product at the same price and quality as Firm Alpha. However, they do not have Firm Alpha's brand name in the marketplace. Should Firm Alpha continue to manufacture this product, or should it outsource it to one of these other firms?

(d) Firm I is convinced that a certain class of technologies holds real economic potential. However, it does not know, for sure, which particular version of this technology is going to dominate the market. There are eight competing versions of this technology currently, but ultimately only one will dominate the market. Should Firm I invest in all eight of these technologies itself? Should it invest in just one of these technologies? Should it partner with other firms that are investing in these different technologies?

MyManagementLab®

Go to **mymanagementlab.com** for the following Assisted-graded writing questions:

✪ **6.13.** How can vertical integration create value by enabling a firm to retain its flexibility?

✪ **6.14.** Describe how both direct duplication and substitution can be used to imitate another firm's valuable and rare vertical integration choices.

End Notes

1. Coase, R. (1937). "The nature of the firm." *Economica*, 4, pp. 386–405.
2. This explanation of vertical integration is known as transactions cost economics in the academic literature. See Williamson, O. (1975). *Markets and hierarchies: Analysis and antitrust implications*. New York: Free Press; Williamson, O. (1985). *The economic institutions of capitalism*.

New York: Free Press; and Klein, B., R. Crawford, and A. Alchian. (1978). "Vertical integration, appropriable rents, and the competitive contracting process." *Journal of Law and Economics*, 21, pp. 297–326.
3. Another option—forming an alliance between these two firms—is discussed in more detail in Chapter 9.

4. This explanation of vertical integration is known as the capabilities-based theory of the firm in the academic literature. It draws heavily from the resource-based view described in Chapter 3. See Barney, J. B. (1991). "Firm resources and sustained competitive advantage." *Journal of Management*, 17, pp. 99–120; Barney, J. B. (1999). "How a firm's capabilities affect boundary decisions." *Sloan Management Review*, 40(3); and Conner, K. R., and C. K. Prahalad. (1996). "A resource-based theory of the firm: Knowledge versus opportunism." *Organization Science*, 7, pp. 477–501.

5. This explanation of vertical integration is known as real-options theory in the academic literature. See Kogut, B. (1991). "Joint ventures and the option to expand and acquire." *Management Science*, 37, pp. 19–33.

6. Kripalani, M., and P. Engardio. (2003). "The rise of India." *BusinessWeek*, December 8, pp. 66+.

7. See Gupta, A. K. (1987). "SBU strategies, corporate-SBU relations and SBU effectiveness in strategy implementation." *Academy of Management Journal*, 30(3), pp. 477–500.

8. Becker, G. S. (1993). *Human capital: A theoretical and empirical analysis, with special reference to education*. Chicago: University of Chicago Press.

9. Barney, J. B. (1991). "Firm resources and sustained competitive advantage." *Journal of Management*, 17, pp. 99–120.

7 Corporate Diversification

LEARNING OBJECTIVES *After reading this chapter, you should be able to:*

1. Define corporate diversification and describe five types of corporate diversification.

2. Specify the two conditions that a corporate diversification strategy must meet in order to create economic value.

3. Define the concept of "economies of scope" and identify eight potential economies of scope a diversified firm might try to exploit.

4. Identify which of these economies of scope a firm's outside equity investors are able to realize on their own at low cost.

5. Specify the circumstances under which a firm's diversification strategy will be rare.

6. Indicate which of the economies of scope identified in this chapter are more likely to be subject to low-cost imitation and which are less likely to be subject to low-cost imitation.

7. Identify two potential substitutes for corporate diversification.

The Worldwide Leader

The breadth of ESPN's diversification has even caught the attention of Hollywood writers. In the 2004 movie *Dodgeball: A True Underdog Story*, the championship game between the underdog Average Joes and the bad guy Purple Cobras is broadcast on the fictitious cable channel ESPN8. Also known as "the Ocho," ESPN8's theme is "If it's almost a sport, we've got it."

Here's the irony: ESPN has way more than eight networks currently in operation.

ESPN was founded in 1979 by Bill and Scott Rasmussen after the father and son duo was fired from positions with the New England Whalers, a National Hockey League team now playing in Raleigh, North Carolina. Their initial idea was to rent satellite space to broadcast sports from Connecticut—the University of Connecticut's basketball games, Whaler's hockey games, and so forth. But they found that it was cheaper to rent satellite space for 24 hours straight than to rent space a few hours during the week, and thus a 24-hour sports channel was born.

ESPN went on the air September 7, 1979. The first event broadcast was a slow-pitch softball game. Initially, the network broadcast sports that, at the time, were not widely known to U.S. consumers—Australian rules football, Davis Cup tennis, professional wrestling, minor league bowling. Early on, ESPN also gained the rights to broadcast early rounds of the NCAA basketball tournament. At the time, the major networks did not broadcast these early round games, even though we now know that some of these early games are among the most exciting in the entire tournament.

The longest-running ESPN program is, of course, *SportsCenter*. Although the first *SportsCenter* contained no highlights and a scheduled interview with the football coach at the University of

Colorado was interrupted by technical difficulties, *SportsCenter* and its familiar theme have become icons in American popular culture. The 50,000th episode of *SportsCenter* was broadcast on September 13, 2012.

ESPN was "admitted" into the world of big-time sports in 1987 when it signed with the National Football League to broadcast Sunday Night Football. Since then, ESPN has broadcast Major League Baseball, the National Basketball Association, and, at various times, the National Hockey League. These professional sports have been augmented by college football, basketball, and baseball games.

ESPN's first expansion was modest—in 1993, it introduced ESPN2. Originally, this station played nothing but rock music and scrolled sports scores. Within a few months, however, ESPN2 was broadcasting a full program of sports.

After this initial slow expansion, ESPN began to diversify its businesses rapidly. In 1996, it added ESPN News (an all-sports news channel); in 1997, it acquired a company and opened ESPN Classics (this channel shows old sporting events); and in 2005, it started ESPNU (a channel dedicated to college athletics).

However, these five ESPN channels represent only a fraction of ESPN's diverse business interests. In 1998, ESPN opened its first restaurant, the ESPN Zone. This chain has continued to expand around the world. Also, in 1998, it started a magazine to compete with the then-dominant *Sports Illustrated*. Called *ESPN The Magazine*, it now has more than 2 million subscribers. In 2001, ESPN went into the entertainment production business when it founded ESPN Original Entertainment. In 2005, ESPN started ESPN Deportes, a Spanish-language 24-hour sports channel. And, in 2006, it founded ESPN on ABC, a company that manages much of the sports content broadcast on ABC. (In 1984, ABC purchased ESPN. Subsequently, ABC was purchased by Capital Cities Entertainment, and most of Capital Cities Entertainment was then sold to Walt Disney Corporation. Currently, 80 percent of ESPN is owned by Disney.)

And none of this counts ESPN HD; ESPN2 HD; ESPN Pay Per View; ESPN3; ESPN Films; ESPN Plus; ESPN America; The Longhorn Network; the SEC Network; the ESPN Web site; city-based ESPN Web sites in Boston, New York, Chicago, and Los Angeles; ESPN Radio; and ESPN's retail operations on the Web—ESPN.com. In addition, ESPN owns 27 international sports networks that reach 190 countries in 11 languages.

Of all the expansion and diversification efforts, so far ESPN has only stumbled once. In 2006, it founded Mobile ESPN, a mobile telephone service. Not only would this service provide its customers mobile telephone service, it would also provide them up-to-the-minute scoring updates and a variety of other sports information. ESPN spent more than $40 million advertising its new service and more than $150 million on the technology required to make this service available. Unfortunately, it never signed up more than 30,000 subscribers. The breakeven point was estimated to be 500,000 subscribers.

Also, all of ESPN's success hasn't gone unnoticed by other broadcasters. Recently, NBC entered the 24-hour sports channel market with NBCSN. CBS also entered this market with the CBS Sports channel.

Despite these challenges, ESPN has emerged from being that odd little cable channel that broadcast odd little games to a multibillion-dollar company with operations around the world in cable and broadcast television, radio, restaurants, magazines, books, and movie and television production. Which of those numerous enterprises could be characterized as "the Ocho" is hard to tell.

Sources: T. Lowry (2006). "ESPN's cell-phone fumble." *BusinessWeek*, October 30, pp. 26+; en.wikipedia.org/wiki/ESPN accessed September 15, 2013; AP Wide World Photos.

ESPN is like most large firms in the United States and the world: It has diversified operations. Indeed, virtually all of the 500 largest firms in the United States and the 500 largest firms in the world are diversified, either by product or geographically. Large single-business firms are very unusual. However, like most of these large diversified firms, ESPN has diversified along some dimensions but not others.

What Is Corporate Diversification?

A firm implements a **corporate diversification strategy** when it operates in multiple industries or markets simultaneously. When a firm operates in multiple industries simultaneously, it is said to be implementing a **product diversification strategy**. When a firm operates in multiple geographic markets simultaneously, it is said to be implementing a **geographic market diversification strategy**. When a firm implements both types of diversification simultaneously, it is said to be implementing a **product-market diversification strategy**.

We have already seen glimpses of these diversification strategies in the discussion of vertical integration strategies in Chapter 6. Sometimes, when a firm vertically integrates backward or forward, it begins operations in a new product or geographic market. This happened to computer software firms when they began manning their own call centers. These firms moved from the "computer software development" business to the "call-center management" business when they vertically integrated forward. In this sense, when firms vertically integrate, they may also be implementing a diversification strategy. However, the critical difference between the diversification strategies studied here and vertical integration (discussed in Chapter 6) is that in this chapter product-market diversification is the primary objective of these strategies, whereas in Chapter 6 such diversification was often a secondary consequence of pursuing a vertical integration strategy.

Types of Corporate Diversification

Firms vary in the extent to which they have diversified the mix of businesses they pursue. Perhaps the simplest way of characterizing differences in the level of corporate diversification focuses on the relatedness of the businesses pursued by a firm. As shown in Figure 7.1, firms can pursue a strategy of **limited corporate diversification**, of **related corporate diversification**, or of **unrelated corporate diversification**.

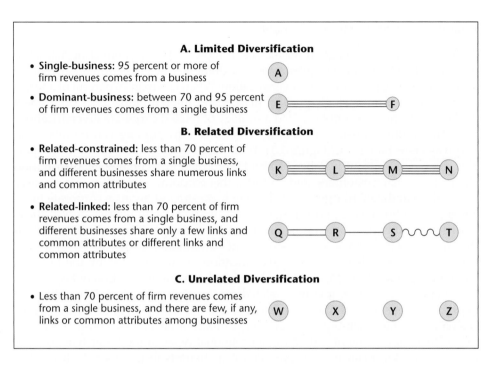

Figure 7.1 Levels and Types of Diversification

Limited Corporate Diversification

A firm has implemented a strategy of **limited corporate diversification** when all or most of its business activities fall within a single industry and geographic market (see Panel A of Figure 7.1). Two kinds of firms are included in this corporate diversification category: **single-business firms** (firms with greater than 95 percent of their total sales in a single-product market) and **dominant-business firms** (firms with between 70 and 95 percent of their total sales in a single-product market).

Differences between single-business and dominant-business firms are represented in Panel A of Figure 7.1. The firm pursuing a single-business corporate diversification strategy engages in only one business, Business A. An example of a single-business firm is the WD-40 Company of San Diego, California. This company manufactures and distributes only one product: the spray cleanser and lubricant WD-40. The dominant-business firm pursues two businesses, Business E and a smaller Business F that is tightly linked to Business E. An example of a dominant-business firm is Donato's Pizza. Donato's Pizza does the vast majority of its business in a single product—pizza—in a single market—the United States. However, Donato's has begun selling non-pizza food products, including sandwiches, and also owns a subsidiary that makes a machine that automatically slices and puts pepperoni on pizzas. Not only does Donato's use this machine in its own pizzerias, it also sells this machine to food manufacturers that make frozen pepperoni pizza.

In an important sense, firms pursuing a strategy of limited corporate diversification are not leveraging their resources and capabilities beyond a single product or market. Thus, the analysis of limited corporate diversification is logically equivalent to the analysis of business-level strategies (discussed in Part 2 of this book). Because these kinds of strategies have already been discussed, the remainder of this chapter focuses on corporate strategies that involve higher levels of diversification.

Related Corporate Diversification

As a firm begins to engage in businesses in more than one product or market, it moves away from being a single-business or dominant-business firm and begins to adopt higher levels of corporate diversification. When less than 70 percent of a firm's revenue comes from a single-product market and these multiple lines of business are linked, the firm has implemented a strategy of **related corporate diversification**.

The multiple businesses that a diversified firm pursues can be related in two ways (see Panel B in Figure 7.1). If all the businesses in which a firm operates share a significant number of inputs, production technologies, distribution channels, similar customers, and so forth, this corporate diversification strategy is called **related-constrained.** This strategy is *constrained* because corporate managers pursue business opportunities in new markets or industries only if those markets or industries share numerous resource and capability requirements with the businesses the firm is currently pursuing. Commonalities across businesses in a strategy of related-constrained diversification are represented by the linkages among Businesses K, L, M, and N in the related-constrained section of Figure 7.1.

PepsiCo is an example of a related-constrained diversified firm. Although PepsiCo operates in multiple businesses around the world, all of its businesses focus on providing snack-type products, either food or beverages. PepsiCo is not in the business of making or selling more traditional types of food—such as pasta or cheese or breakfast cereal. Moreover, PepsiCo attempts to use a single, firm-wide capability to gain competitive advantages in each of its businesses—its ability to develop and exploit well-known brand names. Whether it's Pepsi, Doritos, Mountain Dew, or Big Red, PepsiCo is all about building brand names. In fact, PepsiCo has 16 brands that generate well over $1 billion or more in revenues each year.[1]

If the different businesses that a single firm pursues are linked on only a couple of dimensions or if different sets of businesses are linked along very different dimensions, the corporate diversification strategy is called **related-linked**. For example, Business Q and Business R may share similar production technology, Business R and Business S may share similar customers, Business S and Business T may share similar suppliers, and Business Q and Business T may have no common attributes. This strategy is represented in the related-linked section of Figure 7.1 by businesses with relatively few links between them and with different kinds of links between them (i.e., straight lines and curved lines).

An example of a related-linked diversified firm is Disney. Disney has evolved from a single-business firm (when it did nothing but produce animated motion pictures), to a dominant business firm (when it produced family-oriented motion pictures and operated a theme park), to a related-constrained diversified firm (when it produced family-oriented motion pictures, operated multiple theme parks, and sold products through its Disney Stores). Recently, it has become so diversified that it has taken on the attributes of related-linked diversification. Although much of the Disney empire still builds on characters developed in its animated motion pictures, it also owns and operates businesses—including several hotels and resorts that have little or nothing to do with Disney characters and a television network (ABC) that broadcasts non-Disney-produced content—that are less directly linked to these characters. This is not to suggest that Disney is pursuing an unrelated diversification strategy. After all, most of its businesses are in the entertainment industry, broadly defined. Rather, this is only to suggest that it is no longer possible to find a single thread—like a Mickey Mouse or a Lion King—that connects all of Disney's business enterprises. In this sense, Disney has become a related-linked diversified firm.[2]

Unrelated Corporate Diversification

Firms that pursue a strategy of related corporate diversification have some type of linkages among most, if not all, the different businesses they pursue. However, it is possible for firms to pursue numerous different businesses and for there to be *no* linkages among them (see Panel C of Figure 7.1). When less than 70 percent of a firm's revenues is generated in a single-product market and when a firm's businesses share few, if any, common attributes, then that firm is pursuing a strategy of **unrelated corporate diversification**.

General Electric (GE) is an example of a firm pursuing an unrelated diversification strategy. GE's mix of businesses includes appliances for business, aviation, capital, critical power, energy management, health care, industrial solutions, intelligent platforms, lighting, mining, oil and gas, power and water, software, and transportation. It is difficult to see how these businesses are closely related to each other. Indeed, GE tends to manage each of its businesses as if they were stand-alone entities—a management approach consistent with a firm implementing an unrelated diversified corporate strategy.[3]

The Value of Corporate Diversification

V R I O

For corporate diversification to be economically valuable, two conditions must hold. First, there must be some valuable economy of scope among the multiple businesses in which a firm is operating. Second, it must be less costly for managers in a firm to realize these economies of scope than for outside equity holders on their own. If outside investors could realize the value of a particular economy of scope on their own and at low cost, then they would have few incentives to "hire" managers to realize this economy of scope for them. Each of these requirements for corporate diversification to add value for a firm will be considered below.

What Are Valuable Economies of Scope?

Economies of scope exist in a firm when the value of the products or services it sells increases as a function of the number of businesses in which that firm operates. In this definition, the term *scope* refers to the range of businesses in which a diversified firm operates. For this reason, only diversified firms can, by definition, exploit economies of scope. Economies of scope are valuable to the extent that they increase a firm's revenues or decrease its costs, compared with what would be the case if these economies of scope were not exploited.

A wide variety of potentially valuable sources of economies of scope have been identified in the literature. Some of the most important of these are listed in Table 7.1 and discussed in the following text. How valuable economies of scope actually are, on average, has been the subject of a great deal of research, which we summarize in the Research Made Relevant feature.

Diversification to Exploit Operational Economies of Scope
Sometimes, economies of scope may reflect operational links among the businesses in which a firm engages. **Operational economies of scope** typically take one of two forms: shared activities and shared core competencies.

Shared Activities.   In Chapter 3, it was suggested that value-chain analysis can be used to describe the specific business activities of a firm. This same value-chain

TABLE 7.1 Different Types of Economies of Scope

1. Operational economies of scope
   - Shared activities
   - Core competencies
2. Financial economies of scope
   - Internal capital allocation
   - Risk reduction
   - Tax advantages
3. Anticompetitive economies of scope
   - Multipoint competition
   - Exploiting market power
4. Employee and stakeholder incentives for diversification
   - Maximizing management compensation

Research Made Relevant

In 1994, Lang and Stulz published a sensational article that suggested that, on average, when a firm began implementing a corporate diversification strategy, it destroyed about 25 percent of its market value. Lang and Stulz came to this conclusion by comparing the market performance of firms pursuing a corporate diversification strategy with portfolios of firms pursuing a limited diversification strategy. Taken together, the market performance of a portfolio of firms that were pursuing a limited diversification strategy was about 25 percent higher than the market performance of a single diversified firm operating in all of the businesses included in this portfolio. These results suggested that not only were economies of scope not valuable, but, on average, efforts to realize these economies actually destroyed economic value. Similar results were published by Comment and Jarrell using different measures of firm performance.

How Valuable Are Economies of Scope, on Average?

Not surprisingly, these results generated quite a stir. If Lang and Stulz were correct, then diversified firms—no matter what kind of diversification strategy they engaged in—destroyed an enormous amount of economic value. This could lead to a fundamental restructuring of the U.S. economy.

However, several researchers questioned Lang and Stulz's conclusions. Two new findings suggest that, even if there is a 25 percent discount, diversification can still add value. First, Villalonga and others found that firms pursuing diversification strategies were generally performing more poorly before they began diversifying than firms that never pursued diversification strategies. Thus, although it might appear that diversification leads to a significant loss of economic value, in reality that loss of value occurred before these firms began implementing a diversification strategy. Indeed, some more recent research suggests that these relatively poor-performing firms may actually increase their market value over what would have been the case if they did not diversify.

Second, Miller found that firms that find it in their self-interest to diversify do so in a very predictable pattern. These firms tend to diversify

analysis can also be used to describe the business activities that may be shared across several different businesses within a diversified firm. These **shared activities** are potential sources of operational economies of scope for diversified firms.

Consider, for example, the hypothetical firm presented in Figure 7.2. This diversified firm engages in three businesses: A, B, and C. However, these three businesses share a variety of activities throughout their value chains. For example, all three draw on the same technology development operation. Product design and manufacturing are shared in Businesses A and B and separate for Business C. All three businesses share a common marketing and service operation. Business A has its own distribution system.

These kinds of shared activities are quite common among both related-constrained and related-linked diversified firms. At Texas Instruments, for example, a variety of electronics businesses share some research and development activities and many share common manufacturing locations. Procter & Gamble's numerous consumer products businesses often share common manufacturing locations and rely on a common distribution network (through retail grocery stores).[4] Some of the most common shared activities in diversified firms and their location in the value chain are summarized in Table 7.2.

into the most profitable new business first, the second-most profitable business second, and so forth. Not surprisingly, the fiftieth diversification move made by these firms might not generate huge additional profits. However, these profits—it turns out—are still, on average, positive. Because multiple rounds of diversification increase profits at a decreasing rate, the overall average profitability of diversified firms will generally be less than the overall average profitability of firms that do not pursue a diversification strategy—thus, a substantial difference between the market value of non-diversified and diversified firms might exist. However, this discount, per se, does not mean that the diversified firm is destroying economic value. Rather, it may mean only that a diversifying firm is creating value in smaller increments as it continues to diversify.

However, more recent research suggests that Lang and Stulz's original

"diversification discount" finding may be reemerging. It turns out that all the papers that show that diversification does not, on average, destroy value, and that it sometimes can add value, fail to consider all the investment options open to firms. In particular, firms that are generating free cash flow but have limited growth opportunities in their current businesses—that is, the kinds of firms that Villalonga and Miller suggest will create value through diversification—have other investment options besides diversification. In particular, these firms can return their free cash to their equity holders, either through a direct cash dividend or through buying back stock.

Mackey and Barney show that firms that do not pay out to shareholders destroy value compared with firms that do pay out. In particular, firms that use their free cash flow to pay dividends and buy back stock create value; firms that pay out and diversify

destroy some value; and firms that just diversify destroy significant value.

Of course, these results are "on average." It is possible to identify firms that actually create value from diversification—about 17 percent of diversified firms in the United States create value from diversification. What distinguishes firms that destroy and create value from diversification is likely to be the subject of research for some time to come.

Sources: H. P. Lang and R. M. Stulz (1994). "Tobin's *q*, corporate diversification, and firm performance." *Journal of Political Economy*, 102, pp. 1248–1280; R. Comment and G. Jarrell (1995). "Corporate focus and stock returns." *Journal of Financial Economics*, 37, pp. 67–87; D. Miller (2006). "Technological diversity, related diversification, and firm performance." *Strategic Management Journal*, 27(7), pp. 601–620; B. Villalonga (2004). "Does diversification cause the 'diversification discount'?" *Financial Management*, 33(2), pp. 5–28; T. Mackey and J. Barney (2013). "Incorporating opportunity costs in strategic management research: The value of diversification and payout as opportunities forgone when reinvesting in the firm." *Strategic Organization*, online, May 8 2013.

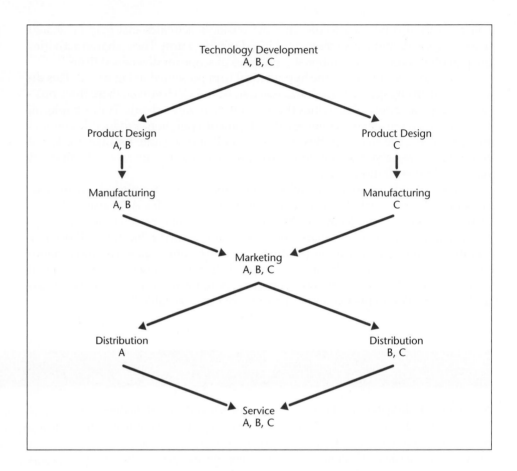

Many of the shared activities listed in Table 7.2 can have the effect of reducing a diversified firm's costs. For example, if a diversified firm has a purchasing function that is common to several of its different businesses, it can often obtain volume discounts on its purchases that would otherwise not be possible. Also, by manufacturing products that are used as inputs into several of a diversified firm's businesses, the total costs of producing these products can be reduced. A single sales force representing the products or services of several different businesses within a diversified firm can reduce the cost of selling these products or services. Firms such as IBM, HP, and General Motors (GM) have all used shared activities to reduce their costs in these ways.

Failure to exploit shared activities across businesses can lead to out-of-control costs. For example, Kentucky Fried Chicken, when it was a division of PepsiCo, encouraged each of its regional business operations in North America to develop its own quality improvement plan. The result was enormous redundancy and at least three conflicting quality efforts—all leading to higher-than-necessary costs. In a similar way, Levi Strauss's unwillingness to centralize and coordinate order processing led to a situation where six separate order-processing computer systems operated simultaneously. This costly redundancy was ultimately replaced by a single, integrated ordering system shared across the entire corporation.[5]

Shared activities can also increase the revenues in diversified firms' businesses. This can happen in at least two ways. First, it may be that shared product development and sales activities may enable two or more businesses in a

Value Chain Activity	Shared Activities
Input activities	Common purchasing
	Common inventory control system
	Common warehousing facilities
	Common inventory delivery system
	Common quality assurance
	Common input requirements system
	Common suppliers
Production activities	Common product components
	Common product components manufacturing
	Common assembly facilities
	Common quality control system
	Common maintenance operation
	Common inventory control system
Warehousing and distribution	Common product delivery system
	Common warehouse facilities
Sales and marketing	Common advertising efforts
	Common promotional activities
	Cross-selling of products
	Common pricing systems
	Common marketing departments
	Common distribution channels
	Common sales forces
	Common sales offices
	Common order processing services
Dealer support and service	Common service network
	Common guarantees and warranties
	Common accounts receivable management systems
	Common dealer training
	Common dealer support services

TABLE 7.2 Possible Shared Activities and Their Place in the Value Chain

Sources: M. E. Porter (1985). *Competitive advantage.* New York: Free Press; R. P. Rumelt (1974). *Strategy, structure, and economic performance.* Cambridge, MA: Harvard University Press; H. I. Ansoff (1965). *Corporate strategy.* New York: McGraw-Hill.

diversified firm to offer a bundled set of products to customers. Sometimes, the value of these "product bundles" is greater than the value of each product separately. This additional customer value can generate revenues greater than would have been the case if the businesses were not together and sharing activities in a diversified firm.

In the telecommunications industry, for example, separate firms sell telephones, access to telephone lines, equipment to route calls in an office, mobile telephones, and paging services. A customer that requires all these services could contact five different companies. Each of these five different firms would likely possess its own unique technological standards and software, making the development of an integrated telecommunications system for the customer difficult at best. Alternatively, a single diversified firm sharing sales activities across these businesses could significantly reduce the search costs of potential customers. This one-stop shopping is likely to be valuable to customers, who might be willing to pay a slightly higher price for this convenience than they would pay if they purchased these services from five separate firms. Moreover, if this diversified firm also shares some technology development activities across its businesses, it might be able to offer an integrated telecommunications network to potential customers. The extra value of this integrated network for customers is very likely to be reflected in prices that are higher than would have been possible if each of these businesses were independent or if activities among these businesses were not shared. Most of the regional telephone operating companies in the United States are attempting to gain these economies of scope.[6]

Such product bundles are important in other firms as well. Many grocery stores now sell prepared foods alongside traditional grocery products in the belief that busy customers want access to all kinds of food products—in the same location.[7]

Second, shared activities can enhance business revenues by exploiting the strong, positive reputations of some of a firm's businesses in other of its businesses. For example, if one business has a strong positive reputation for high-quality manufacturing, other businesses sharing this manufacturing activity will gain some of the advantages of this reputation. And, if one business has a strong positive reputation for selling high-performance products, other businesses sharing sales and marketing activities with this business will gain some of the advantages of this reputation. In both cases, businesses that draw on the strong reputation of another business through shared activities with that business will have larger revenues than they would were they operating on their own.

The Limits of Activity Sharing.   Despite the potential of activity sharing to be the basis of a valuable corporate diversification strategy, this approach has three important limits.[8] First, substantial organizational issues are often associated with a diversified firm's learning how to manage cross-business relationships. Managing these relationships effectively can be very difficult, and failure can lead to excess bureaucracy, inefficiency, and organizational gridlock. These issues are discussed in detail in Chapter 8.

Second, sharing activities may limit the ability of a particular business to meet its specific customers' needs. For example, if two businesses share manufacturing activities, they may reduce their manufacturing costs. However, to gain these cost advantages, these businesses may need to build products using somewhat standardized components that do not fully meet their individual customers' needs. Businesses that share distribution activities may have lower overall distribution costs but be unable to distribute their products to all their customers. Businesses that share sales activities may have lower overall sales costs but be unable to provide the specialized selling required in each business.

One diversified firm that has struggled with the ability to meet the specialized needs of customers in its different divisions is GM. To exploit economies of scope in the design of new automobiles, GM shared the design process across several automobile divisions. The result through much of the 1990s was "cookie-cutter" cars—the traditional distinctiveness of several GM divisions, including Oldsmobile and Cadillac, was all but lost.[9]

Third, if one business in a diversified firm has a poor reputation, sharing activities with that business can reduce the quality of the reputation of other businesses in the firm.

Taken together, these limits on activity sharing can more than offset any possible gains. Indeed, over the past decade more and more diversified firms have been abandoning efforts at activity sharing in favor of managing each business's activities independently. For example, ABB, Inc. (a Swiss engineering firm) and CIBA-Geigy (a Swiss chemicals firm) have adopted explicit corporate policies that restrict almost all activity sharing across businesses.[10] Other diversified firms, including Nestlé and GE, restrict activity sharing to just one or two activities (such as research and development or management training). However, to the extent that a diversified firm can exploit shared activities while avoiding these problems, shared activities can add value to a firm.

Core Competencies.   Recently, a second operational linkage among the businesses of a diversified firm has been described. Unlike shared activities, this linkage is based on different businesses in a diversified firm sharing less tangible resources such as managerial and technical know-how, experience, and wisdom. This source of operational economy of scope has been called a firm's core competence.[11] **Core competence** has been defined by Prahalad and Hamel as "the collective learning in the organization, especially how to coordinate diverse production skills and integrate multiple streams of technologies." Core competencies are complex sets of resources and capabilities that link different businesses in a diversified firm through managerial and technical know-how, experience, and wisdom.[12]

Two firms that have well-developed core competencies are 3M and Johnson & Johnson (J&J). 3M has a core competence in substrates, adhesives, and coatings. Collectively, employees at 3M know more about developing and applying adhesives and coatings on different kinds of substrates than do employees in any other organization. Over the years, 3M has applied these resources and capabilities in a wide variety of products, including Post-it notes, magnetic tape, photographic film, pressure-sensitive tape, and coated abrasives. At first glance, these widely diversified products seem to have little or nothing in common. Yet they all draw on a single core set of resources and capabilities in substrates, adhesives, and coatings.

Johnson & Johnson has a core competence in developing or acquiring pharmaceutical and medical products and then marketing them to the public. Many of J&J's products are dominant in their market segments—J&J's in baby powder, Ethicon in surgical sutures, and Tylenol in pain relievers. And although these products range broadly from those sold directly to consumers (e.g., the Band-Aid brand of adhesive bandages) to highly sophisticated medical technologies sold only to doctors and hospitals (e.g., Ethicon sutures), all of J&J's products build on the same ability to identify, develop, acquire, and market products in the pharmaceutical and medical products industry.

To understand how core competencies can reduce a firm's costs or increase its revenues, consider how core competencies emerge over time. Most firms begin operations in a single business. Imagine that a firm has carefully evaluated all of its current business opportunities and has fully funded all of those with a positive net present value. Any of the above-normal returns that this firm has left over after fully funding all its current positive net present value opportunities can be thought of as **free cash flow**.[13] Firms can spend this free cash in a variety of ways: They can spend it on benefits for managers; they can give it to shareholders through dividends or by buying back a firm's stock; they can use it to invest in new businesses.

Suppose a firm chooses to use this cash to invest in a new business. In other words, suppose this firm chooses to implement a diversification strategy. If this firm is seeking to maximize the return from implementing this diversification strategy, which of all the possible businesses that it could invest in should it invest in? Obviously, a profit-maximizing firm will choose to begin operations in a business in which it has a competitive advantage. What kind of business is likely to generate this competitive advantage for this firm? The obvious answer is a business in which the same underlying resources and capabilities that gave this firm an advantage in its original business are still valuable, rare, and costly to imitate. Consequently, this first diversification move sees the firm investing in a business that is closely related to its original business because both businesses will draw on a common set of underlying resources and capabilities that provide the firm with a competitive advantage.

Put another way, a firm that diversifies by exploiting its resource and capability advantages in its original business will have lower costs than those that begin a new business without these resource and capability advantages, or higher revenues than firms lacking these advantages, or both. As long as this firm organizes itself to take advantage of these resource and capability advantages in its new business, it should earn high profits in its new business, along with the profits it will still be earning in its original business.[14] This can be true for even relatively small firms, as described in the Strategy in the Emerging Enterprise feature.

Of course, over time this diversified firm is likely to develop new resources and capabilities through its operations in the new business. These new resources and capabilities enhance the entire set of skills that a firm might be able to bring to still another business. Using the profits it has obtained in its previous businesses, this firm is likely to enter another new business. Again, choosing from among all the new businesses it could enter, it is likely to begin operations in a business in which it can exploit its now-expanded resource and capability advantages to obtain a competitive advantage, and so forth.

After a firm has engaged in this diversification strategy several times, the resources and capabilities that enable it to operate successfully in several businesses become its core competencies. A firm develops these core competencies by transferring the technical and management knowledge, experience, and wisdom it developed in earlier businesses to its new businesses. A firm that has just begun this diversification process has implemented a dominant-business strategy. If all of a firm's businesses share the same core competencies, then that firm has implemented a strategy of related-constrained diversification. If different businesses exploit different sets of resources and capabilities, that firm has implemented a strategy of related-linked diversification. In any case, these core competencies enable firms to have lower costs or higher revenues as they include more businesses in their diversified portfolio, compared with firms without these competencies.

Of course, not all firms develop core competencies in this logical and rational manner. That is, sometimes a firm's core competencies are examples of the emergent strategies described in Chapter 1. Indeed, as described in Chapter 1, J&J is an example of a firm that has a core competence that emerged over time. However, no matter how a firm develops core competencies, to the extent that they enable a diversified firm to have lower costs or larger revenues in its business operations, these competencies can be thought of as sources of economies of scope.

Strategy in the Emerging Enterprise

W. L. Gore & Associates is best known for manufacturing a waterproof and windproof, but breathable, fabric that is used to insulate winter coats, hiking boots, and a myriad of other outdoor apparel products. This fabric—known as Gore-Tex—has a brand name in its market niche every bit as strong as any of the brand names controlled by PepsiCo or Procter & Gamble. The "Gore-Tex" label attached to any outdoor garment promises waterproof comfort in even the harshest conditions.

But W. L. Gore & Associates did not start out in the outdoor fabric business. Indeed, for the first 10 years of its existence, W. L. Gore sold insulation for wires and similar industrial products using a molecular technology originally developed by DuPont—a technology most of us know as Teflon. Only 10 years after its initial founding did the founder's son, Bob Gore, discover that it was possible to stretch the Teflon molecule to form a strong and porous material that is chemically inert, has a low friction coefficient, functions within a wide temperature range, does not age, and is extremely strong. This is the material called Gore-Tex.

Gore-Tex and Guitar Strings

By extending its basic technology, W. L. Gore and Associates has been able to diversify well beyond its original wire insulation business. With more than 8,000 employees and more than $2 billion in revenues, the company currently has operations in medical products (including synthetic blood vessels and patches for soft tissue regeneration), electronics products (including wiring board materials and computer chip components), industrial products (including filter bags for environmental protection and sealants for chemical manufacturing), and fabrics (including Gore-Tex fabric, Wind-Stopper fabric, and CleanStream filters).

And Gore continues to discover new ways to exploit its competence in the Teflon molecule. In 1997, a team of Gore engineers developed a cable made out of the Teflon molecule to control puppets at Disney's theme parks. Unfortunately, these cables did not perform up to expectations and were not sold to Disney. However, some guitar players discovered these cables and began using them as strings for their guitars. They found out that these "Gore-Tex" strings sounded great and lasted five times as long as alternative guitar strings. So Gore entered yet another market— the $100 million fretted-stringed-instrument business—with its Elixir brand of guitar strings. Currently, W. L. Gore is the second-largest manufacturer in this market.

The flexibility of the Teflon molecule—and W. L. Gore's ability to explore and exploit that flexibility—has created a diversified company whose original objective was simply to sell insulation for wires.

Sources: www.gore.com accessed July 15, 2012; D. Sacks (2003). "The Gore-Tex of guitar strings." *Fast Times,* December, p. 46.

Some diversified firms realize the value of these kinds of core competencies through shared activities. For example, as suggested earlier, 3M has a core competence in substrates, adhesives, and coatings. To exploit this, 3M has adopted a multitiered product innovation process. In addition to product innovations within each business unit separately, 3M also supports a corporate research and development lab that seeks to exploit and expand its core competence in substrates, adhesives, and coatings. Because the corporate research and development laboratory is shared by all of 3M's different businesses, it can be thought of as a shared activity.

However, other firms realize the value of their core competencies without shared activities. Although J&J has a core competence in developing, acquiring, and marketing pharmaceutical and medical products, it does not realize this core competence through shared activities. Indeed, each of J&J's businesses is run very independently. For example, although one of its most successful products is Tylenol, the fact that the company that manufactures and distributes Tylenol—McNeil—is actually a division of J&J and is not printed on any Tylenol packaging. If you did not know that Tylenol was a J&J product, you could not tell from the bottles of Tylenol you buy.

Although J&J does not use shared activities to realize the value of its core competencies, it does engage in other activities to realize this value. For example, it is not uncommon for members of the senior management team of each of the businesses in J&J's portfolio to have obtained managerial experience in some other J&J business. That is, J&J identifies high-potential managers in one of its businesses and uses this knowledge by giving these managers additional responsibilities in another J&J business. This ability to leverage its management talent across multiple businesses is an example of a firm's core competence, although the realization of the value of that competence does not depend on the existence of a shared activity.

Sometimes, because a firm's core competence is not reflected in specific shared activities, it is easy to conclude that it is not exploiting any economies of scope in its diversification strategy. Diversified firms that are exploiting core competencies as an economy of scope but are not doing so with any shared activities are sometimes called **seemingly unrelated diversified firms**. They may appear to be unrelated diversified firms but are, in fact, related diversified firms without any shared activities.

One example of a seemingly unrelated diversified firm is the British company Virgin Group. Operating in a wide variety of businesses—everything from record producing, music retailing, air and rail travel, soft drinks, spirits, mobile phones, cosmetics, retail bridal shops, financial services, and providing gas and electricity to hot air ballooning—the Virgin Group is clearly diversified. The firm has few, if any, shared activities. However, at least two core competencies cut across all the business activities in the group—the brand name "Virgin" and the eccentric marketing and management approach of Virgin's founder, Richard Branson. Branson is the CEO who walked down a "catwalk" in a wedding gown to help publicize the opening of Virgin Brides—the Virgin Group's line of retail bridal shops. Branson is also the CEO who had all of Virgin Air's airplanes repainted with the British "Union Jack" and the slogan "Britain's Real Airline" when British Airways eliminated the British flag from its airplanes. Whether these two core competencies create sufficient value to justify the Virgin Group's continued existence and whether they will continue beyond Branson's affiliation with the group are still open questions.

Limits of Core Competencies.   Just as there are limits to the value of shared activities as sources of economies of scope, so there are limits to core competencies as sources of these economies. The first of these limitations stems from important organizational issues to be discussed in Chapter 8. The way that a diversified firm is organized can either facilitate the exploitation of core competencies or prevent this exploitation from occurring.

A second limitation of core competencies is a result of the intangible nature of these economies of scope. Whereas shared activities are reflected in tangible operations in a diversified firm, core competencies may be reflected only in shared knowledge, experience, and wisdom across businesses. The intangible character of these relationships is emphasized when they are described as a **dominant logic** in a firm, or a common way of thinking about strategy across different businesses.[15]

The intangibility of core competencies can lead diversified firms to make two kinds of errors in managing relatedness. First, intangible core competencies can be illusory inventions by creative managers who link even the most completely unrelated businesses and thereby justify their diversification strategy. A firm that manufactures airplanes and running shoes can rationalize this diversification by claiming to have a core competence in managing transportation businesses. A firm operating in the professional football business and the movie business can rationalize this diversification by claiming to have a core competence in managing entertainment businesses. Such **invented competencies** are not real sources of economies of scope.

Second, a diversified firm's businesses may be linked by a core competence, but this competence may affect these businesses' costs or revenues in a trivial way. Thus, for example, all of a firm's businesses may be affected by government actions, but the impact of these actions on costs and revenues in different businesses may be quite small. A firm may have a core competence in managing relationships with the government, but this core competence will not reduce costs or enhance revenues for these particular businesses very much. Also, each of a diversified firm's businesses may use some advertising. However, if advertising does not have a major impact on revenues for these businesses, core competencies in advertising are not likely to significantly reduce a firm's costs or increase its revenues. In this case, a core competence may be a source of economies of scope, but the value of those economies may be very small.

Diversification to Exploit Financial Economies of Scope

A second class of motivations for diversification shifts attention away from operational linkages among a firm's businesses and toward financial advantages associated with diversification. Three financial implications of diversification have been studied: diversification and capital allocation, diversification and risk reduction, and tax advantages of diversification.

Diversification and Capital Allocation. Capital can be allocated to businesses in one of two ways. First, businesses operating as independent entities can compete for capital in the external capital market. They do this by providing a sufficiently high return to induce investors to purchase shares of their equity, by having a sufficiently high cash flow to repay principal and interest on debt, and in other ways. Alternatively, a business can be part of a diversified firm. That diversified firm competes in the external capital market and allocates capital among its various businesses. In a sense, diversification creates an **internal capital market** in which businesses in a diversified firm compete for corporate capital.[16]

For an internal capital market to create value for a diversified firm, it must offer some efficiency advantages over an external capital market. It has been suggested that a potential efficiency gain from internal capital markets depends on the greater amount and quality of information that a diversified firm possesses about the businesses it owns, compared with the information that external suppliers of capital possess. Owning a business gives a diversified firm access to detailed and accurate information about the actual performance of the business, its true future prospects, and thus the actual amount and cost of the capital that should be allocated to it. External sources of capital, in contrast, have relatively limited access to information and thus have a limited ability to judge the actual performance and future prospects of a business.

Some have questioned whether a diversified firm, as a source of capital, actually has more and better information about a business it owns, compared with external sources of capital. After all, independent businesses seeking capital have a strong incentive to provide sufficient information to external suppliers of capital to obtain required funds. However, a firm that owns a business may have at least two informational advantages over external sources of capital.

First, although an independent business has an incentive to provide information to external sources of capital, it also has an incentive to downplay or even not report any negative information about its performance and prospects. Such negative information would raise an independent firm's cost of capital. External sources of capital have limited ability to force a business to reveal all information about its performance and prospects and thus may provide capital at a lower cost than they would if they had full information. Ownership gives a firm the right to compel more complete disclosure, although even here full disclosure is not guaranteed. With this more complete information, a diversified firm can allocate just the right amount of capital, at the appropriate cost, to each business.

Second, an independent business may have an incentive not to reveal all the positive information about its performance and prospects. In Chapter 3, the ability of a firm to earn economic profits was shown to depend on the imitability of its resources and capabilities. An independent business that informs external sources of capital about all of its sources of competitive advantage is also informing its potential competitors about these sources of advantage. This information sharing increases the probability that these sources of advantage will be imitated. Because of the competitive implications of sharing this information, firms may choose not to share it, and external sources of capital may underestimate the true performance and prospects of a business.

A diversified firm, however, may gain access to this additional information about its businesses without revealing it to potential competitors. This information enables the diversified firm to make more informed decisions about how much capital to allocate to a business and about the cost of that capital, compared with the external capital market.[17]

Over time, there should be fewer errors in funding businesses through internal capital markets, compared with funding businesses through external capital markets. Fewer funding errors, over time, suggest a slight capital allocation advantage for a diversified firm, compared with an external capital market. This advantage should be reflected in somewhat higher rates of return on invested capital for the diversified firm, compared with the rates of return on invested capital for external sources of capital.

However, the businesses within a diversified firm do not always gain cost-of-capital advantages by being part of a diversified firm's portfolio. Several authors have argued that because a diversified firm has lower overall risk (see the following discussion), it will have a lower cost of capital, which it can pass along to the businesses within its portfolio. Although the lower risks associated with a diversified firm may lower the firm's cost of capital, the appropriate cost of capital to businesses within the firm depends on the performance and prospects of each of those businesses. The firm's advantages in evaluating its businesses' performances and prospects result in more appropriate capital allocation, not just in lower cost of capital for those businesses. Indeed, a business's cost of capital may be lower than it could have obtained in the external capital market (because the firm is able to more fully evaluate the positive aspects of that business), or it may be higher than it could have obtained in the external capital market (because the firm is able to more fully evaluate the negative aspects of that business).

Of course, if these businesses also have lower cost or higher revenue expectations because they are part of a diversified firm, then those cost/revenue advantages will be reflected in the appropriate cost of capital for these businesses. In this sense, any operational economies of scope for businesses in a diversified firm may be recognized by a diversified firm exploiting financial economies of scope.

Limits on Internal Capital Markets.   Although internal capital allocation has several potential advantages for a diversified firm, this process also has several limits. First, the level and type of diversification that a firm pursues can affect the efficiency of this allocation process. A firm that implements a strategy of unrelated diversification, whereby managers have to evaluate the performance and prospects of numerous very different businesses, puts a greater strain on the capital allocation skills of its managers than does a firm that implements related diversification. Indeed, in the extreme, the capital allocation efficiency of a firm pursuing broad-based unrelated diversification will probably not be superior to the capital allocation efficiency of the external capital market.

Second, the increased efficiency of internal capital allocation depends on managers in a diversified firm having better information for capital allocation than the information available to external sources. However, this higher-quality information is not guaranteed. The incentives that can lead managers to exaggerate their performance and prospects to external capital sources can also lead to this behavior within a diversified firm. Indeed, several examples of business managers falsifying performance records to gain access to more internal capital have been reported.[18] Research suggests that capital allocation requests by managers are routinely discounted in diversified firms in order to correct for these managers' inflated estimates of the performance and prospects of their businesses.[19]

Finally, not only do business managers have an incentive to inflate the performance and prospects of their business in a diversified firm, but managers in charge of capital allocation in these firms may have an incentive to continue investing in a business despite its poor performance and prospects. The reputation and status of these managers often depend on the success of these business investments because often they initially approved them. These managers often continue throwing good money at these businesses in hope that they will someday improve, thereby justifying their original decision. Organizational psychologists call this process **escalation of commitment** and have presented numerous examples of managers becoming irrationally committed to a particular investment.[20]

Indeed, research on the value of internal capital markets in diversified firms suggests that, on average, the limitations of these markets often outweigh their advantages. For example, even controlling for firm size, excessive investment in poorly performing businesses in a diversified firm reduces the market value of the average diversified firm.[21] However, the fact that many firms do not gain the advantages associated with internal capital markets does not necessarily imply that no firms gain these advantages. If only a few firms are able to obtain the advantages of internal capital markets while successfully avoiding their limitations, this financial economy of scope may be a source of at least a temporary competitive advantage.

Diversification and Risk Reduction.   Another possible financial economy of scope for a diversified firm has already been briefly mentioned—the riskiness of the cash flows of diversified firms is lower than the riskiness of the cash flows of undiversified firms. Consider, for example, the riskiness of two businesses operating separately compared with the risk of a diversified firm operating in those same two businesses simultaneously. If both these businesses are very risky on their own and the cash flows from these businesses are not highly correlated over time, then combining these two businesses into a single firm will generate a lower level of overall risk for the diversified firm than for each of these businesses on their own.

This lower level of risk is due to the low correlation between the cash flows associated with these two businesses. If Business I is having a bad year, Business II might be having a good year, and a firm that operates in both of these businesses simultaneously can have moderate levels of performance. In another year, Business II might be off, while Business I is having a good year. Again, the firm operating in both these businesses can have moderate levels of performance. Firms that diversify to reduce risk will have relatively stable returns over time, especially as they diversify into many different businesses with cash flows that are not highly correlated over time.

Tax Advantages of Diversification.   Another financial economy of scope from diversification stems from possible tax advantages of this corporate strategy. These possible tax advantages reflect one or a combination of two effects. First, a diversified firm can use losses in some of its businesses to offset profits in others, thereby reducing its overall tax liability. Of course, substantial losses in some of its businesses may overwhelm profits in other businesses, forcing businesses that would have remained solvent if they were independent to cease operation. However, as long as business losses are not too large, a diversified firm's tax liability can be reduced. Empirical research suggests that diversified firms do, sometimes, offset profits in some businesses with losses in others, although the tax savings of these activities are usually small.[22]

Second, because diversification can reduce the riskiness of a firm's cash flows, it can also reduce the probability that a firm will declare bankruptcy. This can increase a firm's debt capacity. This effect on debt capacity is greatest when the cash flows of a diversified firm's businesses are perfectly and negatively correlated. However, even when these cash flows are perfectly and positively correlated, there can still be a (modest) increase in debt capacity.

Debt capacity is particularly important in tax environments where interest payments on debt are tax deductible. In this context, diversified firms can increase their leverage up to their debt capacity and reduce their tax liability accordingly. Of course, if interest payments are not tax deductible or if the marginal corporate tax rate is relatively small, then the tax advantages of diversification can be quite small. Empirical work suggests that diversified firms do have greater debt capacity than undiversified firms. However, low marginal corporate tax rates, at least in the United States, make the accompanying tax savings on average relatively small.[23]

Diversification to Exploit Anticompetitive Economies of Scope

A third group of motivations for diversification is based on the relationship between diversification strategies and various anticompetitive activities by firms. Two specific examples of these activities are (1) multipoint competition to facilitate mutual forbearance and tacit collusion and (2) exploiting market power.

Multipoint Competition.   Multipoint competition exists when two or more diversified firms simultaneously compete in multiple markets. For example, HP and

Dell compete in both the personal computer market and the market for computer printers. Michelin and Goodyear compete in both the U.S. automobile tire market and the European automobile tire market. Disney and AOL/Time Warner compete in both the movie production and book publishing businesses.

Multipoint competition can serve to facilitate a particular type of tacit collusion called **mutual forbearance**. Firms engage in **tacit collusion** when they cooperate to reduce rivalry below the level expected under perfect competition. Consider the situation facing two diversified firms, A and B. These two firms operate in the same businesses, I, II, III, and IV (see Figure 7.3). In this context, any decisions that Firm A might make to compete aggressively in Businesses I and III must take into account the possibility that Firm B will respond by competing aggressively in Businesses II and IV and vice versa. The potential loss that each of these firms may experience in some of its businesses must be compared with the potential gain that each might obtain if it exploits competitive advantages in other of its businesses. If the present value of gains does not outweigh the present value of losses from retaliation, then both firms will avoid competitive activity. Refraining from competition is mutual forbearance.[24]

Mutual forbearance as a result of multipoint competition has occurred in several industries. For example, this form of tacit collusion has been described as existing between Michelin and Goodyear, Maxwell House and Folger's, Caterpillar and John Deere, and BIC and Gillette.[25] Another clear example of such cooperation can be found in the airline industry. For example, America West (now part of US Air) began service into the Houston Intercontinental Airport with very low introductory fares. Continental Airlines (now part of United Airlines), the dominant firm at Houston Intercontinental, rapidly responded to America West's low Houston fares by reducing the price of its flights from Phoenix, Arizona, to several cities in the United States. Phoenix is the home airport of America West. Within just a few weeks, America West withdrew its low introductory fares in the Houston market, and Continental withdrew its reduced prices in the Phoenix market. The threat of retaliation across markets apparently led America West and Continental to tacitly collude on prices.[26]

However, sometimes multipoint competition does not lead to mutual forbearance. Consider, for example, a conflict between The Walt Disney Company and Time Warner. As mentioned earlier, Disney operates in the theme park, movie

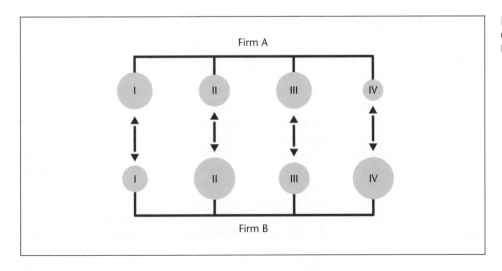

Figure 7.3 Multipoint Competition Between Hypothetical Firms A and B

and television production, and television broadcasting industries. Time Warner operates in the theme park and movie and television production industries and also operates a very large magazine business (*Time*, *People*, *Sports Illustrated*, among others). From 1988 through 1993, Disney spent more than $40 million in advertising its theme parks in Time Warner magazines. Despite this substantial revenue, Time Warner began an aggressive advertising campaign aimed at wooing customers away from Disney theme parks to its own. Disney retaliated by canceling all of its advertising in Time Warner magazines. Time Warner responded to Disney's actions by canceling a corporate meeting to be held in Florida at Disney World. Disney responded to Time Warner's meeting cancellation by refusing to broadcast Time Warner theme park advertisements on its Los Angeles television station.[27]

Some recent research investigates the conditions under which mutual forbearance strategies are pursued, as well as conditions under which multipoint competition does not lead to mutual forbearance.[28] In general, the value of the threat of retaliation must be substantial for multipoint competition to lead to mutual forbearance. However, not only must the payoffs to mutual forbearance be substantial, but the firms pursuing this strategy must have strong strategic linkages among their diversified businesses. This suggests that firms pursuing mutual forbearance strategies based on multipoint competition are usually pursuing a form of related diversification.

Diversification and Market Power.   Internal allocations of capital among a diversified firm's businesses may enable it to exploit in some of its businesses the market power advantages it enjoys in other of its businesses. For example, suppose that a firm is earning monopoly profits in a particular business. This firm can use some of these monopoly profits to subsidize the operations of another of its businesses. This cross-subsidization can take several forms, including **predatory pricing**—that is, setting prices so that they are less than the subsidized business's costs. The effect of this cross-subsidy may be to drive competitors out of the subsidized business and then to obtain monopoly profits in that subsidized business. In a sense, diversification enables a firm to apply its monopoly power in several different businesses. Economists call this a **deep-pockets model** of diversification.[29]

Diversified firms with operations in regulated monopolies have been criticized for this kind of cross-subsidization. For example, most of the regional telephone companies in the United States are engaging in diversification strategies. The consent decree that forced the breakup of the original AT&T expressly forbade cross-subsidies between these regional companies' telephone monopolies and other business activities, under the assumption that such subsidies would give these firms an unfair competitive advantage in their diversified business activities.[30]

Although these market power economies of scope, in principle, may exist, relatively little empirical work documents their existence. Indeed, research on regulated utilities diversifying into nonregulated businesses in the 1980s suggests not that these firms use monopoly profits in their regulated businesses to unfairly subsidize nonregulated businesses, but that non-competition-oriented management skills developed in the regulated businesses tend to make diversification less profitable rather than more profitable.[31] Nevertheless, the potential that large diversified firms have to exercise market power and to behave in socially irresponsible ways has led some observers to call for actions to curtail both the economic and political power of these firms. These issues are discussed in the Ethics and Strategy feature.

Firm Size and Employee Incentives to Diversify

Employees may have incentives to diversify that are independent of any benefits from other sources of economies of scope. This is especially the case for employees in senior management positions and employees with long tenure in a particular firm. These employee incentives reflect the interest of employees to diversify because of the relationship between firm size and management compensation.

Research over the years demonstrates conclusively that the primary determinant of the compensation of top managers in a firm is not the economic performance of the firm but the size of the firm, usually measured in sales.[32] Thus, managers seeking to maximize their income should attempt to grow their firm. One of the easiest ways to grow a firm is through diversification, especially unrelated diversification through mergers and acquisitions. By making large acquisitions, a diversified firm can grow substantially in a short period of time, leading senior managers to earn higher incomes. All of this is independent of any economic profit that diversification may or may not generate. Senior managers need only worry about economic profit if the level of that profit is so low that unfriendly takeovers are a threat or so low that the board of directors may be forced to replace management.

Recently, the traditional relationship between firm size and management compensation has begun to break down. More and more, the compensation of senior managers is being tied to the firm's economic performance. In particular, the use of stock and other forms of deferred compensation makes it in management's best interest to be concerned with a firm's economic performance. These changes in compensation do not necessarily imply that firms will abandon all forms of diversification. However, they do suggest that firms will abandon those forms of diversification that do not generate real economies of scope.

Can Equity Holders Realize These Economies of Scope on Their Own?

Earlier in this chapter, it was suggested that for a firm's diversification strategies to create value, two conditions must hold. First, these strategies must exploit valuable economies of scope. Potentially valuable economies of scope were presented in Table 7.1 and discussed in the previous section. Second, it must be less costly for managers in a firm to realize these economies of scope than for outside equity holders on their own. If outside equity holders could realize a particular economy of scope on their own, without a firm's managers, at low cost, why would they want to hire managers to do this for them by investing in a firm and providing capital to managers to exploit an economy of scope?

Table 7.3 summarizes the discussion on the potential value of the different economies of scope listed in Table 7.1. It also suggests which of these economies of scope will be difficult for outside equity investors to exploit on their own and thus which bases of diversification are most likely to create positive returns for a firm's equity holders.

Most of the economies of scope listed in Table 7.3 cannot be realized by equity holders on their own. This is because most of them require activities that equity holders cannot engage in or information that equity holders do not possess. For example, shared activities, core competencies, multipoint competition, and exploiting market power all require the detailed coordination of business activities across multiple businesses in a firm. Although equity holders may own a portfolio of equities, they are not in a position to coordinate business activities across this portfolio. In a similar way, internal capital allocation requires information about a business's prospects that is simply not available to a firm's outside equity holders.

Ethics and Strategy

In 1999, a loose coalition of union members, environmentalists, youth, indigenous peoples, human rights activists, and small farmers took to the streets of Seattle, Washington, to protest a meeting of the World Trade Organization (WTO) and to fight against the growing global power of corporations. Government officials and corporate officers alike were confused by these protests. After all, hadn't world trade increased 19 times from 1950 to 1995 ($0.4 trillion to $7.6 trillion in constant 2003 dollars), and hadn't the total economic output of the entire world gone from $6.4 trillion in 1950 to $60.7 trillion in 2005 (again, in constant 2003 dollars)? Why protest a global economic system—a system that was enhancing the level of free trade and facilitating global economic efficiency—that was so clearly improving the economic well-being of the world's population? This 1999 protest turned out to be the first of many such demonstrations, culminating in the Occupy Movement after the financial crisis of 2007. And, still, many business and government leaders remain confused. Empirically, globalization has improved the world economy, so why the protests?

The protestors' message to government and big business was that these aggregate growth numbers masked more truth than they told. Yes, there has been economic growth. But that growth has benefited only a small percentage of the world's population. Most of the population still struggles to survive. The combined net worth of 358 U.S. billionaires in the early 1990s ($760 billion) was equal to the combined net worth of the 2.5 billion poorest people on the earth! Eighty-three percent of the world's total income

Globalization and the Threat of the Multinational Firm

goes to the richest fifth of the population while the poorest fifth of the world's population receives only 1.4 percent of the world's total income. Currently, 45 million to 70 million people worldwide have had to leave their home countries to find work in foreign lands, and approximately 1.4 billion people around the world live on less than $1 a day. Even in relatively affluent societies such as the United States, people find it increasingly difficult to meet their financial obligations. Falling real wages, economic insecurity, and corporate downsizing have led many people to work longer hours or to hold two or three jobs. While the number of billionaires in the world continues to grow, the number of people facing mind-numbing and strength-robbing poverty grows even faster.

The causes of this apparent contradiction—global economic growth linked with growing global economic decay—are numerous and complex. However, one explanation focuses on the growing economic power of the diversified multinational corporation.

The size of these institutions can be immense—many international diversified firms are larger than the entire economies of many nations. And these huge institutions, with a single-minded focus on maximizing their performance, can make profit-making decisions that adversely affect their suppliers, their customers, their employees, and the environment, all with relative impunity. Armed with the unspoken mantra that "Greed is good," these corporations can justify almost any action, as long as it increases the wealth of their shareholders.

Of course, even if one accepts this hypothesis—and it is far from being universally accepted—solutions to the growing power of internationally diversified firms are not obvious. The problem is that one way that firms become large and powerful is by being able to meet customer demands effectively. Thus, firm size, per se, is not necessarily an indication that a firm is behaving in ways inconsistent with the public good. Government efforts to restrict the size of firms simply because they are large could easily have the effect of making citizens worse off. However, once firms are large and powerful, they may very well be tempted to exercise that power in ways that benefit themselves at great cost to society.

Whatever the causes and solutions to these problems, protests that began in Seattle in 1999 have at least one clear message: global growth for growth's sake is no longer universally accepted as the correct objective of international economic policy.

Sources: D. C. Korten (2001). *When corporations rule the world*, 2nd ed. Bloomfield, CT: Kumarian Press; H. Demsetz (1973). "Industry structure, market rivalry, and public policy." *Journal of Law and Economics*, 16, pp. 1–9; J. Stiglitz (2007). *Making globalization work*. New York: Norton.

TABLE 7.3 The Competitive Implications of Different Economies of Scope

Types of Economy of Scope	Are They Valuable?	Can They Be Realized by Equity Holders on Their Own?	Positive Returns to Equity Holders?
1. *Operational economies of scope*			
Shared activities	Possible	No	Possible
Core competencies	Possible	No	Possible
2. *Financial economies of scope*			
Internal capital allocation	Possible	No	Possible
Risk reduction	Possible	Yes	No
Tax advantages	Possible—small	No	Possible—small
3. *Anticompetitive economies of scope*			
Multipoint competition	Possible	No	Possible
Exploiting market power	Possible	No	Possible
4. *Employee incentives for diversification*			
Maximizing management compensation	No	No	No

Indeed, the only two economies of scope listed in Table 7.3 that do not have the potential for generating positive returns for a firm's equity holders are diversification in order to maximize the size of a firm—because firm size, per se, is not valuable—and diversification to reduce risk—because equity holders can do this on their own at very low cost by simply investing in a diversified portfolio of stocks. Indeed, although risk reduction is often a published rationale for many diversification moves, this rationale, by itself, is not directly consistent with the interests of a firm's equity holders. However, some scholars have suggested that this strategy may directly benefit other of a firm's stakeholders and thus indirectly benefit its equity holders. This possibility is discussed in detail in the Strategy in Depth feature.

Overall, this analysis of possible bases of diversification suggests that related diversification is more likely to be consistent with the interests of a firm's equity holders than unrelated diversification. This is because the one economy of scope listed in Table 7.3 that is the easiest for outside equity holders to duplicate—risk reduction—is the only economy of scope that an unrelated diversified firm can try to realize. All the other economies of scope listed in Table 7.3 require coordination and information sharing across businesses in a diversified firm that are very difficult to realize in unrelated diversified firms. Indeed, the preponderance of empirical research suggests that related diversified firms outperform unrelated diversified firms.[33]

Corporate Diversification and Sustained Competitive Advantage

Table 7.3 describes those economies of scope that are likely to create real economic value for diversifying firms. It also suggests that related diversification can be valuable, and unrelated diversification is usually not valuable. However, as we have seen with all the other strategies discussed in this book, the fact that a

Strategy in Depth

Although diversifying in order to reduce risk generally does not directly benefit outside equity investors in a firm, it can *indirectly* benefit outside equity investors through its impact on the willingness of other stakeholders in a firm to make firm-specific investments. A firm's **stakeholders** include all those groups and individuals who have an interest in how a firm performs. In this sense, a firm's equity investors are one of a firm's stakeholders. Other firm stakeholders include employees, suppliers, and customers.

Firm stakeholders make **firm-specific investments** when the value of the investments they make in a particular firm is much greater than the value of those same investments would be in other firms. Consider, for example, a firm's employees. An employee with a long tenure in a particular firm has generally made substantial **firm-specific human capital investments.** These investments include understanding a particular firm's culture, policies, and procedures; knowing the "right" people to contact to complete a task; and so forth. Such investments have significant value in the firm where they are made. Indeed, such firm-specific knowledge is generally necessary if an employee is to be able to help a firm conceive and implement valuable

Risk-Reducing Diversification and a Firm's Other Stakeholders

strategies. However, the specific investments that an employee makes in a particular firm have almost no value in other firms. If a firm were to cease operations, employees would instantly lose almost all the value of any of the firm-specific investments they had made in that firm.

Suppliers and customers can also make these firm-specific investments. Suppliers make these investments when they customize their products or services to the specific requirements of a particular customer. They also make firm-specific investments when they forgo opportunities to sell to other firms in order to sell to a particular firm. Customers make firm-specific investments when they customize their operations to fully utilize the products or services

of a particular firm. Also, by developing close relationships with a particular firm, customers may forgo the opportunity to develop relationships with other firms. These, too, are firm-specific investments made by customers. If a firm were to cease operations, suppliers and customers would instantly lose almost the entire value of the specific investments they have made in this firm.

Although the firm-specific investments made by employees, suppliers, and customers are risky—in the sense that almost their entire value is lost if the firm in which they are made ceases operations—they are extremely important if a firm is going to be able to generate economic profits. As was suggested in Chapter 3, valuable, rare, and costly-to-imitate resources and capabilities are more likely to be a source of sustained competitive advantage than resources and capabilities without these attributes. Firm-specific investments are more likely to have these attributes than non-firm-specific investments. Non-firm-specific investments are investments that can generate value in numerous different firms.

Thus, valuable, rare, and costly-to-imitate firm-specific investments made by a firm's employees, suppliers, and customers can be the source of economic profits. And because a

strategy is valuable does not necessarily imply that it will be a source of sustained competitive advantage. In order for diversification to be a source of sustained competitive advantage, it must be not only valuable but also rare and costly to imitate, and a firm must be organized to implement this strategy. The rarity and imitability of diversification are discussed in this section; organizational questions are deferred until the next.

firm's outside equity holders are residual claimants on the cash flows generated by a firm, these economic profits benefit equity holders. Thus, a firm's outside equity holders generally will want a firm's employees, suppliers, and customers to make specific investments in a firm because those investments are likely to be sources of economic wealth for outside equity holders.

However, given the riskiness of firm-specific investments, employees, suppliers, and customers will generally only be willing to make these investments if some of the riskiness associated with making them can be reduced. Outside equity holders have little difficulty managing the risks associated with investing in a particular firm because they can always create a portfolio of stocks that fully diversifies this risk at very low cost. This is why diversification that reduces the riskiness of a firm's cash flows does not generally directly benefit a firm's outside equity holders. However, a firm's employees, suppliers, and customers usually do not have these low-cost diversification opportunities. Employees, for example, are rarely able to make firm-specific human capital investments in a large enough number of different firms to fully diversify the risks associated with making them. And although

suppliers and customers can diversify their firm-specific investments to a greater degree than employees—through selling to multiple customers and through buying from multiple suppliers—the cost of this diversification for suppliers and customers is usually greater than the costs that are borne by outside equity holders in diversifying their risk.

Because it is often very costly for a firm's employees, suppliers, and customers to diversify the risks associated with making firm-specific investments on their own, these stakeholders will often prefer that a firm's managers help manage this risk for them. Managers in a firm can do this by diversifying the portfolio of businesses in which a firm operates. If a firm is unwilling to diversify its portfolio of businesses, then that firm's employees, suppliers, and customers will generally be unwilling to make specific investments in that firm. Moreover, because these firm-specific investments can generate economic profits and because economic profits can directly benefit a firm's outside equity holders, equity holders have an indirect incentive to encourage a firm to pursue a diversification strategy, even though that strategy does not directly benefit them.

Put differently, a firm's diversification strategy can be thought of

as compensation for the firm-specific investments that a firm's employees, suppliers, and customers make in a firm. Outside equity holders have an incentive to encourage this compensation in return for access to some of the economic profits that these firm-specific investments can generate. In general, the greater the impact of the firm-specific investment made by a firm's employees, suppliers, and customers on the ability of a firm to generate economic profits, the more likely that pursuing a corporate diversification strategy is indirectly consistent with the interests of a firm's outside equity holders. In addition, the more limited the ability of a firm's employees, suppliers, and customers to diversify the risks associated with making firm-specific investments at low cost, the more that corporate diversification is consistent with the interests of outside equity investors.

Sources: J. B. Barney (1991). "Firm resources and sustained competitive advantage." *Journal of Management*, 17, pp. 99–120; R. M. Stulz (1996). "Rethinking risk management." *Journal of Applied Corporate Finance*, Fall, pp. 8–24; K. Miller (1998). "Economic exposure and integrated risk management," *Strategic Management Journal*, 33, pp. 756–779; R. Amit and B. Wernerfelt (1990). "Why do firms reduce business risk?" *Academy of Management Journal*, 33, pp. 520–533; H. Wang and J. Barney (2006), "Employee incentives to make firm specific investments: Implications for resource-based theories of diversification." *Academy of Management Review*, 31(2), pp. 466–476.

The Rarity of Diversification

At first glance, it seems clear that diversification per se is usually not a rare firm strategy. Most large firms have adopted some form of diversification, if only the limited diversification of a dominant-business firm. Even many small and medium-sized firms have adopted different levels of diversification strategy.

However, the rarity of diversification depends not on diversification per se but on how rare the particular economies of scope associated with that diversification are. If only a few competing firms have exploited a particular economy of scope, that economy of scope can be rare. If numerous firms have done so, it will be common and not a source of competitive advantage.

The Imitability of Diversification

Both forms of imitation—direct duplication and substitution—are relevant in evaluating the ability of diversification strategies to generate sustained competitive advantages, even if the economies of scope that they create are rare.

Direct Duplication of Diversification

The extent to which a valuable and rare corporate diversification strategy is immune from direct duplication depends on how costly it is for competing firms to realize this same economy of scope. As suggested in Table 7.4, some economies of scope are, in general, more costly to duplicate than others.

Shared activities, risk reduction, tax advantages, and employee compensation as bases for corporate diversification are usually relatively easy to duplicate. Because shared activities are based on tangible assets that a firm exploits across multiple businesses, such as common research and development labs, common sales forces, and common manufacturing, they are usually relatively easy to duplicate. The only duplication issues for shared activities concern developing the cooperative cross-business relationships that often facilitate the use of shared activities—issues discussed in the next chapter. Moreover, because risk reduction, tax advantages, and employee compensation motives for diversifying can be accomplished through both related and unrelated diversification, these motives for diversifying tend to be relatively easy to duplicate.

Other economies of scope are much more difficult to duplicate. These difficult-to-duplicate economies of scope include core competencies, internal capital allocation efficiencies, multipoint competition, and exploitation of market power. Because core competencies are more intangible, their direct duplication is often challenging. The realization of capital allocation economies of scope requires very substantial information-processing capabilities. These capabilities are often very difficult to develop. Multipoint competition requires very close coordination between the different businesses in which a firm operates. This kind of coordination is socially complex and thus often immune from direct duplication. Finally, exploitation of market power may be costly to duplicate because it requires that a firm must possess significant market power in one of its lines of business. A firm that does not have this market power advantage would have to obtain it. The cost of doing so, in most situations, would be prohibitive.

TABLE 7.4 Costly Duplication of Economies of Scope

Less Costly-to-Duplicate Economies of Scope	Costly-to-Duplicate Economies of Scope
Shared activities	Core competencies
Risk reduction	Internal capital allocation
Tax advantages	Multipoint competition
Employee compensation	Exploiting market power

Substitutes for Diversification

Two obvious substitutes for diversification exist. First, instead of obtaining cost or revenue advantages from exploiting economies of scope *across* businesses in a diversified firm, a firm may decide to simply grow and develop each of its businesses separately. In this sense, a firm that successfully implements a cost leadership strategy or a product differentiation strategy in a single business can obtain the same cost or revenue advantages it could have obtained by exploiting economies of scope but without having to develop cross-business relations. Growing independent businesses within a diversified firm can be a substitute for exploiting economies of scope in a diversification strategy.

One firm that has chosen this strategy is Nestlé. Nestlé exploits few, if any, economies of scope among its different businesses. Rather, it has focused its efforts on growing each of its international operations to the point that they obtain cost or revenue advantages that could have otherwise been obtained in some form of related diversification. Thus, for example, Nestlé's operation in the United States is sufficiently large to exploit economies of scale in production, sales, and marketing, without reliance on economies of scope between U.S. operations and operations in other countries.[34]

A second substitute for exploiting economies of scope in diversification can be found in strategic alliances. By using a strategic alliance, a firm may be able to gain the economies of scope it could have obtained if it had carefully exploited economies of scope across its businesses. Thus, for example, instead of a firm exploiting research and development economies of scope between two businesses it owns, it could form a strategic alliance with a different firm and form a joint research and development lab. Instead of a firm exploiting sales economies of scope by linking its businesses through a common sales force, it might develop a sales agreement with another firm and obtain cost or revenue advantages in this way.

Summary

Firms implement corporate diversification strategies that range from limited diversification (single-business, dominant-business) to related diversification (related-constrained, related-linked) to unrelated diversification. In order to be valuable, corporate diversification strategies must reduce costs or increase revenues by exploiting economies of scope that outside equity holders cannot realize on their own at low cost.

Several motivations for implementing diversification strategies exist, including exploiting operational economies of scope (shared activities, core competencies), exploiting financial economies of scope (internal capital allocation, risk reduction, obtaining tax advantages), exploiting anticompetitive economies of scope (multipoint competition, market power advantages), and employee incentives to diversify (maximizing management compensation). All these reasons for diversifying, except diversifying to maximize management compensation, have the potential to create economic value for a firm. Moreover, a firm's outside equity holders will find it costly to realize all of these bases for diversification, except risk reduction. Thus, diversifying to maximize management compensation or diversifying to reduce risk is not consistent with the wealth-maximizing interests of a firm's equity holders. This analysis also suggests that, on average, related diversified firms will outperform unrelated diversified firms.

The ability of a diversification strategy to create sustained competitive advantages depends not only on the value of that strategy, but also on its rarity and imitability. The rarity of a diversification strategy depends on the number of competing firms that are exploiting the same economies of scope through diversification. Imitation can occur either through direct duplication or through substitutes. Costly-to-duplicate economies of scope include core competencies, internal capital allocation, multipoint competition, and exploitation of market power. Other economies of scope are usually less costly to duplicate. Important substitutes for diversification are when relevant economies are obtained through the independent actions of businesses within a firm and when relevant economies are obtained through strategic alliances. This discussion set aside important organizational issues in implementing diversification strategies. These issues are examined in detail in the next chapter.

MyManagementLab®

Go to **mymanagementlab.com** to complete the problems marked with this icon ✪.

Challenge Questions

7.1. One simple way to think about relatedness is to look at the products or services a firm manufactures. The more similar these products or services are, the more related is the firm's diversification strategy. Why or why not would firms that exploit core competencies in their diversification strategies always produce products or services that are similar to each other?

7.2. Unrelated corporate diversification involves entering an unfamiliar industry. Is the economies of scope analysis enough to make a decision on unrelated diversification? Is the five forces analysis also needed? If not, why not? If so, then how

should the two analyses be used in combination?

✪ **7.3.** One of the reasons why internal capital markets may be more efficient than external capital markets is that firms may not want to reveal full information about their sources of competitive advantage to external capital markets in order to reduce the threat of competitive imitation. This suggests that external capital markets may systematically undervalue firms with competitive advantages that are subject to imitation. If you agree with this analysis, how could you trade on this information in your own investment activities?

7.4. Almost all firms share certain value chain activities. For example, most firms have a centralized finance and accounting department, a procurement, an MIS and an HR function. Given this fact, two firms from unrelated industries are planning to merge simply to combine their overhead functions, which constitute a large fraction (e.g., > 40%) of their individual cost basis. Is the logic sound? Why or why not?

✪ **7.5.** Under what conditions will a related diversification strategy not be a source of competitive advantage for a firm?

Problem Set

7.6. Visit the corporate Web sites of the following firms. How would you characterize their corporate strategies? Are they following a strategy of limited diversification, related diversification, or unrelated diversification?

(a) Dangote
(b) América Móvil
(c) LVMH
(d) Tata
(e) Baidu
(f) SAP
(g) Cheung Kong Holdings
(h) Embraer
(i) Rovio Entertainment

7.7. Consider the following list of strategies. In your view, which of these strategies are examples of potential economies of scope underlying a corporate diversification strategy? For those strategies that are an economy of scope, which economy of scope are they? For those strategies that are not an economy of scope, why aren't they?

(a) Tata launches Swach, its water purifier for the Indian market, developed with the help of Tata Chemicals, Tata Autocomp Systems, Tata Consulting Services and other Tata Group companies.

(b) Medtronic, US medical device maker (strongest in pacemakers and spinal treatment), announces acquisition of Ireland-based Covidien (strongest in surgical equipment) and plans to relocate its headquarters to Ireland to lower corporate tax.

(c) GE Capital announces intent to spin off its retail lending business to focus on its industrial segment with products such as fleet finance, commercial loans and leases.

(d) Robinsons Retail, a leading retailer in the Phillipines, announces the purchase of A.M. Builders' Depot. This deal will make available to A.M. Builders' Depot, a wide range of home improvement products and appliances from Robinsons.

(e) Oracle's acquisition of PeopleSoft: both are global leaders in business software.

(f) FedEx Corp, a global courier service, announced that its FedEx Express subsidiary has acquired an African courier, Supaswift, with businesses in South Africa and six other countries in order to extend the Fedex network in Africa.

(g) Omron Healthcare, a popular maker of medical devices for use at home, announced the launch of its latest pain relief device, the Pain Relief Pro, which now comes with a massage feature and more pain modes (arm, lower back, leg, foot and joint).

(h) InternetQ, a global mobile marketing services company announces the acquisition of Interacel, a growing mobile service provider in Latin America. The merger is expected to enable InternetQ to upsell its mobile marketing, Akazoo music streaming and Minimob smart advertising services directly to mobile network operators and media brands in Latin America.

(i) A venture capital firm invests in a firm in the biotechnology industry and a firm in the entertainment industry.

(j) Another venture capital firm invests in two firms in the biotechnology industry.

7.8. Consider the following facts. The standard deviation of the cash flows associated with Business I is 0.8. The larger this standard deviation, the riskier a business's future cash flows are likely to be. The standard deviation of the cash flows associated with Business II is 1.3. That is, Business II is riskier than Business I. Finally, the correlation between the cash flows of these two businesses over time is 0.8. This means that when Business I is up, Business II tends to be down, and vice versa. Suppose one firm owns both of these businesses.

(a) Assuming that Business I constitutes 40 percent of this firm's revenues and Business II constitutes 60 percent of its revenues, calculate the riskiness of this firm's total revenues using the following equation:

$$sd_{I,II} = \sqrt{w^2 sd_I^2 + (1 - w)^2 sd_{II}^2 + 2w(1 + w)(r_{I,II} sd_I sd_{II})}$$

Where $w = 0.40$; $sd_I = 0.8$, $sd_{II} = 1.3$, and $r_{I,\,II} = -8$.

(b) Given this result, does it make sense for this firm to own both Business I and Business II? Why or why not?

MyManagementLab®

Go to **mymanagementlab.com** for the following Assisted-graded writing questions:

⭐ **7.9.** Not all firms will choose corporate diversification. Describe the benefits and challenges of the alternatives.

⭐ **7.10.** Internal capital markets have several limitations. When a firm is confronted by these limitations, what is it likely to do?

End Notes

1. See Sellers, P. (2004). "The brand king's challenge." *Fortune*, April 5, pp. 192+.
2. The Walt Disney Company. (1995). Harvard Business School Case No. 1-388-147.
3. Useem, J. (2004). "Another boss, another revolution." *Fortune*, April 5, pp. 112+.
4. See Rogers, A. (1992). "It's the execution that counts." *Fortune*, November 30, pp. 80–83; and Porter, M. E. (1981). "Disposable diaper industry in 1974." Harvard Business School Case No. 9-380-175. A more general discussion of the value of shared activities can be found in St. John, C. H., and J. S. Harrison. (1999). "Manufacturing-based relatedness, synergy, and coordination." *Strategic Management Journal*, 20, pp. 129–145.
5. See Fuchsberg, G. (1992). "Decentralized management can have its drawbacks." *The Wall Street Journal*, December 9, p. B1.
6. See Crockett, R. (2000). "A Baby Bell's growth formula." *BusinessWeek*, March 6, pp. 50–52; and Crockett, R. (1999). "The last monopolist." *BusinessWeek*, April 12, p. 76.
7. de Lisser, E. (1993). "Catering to cooking-phobic customers, supermarkets stress carryout." *The Wall Street Journal*, April 5, p. B1.
8. See, for example, Davis, P., R. Robinson, J. Pearce, and S. Park. (1992). "Business unit relatedness and performance: A look at the pulp and paper industry." *Strategic Management Journal*, 13, pp. 349–361.
9. Loomis, C. J. (1993). "Dinosaurs?" *Fortune*, May 3, pp. 36–42.
10. Rapoport, C. (1992). "A tough Swede invades the U.S." *Fortune*, June 29, pp. 776–779.
11. Prahalad, C. K., and G. Hamel. (1990). "The core competence of the organization." *Harvard Business Review*, 90, p. 82.
12. See also Grant, R. M. (1988). "On 'dominant logic' relatedness and the link between diversity and performance." *Strategic Management Journal*, 9, pp. 639–642; Chatterjee, S., and B. Wernerfelt. (1991). "The link between resources and type of diversification: Theory and evidence." *Strategic Management Journal*, 12, pp. 33–48; Markides, C., and P. J. Williamson. (1994). "Related diversification, core competencies, and corporate performance." *Strategic Management Journal*, 15, pp. 149–165; Montgomery, C. A., and B. Wernerfelt. (1991). "Sources of superior performance: Market share versus industry effects in the U.S. brewing industry." *Management Science*, 37, pp. 954–959; Liedtka, J. M. (1996). "Collaborating across lines of business for competitive advantage." *Academy of Management Executive*, 10(2), pp. 20–37; and Farjoun, M. (1998). "The independent and joint effects of the skill and physical bases of relatedness in diversification." *Strategic Management Journal*, 19, pp. 611–630.
13. Jensen, M. C. (1986). "Agency costs of free cash flow, corporate finance, and takeovers." *American Economic Review*, 76, pp. 323–329.
14. See Nayyar, P. (1990). "Information asymmetries: A source of competitive advantage for diversified service firms." *Strategic Management Journal*, 11, pp. 513–519; and Robins, J., and M. Wiersema. (1995). "A resource-based approach to the multibusiness firm: Empirical analysis of portfolio interrelationships and corporate financial performance." *Strategic Management Journal*, 16, pp. 277–299, for a discussion of the evolution of core competencies.
15. Prahalad, C. K., and R. A. Bettis. (1986). "The dominant logic: A new linkage between diversity and performance." *Strategic Management Journal*, 7(6), pp. 485–501.
16. See Williamson, O. E. (1975). *Markets and hierarchies: Analysis and antitrust implications*. New York: Free Press.
17. See Liebeskind, J. P. (1996). "Knowledge, strategy, and the theory of the firm." *Strategic Management Journal*, 17 (Winter Special Edition), pp. 93–107.
18. Perry, L. T., and J. B. Barney. (1981). "Performance lies are hazardous to organizational health." *Organizational Dynamics*, 9(3), pp. 68–80.
19. Bethel, J. E. (1990). *The capital allocation process and managerial mobility: A theoretical and empirical investigation*. Unpublished doctoral dissertation, University of California at Los Angeles.
20. Staw, B. M. (1981). "The escalation of commitment to a course of action." *Academy of Management Review*, 6, pp. 577–587.
21. See Comment, R., and G. Jarrell. (1995). "Corporate focus and stock returns." *Journal of Financial Economics*, 37, pp. 67–87; Berger, P. G., and E. Ofek. (1995). "Diversification's effect on firm value." *Journal of Financial Economics*, 37, pp. 39–65; Maksimovic, V., and G. Phillips. (1999). "Do conglomerate firms allocate resources inefficiently?" Working paper, University of Maryland; Matsusaka, J. G., and V. Nanda. (1998). "Internal capital markets and corporate refocusing." Working paper, University of Southern California; Palia, D. (1998). "Division-level overinvestment and agency conflicts in diversified firms." Working paper, Columbia University; Rajan, R., H. Servaes, and L. Zingales. (1997). "The cost of diversity: The diversification discount and inefficient investment." Working paper, University of Chicago; Scharfstein, D. S. (1997). "The dark side of internal capital markets II: Evidence from diversified conglomerates." NBER [National Bureau of Economic Research]. Working paper; Shin, H. H., and R. M. Stulz. (1998). "Are internal capital markets efficient?" *The Quarterly Journal of Economics*, May, pp. 551–552. But Houston and James (1998) show that internal capital markets can create competitive advantages for firms: Houston, J., and C. James. (1998). "Some evidence that banks use internal capital markets to lower capital costs." *Journal of Applied Corporate Finance*, 11(2), pp. 70–78.
22. Scott, J. H. (1977). "On the theory of conglomerate mergers." *Journal of Finance*, 32, pp. 1235–1250.
23. See Brennan, M. (1979). "The pricing of contingent claims in discrete time models." *Journal of Finance*, 34, pp. 53–68; Cox, J., S. Ross, and M. Rubinstein. (1979). "Option pricing: A simplified approach." *Journal of Financial Economics*, 7, pp. 229–263; Stapleton, R. C. (1982). "Mergers, debt capacity, and the valuation of corporate loans." In M. Keenan and L. J. White. (eds.), *Mergers and acquisitions*. Lexington, MA: D. C. Heath, Chapter 2; and Galai, D., and R. W. Masulis. (1976). "The option pricing model and the risk factor of stock." *Journal of Financial Economics*, 3, pp. 53–82.
24. See Karnani, A., and B. Wernerfelt. (1985). "Multiple point competition." *Strategic Management Journal*, 6, pp. 87–96; Bernheim, R. D., and M. D. Whinston. (1990). "Multimarket contact and collusive behavior." *Rand Journal of Economics*, 12, pp. 605–617; Tirole, J. (1988). *The theory of industrial organization*. Cambridge, MA: MIT Press; Gimeno, J., and C. Y. Woo. (1999). "Multimarket contact, economies of scope, and firm performance." *Academy of Management Journal*, 43(3), pp. 239–259; Korn, H. J., and J. A. C. Baum. (1999). "Chance, imitative, and strategic antecedents to multimarket contact." *Academy of Management Journal*, 42(2), pp. 171–193; Baum, J. A. C., and H. J. Korn. (1999). "Dynamics of dyadic competitive interaction." *Strategic Management Journal*, 20, pp. 251–278; Gimeno, J. (1999). "Reciprocal threats in multimarket rivalry: Staking our 'spheres of influence' in the U.S. airline industry." *Strategic Management Journal*, 20, pp. 101–128; Gimeno, J., and C. Y. Woo. (1996). "Hypercompetition in a multimarket environment:

The role of strategic similarity and multimarket contact in competitive de-escalation." *Organization Science*, 7(3), pp. 322–341; Ma, H. (1998). "Mutual forbearance in international business." *Journal of International Management*, 4(2), pp. 129–147; McGrath, R. G., and M.-J. Chen. (1998). "Multimarket maneuvering in uncertain spheres of influence: Resource diversion strategies." *Academy of Management Review*, 23(4), pp. 724–740; Chen, M.-J. (1996). "Competitor analysis and interfirm rivalry: Toward a theoretical integration." *Academy of Management Review*, 21(1), pp. 100–134; Chen, M.-J., and K. Stucker. (1997). "Multinational management and multimarket rivalry: Toward a theoretical development of global competition." *Academy of Management Proceedings 1997*, pp. 2–6; and Young, G., K. G. Smith, and C. M. Grimm. (1997). "Multimarket contact, resource heterogeneity, and rivalrous firm behavior." *Academy of Management Proceedings 1997*, pp. 55–59. This idea was originally proposed by Edwards, C. D. (1955). "Conglomerate bigness as a source of power." In *Business concentration and price policy*. NBER Conference Report. Princeton, NJ: Princeton University Press.

25. See Karnani, A., and B. Wernerfelt. (1985). "Multiple point competition." *Strategic Management Journal*, 6, pp. 87–96.

26. This was documented by Gimeno, J. (1994). "Multipoint competition, market rivalry and firm performance: A test of the mutual forbearance hypothesis in the United States airline industry, 1984–1988." Unpublished doctoral dissertation, Purdue University.

27. See Landro, L., P. M. Reilly, and R. Turner. (1993). "Cartoon clash: Disney relationship with Time Warner is a strained one." *The Wall Street Journal*, April 14, p. A1; and Reilly, P. M., and R. Turner. (1993). "Disney pulls ads in tiff with *Time*." *The Wall Street Journal*, April 2, p. B1. The growth and consolidation of the entertainment industry since the early 1990s have made Disney and Time Warner (especially after its merger with AOL) large entertainment conglomerates. It will be interesting to see if these two larger firms will be able to find ways to tacitly collude or will continue the competition begun in the early 1990s.

28. The best work in this area has been done by Gimeno, J. (1994). "Multipoint competition, market rivalry and firm performance: A test of the mutual forbearance hypothesis in the United States airline industry, 1984–1988." Unpublished doctoral dissertation, Purdue University. See also Smith, F., and R. Wilson. (1995). "The predictive validity of the Karnani and Wernerfelt model of multipoint competition." *Strategic Management Journal*, 16, pp. 143–160.

29. See Tirole, J. (1988). *The theory of industrial organization*. Cambridge, MA: MIT Press.

30. Carnevale, M. L. (1993). "Ring in the new: Telephone service seems on the brink of huge innovations." *The Wall Street Journal*, February 10, p. A1. SBC acquired the remaining assets of the original AT&T and renamed the newly merged company AT&T.

31. See Russo, M. V. (1992). "Power plays: Regulation, diversification, and backward integration in the electric utility industry." *Strategic Management Journal*, 13, pp. 13–27. Work by Jandik and Makhija (1999) indicates that when a regulated utility diversifies out of a regulated industry, it often earns a more positive return than when an unregulated firm does this. Jandik, T., and A. K. Makhija. (1999). "An empirical examination of the atypical diversification practices of electric utilities: Internal capital markets and regulation." Fisher College of Business, Ohio State University, working paper (September). This work shows that regulators have the effect of making a regulated firm's internal capital market more efficient. Differences between Russo's (1992) findings and Jandik and Makhija's (1999) findings may have to do with when this work was done. Russo's (1992) research may have focused on a time period before regulatory agencies had learned how to improve a firm's internal capital market. However, even though Jandik and Makhija (1999) report positive returns from regulated firms diversifying, these positive returns do not reflect the market power advantages of these firms.

32. Finkelstein, S., and D. C. Hambrick. (1989). "Chief executive compensation: A study of the intersection of markets and political processes." *Strategic Management Journal*, 10, pp. 121–134.

33. See William, J., B. L. Paez, and L. Sanders. (1988). "Conglomerates revisited." *Strategic Management Journal*, 9, pp. 403–414; Geringer, J. M., S. Tallman, and D. M. Olsen. (2000). "Product and international diversification among Japanese multinational firms." *Strategic Management Journal*, 21, pp. 51–80; Nail, L. A., W. L. Megginson, and C. Maquieira. (1998). "How stock-swap mergers affect shareholder (and bondholder) wealth: More evidence of the value of corporate 'focus.'" *Journal of Applied Corporate Finance*, 11(2), pp. 95–106; Carroll, G. R., L. S. Bigelow, M.-D. L. Seidel, and L. B. Tsai. (1966). "The fates of *De Novo* and *De Alio* producers in the American automobile industry 1885–1981." *Strategic Management Journal*, 17 (Special Summer Issue), pp. 117–138; Nguyen, T. H., A. Seror, and T. M. Devinney. (1990). "Diversification strategy and performance in Canadian manufacturing firms." *Strategic Management Journal*, 11, pp. 411–418; and Amit, R., and J. Livnat. (1988). "Diversification strategies, business cycles and economic performance." *Strategic Management Journal*, 9, pp. 99–110, for a discussion of corporate diversification in the economy over time.

34. The Nestlé story is summarized in Templeman, J. (1993). "Nestlé: A giant in a hurry." *BusinessWeek*, March 22, pp. 50–54.

Organizing to Implement Corporate Diversification

1. Describe the multidivisional, or M-form, structure and how it is used to implement a corporate diversification strategy.

2. Describe the roles of the board of directors, institutional investors, the senior executive, corporate staff, division general managers, and shared activity managers in making the M-form structure work.

3. Describe how three management control processes—measuring divisional performance, allocating corporate capital, and transferring intermediate products—are used to help implement a corporate diversification strategy.

4. Describe the role of management compensation in helping to implement a corporate diversification strategy.

MyManagementLab®

⭐ **Improve Your Grade!**

Over 10 million students improved their results using the Pearson MyLabs.

Visit **mymanagementlab.com** for simulations, tutorials, and end-of-chapter problems.

And Then There Is Berkshire Hathaway

Berkshire Hathaway is one of the largest and most profitable publicly traded diversified corporations in the world. With sales in excess of $162 billion, Berkshire Hathaway operates in four large segments: insurance; railroads; utilities and energy; and manufacturing, services, and retail. However, its businesses are run through literally hundreds of wholly owned subsidiaries. Some of these subsidiaries are relatively obscure and sell only to other companies—TTI, a Texas company that distributes components to electronics manufacturing firms. Other subsidiaries are well-known—GEICO, Fruit of the Loom, Russell Brands, Justin Brands, Benjamin Moore, Dairy Queen, RC Wiley, Helzberg Diamonds, and Net Jets to name just a few.

In addition to owning hundreds of businesses outright, Berkshire Hathaway also invests cash from its insurance businesses to take substantial, but not controlling, investments in a variety of other companies, including Mars, American Express, Coca-Cola, Wells Fargo, and IBM.

However, unlike many diversified firms, Berkshire Hathaway does not look to realize economics of scope across its businesses. According to its 2012 10K report: "Berkshire's operating businesses are managed on an unusually decentralized basis. There are essentially no centralized or integrated business functions (such as sales, marketing, purchasing, legal, or human resources) and there is minimal involvement by Berkshire's corporate headquarters in the day to day business activities of the operating businesses."

Thus, Berkshire Hathaway is an unrelated diversified firm. And, yet, it is so effectively managed as an unrelated diversified firm that it is able to generate significant value. For example, Berkshire employs 288,500 people worldwide, but—consistent with its unrelated diversification strategy—has only 24 employees at corporate headquarters.

In describing Berkshire's operating principles, founder and chair, Warren Buffett, has written: "Although our form is corporate, our attitude is partnership. Charlie Munger (Vice Chair of the Board) and I think of our shareholders as owner-partners, and ourselves as managing partners… We do not view the company as the ultimate owner of our business assets but instead view the company as a conduit through which our shareholders own the assets… Our long term economic goal is to maximize Berkshire's average annual rate of gain in intrinsic business value on a per-share basis. We do not measure the economic significance or performance of Berkshire by its size; we measure by per-share progress… Our preference would be to reach our goal by directly

© ZUMA Press, Inc./Alamy

owning a diversified group of businesses…our second preference is to own parts of similar businesses… Accounting consequences do not influence our operating or capital allocation decisions. When acquisition costs are similar, we much prefer to purchase $2 of earnings that is not reportable by us under standard accounting procedures than to buy $1 of earnings that are reportable…Regardless of price, we have no interest in selling any good business Berkshire owns. We are also reluctant to sell sub-par businesses as long as we expect them to generate at least some cash… Gin Rummy managerial behavior (discard your least-promising business at each turn) is not our style."

These operating principles are quite different from many other diversified firms. General Electric, for example, for some time followed a simple operating principle: If a business unit was not number one or number two in a growing business, it would be divested. This is very much the "gin rummy" approach to management described by Warren Buffett. Also, most diversified firms seek to realize as many "integrated business activities" as they can. Certainly, ESPN—the diversified firm discussed at the beginning of Chapter 7—has many shared activities across its numerous networks.

But what works for GE or for ESPN may simply not work for Berkshire Hathaway, and vice versa. One of the many things we can learn from Berkshire Hathaway is how important it is to match a firm's corporate strategy with its organizing principles. One could argue that Berkshire Hathaway does this match very well.

Sources: (2012). *10K report for Berkshire Hathaway*; W. Buffet (2013). "An owner's manual, revised." www.berkshirehathaway.com. Accessed July 26, 2013.

This chapter is about how large diversified firms—like Berkshire Hathaway—are managed and governed efficiently. The chapter explains how these kinds of firms are managed in a way that is consistent with the interests of their owners—equity holders—as well as the interests of their other stakeholders. The three components of organizing to implement any strategy, which were first identified in Chapter 3—organizational structure, management controls, and compensation policy—are also important in implementing corporate diversification strategies.

VRIO Organizational Structure and Implementing Corporate Diversification

The most common organizational structure for implementing a corporate diversification strategy is the **M-form,** or **multidivisional,** structure. A typical M-form structure, as it would appear in a firm's annual report, is presented in Figure 8.1. This same structure is redrawn in Figure 8.2 to emphasize the roles and responsibilities of each of the major components of the M-form organization.[1]

In the multidivisional structure, each business that the firm engages in is managed through a **division.** Different firms have different names for these divisions—strategic business units (SBUs), business groups, companies. Whatever their names, the divisions in an M-form organization are true **profit-and-loss centers:** Profits and losses are calculated at the level of the division in these firms.

Different firms use different criteria for defining the boundaries of profit-and-loss centers. For example, General Electric defines its divisions in terms of the types of products each one manufactures and sells (e.g., aviation, capital, energy management, and health care). Nestlé defines its divisions with reference to the

Figure 8.1   An Example of M-Form Organizational Structure as Depicted in a Firm's Annual Report

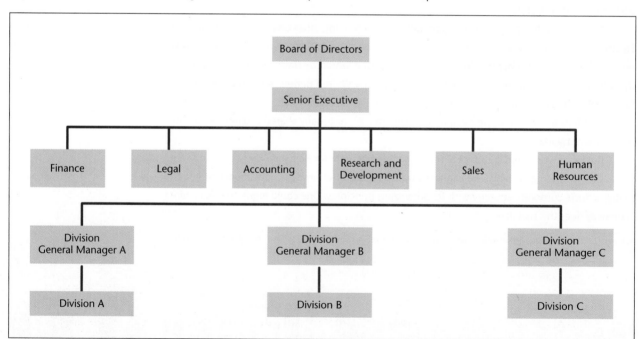

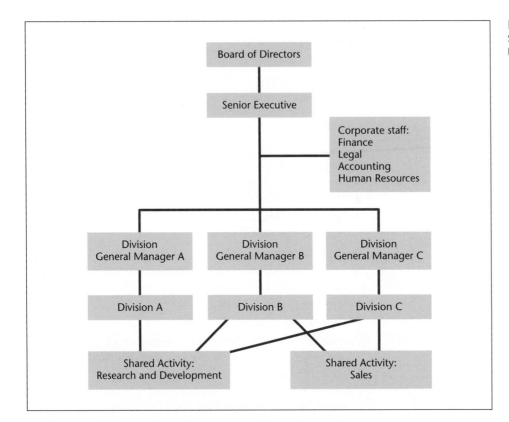

Figure 8.2   An M-Form Structure Redrawn to Emphasize Roles and Responsibilities

geographic scope of each of its businesses (North America, South America, and so forth). General Motors defines its divisions in terms of the brand names of its products (Cadillac, Chevrolet, and so forth). However they are defined, divisions in an M-form organization should be large enough to represent identifiable business entities but small enough so that each one can be managed effectively by a division general manager. Indeed, each division in an M-form organization typically adopts a U-form structure (see the discussion of the U-form structure in Chapters 4, 5, and 6), and the division general manager takes on the role of a U-form senior executive for his or her division.

The M-form structure is designed to create checks and balances for managers that increase the probability that a diversified firm will be managed in ways consistent with the interests of its equity holders. The roles of each of the major elements of the M-form structure in accomplishing this objective are summarized in Table 8.1 and discussed in the following text. Some of the conflicts of interest that might emerge between a firm's equity holders and its managers are described in the Strategy in Depth feature.

The Board of Directors

One of the major components of an M-form organization is a firm's **board of directors.** In principle, all of a firm's senior managers report to the board. The board's primary responsibility is to monitor decision making in the firm, ensuring that it is consistent with the interests of outside equity holders.

A board of directors typically consists of 10 to 15 individuals drawn from a firm's top management group and from individuals outside the firm. A firm's

Component	Activity
Board of directors	Monitor decision making in a firm to ensure that it is consistent with the interests of outside equity holders
Institutional investors	Monitor decision making to ensure that it is consistent with the interests of major institutional equity investors
Senior executives	Formulate corporate strategies consistent with equity holders' interests and assure strategy implementation
	Strategy formulation: ■ Decide the businesses in which the firm will operate ■ Decide how the firm should compete in those businesses ■ Specify the economies of scope around which the diversified firm will operate
	Strategy implementation: ■ Encourage cooperation across divisions to exploit economies of scope ■ Evaluate performance of divisions ■ Allocate capital across divisions
Corporate staff	Provide information to the senior executive about internal and external environments for strategy formulation and implementation
Division general managers	Formulate divisional strategies consistent with corporate strategies and assure strategy implementation
	Strategy formulation: ■ Decide how the division will compete in its business, given the corporate strategy
	Strategy implementation: ■ Coordinate the decisions and actions of functional managers reporting to the division general manager to implement divisional strategy ■ Compete for corporate capital allocations ■ Cooperate with other divisions to exploit corporate economies of scope
Shared activity managers	Support the operations of multiple divisions

senior executive (often identified by the title *president* or *chief executive officer* or *CEO*), its chief financial officer (CFO), and a few other senior managers are usually on the board—although managers on the board are typically outnumbered by outsiders. The firm's senior executive is often, but not always, the **chairman of the board** (a term used here to denote both female and male senior executives). The task of managerial board members—including the board chairman—is to provide other board members information and insights about critical decisions being made in the firm and the effect those decisions are likely to have on a firm's equity holders. The task of outsiders on the board is to evaluate the past, current, and future performance of the firm and of its senior managers to ensure that the actions taken in the firm are consistent with equity holders' interests.[2]

Strategy in Depth

In Chapter 7, it was suggested that sometimes it is in the best interest of equity holders to delegate to managers the day-to-day management of their equity investments in a firm. This will be the case when equity investors cannot realize a valuable economy of scope on their own, while managers *can* realize that economy of scope.

Several authors have suggested that whenever one party in an exchange delegates decision-making authority to a second party, an **agency relationship** has been created between these parties. The party delegating this decision-making authority is called the **principal;** the party to whom this authority is delegated is called the **agent.** In the context of corporate diversification, an agency relationship exists between a firm's outside equity holders (as principals) and its managers (as agents) to the extent that equity holders delegate the day-to-day management of their investment to those managers.

The agency relationship between equity holders and managers can be very effective as long as managers make investment decisions that are consistent with equity holders' interests. Thus, if equity holders are interested in maximizing the rate of return on their investment in a firm and if managers make their investment decisions with this objective in mind, then equity holders will have few concerns about delegating the day-to-day management of their investments to managers. Unfortunately, in numerous situations the interests of a firm's outside equity holders and its managers do not coincide. When parties in an agency relationship differ in their decision-making objectives,

Agency Conflicts Between Managers and Equity Holders

agency problems arise. Two common agency problems have been identified: investment in managerial perquisites and managerial risk aversion.

Managers may decide to take some of a firm's capital and invest it in **managerial perquisites** that do not add economic value to the firm but do directly benefit those managers. Examples of such investments include lavish offices, fleets of corporate jets, and corporate vacation homes. Dennis Kozlowski, former CEO of Tyco International, is accused of "stealing" $600 million in these kinds of managerial perquisites from his firm. The list of goods and services that Kozlowski lavished on himself and those close to him is truly astounding—a multimillion-dollar birthday party for his wife, a $6,000 wastebasket, a $15,000 umbrella stand, a $144,000 loan to a board member, toga-clad waiters at an event, and so on.

As outrageous as some of these managerial perquisites can be, the

second source of agency problems—**managerial risk aversion**—is probably more important in most diversified firms. As discussed in Chapter 7, equity holders can diversify their portfolio of investments at very low cost. Through their diversification efforts, they can eliminate all firm-specific risk in their portfolios. In this setting, equity holders would prefer that managers make more risky rather than less risky investments because the expected return on risky investments is usually greater than the expected return on less risky investments.

Managers, in contrast, have limited ability to diversify their human capital investments in their firm. Some portion of these investments is specific to a particular firm and has limited value in alternative uses. The value of a manager's human capital investment in a firm depends critically on the continued existence of the firm. Thus, managers are *not* indifferent to the riskiness of investment opportunities in a firm. Very risky investments may jeopardize a firm's survival and thus eliminate the value of a manager's human capital investments. These incentives can make managers more risk averse in their decision making than equity holders would like them to be.

One of the purposes of the M-form structure, and indeed of all aspects of organizing to implement corporate diversification, is to reduce these agency problems.

Sources: M. C. Jensen and W. H. Meckling (1976). "Theory of the firm: Managerial behavior, agency costs, and ownership structure." *Journal of Financial Economics*, 3, pp. 305–360; J. Useem (2003). "The biggest show." *Fortune*, December 8, pp. 157+; R. Lambert (1986). "Executive effort and selection of risky projects." *Rand Journal of Economics*, 13(2), pp. 369–378.

Research Made Relevant

A great deal of research has tried to determine when boards of directors are more or less effective in ensuring that firms are managed in ways consistent with the interests of equity holders. Three issues have received particular attention: (1) the roles of insiders (i.e., managers) and outsiders on the board, (2) whether the board chair and the senior executive should be the same or different people, and (3) whether the board should be active or passive.

With respect to insiders and outsiders on the board, in one way this seems like a simple problem. Because the primary role of the board of directors is to monitor managerial decisions to ensure that they are consistent with the interests of equity holders, it follows that the board should consist primarily of outsiders because they face no conflict of interest in evaluating managerial performance. Obviously, managers, as inside members of the board, face significant conflicts of interest in evaluating their own performance.

Research on outsider members of boards of directors tends to support this point of view. Outside directors,

The Effectiveness of Boards of Directors

as compared with insiders, tend to focus more on monitoring a firm's economic performance than on other measures of firm performance. Obviously, a firm's economic performance is most relevant to its equity investors. Outside board members are also more likely than inside members to dismiss CEOs for poor performance. Also, outside board members have a stronger incentive than inside members to maintain their reputations as effective monitors. This incentive by itself can lead to more effective monitoring by outside board members. Moreover, the monitoring effectiveness of outside

board members seems to be enhanced when they personally own a substantial amount of a firm's equity.

However, the fact that outside members face fewer conflicts of interest in evaluating managerial performance compared with management insiders on the board does not mean that there is no appropriate role for inside board members. Managers bring something to the board that cannot be easily duplicated by outsiders— detailed information about the decision-making activities inside the firm. This is precisely the information that outsiders need to effectively monitor the activities of a firm, and it is information available to them only if they work closely with insiders (managers). One way to gain access to this information is to include managers as members of the board of directors. Thus, while most research suggests that a board of directors should be composed primarily of outsiders, there is an important role for insiders/managers to play as members of a firm's board.

There is currently some debate about whether the roles of board chair and CEO should be combined

Boards of directors are typically organized into several subcommittees. An **audit committee** is responsible for ensuring the accuracy of accounting and financial statements. A **finance committee** maintains the relationship between the firm and external capital markets. A **nominating committee** nominates new board members. A **personnel and compensation committee** evaluates and compensates the performance of a firm's senior executive and other senior managers. Often, membership on these standing committees is reserved for external board members. Other standing committees reflect specific issues for a particular firm and are typically open to external and internal board members.[3]

Over the years, a great deal of research has been conducted about the effectiveness of boards of directors in ensuring that a firm's managers make decisions in ways consistent with the interests of its equity holders. Some of this work is summarized in the Research Made Relevant feature.

or separated and, if separated, what kinds of people should occupy these positions. Some have argued that the roles of CEO and board chair should definitely be separated and that the role of the chair should be filled by an outside (nonmanagerial) member of the board of directors. These arguments are based on the assumption that only an outside member of the board can ensure the independent monitoring of managerial decision making. Others have argued that effective monitoring often requires more information than would be available to outsiders, and thus the roles of board chair and CEO should be combined and filled by a firm's senior manager.

Empirical research on this question suggests that whether these roles of CEO and chairman should be combined depends on the complexity of the information analysis and monitoring task facing the CEO and board chair. Brian Boyd has found that combining the roles of CEO and chair is positively correlated with firm performance when firms operate in slow-growth and simple competitive environments—environments that do not overtax the cognitive capability

of a single individual. This finding suggests that combining these roles does not necessarily increase conflicts between a firm and its equity holders. This research also found that separating the roles of CEO and board chair is positively correlated with firm performance when firms operate in high-growth and very complex environments. In such environments, a single individual cannot fulfill all the responsibilities of both CEO and board chair, and thus the two roles need to be held by separate individuals.

Finally, with respect to active versus passive boards, historically the boards of major firms have been relatively passive and would take dramatic action, such as firing the senior executive, only if a firm's performance was significantly below expectations for long periods of time. However, more recently, boards have become more active proponents of equity holders' interests. This recent surge in board activity reflects a new economic reality: If a board does not become more active in monitoring firm performance, then other monitoring mechanisms will.

Consequently, the board of directors has become progressively more influential in representing the interests of a firm's equity holders.

However, board activity can go too far. To the extent that the board begins to operate a business on a day-to-day basis, it goes beyond its capabilities. Boards rarely have sufficient detailed information to manage a firm directly. When it is necessary to change a firm's senior executive, boards will usually not take on the responsibilities of that executive, but rather will rapidly identify a single individual—either an insider or outsider—to take over this position.

Sources: E. Zajac and J. Westphal (1994). "The costs and benefits of managerial incentives and monitoring in large U.S. corporations: When is more not better?" *Strategic Management Journal*, 15, pp. 121–142; P. Rechner and D. Dalton (1991). "CEO duality and organizational performance: A longitudinal analysis." *Strategic Management Journal*, 12, pp. 155–160; S. Finkelstein and R. D'Aveni (1994). "CEO duality as a double-edged sword: How boards of directors balance entrenchment avoidance and unity of command." *Academy of Management Journal*, 37, pp. 1079–1108; B. K. Boyd (1995). "CEO duality and firm performance: A contingency model." *Strategic Management Journal*, 16, pp. 301–312; I. F. Kesner and R. B. Johnson (1990). "An investigation of the relationship between board composition and stockholder suits." *Strategic Management Journal*, 11, pp. 327–336.

Institutional Owners

Historically, the typical large diversified firm has had its equity owned in small blocks by millions of individual investors. The exception to this general rule was family-owned or -dominated firms, a phenomenon that is relatively more common outside the United States. When a firm's ownership is spread among millions of small investors, it is difficult for any one of these investors to have a large enough ownership position to influence management decisions directly. The only course of action open to such investors if they disagree with management decisions is to sell their stock.

However, the growth of institutional owners has changed the ownership structure of many large diversified firms over the past several years. **Institutional owners** are usually pension funds, mutual funds, insurance companies, or other groups of individual investors that have joined together to manage their investments. In 1970, institutions owned 32 percent of the equity traded in the United States. By 1990, institutions owned 48 percent of this equity. In 2005, they owned 59 percent of all equity traded in the United States and 69 percent of the equity of the 1,000 largest firms in the United States.[4]

Institutional investors can use their investment clout to insist that a firm's management behaves in ways consistent with the interests of equity holders. Observers who assume that institutional investors are interested more in maximizing the short-term value of their portfolios than in the long-term performance of firms in those portfolios fear that such power will force firms to make only short-term investments. Research in the United States and Japan, however, suggests that institutional investors are not unduly myopic. Rather, as suggested earlier, these investors use approximately the same logic equity investors use when evaluating the performance of a firm. For example, one group of researchers examined the impact of institutional ownership on research and development investments in research and development (R&D)–intensive industries. R&D investments tend to be longer term in orientation. If institutional investors are myopic, they should influence firms to invest in relatively less R&D in favor of investments that generate shorter-term profits. This research showed that high levels of institutional ownership did not adversely affect the level of R&D in a firm. These findings are consistent with the notion that institutional investors are not inappropriately concerned with the short term in their monitoring activities.[5]

More generally, other researchers have shown that high levels of institutional ownership lead firms to sell strategically unrelated businesses. This effect of institutional investors is enhanced if, in addition, outside directors on a firm's board have substantial equity investments in the firm. Given the discussion of the value of unrelated diversification in Chapter 7, it seems clear that these divestment actions are typically consistent with maximizing the present value of a firm.[6]

The Senior Executive

As suggested in Table 8.1, the senior executive (the president or CEO) in an M-form organization has two responsibilities: strategy formulation and strategy implementation. *Strategy formulation* entails deciding which set of businesses a diversified firm will operate in; *strategy implementation* focuses on encouraging behavior in a firm that is consistent with this strategy. Each of these responsibilities of the senior executive is discussed in turn.

Strategy Formulation
At the broadest level, deciding which businesses a diversified firm should operate in is equivalent to discovering and developing valuable economies of scope among a firm's current and potential businesses. If these economies of scope are also rare and costly to imitate, they can be a source of sustained competitive advantage for a diversified firm.

The senior executive is uniquely positioned to discover, develop, and nurture valuable economies of scope in a diversified firm. Every other manager in this kind of firm either has a divisional point of view (e.g., division general managers and shared activity managers) or is a functional specialist (e.g., corporate staff and functional managers within divisions). Only the senior executive has a truly corporate perspective. However, the senior executive in an M-form organization should involve numerous other divisional and functional managers in strategy formulation to ensure complete and accurate information as input to the process and a broad understanding of and commitment to that strategy once it has been formulated.

Strategy Implementation

As is the case for senior executives in a U-form structure, strategy implementation in an M-form structure almost always involves resolving conflicts among groups of managers. However, instead of simply resolving conflicts between functional managers (as is the case in a U-form), senior executives in M-form organizations must resolve conflicts within and between each of the major managerial components of the M-form structure: corporate staff, division general managers, and shared activity managers. Various corporate staff managers may disagree about the economic relevance of their staff functions, corporate staff may come into conflict with division general managers over various corporate programs and activities, division general managers may disagree with how capital is allocated across divisions, division general managers may come into conflict with shared activity managers about how shared activities should be managed, shared activity managers may disagree with corporate staff about their mutual roles and responsibilities, and so forth.

Obviously, the numerous and often conflicting relationships among groups of managers in an M-form organization can place significant strategy implementation burdens on the senior executive.[7] While resolving these numerous conflicts, however, the senior executive needs to keep in mind the reasons why the firm began pursuing a diversification strategy in the first place: to exploit real economies of scope that outside investors cannot realize on their own. Any strategy implementation decisions that jeopardize the realization of these real economies of scope are inconsistent with the underlying strategic objectives of a diversified firm. These issues are analyzed in detail later in this chapter, in the discussion of management control systems in the M-form organization.

The Office of the President: Board Chair, CEO, and COO

It is often the case that the roles and responsibilities of the senior executive in an M-form organization are greater than can be reasonably managed by a single individual. This is especially likely if a firm is broadly diversified across numerous complex products and markets. In this situation, it is not uncommon for the tasks of the senior executive to be divided among two or three people: the **board chair,** the **chief executive officer,** and the **chief operating officer (COO).** The primary responsibilities of each of these roles in an M-form organization are listed in Table 8.2. Together, these roles are known as the **office of the president.** In general, as the tasks facing the office of the president become more demanding and complex, the more likely it is that the roles and responsibilities of this office will be divided among two or three people.

Corporate Staff

The primary responsibility of **corporate staff** is to provide information about the firm's external and internal environments to the firm's senior executive. This information is vital for both the strategy formulation and the strategy implementation responsibilities of the senior executive. Corporate staff functions that provide

Board chair	Supervision of the board of directors in its monitoring role
Chief executive officer	Strategy formulation
Chief operating officer	Strategy implementation

TABLE 8.2 Responsibilities of Three Different Roles in the Office of the President

information about a firm's external environment include finance, investor relations, legal affairs, regulatory affairs, and corporate advertising. Corporate staff functions that provide information about a firm's internal environment include accounting and corporate human resources. These corporate staff functions report directly to a firm's senior executive and are a conduit of information to that executive.

Corporate and Divisional Staff

Many organizations re-create some corporate staff functions within each division of the organization. This is particularly true for internally oriented corporate staff functions such as accounting and human resources. At the division level, divisional staff managers usually have a direct "solid-line" reporting relationship to their respective corporate staff functional managers and a less formal "dotted-line" reporting relationship to their division general manager. The reporting relationship between the divisional staff manager and the corporate staff manager is the link that enables the corporate staff manager to collect the information that the senior executive requires for strategy formulation and implementation. The senior executive can also use this corporate staff–division staff relationship to communicate corporate policies and procedures to the divisions, although these policies can also be communicated directly by the senior executive to division general managers.

Although divisional staff managers usually have a less formal relationship with their division general managers, in practice division general managers can have an important influence on the activities of divisional staff. After all, divisional staff managers may formally report to corporate staff managers, but they spend most of their time interacting with their division general managers and with the other functional managers who report to their division general managers. These divided loyalties can sometimes affect the timeliness and accuracy of the information transmitted from divisional staff managers to corporate staff managers and thus affect the timeliness and accuracy of the information the senior executive uses for strategy formulation and implementation.

Nowhere are these divided loyalties potentially more problematic than in accounting staff functions. Obviously, it is vitally important for the senior executive in an M-form organization to receive timely and accurate information about divisional performance. If the timeliness and accuracy of that information are inappropriately affected by division general managers, the effectiveness of senior management can be adversely affected. Moreover, in some situations division general managers can have very strong incentives to affect the timeliness and accuracy of divisional performance information, especially if a division general manager's compensation depends on this information or if the capital allocated to a division depends on this information.

Efficient monitoring by the senior executive requires that corporate staff, and especially the accounting corporate staff function, remains organizationally independent of division general managers—thus, the importance of the solid-line relationship between divisional staff managers and corporate staff managers. Nevertheless, the ability of corporate staff to obtain accurate performance information from divisions also depends on close cooperative working relationships between corporate staff, divisional staff, and division general managers—hence, the importance of the dotted-line relationship between divisional staff managers and division general managers. How one maintains the balance between the distance and objectivity needed to evaluate a division's performance on the one hand, and, on the other hand, the cooperation and teamwork needed to gain access to the information required to evaluate a division's performance distinguishes excellent from mediocre corporate staff managers.

Overinvolvement in Managing Division Operations

Over and above the failure to maintain a balance between objectivity and cooperation in evaluating divisional performance, the one sure way that corporate staff can fail in a multidivisional firm is to become too involved in the day-to-day operations of divisions. In an M-form structure, the management of such day-to-day operations is delegated to division general managers and to functional managers who report to division general managers. Corporate staff managers collect and transmit information; they do not manage divisional operations.

One way to ensure that corporate staff does not become too involved in managing the day-to-day operations of divisions is to keep corporate staff small. This is certainly true for some of the best-managed diversified firms in the world including (and described in the opening case) Berkshire Hathaway. For example, just 1.5 percent of Johnson & Johnson's more than 80,000 employees work at the firm's headquarters, and only some of those individuals are members of the corporate staff. Hanson Industries has in its U.S. headquarters 120 people who help manage a diversified firm with $8 billion in revenues. Clayton, Dubilier, and Rice, a management buyout firm, has only 11 headquarters staff members overseeing eight businesses with collective sales of more than $6 billion.[8]

Division General Manager

Division general managers in an M-form organization have primary responsibility for managing a firm's businesses from day to day. Division general managers have full profit-and-loss responsibility and typically have multiple functional managers reporting to them. As general managers, they have both strategy formulation and strategy implementation responsibilities. On the strategy formulation side, division general managers choose strategies for their divisions, within the broader strategic context established by the senior executive of the firm. Many of the analytical tools described in Parts 1 and 2 of this book can be used by division general managers to make these strategy formulation decisions.

The strategy implementation responsibilities of division general managers in an M-form organization parallel the strategy implementation responsibilities of senior executives in U-form organizations. In particular, division general managers must be able to coordinate the activities of often-conflicting functional managers in order to implement a division's strategies.

In addition to their responsibilities as a U-form senior executive, division general managers in an M-form organization have two additional responsibilities: to compete for corporate capital and to cooperate with other divisions to exploit corporate economies of scope. Division general managers compete for corporate capital by promising high rates of return on capital invested by the corporation in their business. In most firms, divisions that have demonstrated the ability to generate high rates of return on earlier capital investments gain access to more capital or to lower-cost capital, compared with divisions that have not demonstrated a history of such performance.

Division general managers cooperate to exploit economies of scope by working with shared activity managers, corporate staff managers, and the senior executive in the firm to isolate, understand, and use the economies of scope around which the diversified firm was originally organized. Division general managers can even become involved in discovering new economies of scope that were not anticipated when the firm's diversification strategy was originally implemented but nevertheless may be both valuable and costly for outside investors to create on their own.

Of course, a careful reader will recognize a fundamental conflict between the last two responsibilities of division general managers in an M-form organization. These managers are required to compete for corporate capital and to cooperate to exploit economies of scope at the same time. Competition is important because it leads division general managers to focus on generating high levels of economic performance from their divisions. If each division is generating high levels of economic performance, then the diversified firm as a whole is likely to do well also. However, cooperation is important to exploit economies of scope that are the economic justification for implementing a diversification strategy in the first place. If divisions do not cooperate in exploiting these economies, there are few, if any, justifications for implementing a corporate diversification strategy, and the diversified firm should be split into multiple independent entities. The need to simultaneously compete and cooperate puts significant managerial burdens on division general managers. It is likely that this ability is both rare and costly to imitate across most diversified firms.[9]

Shared Activity Managers

One of the potential economies of scope identified in Chapter 7 was shared activities. Divisions in an M-form organization exploit this economy of scope when one or more of the stages in their value chains are managed in common. Typical examples of activities shared across two or more divisions in a multidivisional firm include common sales forces, common distribution systems, common manufacturing facilities, and common research and development efforts (also see Table 7.2). The primary responsibility of the individuals who manage shared activities is to support the operations of the divisions that share the activity.

The way in which M-form structure is often depicted in company annual reports (as in Figure 8.1) tends to obscure the operational role of shared activities. In this version of the M-form organizational chart, no distinction is made between corporate staff functions and shared activity functions. Moreover, it appears that managers of shared activities report directly to a firm's senior executive, just like corporate staff. These ambiguities are resolved by redrawing the M-form organizational chart to emphasize the roles and responsibilities of different units within the M-form (as in Figure 8.2). In this more accurate representation of how an M-form actually functions, corporate staff groups are separated from shared activity managers, and each is shown reporting to its primary internal "customer." That "internal customer" is the senior executive for corporate staff groups and two or more division general managers for shared activity managers.

Shared Activities as Cost Centers

Shared activities are often managed as cost centers in an M-form structure. That is, rather than having profit-and-loss responsibility, **cost centers** are assigned a budget and manage their operations to that budget. When this is the case, shared activity managers do not attempt to create profits when they provide services to the divisions they support. Rather, these services are priced to internal customers in such a way that the shared activity just covers its cost of operating.

Because cost center shared activities do not have to generate profits from their operations, the cost of the services they provide to divisions can be less than the cost of similar services provided either by a division itself or by outside suppliers. If a shared activity is managed as a cost center, and the cost of services from this shared activity is *greater than* the cost of similar services provided by alternative sources, then either this shared activity is not being well managed or it was not a real economy of scope in the first place. However, when the cost of services from a shared activity is *less than* the cost of comparable services provided by a division itself or by an outside supplier, then division general managers have a strong incentive to use the services of shared activities, thereby exploiting an economy of scope that may have been one of the original reasons why a firm implemented a corporate diversification strategy.

Shared Activities as Profit Centers

Some diversified firms are beginning to manage shared activities as profit centers, rather than as cost centers. Moreover, rather than requiring divisions to use the services of shared activities, divisions retain the right to purchase services from internal shared activities or from outside suppliers or to provide services for themselves. In this setting, managers of shared activities are required to compete for their internal customers on the basis of the price and quality of the services they provide.[10]

One firm that has taken this profit-center approach to managing shared activities is ABB, Inc., a Swiss engineering firm. ABB eliminated almost all its corporate staff and reorganized its remaining staff functions into shared activities. Shared activities in ABB compete to provide services to ABB divisions. Not only do some traditional shared activities—such as research and development and sales—compete for internal customers, but many traditional corporate staff functions—such as human resources, marketing, and finance—do as well. ABB's approach to managing shared activities has resulted in a relatively small corporate staff and in increasingly specialized and customized shared activities.[11]

Of course, the greatest risk associated with treating shared activities as profit centers and letting them compete for divisional customers is that divisions may choose to obtain no services or support from shared activities. Although this course of action may be in the self-interest of each division, it may not be in the best interest of the corporation as a whole if, in fact, shared activities are an important economy of scope around which the diversified firm is organized.

In the end, the task facing the managers of shared activities is the same: to provide such highly customized and high-quality services to divisional customers at a reasonable cost that those internal customers will not want to seek alternative suppliers outside the firm or provide those services themselves. In an M-form organization, the best way to ensure that shared activity economies of scope are realized is for shared activity managers to satisfy their internal customers.

Management Controls and Implementing Corporate Diversification

The M-form structure presented in Figures 8.1 and 8.2 is complex and multifaceted. However, no organizational structure by itself is able to fully implement a corporate diversification strategy. The M-form structure must be supplemented with a variety of management controls. Three of the most important management controls in an M-form structure—systems for evaluating divisional performance, for allocating capital across divisions, and for transferring intermediate products between divisions—are discussed in this section.[12]

Evaluating Divisional Performance

Because divisions in an M-form structure are profit-and-loss centers, evaluating divisional performance should, in principle, be straightforward: Divisions that are very profitable should be evaluated more positively than divisions that are less profitable. In practice, this seemingly simple task is surprisingly complex. Two problems typically arise: (1) How should division profitability be measured? and (2) How should economy-of-scope linkages between divisions be factored into divisional performance measures?

Measuring Divisional Performance

Divisional performance can be measured in at least two ways. The first focuses on a division's accounting performance; the second on a division's economic performance.

Accounting Measures of Divisional Performance.   Both accounting and economic measures of performance can be used in measuring the performance of divisions within a diversified firm. Common accounting measures of divisional performance include the return on the assets controlled by a division, the return on a division's sales, and a division's sales growth. These accounting measures of divisional performance are then compared with some standard to see if a division's performance exceeds or falls short of that standard. Diversified firms use three different standards of comparison when evaluating the performance of a division: (1) a hurdle rate that is common across all the different business units in a firm, (2) a division's budgeted level of performance (which may vary by division), and (3) the average level of profitability of firms in a division's industry.

Each of these standards of comparison has its strengths and weaknesses. For example, if a corporation has a single hurdle rate of profitability that all divisions must meet or exceed, there is little ambiguity about the performance objectives of divisions. However, a single standard ignores important differences in performance that might exist across divisions.

Comparing a division's actual performance to its budgeted performance allows the performance expectations of different divisions to vary, but the budgeting process is time-consuming and fraught with political intrigue. One study showed that corporate managers routinely discount the sales projections and capital requests of division managers on the assumption that division managers are trying to "game" the budgeting system.[13] Moreover, division budgets are usually based on a single set of assumptions about how the economy is going to evolve, how competition in a division's industry is going to evolve, and what actions that division is going to take in its industry. When these assumptions no longer hold, budgets are redone—a costly and time-consuming process that has little to do with generating value in a firm.

Finally, although comparing a division's performance with the average level of profitability of firms in a division's industry also allows performance expectations to vary across divisions within a diversified firm, this approach lets other firms determine what is and is not excellent performance for a division within a diversified firm. This approach can also be manipulated: By choosing just the "right" firms with which to compare a division's performance, almost any division can be made to look like it's performing better than its industry average.[14]

No matter what standard of comparison is used to evaluate a division's accounting performance, most accounting measures of divisional performance have a common limitation. All these measures have a short-term bias. This short-term bias reflects the fact that all these measures treat investments in resources and capabilities that have the potential for generating value in the long run as costs during a particular year. In order to reduce costs in a given year, division managers may sometimes forgo investing in these resources and capabilities, even if they could be a source of sustained competitive advantage for a division in the long run.

Economic Measures of Divisional Performance.   Given the limitations of accounting measures of divisional performance, several firms have begun adopting economic methods of evaluating this performance. Economic methods build on accounting methods but adjust those methods to incorporate short-term investments that may generate long-term benefits. Economic methods also compare a division's performance with a firm's cost of capital (see Chapter 1). This avoids some of the gaming that can characterize the use of other standards of comparison in applying accounting measures of divisional performance.

Perhaps the most popular of these economically oriented measures of division performance is known as **economic value added (EVA).**[15] EVA is calculated by subtracting the cost of capital employed in a division from that division's earnings in the following manner:

$$EVA = \text{adjusted accounting earnings}$$
$$(\text{weighted average cost of capital} \times \text{total capital employed by a division})$$

Several of the terms in the EVA formula require some discussion. For example, the calculation of economic value added begins with a division's "adjusted" accounting earnings. These are a division's traditional accounting earnings, adjusted so that they approximate a division's economic earnings. Several adjustments to a division's accounting statements have been described in the literature. For example, traditional accounting practices require R&D spending to be deducted each year from a division's earnings. This can lead division general managers to under-invest in longer-term R&D efforts. In the EVA measure of divisional performance, R&D spending is added back into a division's performance, and R&D is then treated as an asset and depreciated over some period of time.

One consulting firm (Stern Stewart) that specializes in implementing EVA-based divisional evaluation systems in multidivisional firms makes up to 40 "adjustments" to a division's standard accounting earnings so that they more closely approximate economic earnings. Many of these adjustments are proprietary to this consulting firm. However, the most important adjustments—such as how R&D should be treated—are broadly known.

The terms in parentheses in the EVA equation reflect the cost of investing in a division. Rather than using some alternative standard of comparison, EVA applies financial theory and multiplies the amount of money invested in a division by a firm's weighted average cost of capital. A firm's weighted average cost of capital is the amount of money a firm could earn if it invested in any of its other divisions. In this sense, a firm's weighted average cost of capital can be thought of as the opportunity cost of investing in a particular division, as opposed to investing in any other division in the firm.

By adjusting a division's earnings and accounting for the cost of investing in a division, EVA is a much more accurate estimate of a division's economic performance than are traditional accounting measures of performance. The number of diversified firms evaluating their divisions with EVA-based measures of divisional performance is impressive and growing. These firms include AT&T, Coca-Cola, Quaker Oats, CSX, Briggs and Stratton, and Allied Signal. At Allied Signal, divisions that do not earn their cost of capital are awarded the infamous "leaky bucket" award. If this performance is not improved, division general managers are replaced. The use of EVA has been touted as the key to creating economic wealth in a diversified corporation.[16]

Economies of Scope and the Ambiguity of Divisional Performance

Whether a firm uses accounting measures to evaluate the performance of a division or uses economic measures of performance such as EVA, divisional performance in a well-managed diversified firm can never be evaluated unambiguously. Consider a simple example.

Suppose that in a particular multidivisional firm there are only two divisions (Division A and Division B) and one shared activity (R&D). Also, suppose that the two divisions are managed as profit-and-loss centers and that the R&D shared activity is managed as a cost center. To support this R&D effort, each division pays $10 million per year and has been doing so for 10 years. Finally, suppose that after 10 years of effort (and investment) the R&D group develops a valuable new technology that perfectly addresses Division A's business needs.

Obviously, no matter how divisional performance is measured it is likely to be the case that Division A's performance will rise relative to Division B's performance. In this situation, what percentage of Division A's improved performance should be allocated to Division A, what percentage should be allocated to the R&D group, and what percentage should be allocated to Division B?

The managers in each part of this diversified firm can make compelling arguments in their favor. Division general manager A can reasonably argue that without Division A's efforts to exploit the new technology, the full value of the technology would never have been realized. The R&D manager can reasonably argue that, without the R&D effort, there would not have been a technology to exploit in the first place. Finally, division general manager B can reasonably argue that, without the dedicated long-term investment of Division B in R&D, there would have been no new technology and no performance increase for Division A.

That all three of these arguments can be made suggests that, to the extent that a firm exploits real economies of scope in implementing a diversification strategy, it will not be possible to unambiguously evaluate the performance of individual divisions in that firm. The fact that there are economies of scope in a diversified firm means that all of the businesses a firm operates in are more valuable bundled together than they would be if kept separate from one another. Efforts to evaluate the performance of these businesses as if they were separate from one another are futile.

One solution to this problem is to force businesses in a diversified firm to operate independently of each other. If each business operates independently, then it will be possible to unambiguously evaluate its performance. Of course, to the extent that this independence is enforced, the diversified firm is unlikely to be able to realize the very economies of scope that were the justification for the diversification strategy in the first place.

Divisional performance ambiguity is bad enough when shared activities are the primary economy of scope that a diversified firm is trying to exploit. This ambiguity increases dramatically when the economy of scope is based on intangible core competencies. In this situation, it is shared learning and experience that justify a firm's diversification efforts. The intangible nature of these economies of scope multiplies the difficulty of the divisional evaluation task.

Even firms that apply rigorous EVA measures of divisional performance are unable to fully resolve these performance ambiguity difficulties. For example, the Coca-Cola division of the Coca-Cola Company has made enormous investments in the Coke brand name over the years, and the Diet Coke division has exploited some of that brand name capital in its own marketing efforts. Of course, it is not clear that all of Diet Coke's success can be attributed to the Coke brand name. After all, Diet Coke has developed its own creative advertising, its own loyal group of customers, and so forth. How much of Diet Coke's success—as measured through that division's economic value added—should be allocated to the Coke brand name (an investment made long before Diet Coke was even conceived) and how much should be allocated to the Diet Coke division's efforts? EVA measures of divisional performance do not resolve ambiguities created when economies of scope exist across divisions.[17]

In the end, the quantitative evaluation of divisional performance—with either accounting or economic measures—must be supplemented by the experience and judgment of senior executives in a diversified firm. Only by evaluating a division's performance numbers in the context of a broader, more subjective evaluation of the division's performance can a true picture of divisional performance be developed.

Allocating Corporate Capital

Another potentially valuable economy of scope outlined in Chapter 7 (besides shared activities and core competencies) is internal capital allocation. In that discussion, it was suggested that for internal capital allocation to be a justification for diversification the information made available to senior executives allocating capital in a diversified firm must be superior, in both amount and quality, to the information available to external sources of capital in the external capital market. Both the quality and the quantity of the information available in an internal capital market depend on the organization of the diversified firm.

One of the primary limitations of internal capital markets is that division general managers have a strong incentive to overstate their division's prospects and understate its problems in order to gain access to more capital at lower costs. Having an independent corporate accounting function in a diversified firm can help address this problem. However, given the ambiguities inherent in evaluating divisional performance in a well-managed diversified firm, independent corporate accountants do not resolve all these informational problems.

In the face of these challenges, some firms use a process called **zero-based budgeting** to help allocate capital. In zero-based budgeting, corporate executives create a list of all capital allocation requests from divisions in a firm, rank them from "most important" to "least important," and then fund all the projects a firm can afford, given the amount of capital it has available. In principle, no project will receive funding for the future simply because it received funding in the past. Rather, each project has to stand on its own merits each year by being included among the important projects the firm can afford to fund.

Although zero-based budgeting has some attractive features, it has some important limitations as well. For example, evaluating and ranking all projects in a diversified firm from "most important" to "least important" is a very difficult task. It requires corporate executives to have a very complete understanding of the strategic role of each of the projects being proposed by a division, as well as an understanding of how these projects will affect the short-term performance of divisions.

In the end, no matter what process firms use to allocate capital, allocating capital inside a firm in a way that is more efficient than could be done by external capital markets requires the use of information that is not available to those external markets. Typically, that information will be intangible, tacit, and complex. Corporate managers looking to realize this economy of scope must find a way to use this kind of information effectively.[18] The difficulty of managing this process effectively may be one of the reasons why internal capital allocation often fails to qualify as a valuable economy of scope in diversified firms.[19]

Transferring Intermediate Products

The existence of economies of scope across multiple divisions in a diversified firm often means that products or services produced in one division are used as inputs for products or services produced by a second division. Such products or services are called **intermediate products or services.** Intermediate products or services can be transferred between any of the units in an M-form organization. This transfer is perhaps most important and problematic when it occurs between profit center divisions.

The transfer of intermediate products or services among divisions is usually managed through a **transfer-pricing system:** One division "sells" its product or service to a second division for a transfer price. Unlike a market price, which is typically determined by market forces of supply and demand, transfer prices are set by a firm's corporate management to accomplish corporate objectives.

Setting Optimal Transfer Prices

From an economic point of view, the rule for establishing the optimal transfer price in a diversified firm is quite simple: The transfer price should be the value of the opportunities forgone when one division's product or service is transferred to another division. Consider the following example. Division A's marginal cost of production is $5 per unit, but Division A can sell all of its output to outside customers for $6 per unit. If Division A can sell all of its output to outside customers for $6 per unit, the value of the opportunity forgone of transferring a unit of production from Division A to Division B is $6—the amount of money that Division A forgoes by transferring its production to Division B instead of selling it to the market.

However, if Division A is selling all the units it can to external customers for $6 per unit but still has some excess manufacturing capacity, the value of the opportunity forgone in transferring the product from Division A to Division B is only $5 per unit—Division A's marginal cost of production. Because the external market cannot absorb any more of Division A's product at $6 per unit, the value of the opportunity forgone when Division A transfers units of production to Division B is not $6 per unit (Division A can't get that price), but only $5 per unit.[20]

When transfer prices are set equal to opportunity costs, selling divisions will produce output up to the point that the marginal cost of the last unit produced equals the transfer price. Moreover, buying divisions will buy units from other divisions in the firm as long as the net revenues from doing so just cover the transfer price. These transfer prices will lead profit-maximizing divisions to optimize the diversified firm's profits.

Difficulties in Setting Optimal Transfer Prices

Setting transfer prices equal to opportunity costs sounds simple enough, but it is very difficult to do in real diversified firms. Establishing optimal transfer prices requires information about the value of the opportunities forgone by the "selling" division. This, in turn, requires information about this division's marginal costs, its manufacturing capacity, external demand for its products, and so forth. Much of this information is difficult to obtain. Moreover, it is rarely stable. As market conditions change, demand for a division's products can change, marginal costs can change, and the value of opportunities forgone can change. Also, to the extent that a selling division customizes the products or services it transfers to other divisions in a diversified firm, the value of the opportunities forgone by this selling division become even more difficult to calculate.

Even if this information could be obtained and updated rapidly, division general managers in selling divisions have strong incentives to manipulate the information in ways that increase the perceived value of the opportunities forgone by their division. These division general managers can thus increase the transfer price for the products or services they sell to internal customers and thereby appropriate for their division profits that should have been allocated to buying divisions.

Setting Transfer Prices in Practice

Because it is rarely possible for firms to establish an optimal transfer-pricing scheme, most diversified firms must adopt some form of transfer pricing that attempts to approximate optimal prices. Several of these transfer-pricing schemes are described in Table 8.3. However, no matter what particular scheme a firm uses, the transfer prices it generates will, at times, create inefficiencies and conflicts in a diversified firm. Some of these inefficiencies and conflicts are described in Table 8.4.[21]

The inefficiencies and conflicts created by transfer-pricing schemes that only approximate optimal transfer prices mean that few diversified firms are ever fully satisfied with how they set transfer prices. Indeed, one study found that as the level of resource sharing in a diversified firm increases (thereby increasing the importance of transfer-pricing mechanisms) the level of job satisfaction for division general managers decreases.[22]

Exchange autonomy	■ Buying and selling division general managers are free to negotiate transfer price without corporate involvement.	**TABLE 8.3** Alternative Transfer-Pricing Schemes
	■ Transfer price is set equal to the selling division's price to external customers.	
Mandated full cost	■ Transfer price is set equal to the selling division's actual cost of production.	
	■ Transfer price is set equal to the selling division's standard cost (i.e., the cost of production if the selling division were operating at maximum efficiency).	
Mandated market based	■ Transfer price is set equal to the market price in the selling division's market.	
Dual pricing	■ Transfer price for the buying division is set equal to the selling division's actual or standard costs.	
	■ Transfer price for the selling division is set equal to the price to external customers or to the market price in the selling division's market.	

Source: R. Eccles (1985). *The transfer pricing problem: A theory for practice.* Lexington Books: Lexington, MA. Used with permission of Rowman and Littlefield Publishing Group.

TABLE 8.4 Weaknesses of Alternative Transfer-Pricing Schemes

1. Buying and selling divisions negotiate transfer price.
   - What about the negotiating and haggling costs?
   - The corporation risks not exploiting economies of scope if the right transfer price cannot be negotiated.
2. Transfer price is set equal to the selling division's price to external customers.
   - Which customers? Different selling division customers may get different prices.
   - Shouldn't the volume created by the buying division for a selling division be reflected in a lower transfer price?
   - The selling division doesn't have marketing expenses when selling to another division. Shouldn't that be reflected in a lower transfer price?
3. Transfer price is set equal to the selling division's actual costs.
   - What are those actual costs and who gets to determine them?
   - *All* the selling division's costs or only the costs relevant to the products being purchased by the buying division?
4. Transfer price is set equal to the selling division's standard costs.
   - Standard costs are the costs the selling division would incur if it were running at maximum efficiency. This hypothetical capacity subsidizes the buying division.
5. Transfer price is set equal to the market price.
   - If the product in question is highly differentiated, there is no simple "market price."
   - Shouldn't the volume created by the buying division for a selling division be reflected in a lower transfer price?
   - The selling division doesn't have marketing expenses when selling to a buying division. Shouldn't that be reflected in a lower transfer price?
6. Transfer price is set equal to actual costs for the selling division and to market price for the buying division.

   - This combination of schemes simply combines other problems of setting transfer prices.

It is not unusual for a diversified firm to change its transfer-pricing mechanisms every few years in an attempt to find the "right" transfer-pricing mechanism. Economic theory tells us what the "right" transfer-pricing mechanism is: Transfer prices should equal opportunity cost. However, this "correct" transfer-pricing mechanism cannot be implemented in most firms. Firms that continually change their transfer-pricing mechanisms generally find that all these systems have some weaknesses. In deciding which system to use, a firm should be less concerned about finding the right transfer-pricing mechanism and more concerned about choosing a transfer-pricing policy that creates the fewest management problems—or at least the kinds of problems that the firm can manage effectively. Indeed, some scholars have suggested that the search for optimal transfer pricing should be abandoned in favor of treating transfer pricing as a conflict-resolution process. Viewed in this way, transfer pricing highlights differences between divisions and thus makes it possible to begin to resolve those differences in a mutually beneficial way.[23]

Overall, the three management control processes described here—measuring divisional performance, allocating corporate capital, and transferring intermediate products—suggest that the implementation of a corporate diversification strategy requires a great deal of management skill and experience. They also suggest that sometimes diversified firms may find themselves operating businesses that no

Strategy in the Emerging Enterprise

A **corporate spin-off** exists when a large, typically diversified firm divests itself of a business in which it has historically been operating and the divested business operates as an independent entity. Thus, corporate spin-offs are different from asset divestitures, where a firm sells some of its assets, including perhaps a particular business, to another firm. Spin-offs are a way that new firms can enter into the economy.

Spin-offs can occur in numerous ways. For example, a business might be sold to its managers and employees who then manage and work in this independently operating firm. Alternatively, a business unit within a diversified firm may be sold to the public through an **initial public offering (IPO).** Sometimes, the corporation spinning off a business unit will retain some ownership stake in the spin-off; other times, this corporation will sever all financial links with the spun-off firm.

In general, large diversified firms might spin off businesses they own for three reasons. First, the efficient management of these businesses may require very specific skills that are not available in a diversified firm. For example, suppose a diversified manufacturing firm finds itself operating in an R&D-intensive industry. The management skills required to manage manufacturing efficiently can be very different from the management skills required to manage R&D. If a diversified firm's skills do not match the skills required in a particular business, that business might be spun off.

Second, anticipated economies of scope between a business and the rest

Transforming Big Business into Entrepreneurship

of a diversified firm may turn out to not be valuable. For example, PepsiCo acquired Kentucky Fried Chicken, Pizza Hut, and Taco Bell, anticipating important marketing synergies between these fast-food restaurants and PepsiCo's soft drink business. Despite numerous efforts to realize these synergies, they were not forthcoming. Indeed, several of these fast-food restaurants began losing market share because they were forced to sell Pepsi rather than Coca-Cola products. After a few years, PepsiCo spun off its restaurants into a separate business.

Finally, it may be necessary to spin a business off in order to fund a firm's other businesses. Large diversified firms may face capital constraints due to, among other things, their high level of debt. In this setting, firms may need to spin off a business in order to raise capital to invest in other parts of the firm. Moreover, spinning off a part of the business that is particularly costly in terms of the capital it consumes may not only be a source of funds for other parts of this firm's business, it can also reduce the demand for that capital within a firm.

Research in corporate finance suggests that corporations are most likely to spin off businesses that are unrelated to a firm's corporate diversification strategy; those that are performing poorly compared with other businesses a firm operates in; and relatively small businesses. Also, the amount of merger and acquisition activity in a particular industry will determine which businesses are spun off. The greater the level of this activity in an industry, the more likely that a business owned by a corporation in such an industry will be spun off. This is because the level of merger and acquisition activity in an industry is an indicator of the number of people and firms that might be interested in purchasing a spun-off business. However, when there is not much merger and acquisition activity in an industry, businesses in that industry are less likely to be spun off, even if they are unrelated to a firm's corporate diversification strategy, are performing poorly, or are small. In such settings, large firms are not likely to obtain the full value associated with spinning off a business and thus are reluctant to do so.

Whatever the conditions that lead a large diversified firm to spin off one of its businesses, this process is important for creating new firms in the economy.

Sources: F. Schlingemann, R. M. Stulz, and R. Walkling (2002). "Divestitures and the liquidity of the market for corporate assets." *Journal of Financial Economics,* 64, pp. 117–144; G. Hite, J. Owens, and R. Rogers (1987). "The market for inter-firm asset sales: Partial sell-offs and total liquidations." *Journal of Financial Economics,* 18, pp. 229–252; P. Berger and E. Ofek (1999). "Causes and consequences of corporate focusing programs." *Review of Financial Studies,* 12, pp. 311–345.

longer fit with the firm's overall corporate strategy. What happens when a division no longer fits with a firm's corporate strategy is described in the Strategy in the Emerging Enterprise feature.

Compensation Policies and Implementing Corporate Diversification

A firm's compensation policies constitute a final set of tools for implementing diversification. Traditionally, the compensation of corporate managers in a diversified firm has been only loosely connected to the firm's economic performance. One important study examined the relationship between executive compensation and firm performance and found that differences in CEO cash compensation (salary plus cash bonus) are not very responsive to differences in firm performance.[24] In particular, this study showed that a CEO of a firm whose equity holders lost, collectively, $400 million in a year earned average cash compensation worth $800,000, while a CEO of a firm whose equity holders gained, collectively, $400 million in a year earned average cash compensation worth $1,040,000. Thus, an $800 million difference in the performance of a firm only had, on average, a $204,000 impact on the size of a CEO's salary and cash bonus. Put differently, for every million dollars of improved firm performance, CEOs, on average, get paid an additional $255. After taxes, increasing a firm's performance by a million dollars is roughly equal in value to a good dinner at a nice restaurant.

However, this same study was able to show that if a substantial percentage of a CEO's compensation came in the form of stock and stock options in the

Ethics and Strategy

Nothing in business gets as much negative press as CEO salaries. In 2012, for example, Larry Ellison, CEO of Oracle, was paid $96.2 million; Robert Kotick, CEO of Activision Blizzard, was paid $64.9 million; Leslie Moonves of CBS $60.3 million; David Zaslay of Discovery Communications $49.9 million; and James Crowe, CEO of Level 3 Communications, $40.7 million. Marissa Mayer, CEO of Yahoo, was the highest-compensated woman in 2012—she was paid $36.6 million (ranked ninth on the list). Reasonable people ask: Is anyone worth this much money?

But determining what CEOs "should" be paid is a difficult question.

Do CEOs Get Paid Too Much?

Some firms adopt policies that state that their CEOs cannot make more than some multiple of the lowest-paid employee in a firm. In Chapter 1, it was suggested that such a compensation policy at Ben & Jerry's Ice Cream may have cost its shareholders millions of dollars because it prevented Ben & Jerry's from recruiting a CEO who would have facilitated Ben & Jerry's acquisition by a firm that could effectively leverage the Ben & Jerry's brand.

Many firms delegate the responsibility of determining CEO salary to the compensation committee on the board of directors. The compensation committee often identifies a set of comparable firms (i.e., firms about the same size and in the same industry) as its firm and

firm, changes in compensation would be closely linked with changes in the firm performance. In particular, the $800 million difference in firm performance just described would be associated with a $1.2 million difference in the value of CEO compensation if CEO compensation included stock and stock options in addition to cash compensation. In this setting, an additional million dollars of firm performance increases a CEO's salary by $667.

These and similar findings reported elsewhere have led more and more diversified firms to include stock and stock options as part of the compensation package for the CEO. As important, many firms now extend this non-cash compensation to other senior managers in a diversified firm, including division general managers. For example, the top 1,300 managers at General Dynamics receive stock and stock options as part of their compensation package. Moreover, the cash bonuses of these managers also depend on General Dynamics' stock market performance. At Johnson & Johnson, all division general managers receive a five-component compensation package. The level of only one of those components, salary, does not vary with the economic profitability of the business over which a division general manager presides. The level of the other four components—a cash bonus, stock grants, stock options, and a deferred income package—varies with the economic performance of a particular division. Moreover, the value of some of these variable components of compensation also depends on Johnson & Johnson's long-term economic performance.[25]

To the extent that compensation in diversified firms gives managers incentives to make decisions consistent with stockholders' interests, they can be an important part of the process of implementing corporate diversification. However, the sheer size of the compensation paid to some CEOs raises ethical issues for some. These ethical issues are discussed in the Ethics and Strategy feature.

then calculates the average compensation of CEOs in these firms. Of course, because no firm wants to think that its CEO is in the "bottom half" of its comparable firms, most firms pay their CEOs something over this average—a decision-making process that ensures that, in the long run, CEO pay will continue to rise.

The mix of compensation also makes it difficult to know how much a CEO should get paid. For example, most of the "big bucks" in CEO compensation come not from salary but from bonuses, stock, stock options, and other perquisites. Most of these non-salary forms of compensation depend on the performance of a firm and are designed to align the financial interests of CEOs and a firm's shareholders. This is the case at Berkshire Hathaway, where a key operating principle is that most of the personal wealth of Warren Buffett and his senior management team is held in Berkshire Hathaway stock. In fact, one study showed that, on average, CEO compensation in excess of what would be expected based on a CEO's business experience is positively correlated with a firm's performance.

Of course, correlation is not causation. The question remains open: Does a CEO have to receive massive incentive compensation—literally hundreds of millions of dollars over time—just so he (or she) will do his (or her) job: to maximize returns to shareholders? And what are the implications of this compensation for the other employees in a firm—does it encourage their ambitions to seek employment among the senior ranks of a firm, or does it discourage and demoralize them that one person can get paid so much while they get paid so little?

Sources: Russell, Karl. "Executive Pay by the Numbers" www.nytimes.com/interactive/2013 /06/30/business/executive/compensation. Accessed August 23, 2013; A. Mackey (2006). "Dynamics in executive labor markets: CEO effects, executive-firm matching, and rent sharing." Dissertation, The Ohio State University.

Summary

To be valuable, diversification strategies must exploit valuable economies of scope that cannot be duplicated by outside investors at low cost. However, to realize the value of these economies of scope, firms must organize themselves appropriately. A firm's organizational structure, its management control processes, and its compensation policies are all relevant in implementing a corporate diversification strategy.

The best organizational structure for implementing a diversification leveraging strategy is the multidivisional, or M-form, structure. The M-form structure has several critical components, including the board of directors, institutional investors, the senior executive, corporate staff, division general managers, and shared activity managers.

This organizational structure is supported by a variety of management control processes. Three critical management control processes for firms implementing diversification strategies are (1) evaluating the performance of divisions, (2) allocating capital across divisions, and (3) transferring intermediate products between divisions. The existence of economies of scope in firms implementing corporate diversification strategies significantly complicates the management of these processes.

Finally, a firm's compensation policies are also important for firms implementing a diversification strategy. Historically, management compensation has been only loosely connected to a firm's economic performance, but recently the increased popularity of using stock and stock options to help compensate managers. Such compensation schemes help reduce conflicts between managers and outside investors, but the absolute level of CEO compensation is still very high, at least in the United States.

MyManagementLab®

Go to **mymanagementlab.com** to complete the problems marked with this icon ✪.

Challenge Questions

8.1. Agency theory has been criticized for assuming that managers, left on their own, will behave in ways that reduce the wealth of outside equity holders when, in fact, most managers are highly responsible stewards of the assets they control. This alternative view of managers has been called *stewardship theory*. Why would you agree with this criticism of agency theory?

✪ **8.2.** Suppose that the concept of the stewardship theory is correct and that most managers, most of the time, behave responsibly and make decisions that maximize the present

value of the assets they control. What implications, if any, would this supposition have on organizing to implement diversification strategies?

8.3. The M-form structure enables firms to pursue complex corporate diversification strategies by delegating different management responsibilities to different individuals and groups within a firm. Based on the concept of the M-form structure is there a natural limit to the efficient size of a diversified firm?

8.4. Due to their sizeable financial prowess, institutional investors

can sometimes own substantial stakes in public listed firms. To what extent should institutional investors influence the executive management in an organization, especially if its vision differs substantially from that of the board and CEO?

8.5. Within conglomerates, some large divisions or strategic business units (SBUs) operate almost like standalone companies, given their size in their respective markets. While senior managers of such divisions should have autonomy, how can corporate level staff, such as the board and CEO, have the company level strategy imprinted on these large divisions?

⭐ **8.6.** Suppose that the optimal transfer price between one business and all other business activities in a firm is the market price. What does this condition say about whether this firm should own this business?

Problem Set

8-7. Which elements of the M-form structure (the board of directors, the office of the CEO, corporate staff, division general managers, shared activity managers) should be involved in the following business activities? If more than one of these groups should be involved, indicate their relative level of involvement (e.g., 20 percent office of the CEO, 10 percent shared activity manager, 70 percent division general manager). Justify your answers.

(a) Determining the compensation of the CEO
(b) Determining the compensation of the corporate vice president of human resources
(c) Determining the compensation of a vice president of human resources in a particular business division
(d) Deciding to sell a business division
(e) Deciding to buy a relatively small firm whose activities are closely related to the activities of one of the firm's current divisions
(f) Deciding to buy a larger firm that is not closely related to the activities of any of a firm's current divisions
(g) Evaluating the performance of the vice president of sales, a manager whose sales staff sells the products of three divisions in the firm
(h) Evaluating the performance of the vice president of sales, a manager whose sales staff sells the products of only one division in the firm
(i) Determining how much money to invest in a corporate R&D function
(j) Deciding how much money to invest in an R&D function that supports the operations of two divisions within the firm
(k) Deciding whether to fire an R&D scientist
(l) Deciding whether to fire the vice president of accounting in a particular division
(m) Deciding whether to fire the corporation's vice president of accounting
(n) Deciding whether to take a firm public by selling stock in the firm to the general public for the first time

8-8. Consider the following facts. Division A in a firm has generated $847,000 of profits on $24 million worth of sales, using $32 million worth of dedicated assets. The cost of capital for this firm is 9 percent, and the firm has invested $7.3 million in this division.

(a) Calculate the Return on Sales (ROS) and Return on Total Assets (ROA) of Division A. If the hurdle rates for ROS and ROA in this firm are, respectively, 0.06 and 0.04, has this division performed well?
(b) Calculate the EVA of Division A (assuming that the reported profits have already been adjusted). Based on this EVA, has this division performed well?
(c) Suppose you were CEO of this firm. How would you choose between ROS/ROA and EVA for evaluating this division?

8-9. Suppose that Division A sells an intermediate product to Division B. Choose one of the ways of determining transfer prices described in this chapter (not setting transfer prices equal to the selling firm's opportunity costs) and show how Division Manager A can use this mechanism to justify a higher transfer price while Division Manager B can use this mechanism to justify a lower transfer price. Repeat this exercise with another approach to setting transfer prices described in the chapter.

MyManagementLab®

Go to **mymanagementlab.com** for the following Assisted-graded writing questions:

⭐ **8.10.** How are the roles of senior executives and shared activity managers different in making the M-form structure work?

⭐ **8.11.** What are the implications for a multidivisional firm when the corporate staff become too involved in the day-to-day operations of divisions?

End Notes

1. The structure and function of the multidimensional firm were first described by Chandler, A. (1962). *Strategy and structure: Chapters in the history of the industrial enterprise.* Cambridge, MA: MIT Press. The economic logic underlying the multidimensional firm was first described by Williamson, O. E. (1975). *Markets and hierarchies: Analysis and antitrust implications.* New York: Free Press. Empirical examinations of the impact of the M-form or firm performance include Armour, H. O., and D. J. Teece. (1980). "Vertical integration and technological innovation." *Review of Economics and Statistics*, 60, pp. 470–474. There continues to be some debate about the efficiency of the M-form structure. See Freeland, R. F. (1966). "The myth of the M-form? Governance, consent, and organizational change." *American Journal of Sociology*, 102(2), pp. 483–626; and Shanley, M. (1996). "Straw men and M-form myths: Comment on Freeland." *American Journal of Sociology*, 102(2), pp. 527–536.
2. See Finkelstein, S., and R. D'Aveni. (1994). "CEO duality as a double-edged sword: How boards of directors balance entrenchment avoidance and unity of command." *Academy of Management Journal*, 37, pp. 1079–1108.
3. Kesner, I. F. (1988). "Director's characteristics and committee membership: An investigation of type, occupation, tenure and gender." *Academy of Management Journal*, 31, pp. 66–84; and Zahra, S. A., and J. A. Pearce II. (1989). "Boards of directors and corporate financial performance: A review and integrative model." *Journal of Management*, 15, pp. 291–334.
4. Investor Relations Business. (2000). "Reversal of fortune: Institutional ownership is declining." *Investor Relations Business*, May 1, pp. 8–9; and Federal Reserve Board. (2006). "Flow of funds report." www.corpgov.net.
5. See Hansen, G. S., and C. W. L. Hill. (1991). "Are institutional investors myopic? A time-series study of four technology-driven industries." *Strategic Management Journal*, 12, pp. 1–16.
6. See Bergh, D. (1995). "Size and relatedness of units sold: An agency theory and resource-based perspective." *Strategic Management Journal*, 16, pp. 221–239; and Bethel, J., and J. Liebeskind. (1993). "The effects of ownership structure on corporate restructuring." *Strategic Management Journal*, 14, pp. 15–31.
7. Burdens that are well described by Westley, F., and H. Mintzberg. (1989). "Visionary leadership and strategic management." *Strategic Management Journal*, 10, pp. 17–32.
8. See Dumaine, B. (1992). "Is big still good?" *Fortune*, April 20, pp. 50–60.
9. See Golden, B. (1992). "SBU strategy and performance: The moderating effects of the corporate–SBU relationship." *Strategic Management Journal*, 13, pp. 145–158; Berger, P., and E. Ofek. (1995). "Diversification effect on firm value." *Journal of Financial Economics*, 37, pp. 36–65;

Lang, H. P., and R. M. Stulz. (1994). "Tobin's q, corporate diversification, and firm performance." *Journal of Political Economy*, 102, pp. 1248–1280; and Rumelt, R. (1991). "How much does industry matter?" *Strategic Management Journal*, 12, pp. 167–185.
10. See Halal, W. (1994). "From hierarchy to enterprise: Internal markets are the new foundation of management." *The Academy of Management Executive*, 8(4), pp. 69–83.
11. Bartlett, C., and S. Ghoshal. (1993). "Beyond the M-form: Toward a managerial theory of the firm." *Strategic Management Journal*, 14, pp. 23–46.
12. See Simons, R. (1994). "How new top managers use control systems as levers of strategic renewal." *Strategic Management Journal*, 15, pp. 169–189.
13. Bethel, J. E. (1990). "The capital allocation process and managerial mobility: A theoretical and empirical investigation." Unpublished doctoral dissertation, UCLA.
14. Some of these are described in Duffy, M. (1989). "ZBB, MBO, PPB, and their effectiveness within the planning/marketing process." *Strategic Management Journal*, 12, pp. 155–160.
15. See Stern, J., B. Stewart, and D. Chew. (1995). "The EVA financial management system." *Journal of Applied Corporate Finance*, 8, pp. 32–46; and Tully, S. (1993). "The real key to creating wealth." *Fortune*, September 20, pp. 38–50.
16. Applications of EVA are described in Tully, S. (1993). "The real key to creating wealth." *Fortune*, September 20, pp. 38–50; Tully, S. (1995). "So, Mr. Bossidy, we know you can cut. Now show us how to grow." *Fortune*, August 21, pp. 70–80; and Tully, S. (1995). "Can EVA deliver profits to the post office?" *Fortune*, July 10, p. 22.
17. A special issue of the *Journal of Applied Corporate Finance* in 1994 addressed many of these issues.
18. See Priem, R. (1990). "Top management team group factors, consensus, and firm performance." *Strategic Management Journal*, 11, pp. 469–478; and Wooldridge, B., and S. Floyd. (1990). "The strategy process, middle management involvement, and organizational performance." *Strategic Management Journal*, 11, pp. 231–241.
19. A point made by Westley, F. (1900). "Middle managers and strategy: Microdynamics of inclusion." *Strategic Management Journal*, 11, pp. 337–351; Lamont, O. (1997). "Cash flow and investment: Evidence from internal capital markets." *The Journal of Finance*, 52(1), pp. 83–109; Shin, H. H., and R. M. Stulz. (1998). "Are internal capital markets efficient?" *Quarterly Journal of Economics*, May, pp. 531–552; and Stein, J. C. (1997). "Internal capital markets and the competition for corporate resources." *The Journal of Finance*, 52(1), pp. 111–133.
20. See Brickley, J., C. Smith, and J. Zimmerman. (1996). *Organizational architecture and managerial economics approach.* Homewood, IL: Irwin;

and Eccles, R. (1985). *The transfer pricing problem: A theory for practice.* Lexington, MA: Lexington Books.

21. See Cyert, R., and J. G. March. (1963). *A behavioral theory of the firm.* Upper Saddle River, NJ: Prentice Hall; Swieringa, R. J., and J. H. Waterhouse. (1982). "Organizational views of transfer pricing." *Accounting, Organizations & Society*, 7(2), pp. 149–165; and Eccles, R. (1985). *The transfer pricing problem: A theory for practice.* Lexington, MA: Lexington Books.

22. Gupta, A. K., and V. Govindarajan. (1986). "Resource sharing among SBUs: Strategic antecedents and administrative implications." *Academy of Management Journal*, 29, pp. 695–714.

23. A point made by Swieringa, R. J., and J. H. Waterhouse. (1982). "Organizational views of transfer pricing." *Accounting, Organizations and Society*, 7(2), pp. 149–165.

24. Jensen, M. C., and K. J. Murphy. (1990). "Performance pay and top management incentives." *Journal of Political Economy*, 98, pp. 225–264.

25. See Dial, J., and K. J. Murphy. (1995). "Incentive, downsizing, and value creation at General Dynamics." *Journal of Financial Economics*, 37, pp. 261–314, on General Dynamics' compensation scheme; and Aguilar, F. J., and A. Bhambri. (1983). "Johnson & Johnson (A)." Harvard Business School Case No. 9-384-053, on Johnson & Johnson's compensation scheme.

9 Strategic Alliances

LEARNING OBJECTIVES *After reading this chapter, you should be able to:*

1. Define a strategic alliance and give three specific examples of strategic alliances.

2. Describe nine different ways that alliances can create value for firms and how these nine sources of value can be grouped into three large categories.

3. Describe how adverse selection, moral hazard, and holdup can threaten the ability of alliances to generate value.

4. Describe the conditions under which a strategic alliance can be rare and costly to duplicate.

5. Describe the conditions under which "going it alone" and acquisitions are not likely to be substitutes for alliances.

6. Describe how contracts, equity investments, firm reputations, joint ventures, and trust can all reduce the threat of cheating in strategic alliances.

MyManagementLab®

⭐ **Improve Your Grade!**
Over 10 million students improved their results using the Pearson MyLabs.
Visit **mymanagementlab.com** for simulations, tutorials, and end-of-chapter problems.

Breaking Up Is Hard to Do: Apple and Samsung

On the one hand, Samsung and Apple are very close business partners. Apple depends on technologies developed and built by Samsung to build its smart phones, iPods, and iPads. In turn, Apple is one of Samsung's largest, and most profitable, customers. In 2012, Samsung sold $10 billion in electronic components to Apple, one-sixth of Samsung's total component sales.

On the other hand, Apple and Samsung have sued and countersued each other over the look and feel of their respective smart phones and related products. Courts around the world are weighing in on these issues. Initially, Samsung was ordered to pay $1 billion (later reduced to $500 million) to Apple for infringing on some Apple patents. Then the U.S. International Trade Commission concluded that Apple had infringed on a Samsung patent and ordered a ban on some older model Apple smart phones (later rescinded by the Obama administration). Not a great way to maintain a business partnership.

For many years, Samsung and Apple had a very functional alliance. Samsung made the kinds of technologies—including microprocessors, memory chips, and displays—that Apple needed to fuel its growth in smart phones and related products. Not only did Samsung supply these technologies to Apple, it was the best supplier of these technologies—both in terms of quality and cost—in the world. Apple was only too happy to source its components to such a supplier.

Then Samsung entered the smart phone market and began to produce phones that ran Google's Android system. Apple and Samsung became competitors. Indeed, there are now more Android phones sold each year—mostly made by Samsung—than Apple iPhones.

Not surprisingly, Apple is looking around the world to find alternative suppliers of its essential electronic components. The problem is: Finding suppliers that are as competent as Samsung in providing these state-of-the-art technologies has turned out to be quite difficult. While Apple has found second sources for memory chips and some displays, Samsung continues to be an almost exclusive supplier of the microprocessors that run Apple's iPods, iPhones, and iPads.

For example, Apple began working with Taiwan Semiconductor Manufacturing Company (TSMC) to create a new source for microprocessors in 2011. It took two years for TSMC to develop chips that met Apple's (and Samsung's) standards. It will take at least another year for TSMC to ramp up its production of this new technology, all while Samsung remains the only viable supplier of this critical component for Apple.

And Samsung isn't just standing pat, waiting for Apple to find new suppliers. For example, Apple tried to develop a contract with the Japanese firm Sharp for certain displays it currently buys from Samsung. This may have become more difficult since Samsung purchased 3 percent of Sharp's stock and became Sharp's fifth-largest shareholder!

Sometimes, breaking up really is hard to do.

Sources: J. Lessin, L. Luk, and J. Osawa (2013). "Apple finds it difficult to divorce Samsung." *The Wall Street Journal,* August 16, 2013//online.wsj.com/articles/SB10 001424127887324682204045785151882349940500 Accessed August 25, 2013; B. Kendall and I. Sherr (2013). "Patent war adds front in U.S." *The Wall Street Journal,* online, August 23, online.wsj.com/article/SB10001424127887324170004578633702773124388 Accessed August 25, 2013; P. Elias (2013). "Apple's Samsung verdict nearly cut in half by federal judge." *Huffington Post,* January 3, huffingtonpost.com/2013/03/01/half-a-billion-cut-from-Apple. Accessed November 4, 2013.

© MaxPayne/Alamy

The use of strategic alliances to manage economic exchanges has grown substantially over the past several years. In the early 1990s, strategic alliances were relatively uncommon, except in a few industries. However, by the late 1990s they had become much more common in a wide variety of industries. Indeed, more than 20,000 alliances were created worldwide in 2000 and 2001. In the computer technology–based industries, more than 2,200 alliances were created between 2001 and 2005. This, the complex web of relationships that characterizes the links between Apple and Samsung, is becoming increasingly more common.[1]

What Is a Strategic Alliance?

A **strategic alliance** exists whenever two or more independent organizations cooperate in the development, manufacture, or sale of products or services. As shown in Figure 9.1, strategic alliances can be grouped into three broad categories: nonequity alliances, equity alliances, and joint ventures.

In a **nonequity alliance,** cooperating firms agree to work together to develop, manufacture, or sell products or services, but they do not take equity positions in each other or form an independent organizational unit to manage their cooperative efforts. Rather, these cooperative relations are managed through the use of various contracts. **Licensing agreements** (where one firm allows others to use its brand name to sell products), **supply agreements** (where one firm agrees to supply others), and **distribution agreements** (where one firm agrees to distribute the products of others) are examples of nonequity strategic alliances. Most of the alliances between Tony Hawk and his partners take the form of nonequity licensing agreements.

In an **equity alliance,** cooperating firms supplement contracts with equity holdings in alliance partners. For example, when GM began importing small cars manufactured by Isuzu, not only did these partners have supply contracts in place, but GM purchased 34.2 percent of Isuzu's stock. Ford had a similar relationship with Mazda, and Chrysler had a similar relationship with Mitsubishi.[2] Equity alliances are also very common in the biotechnology industry. Large pharmaceutical firms such as Pfizer and Merck often own equity positions in several startup biotechnology companies.

Figure 9.1   Types of Strategic Alliances

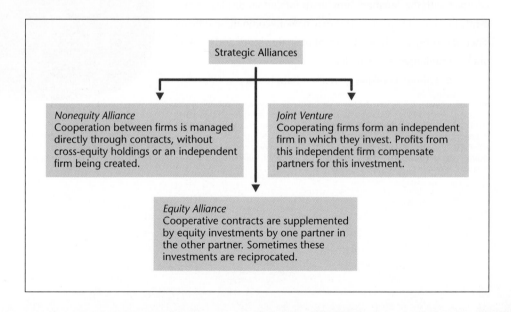

In a **joint venture,** cooperating firms create a legally independent firm in which they invest and from which they share any profits that are created. Some of these joint ventures can be very large. For example, Dow and Corning's joint venture, Dow-Corning, is a *Fortune 500* company on its own. Before they merged, AT&T and BellSouth were co-owners of the joint venture Cingular, one of the largest wireless phone companies in the United States. And CFM—a joint venture between General Electric and SNECMA (a French aerospace firm)—is one of the world's leading manufacturers of jet engines for commercial aircraft. If you have ever flown on a Boeing 737, then you have placed your life in the hands of this joint venture because it manufactures the engines for virtually all of these aircraft.

How Do Strategic Alliances Create Value?

VRIO

Like all the strategies discussed in this book, strategic alliances create value by exploiting opportunities and neutralizing threats facing a firm. Some of the most important opportunities that can be exploited by strategic alliances are listed in Table 9.1. Threats to strategic alliances are discussed later in this chapter.

Strategic Alliance Opportunities

Opportunities associated with strategic alliances fall into three large categories. First, these alliances can be used by a firm to improve the performance of its current operations. Second, alliances can be used to create a competitive environment favorable to superior firm performance. Finally, they can be used to facilitate a firm's entry into or exit from new markets or industries.

Improving Current Operations

One way that firms can use strategic alliances to improve their current operations is to use alliances to realize economies of scale. The concept of economies of scale was first introduced in Chapter 2. **Economies of scale** exist when the per-unit cost of production falls as the volume of production increases. Thus, for example, although the per-unit cost of producing one BIC pen is very high, the per-unit cost of producing 50 million BIC pens is very low.

To realize economies of scale, firms have to have a large volume of production, or at least a volume of production large enough so that the cost advantages

---

TABLE 9.1 Ways Strategic Alliances Can Create Economic Value

Helping firms improve the performance of their current operations

1. Exploiting economies of scale
2. Learning from competitors
3. Managing risk and sharing costs
4. Creating a competitive environment favorable to superior performance
5. Facilitating the development of technology standards
6. Facilitating tacit collusion
7. Facilitating entry and exit
8. Low-cost entry into new industries and new industry segments
9. Low-cost exit from industries and industry segments
10. Managing uncertainty
11. Low-cost entry into new markets

associated with scale can be realized. Sometimes—as was described in Chapters 2 and 4—a firm can realize these economies of scale by itself; other times, it cannot. When a firm cannot realize the cost savings from economies of scale all by itself, it may join in a strategic alliance with other firms. Jointly, these firms may have sufficient volume to be able to gain the cost advantages of economies of scale.

But why wouldn't a firm be able to realize these economies all by itself? A firm may have to turn to alliance partners to help realize economies of scale for a number of reasons. For example, if the volume of production required to realize these economies is very large, a single firm might have to dominate an entire industry in order to obtain these advantages. It is often very difficult for a single firm to obtain such a dominant position in an industry. And even if it does so, it may be subject to anti-monopoly regulation by the government. Also, although a particular part or technology may be very important to several firms, no one firm may generate sufficient demand for this part or technology to realize economies of scale in its development and production. In this setting as well, independent firms may join together to form an alliance to realize economies of scale in the development and production of the part or technology.

Firms can also use alliances to improve their current operations by learning from their competitors. As suggested in Chapter 3, different firms in an industry may have different resources and capabilities. These resources can give some firms competitive advantages over others. Firms that are at a competitive disadvantage may want to form alliances with the firms that have an advantage in order to learn about their resources and capabilities.

General Motors formed this kind of alliance with Toyota. In the early 1990s, GM and Toyota jointly invested in a previously closed GM plant in Fremont, California. This joint venture—called NUMI—was to build compact cars to be distributed through GM's distribution network. But why did GM decide to build these cars in an alliance with Toyota? Obviously, it could have built them in any of its own plants. However, GM was very interested in learning about how Toyota was able to manufacture high-quality small cars at a profit. Indeed, in the NUMI plant, Toyota agreed to take total responsibility for the manufacturing process, using former GM employees to install and operate the "lean manufacturing" system that had enabled Toyota to become the quality leader in the small-car segment of the automobile industry. However, Toyota also agreed to let GM managers work in the plant and directly observe how Toyota managed this production process. Since its inception, GM has rotated thousands of its managers from other GM plants through the NUMI plant so that they can be exposed to Toyota's lean manufacturing methods.

It is clear why GM would want this alliance with Toyota. But why would Toyota want this alliance with GM? Certainly, Toyota was not looking to learn about lean manufacturing, per se. However, because Toyota was contemplating entering the United States by building its own manufacturing facilities, it did need to learn how to implement lean manufacturing in the United States with U.S. employees. Thus, Toyota also had something to learn from this alliance.

When both parties to an alliance are seeking to learn something from that alliance, an interesting dynamic called a **learning race** can evolve. This dynamic is described in more detail in the Strategy in Depth feature.

Finally, firms can use alliances to improve their current operations through sharing costs and risks. For example, HBO produces most of its original programs in alliances with independent producers. Most of these alliances are created to share costs and risks. Producing new television shows can be costly. Development and production costs can run into the hundreds of millions of dollars, especially for long and complicated series like HBO's *Deadwood, Entourage,* and *The Sopranos.* And, despite audience testing and careful market analyses, the production of these new shows is also very risky. Even a bankable star like Johnny Depp—remember *The Lone Ranger*—cannot guarantee success.

In this context, it is not surprising that HBO decides to not "go it alone" in its production efforts. If HBO was to be the sole producer of its original programming, not only would it have to absorb all the production costs, but it would also bear all the risk if a production turned out not to be successful. Of course, by getting other firms involved in its production efforts, HBO also has to share whatever profits a particular production generates. Apparently, HBO has concluded that sharing this upside potential is more than compensated for by sharing the costs and risks of these productions.

Creating a Favorable Competitive Environment

Firms can also use strategic alliances to create a competitive environment that is more conducive to superior performance. This can be done in at least two ways. First, firms can use alliances to help set technology standards in an industry. With these standards in place, technology-based products can be developed and consumers can be confident that the products they buy will be useful for some time to come.

Such technological standards are particularly important in what are called **network industries.** Such industries are characterized by **increasing returns to scale.** Consider, for example, fax machines. How valuable is one fax machine, all by itself? Obviously, not very valuable. Two fax machines that can talk to each other are a little more valuable, three that can talk to each other are still more valuable, and so forth. The value of each individual fax machine depends on the total number of fax machines in operation that can talk to each other. This is what is meant by increasing returns to scale—the value (or returns) on each product increases as the number of these products (or scale) increases.

If there are 100 million fax machines in operation but none of these machines can talk to each other, none of these machines has any value whatsoever—except as a large paperweight. For their full value to be realized, they must be able to talk to each other. And to talk to each other, they must all adopt the same—or at least compatible—communication standards. This is why setting technology standards is so important in network industries.

Standards can be set in two ways. First, different firms can introduce different standards, and consumers can decide which they prefer. This is how the standard for high-definition DVDs was set. Initially, two formats competed: HD DVD (supported by Toshiba) and Blu-ray DVD (supported by the Blu-ray Disc Association, a group of 50 or so electronics firms and content providers). Both formats had attractive features, but they could not be played on each other's players. Competition between the two formats continued for some time, until firms like Panasonic (in 2004), Samsung (in 2005), Disney (in 2004), and Paramount (in 2005) committed to the Blu-ray Disc format. By 2008, even Toshiba had to acknowledge the dominance of Blu-ray Discs. Toshiba released its own Blu-ray Disc player in 2009.[3]

Of course, the biggest problem with letting customers and competition set technology standards is that customers may end up purchasing technologies that are incompatible with the standard that is ultimately set in the industry. What about all those consumers who purchased HD products? For this reason, customers may be unwilling to invest in a new technology until the standards of that technology are established.

Strategy in Depth

A learning race exists in a strategic alliance when both parties to that alliance seek to learn from each other but the rate at which these two firms learn varies. In this setting, the first firm to learn what it wants to learn from an alliance has the option to begin to underinvest in, and perhaps even withdraw from, an alliance. In this way, the firm that learns faster is able to prevent the slower-learning firm from learning all it wanted from an alliance. If, outside of this alliance, these firms are competitors, winning a learning race can create a sustained competitive advantage for the faster-learning firm over the slower-learning firm.

Firms in an alliance may vary in the rate they learn from each other for a variety of reasons. First, they may be looking to learn different things, some of which are easier to learn than others. For example, in the GM–Toyota example, GM wanted to learn about how to use "lean manufacturing" to build high-quality small cars profitably. Toyota wanted to learn how to apply the "lean manufacturing" skills it already possessed in the United States. Which of these is easier to learn—"lean manufacturing" or how to apply "lean manufacturing" in the United States?

An argument can be made that GM's learning task was much more complicated than Toyota's. At the very least, in order for GM to apply knowledge about "lean manufacturing" gleaned from Toyota it would have to transfer that knowledge to several of its currently operating plants. Using this knowledge would require these plants to change their current operations—a difficult and time-consuming process. Toyota, however, only had to transfer its knowledge of how to operate a

Winning Learning Races

"lean manufacturing" operation in the United States to its other U.S. plants—plants that at the time this alliance was first created had yet to be built. Because GM's learning task was more complicated than Toyota's, it is very likely that Toyota's rate of learning was greater than GM's.

Second, firms may differ in terms of their ability to learn. This ability has been called a firm's **absorptive capacity.** Firms with high levels of absorptive capacity will learn at faster rates than firms with low levels of absorptive capacity, even if these two firms are trying to learn exactly the same things in an alliance. Absorptive capacity has been shown to be an important organizational capability in a wide variety of settings.

Third, firms can engage in activities to try to slow the rate of learning of their alliance partners. For example, although a firm might make its technology available to an alliance partner—thereby fulfilling the alliance agreement—it may not provide all the know-how necessary to

exploit this technology. This can slow a partner's learning. Also, a firm might withhold critical employees from an alliance, thereby slowing the learning of an alliance partner. All these actions, to the extent that they slow the rate of a partner's learning without also slowing the rate at which the firm engaging in these activities learns, can help this firm win a learning race.

Although learning race dynamics have been described in a wide variety of settings, they are particularly common in relations between entrepreneurial and large firms. In these alliances, entrepreneurial firms are often looking to learn about all the managerial functions required to bring a product to market, including manufacturing, sales, distribution, and so forth. This is a difficult learning task. Large firms in these alliances often are only looking to learn about the entrepreneurial firm's technology. This is a less difficult learning task. Because the learning task facing entrepreneurial firms is more challenging than that facing their large-firm partners, larger firms in these alliances typically win the learning race. Once these large firms learn what they want from their alliance partners, they often underinvest or even withdraw from these alliances. This is why, in one study, almost 80 percent of the managers in entrepreneurial firms felt unfairly exploited by their large-firm alliance partners.

Sources: S. A. Alvarez and J. B. Barney (2001). "How entrepreneurial firms can benefit from alliances with large partners." *Academy of Management Executive,* 15, pp. 139–148; G. Hamel (1991). "Competition for competence and inter-partner learning within international alliances." *Strategic Management Journal,* 12, pp. 83–103; W. Cohen and D. Levinthal (1990). "Absorptive capacity: A new perspective on learning and innovation." *Administrative Science Quarterly,* 35, pp. 128–152.

This is where strategic alliances come in. Sometimes, firms form strategic alliances with the sole purpose of evaluating and then choosing a technology standard. With such a standard in place, technologies can be turned into products that customers are likely to be more willing to purchase because they know that they will be compatible with industry standards for at least some period of time. Thus, in this setting, strategic alliances can be used to create a more favorable competitive environment.

Another incentive for cooperating in strategic alliances is that such activities may facilitate the development of tacit collusion. As explained in Chapter 3, **collusion** exists when two or more firms in an industry coordinate their strategic choices to reduce competition in an industry. This reduction in competition usually makes it easier for colluding firms to earn high levels of performance. A common example of collusion is when firms cooperate to reduce the quantity of products being produced in an industry in order to drive prices up. **Explicit collusion** exists when firms directly communicate with each other to coordinate their levels of production, their prices, and so forth. Explicit collusion is illegal in most countries.

Because managers that engage in explicit collusion can end up in jail, most collusion must be tacit in character. **Tacit collusion** exists when firms coordinate their production and pricing decisions not by directly communicating with each other, but by exchanging signals with other firms about their intent to cooperate. Examples of such signals might include public announcements about price increases, public announcements about reductions in a firm's productive output, public announcements about decisions not to pursue a new technology, and so forth.

Sometimes, signals of intent to collude are very ambiguous. For example, when firms in an industry do not reduce their prices in response to a decrease in demand, they may be sending a signal that they want to collude, or they may be attempting to exploit their product differentiation to maintain high margins. When firms do not reduce their prices in response to reduced supply costs, they may be sending a signal that they want to collude, or they may be individually maximizing their economic performance. In both these cases, a firm's intent to collude or not, as implied by its activities, is ambiguous at best.

In this context, strategic alliances can facilitate tacit collusion. Separate firms, even if they are in the same industry, can form strategic alliances. Although communication between these firms cannot legally include sharing information about prices and costs for products or services that are produced outside the alliance, such interaction does help create the social setting within which tacit collusion may develop.[4] As suggested in the Research Made Relevant feature, most early research on strategic alliances focused on their implications for tacit collusion. More recently, research suggests that alliances do not usually facilitate tacit collusion.

Facilitating Entry and Exit

A final way that strategic alliances can be used to create value is by facilitating a firm's entry into a new market or industry or its exit from a market or industry. Strategic alliances are particularly valuable in this context when the value of market entry or exit is uncertain. Entry into an industry can require skills, abilities, and products that a potential entrant does not possess. Strategic alliances can help a firm enter a new industry by avoiding the high costs of creating these skills, abilities, and products.

For example, DuPont wanted to enter into the electronics industry. However, building the skills and abilities needed to develop competitive products in this industry can be very difficult and costly. Rather than absorb these costs, DuPont developed a strategic alliance (DuPont/Philips Optical) with an established electronics firm, Philips, to distribute some of Philips's products in the United States. In this way, DuPont was able to enter into a new industry (electronics) without having to absorb all the costs of creating electronics resources and abilities from the ground up.

Of course, for this joint venture to succeed, Philips must have had an incentive to cooperate with DuPont. Whereas DuPont was looking to reduce its cost of entry into a new industry, Philips was looking to reduce its cost of continued entry into a new market—the United States. Philips used its alliance with DuPont to sell in the United States the compact discs it already was selling in Europe.[5] The role of alliances in facilitating entry into new geographic markets will be discussed in more detail later in this chapter.

Alliances to facilitate entry into new industries can be valuable even when the skills needed in these industries are not as complex and difficult to learn as skills in the electronics industry. For example, rather than develop their own frozen novelty foods, Welch Foods, Inc., and Leaf, Inc. (maker of Heath candy bars) asked Eskimo Pie to formulate products for this industry. Eskimo Pie developed Welch's frozen grape juice bar and the Heath toffee ice cream bar. These firms then split the profits derived from these products.[6] As long as the cost of using an alliance to enter a new industry is less than the cost of learning new skills and capabilities, an alliance can be a valuable strategic opportunity.

Some firms use strategic alliances as a mechanism to withdraw from industries or industry segments in a low-cost way. Firms are motivated to withdraw from an industry or industry segment when their level of performance in that business is less than expected and when there are few prospects of it improving. When a firm desires to exit an industry or industry segment, often it will need to dispose of the assets it has developed to compete in that industry or industry segment. These assets often include tangible resources and capabilities, such as factories, distribution centers, and product technologies, and intangible resources and capabilities, such as brand name, relationships with suppliers and customers, a loyal and committed workforce, and so forth.

Firms will often have difficulty in obtaining the full economic value of these tangible and intangible assets as they exit an industry or industry segment. This reflects an important information asymmetry that exists between the firms that currently own these assets and firms that may want to purchase these assets. By forming an alliance with a firm that may want to purchase its assets, a firm is giving its partner an opportunity to directly observe how valuable those assets are. If those assets are actually valuable, then this "sneak preview" can lead the assets to be more appropriately priced and thereby facilitate the exit of the firm that is looking to sell its assets. These issues will be discussed in more detail in Chapter 10's discussion of mergers and acquisitions.

One firm that has used strategic alliances to facilitate its exit from an industry or industry segment is Corning. In the late 1980s, Corning entered the medical diagnostics industry. After several years, however, Corning concluded that its resources and capabilities could be more productively used in other businesses. For this reason, it began to extract itself from the medical diagnostics business. However, to ensure that it received the full value of the assets it had created in the medical diagnostics business upon exiting, it formed a strategic alliance with the Swiss specialty chemical company Ciba-Geigy. Ciba-Geigy paid $75 million to purchase half of Corning's medical diagnostics business. A couple of years later, Corning finished exiting from the medical diagnostics business by selling its remaining assets in this industry to Ciba-Geigy. However, whereas Ciba-Geigy had paid $75 million for the first half of Corning's assets, it paid $150 million for the second half. Corning's alliance with Ciba-Geigy had made it possible for Ciba-Geigy to fully value Corning's medical diagnostics capabilities. Any information asymmetry that might have existed was reduced, and Corning was able to get more of the full value of its assets upon exiting this industry.[7]

Finally, firms may use strategic alliances to manage **uncertainty.** Under conditions of high uncertainty, firms may not be able to tell at a particular point in time which of several different strategies they should pursue. Firms in this setting have an incentive to retain the flexibility to move quickly into a particular market

Research Made Relevant

Several authors have concluded that joint ventures, as a form of alliance, do increase the probability of tacit collusion in an industry. As reviewed in books by Scherer and Barney, one study found that joint ventures created two industrial groups, besides U.S. Steel, in the U.S. iron and steel industry in the early 1900s. In this sense, joint ventures in the steel industry were a substitute for U.S. Steel's vertical integration and had the effect of creating an oligopoly in what (without joint ventures) would have been a more competitive market. Other studies found that more than 50 percent of joint venture parents belong to the same industry. After examining 885 joint venture bids for oil and gas leases, yet another study found only 16 instances where joint venture parents competed with one another on another tract in the same sale. These results suggest that joint ventures might encourage subsequent tacit collusion among firms in the same industry.

In a particularly influential study, Pfeffer and Nowak found that joint ventures were most likely in industries of moderate concentration. These authors argued that in highly

Do Strategic Alliances Facilitate Tacit Collusion?

concentrated industries—where there were only a small number of competing firms—joint ventures were not necessary to create conditions conducive to collusion. In highly fragmented industries, the high levels of industry concentration conducive to tacit collusion could not be created by joint ventures. Only when joint venture activity could effectively create concentrated industries—that is, only when industries were moderately concentrated—were joint ventures likely.

Scherer and Barney also reviewed more recent work that disputes these findings. Joint ventures between firms in the same industry may be valuable for a variety of reasons that have little or nothing to do with collusion. Moreover, by using a lower level of aggregation, several authors have disputed the finding that joint ventures are most likely in moderately concentrated industries. The original study defined industries using very broad industry categories— "the electronics industry," "the automobile industry," and so forth. By defining industries less broadly—"consumer electronics" and "automobile part manufacturers"—subsequent work found that 73 percent of the joint ventures had parent firms coming from different industries. Although joint ventures between firms in the same industry (defined at this lower level of aggregation) may have collusive implications, subsequent work has shown that these kinds of joint ventures are relatively rare.

Sources: F. M. Scherer (1980). *Industrial market structure and economic performance.* Boston: Houghton Mifflin; J. B. Barney (2006). *Gaining and sustaining competitive advantage*, 3rd ed. Upper Saddle River, NJ: Prentice Hall; J. Pfeffer and P. Nowak (1976). "Patterns of joint venture activity: Implications for anti-trust research." *Antitrust Bulletin*, 21, pp. 315–339.

or industry once the full value of that strategy is revealed. In this sense, strategic alliances enable a firm to maintain a point of entry into a market or industry, without incurring the costs associated with full-scale entry.

Based on this logic, strategic alliances have been analyzed as **real options.**[8] In this sense, a joint venture is an option that a firm buys, under conditions of uncertainty, to retain the ability to move quickly into a market or industry if valuable opportunities present themselves. One way in which firms can move quickly into a market is simply to buy out their partner(s) in the joint venture. Moreover, by investing in a joint venture a firm may gain access to the information it needs to evaluate full-scale entry into a market. In this approach to analyzing strategic alliances, firms that invest in alliances as options will acquire their alliance partners only after the market signals an unexpected increase in value of the venture; that is, only after uncertainty is reduced and the true, positive value of entering into a market is known. Empirical findings are consistent with these expectations.[9]

Given these observations, it is not surprising to see firms in new and uncertain environments develop numerous strategic alliances. This is one of the reasons that strategic alliances are so common in the biotechnology industry. Although there is relatively little uncertainty that at least some drugs created through biotechnology will ultimately prove to be very valuable, which specific drugs will turn out to be the most valuable is very uncertain. Rather than investing in a small number of biotechnology drugs on their own, pharmaceutical companies have invested in numerous strategic alliances with small biotechnology firms. Each of these smaller firms represents a particular "bet" about the value of biotechnology in a particular class of drugs. If one of these "bets" turns out to be valuable, then the large pharmaceutical firm that has invested in that firm has the right, but not the obligation, to purchase the rest of this company. In this sense, from the point of view of the pharmaceutical firms, alliances between large pharmaceutical firms and small biotechnology firms can be thought of as real options.

Alliance Threats: Incentives to Cheat on Strategic Alliances

Just as there are incentives to cooperate in strategic alliances, there are also incentives to cheat on these cooperative agreements. Indeed, research shows that as many as one-third of all strategic alliances do not meet the expectations of at least one alliance partner.[10] Although some of these alliance "failures" may be due to firms forming alliances that do not have the potential for creating value, some are also due to parties to an alliance cheating—that is, not cooperating in a way that maximizes the value of the alliance. Cheating can occur in at least the three different ways presented in Table 9.2: adverse selection, moral hazard, and holdup.[11]

TABLE 9.2 Ways to Cheat in Strategic Alliances

- *Adverse selection*: Potential partners misrepresent the value of the skills and abilities they bring to the alliance.
- *Moral hazard*: Partners provide to the alliance skills and abilities of lower quality than they promised.
- *Holdup*: Partners exploit the transaction-specific investments made by others in the alliance.

Adverse Selection

Potential cooperative partners can misrepresent the skills, abilities, and other resources that they will bring to an alliance. This form of cheating, called **adverse selection,** exists when an alliance partner promises to bring to an alliance certain resources that it either does not control or cannot acquire. For example, a local firm engages in adverse selection when it promises to make available to alliance partners a local distribution network that does not currently exist. Firms that engage in adverse selection are not competent alliance partners.

Adverse selection in a strategic alliance is likely only when it is difficult or costly to observe the resources or capabilities that a partner brings to an alliance. If potential partners can easily see that a firm is misrepresenting the resources and capabilities it possesses, they will not create a strategic alliance with that firm. Armed with such understanding, they will seek a different alliance partner, develop the needed skills and resources internally, or perhaps forgo this particular business opportunity.

However, evaluating the veracity of the claims of potential alliance partners is often not easy. The ability to evaluate these claims depends on information that a firm may not possess. To fully evaluate claims about a potential partner's political contacts, for example, a firm needs its own political contacts; to fully evaluate claims about potential partners' market knowledge, a firm needs significant market knowledge. A firm that can completely, and at low cost, evaluate the resources and capabilities of potential alliance partners probably does not really need these partners in a strategic alliance. The fact that a firm is seeking an alliance partner is in some sense an indication that the firm has limited abilities to evaluate potential partners.

In general, the less tangible the resources and capabilities that are to be brought to a strategic alliance, the more costly it will be to estimate their value before an alliance is created, and the more likely it is that adverse selection will occur. Firms considering alliances with partners that bring intangible resources such as "knowledge of local conditions" or "contacts with key political figures" will need to guard against this form of cheating.

Moral Hazard

Partners in an alliance may possess high-quality resources and capabilities of significant value in an alliance but fail to make those resources and capabilities available to alliance partners. This form of cheating is called **moral hazard.** For example, a partner in an engineering strategic alliance may agree to send only its most talented and best-trained engineers to work in the alliance but then actually send less talented, poorly trained engineers. These less qualified engineers may not be able to contribute substantially to making the alliance successful, but they may be able to learn a great deal from the highly qualified engineers provided by other alliance partners. In this way, the less qualified engineers effectively transfer wealth from other alliance partners to their own firm.[12]

Often both parties in a failed alliance accuse each other of moral hazard. This was the case in the abandoned alliance between Disney and Pixar, described in the Strategy in the Emerging Enterprise feature.

The existence of moral hazard in a strategic alliance does not necessarily mean that any of the parties to that alliance are malicious or dishonest. Rather, what often happens is that market conditions change after an alliance is formed, requiring one or more partners to an alliance to change their strategies.

For example, in the early days of the personal computer industry Compaq Computer Corporation relied on a network of independent distributors to sell its computers. However, as competition in the personal computer industry increased, Internet, mail order, and so-called computer superstores became much more valuable distribution networks, and alliances between Compaq and its traditional distributors became strained. Over time, Compaq's traditional distributors were unable to obtain the inventory they wanted in a timely manner. Indeed, to satisfy the needs of large accounts, some traditional distributors actually purchased Compaq computers from local computer superstores and then shipped them to their customers. Compaq's shift from independent dealers to alternative distributors looked like moral hazard—at least from the point of view of the independent dealers. However, from Compaq's perspective, this change simply reflected economic realities in the personal computer industry.[13]

Holdup

Even if alliance partners do not engage in either adverse selection or moral hazard, another form of cheating may evolve. Once a strategic alliance has been created, partner firms may make investments that have value only in the context of that alliance and in no other economic exchanges. These are the transaction-specific investments mentioned in Chapter 6. For example, managers from one alliance partner may have to develop close, trusting relationships with managers from other alliance partners. These close relationships are very valuable in the context of the alliance, but they have limited economic value in other economic exchanges. Also, one partner may have to customize its manufacturing equipment, distribution network, and key organizational policies to cooperate with other partners. These modifications have significant value in the context of the alliance, but they do not help the firm, and may even hurt it, in economic exchanges outside the alliance. As was the case in Chapter 6, whenever an investment's value in its first-best use (in this case, within the alliance) is much greater than its value in its second-best use (in this case, outside the alliance), that investment is said to be **transaction specific.**[14]

When one firm makes more transaction-specific investments in a strategic alliance than partner firms make, that firm may be subject to the form of cheating called **holdup.** Holdup occurs when a firm that has not made significant transaction-specific investments demands returns from an alliance that are higher than the partners agreed to when they created the alliance.

For example, suppose two alliance partners agree to a 50–50 split of the costs and profits associated with an alliance. To make the alliance work, Firm A has to customize its production process. Firm B, however, does not have to modify itself to cooperate with Firm A. The value to Firm A of this customized production process, if it is used in the strategic alliance, is $5,000. However, outside the alliance, this customized process is only worth $200 (as scrap).

Obviously, Firm A has made a transaction-specific investment in this alliance and Firm B has not. Consequently, Firm A may be subject to holdup by Firm B. In particular, Firm B may threaten to leave the alliance unless Firm A agrees to give Firm B part of the $5,000 value that Firm A obtains by using the modified production process in the alliance. Rather than lose all the value that could be generated by its investment, Firm A may be willing to give up some of its $5,000 to avoid gaining only $200. Indeed, if Firm B extracts up to the value of Firm A's production process in its next-best use (here, only $200), Firm A will still be better off continuing in this relationship rather than dissolving it. Thus, even though Firm A and Firm B initially agreed on a 50–50 split from this strategic alliance, the agreement may be modified if one party to the alliance makes significant transaction-specific investments. Research on international joint ventures suggests that the existence of transaction-specific investments in these relationships often leads to holdup problems.[15]

Strategy in the Emerging Enterprise

In 1994, Pixar was a struggling startup company in northern California that was trying to compete in an industry that really didn't yet exist—the computer graphics animated motion picture industry. Headed by the founder of Apple Computer, Steve Jobs, Pixar was desperately looking for a partner that could help finance and distribute its new brand of animated movies. Who better, Pixar thought, than the world's leader in animated feature-length films: Disney. And, thus, a strategic alliance between Pixar and Disney was formed.

In the alliance, Disney agreed to help finance and distribute Pixar's films. In return, it would share in any profits these films generated. Also, Disney would retain the right to produce any sequels to Pixar's films—after first offering Pixar the right to make these sequels. This agreement gave Disney a great deal of control over any characters that Pixar created in movies distributed through Pixar's alliance with Disney. Of course, at the time the alliance was originally formed there were no such characters. Indeed, Pixar had yet to produce any movies. So, because Pixar was a weak alliance partner, Disney was able to gain control of any characters Pixar developed in the future. Disney, after all, had the track record of success.

A funny thing happened over the next 10 years. Pixar produced blockbuster animated features such as *Toy Story* (total revenues of $419.9 million); *A Bug's Life* (total revenues of $358 million); *Toy Story 2* (total revenues of

Disney and Pixar

$629.9 million); *Monsters, Inc.* (total revenues of $903.1 million); *Finding Nemo* (total revenues of $1,281.4 million); *The Incredibles* (total revenues of $946.6 million); and *Cars* (total revenues of $331.9 million). And these revenue numbers do not include sales of merchandise associated with these films. During this same time period, Disney's traditional animated fare performed much more poorly—*Treasure Planet* generated only $112 million in revenues, *The Emperor's New Groove* only $169 million, and *Brother Bear* only $126 million. Disney's "big hit" during this time period was *Lilo & Stitch*, with revenues of $269 million—less than any of the movies produced by Pixar.

Oops! The firm with the "proven track record" of producing hit animated features—Disney—stumbled badly, and the upstart company with no track record—Pixar—had all the success. Because Disney did not have many of its own characters upon which to base sequels, it began to eye Pixar's characters.

Fast-forward to 2004. It's time to renew this alliance. But now Pixar has the upper hand because it has the track record. Disney comes knocking and asks Pixar to redo the alliance. What does Pixar say? "OK, but … we want control of our characters, we want Disney to act just as a distributor"—in other words, "We want Disney out of our business!" Disney balks at these demands, and Pixar—well, Pixar just canceled the alliance.

But Pixar still needed a distribution partner. Pixar simply does not produce enough films to justify the expense of building its own distribution system. After a several-month search, Pixar found what it considered to be its best distribution partner. The only problem was—it was Disney.

Reestablishing the alliance between Pixar and Disney seemed out of the question. After all, such an alliance would have all the same challenges as the previous alliance.

Instead, Disney decided to buy Pixar. On January 25, 2006, Disney announced that it was buying Pixar in a deal worth $7.4 billion. Steve Jobs became Disney's single largest investor and became a member of Disney's board of directors. John Lasseter—the creative force behind Pixar's success—became chief creative officer at Disney.

Sources: S. Levy and D. Jefferson (2004). "Hey Mickey, buzz off!" *BusinessWeek*, February 9, p. 4; T. Lowry et al. (2004). "Megamedia mergers: How dangerous?" *BusinessWeek*, February 23, pp. 34+; and money.cnn.com/2006/01/24/newscompanies/disney_pixar_deal.

Although holdup is a form of cheating in strategic alliances, the threat of holdup can also be a motivation for creating an alliance. Bauxite-smelting companies often join in joint ventures with mining companies in order to exploit economies of scale in mining. However, these firms have another option: They could choose to operate large and efficient mines by themselves and then sell the excess bauxite (over and above their needs for their own smelters) on the open market. Unfortunately, bauxite is not a homogeneous commodity. Moreover, different kinds of bauxite require different smelting technologies. In order for one firm to sell its excess bauxite on the market, other smelting firms would have to make enormous investments, the sole purpose of which would be to refine that particular firm's bauxite. These investments would be transaction specific and subject these other smelters to holdup problems.

In this context, a strategic alliance can be thought of as a way of reducing the threat of holdup by creating an explicit management framework for resolving holdup problems. In other words, although holdup problems might still exist in these strategic alliances, the alliance framework may still be a better way in which to manage these problems than attempting to manage them in arm's-length market relationships. Some of the ethical dimensions of adverse selection, moral hazard, and holdup are discussed in the Ethics and Strategy feature.

Strategic Alliances and Sustained Competitive Advantage

The ability of strategic alliances to be sources of sustained competitive advantage, like all the other strategies discussed in this book, can be analyzed with the VRIO framework developed in Chapter 3. An alliance is economically valuable when it exploits any of the opportunities listed in Table 9.1 but avoids the threats in Table 9.2. In addition, for a strategic alliance to be a source of sustained competitive advantage it must be rare and costly to imitate.

The Rarity of Strategic Alliances

The rarity of strategic alliances does not only depend on the number of competing firms that have already implemented an alliance. It also depends on whether the benefits that firms obtain from their alliances are common across firms competing in an industry.

Consider, for example, the U.S. automobile industry. Over the past several years, strategic alliances have become very common in this industry, especially with Japanese auto firms. General Motors developed an alliance with Toyota that has already been described; Ford developed an alliance with Mazda before it purchased this Japanese firm outright; and Chrysler developed an alliance with Mitsubishi. Given the frequency with which alliances have developed in this industry, it is tempting to conclude that strategic alliances are not rare and thus not a source of competitive advantage.

Closer examination, however, suggests that these alliances may have been created for different reasons. For example, until recently, GM and Toyota have cooperated only in building a single line of cars, the Chevrolet Nova. General Motors has been less interested in learning design skills from Toyota and has been more interested in learning about manufacturing high-quality small cars profitably. Ford and Mazda, in contrast, worked closely together in designing new cars and had joint manufacturing operations. Indeed, Ford and Mazda worked so closely together that Ford finally once purchased 33 percent of Mazda's stock. Since 2008, Ford has reduced its investment in Mazda dramatically. Mitsubishi has acted primarily as a supplier to Chrysler, and (until recently) there has been relatively little joint development or manufacturing. Thus, although all three U.S. firms have strategic alliances, the alliances serve different purposes, and therefore each may be rare.[16]

One of the reasons why the benefits that accrue from a particular strategic alliance may be rare is that relatively few firms may have the complementary resources and abilities needed to form an alliance. This is particularly likely when an alliance is formed to enter into a new market, especially a new foreign market. In many less-developed economies, only one local firm or very few local firms may exist with the local knowledge, contacts, and distribution network needed to facilitate entry into that market. Moreover, sometimes the government acts to limit the number of these local firms. Although several firms may seek entry into this market, only a very small number will be able to form a strategic alliance with the local entity, and therefore the benefits that accrue to the allied firms will likely be rare.

The Imitability of Strategic Alliances

As discussed in Chapter 3, the resources and capabilities that enable firms to conceive and implement valuable strategies may be imitated in two ways: direct duplication and substitution. Both duplication and substitution are important considerations in analyzing the imitability of strategic alliances.

Direct Duplication of Strategic Alliances

Research suggests that successful strategic alliances are often based on socially complex relations among alliance partners.[17] In this sense, successful strategic alliances often go well beyond simple legal contracts and are characterized by socially complex phenomena such as a trusting relationship between alliance partners, friendship, and even (perhaps) a willingness to suspend narrow self-interest for the longer-term good of the relationship.

Some research has shown that the development of trusting relationships between alliance partners is both difficult and essential to the success of strategic alliances. In one study, the most common reason that alliances failed to meet the expectations of partner firms was the partners' inability to trust one another. Interpersonal communication, tolerance for cultural differences, patience, and willingness to sacrifice short-term profits for longer-term success were all important determinants of the level of trust among alliance partners.[18]

Of course, not all firms in an industry are likely to have the organizational and relationship-building skills required for successful alliance building. If these skills and abilities are rare among a set of competing firms and costly to develop, then firms that are able to exploit these abilities by creating alliances may gain competitive advantages. Examples of firms that have developed these specialized skills include Corning and Cisco, with several hundred strategic alliances each.[19]

Ethics and Strategy

Firms in strategic alliances can cheat on their alliance partners by engaging in adverse selection, moral hazard, or holdup. These three activities all have at least one thing in common—they all involve one alliance partner lying to another. And these lies can often pay off big in the form of the lying firm appropriating more than its "fair share" of the value created in an alliance. Are alliances one place in the economy where the adage "cheaters never prosper" does not hold?

There is little doubt that, in the short run, firms that cheat on their alliance partners can gain some advantages. But research suggests that cheating does not pay in the long run because firms that cheat on their alliance partners will find it difficult to form alliances with new partners and thus have many valuable exchange opportunities foreclosed to them.

One study that examined the long-term return to "cheaters" in strategic alliances analyzed alliances using a simple game called the "Prisoner's Dilemma." In a "Prisoner's Dilemma" game, firms have two options: to continue cooperating in a strategic alliance or to "cheat" on that alliance through adverse selection, moral hazard, or holdup. The payoffs to firms in this game depend on the decisions made by both firms. As shown in Table 9.3, if both firms decide to cooperate, they

When It Comes to Alliances, Do "Cheaters Never Prosper"?

each get a good size payoff from the alliance ($3,000 in Table 9.3); if they both decide to cheat on the alliance, they each get a very small payoff ($1,000 in Table 9.3); and if one decides to cheat while the other decides to cooperate, then the cheating firm gets a very big payoff ($5,000 in Table 9.3) while the co-operating firm gets a very small payoff ($0 in Table 9.3).

If Firm 1 and Firm 2 in this game are going to engage in only one strategic alliance, then they have a very strong incentive to "cheat." The worst that could happen if they cheat is that they earn a $1,000 payoff, but there is a possibility of a $5,000 payoff. However, research has shown that if

a firm is contemplating engaging in multiple strategic alliances over time, then the optimal strategy is to cooperate in all its alliances. This is true even if all these alliances are not with the same partner firm.

The specific "winning" strategy in repeated "Prisoner Dilemma" games is called a "tit-for-tat" strategy. "Tit-for-tat" means that Firm 1 will cooperate in an alliance as long as Firm 2 cooperates. However, as soon as Firm 2 cheats on an alliance, Firm 1 cheats as well. "Tit-for-tat" works well in this setting because adopting a cooperative posture in an alliance ensures that, most of the time, the alliance will generate a high payoff (of $3,000 in Table 9.3). However, by immediately responding to cheaters by cheating, the firm implementing a "tit-for-tat" strategy also minimizes the times when it will earn the lowest payoff in the table ($0). So, "tit-for-tat" maximizes the upside potential of an alliance while minimizing its downside.

All this analysis suggests that although cheating on an alliance can give a firm competitive advantages in the short to medium term, in the long run, "cheaters never prosper."

Sources: R. M. Axelrod (1984). *The evolution of cooperation.* New York: Basic Books; D. Ernst and J. Bleeke (1993). *Collaborating to compete.* New York: Wiley.

TABLE 9.3 Returns from Cooperating and Cheating in a "Prisoner's Dilemma"

		Strategic Alliance	
Firm 1			
		Cooperates	Cheats
	Cooperates	1: $3,000	1: $5,000
		2: $3,000	2: $0
Firm 2			
	Cheats	1: $0	1: $1,000
		2: $5,000	2: $1,000

Substitutes for Strategic Alliances

Even if the purpose and objectives of a strategic alliance are valuable and rare and even if the relationships on which an alliance is created are socially complex and costly to imitate, that alliance will still not generate a sustained competitive advantage if low-cost substitutes are available. At least two possible substitutes for strategic alliances exist: "going it alone" and acquisitions.[20]

"Going It Alone."   Firms "go it alone" when they attempt to develop all the resources and capabilities they need to exploit market opportunities and neutralize market threats by themselves. Sometimes "going it alone" can create the same—or even more—value than using alliances to exploit opportunities and neutralize threats. In these settings, "going it alone" is a substitute for a strategic alliance. However, in other settings using an alliance can create substantially more value than "going it alone." In these settings, "going it alone" is not a substitute for a strategic alliance.

So, when will firms prefer an alliance over "going it alone"? Not surprisingly, the three explanations of vertical integration, discussed in Chapter 6, are relevant here as well. These three explanations focused on the threat of opportunism, the impact of firm resources and capabilities, and the role of uncertainty. If you need to review these three explanations, they are described in detail in Chapter 6. They are relevant here because "going it alone"—as a potential substitute for a strategic alliance—is an example of vertical integration. The implications of these three explanations for when strategic alliances will be preferred over "going it alone" are summarized in Table 9.4. If any of the conditions listed in Table 9.4 exist, then "going it alone" will not be a substitute for strategic alliances.

Recall from Chapter 6 that opportunism-based explanations of vertical integration suggest that firms will want to vertically integrate an economic exchange when they have made high levels of transaction-specific investment in that exchange. That is, using language developed in this chapter, firms will want to vertically integrate an economic exchange when using an alliance to manage that exchange could subject them to holdup. Extending this logic to strategic alliances suggests that strategic alliances will be preferred over "going it alone" and other alternatives when the level of transaction-specific investment required to complete an exchange is moderate. If the level of this specific investment is low, then market forms of exchange will be preferred; if the level of this specific investment is high, then "going it alone" in a vertically integrated way will be preferred; if the level of this specific investment is moderate, then some sort of strategic alliance will be preferred. Thus, when the level of specific exchange in a transaction is moderate, then "going it alone" is not a substitute for a strategic alliance.

Alliances will be preferred over "going it alone" when:

1. The level of transaction-specific investment required to complete an exchange is moderate.
2. An exchange partner possesses valuable, rare, and costly-to-imitate resources and capabilities.
3. There is great uncertainty about the future value of an exchange.

TABLE 9.4 When Alliances Will Be Preferred Over "Going It Alone"

Capabilities-based explanations suggest that an alliance will be preferred over "going it alone" when an exchange partner possesses valuable, rare, and costly-to-imitate resources and capabilities. A firm without these capabilities may find them to be too costly to develop on its own. If a firm must have access to capabilities it cannot develop on its own, it must use an alliance to gain access to those capabilities. In this setting, "going it alone" is not a substitute for a strategic alliance.[21]

Finally, it has already been suggested that, under conditions of high uncertainty, firms may be unwilling to commit to a particular course of action by engaging in an exchange within a firm. In such settings, firms may choose the strategic flexibility associated with alliances. As suggested earlier in this chapter, alliances can be thought of as real options that give a firm the right, but not the obligation, to invest further in an exchange—perhaps by bringing it within the boundaries of a firm—if that exchange turns out to be valuable sometime in the future. Thus, under conditions of high uncertainty, "going it alone" is not a substitute for strategic alliances.

Acquisitions.   The acquisition of other firms can also be a substitute for alliances. In this case, rather than developing a strategic alliance or attempting to develop and exploit the relevant resources by "going it alone," a firm seeking to exploit the opportunities listed in Table 9.1 may simply acquire another firm that already possesses the relevant resources and capabilities. However, such acquisitions have four characteristics that often limit the extent to which they can act as substitutes for strategic alliances. These are summarized in Table 9.5.[22]

First, there may be legal constraints on acquisitions. These are especially likely if firms are seeking advantages by combining with other firms in their own industry. Thus, for example, using acquisitions as a substitute for strategic alliances in the aluminum industry would lead to a very concentrated industry and subject some of these firms to serious antitrust liabilities. These firms have acquisitions foreclosed to them and must look elsewhere to gain advantages from cooperating with their competition.

Second, as has already been suggested, strategic alliances enable a firm to retain its flexibility either to enter or not to enter into a new business. Acquisitions limit that flexibility because they represent a strong commitment to engage in a certain business activity. Consequently, under conditions of high uncertainty firms may choose strategic alliances over acquisitions as a way to exploit opportunities while maintaining the flexibility that alliances create.

Third, firms may choose strategic alliances over acquisitions because of the unwanted organizational baggage that often comes with an acquisition. Sometimes, the value created by combining firms depends on combining particular functions, divisions, or other assets in the firms. A strategic alliance can focus on exploiting the value of combining just those parts of firms that create the most

TABLE 9.5 Reasons Why Strategic Alliances May Be More Attractive Than Acquisitions to Realize Exchange Opportunities

Alliances will be preferred to acquisitions when:

1. There are legal constraints on acquisitions.
2. Acquisitions limit a firm's flexibility under conditions of high uncertainty.
3. There is substantial unwanted organizational "baggage" in an acquired firm.
4. The value of a firm's resources and capabilities depends on its independence.

value. Acquisitions, in contrast, generally include the entire organization, both the parts of a firm where value is likely to be created and parts of a firm where value is not likely to be created.

From the point of view of the acquiring firm, parts of a firm that do not create value are essentially unwanted baggage. These parts of the firm may be sold off subsequent to an acquisition. However, this sell-off may be costly and time consuming. If enough baggage exists, firms may determine that an acquisition is not a viable option, even though important economic value could be created between a firm and a potential acquisition target. To gain this value, an alternative approach—a strategic alliance—may be preferred. These issues will be explored in more detail in Chapter 10.

Finally, sometimes a firm's resources and capabilities are valuable because that firm is independent. In this setting, the act of acquiring a firm can actually reduce the value of a firm. When this is the case, any value between two firms is best realized through an alliance, not an acquisition. For example, the international growth of numerous marketing-oriented companies in the 1980s led to strong pressures for advertising agencies to develop global marketing capabilities. During the 1990s, many domestic-only advertising firms acquired nondomestic agencies to form a few large international advertising agencies. However, one firm that was reluctant to be acquired in order to be part of an international advertising network was the French advertising company Publicis. Over and above the personal interests of its owners to retain control of the company, Publicis wanted to remain an independent French agency in order to retain its stable of French and French-speaking clients—including Renault and Nestlé. These firms had indicated that they preferred working with a French advertising agency and that they would look for alternative suppliers if Publicis were acquired by a foreign firm. Because much of the value that Publicis created in a potential acquisition depended on obtaining access to its stable of clients, the act of acquiring Publicis would have had the effect of destroying the very thing that made the acquisition attractive. For this reason, rather than allowing itself to be acquired by foreign advertising agencies, Publicis developed a complex equity strategic alliance and joint venture with a U.S. advertising firm, Foote, Coyne, and Belding. Although, ultimately, this alliance was not successful in providing an international network for either of these two partner firms, an acquisition of Publicis by Foote, Coyne, and Belding would almost certainly have destroyed some of the economic value that Publicis enjoyed as a stand-alone company.

Organizing to Implement Strategic Alliances

V R I O

One of the most important determinants of the success of strategic alliances is their organization. The primary purpose of organizing a strategic alliance is to enable partners in the alliance to gain all the benefits associated with cooperation while minimizing the probability that cooperating firms will cheat on their cooperative agreements. The organizing skills required in managing alliances are, in many ways, unique. It often takes some time for firms to learn these skills and realize the full potential of their alliances. This is why some firms are able to gain competitive advantages from managing alliances more effectively than their competitors. Indeed, sometimes firms may have to choose alternatives to alliances—including "going it alone" and acquisitions—even when those alternatives are not preferred, simply because they do not have the skills required to organize and manage alliances.

A variety of tools and mechanisms can be used to help realize the value of alliances and minimize the threat of cheating. These include contracts, equity investments, firm reputations, joint ventures, and trust.

Explicit Contracts and Legal Sanctions

One way to avoid cheating in strategic alliances is for the parties to an alliance to anticipate the ways in which cheating may occur (including adverse selection, moral hazard, and holdup) and to write explicit contracts that define legal liability if cheating does occur. Writing these contracts, together with the close monitoring of contractual compliance and the threat of legal sanctions, can reduce the probability of cheating. Earlier in this chapter, such strategic alliances were called nonequity alliances.

However, contracts sometimes fail to anticipate all forms of cheating that might occur in a relationship—and firms may cheat on cooperative agreements in subtle ways that are difficult to evaluate in terms of contractual requirements. Thus, for example, a contract may require parties in a strategic alliance to make available to the alliance certain proprietary technologies or processes. However, it may be very difficult to communicate the subtleties of these technologies or processes to alliance partners. Does this failure in communication represent a clear violation of contractual requirements, or does it represent a good-faith effort by alliance partners? Moreover, how can one partner tell whether it is obtaining all the necessary information about a technology or process when it is unaware of all the information that exists in another firm? Hence, although contracts are an important component of most strategic alliances, they do not resolve all the problems associated with cheating.

Although most contracts associated with strategic alliances are highly customized, these different contracts do have some common features. These common features are described in detail in Table 9.6. In general, firms contemplating a strategic alliance that will be at least partially governed by a contract will have to include clauses that address the issues presented in Table 9.6.

Equity Investments

The effectiveness of contracts can be enhanced by having partners in an alliance make equity investments in each other. When Firm A buys a substantial equity position in its alliance partner, Firm B, the market value of Firm A now depends, to some extent, on the economic performance of that partner. The incentive of Firm A to cheat Firm B falls, for to do so would be to reduce the economic performance of Firm B and thus the value of Firm A's investment in its partner. These kinds of strategic alliances are called equity alliances.

Many firms use cross-equity investments to help manage their strategic alliances. These arrangements are particularly common in Japan, where a firm's largest equity holders often include several of its key suppliers, including its main banks. These equity investments, because they reduce the threat of cheating in alliances with suppliers, can reduce these firms' supply costs. In turn, not only do firms have equity positions in their suppliers, but suppliers often have substantial equity positions in the firms to which they sell.[23]

TABLE 9.6 Common Clauses in Contracts Used to Govern Strategic Alliances

Establishment Issues

Shareholdings: Percentage of JV owned by various partners

Voting rights: Votes held by various partners

Dividend percentage: How profits are to be allocated

Minority protection: How minority owner interests are protected

Board of directors: Initial board and rules for modifying the board

Articles of association: Processes for making decisions

Place of incorporation

Accountants, lawyers, and other advisors

Operating Issues

Performance expectations

Noncompete agreements

Nonsolicitation clauses: Partners cannot recruit employees from each other

Confidentiality clauses

Licensing intellectual property rights: Who owns the intellectual property created by a joint venture?

Liability of the alliance and liability of cooperating partners

Process of changing the contract

Process of resolving disputes

Termination Issues

Preemption rights: If one partner wishes to sell its shares, it must first offer them to the other partner

When one partner can force the other partner to sell its shares to it

When a partner has the right to force another partner to buy its alliance shares

Drag-along rights: When one partner can arrange a sale to an outside firm and force the other partner to sell shares as well

Tag-along rights: When one partner can prevent the sale of the second partner's shares to an outside firm unless that outside firm also buys the first partner's shares

When an initial public offering (IPO) will be pursued

Termination: When the JV can be terminated

Source: Based on E. Campbell and J. Reuer (2001). "Note on the legal negotiation of strategic alliance agreements." Copyright © 2000 INSEAD.

Firm Reputations

A third constraint on incentives to cheat in strategic alliances exists in the effect that a reputation for cheating has on a firm's future opportunities. Although it is often difficult to anticipate all the different ways in which an alliance partner may cheat, it is often easier to describe after the fact how an alliance partner has cheated. Information about an alliance partner that has cheated is likely to become widely known. A firm with a reputation as a cheater is not likely to be able to develop strategic alliances with other partners in the future, despite any special resources or capabilities that it might be able to bring to an alliance. In this way, cheating in a current alliance may foreclose opportunities for developing other valuable alliances. For this reason, firms may decide not to cheat in their current alliances.[24]

Substantial evidence suggests that the effect of reputation on future business opportunities is important. Firms go to great lengths to make sure that they do not develop a negative reputation. Nevertheless, this reputational control of cheating in strategic alliances does have several limitations.[25]

First, subtle cheating in a strategic alliance may not become public, and if it does become public, the responsibility for the failure of the strategic alliance may be very ambiguous. In one equity joint venture attempting to perfect the design of a new turbine for power generation, financial troubles made one partner considerably more anxious than the other partner to complete product development. The financially healthy, and thus patient, partner believed that if the alliance required an additional infusion of capital, the financially troubled partner would have to abandon the alliance and would have to sell its part of the alliance at a relatively low price. The patient partner thus encouraged alliance engineers to work slowly and carefully in the guise of developing the technology to reach its full potential. The financially troubled, and thus impatient, partner encouraged alliance engineers to work quickly, perhaps sacrificing some quality to develop the technology sooner. Eventually, the impatient partner ran out of money, sold its share of the alliance to the patient partner at a reduced price, and accused the patient partner of not acting in good faith to facilitate the rapid development of the new technology. The patient partner accused the other firm of pushing the technology too quickly, thereby sacrificing quality and, perhaps, worker safety. In some sense, both firms were cheating on their agreement to develop the new technology cooperatively. However, this cheating was subtle and difficult to spot and had relatively little impact on the reputation of either firm or on the ability of either firm to establish alliances in the future. It is likely that most observers would simply conclude that the patient partner obtained a windfall because of the impatient partner's bad luck.[26]

Second, although one partner to an alliance may be unambiguously cheating on the relationship, one or both of the firms may not be sufficiently connected into a network with other firms to make this information public. When information about cheating remains private, public reputations are not tarnished and future opportunities are not forgone. This is especially likely to happen if one or both alliance partners operate in less-developed economies where information about partner behavior may not be rapidly diffused to other firms or to other countries.

Finally, the effect of a tarnished reputation, as long as cheating in an alliance is unambiguous and publicly known, may foreclose future opportunities for a firm, but it does little to address the current losses experienced by the firm that was cheated. Moreover, any of the forms of cheating discussed earlier—adverse selection, moral hazard, or holdup—can result in substantial losses for a firm currently in an alliance. Indeed, the wealth created by cheating in a current alliance may be large enough to make a firm willing to forgo future alliances. In this case, a tarnished reputation may be of minor consequence to a cheating firm.[27]

Joint Ventures

A fourth way to reduce the threat of cheating is for partners in a strategic alliance to invest in a joint venture. Creating a separate legal entity, in which alliance partners invest and from whose profits they earn returns on their investments, reduces some of the risks of cheating in strategic alliances. When a joint venture is created, the ability of partners to earn returns on their investments depends on the economic success of the joint venture. Partners in joint ventures have limited interests in behaving in ways that hurt the performance of the joint venture because such behaviors end up hurting both partners. Moreover, unlike reputational consequences of cheating, cheating in a joint venture does not just foreclose future alliance opportunities; it can hurt the cheating firm in the current period as well.

Given the advantages of joint ventures in controlling cheating, it is not surprising that when the probability of cheating in a cooperative relationship is greatest, a joint venture is usually the preferred form of cooperation. For example, bauxite mining has some clear economies of scale. However, transaction-specific investments would lead to significant holdup problems in selling excess bauxite in the open market, and legal constraints prevent the acquisition of other smelter companies to create an intraorganizational demand for excess bauxite. Holdup problems would continue to exist in any mining strategic alliances that might be created. Nonequity alliances, equity alliances, and reputational effects are not likely to restrain cheating in this situation because the returns on holdup, once transaction-specific investments are in place, can be very large. Thus, most of the strategic alliances created to mine bauxite take the form of joint ventures. Only this form of strategic alliance is likely to create incentives strong enough to significantly reduce the probability of cheating.[28]

Despite these strengths, joint ventures are not able to reduce all cheating in an alliance without cost. Sometimes the value of cheating in a joint venture is sufficiently large that a firm cheats even though doing so hurts the joint venture and forecloses future opportunities. For example, a particular firm may gain access to a technology through a joint venture that would be valuable if used in another of its lines of business. This firm may be tempted to transfer this technology to this other line of business even if it has agreed not to do so and even if doing so would limit the performance of its joint venture. Because the profits earned in this other line of business may have a greater value than the returns that could have been earned in the joint venture and the returns that could have been earned in the future with other strategic alliances, cheating may occur.

Trust

It is sometimes the case that alliance partners rely only on legalistic and narrowly economic approaches to manage their alliance. However, recent work seems to suggest that although successful alliance partners do not ignore legal and economic disincentives to cheating, they strongly support these narrower linkages with a rich set of interpersonal relations and trust. Trust, in combination with contracts, can help reduce the threat of cheating. More important, trust may enable partners to explore exchange opportunities that they could not explore if only legal and economic organizing mechanisms were in place.[29]

At first glance, this argument may seem far-fetched. However, some research offers support for this approach to managing strategic alliances, suggesting that successful alliance partners typically do not specify all the terms and conditions in their relationship in a legal contract and do not specify all possible forms of cheating and their consequences. Moreover, when joint ventures are formed, partners do not always insist on simple 50–50 splits of equity ownership and profit sharing. Rather, successful alliances involve trust, a willingness to be flexible, a willingness to learn, and a willingness to let the alliance develop in ways that the partners could not have anticipated.[30]

Commitment, coordination, and trust are all important determinants of alliance success. Put another way, a strategic alliance is a relationship that evolves over time. Allowing the lawyers and economists to too rigorously define, a priori, the boundaries of that relationship may limit it and stunt its development.[31]

This "trust" approach also has implications for the extent to which strategic alliances may be sources of sustained competitive advantage for firms. The ability to move into strategic alliances in this trusting way may be very valuable over the long run. There is strong reason to believe that this ability is not uniformly distributed across all firms that might have an interest in forming strategic alliances and that this ability may be history-dependent and socially complex and thus costly to imitate. Firms with these skills may be able to gain sustained competitive advantages from their alliance relationships. The observation that just a few firms, including Corning and Cisco, are well-known for their strategic alliance successes is consistent with the observation that these alliance management skills may be valuable, rare, and costly to imitate.

Summary

Strategic alliances exist whenever two or more organizations cooperate in the development, manufacture, or sale of products or services. Strategic alliances can be grouped into three large categories: nonequity alliances, equity alliances, and joint ventures.

Firms join in strategic alliances for three broad reasons: to improve the performance of their current operations, to improve the competitive environment within which they are operating, and to facilitate entry into or exit from markets and industries. Just as there are incentives to cooperate in strategic alliances, there are also incentives to cheat. Cheating generally takes one or a combination of three forms: adverse selection, moral hazard, or holdup.

Strategic alliances can be a source of sustained competitive advantage. The rarity of alliances depends not only on the number of competing firms that have developed an alliance, but also on the benefits that firms gain through their alliances.

Imitation through direct duplication of an alliance may be costly because of the socially complex relations that underlie an alliance; however, imitation through substitution is more likely. Two substitutes for alliances may be "going it alone," where firms develop and exploit the relevant sets of resources and capabilities on their own, and acquisitions. Opportunism, capabilities, and uncertainty all have an impact on when "going it alone" will be a substitute for a strategic alliance. Acquisitions may be a substitute for strategic alliances when there are no legal constraints, strategic flexibility is not an important consideration, when the acquired firm has relatively little unwanted "organizational baggage," and when the value of a firm's resources and capabilities does not depend on its remaining independent. However, when these conditions do not exist, acquisitions are not a substitute for alliances.

The key issue facing firms in organizing their alliances is to facilitate cooperation while avoiding the threat of cheating. Contracts, equity investments, firm reputations, joint ventures, and trust can all reduce the threat of cheating in different contexts.

MyManagementLab®

Go to **mymanagementlab.com** to complete the problems marked with this icon ⊗ .

Challenge Questions

9.1. In strategic alliances, organizations have several options beyond that of an equity alliance, such as joint ventures and a spectrum of non-equity alliance choices. Then why would a company want to participate in an equity alliance by investing in a partner's firm?

9.2. In the 21st century, many organizations feel compelled to partner for expansion, particularly in an international situation. Options include exporting or licensing one's intellectual property in a low risk exercise where royalties can have high profit margins. In addition, franchising can provide very lucrative continuous cash flow opportunities as a fraction of the franchisee's revenue. Why do companies engage in joint ventures when there exist many other forms of non-equity options for expansion?

9.3. Consider the joint venture between General Motors and Toyota. GM has been interested in learning how to profitably manufacture high-quality small cars from its alliance with Toyota. Toyota has been interested in gaining access to GM's U.S. distribution network and in reducing the political liability associated with local content laws. What implications, if any, does this alliance have for a possible "learning race?"

9.4. An exclusive distributorship agreement entered into by a manufacturer (the principal) with an organization can constitute a strategic alliance. On the other hand, some companies appoint a huge number of partners to resell their product, in a form known as intensive distribution. Why would a principal restrict themselves to one partner alone when more distributors may provide a wider breadth of coverage?

⭐ **9.5.** How can one tell whether two firms are engaging in an alliance to facilitate collusion or are engaging in an alliance for other purposes?

9.6. Partnerships can range from simple principal-reseller relationships to equity joint ventures. In the latter makeup, partners have real and often long-term financial interests in the project. There are others that sit somewhere in the middle, such as franchising or trademark license agreements. In what ways can such alliances turn out badly?

9.7. Some researchers have argued that alliances can be used to help firms evaluate the economic potential of entering into a new industry or market. Why couldn't such a firm simply hire some smart managers, consultants, and industry experts to evaluate the economic potential of entering into a new industry?

⭐ **9.8.** Some researchers have argued that alliances can be used to help firms evaluate the economic potential of entering into a new industry or market. What, if anything, about an alliance makes this a better way to evaluate entry opportunities than alternative methods?

9.9. If adverse selection, moral hazard, and holdup are such significant problems for firms pursuing alliance strategies, why do firms even bother with alliances?

9.10. If adverse selection, moral hazard, and holdup are such significant problems for firms pursuing alliance strategies, why don't they instead adopt a "go it alone" strategy to replace strategic alliances?

Problem Set

9.11. Which of the following firms faces the greater threat of "cheating" in the alliances described, and why?

(a) Firm I and Firm II form a strategic alliance. As part of the alliance, Firm I agrees to build a new plant right next to Firm II's primary facility. In return, Firm II promises to buy most of the output of this new plant. Which is at risk, Firm I or Firm II?

(b) Firm A and Firm B form a strategic alliance. As part of the alliance, Firm A promises to begin selling products it already sells around the world in the home country of Firm B. In return, Firm B promises to provide Firm A with crucial contacts in its home country's government. These contacts are essential if Firm A is going to be able to sell in Firm B's home country. Which is at risk, Firm A or Firm B?

(c) Firm 1 and Firm 2 form a strategic alliance. As part of the alliance, Firm 1 promises to provide Firm 2 access to some new and untested technology that Firm 2 will use in its products. In return, Firm 2 will share some of the profits from its sales with Firm 1. Which is at risk, Firm 1 or Firm 2?

9.12. Are all strategic alliances used for entry into a market? Explain with examples.

9.13. Examine the Web sites of the following strategic alliances and determine which of the sources of value presented in Table 9.1 are present:

(a) Dow-Corning (an alliance between Dow Chemical and Corning)
(b) CFM (an alliance between General Electric and SNECMA)
(c) NCAA (an alliance among colleges and universities in the United States)
(d) Visa (an alliance among banks in the United States)
(e) The alliance among United, Delta, Singapore Airlines, AeroMexico, Alitalia, and Korean Air

MyManagementLab®

Go to **mymanagementlab.com** for the following Assisted-graded writing questions:

✪ **9.14.** How would a firm's reputation reduce the threat of cheating in a strategic alliance?

✪ **9.15.** How can holdup be considered a form of cheating in strategic alliances and threat of holdup be considered a motivation for creating an alliance?

End Notes

1. See www.pwc.com/extweb/exccps.nsf/docid; www.addme.com/issue208; McCracken, J. (2006). "Ford doubles reported loss for second quarter." *The Wall Street Journal*, August 3, p. A3; and www.msnbc.msn.com/id/13753688.
2. Badaracco, J. L., and N. Hasegawa. (1988). "General Motors' Asian alliances." Harvard Business School Case No. 9-388-094.
3. See www.blu-ray.com.
4. See Burgers, W. P., C. W. L. Hill, and W. C. Kim. (1993). "A theory of global strategic alliances: The case of the global auto industry." *Strategic Management Journal*, 14, pp. 419–432.
5. See Freeman, A., and R. Hudson. (1980). "DuPont and Philips plan joint venture to make, market laser disc products." *The Wall Street Journal*, December 22, p. 10.
6. Teitelbaum, R. S. (1992). "Eskimo pie." *Fortune*, June 15, p. 123.
7. Nanda, A., and C. A. Bartlett. (1990). "Corning Incorporated: A network of alliances." Harvard Business School Case No. 9-391-102.
8. See Knight, F. H. (1965). *Risk, uncertainty, and profit*. New York: John Wiley & Sons, Inc., on uncertainty; Kogut, B. (1991). "Joint ventures and the option to expand and acquire." *Management Science*, 37, pp. 19–33; Burgers, W. P., C. W. L. Hill, and W. C. Kim. (1993). "A theory of global strategic alliances: The case of the global auto industry." *Strategic Management Journal*, 14, pp. 419–432; Noldeke, G., and K. M. Schmidt. (1998). "Sequential investments and options to own." *Rand Journal of Economics*, 29(4), pp. 633–653; and Folta, T. B. (1998). "Governance and uncertainty: The tradeoff between administrative control and commitment." *Strategic Management Journal*, 19, pp. 1007–1028.
9. See Kogut, B. (1991). "Joint ventures and the option to expand and acquire." *Management Science*, 37, pp. 19–33; and Balakrishnan, S., and M. Koza. (1993). "Information asymmetry, adverse selection and joint-ventures." *Journal of Economic Behavior & Organization*, 20, pp. 99–117.
10. See, for example, Ernst, D., and J. Bleeke. (1993). *Collaborating to compete: Using strategic alliances and acquisition in the global marketplace*. New York: John Wiley & Sons, Inc.
11. These terms are defined in Barney, J. B., and W. G. Ouchi. (1986). *Organizational economics*. San Francisco: Jossey-Bass; and Holmstrom, B. (1979). "Moral hazard and observability." *Bell Journal of Economics*, 10(1), pp. 74–91. Problems of cheating in economic exchanges in

general, and in alliances in particular, are discussed by Gulati, R., and H. Singh. (1998). "The architecture of cooperation: Managing coordination costs and appropriation concerns in strategic alliances." *Administrative Science Quarterly*, 43, pp. 781–814; Williamson, O. E. (1991). "Comparative economic organization: The analysis of discrete structural alternatives." *Administrative Science Quarterly*, 36, pp. 269–296; Osborn, R. N., and C. C. Baughn. (1990). "Forms of interorganizational governance for multinational alliances." *Academy of Management Journal*, 33(3), pp. 503–519; Hagedoorn, J., and R. Narula. (1996). "Choosing organizational modes of strategic technology partnering: International and sectoral differences." *Journal of International Business Studies*, second quarter, pp. 265–284; Hagedorn, J. (1996). "Trends and patterns in strategic technology partnering since the early seventies." *Review of Industrial Organization*, 11, pp. 601–616; Kent, D. H. (1991). "Joint ventures vs. non-joint ventures: An empirical investigation." *Strategic Management Journal*, 12, pp. 387–393; and Shane, S. A. (1998). "Making new franchise systems work." *Strategic Management Journal*, 19, pp. 697–707.
12. Such alliance difficulties are described in Ouchi, W. G. (1984). *The M-form society: How American teamwork can capture the competitive edge*. Reading, MA: Addison-Wesley; and Bresser, R. K. (1988). "Cooperative strategy." *Strategic Management Journal*, 9, pp. 475–492.
13. Pope, K. (1993). "Dealers accuse Compaq of jilting them." *The Wall Street Journal*, February 26, pp. 8, B1+.
14. Williamson, O. E. (1975). *Markets and hierarchies: Analysis and antitrust implications*. New York: Free Press; Klein, B., R. Crawford, and A. Alchian. (1978). "Vertical integration, appropriable rents, and the competitive contracting process." *Journal of Law and Economics*, 21, pp. 297–326.
15. See, for example, Yan, A., and B. Gray. (1994). "Bargaining power, management control, and performance in United States–China joint ventures: A comparative case study." *Academy of Management Journal*, 37, pp. 1478–1517.
16. See Badaracco, J. L., and N. Hasegawa. (1988). "General Motors' Asian alliances." Harvard Business School Case No. 9-388-094, on GM and Toyota; Patterson, G. A. (1991). "Mazda hopes to crack Japan's top tier." *The Wall Street Journal*, September 20, pp. B1+; and Williams, M., and M. Kanabayashi. (1993). "Mazda and Ford drop proposal to build

cars together in Europe." *The Wall Street Journal*, March 4, p. A14, on Ford and Mazda; and Ennis, P. (1991). "Mitsubishi group wary of deeper ties to Chrysler." *Tokyo Business Today*, 59, July, p. 10, on DaimlerChrysler and Mitsubishi.

17. See, for example, Ernst, D., and J. Bleeke. (1993). *Collaborating to compete: Using strategic alliances and acquisition in the global marketplace.* New York: John Wiley & Sons, Inc.; and Barney, J. B., and M. H. Hansen. (1994). "Trustworthiness as a source of competitive advantage." *Strategic Management Journal*, 15, winter (special issue), pp. 175–190.

18. Ernst, D., and J. Bleeke. (1993). *Collaborating to compete: Using strategic alliances and acquisition in the global marketplace.* New York: John Wiley & Sons, Inc.

19. Bartlett, C., and S. Ghoshal. (1993). "Beyond the M-form: Toward a managerial theory of the firm." *Strategic Management Journal*, 14, pp. 23–46.

20. See Nagarajan, A., and W. Mitchell. (1998). "Evolutionary diffusion: Internal and external methods used to acquire encompassing, complementary, and incremental technological changes in the lithotripsy industry." *Strategic Management Journal*, 19, pp. 1063–1077; Hagedoorn, J., and B. Sadowski. (1999). "The transition from strategic technology alliances to mergers and acquisitions: An exploratory study." *Journal of Management Studies*, 36(1), pp. 87–107; and Newbury, W., and Y. Zeira. (1997). "Generic differences between equity international joint ventures (EIJVs), international acquisitions (IAs) and International Greenfield investments (IGIs): Implications for parent companies." *Journal of World Business*, 32(2), pp. 87–102, on alliance substitutes.

21. Barney, J. B. (1999). "How a firm's capabilities affect boundary decisions." *Sloan Management Review*, 40(3), pp. 137–145.

22. See Hennart, J. F. (1988). "A transaction cost theory of equity joint ventures." *Strategic Management Journal*, 9, pp. 361–374; Kogut, B. (1988). "Joint ventures: Theoretical and empirical perspectives." *Strategic Management Journal*, 9, pp. 319–332; and Barney, J. B. (1999). "How a firm's capabilities affect boundary decisions." *Sloan Management Review*, 40(3), pp. 137–145, for a discussion of these limitations.

23. See Ouchi, W. G. (1984). *The M-form society: How American teamwork can capture the competitive edge.* Reading, MA: Addison-Wesley; and Barney, J. B. (1990). "Profit sharing bonuses and the cost of debt: Business finance and compensation policy in Japanese electronics firms." *Asia Pacific Journal of Management*, 7, pp. 49–64.

24. This is an argument developed by Barney, J. B., and M. H. Hansen. (1994). "Trustworthiness as a source of competitive advantage." *Strategic Management Journal*, 15, winter (special issue), pp. 175–190; Weigelt, K., and C. Camerer. (1988). "Reputation and corporate strategy: A review of recent theory and applications." *Strategic Management Journal*, 9, pp. 443–454; and Granovetter, M. (1985). "Economic action and social structure: The problem of embeddedness." *American Journal of Sociology*, 3, pp. 481–510.

25. See, for example, Eichenseher, J., and D. Shields. (1985). "Reputation and corporate strategy: A review of recent theory and applications." *Strategic Management Journal*, 9, pp. 443–454; Beatty, R., and R. Ritter. (1986). "Investment banking, reputation, and the underpricing of initial public offerings." *Journal of Financial Economics*, 15, pp. 213–232; Kalleberg, A. L., and T. Reve. (1992). "Contracts and commitment: Economic and Sociological Perspectives on Employment Relations." *Human Relations*,

45(9), pp. 1103–1132; Larson, A. (1992). "Network dyads in entrepreneurial settings: A study of the governance of exchange relationships." *Administrative Science Quarterly*, March, pp. 76–104; Stuart, T. E., H. Hoang, and R. C. Hybels. (1999). "Interorganizational endorsements and the performance of entrepreneurial ventures." *Administrative Science Quarterly*, 44, pp. 315–349; Stuart, T. E. (1998). "Network positions and propensities to collaborate: An investigation of strategic alliance formation in a high-technology industry." *Administrative Science Quarterly*, 43(3), pp. 668–698; and Gulati, R. (1998). "Alliances and networks." *Strategic Management Journal*, 19, pp. 293–317.

26. Personal communication, April 8, 1986.

27. This same theoretic approach to firm reputation is discussed in Tirole, J. (1988). *The theory of industrial organization.* Cambridge, MA: MIT Press.

28. Scherer, F. M. (1980). *Industrial market structure and economic performance.* Boston: Houghton Mifflin.

29. See, again, Ernst, D., and J. Bleeke. (1993). *Collaborating to compete: Using strategic alliances and acquisition in the global marketplace.* New York: John Wiley & Sons, Inc.; and Barney, J. B., and M. H. Hansen. (1994). "Trustworthiness as a source of competitive advantage." *Strategic Management Journal*, 15, winter (special issue), pp. 175–190. In fact, there is a great deal of literature on the role of trust in strategic alliances. Some of the most interesting of this work can be found in Holm, D. B., K. Eriksson, and J. Johanson. (1999). "Creating value through mutual commitment to business network relationships." *Strategic Management Journal*, 20, pp. 467–486; Lorenzoni, G., and A. Lipparini. (1999). "The leveraging of interfirm relationships as a distinctive organizational capability: A longitudinal study." *Strategic Management Journal*, 20(4), pp. 317–338; Blois, K. J. (1999). "Trust in business to business relationships: An evaluation of its status." *Journal of Management Studies*, 36(2), pp. 197–215; Chiles, T. H., and J. F. McMackin. (1996). "Integrating variable risk preferences, trust, and transaction cost economics." *Academy of Management Review*, 21(1), pp. 73–99; Larzelere, R. E., and T. L. Huston. (1980). "The dyadic trust scale: Toward understanding interpersonal trust in close relationships." *Journal of Marriage and the Family*, August, pp. 595–604; Butler, J. K., Jr. (1983). "Reciprocity of trust between professionals and their secretaries." *Psychological Reports*, 53, pp. 411–416; Zaheer, A., and N. Venkatraman. (1995). "Relational governance as an interorganizational strategy: An empirical test of the role of trust in economic exchange." *Strategic Management Journal*, 16, pp. 373–392; Butler, J. K., Jr., and R. S. Cantrell. (1984). "A behavioral decision theory approach to modeling dyadic trust in superiors and subordinates." *Psychological Reports*, 55, pp. 19–28; Carney, M. (1998). "The competitiveness of networked production: The role of trust and asset specificity." *Journal of Management Studies*, 35(4), pp. 457–479.

30. Ernst, D., and J. Bleeke. (1993). *Collaborating to compete: Using strategic alliances and acquisition in the global marketplace.* New York: John Wiley & Sons, Inc.

31. See Mohr, J., and R. Spekman. (1994). "Characteristics of partnership success: Partnership attributes, communication behavior, and conflict resolution techniques." *Strategic Management Journal*, 15, pp. 135–152; and Zaheer, A., and N. Venkatraman. (1995). "Relational governance as an interorganizational strategy: An empirical test of the role of trust in economic exchange." *Strategic Management Journal*, 16, pp. 373–392.

10 Mergers and Acquisitions

LEARNING OBJECTIVES *After reading this chapter, you should be able to:*

1. Describe different types of mergers and acquisitions.

2. Estimate the return to the stockholders of bidding and target firms when there is no strategic relatedness between firms.

3. Describe different sources of relatedness between bidding and target firms.

4. Estimate the return to stockholders of bidding and target firms when there is strategic relatedness between firms.

5. Describe five reasons why bidding firms might still engage in acquisitions, even if, on average, they do not create value for a bidding firm's stockholders.

6. Describe three ways that bidding firms might be able to generate high returns for their equity holders through implementing mergers or acquisitions.

7. Describe the major challenges that firms integrating acquisitions are likely to face.

The Google Acquistion Machine

Google spent almost $6.8 billion on research and development in 2012. More than 19,700 of its 54,000 employees work in R&D, which generated 13.5 percent of all of its costs in 2012 and constituted the largest expense item on its annual income statement. In public statements, Google justified this expense as necessary to keep up with the rapidly changing technological environment within which it competes.

But Google also uses another strategy to try to keep up with technological change: acquisitions. Since 2010, Google has acquired other companies at the rate of one company per week. These acquisitions ranged from extremely small to very large, the largest being the $12.5 billion acquisition of Motorola's mobile phone business. Some other large Google acquisitions included YouTube (in 2006 for $1.65 billion), DoubleClick (in 2007 for $3.2 billion), and Waze (in 2013 for $1 billion).

If Google is spending so much money on R&D, why does it also have to spend so much money on acquisitions? After all, if Google is inventing lots of cool technology internally, why does it also have to buy technology on the market? Or, alternatively, if Google is buying lots of cool technology on the market—by buying other companies—why does it have to spend so much money on R&D?

Of course, for Google, there is a direct link between its external acquisitions and its internal R&D. In particular, Google's internal R&D not only develops new products from scratch—like

the Android operating system for smart phones—it also invests in integrating the technologies it purchases into upgrading established Google products. Indeed, some observers believe that Google is unusually skilled in creating economic value by integrating the technologies it acquires into its products. Of the hundred or so technologies that Google has gained access to through its acquisitions, only a handful have not been integrated into current Google products—including, to name just a few, Google Wallet, Google Docs, Gmail, Google+, and Google TV—or have become established as new products within the Google portfolio—including, for example, YouTube.

In fact, Google has only divested three of its hundreds of acquisitions: Dodgeball (a mobile phone service divested in 2005), Slide (a social gaming company divested in 2010), and Frommer's (a travel guide company divested in 2012). These three acquisitions are widely seen as failures.

But three "failures" out of hundreds of deals is a much higher success rate than other firms in high-technology industries. It is even a higher success rate than firms in other industries. While the corporate strategy of acquisitions often does not generate superior performance for acquiring firms, Google seems to have found a way to create enough value from its acquisitions to justify their prices while still investing in its own research and development projects. Of course, the big question mark facing Google is its acquisition of Motorola. Recently, Motorola introduced its first new line of mobile phones designed and manufactured under Google's ownership—the Moto X. Reviews of these phones were mixed. Commentators were particularly surprised that Motorola's latest phones did not run the most up-to-date version of Android, Google's smart phone operating system. Perhaps Google did not want to disadvantage other users of its Android system, including Samsung, by making the latest version available on the Moto X. At the very least, that Motorola's most advanced phone did not use Android's most advanced system suggests some challenges in integrating Motorola into Google's technology family.

Sources: Google 2013 10K http://www.sec.gov/Archives/edgar/data/1288776/000119312513028362/d452134d10k.htm; A. Efrati (2013). "Google nears deal for Waze." *The Wall Street Journal*, June 10, pp. B1+; R. Knutson and S. Ante (2013). "Google leans on Motorola with hardware push." *The Wall Street Journal*, April 1, p. B2.

Google is not the only firm that engages in mergers and acquisitions. Indeed, mergers and acquisitions are one very common way that a firm can accomplish its vertical integration and diversification objectives. However, although a firm may be able to accomplish its vertical integration and diversification objectives through mergers or acquisitions, it is sometimes difficult to generate real economic profit from doing so. Indeed, one of the strongest empirical findings in the fields of strategic management and finance is that, on average, the equity holders of target firms in mergers and acquisitions make money while the equity holders of bidding firms in these same mergers and acquisitions usually only "break even."

What Are Mergers and Acquisitions?

The terms *mergers* and *acquisitions* are often used interchangeably, even though they are not synonyms. A firm engages in an **acquisition** when it purchases a second firm. The form of this purchase can vary. For example, an acquiring firm can use cash it has generated from its ongoing businesses to purchase a target firm; it can go into debt to purchase a target firm; it can use its own equity to purchase a target firm; or it can use a mix of these mechanisms to purchase a target firm. Also, an acquiring firm can purchase all of a target firm's assets; it can purchase a majority of those assets (greater than 51 percent); or it can purchase a **controlling share** of those assets (i.e., enough assets so that the acquiring firm is able to make all the management and strategic decisions in the target firm).

Acquisitions also vary on several other dimensions. For example, **friendly acquisitions** occur when the management of the target firm wants the firm to be acquired. **Unfriendly acquisitions** occur when the management of the target firm does not want the firm to be acquired. Some unfriendly acquisitions are also known as **hostile takeovers**. Some acquisitions are accomplished through direct negotiations between an acquiring firm's managers and the managers of a target firm. This is especially common when a target firm is **privately held** (i.e., when it has not sold shares on the public stock market) or **closely held** (i.e., when it has not sold very many shares on the public stock market). Other acquisitions are accomplished by the acquiring firm publicly announcing that it is willing to purchase the outstanding shares of a potential target for a particular price. This price is normally greater than the current market price of the target firm's shares. The difference between the current market price of a target firm's shares and the price a potential acquirer offers to pay for those shares is known as an **acquisition premium**. This approach to purchasing a firm is called a **tender offer**. Tender offers can be made either with or without the support of the management of the target firm. Obviously, tender offers with the support of the target firm's management are typically friendly in character; those made without the support of the target firm's management are typically unfriendly.

It is usually the case that larger firms—in terms of sales or assets—acquire smaller firms. For example, Google has been larger than all of its intended targets, including Motorola Mobile. In contrast, when the assets of two similar-sized firms are combined, this transaction is called a **merger**. Mergers can be accomplished in many of the same ways as acquisitions, that is, using cash or stock to purchase a percentage of another firm's assets. Typically, however, mergers will not be unfriendly. In a merger, one firm purchases some percentage of a second firm's assets while the second firm simultaneously purchases some percentage of the first firm's assets. For example, DaimlerChrysler was created as a merger between Daimler-Benz (the maker of Mercedes-Benz) and Chrysler. Daimler-Benz invested some of its capital in Chrysler, and Chrysler invested some of its capital in Daimler-Benz. More recently, these merged companies split into two firms again. Then, after the financial crisis of 2007, Chrysler merged with Fiat.

Although mergers typically begin as a transaction between equals—that is, between firms of equal size and profitability—they often evolve after a merger such that one firm becomes more dominant in the management of the merged firm than the other. For example, most observers believe that Daimler (the German part of DaimlerChrysler) became more dominant in the management of the combined firm than Chrysler (the American part). And now, most believe that Fiat is more dominate.[1] Put differently, although mergers usually start out as something different from acquisitions, they usually end up looking more like acquisitions than mergers.

The Value of Mergers and Acquisitions

V R I O

That merger and acquisition strategies are an important strategic option open to firms pursuing diversification and vertical integration strategies can hardly be disputed. The number of firms that have used merger and acquisition strategies to become diversified over the past few years is staggering. This is the case even though the credit crunch crisis in 2008 reduced M&A activity somewhat. For example, in 2010, there were 10,108 acquistions or mergers in the United States, valued at $898 billion. In 2011, there were 10,518 deals valued at $1 trillion, and in 2012, 12,192 deals valued at $482 billion.[2]

The list of firms that have recently engaged in mergers and acquisitions is long and varied. For example, in 2012 SAP (an enterprise software company) purchased Ariba (a cloud computing firm) for $4.3 billion; Cisco (a computer server company) bought NDS Group (a video software and security company) for $5 billion; and Softbank (the third-largest mobile phone company in Japan) bought SprintNextel (a U.S. mobile provider) for $20.1 billion.

That mergers and acquisitions are common is clear. What is less clear is that they actually generate value for firms implementing these strategies. Two cases will be examined here: mergers and acquisitions between strategically unrelated firms and mergers and acquisitions between strategically related firms.

Mergers and Acquisitions: The Unrelated Case

Imagine the following scenario: One firm (the target) is the object of an acquisition effort, and 10 firms (the bidders) are interested in making this acquisition. Suppose the **current market value** of the target firm is $10,000—that is, the price of each of this firm's shares times the number of shares outstanding equals $10,000. Also, suppose the current market value of each of the bidding firms is $15,000.[3] Finally, suppose there is no strategic relatedness between these bidding firms and the target. This means that the value of any one of these bidding firms when combined with the target firm exactly equals the sum of the value of these firms as separate entities. In this example, because the current market value of the target is $10,000 and the current market value of the bidding firms is $15,000, the value of this target when combined with any of these bidders would be $25,000 ($10,000 + $15,000). Given this information, at what price will this target be acquired, and what are the economic performance implications for bidding and target firms at this price?

In this and all acquisition situations, bidding firms will be willing to pay a price for a target up to the value that the target firm adds to the bidder once it is acquired. This price is simply the difference between the value of the two firms combined (in this case, $25,000) and the value of the bidding firm by itself (in this case, $15,000). Notice that this price does not depend on the value of the target firm acting as an independent business; rather, it depends on the value that the target firm creates when it is combined with the bidding firm. Any price for a target less than this value (i.e., less than $10,000) will be a source of economic profit for a bidding firm; any price equal to this value (i.e., equal to $10,000) will be a source of zero economic profits; and any price greater than this value (i.e., greater than $10,000) will be a source of economic losses for the bidding firm that acquires the target.

It is not hard to see that the price of this acquisition will quickly rise to $10,000 and that at this price the bidding firm that acquires the target will earn zero economic profits. The price of this acquisition will quickly rise to $10,000 because any bid less than $10,000 will generate economic profits for a successful bidder. These potential profits, in turn, will generate entry into the bidding war for a target. Because entry into the acquisition contest is very likely, the price of the acquisition will quickly rise to its value, and economic profits will not be created.

Moreover, at this $10,000 price the target firm's equity holders will also gain zero economic profits. Indeed, for them, all that has occurred is that the market value of the target firm has been capitalized in the form of a cash payment from the bidder to the target. The target was worth $10,000, and that is exactly what these equity holders will receive.

Mergers and Acquisitions: The Related Case

The conclusion that the acquisition of strategically unrelated targets will generate only zero economic profits for both the bidding and the target firms is not surprising. It is very consistent with the discussion of the economic consequences of unrelated diversification in Chapter 7. There it was argued that there is no economic justification for a corporate diversification strategy that does not build on some type of economy of scope across the businesses within which a firm operates, and therefore unrelated diversification is not an economically viable corporate strategy. So, if there is any hope that mergers and acquisitions will be a source of superior performance for bidding firms, it must be because of some sort of strategic relatedness or economy of scope between bidding and target firms.

Types of Strategic Relatedness

Of course, bidding and target firms can be strategically related in a wide variety of ways. Three particularly important lists of these potential linkages are discussed here.[4]

The Federal Trade Commission Categories.   Because mergers and acquisitions can have the effect of increasing (or decreasing) the level of concentration in an industry, the Federal Trade Commission (FTC) is charged with the responsibility of evaluating the competitive implications of proposed mergers or acquisitions. In principle, the FTC will disallow any acquisition involving firms with headquarters in the United States that could have the potential for generating monopoly

■ Vertical merger	A firm acquires former suppliers or customers.
■ Horizontal merger	A firm acquires a former competitor.
■ Product extension merger	A firm gains access to complementary products through an acquisition.
■ Market extension merger	A firm gains access to complementary markets through an acquisition.
■ Conglomerate merger	There is no strategic relatedness between a bidding and a target firm.

TABLE 10.1 Federal Trade Commission Categories of Mergers and Acquisitions

(or oligopoly) profits in an industry. To help in this regulatory effort, the FTC has developed a typology of mergers and acquisitions (see Table 10.1). Each category in this typology can be thought of as a different way in which a bidding firm and a target firm can be related in a merger or acquisition.

According to the FTC, a firm engages in a **vertical merger** when it vertically integrates, either forward or backward, through its acquisition efforts. Vertical mergers could include a firm purchasing critical suppliers of raw materials (backward vertical integration) or acquiring customers and distribution networks (forward vertical integration). eBay's acquisition of Skype is an example of a backward vertical integration as eBay tries to assemble all the resources to compete in the Internet telephone industry. Disney's acquisition of Capital Cities/ABC can be understood as an attempt by Disney to forward vertically integrate into the entertainment distribution industry, and its acquisition of ESPN can be seen as backward vertical integration into the entertainment production business.[5]

A firm engages in a **horizontal merger** when it acquires a former competitor; Adidas's acquisition of Reebok is an example of a horizontal merger, as the number 2 and number 3 sneaker manufacturers in the world combined their efforts. Obviously, the FTC is particularly concerned with the competitive implications of horizontal mergers because these strategies can have the most direct and obvious anticompetitive implications in an industry. For example, the FTC raised antitrust concerns in the $10 billion merger between Oracle and PeopleSoft because these firms, collectively, dominated the enterprise software market. Similar concerns were raised in the $16.4 billion merger between ChevronTexaco and Unocal and the merger between Mobil and Exxon.

The third type of merger identified by the FTC is a **product extension merger**. In a product extension merger, firms acquire complementary products through their merger and acquisition activities. Examples include Google's acquisition of Motorola Mobile.

The fourth type of merger identified by the FTC is a **market extension merger**. Here the primary objective is to gain access to new geographic markets. Examples include SABMiller's acquisition of Bavaria Brewery Company in Columbia, South America.

The final type of merger or acquisition identified by the FTC is a **conglomerate merger**. For the FTC, conglomerate mergers are a residual category. If there are no vertical, horizontal, product extension, or market extension links between firms, the FTC defines the merger or acquisition activity between firms as a conglomerate merger. Given our earlier conclusion that mergers or acquisitions between strategically *unrelated* firms will not generate economic profits for either bidders or targets, it should not be surprising that there are currently relatively few examples of conglomerate mergers or acquisitions; however, at various times in history, they have been relatively common. In the 1960s, for example, many acquisitions took the form of conglomerate mergers. Research has shown that the fraction of single-business firms in the Fortune 500 dropped from 22.8 percent in 1959 to 14.8 percent in 1969, while the fraction of firms in the *Fortune 500* pursuing unrelated diversification strategies rose from 7.3 to 18.7 percent during the same time period. These findings are consistent with an increase in the number of conglomerate mergers and acquisitions during the 1960s.[6]

Despite the popularity of conglomerate mergers in the 1960s, many mergers or acquisitions among strategically unrelated firms are divested shortly after they are completed. One study estimated that more than one-third of the conglomerate mergers of the 1960s were divested by the early 1980s. Another study showed that more than 50 percent of these acquisitions were subsequently divested. These results are all consistent with our earlier conclusion that mergers or acquisitions involving strategically unrelated firms are not a source of economic profits.[7]

Other Types of Strategic Relatedness. Although the FTC categories of mergers and acquisitions provide some information about possible motives underlying these corporate strategies, they do not capture the full complexity of the links that might exist between bidding and target firms. Several authors have attempted to develop more complete lists of possible sources of relatedness between bidding and target firms. One of these lists, developed by Professor Michael Lubatkin, is summarized in Table 10.2. This list includes **technical economies** (in marketing, production, and similar forms of relatedness), **pecuniary economies** (market power), and **diversification economies** (in portfolio management and risk reduction) as possible bases of strategic relatedness between bidding and target firms.

A second important list of possible sources of strategic relatedness between bidding and target firms was developed by Michael Jensen and Richard Ruback after a comprehensive review of empirical research on the economic returns to mergers and acquisitions. This list is summarized in Table 10.3 and includes the following factors as possible sources of economic gains in mergers and acquisitions: potential reductions in production or distribution costs (from economies of scale, vertical integration, reduction in agency costs, and so forth); the realization of financial opportunities (such as gaining access to underutilized tax shields, avoiding bankruptcy costs); the creation of market power; and the ability to eliminate inefficient management in the target firm.

TABLE 10.2 Lubatkin's List of Potential Sources of Strategic Relatedness Between Bidding and Target Firms

Technical economies	Scale economies that occur when the physical processes inside a firm are altered so that the same amounts of input produce a higher quantity of outputs. Sources of technical economies include marketing, production, experience, scheduling, banking, and compensation.
Pecuniary economies	Economies achieved by the ability of firms to dictate prices by exerting market power.
Diversification economies	Economies achieved by improving a firm's performance relative to its risk attributes or lowering its risk attributes relative to its performance. Sources of diversification economies include portfolio management and risk reduction.

Source: M. Lubatkin (1983). "Mergers and the performance of the acquiring firm." *Academy of Management Review*, 8, pp. 218–225. © 1983 by the Academy of Management. Reproduced with permission.

TABLE 10.3 Jensen and Ruback's List of Reasons Why Bidding Firms Might Want to Engage in Merger and Acquisition Strategies

To reduce production or distribution costs:
1. Through economies of scale.
2. Through vertical integration.
3. Through the adoption of more efficient production or organizational technology.
4. Through the increased utilization of the bidder's management team.
5. Through a reduction of agency costs by bringing organization-specific assets under common ownership.

Financial motivations:
1. To gain access to underutilized tax shields.
2. To avoid bankruptcy costs.
3. To increase leverage opportunities.
4. To gain other tax advantages.
5. To gain market power in product markets.
6. To eliminate inefficient target management.

Source: Reprinted from Jensen, M. C., and R. S. Ruback (1983). "The Market for Corporate Control: The Scientific Evidence." *Journal of Financial Economics*, 11, pp. 5–50. Vol. II. Copyright © with permission from Elsevier.

To be economically valuable, links between bidding and target firms must meet the same criteria as diversification strategies (see Chapter 7). First, these links must build on real economies of scope between bidding and target firms. These economies of scope can reflect either cost savings or revenue enhancements that are created by combining firms. Second, not only must this economy of scope exist, but it must be less costly for the merged firm to realize than for outside equity holders to realize on their own. As is the case with corporate diversification strategies, by investing in a diversified portfolio of stocks, outside equity investors can gain many of the economies associated with a merger or acquisition on their own. Moreover, investors can realize some of these economies of scope at almost zero cost. In this situation, it makes little sense for investors to "hire" managers in firms to realize these economies of scope for them through a merger or acquisition. Rather, firms should pursue merger and acquisition strategies only to obtain valuable economies of scope that outside investors find too costly to create on their own.

Economic Profits in Related Acquisitions
If bidding and target firms are strategically related, then the economic value of these two firms combined is greater than their economic value as separate entities. To see how this changes returns to merger and acquisition strategies, consider the following scenario: As before, there is one target firm and 10 bidding firms. The market value of the target firm as a stand-alone entity is $10,000, and the market value of the bidding firms as stand-alone entities is $15,000. However, unlike the earlier scenario in this chapter, the bidding and target firms are strategically related. Any of the types of relatedness identified in Table 10.1, Table 10.2, or Table 10.3 could be the source of these economies of scope. They imply that when any of the bidding firms and the target are combined, the market value of this combined entity will be $32,000—note that $32,000 is greater than the sum of $15,000 and $10,000. At what price will this target firm be acquired, and what are the economic profit implications for bidding and target firms at this price?

As before, bidding firms will be willing to pay a price for a target up to the value that a target firm adds once it is acquired. Thus, the maximum price bidding firms are willing to pay is still the difference between the value of the combined entity (here, $32,000) and the value of a bidding firm on its own (here, $15,000), or $17,000.

As was the case for the strategically unrelated acquisition, it is not hard to see that the price for actually acquiring the target firm in this scenario will rapidly rise to $17,000 because any bid less than $17,000 has the potential for generating profits for a bidding firm. Suppose that one bidding firm offers $13,000 for the target. For this $13,000, the bidding firm gains access to a target that will generate $17,000 of value once it is acquired. Thus, to this bidding firm, the target is worth $17,000, and a bid of $13,000 will generate $4,000 economic profit. Of course, these potential profits will motivate entry into the competitive bidding process. Entry will continue until the price of this target equals $17,000. Any price greater than $17,000 would mean that a bidding firm is actually losing money on its acquisition.[8]

At this $17,000 price, the successful bidding firm earns zero economic profits. After all, this firm has acquired an asset that will generate $17,000 of value and has paid $17,000 to do so. However, the owners of the target firm will earn an economic profit worth $7,000. As a stand-alone firm, the target is worth $10,000; when combined with a bidding firm, it is worth $17,000. The difference between the value of the target as a stand-alone entity and its value in combination with a bidding firm is the value of the economic profit that can be appropriated by the owners of the target firm.

Thus, the existence of strategic relatedness between bidding and target firms is not a sufficient condition for the equity holders of bidding firms to earn economic profits from their acquisition strategies. If the economic potential of acquiring a particular target firm is widely known and if several potential bidding firms can all obtain this value by acquiring a target, the equity holders of bidding firms will, at best, earn only zero economic profits from implementing an acquisition strategy. In this setting, a "strategically related" merger or acquisition will create economic value, but this value will be distributed in the form of economic profits to the equity holders of acquired target firms.

Because so much of the value created in a merger or acquisition is appropriated by the stockholders of the target firm, it is not surprising that many small and entrepreneurial firms look to be acquired as one way to compensate their owners for taking the risks associated with founding these firms. This phenomenon is discussed in more detail in the Strategy in the Emerging Enterprise feature.

What Does Research Say About Returns to Mergers and Acquisitions?

The empirical implications of this discussion of returns to bidding and target firms in strategically related and strategically unrelated mergers and acquisitions have been examined in a variety of academic literatures. One study reviewed more than 40 empirical merger and acquisition studies in the finance literature. This study concluded that acquisitions, on average, increased the market value of target firms by about 25 percent and left the market value of bidding firms unchanged. The authors of this report concluded that "corporate takeovers generate positive gains,...target firm equity holders benefit, and...bidding firm equity holders do not lose."[9] The way these studies evaluate the return to acquisition strategies is discussed in the Strategy in Depth feature.

Strategy in the Emerging Enterprise

Imagine you are an entrepreneur. You have mortgaged your home, taken out loans, run up your credit cards, and put all you own on the line in order to help grow a small company. And, finally, after years of effort, things start going well. Your product or service starts to sell, customers start to appreciate your unique value proposition, and you actually begin to pay yourself a reasonable salary. What do you do next to help grow your company?

Some entrepreneurs in this situation decide that maintaining control of the firm is very important. These entrepreneurs may compensate certain critical employees with equity in the firm, but typically limit the number of outsiders who make equity investments in their firm. To grow these closely held firms, these entrepreneurs must rely on capital generated from their ongoing operations (called **retained earnings**) and debt capital provided by banks, customers, and suppliers. Entrepreneurs who decide to maintain control of their companies are compensated for taking the risks associated with starting a firm through the salary they pay themselves.

Other entrepreneurs get more outside equity investors involved in providing the capital a firm needs to grow. These outside investors might include wealthy individuals—called **business angels**—looking to invest in entrepreneurial ventures or **venture capital firms**. Venture capital firms

Cashing Out

typically raise money from numerous smaller investors that they then invest in a portfolio of entrepreneurial firms. Over time, many of these firms decide to "go public" by engaging in what is called an **initial public offering (IPO).** In an IPO, a firm, typically working with an investment banker, sells its equity to the public at large. Entrepreneurs who decide to sell equity in their firm are compensated for taking the risks associated with starting a firm through the sale of their equity on the public markets through an IPO. An entrepreneur who receives compensation for risk-taking in this manner is said to be **cashing out.**

Finally, still other entrepreneurs may decide to not use an IPO to cash out, but rather to have their firm acquired by another, typically larger firm. In this scenario, entrepreneurs are compensated by the acquiring firm for taking the risks associated with starting a firm. Indeed, because the demand for IPOs has been volatile

since the technology-bubble burst of 2000, more and more small and entrepreneurial firms are looking to be acquired as a way for their founders to cash out. Moreover, because the stockholders of target firms typically appropriate a large percentage of the total value created by an acquisition and because the founders of these entrepreneurial firms are also often large stockholders, being acquired is often a source of great wealth for an entrepreneurial firm's founders.

The choice between keeping a firm private, going public, or being acquired is a difficult and multidimensional one. Issues such as the personal preferences of a firm's founders, demand for IPOs, how much capital a firm will need in order to continue to grow its business, and what other resources—besides capital—the firm will need to create additional value all play a role. In general, firms that do not need a great deal of money or other resources to grow will choose to remain private. Those that need only money to grow will choose IPOs, whereas those that need managerial or technical resources controlled by another firm to grow will typically be acquired. Of course, this changes if the entrepreneurs decide to maintain control of their firms because they want to.

Sources: R. Hennessey (2004). "Underwriters cut prices on IPOs as market softens." *The Wall Street Journal*, May 27, p. C4; F. Vogelstein (2003). "Can Google grow up?" *Fortune*, December 8, pp. 102+.

Strategy researchers have also attempted to examine in more detail the sources of value creation in mergers and acquisitions and the question of whether these sources of value creation affect whether bidders or targets appropriate this value. For example, two well-known studies examined the impact of the type and degree of strategic relatedness (defined using the FTC typology summarized in Table 10.1) between bidding and target firms on the economic consequences of mergers and acquisitions.[10] These studies found that the more strategically related bidding and target firms are, the more economic value mergers and acquisitions create. However, like the finance studies, this work found that this economic value was appropriated by the owners of the target firm, regardless of the type or degree of relatedness between the bidding and target firms. Bidding firms—even when they attempt to acquire strategically related targets—earn, on average, zero economic profits from their merger and acquisition strategies.

Why Are There So Many Mergers and Acquisitions?

Given the overwhelming empirical evidence that most of the economic value created in mergers and acquisitions is appropriated by the owners of the target firm most of the time, an important question becomes: "Why do managers of bidding firms continue to engage in merger and acquisition strategies?" Some possible explanations are summarized in Table 10.4 and discussed in this section.

To Ensure Survival

Even if mergers and acquisitions, on average, generate only zero economic profits for bidding firms, it may be necessary for bidding firms to engage in these activities to ensure their survival. In particular, if all of a bidding firm's competitors have been able to improve their efficiency and effectiveness through a particular type of acquisition, then failing to make such an acquisition may put a firm at a competitive disadvantage. Here the purpose of a merger or acquisition is not to gain competitive advantages, but rather to gain competitive parity.

Many recent mergers among banks in the United States seem to have competitive parity and normal economic profits as an objective. Most bank managers recognize that changing bank regulations, increased competition from nonbanking financial institutions, and soft demand are likely to lead to a consolidation of the U.S. banking industry. To survive in this consolidated industry, many U.S. banks will have to merge. As the number of banks engaging in mergers and acquisitions goes up, the ability to earn superior profits from those strategies goes down. These lower returns from acquisitions have already reduced the economic value of some of the most aggressive acquiring banks. Despite these lower returns, acquisitions are likely to continue for the foreseeable future, as banks seek survival opportunities in a consolidated industry.[11]

Free Cash Flow

Another reason why firms may continue to invest in merger and acquisition strategies is that these strategies, on average, can be expected to generate at least competitive parity for bidding firms. This zero economic profit may be a more attractive investment for some firms than alternative strategic investments. This is particularly the case for firms that generate free cash flow.[12]

TABLE 10.4 Possible Motivations to Engage in Mergers and Acquisitions Even Though They Usually Do Not Generate Profits for Bidding Firms

1. To ensure survival
2. Free cash flow
3. Agency problems
4. Managerial hubris
5. The potential for above-normal profits

Free cash flow is simply the amount of cash a firm has to invest after all positive net present-value investments in its ongoing businesses have been funded. Free cash flow is created when a firm's ongoing business operations are very profitable but offer few opportunities for additional investment. One firm that seems to have generated a great deal of free cash flow over the past several years is Philip Morris. Philip Morris's retail tobacco operations are extremely profitable. However, regulatory constraints, health concerns, and slowing growth in demand limit investment opportunities in the tobacco industry. Thus, the amount of cash generated by Philip Morris's ongoing tobacco business has probably been larger than the sum of its positive net present-value investments in that business. This difference is free cash flow for Philip Morris.[13]

A firm that generates a great deal of free cash flow must decide what to do with this money. One obvious alternative would be to give it to stockholders in the form of dividends or stock buybacks. However, in some situations (e.g., when stockholders face high marginal tax rates), stockholders may prefer a firm to retain this cash flow and invest it for them. When this is the case, how should a firm invest its free cash flow?

Because (by definition) no positive net present-value investment opportunities in a firm's ongoing business operations are available, firms have only two investment options: to invest their free cash flow in strategies that generate competitive parity or in strategies that generate competitive disadvantages. In this context, merger and acquisition strategies are a viable option because bidding firms, on average, can expect to generate at least competitive parity. Put differently, although mergers and acquisitions may not be a source of superior profits, there are worse things you could do with your free cash flow.

Agency Problems

Another reason why firms might continue to engage in mergers and acquisitions, despite earning only competitive parity from doing so, is that mergers and acquisitions benefit managers directly, independent of any value they may or may not create for a bidding firm's stockholders. As suggested in Chapter 8, these conflicts of interest are a manifestation of agency problems between a firm's managers and its stockholders.

Merger and acquisition strategies can benefit managers—even if they do not directly benefit a bidding firm's equity holders—in at least two ways. First, managers can use mergers and acquisitions to help diversify their human capital investments in their firm. As discussed in Chapter 7, managers have difficulty diversifying their firm-specific human capital investments when a firm operates in a narrow range of businesses. By acquiring firms with cash flows that are not perfectly correlated with the cash flows of a firm's current businesses, managers can reduce the probability of bankruptcy for their firm and thus partially diversify their human capital investments in their firm.

Second, managers can use mergers and acquisitions to quickly increase firm size, measured in either sales or assets. If management compensation is closely linked to firm size, managers who increase firm size are able to increase their compensation. Of all the ways to increase the size of a firm quickly, growth through mergers and acquisitions is perhaps the easiest. Even if there are no economies of scope between a bidding and a target firm, an acquisition ensures that the bidding firm will grow by the size of the target (measured in either sales or assets). If there are economies of scope between a bidding and a target firm, the size of the bidding firm can grow at an even faster rate, as can the value of management's compensation, even though, on average, acquisitions do not generate wealth for the owners of the bidding firm.

Strategy in Depth

By far, the most popular way to evaluate the performance effects of acquisitions for bidding firms is called **event study analysis**. Rooted in the field of financial economics, event study analysis compares the actual performance of a stock after an acquisition has been announced with the expected performance of that stock if no acquisition had been announced. Any performance greater (or less) than what was expected in a short period of time around when an acquisition is announced is attributed to that acquisition. This **cumulative abnormal return (CAR)** can be positive or negative depending on whether the stock in question performs better or worse than expected without an acquisition.

The CAR created by an acquisition is calculated in several stages. First, the expected performance of a stock, without an acquisition, is estimated with the following regression equation:

$$E(R_{j,t}) = a_j + b_j R_{m,t} + e_{j,t}$$

where $E(R_{j,t})$ is the expected return of stock j during time t; a_j is a constant (approximately equal to the rate of return on risk-free equities); b_j is an empirical estimate of the financial parameter β (equal to the covariance between the returns of a particular firm's stock and the average return of all stocks in the market, over time); $R_{m,t}$ is the actual average rate of return of all stocks in the market over time; and $e_{j,t}$ is an error term. The form of this equation is derived from the capital asset pricing model in finance. In this model, $E(R_{j,t})$ is simply the expected

Evaluating the Performance Effects of Acquisitions

performance of a stock, given the historical relationship between that stock and the overall performance of the stock market.

To calculate the unexpected performance of a stock, this expected level of performance is simply subtracted from the actual level of performance for a stock. This is done in the following equation:

$$XR_{j,t} = R_{j,t} - (a_j + b_j R_{m,t})$$

where $R_{j,t}$ is the actual performance of stock j during time t, and $XR_{j,t}$ is the unexpected performance of stock j during time t.

In calculating the CAR for a particular acquisition, it is necessary to sum the unexpected returns ($XR_{j,t}$) for a stock across the t periods when the stock market is responding to news about this acquisition. Most analyses of acquisitions examine the market's reaction one day before an acquisition is formally announced to three days after it is announced. The sum of these unexpected returns over this

time period is the CAR attributable to this acquisition.

This methodology has been applied to literally thousands of acquisition episodes. For example, when Manulife Financial purchased John Hancock Financial, Manulife's CAR was –10 percent, whereas John Hancock's CAR was 6 percent; when Anthem acquired Wellpoint, Anthem's CAR was –10 percent, and Wellpoint's was 7 percent; when Bank of America acquired FleetBoston Financial, Bank of America's CAR was –9 percent, and FleetBoston's was 24 percent; and when UnitedHealth acquired Mid Atlantic Medical, UnitedHealth's CAR was –4 percent, and Mid Atlantic Medical's was 11 percent.

Although the event study method has been used widely, it does have some important limitations. First, it is based entirely on the capital asset pricing model, and there is some reason to believe that this model is not a particularly good predictor of a firm's expected stock price. Second, it assumes that a firm's equity holders can anticipate all the benefits associated with making an acquisition at the time that acquisition is made. Some scholars have argued that value creation continues long after an acquisition is announced as parties in this exchange discover value-creating opportunities that could not have been anticipated.

Sources: A. Arikan (2004). "Long-term returns to acquisitions: The case of purchasing tangible and intangible assets." Unpublished, Fisher College of Business, Ohio State University; S. J. Brown and J. B. Warner (1985). "Using daily stock returns: The case of event studies." *Journal of Financial Economics*, 14, pp. 3–31; D. Henry, M. Der Hovanseian, and D. Foust (2003). "M&A deals: Show me." *BusinessWeek*, November 10, pp. 38+.

Managerial Hubris

Another reason why managers may choose to continue to invest in mergers and acquisitions, despite the fact that, on average, they gain no profits from doing so, is the existence of what has been called **managerial hubris**.[14] This is the unrealistic belief held by managers in bidding firms that they can manage the assets of a target firm more efficiently than the target firm's current management. This notion can lead bidding firms to engage in acquisition strategies even though there may not be positive economic profits from doing so.

The existence of managerial hubris suggests that the economic value of bidding firms will fall once they announce a merger or acquisition strategy. Although managers in bidding firms might truly believe that they can manage a target firm's assets more efficiently than the target firm's managers, investors in the capital markets are much less likely to be caught up in this hubris. In this context, a commitment to a merger or acquisition strategy is a strong signal that a bidding firm's management has deluded itself about its abilities to manage a target firm's assets. Such delusions will certainly adversely affect the economic value of the bidding firm.

Of course, empirical work on mergers and acquisitions discussed earlier in this chapter has concluded that although bidding firms do not obtain profits from their merger and acquisition strategies, they also do not, on average, reduce their economic value from implementing these strategies. This is inconsistent with the "hubris hypothesis." However, the fact that, on average, bidding firms do not lose economic value does not mean that some bidding firms do not lose economic value. Thus, although it is unlikely that all merger and acquisition strategies are motivated by managerial hubris, it is likely that at least some of them are.[15]

The Potential for Economic Profits

A final reason why managers might continue to pursue merger and acquisition strategies is the potential that these strategies offer for generating profits for at least some bidding firms. The empirical research on returns to bidding firms in mergers and acquisitions is very strong. On average, bidding firms do not gain profits from their merger and acquisition strategies. However, the fact that bidding firms, *on average*, do not earn profits on these strategies does not mean that *all* bidding firms will *always* fail to earn profits. In some situations, bidding firms may be able to gain competitive advantages from merger and acquisition activities. These situations are discussed in the following section.

Mergers and Acquisitions and Sustained Competitive Advantage

V R I O

We have already seen that the economies of scope that motivate mergers and acquisitions between strategically related bidding and target firms can be valuable. However, the ability of these economies to generate profits and competitive advantages for bidding firms depends not only on their economic value, but also on the competitiveness of the market for corporate control through which these valuable economies are realized. The **market for corporate control** is the market that is created when multiple firms actively seek to acquire one or several firms. Only when the market for corporate control is imperfectly competitive might it be possible for bidding firms to earn profits from implementing a merger or acquisition strategy. To see how the competitiveness of the market for corporate control can affect returns to merger and acquisition strategies, we will consider three scenarios involving bidding and target firms and examine their implications for the managers of these firms.[16]

Valuable, Rare, and Private Economies of Scope

An imperfectly competitive market for corporate control can exist when a target is worth more to one bidder than it is to any other bidders and when no other firms—including bidders and targets—are aware of this additional value. In this setting, the price of a target will rise to reflect public expectations about the value of the target. Once the target is acquired, however, the performance of the special bidder that acquires the target will be greater than generally expected, and this level of performance will generate profits for the equity holders of the bidding firm.

Consider a simple case. Suppose the market value of bidder Firm A combined with target firms is $12,000, whereas the market value of all other bidders combined with targets is $10,000. No other firms (bidders or targets) are aware of Firm A's unique relationship with these targets, but they are aware of the value of all other bidders combined with targets (i.e., $10,000). Suppose also that the market value of all bidding firms, as stand-alone entities, is $7,000. In this setting, Firm A will be willing to pay up to $5,000 to acquire a target ($12,000 − $7,000), and all other bidders will only be willing to pay up to $3,000 to acquire a target ($10,000 − $7,000).

Because publicly available information suggests that acquiring a target is worth $3,000 more than the target's stand-alone price, the price of targets will rapidly rise to this level, ensuring that, if bidding firms, apart from Firm A, acquire a target, they will obtain no profits. If there is only one target in this market for corporate control, then Firm A will be able to bid slightly more than $3,000 (perhaps $3,001) for this target. No other firms will bid higher than Firm A because, from their point of view, the acquisition is simply not worth more than $3,000. At this $3,001 price, Firm A will earn a profit of $1,999—Firm A had to spend only $3,001 for a firm that brings $5,000 in value above its stand-alone market price. Alternatively, if there are multiple targets, then several bidding firms, including Firm A, will pay $3,000 for their targets. At this price, these bidding firms will all earn zero economic profits, except for Firm A, which will earn an economic profit equal to $2,000. That is, only Firm A will gain a competitive advantage from acquiring a target in this market.

In order for Firm A to obtain this profit, the value of Firm A's economy of scope with target firms must be greater than the value of any other bidding firms with that target. This special value will generally reflect unusual resources and capabilities possessed by Firm A—resources and capabilities that are more valuable in combination with target firms than are the resources and capabilities that other bidding firms possess. Put differently, to be a source of economic profits and competitive advantage, Firm A's link with targets must be based on resources and capabilities that are rare among those firms competing in this market for corporate control.

However, not only does Firm A have to possess valuable and rare links with bidding firms to gain economic profits and competitive advantages from its acquisition strategies, but information about these special economies of scope must not be known by other firms. If other bidding firms know about the additional value associated with acquiring a target, they are likely to try to duplicate this value for themselves. Typically, they would accomplish this by imitating the type of relatedness that exists between Firm A and its targets by developing the resources and capabilities that enabled Firm A to have its valuable economies of scope with targets. Once other bidders developed the resources and capabilities necessary to obtain this more valuable economy of scope, they would be able to enter into bidding, thereby increasing the likelihood that the equity holders of successful bidding firms would earn no economic profits.

Target firms must also be unaware of Firm A's special resources and capabilities if Firm A is to obtain competitive advantages from an acquisition. If target firms were aware of this extra value available to Firm A, along with the sources of this value, they could inform other bidding firms. These bidding firms could then adjust their bids to reflect this higher value, and competitive bidding would reduce profits to bidders. Target firms are likely to inform bidding firms in this way because increasing the number of bidders with more valuable economies of scope increases the likelihood that target firms will extract all the economic value created in a merger or acquisition.[17]

Valuable, Rare, and Costly-to-Imitate Economies of Scope

The existence of firms that have valuable, rare, and private economies of scope with targets is not the only way that the market for corporate control can be imperfectly competitive. If other bidders cannot imitate one bidder's valuable and rare economies with targets, then competition in this market for corporate control will be imperfect, and the equity holders of this special bidding firm will earn economic profits. In this case, the existence of valuable and rare economies does not need to be private because other bidding firms cannot imitate these economies, and therefore bids that substantially reduce the profits for the equity holders of the special bidding firm are not forthcoming.

Typically, bidding firms will be unable to imitate one bidder's valuable and rare economies of scope with targets when the strategic relatedness between the special bidder and the targets stems from some rare and costly-to-imitate resources or capabilities controlled by the special bidding firm. Any of the costly-to-imitate resources and capabilities discussed in Chapter 3 could create costly-to-imitate economies of scope between a firm and a target. If, in addition, these economies are valuable and rare, they can be a source of profits to the equity holders of the special bidding firm. This can happen even if all firms in this market for corporate control are aware of the more valuable economies of scope available to this firm and its sources. Although information about this special economy of scope is publicly available, equity holders of special bidding firms will earn a profit when acquisition occurs. The equity holders of target firms will not obtain all of this profit because competitive bidding dynamics cannot unfold when the sources of a more valuable economy of scope are costly to imitate.

Of course, it may be possible for a valuable, rare, and costly-to-imitate economy of scope between a bidding and a target firm to also be private. Indeed, it is often the case that those attributes of a firm that are costly to imitate are also difficult to describe and thus can be held as proprietary information. In that case, the analysis of profits associated with valuable, rare, and private economies of scope presented earlier applies.

Unexpected Valuable Economies of Scope Between Bidding and Target Firms

Thus far, this discussion has adopted, for convenience, the strong assumption that the present value of the strategic relatedness between bidders and targets is known with certainty by individual bidders. This is, in principle, possible, but certainly not likely. Most modern acquisitions and mergers are massively complex, involving numerous unknown and complicated relationships between firms. In these settings, unexpected events after an acquisition has been completed may make an acquisition or merger more valuable than bidders and targets anticipated it would be. The price that bidding firms will pay to acquire a target will equal the expected value of the target only when the target is combined with the bidder. The difference between the unexpected value of an acquisition actually obtained by a bidder and the price the bidder paid for the acquisition is a profit for the equity holders of the bidding firm.

Of course, by definition, bidding firms cannot expect to obtain unexpected value from an acquisition. Unexpected value, in this context, is a surprise, a manifestation of a bidding firm's good luck, not its skill in acquiring targets. For example, when the British advertising firm WPP acquired J. Walter Thompson for $550 million, it discovered some property owned by J. Walter Thomson in Tokyo. No one knew of this property when the firm was acquired. It turned out to be worth more than $100 million after taxes, a financial windfall that helped offset the high cost of this acquisition. When asked, Martin Sorrel, president of WPP and the architect of this acquisition, admitted that this $100 million windfall was simply good luck.[18]

Implications for Bidding Firm Managers

The existence of valuable, rare, and private economies of scope between bidding and target firms and of valuable, rare, and costly-to-imitate economies of scope between bidding and target firms suggests that although, on average, most bidding firms do not generate competitive advantages from their acquisition strategies, in some special circumstances it may be possible for them to do so. Thus, the task facing managers in firms contemplating merger and acquisition strategies is to choose strategies that have the greatest likelihood of being able to generate profits for their equity holders. Several important managerial prescriptions can be derived from this discussion. These "rules" for bidding firm managers are summarized in Table 10.5.

TABLE 10.5 Rules for Bidding Firm Managers

1. Search for valuable and rare economies of scope.
2. Keep information away from other bidders.
3. Keep information away from targets.
4. Avoid winning bidding wars.
5. Close the deal quickly.
6. Operate in "thinly traded" acquisition markets.

Search for Valuable and Rare Economies of Scope

One of the main reasons why bidding firms do not obtain competitive advantages from acquiring strategically related target firms is that several other bidding firms value the target firm in the same way. When multiple bidders all value a target in the same way, competitive bidding is likely. Competitive bidding, in turn, drives out the potential for superior performance. To avoid this problem, bidding firms should seek to acquire targets with which they enjoy valuable and rare linkages.

Operationally, the search for rare economies of scope suggests that managers in bidding firms need to consider not only the value of a target firm when combined with their own company, but also the value of a target firm when combined with other potential bidders. This is important because it is the difference between the value of a particular bidding firm's relationship with a target and the value of other bidding firms' relationships with that target that defines the size of the potential economic profits from an acquisition.

In practice, the search for valuable and rare economies of scope is likely to become a search for valuable and rare resources already controlled by a firm that are synergistically related to a target. For example, if a bidding firm has a unique reputation in its product market and if the target firm's products could benefit by association with that reputation, then the target firm may be more valuable to this particular bidder than to other bidders (firms that do not possess this special reputation). Also, if a particular bidder possesses the largest market share in its industry, the best distribution system, or restricted access to certain key raw materials and if the target firm would benefit from being associated with these valuable and rare resources, then the acquisition of this target may be a source of economic profits.

The search for valuable and rare economies of scope as a basis of mergers and acquisitions tends to rule out certain interfirm linkages as sources of economic profits. For example, most acquisitions can lead to a reduction in overhead costs because much of the corporate overhead associated with the target firm can be eliminated subsequent to acquisition. However, the ability to eliminate these overhead costs is not unique to any one bidder, and thus the value created by these reduced costs will usually be captured by the equity holders of the target firm.

Keep Information Away from Other Bidders

One of the keys to earning superior performance in an acquisition strategy is to avoid multiple bidders for a single target. One way to accomplish this is to keep information about the bidding process, and about the sources of economies of scope between a bidder and target that underlie this bidding process, as private as possible. In order for other firms to become involved in bidding for a target, they must be aware of the value of the economies of scope between themselves and that target. If only one bidding firm knows this information and if this bidding firm can close the deal before the full value of the target is known, then it may gain a competitive advantage from completing this acquisition.

Of course, in many circumstances, keeping all this information private is difficult. Often, it is illegal. For example, when seeking to acquire a publicly traded firm, potential bidders must meet disclosure requirements that effectively reduce the amount of private information a bidder can retain. In these circumstances, unless a bidding firm has some valuable, rare, and costly-to-imitate economy of scope with a target firm, the possibility of economic profits coming from an acquisition is very low. It is not surprising that the research conducted on mergers and acquisitions of firms traded on public stock exchanges governed by the U.S. Securities and Exchange Commission (SEC) disclosure rules suggests that, most of the time, bidding firms do not earn economic profits from implementing their acquisition strategies.

However, not all potential targets are publicly traded. Privately held firms may be acquired in an information environment that can create opportunities for above-normal performance for bidding firms. Moreover, even when acquiring a publicly traded firm, a bidder does not have to release all the information it has about the potential value of that target in combination with itself. Indeed, if some of this value reflects a bidding firm's taken-for-granted "invisible" assets, it may not be possible to communicate this information. In this case, as well, there may be opportunities for competitive advantages for bidding firms.

Keep Information Away from Targets

Not only should bidding firms keep information about the value of their economy of scope with a target away from other bidders, they should also keep this information away from target firms. Suppose that the value of a target firm to a bidding firm is $8,000, but the bidding firm, in an attempt to earn economic profits, has bid only $5,000 for the target. If the target knows that it is actually worth $8,000, it is very likely to hold out for a higher bid. In fact, the target may contact other potential bidding firms and tell them of the opportunity created by the $5,000 bid. As the number of bidders goes up, the possibility of superior economic performance for bidders goes down. Therefore, to keep the possibility of these profits alive, bidding firms must not fully reveal the value of their economies of scope with a target firm. Again, in some circumstances, it is very difficult, or even illegal, to attempt to limit the flow of information to target firms. In these settings, superior economic performance for bidding firms is very unlikely.

Limiting the amount of information that flows to the target firm may have some other consequences as well. For example, it has been shown that a complete sharing of information, insights, and perspectives before an acquisition is completed increases the probability that economies of scope will actually be realized once it is completed.[19] By limiting the flow of information between itself and a target, a bidding firm may actually be increasing the cost of integrating the target into its ongoing business, thereby jeopardizing at least some of the superior economic performance that limiting information flow is designed to create. Bidding firms will need to carefully balance the economic benefits of limiting the information they share with the target firm against the costs that limiting information flow may create.

Avoid Winning Bidding Wars

It should be reasonably clear that if a number of firms bid for the same target, the probability that the firm that successfully acquires the target will gain competitive advantages is very low. Indeed, to ensure that competitive bidding occurs, target firms can actively encourage other bidding firms to enter into the bidding process. The implications of these arguments are clear: Bidding firms should generally avoid winning a bidding war. To "win" a bidding war, a bidding firm will often have to pay a price at least equal to the full value of the target. Many times, given the emotions of an intense bidding contest, the winning bid may actually be larger than the true value of the target. Completing this type of acquisition will certainly reduce the economic performance of the bidding firm.

The only time it might make sense to "win" a bidding war is when the winning firm possesses a rare and private or a rare and costly-to-imitate economy of scope with a target that is more valuable than the strategic relatedness that exists between any other bidders and that target. In this setting, the winning firm may be able to earn a profit if it is able to fully realize the value of its relationship with the target.

Close the Deal Quickly

Another rule of thumb for obtaining superior performance from implementing merger and acquisition strategies is to close the deal quickly. All the economic processes that make it difficult for bidding firms to earn economic profits from acquiring a strategically related target take time to unfold. It takes time for other bidders to become aware of the economic value associated with acquiring a target; it takes time for the target to recruit other bidders; information leakage becomes more of a problem over time; and so forth. A bidding firm that begins and ends the bidding process quickly may forestall some of these processes and thereby retain some superior performance for itself.

The admonition to close the deal quickly should not be taken to mean that bidding firms need to make their acquisition decisions quickly. Indeed, the search for valuable and rare economies of scope should be undertaken with great care. There should be little rush in isolating and evaluating acquisition candidates. However, once a target firm has been located and valued, bidding firms have a strong incentive to reduce the period of time between the first bid and the completion of the deal. The longer this period of negotiation, the less likely it is that the bidding firm will earn economic profits from the acquisition.

Complete Acquisitions in "Thinly Traded" Markets

Finally, an acquisition strategy can be a source of economic profits to bidding firms if these firms implement this corporate strategy in what could be described as "thinly traded markets." In general, a **thinly traded market** is a market where there are only a small number of buyers and sellers, where information about opportunities in this market is not widely known, and where interests besides purely maximizing the value of a firm can be important. In the context of mergers and acquisitions, thinly traded markets are markets where only a few (often only one) firms are implementing acquisition strategies. These unique firms may be the only firms that understand the full value of the acquisition opportunities in this market. Even target firm managers may not fully understand the value of the economic opportunities in these markets, and, if they do, they may have other interests besides maximizing the value of their firm if it becomes the object of a takeover.

In general, thinly traded merger and acquisition markets are highly fragmented. Competition in these markets occurs at the local level, as one small local firm competes with other small local firms for a common group of geographically defined customers. Most of these small firms are privately held. Many are sole proprietorships. Examples of these thinly traded markets have included, at various points in history, the printing industry, the fast-food industry, the used-car industry, the dry-cleaning industry, and the barber shop/hair salon industry.

As was suggested in Chapter 2, the major opportunity in all highly fragmented industries is consolidation. In the context of mergers and acquisitions, consolidation can occur by one firm (or a small number of firms) buying numerous independent firms to realize economies of scope in these industries. Often, these economies of scope reflect economies of scale in these industries—economies of scale that were not realized in a highly fragmented setting. As long as the number of firms implementing this consolidation strategy is small, then the market for corporate control in these markets will probably be less than perfectly competitive, and opportunities for profits from implementing an acquisition strategy may be possible.

More generally, if a merger or acquisition contest is played out through full-page ads in *The Wall Street Journal*, the ability of bidding firms to gain competitive advantages from their acquisitions is limited. Such highly public acquisitions are likely to lead to very competitive markets for corporate control. Competitive markets for corporate control, in turn, assure that the equity holders of the target firm will appropriate any value that could be created by an acquisition. However, if these contests occur in obscure, out-of-the-way industries, it is more likely that bidding firms will be able to earn profits from their acquisitions.

Service Corporation International: An Example

Empirical research on mergers and acquisitions suggests that it is not easy for bidding firms to earn economic profits from these strategies. However, it may be possible for some bidding firms, some of the time, to do so. One firm that has been successful in gaining competitive advantages from its merger and acquisition strategies is Service Corporation International (SCI). Service Corporation International is in the funeral home and cemetery business. It grew from a collection of five funeral homes in 1967 to being the largest owner of cemeteries and funeral homes in the United States today. It has done this through an aggressive and what was until recently a highly profitable acquisitions program in this historically fragmented industry.

The valuable and rare economy of scope that SCI brought to the funeral home industry is the application of traditional business practices in a highly fragmented and not often professionally managed industry. Service Corporation International–owned funeral homes operate with gross margins approaching 30 percent, nearly three times the gross margins of independently owned funeral homes. Among other things, higher margins reflected savings from centralized purchasing services, centralized embalming and professional services, and the sharing of underutilized resources (including hearses) among funeral homes within geographic regions. Service Corporation International's scale advantages made a particular funeral home more valuable to SCI than to one of SCI's smaller competitors and more valuable than if a particular funeral home was left as a stand-alone business.

Moreover, the funeral homes that SCI targeted for acquisition were, typically, family-owned and lacked heirs to continue the business. Many of the owners or operators of these funeral homes were not fully aware of the value of their operations to SCI (they are morticians more than business managers), nor were they just interested in maximizing the sale price of their funeral homes. Rather, they were often looking to maintain continuity of service in a community, secure employment for their loyal employees, and ensure a comfortable (if not lavish) retirement for themselves. Being acquired by SCI was likely to be the only alternative to closing the funeral home once an owner or operator retired. Extracting less than the full value of the funeral home when selling to SCI often seemed preferable to other alternatives.

Because SCI's acquisition of funeral homes exploited real and valuable economies of scope, this strategy had the potential for generating superior economic performance. Because SCI was, for many years, the only firm implementing this strategy in the funeral home industry, because the funeral homes that SCI acquired were generally not publicly traded, and because the owners or operators of these funeral homes often had interests besides simply maximizing the price of their operations when they sold them, it seems likely that SCI's acquisition strategy generated superior economic performance for many years. However, information about SCI's acquisition strategy has become widely known. This has led other funeral homes to begin bidding to acquire formerly independent funeral homes. Moreover, independent funeral home owners have become more aware of their full value to SCI. Although SCI's economy of scope with independent funeral homes is still valuable, it is no longer rare, and thus it is no longer a source of economic profits to SCI. Put differently, the imperfectly competitive market for corporate control that SCI was able to exploit for almost 10 years has become more perfectly competitive. Future acquisitions in this market by SCI are not likely to be a source of sustained competitive advantage and economic profit. In response, SCI now focuses on managing its more than 1,800 funeral homes in the United States.[20]

Implications for Target Firm Managers

Although bidding firm managers can do several things to attempt to maximize the probability of earning economic profits from their merger and acquisition strategies, target firm managers can attempt to counter these efforts to ensure that the owners of target firms appropriate whatever value is created by a merger or acquisition. These "rules" for target firm managers are summarized in Table 10.6.

Seek Information from Bidders

One way a bidder can attempt to obtain superior performance from implementing an acquisition strategy is to keep information about the source and value of the strategic relatedness that exists between the bidder and target private. If that relationship is actually worth $12,000, but targets believe it is only worth $8,000, then a target might be willing to settle for a bid of $8,000 and, thereby, forgo the extra $4,000 it could have extracted from the bidder. Once the target knows that its true value to the bidder is $12,000, it is in a much better position to obtain this full value when the acquisition is completed. Therefore, not only should a bidding firm inform itself about the value of a target, target firms must inform themselves about their value to potential bidders. In this way, they can help obtain the full value of their assets.

TABLE 10.6 Rules for Target Firm Managers

1. Seek information from bidders.
2. Invite other bidders to join the bidding competition.
3. Delay, but do not stop, the acquisition.

Invite Other Bidders to Join the Bidding Competition

Once a target firm is fully aware of the nature and value of the economies of scope that exist between it and current bidding firms, it can exploit this information by seeking other firms that may have the same relationship with it and then informing these firms of a potential acquisition opportunity. By inviting other firms into the bidding process, the target firm increases the competitiveness of the market for corporate control, thereby increasing the probability that the value created by an acquisition will be fully captured by the target firm.

Delay, but Do Not Stop, the Acquisition

As suggested earlier, bidding firms have a strong incentive to expedite the acquisition process in order to prevent other bidders from becoming involved in an acquisition. Of course, the target firm wants other bidding firms to enter the process. To increase the probability of receiving more than one bid, target firms have a strong incentive to delay an acquisition.

The objective, however, should be to delay an acquisition to create a more competitive market for corporate control, not to stop an acquisition. If a valuable economy of scope exists between a bidding firm and a target firm, the merger of these two firms will create economic value. If the market for corporate control within which this merger occurs is competitive, then the equity holders of the target firm will appropriate the full value of this economy of scope. Preventing an acquisition in this setting can be very costly to the equity holders of the target firm.

Target firm managers can engage in a wide variety of activities to delay the completion of an acquisition. Some common responses of target firm management to takeover efforts, along with their economic implications for the equity holders of target firms, are discussed in the Research Made Relevant feature.

V R I O   Organizing to Implement a Merger or Acquisition

To realize the full value of any strategic relatedness that exists between a bidding firm and a target firm, the merged organizations must be organized appropriately. The realization of each of the types of strategic relatedness discussed earlier in this chapter requires at least some coordination and integration between the bidding and target firms after an acquisition has occurred. For example, to realize economies of scale from an acquisition, bidding and target firms must coordinate in the combined firm the functions that are sensitive to economies of scale. To realize the value of any technology that a bidding firm acquires from a target firm, the combined firm must use this technology in developing, manufacturing, or selling its products. To exploit underutilized leverage capacity in the target firm, the balance sheets of the bidding and target firms must be merged, and the resulting firm must then seek additional debt funding. To realize the opportunity of replacing the target firm's inefficient management with more efficient management from the bidding firm, these management changes must actually take place.

Post-acquisition coordination and integration is essential if bidding and target firms are to realize the full potential of the strategic relatedness that drove the acquisition in the first place. If a bidding firm decides not to coordinate or integrate any of its business activities with the activities of a target firm, then why was this target firm acquired? Just as corporate diversification requires the active management of linkages among different parts of a firm, mergers and acquisitions (as one way in which corporate diversification strategies can be created) require the active management of linkages between a bidding and a target firm.

Post-Merger Integration and Implementing a Diversification Strategy

Given that most merger and acquisition strategies are used to create corporate diversification strategies, the organizational approaches previously described for implementing diversification are relevant for implementing merger and acquisition strategies as well. Thus, mergers and acquisitions designed to create diversification strategies should be managed through the M-form structure. The management control systems and compensation policies associated with implementing diversification strategies should also be applied in organizing to implement merger and acquisition strategies. In contrast, mergers and acquisitions designed to create vertical integration strategies should be managed through the U-form structure and have management controls and compensation policies consistent with this strategy.

Special Challenges in Post-Merger Integration

Although, in general, organizing to implement merger and acquisition strategies can be seen as a special case of organizing to implement corporate diversification strategies or vertical integration strategies, implementing merger and acquisition strategies can create special problems. Most of these problems reflect the fact that operational, functional, strategic, and cultural differences between bidding and target firms involved in a merger or acquisition are likely to be much greater than these same differences between the different parts of a diversified or vertically integrated business that was not created through acquisition. The reason for this difference is that the firms involved in a merger or acquisition have had a separate existence, separate histories, separate management philosophies, and separate strategies.

Differences between bidding and target firms can manifest themselves in a wide variety of ways. For example, the firms may own and operate different computer systems, different telephone systems, and other conflicting technologies. These firms might have very different human resource policies and practices. One firm might have a very generous retirement and health care program; the other, a less generous program. One firm's compensation system might focus on high salaries; the other firm's compensation system might focus on large cash bonuses and stock options. Also, these firms might have very different relationships with customers. At one firm, customers might be thought of as business partners; in another, the relationship with customers might be more arm's-length in character. Integrating bidding and target firms may require the resolution of numerous differences.

Perhaps the most significant challenge in integrating bidding and target firms has to do with cultural differences.[21] In Chapter 3, it was suggested that it can often be difficult to change a firm's organizational culture. The fact that a firm has been acquired does not mean that the culture in that firm will rapidly change to become more like the culture of the bidding firm; cultural conflicts can last for very long periods of time.

Research Made Relevant

Managers in potential target firms can respond to takeover attempts in a variety of ways. As suggested in Table 10.7, some of these responses increase the wealth of target firm shareholders, some have no impact on target firm shareholders, and others decrease the wealth of target firm shareholders.

Management responses that have the effect of reducing the value of target firms include greenmail, standstill agreements, and "poison pills." Each of these is an anti-takeover action that target firm managers can take to reduce the wealth of target firm equity holders. **Greenmail** is a maneuver in which a target firm's management purchases any of the target firm's stock owned by a bidder and does so for a price that is greater than the current market value of that stock. Greenmail effectively ends a bidding firm's effort to acquire a particular target and does so in a way that can greatly reduce the wealth of a target firm's equity holders. Not only do these equity holders not appropriate any economic value that could have been created if

The Wealth Effects of Management Responses to Takeover Attempts

an acquisition had been completed, but they have to bear the cost of the premium price that management pays to buy its stock back from the bidding firm.

Not surprisingly, target firms that resort to greenmail substantially reduce the economic wealth of their equity holders. One study found that the value of target firms that pay greenmail drops, on average, 1.76 percent. Another study reported a 2.85 percent drop in the value of such firms. These reductions in value are greater if

greenmail leads to the cancellation of a takeover effort. Indeed, this second study found that such episodes led to a 5.50 percent reduction in the value of target firms. These reductions in value as a response to greenmail activities stand in marked contrast to the generally positive market response to efforts by a firm to repurchase its own shares in nongreenmail situations.

Standstill agreements are often negotiated in conjunction with greenmail. A standstill agreement is a contract between a target and a bidding firm wherein the bidding firm agrees not to attempt to take over the target for some period of time. When a target firm negotiates a standstill agreement, it prevents the current acquisition effort from being completed, and it reduces the number of bidders that might become involved in future acquisition efforts. Thus, the equity holders of this target firm forgo any value that could have been created if the current acquisition had occurred, and they also lose some of the value that they could have appropriated in future acquisition episodes by the

TABLE 10.7 The Wealth Effects of Target Firm Management Responses to Acquisition Efforts

1. Responses that reduce the wealth of target firm equity holders:
   - Greenmail
   - Standstill agreements
   - Poison pills
2. Responses that do not affect the wealth of target firm equity holders:
   - Shark repellents
   - Pac Man defense
   - Crown jewel sale
   - Lawsuits
3. Responses that increase the wealth of target firm equity holders:
   - Search for white knights
   - Creation of bidding auctions
   - Golden parachutes

target's inviting multiple bidders into a market for corporate control.

Standstill agreements, either alone or in conjunction with greenmail, reduce the economic value of a target firm. One study found that standstill agreements that were unaccompanied by stock repurchase agreements reduced the value of a target firm by 4.05 percent. Such agreements, in combination with stock repurchases, reduced the value of a target firm by 4.52 percent.

So-called **poison pills** include any of a variety of actions that target firm managers can take to make the acquisition of the target prohibitively expensive. In one common poison-pill maneuver, a target firm issues rights to its current stockholders indicating that if the firm is acquired in an unfriendly takeover, it will distribute a special cash dividend to stockholders. This cash dividend effectively increases the cost of acquiring the target and can discourage otherwise interested bidding firms from attempting to acquire this target. Another poison-pill tactic substitutes the distribution of additional shares of a target firm's stock, at very low prices, for the special cash dividend. Issuing this low-price stock to current stockholders effectively undermines the value of a bidding firm's equity investment in a target and thus increases the cost of the acquisition. Other poison pills involve granting current stockholders other rights—rights that effectively increase the cost of an unfriendly takeover.

Although poison pills are creative devices that target firms can use to prevent an acquisition, they generally have not been very effective. If

a bidding firm and a target firm are strategically related, the value that can be created in an acquisition can be substantial, and most of this value will be appropriated by the stockholders of the target firm. Thus, target firm stockholders have a strong incentive to see that the target firm is acquired, and they are amenable to direct offers made by a bidding firm to them as individual investors; these are called **tender offers**. However, to the extent that poison pills actually do prevent mergers and acquisitions, they are usually bad for the equity holders of target firms.

Target firm management can also engage in a wide variety of actions that have little or no impact on the wealth of a target firm's equity holders. One class of these responses is known as shark repellents. **Shark repellents** include a variety of relatively minor corporate governance changes that, in principle, are supposed to make it somewhat more difficult to acquire a target firm. Common examples of shark repellents include **supermajority voting rules** (which specify that more than 50 percent of the target firm's board of directors must approve a takeover) and state incorporation laws (in some states, incorporation laws make it difficult to acquire a firm incorporated in that state). However, if the value created by an acquisition is sufficiently large, these shark repellents will neither slow an acquisition attempt significantly nor prevent it from being completed.

Another response that does not affect the wealth of target firm equity holders is known as the **Pac Man defense**. Targets using this tactic fend

off an acquisition by taking over the firm or firms bidding for them. Just as in the old video game, the hunted becomes the hunter; the target turns the tables on current and potential bidders. It should not be too surprising that the Pac Man defense does not, on average, either hurt or help the stockholders of target firms. In this defense, targets become bidders, and we know from empirical literature that, on average, bidding firms earn only zero economic profits from their acquisition efforts. Thus, one would expect that, on average, the Pac Man defense would generate only zero economic profits for the stockholders of target firms implementing it.

Another ineffective and inconsequential response is called a **crown jewel sale**. The idea behind a crown jewel sale is that sometimes a bidding firm is interested in just a few of the businesses currently being operated by the target firm. These businesses are the target firm's "crown jewels." To prevent an acquisition, the target firm can sell off these crown jewels, either directly to the bidding firm or by setting up a separate company to own and operate these businesses. In this way, the bidding firm is likely to be less interested in acquiring the target.

A final, relatively ineffective defense that most target firm managers pursue is filing lawsuits against bidding firms. Indeed, at least in the United States, the filing of a lawsuit has been almost automatic as soon as an acquisition effort is announced. These suits, however, usually do not delay or stop an acquisition or merger.

(Continued)

Finally, as suggested in Table 10.7, some of the actions that the management of target firms can take to delay (but not stop) an acquisition actually benefit target firm equity holders. The first of these is the search for a **white knight**—another bidding firm that agrees to acquire a particular target in the place of the original bidding firm. Target firm management may prefer to be acquired by some bidding firms over others. For example, it may be that some bidding firms possess much more valuable economies of scope with a target firm than other bidding firms. It may also be that some bidding firms will take a longer-term view in managing a target firm's assets than other bidding firms. In both cases, target firm managers are likely to prefer some bidding firms over others.

Whatever motivation a target firm's management has, inviting a white knight to bid on a target firm has the effect of increasing the number of firms bidding for a target by at least one. If there is currently only one bidder, inviting a white knight into the bidding competition doubles the number of firms bidding for a target. As the number of bidders increases, the competitiveness of the market for corporate control and the likelihood that the equity holders of the target firm will appropriate all the value created by an acquisition also increase. On average, the entrance of a white knight into a competitive bidding contest for a target firm increases the wealth of target firm equity holders by 17 percent.

If adding one firm into the competitive bidding process increases the wealth of target firm equity holders some, then adding more firms to the process is likely to increase this wealth even more. Target firms can accomplish this outcome by creating an **auction** among bidding firms. On average, the creation of an auction among multiple bidders increases the wealth of target firm equity holders by 20 percent.

A third action that the managers of a target firm can take to increase the wealth of their equity holders from an acquisition effort is the institution of **golden parachutes.** A golden parachute is a compensation arrangement between a firm and its senior management team that promises these individuals a substantial cash payment if their firm is acquired and they lose their jobs in the process. These cash payments can appear to be very large, but they are actually quite small in comparison to the total value that can be created if a merger or acquisition is completed. In this sense, golden parachutes are a small price to pay to give a potential target firm's top managers incentives not to stand in the way of completing a takeover of their firm. Put differently, golden parachutes reduce agency problems for the equity holders of a potential target firm by aligning the interests of top managers with the interests of that firm's stockholders. On average, when a firm announces golden parachute compensation packages for its top management team, the value of this potential target firm's equity increases by 7 percent.

Overall, substantial evidence suggests that delaying an acquisition long enough to ensure that a competitive market for corporate control emerges can significantly benefit the equity holders of target firms. One study found that when target firms did not delay the completion of an acquisition, their equity holders experienced, on average, a 36 percent increase in the value of their stock once the acquisition was complete. If, however, target firms did delay the completion of the acquisition, this average increase in value jumped to 65 percent.

Of course, target firm managers can delay too long. Delaying too long can create opportunity costs for their firm's equity holders because these individuals do not actually realize the gain from an acquisition until it has been completed. Also, long delays can jeopardize the completion of an acquisition, in which case the equity holders of the target firm do not realize any gains from the acquisition.

Sources: R. Walkling and M. Long (1984). "Agency theory, managerial welfare, and takeover bid resistance." *Rand Journal of Economics,* 15(1), pp. 54–68; R. D. Kosnik (1987). "Greenmail: A study of board performance in corporate governance." *Administrative Science Quarterly,* 32, pp. 163–185; J. Walsh (1989). "Doing a deal: Merger and acquisition negotiations and their impact upon target company top management turnover." *Strategic Management Journal,* 10, pp. 307–322; L. Y. Dann and H. DeAngelo (1983). "Standstill agreements, privately negotiated stock repurchases, and the market for corporate control." *Journal of Financial Economics,* 11, pp. 275–300; M. Bradey and L. Wakeman (1983). "The wealth effects of targeted share repurchases." *Journal of Financial Economics,* 11, pp. 301–328; H. Singh and F. Haricento (1989). "Top management tenure, corporate ownership and the magnitude of golden parachutes." *Strategic Management Journal,* 10, pp. 143–156; T. A. Turk (1987). "The determinants of management responses to interfirm tender offers and their effect on shareholder wealth." Unpublished doctoral dissertation, Graduate School of Management, University of California at Irvine.

The failures of what some observers believe are some of the worst acquisitions ever have all been attributed to cultural clashes.[22] For example, the merger between Daimler (the maker of Mercedes-Benz) and Chrysler pitted the culture of a German company that focused on luxury vehicles with a midwestern U.S. company that sold lower-prestige cars and Jeeps. The merger became the source of a widely known joke: "How do you pronounce DaimlerChrysler? Daimler. The Chrysler is silent." These two firms split after only a few painful years.

Also, Novell's acquisition of Word Perfect brought together two management teams that refused to cooperate. While Novell and Word Perfect managers fought each other, Microsoft emerged as the dominant firm in the word processing industry with Microsoft Word. After two years, Novell sold Word Perfect for $1 billion less than its purchase price.

Another disastrous acquisition involved the combination of America Online (AOL) and Time Warner. In 2000, before the merger, AOL's shares sold for more than $75; in 2008, after the merger, they sold for $15. The problem: the clash between the "new media" AOL culture with the "old media" Time Warner culture.

Sprint's acquisition of Nextel was also a spectacular failure. In 2005, the deal cost Sprint $35 billion. Within three years, 80 percent of Sprint's investment in Nextel was written off. The culprit, once again, was the clash between the cultures of these two firms: Sprint was a "button-down" bureaucratic culture that could not tolerate Nextel's more freewheeling entrepreneurial culture. The two management teams fought about everything from advertising strategy to cell phone technology. Not surprisingly, in 2012, SprintNextel was purchased by the third-largest Japanese mobile phone company, Softbank, for $20.1 billion—almost $15 billion less than Sprint had paid for Nextel seven years earlier.

Finally, HP's acquisition of Compaq reduced the market capitalization of HP by approximately $13 billion. HP's engineering- and consensus-driven culture clashed with Compaq's quick-decision, sales-driven culture. After several years, HP has been able to make cultural and leadership changes that have improved the performance of this acquisition, but this integration has been long in coming.

Operational, functional, strategic, and cultural differences between bidding and target firms can all be compounded by the merger and acquisition process—especially if that process was unfriendly. Unfriendly takeovers can generate anger and animosity among the target firm management that is directed toward the management of the bidding firm. Research has shown that top management turnover is much higher in firms that have been taken over compared with firms not subject to takeovers, reflecting one approach to resolving these management conflicts.[23]

The difficulties often associated with organizing to implement a merger and acquisition strategy can be thought of as an additional cost of the acquisition process. Bidding firms, in addition to estimating the value of the strategic relatedness between themselves and a target firm, also need to estimate the cost of organizing to implement an acquisition. The value that a target firm brings to a bidding firm through an acquisition should be discounted by the cost of organizing to implement this strategy. In some circumstances, it may be the case that the cost of organizing to realize the value of strategic relatedness between a bidding firm and a target may be greater than the value of that strategic relatedness, in which case the acquisition should not occur. For this reason, many observers argue that potential economies of scope between bidding and target firms are often not fully realized.

Although organizing to implement mergers and acquisitions can be a source of significant cost, it can also be a source of value and opportunity. Some scholars have suggested that value creation can continue to occur in a merger or acquisition long after the formal acquisition is complete.[24] As bidding and target firms continue to coordinate and integrate their operations, unanticipated opportunities for value creation can be discovered. These sources of value could not have been anticipated at the time a firm was originally acquired (and thus are, at least partially, a manifestation of a bidding firm's good luck), but bidding firms can influence the probability of discovering these unanticipated sources of value by learning to cooperate effectively with target firms while organizing to implement a merger or acquisition strategy.

Summary

Firms can use mergers and acquisitions to create corporate diversification and vertical integration strategies. Mergers or acquisitions between strategically unrelated firms can be expected to generate only competitive parity for both bidders and targets. Thus, firms contemplating merger and acquisition strategies must search for strategically related targets.

Several sources of strategic relatedness have been discussed in literature. On average, the acquisition of strategically related targets does create economic value, but most of that value is captured by the equity holders of target firms. The equity holders of bidding firms generally gain competitive parity even when bidding firms acquire strategically related targets. Empirical research on mergers and acquisitions is consistent with these expectations. On average, acquisitions do create value, but that value is captured by target firms, and acquisitions do not hurt bidding firms.

Given that most mergers and acquisitions generate only zero economic profits for bidding firms, an important question becomes: "Why are there so many mergers and acquisitions?" Explanations include (1) the desire to ensure firm survival, (2) the existence of free cash flow, (3) agency problems between bidding firm managers and equity holders, (4) managerial hubris, and (5) the possibility that some bidding firms might earn economic profits from implementing merger and acquisition strategies.

To gain competitive advantages and economic profits from mergers or acquisitions, these strategies must be either valuable, rare, and private or valuable, rare, and costly to imitate. In addition, a bidding firm may exploit unanticipated sources of strategic relatedness with a target. These unanticipated sources of relatedness can also be a source of economic profits for a bidding firm. These observations have several implications for the managers of bidding and target firms.

Organizing to implement a merger or acquisition strategy can be seen as a special case of organizing to implement a corporate diversification or vertical integration strategy. However, historical differences between bidding and target firms may make the integration of different parts of a firm created through acquisitions more difficult than if a firm is not created through acquisitions. Cultural differences between bidding and target firms are particularly problematic. Bidding firms need to estimate the cost of organizing to implement a merger or acquisition strategy and discount the value of a target by that cost. However, organizing to implement a merger or acquisition can also be a way that bidding and target firms can discover unanticipated economies of scope.

MyManagementLab®

Go to **mymanagementlab.com** to complete the problems marked with this icon ✪.

Challenge Questions

10.1. The terms merger and acquisition are often used interchangeably to describe the combination of two corporate entities. Whilst there are no specific definitions as to what makes a process more of one rather than the other, discuss when distinctions can be made between a merger and an acquisition.

✪**10.2.** Consider this scenario: A firm acquires a strategically related target; there were no other bidding firms. Under what conditions, if any, can the firm that acquired this target expect to earn an economic profit from doing so?

10.3. Some researchers have argued that the existence of free cash flow can lead managers in a firm to make inappropriate acquisition decisions. To avoid these problems, these authors have argued that firms should increase their debt-to-equity ratio and "soak up" free cash flow through interest and principal payments. Is free cash flow a significant problem for many firms?

10.4. What are the strengths and weaknesses of increased leverage as a response to free cash flow problems in a firm?

10.5. The hubris hypothesis suggests that managers continue to engage in acquisitions, even though, on average, they do not generate economic profits, because of the unrealistic belief on the part of these managers that they can manage a target firm's assets more efficiently than that firm's current management. This type of systematic nonrationality usually does not last too long in competitive market conditions: Firms led by managers with these unrealistic beliefs change, are acquired, or go bankrupt in the long run. What are the attributes of the market for corporate control that suggest that managerial hubris could exist in this market, despite its performance-reducing implications for bidding firms?

10.6. The hubris hypothesis suggests that managers continue to engage in acquisitions, even though, on average, they do not generate economic profits, because of the unrealistic belief on the part of these managers that they can manage a target firm's assets more efficiently than that firm's current management. This type of systematic nonrationality usually does not last too long in competitive market conditions: Firms led by managers with these unrealistic beliefs change, are acquired, or go bankrupt in the long run. Can the hubris hypothesis be a legitimate explanation for continuing acquisition activity?

✪**10.7.** It has been shown that so-called poison pills rarely prevent a takeover from occurring. In fact, sometimes when a firm announces that it is instituting a poison pill, its stock price goes up. Why?

10.8. A merger between companies of equal standing is often fraught with peril. This is especially so in the case of large entities, for example, the merger between HP and Compaq, and that of Citicorp and Travelers Group. Whilst the valuation and bidding processes can be challenging, post-merger operations can prove to be even more painful. Enumerate and expand on some of the difficulties that large companies can encounter after corporate consummation.

Problem Set

10.9. For each of the following scenarios, estimate how much value an acquisition will create, how much of that value will be appropriated by each of the bidding firms, and how much of that value will be appropriated by each of the target firms. In each of these scenarios, assume that firms do not face significant capital constraints.

(a) A bidding firm, A, is worth $27,000 as a stand-alone entity. A target firm, B, is worth $12,000 as a stand-alone entity, but $18,000 if it is acquired and integrated with Firm A. Several other firms are interested in acquiring Firm B, and Firm B is also worth $18,000 if it is acquired by these other firms. If Firm A acquired Firm B, would this acquisition create value? If yes, how much? How much of this value would the equity holders of Firm A receive? How much would the equity holders of Firm B receive?

(b) The same scenario as above except that the value of Firm B, if it is acquired by the other firms interested in it, is only $12,000.

(c) The same scenario in part (a), except that the value of Firm B, if it is acquired by the other firms interested in it, is $16,000.

(d) The same scenario as in part (b), except that Firm B contacts several other firms and explains to them how they can create the same value with Firm B that Firm A does.

(e) The same scenario as in part (b), except that Firm B sues Firm A. After suing Firm A, Firm B installs a "supermajority" rule in how its board of directors operates. After putting this new rule in place, Firm B offers to buy back any stock purchased by Firm A for 20 percent above the current market price.

MyManagementLab®

Go to **mymanagementlab.com** for the following Assisted-graded writing questions:

✪ **10.9.** How can product differentiation be used to neutralize environmental threats and exploit environmental opportunities?

✪ **10.10.** How would a firm's investment in merger and acquisition strategies, on average, be expected to generate at least competitive parity for bidding firms?

End Notes

1. See Welch, D., and G. Edmondson. (2004). "A shaky automotive *ménage à trois.*" *BusinessWeek*, May 10, pp. 40–41.
2. (2013). "S&P, Nasdaq set marks as merger activity boosts stocks." *Salt Lake Tribune*, February 20, p. E3.
3. Here, and throughout this chapter, it is assumed that capital markets are semi-strong efficient, that is, all publicly available information about the value of a firm's assets is reflected in the market price of those assets. One implication of semi-strong efficiency is that firms will be able to gain access to the capital they need to pursue any strategy that generates positive present value. See Fama, E. F. (1970). "Efficient capital markets: A review of theory and empirical work." *Journal of Finance*, 25, pp. 383–417.
4. See Trautwein, I. (1990). "Merger motives and merger prescriptions." *Strategic Management Journal*, 11, pp. 283–295; and Walter, G., and J. B. Barney. (1990). "Management objectives in mergers and acquisitions." *Strategic Management Journal*, 11, pp. 79–86. The three lists of potential links between bidding and target firms were developed by the Federal Trade Commission; Lubatkin, M. (1983). "Mergers and the performance of the acquiring firm." *Academy of Management Review*, 8, pp. 218–225; and Jensen, M. C., and R. S. Ruback. (1983). "The market for corporate control: The scientific evidence." *Journal of Financial Economics*, 11, pp. 5–50.
5. See Huey, J. (1995). "Eisner explains everything." *Fortune*, April 17, pp. 44–68; and Lefton, T. (1996). "Fitting ABC and ESPN into Disney: Hands in glove." *Brandweek*, 37(18), April 29, pp. 30–40.
6. See Rumelt, R. (1974). *Strategy, structure, and economic performance.* Cambridge, MA: Harvard University Press.
7. The first study was by Ravenscraft, D. J., and F. M. Scherer. (1987). *Mergers, sell-offs, and economic efficiency.* Washington, DC: Brookings Institution. The second study was by Porter, M. E. (1987). "From competitive advantage to corporate strategy." *Harvard Business Review*, 3, pp. 43–59.
8. This is because if the combined firm is worth $32,000 the bidder firm is worth $15,000 on its own. If a bidder pays, say, $20,000 for this target, it will be paying $20,000 for a firm that can only add $17,000 in value. So, a $20,000 bid would lead to a $3,000 economic loss.
9. This is Jensen, M. C., and R. S. Ruback. (1983). "The market for corporate control: The scientific evidence." *Journal of Financial Economics*, 11, pp. 5–50.
10. See Lubatkin, M. (1987). "Merger strategies and stockholder value." *Strategic Management Journal*, 8, pp. 39–53; and Singh, H., and C. A. Montgomery. (1987). "Corporate acquisition strategies and economic performance." *Strategic Management Journal*, 8, pp. 377–386.
11. See Grant, L. (1995). "Here comes Hugh." *Fortune*, August 21, pp. 43–52; Serwer, A. E. (1995). "Why bank mergers are good for your savings account." *Fortune*, October 2, p. 32; and Deogun, N. (2000). "Europe catches merger fever as global volume sets record." *The Wall Street Journal*, January 3, p. R8.
12. The concept of free cash flow has been emphasized in Jensen, M. C. (1986). "Agency costs of free cash flow, corporate finance, and takeovers." *American Economic Review*, 76, pp. 323–329; and Jensen, M. (1988). "Takeovers: Their causes and consequences." *Journal of Economic Perspectives*, 2, pp. 21–48.
13. See Miles, R. H., and K. S. Cameron. (1982). *Coffin nails and corporate strategies.* Upper Saddle River, NJ: Prentice Hall.
14. Roll, R. (1986). "The hubris hypothesis of corporate takeovers." *Journal of Business*, 59, pp. 205–216.
15. See Dodd, P. (1980). "Merger proposals, managerial discretion and stockholder wealth." *Journal of Financial Economics*, 8, pp. 105–138; Eger, C. E. (1983). "An empirical test of the redistribution effect in pure exchange mergers." *Journal of Financial and Quantitative Analysis*, 18, pp. 547–572; Firth, M. (1980). "Takeovers, shareholder returns, and the theory of the firm." *Quarterly Journal of Economics*, 94, pp. 235–260; Varaiya, N. (1985). "A test of Roll's hubris hypothesis of corporate takeovers." Working paper, Southern Methodist University, School of Business; Ruback, R. S., and W. H. Mikkelson. (1984). "Corporate investments in common stock." Working paper, Massachusetts Institute of Technology, Sloan School of Business; and Ruback, R. S. (1982). "The Conoco takeover and stockholder returns." *Sloan Management Review*, 14, pp. 13–33.
16. This section of the chapter draws on Barney, J. B. (1988). "Returns to bidding firms in mergers and acquisitions: Reconsidering the relatedness hypothesis." *Strategic Management Journal*, 9, pp. 71–78.
17. See Turk, T. A. (1987). "The determinants of management responses to interfirm tender offers and their effect on shareholder wealth." Unpublished doctoral dissertation, Graduate School of Management, University of California at Irvine. In fact, this is an example of an anti-takeover action that can increase the value

of a target firm. These anti-takeover actions are discussed later in this chapter.

18. See Bower, J. (1996). "WPP-integrating icons." Harvard Business School Case No. 9-396-249.

19. See Jemison, D. B., and S. B. Sitkin. (1986). "Corporate acquisitions: A process perspective." *Academy of Management Review*, 11, pp. 145–163.

20. Blackwell, R. D. (1998). "Service Corporation International." Presented to The Cullman Symposium, October, Columbus, OH.

21. Cartwright, S., and C. Cooper. (1993). "The role of culture compatibility in successful organizational marriage." *The Academy of Management Executive*, 7(2), pp. 57–70; Chatterjee, S., M. Lubatkin, D. Schweiger,

and Y. Weber. (1992). "Cultural differences and shareholder value in related mergers: Linking equity and human capital." *Strategic Management Journal*, 13, pp. 319–334.

22. Jacobsen, D. (2012). "Six big mergers killed by culture." *Globoforce*, September 22.

23. See Walsh, J., and J. Ellwood. (1991). "Mergers, acquisitions, and the pruning of managerial deadwood." *Strategic Management Journal*, 12, pp. 201–217; and Walsh, J. (1988). "Top management turnover following mergers and acquisitions." *Strategic Management Journal*, 9, pp. 173–183.

24. See Haspeslagh, P., and D. Jemison. (1991). *Managing acquisitions: Creating value through corporate renewal*. New York: Free Press.

11 International Strategies

LEARNING OBJECTIVES *After reading this chapter, you should be able to:*

1. Define international strategy.

2. Describe the relationship between international strategy and other corporate strategies, including vertical integration and diversification.

3. Describe five ways that international strategies can create economic value.

4. Discuss the trade-off between local responsiveness and international integration and transnational strategies as a way to manage this trade-off.

5. Discuss the political risks associated with international strategies and how they can be measured.

6. Discuss the rarity and imitability of international strategies.

7. Describe four different ways to organize to implement international strategies.

MyManagementLab®

⭐ **Improve Your Grade!**

More than 10 million students improved their results using the Pearson MyLabs.
Visit **mymanagementlab.com** for simulations, tutorials, and end-of-chapter problems.

The Baby Formula Problem

It began in 2008, when most of the domestic dairy producers in China were found to be selling baby formula tainted with the toxic chemical melamine. Melamine—a chemical used in plastics and fertilizers—makes baby formula appear less watery than it actually is. Six babies died, and 300,000 became sick. Not surprisingly, demand among Chinese consumers for baby formula produced by Chinese firms dropped dramatically.

Enter foreign companies. Recognizing a market opportunity, companies headquartered outside China began importing baby formula into China. These included Mead Johnson, Dumex, Abbott Laboratories, Royal FrieslandCampina, and Fonterra. By 2012, non-Chinese producers of baby formula had 60 percent of the Chinese market, even though they charged prices that were 30 percent higher than formula produced by Chinese firms.

Even at these prices, supply of non-Chinese formula was not enough to satisfy Chinese demand. Visitors from China to Hong Kong began loading up on non-Chinese formula and bringing it into the mainland, where they used it for their own children or sold it. This continued until quotas on importing formula from Hong Kong to China were implemented. Shortages of non-Chinese formula began showing up around the world. In the United Kingdom, Tesco and Sainsbury—two leading grocery store chains—had to put restrictions on the amount of baby formula that could be purchased because people were buying numerous boxes of non-Chinese formula and selling it online to consumers in China.

Apparently, even though the melamine poisonings took place in 2008, Chinese consumers still don't trust Chinese producers—and with some reason. Most of the dairy companies that put melamine in their milk in 2008 are still operating. Mengniu Dairy, a state-owned dairy, discovered cancer-causing toxins in its milk in 2011. Yili Dairy had to recall some of its formula, tainted with mercury, in 2012, and in 2013, it sold formula with more trans-fat than is deemed safe.

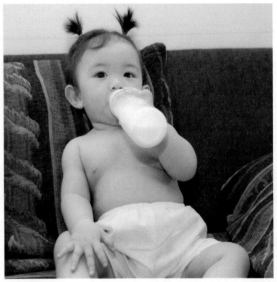

In this setting, the decision taken by the National Development and Reform Commission was a bit surprising—it levied fines amounting to $108 million on five international producers of baby formula—the five listed earlier—and one domestic producer. This agency concluded that these producers set minimum resale prices and punished distributors who sold at lower prices. Xu Kunlin, a spokesperson for the commission, was quoted as saying, "These practices caused milk powder prices to remain at a high level, restricted competition in the market, and harmed the interests of consumers."

Another interpretation of the commission's decision was that it concluded it was time for China to "reclaim" the domestic baby formula market and that one way to do this would be to punish foreign producers. Indeed, this motive was hinted at in an article published in *The People's Daily* that emphasized that Chinese firms needed to take advantage of this situation by producing "high-quality low-cost products." The article went on to say, "In fact, it is very possible for China-made milk powder to replace imported ones or even defeat their foreign counterparts and sell their products to the overseas market by improving the quality and regaining consumer confidence."

Did non-Chinese producers engage in anticompetitive activities to artificially inflate the price of baby formula in China? Did the Chinese government, for its own reasons, decide to help reestablish the domestic baby formula industry by fining non-Chinese producers? It is difficult to know, but this kind of interaction between business and industry is the kind of thing that can make international strategies very complicated.

Sources: E. Wong (2013). "China says foreign makers of baby formula may be fixing prices." *The New York Times,* July 3, www.nytimes.com/2013/07/04/business/global/china-says-its-investigating-price-fixing. Accessed August 26, 2013; B. Demick (2013). "China fines baby formula companies $108 million in price-fixing case." *The Los Angeles Times,* August 7, www.latimes.com/new/world/worldnow/la-fg-china-fines-babyformula-companies. Accessed August 26, 2013; C. Riley (2013). "China fines six companies for baby formula price fixing." *CNN Money,* August 7, money.cnn.com/2013/08/07/news/china-baby-formula/index.html. Accessed August 26, 2013; L. Kuo (2013). "Why Chinese parents are still so paranoid about made-in-China baby formula." *Quartz,* August 9, qz.com/113508/why-chinese-parents-are-still-so-paranoid-about-made-in-china-babyformula. Accessed August 26, 2013.

As the five non-Chinese baby formula firms have discovered, operating internationally can sometimes create unexpected strategic challenges.

Firms that operate in multiple countries simultaneously are implementing **international strategies**. International strategies are actually a special case of the corporate strategies already discussed in Part 3 of this book. That is, firms can vertically integrate, diversify, form strategic alliances, and implement mergers and acquisitions, all across national borders. Thus, the reasons why firms might want to pursue these corporate strategies identified in Chapters 6 through 10 also apply to firms pursuing international strategies. For this reason, this chapter emphasizes the unique characteristics of international strategies.

At some level, international strategies have existed since before the beginning of recorded time. Certainly, trade across country borders has been an important determinant of the wealth of individuals, companies, and countries throughout history. The search for trading opportunities and trade routes was a primary motivation for the exploration of much of the world. Therefore, it would be inappropriate to argue that international strategies are an invention of the late twentieth century.

Strategy in the Emerging Enterprise

Logitech is a leader in peripheral devices for personal computers and related digital technology. With 2013 sales of $2.1 billion, Logitech sells computer pointing devices (e.g., computer mice and trackballs), regular and cordless computer keyboards, webcam cameras, PC headsets and VoIP (voice over Internet protocol) handsets, PC game controllers, and speakers and headphones for PCs in virtually every country in the world. Headquartered in Switzerland and with offices in California, Switzerland, China, Hong Kong, Taiwan, and Japan, Logitech is a classic example of a firm pursuing an international strategy.

And it has always been this way—not that Logitech had sales of $2.1 billion when it was first founded, in 1981. But Logitech was one of the first entrepreneurial firms that began its operations—way back in 1981—by pursuing an international strategy. At its founding, for example, Logitech had offices in Switzerland and the United States. Within two years of its founding, it had research and development

International Entrepreneurial Firms: The Case of Logitech

and manufacturing operations in Taiwan and Ireland. In short, Logitech was "born global."

Of course, not all entrepreneurial firms pursue international strategies from their inception. But this is less unusual for firms in high-technology industries, where global technical standards make it possible for products made in one market to be sold as "plug and play" products in markets around the world. Because Logitech's pointing devices and other peripherals could be used by any personal computer

around the world, their market—from day one—was global in scope. Indeed, in one study of firms that were "born global," most of these firms were operating in high-technology markets with well-developed technical standards.

More recently, entrepreneurial firms have begun exploiting international opportunities in sourcing the manufacturing of their products. The rise of low-cost manufacturing in China, Vietnam, and the Philippines—among other places—has led increased numbers of firms, including many small and entrepreneurial firms, to outsource their manufacturing operations to these countries. In this global environment, even the smallest entrepreneurial firms must become aware of and manage the challenges associated with implementing international strategies discussed in this chapter.

Sources: www.logitech.com; (2013). Logitech 10 K Report; B. Oviatt and P. McDougall (1995). "Global start-ups: Entrepreneurs on a worldwide stage." *Academy of Management Executive,* 9, pp. 30–44.

In the past, however, the implementation of international strategies was limited to relatively small numbers of risk-taking individuals and firms. Today these strategies are becoming remarkably common. For example, in 2012, almost a third of Wal-Mart's sales revenues came from outside the United States; only about a third of ExxonMobil's profits came from its U.S. operations; almost 50 percent of General Motors' automobile sales came from outside the United States; and about half of General Electric's revenues came from non-U.S. operations. And it's not only U.S-based firms that have invested in non-U.S. operations. Numerous non-U.S. firms have invested around the world as well. For example, the U.S. market provides the largest percentage of the sales of such firms as Nestlé (a Swiss food company), Toyota (a Japanese car company), and Royal Dutch/Shell Group (an energy company headquartered in both the United Kingdom and the Netherlands). Moreover, as described in the Strategy in the Emerging Enterprise feature, international strategies are not limited to just huge multinational companies.

The increased use of international strategies by both large and small firms suggests that the economic opportunities associated with operating in multiple geographic markets can be substantial. However, to be a source of sustained competitive advantages for firms, these strategies must exploit a firm's valuable, rare, and costly to imitate resources and capabilities. Moreover, a firm must be appropriately organized to realize the full competitive potential of these resources and capabilities. This chapter examines the conditions under which international strategies can create economic value, as well as the conditions under which they can be sources of sustained competitive advantages.

The Value of International Strategies

V R I O

As suggested earlier, international strategies are an example of corporate strategies. So to be economically valuable, they must meet the two value criteria originally introduced in Chapter 7: They must exploit real economies of scope, and it must be costly for outside investors to realize these economies of scope on their own. Many of the economies of scope discussed in the context of vertical integration, corporate diversification, strategic alliances, and merger and acquisition strategies can be created when firms operate across multiple businesses. These same economies can also be created when firms operate across multiple geographic markets.

More generally, like all the strategies discussed in this book, to be valuable, international strategies must enable a firm to exploit environmental opportunities or neutralize environmental threats. To the extent that international strategies enable a firm to respond to its environment, they will also enable a firm to reduce its costs or increase the willingness of its customers to pay compared to what would have been the case if that firm did not pursue these strategies. Several potentially valuable economies of scope particularly relevant for firms pursuing international strategies are summarized in Table 11.1.

1. To gain access to new customers for current products or services
2. To gain access to low-cost factors of production
3. To develop new core competencies
4. To leverage current core competencies in new ways
5. To manage corporate risk

TABLE 11.1 Potential Sources of Economies of Scope for Firms Pursuing International Strategies

To Gain Access to New Customers for Current Products or Services

The most obvious economy of scope that may motivate firms to pursue an international strategy is the potential new customers for a firm's current products or services that such a strategy might generate. To the extent that customers outside a firm's domestic market are willing and able to buy a firm's current products or services, implementing an international strategy can directly increase a firm's revenues.

Internationalization and Firm Revenues

If customers outside a firm's domestic market are willing and able to purchase its products or services, then selling into these markets will increase the firm's revenues. However, it is not always clear that the products and services that a firm sells in its domestic market will also sell in foreign markets.

Are Nondomestic Customers Willing to Buy?

It may be the case that customer preferences vary significantly in a firm's domestic and foreign markets. These different preferences may require firms seeking to internationalize their operations to substantially change their current products or services before nondomestic customers are willing to purchase them.

This challenge faced many U.S. home appliance manufacturers as they looked to expand their operations into Europe and Asia. In the United States, the physical size of most home appliances (washing machines, dryers, refrigerators, dishwashers, and so forth) has become standardized, and these standard sizes are built into new homes, condominiums, and apartments. Standard sizes have also emerged in Europe and Asia. However, these non-U.S. standard sizes are much smaller than the U.S. sizes, requiring U.S. manufacturers to substantially retool their manufacturing operations in order to build products that might be attractive to Asian and European customers.[1]

Different physical standards can require a firm pursuing international opportunities to change its current products or services to sell them into a nondomestic market. Physical standards, however, can easily be measured and described. Differences in tastes can be much more challenging for firms looking to sell their products or services outside the domestic market.

The inability to anticipate differences in tastes around the world has sometimes led to very unfortunate, and often humorous, marketing blunders. For example, General Motors once introduced the Chevrolet Nova to South America, even though "No va" in Spanish means "it won't go." When Coca-Cola was first introduced in China, it was translated into Ke-kou-ke-la, which turns out to mean either "bite the wax tadpole" or "female horse stuffed with wax," depending on which dialect one speaks. Coca-Cola reintroduced its product with the name Ke-kou-ko-le, which roughly translates into "happiness in the mouth."

Coca-Cola is not the only beverage firm to run into problems internationally. Pepsi's slogan "Come alive with the Pepsi generation" was translated into "Pepsi will bring your ancestors back from the dead" in Taiwan. In Italy, a marketing campaign for Schweppes tonic water was translated into Schweppes toilet water—not a terribly appealing drink. Bacardi developed a fruity drink called "Pavian." Unfortunately, "Pavian" means baboon in German. Coors used its "Turn it loose" slogan when selling beer in Spain and Latin America. Unfortunately, "Turn it loose" was translated into "Suffer from diarrhea."

Food companies have had similar problems. Kentucky Fried Chicken's slogan "Finger-lickin' good" translates into "eat your fingers off" in Chinese. In Arabic, the "Jolly Green Giant" translates into "Intimidating Green Ogre." Frank Perdue's famous catch phrase—"It takes a tough man to make a tender chicken"—takes on a slightly different meaning when translated into Spanish—"It takes a sexually stimulated man to make a chicken affectionate." And Gerber found that it was unable to sell its baby food in Africa—with pictures of cute babies on the jar—because the tradition in Africa is to put pictures of what is inside the jar on the label. Think about it.

Other marketing blunders include Colgate's decision to introduce Cue toothpaste in France, even though Cue is the name of a French pornographic magazine; an American T-shirt manufacturer that wanted to print T-shirts in Spanish that said "I saw the Pope" (el Papa) but instead printed T-shirts that said "I saw the potato" (la papa); and Salem cigarettes, whose slogan "Salem—feeling free" translated into Japanese as "When smoking Salem, you feel so refreshed that your mind seems to be free and empty." What were they smoking?

However, of all these blunders, perhaps none tops Electrolux—a Scandinavian vacuum cleaner manufacturer. While its marketing slogan for the U.S. market does rhyme—"Nothing sucks like an Electrolux"—it doesn't really communicate what the firm had in mind.[2]

It's not just these marketing blunders that can limit sales in nondomestic markets. For example, Yugo had difficulty selling its automobiles in the United States. Apparently, U.S. consumers were unwilling to accept poor-performing, poor-quality automobiles, despite their low price. Sony, despite its success in Japan, was unable to carve out significant market share in the U.S. video market with its Betamax technology. Most observers blame Sony's reluctance to license this technology to other manufacturers, together with the shorter recording time available on Betamax, for this product failure. The British retail giant Marks and Spencer's efforts to enter the Canadian and U.S. retail markets with its traditional mix of clothing and food stores also met with stiff consumer resistance.[3]

In order for the basis of an international strategy to attract new customers, those products or services must address the needs, wants, and preferences of customers in foreign markets at least as well as, if not better than, alternatives. Firms pursuing international opportunities may have to implement many of the cost-leadership and product differentiation business strategies discussed in Chapters 4 and 5, modified to address the specific market needs of a nondomestic market. Only then will customers in nondomestic markets be willing to buy a firm's current products or services.

Are Nondomestic Customers Able to Buy?

Customers in foreign markets might be willing to buy a firm's current products or services but be unable to buy them. This can occur for at least three reasons: inadequate distribution channels, trade barriers, and insufficient wealth to make purchases.

Inadequate distribution channels may make it difficult, if not impossible, for a firm to make its products or services available to customers outside its domestic market. In some international markets, adequate distribution networks exist but are tied up by firms already operating in these markets. Many European firms face this situation as they try to enter the U.S. market. In such a situation, firms pursuing international opportunities must either build their own distribution networks from scratch (a very costly endeavor) or work with a local partner to utilize the networks that are already in place.

However, the problem facing some firms pursuing international opportunities is not that distribution networks are tied up by firms already operating in a market. Rather, the problem is that distribution networks do not exist or operate in ways that are very different from the operation of the distribution networks in a firm's domestic market. This problem can be serious when firms seek to expand their operations into developing economies. Inadequate transportation, warehousing, and retail facilities can make it difficult to distribute a firm's products or services into a new geographic market. These kinds of problems have hampered investment in Russia, China, and India. For example, when Nestlé entered the Chinese dairy market, it had to build a network of gravel roads connecting the villages where dairy farmers produce milk and factory collection points. Obtaining the right to build this network of roads took 13 years of negotiations with Chinese government officials.[4]

Such distribution problems are not limited to developing economies. For example, Japanese retail distribution has historically been much more fragmented, and much less efficient, than the system that exists in either the United States or Western Europe. Rather than being dominated by large grocery stores, discount retail operations, and retail superstores, the Japanese retail distribution network has been dominated by numerous small "mom-and-pop" operations. Many Western firms find this distribution network difficult to use because its operating principles are so different from what they have seen in their domestic markets. However, Procter & Gamble and a few other firms have been able to crack open this Japanese distribution system and exploit significant sales opportunities in Japan.[5]

Even if distribution networks exist in nondomestic markets and even if international firms can operate through those networks if they have access to them, it still might be the case that entry into these markets can be restricted by various tariff and nontariff trade barriers. A list of such trade barriers is presented in Table 11.2. Trade barriers, no matter what their specific form, have the effect

TABLE 11.2 Tariffs, Quotas, and Nontariff Trade Barriers

Tariffs: Taxes levied on imported goods or services	Quotas: Quantity limits on the number of products or services that can be imported	Nontariff barriers: Rules, regulations, and policies that increase the cost of importing products or services
Import duties	Voluntary quotas	Government policies
Supplemental duties	Involuntary quotas	Government procurement policies
Variable levies	Restricted import licenses	Government-sponsored exports
Subsidies	Minimum import limits	Domestic assistance programs
Border levies	Embargoes	Custom policies
Countervailing duties		Valuation systems
		Tariff classifications
		Documentation requirements
		Fees
		Quality standards
		Packaging standards
		Labeling standards

of increasing the cost of selling a firm's current products or services in a new geographic market and thus make it difficult for a firm to realize this economy of scope from its international strategy.

Despite a worldwide movement toward free trade and reduction in trade barriers, trade barriers are still an important economic phenomenon for many firms seeking to implement an international strategy. Japanese automobile manufacturers have faced voluntary quotas and various other trade barriers as they have sought to expand their presence in the U.S. market; U.S. automobile firms have argued that Japan has used a series of tariff and nontariff trade barriers to restrict their entry into the Japanese market. Kodak once asked the U.S. government to begin negotiations to facilitate Kodak's entry into the Japanese photography market—a market that Kodak argued was controlled, through a government-sanctioned monopoly, by Fuji. Historically, beginning operations in India was hampered by a variety of tariff and nontariff trade barriers. Tariffs in India had averaged more than 80 percent; foreign firms have been restricted to a 40 percent ownership stake in their operations in India; and foreign imports had required government approvals and licenses that could take up to three years to obtain. Many of these trade barriers in India have been reduced but not eliminated. The same is true for the United States. The tariff on imported goods and services imposed by the U.S. government reached an all-time high of 60 percent in 1932. It averaged from 12 to 15 percent after the Second World War and now averages about 5 percent for most imports into the United States. Thus, U.S. trade barriers have been reduced but not eliminated.[6]

Governments create trade barriers for a wide variety of reasons: to raise government revenue, to protect local employment, to encourage local production to replace imports, to protect new industries from competition, to discourage foreign direct investment, and to promote export activity. However, for firms seeking to implement international strategies, trade barriers, no matter why they are erected, have the effect of increasing the cost of implementing these strategies. Indeed, trade barriers can be thought of as a special case of artificial barriers to entry, as discussed in Chapter 2. Such barriers to entry can turn what could have been economically viable strategies into nonviable strategies.

Finally, customers may be willing but unable to purchase a firm's current products or services even if distribution networks are in place and trade barriers are not making internationalization efforts too costly. If these customers lack the wealth or sufficient hard currency to make these purchases, then the potential value of this economy of scope can go unrealized.

Insufficient consumer wealth limits the ability of firms to sell products into a variety of markets. For example, per capita gross national product is $270 in Bangladesh, $240 in Chad, and $110 in the Congo. In these countries, it is unlikely that there will be significant demand for many products or services originally designed for affluent Western economies. This situation also exists in India. The middle class in India is large and growing (164 million people with the highest 20 percent of income in 1998), but the income of this middle class is considerably lower than the income of the middle class in other economies. These income levels are sufficient to create demand for some consumer products. For example, Gillette estimates the market in India for its shaving products could include 240 million consumers, and Nestlé believes that the market in India for its noodles, ketchup, and instant coffee products could include more than 100 million people. However, the potential market for higher-end products in India is somewhat smaller. For example, Bausch & Lomb believes that only about 30 million consumers in India can afford to purchase its high-end sunglasses and soft contact lenses. The level of consumer wealth is such an important determinant of the economic potential of beginning operations in a new country that McDonald's adjusts the number of restaurants it expects to build in a new market by the per capita income of people in that market.[7]

Even if there is sufficient wealth in a country to create market demand, lack of hard currency can hamper internationalization efforts. **Hard currencies** are currencies that are traded, and thus have value, on international money markets. When an international firm does business in a country with hard currency, the firm can take whatever after-tax profits it earns in that country and translate those profits into other hard currencies—including the currency of the country in which the firm has headquarters. Moreover, because the value of hard currencies can fluctuate in the world economy, firms can also manage their currency risk by engaging in various hedging strategies in world money markets.

When firms begin operations in countries without hard currency, they are able to obtain few of these advantages. Indeed, without hard currency, cash payments to these firms are made with a currency that has essentially no value

Strategy in Depth

When international firms engage in countertrade, they receive payment for the products or services they sell into a country, but not in the form of currency. They receive payment in the form of other products or services that they can sell on the world market. Countertrade has been a particularly important way by which firms have tried to gain access to the markets in the former Soviet Union. For example, Marc Rich and Company (a Swiss commodity-trading firm) once put together the following deal: Marc Rich purchased 70,000 tons of raw sugar from Brazil on the open market; shipped this sugar to Ukraine, where it was refined; then transported 30,000 tons of refined sugar (after using some profits to pay the refineries) to Siberia, where it was sold for 130,000 tons of oil products that, in turn, were shipped to Mongolia in exchange for 35,000 tons of copper concentrate, which was moved to Kazakhstan, where it was refined into copper and, finally, sold on the world

Countertrade

market to obtain hard currency. This complicated countertrade deal is typical of the kinds of actions that international firms must take if they are to engage in business in countries without hard currency and if they desire to extract their profits out of those countries. Indeed, countertrade in various forms is actually quite common. One estimate suggests that countertrade accounts for between 10 and 20 percent of world trade.

Although countertrade can enable a firm to begin operations in countries without hard currency, it can create difficulties as well. In particular, in order to do business, a firm must be willing to accept payment in the form of some good or commodity that it must sell in order to obtain hard currency. This is not likely to be a problem for a firm that specializes in buying and selling commodities. However, a firm that does not have this expertise may find itself taking possession of natural gas, sesame seeds, or rattan in order to sell its products or services in a country. If this firm has limited expertise in marketing these kinds of commodities, it may have to use brokers and other advisers to complete these transactions. This, of course, increases the cost of using countertrade as a way to facilitate international operations.

Source: A. Ignatius (1993). "Commodity giant: Marc Rich & Co. does big deals at big risk in former U.S.S.R." *The Wall Street Journal*, May 13, p. A1; D. Marin (1990). "Tying in trade: Evidence on countertrade." *World Economy*, 13(3), p. 445.

outside the country where the payments are made. Although these payments can be used for additional investments inside that country, an international firm has limited ability to extract profits from countries without hard currencies and even less ability to hedge currency fluctuation risks in this context. The lack of hard currency has discouraged firms from entering a wide variety of countries at various points in time despite the substantial demand for products and services in those countries.[8] One solution to this problem, called **countertrade**, is discussed in the Strategy in Depth feature.

Internationalization and Product Life Cycles

Gaining access to new customers not only can directly increase a firm's revenues but also can enable a firm to manage its products or services through their life cycle. A typical **product life cycle** is depicted in Figure 11.1. Different stages in this life cycle are defined by different growth rates in demand for a product. Thus, in the first emerging stage (called **introduction** in the figure), relatively few firms are producing a product, there are relatively few customers, and the rate of growth in demand for the product is relatively low. In the second stage (**growth**) of the product life cycle, demand increases rapidly, and many new firms enter to begin producing the product or service. In the third phase of the product life cycle (**maturity**), the number of firms producing a product or service remains stable, demand growth levels off, and firms direct their investment efforts toward refining the process by which a product or service is created and away from developing entirely new products. In the final phase of the product life cycle (**decline**), demand drops off when a technologically superior product or service is introduced.[9]

From an international strategy perspective, the critical observation about product life cycles is that a product or service can be at different stages of its life cycle in different countries. Thus, a firm can use the resources and capabilities it developed during a particular stage of the life cycle in its domestic market during that same stage of the life cycle in a nondomestic market. This can substantially enhance a firm's economic performance.

One firm that has been very successful in managing its product life cycles through its international efforts is Crown Cork & Seal. This firm had a traditional

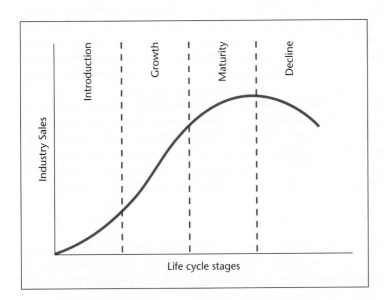

Figure 11.1 The Product Life Cycle

strength in the manufacturing of three-piece metal containers when the introduction of two-piece metal cans into the U.S. market rapidly made three-piece cans obsolete. However, rather than abandoning its three-piece manufacturing technology, Crown Cork & Seal moved many of its three-piece manufacturing operations overseas into developing countries where demand for three-piece cans was just emerging. In this way, Crown Cork & Seal was able to extend the effective life of its three-piece manufacturing operations and substantially enhance its economic performance.[10]

Internationalization and Cost Reduction

Gaining access to new customers for a firm's current products or services can increase a firm's sales. If aspects of a firm's production process are sensitive to economies of scale, this increased volume of sales can also reduce the firm's costs and enable the firm to gain cost advantages in both its nondomestic and its domestic markets.

    Many firms in the worldwide automobile industry have attempted to realize manufacturing economies of scale through their international operations. According to one estimate, the minimum efficient scale of a single compact-car manufacturing plant is 400,000 units per year.[11] Such a plant would produce approximately 20 percent of all the automobiles sold in Britain, Italy, or France. Obviously, to exploit this 400,000 car-per-year manufacturing efficiency, European automobile firms have had to sell cars in more than just a single country market. Thus, the implementation of an international strategy has enabled these firms to realize an important manufacturing economy of scale.[12]

To Gain Access to Low-Cost Factors of Production

Just as gaining access to new customers can be an important economy of scope for firms pursuing international opportunities, so is gaining access to low-cost factors of production such as raw materials, labor, and technology.

Raw Materials

Gaining access to low-cost raw materials is, perhaps, the most traditional reason why firms begin international operations. For example, in 1600, the British East India Company was formed with an initial investment of $70,000 to manage trade between England and the Far East, including India. In 1601, the third British East India Company fleet sailed for the Indies to buy cloves, pepper, silk, coffee, saltpeter, and other products. This fleet generated a return on investment of 234 percent. These profits led to the formation of the Dutch East India Company in 1602 and the French East India Company in 1664. Similar firms were organized to manage trade in the New World. The Hudson Bay Company was chartered in 1670 to manage the fur trade, and the rival North West Company was organized in 1784 for the same purpose. All these organizations were created to gain access to low-cost raw materials that were available only in nondomestic markets.[13]

Labor

In addition to gaining access to low-cost raw materials, firms also begin international operations in order to gain access to low-cost labor. After World War II, Japan had some of the lowest labor costs, and highest labor productivity, in the

Ethics and Strategy

There is little doubt that globalization has improved lives of both producers in developing economies and consumers in more developed economies. Individuals working in companies that make, for example, clothing in countries like Bangladesh, China, the Philippines, and Vietnam have jobs that pay good wages—compared to alternatives in those countries—and are able to move their families out of abject poverty. Consumers in developed economies are able to buy good quality clothes at relatively low prices.

But this seemingly virtuous trade is not without its personal and social costs. A series of disasters in factories in Bangladesh reminds us that low-cost clothes for consumers in developed countries can sometimes be manufactured in grossly unsafe factories in less-developed countries. One fire in a Bangladeshi factory killed 112 workers. At least some of the fire escape doors built in this factory had been locked to prevent workers from taking unauthorized breaks. Then a complex of clothing factories in Bangladesh collapsed, killing 892 workers. It turns out that the top four floors of this complex had been built illegally without the proper permits. And even though cracks in the building led the manager of a bank located on the first floor to close and send all his employees home for their safety, the owners of the factories in the top floors insisted that their employees go to work. Shortly thereafter,

Manufacturing Tragedies and International Business

the building collapsed, and almost 900 people died.

These factories all produced clothing for well-known U.S. and Western European stores, including H&M, Wal-Mart, Target, Benetton, Primark (in the United Kingdom), and Mango (in Spain)—to name just a few. Indeed, because Bangladesh is the second-largest producer of garments in the world, behind China, it is very likely that at least some of the clothing that each of us wear each day is made by Bangladeshi workers operating in marginally safe factories.

Of course, these Western firms do not have managers on site at these factories insisting that fire doors are locked and unsafe buildings are built. Indeed, after the building collapse, many firms in developed economies pledged to work with suppliers to ensure safer

working conditions. This will take some time, of course. And, in the meantime, at least some workers' lives may be at risk. For example, shortly after these firms announced their commitment to improved worker safety, a fire in another Bangladeshi factory that makes clothing for Wal-Mart, Benetton, and other companies killed eight employees.

Some have argued that the intense cost pressures put on Bangladeshi factory owners by their developed economy customers force these factory owners to locate their factories in inexpensive but dangerous locations. It would be convenient for these factory owners if all the blame for these terrible tragedies could be placed on their customers from developed countries—and by implication on all who purchase clothes from these retailers. Of course, things are rarely that simple. While these retail firms do put cost pressures on their suppliers, it is the factory owners and factory managers who lock fire doors and insist on production in a building that appears likely to collapse at any time.

Nevertheless, the growing number of tragedies in Bangladesh, China, and elsewhere in garment manufacturing may require firms in developed economies to rethink at least some aspects of their international business strategies.

Sources: J. Yardley (2013). "Fire at Bangladeshi factory kills eight." *NYTimes,* May 9; J. Juliflar, A. Monik, and J. Yardley (2013). "Building collapses in Bangladesh, leaves scores dead." *NYTimes,* April 24.

world. Over time, however, the improving Japanese economy and the increased value of the yen have had the effect of increasing labor costs in Japan, and South Korea, Taiwan, Singapore, and Malaysia all emerged as geographic areas with inexpensive and highly productive labor. More recently, China, Mexico, and Vietnam have taken this role in the world economy.[14]

Numerous firms have attempted to gain the advantages of low labor costs by moving their manufacturing operations. For example, Minebea, a Japanese ball-bearing and semiconductor manufacturer, attempted to exploit low labor costs by manufacturing ball bearings in Japan in the 1950s and early 1960s, in Singapore in the 1970s, and since 1980 has been manufacturing them in Thailand. Hewlett-Packard operates manufacturing and assembly operations in Malaysia and Mexico, Japan's Mitsubishi Motors opened an automobile assembly plant in Vietnam, General Motors operates assembly plants in Mexico, and Motorola has begun operations in China. All these investments were motivated, at least partly, by the availability of low-cost labor in these countries.[15] Some of the ethical issues associated with the search for low-cost labor are discussed in the Ethics and Strategy feature.

Although gaining access to low-cost labor can be an important determinant of a firm's international efforts, this access by itself is usually not sufficient to motivate entry into particular countries. After all, relative labor costs can change over time. For example, South Korea used to be the country in which most sports shoes were manufactured. In 1990, Korean shoe manufacturers employed 130,000 workers in 302 factories. However, by 1993, only 80,000 Koreans were employed in the shoe industry, and only 244 factories (most employing fewer than 100 people) remained. A significant portion of the shoe-manufacturing industry had moved from Korea to China because of the labor-cost advantages of China (approximately $40 per employee per month) compared with Korea (approximately $800 per employee per month).[16]

Moreover, low labor costs are not beneficial if a country's workforce is not able to produce high-quality products efficiently. In the sport shoe industry, China's access to some of the manufacturing technology and supporting industries (for example, synthetic fabrics) to efficiently produce high-end sports shoes and high-technology hiking boots was delayed for several years. As a result, Korea was able to maintain a presence in the shoe-manufacturing industry—even though most of that industry had been outsourced to China.

One interesting example of firms gaining access to low-cost labor through their international strategies is maquiladoras—manufacturing plants that are owned by non-Mexican companies and operated in Mexico near the U.S. border. The primary driver behind maquiladora investments is lower labor costs than similar plants located in the United States. In addition, firms exporting from maquiladoras to the United States have to pay duties only on the value added that was created in Mexico; maquiladoras do not have to pay Mexican taxes on the goods processed in Mexico; and the cost of land on which plants are built in Mexico is substantially lower than would be the case in the United States. However, a study by the Banco de Mexico suggests that without the 20 percent cost-of-labor advantage, most maquildoras would not be profitable.[17]

Technology

Another factor of production that firms can gain low-cost access to through operations is technology. Historically, Japanese firms have tried to gain access to technology by partnering with non-Japanese firms. Although the non-Japanese firms have often been looking to gain access to new customers for their current products or services by operating in Japan, Japanese firms have used this entry into the Japanese market to gain access to foreign technology.[18]

To Develop New Core Competencies

One of the most compelling reasons for firms to begin operations outside their domestic markets is to refine their current core competencies and to develop new core competencies. By beginning operations outside their domestic markets, firms can gain a greater understanding of the strengths and weaknesses of their core competencies. By exposing these competencies to new competitive contexts, traditional competencies can be modified, and new competencies can be developed.

Of course, for international operations to affect a firm's core competencies, firms must learn from their experiences in nondomestic markets. Moreover, once these new core competencies are developed, they must be exploited in a firm's other operations in order to realize their full economic potential.

Learning from International Operations

Learning from international operations is anything but automatic. Many firms that begin operations in a nondomestic market encounter challenges and difficulties and then immediately withdraw from their international efforts. Other firms continue to try to operate internationally but are unable to learn how to modify and change their core competencies.

One study examined several strategic alliances in an effort to understand why some firms in these alliances were able to learn from their international operations, modify their core competencies, and develop new core competencies while others were not. This study identified the intent to learn, the transparency of business partners, and receptivity to learning as determinants of a firm's ability to learn from its international operations (see Table 11.3).

The Intent to Learn

A firm that has a strong intent to learn from its international operations is more likely to learn than a firm without this intent. Moreover, this intent must be communicated to all those who work in a firm's international activities. Compare, for example, a quote from a manager whose firm failed to learn from its international operations with a quote from a manager whose firm was able to learn from these operations.[19]

> *Our engineers were just as good as [our partner's]. In fact, theirs were narrower technically, but they had a much better understanding of what the company was trying to accomplish. They knew they were there to learn; our people didn't.*
>
> *We wanted to make learning an automatic discipline. We asked the staff every day, "What did you learn from [our partner] today?" Learning was carefully monitored and recorded.*

Obviously, the second firm was in a much better position than the first to learn from its international operations and to modify its current core competencies and

---

1. The intent to learn
2. The transparency of business partners
3. Receptivity to learning

Source: G. Hamel (1991). "Competition for competence and inter-partner learning within international strategic alliances." *Strategic Management Journal*, 12, pp. 83–103.

TABLE 11.3 Determinants of the Ability of a Firm to Learn from Its International Operations

develop new core competencies. Learning from international operations takes place by design, not by default.

Transparency and Learning

It has also been shown that firms were more likely to learn from their international operations when they interacted with what have been called **transparent business partners**. Some international business partners are more open and accessible than others. This variance in accessibility can reflect different organizational philosophies, practices, and procedures, as well as differences in the culture of a firm's home country. For example, knowledge in Japanese and most other Asian cultures tends to be context specific and deeply embedded in the broader social system. This makes it difficult for many Western managers to understand and appreciate the subtlety of Japanese business practices and Japanese culture. This, in turn, limits the ability of Western managers to learn from their operations in the Japanese market or from their Japanese partners.[20]

In contrast, knowledge in most Western cultures tends to be less context specific, less deeply embedded in the broader social system. Such knowledge can be written down, can be taught in classes, and can be transmitted, all at a relatively low cost. Japanese managers working in Western economies are more likely to be able to appreciate and understand Western business practices and thus are more able to learn from their operations in the West and from their Western partners.

Receptivity to Learning

Firms also vary in their receptiveness to learning. A firm's receptiveness to learning is affected by its culture, its operating procedures, and its history. Research on organizational learning suggests that, before firms can learn from their international operations, they must be prepared to unlearn. **Unlearning** requires a firm to modify or abandon traditional ways of engaging in business. Unlearning can be difficult, especially if a firm has a long history of success using old patterns of behavior and if those old patterns of behavior are reflected in a firm's organizational structure, its management control systems, and its compensation policies.[21]

Even if unlearning is possible, a firm may not have the resources it needs to learn. If a firm is using all of its available managerial time and talent, capital, and technology just to compete on a day-to-day business, the additional task of learning from international operations can go undone. Although managers in this situation often acknowledge the importance of learning from their international operations in order to modify their current core competencies or build new ones, they simply may not have the time or energy to do so.[22]

The ability to learn from operations can also be hampered if managers perceive that there is too much to be learned. It is often difficult for a firm to understand how it can evolve from its current state to a position where it operates with new and more valuable core competencies. This difficulty is exacerbated when the distance between where a firm is and where it needs to be is large. One Western manager who perceived this large learning gap after visiting a state-of-the-art manufacturing facility operated by a Japanese partner was quoted as saying:[23]

> It's no good for us to simply observe where they are today, what we have to find out is how they got from where we are to where they are. We need to experiment and learn with intermediate technologies before duplicating what they've done.

Leveraging New Core Competencies in Additional Markets

Once a firm has been able to learn from its international operations and modify its traditional core competencies or develop new core competencies, it must then leverage those competencies across its operations, both domestic and international, in order to realize their full value. Failure to leverage these "lessons learned" can substantially reduce the return associated with implementing an international strategy.

To Leverage Current Core Competencies in New Ways

International operations can also create opportunities for firms to leverage their traditional core competencies in new ways. This ability is related to, though different from, using international operations to gain access to new customers for a firm's current products or services. When firms gain access to new customers for their current products, they often leverage their domestic core competencies across country boundaries. When they leverage core competencies in *new* ways, they not only extend operations across country boundaries but also leverage their competencies across products and services in ways that would not be economically viable in their domestic market.

Consider, for example, Honda. There is widespread agreement that Honda has developed core competencies in the design and manufacture of power trains. Honda has used this core competence to facilitate entry into a variety of product markets—including motorcycles, automobiles, and snow blowers—both in its domestic Japanese market and in nondomestic markets such as the United States. However, Honda has begun to explore some competence-leverage opportunities in the United States that are not available in the Japanese market. For example, Honda has begun to design and manufacture lawn mowers of various sizes for the home in the U.S. market—lawn mowers clearly build on Honda's traditional power train competence. However, given the crowded living conditions in Japan, consumer demand for lawn mowers in that country has never been very great. Lawns in the United States, however, can be very large, and consumer demand for high-quality lawn mowers in that market is substantial. The opportunity for Honda to begin to leverage its power train competencies in the sale of lawn mowers to U.S. homeowners exists only because Honda operates outside its Japanese home market.

To Manage Corporate Risk

The value of risk reduction for firms pursuing a corporate diversification strategy was evaluated previously. It was suggested that, although diversified operations across businesses with imperfectly correlated cash flows can reduce a firm's risk, outside equity holders can manage this risk more efficiently on their own by investing in a diversified portfolio of stocks. Consequently equity holders have little direct interest in hiring managers to operate a diversified portfolio of businesses, the sole purpose of which is risk diversification.

Similar conclusions apply to firms pursuing international strategies—with two qualifications. First, in some circumstances, it may be difficult for equity holders in one market to diversify their portfolio of investments across multiple markets. To the extent that such barriers to diversification exist for individual equity holders but not for firms pursuing international strategies, risk reduction can directly benefit equity holders. In general, whenever barriers to international capital flows exist, individual investors may not be able to diversify their portfolios across country boundaries optimally. In this context, individual investors can indirectly diversify their portfolio of investments by purchasing shares in diversified multinationals.[24]

Research Made Relevant

Firms whose ownership is dominated by a single family are surprisingly common around the world. In the United States, for example, Marriott, Walgreens, Wrigley, Alberto-Culver, Campbell Soup, Dell, and Wal-Mart are all family dominated. However, only four of the 20 largest firms in the United States are family dominated, and only one of the 20 largest firms in the United Kingdom is family dominated.

Though not uncommon in the United States and the United Kingdom, family-dominated firms are the rule, not the exception, in most economies around the world. For example, in New Zealand, nine of the 20 largest firms are family dominated; in Argentina, 13 of the 20 largest firms are family dominated; and in Mexico, all 20 of the 20 largest firms are family dominated. In many countries, including Argentina, Belgium, Canada, Denmark, Greece, Hong Kong, Israel, Mexico, New Zealand, Portugal, Singapore, South Korea, Sweden, and Switzerland, more than one-third of the largest 20 firms are dominated by family owners.

A variety of explanations of why family-dominated firms continue to be an important part of the world economy have been proposed. For example, some researchers have argued that family owners obtain private benefits of ownership—over and above the financial benefits they might receive. Such private benefits include high social status in their countries. Other researchers

Family Firms in the Global Economy

have argued that family ownership helps guarantee that family members will be able to control their property in countries with less-well-developed property rights. And still others have argued that concentrated family owners help a firm gain political clout in its negotiations with the government.

On the positive side, family ownership may reduce conflicts that might otherwise arise between a firm's managers and its outside equity holders—the agency costs discussed in the Strategy in Depth feature in Chapter 8. Managers of family firms are "playing with" their own money, not "other people's money," and thus are less likely to pursue strategies that benefit themselves but hurt the firm's owners because they are the firm's owners.

On the negative side, family firms may become starved for capital, and especially equity capital. Non-family

members will often be reluctant to invest in family firms because the interests of the family are often likely to take precedence over the interests of outsiders. Also, family firms must limit their search for senior leadership to family members. It may well be the case that the best leaders of a family firm are not members of the family, but family ownership can prevent a firm from gaining access to the entire labor market. Finally, for reasons explained in the text, family firms may need to pursue a broad diversification strategy in order to reduce the risk borne by their family owners. As suggested in Chapter 8, such unrelated diversification strategies can sometimes be difficult to manage.

From a broader perspective, the importance of family-dominated firms throughout the world suggests that the "standard" model of corporate governance—with numerous anonymous stockholders, an independent board of directors, and senior managers chosen only for their ability to lead and create economic value—may not apply that broadly. This approach to corporate governance, so dominant in the United States and the United Kingdom, may actually be the exception, not the rule.

Sources: R. Morck and B. Yeung (2004). "Family control and the rent-seeking society." *Entrepreneurship: Theory and Practice*, Summer, pp. 391–409; R. LaPorta, F. Lopez-de-salina, A. Shleifer, and R. Vishny (1999). "Corporate ownership around the world." *Journal of Finance*, 54, pp. 471–520; J. Weber, L. Lavelle, T. Lowry, W. Zellner, and A. Barrett (2003). "Family, Inc.," *BusinessWeek*, November 10, pp. 100+.

Second, large privately held firms may find it in their wealth maximizing interests to broadly diversify to reduce risk. In order to gain the risk reduction advantages of diversifying their investments by owning a portfolio of stocks, the owners of these firms would have to "cash out" their ownership position in their firm—by, for example, taking their firm public—and then use this cash to invest in a portfolio of stocks. However, these individuals may gain other advantages from owning their firms and may not want to cash out. In this setting, the only way that owners can gain the risk-reducing benefits of broad diversification is for the firm that they own to broadly diversify.

This justification of diversification for risk reduction purposes is particularly relevant in the international context because, as described in the Research Made Relevant feature, many of the economies of countries around the world are dominated by private companies owned by large families. Not surprisingly, these family-owned firms tend to be much more diversified than the publicly traded firms that are more common in the United States and the United Kingdom.

The Local Responsiveness/International Integration Trade-Off

As firms pursue the economies of scope listed in Table 11.1, they constantly face a trade-off between the advantages of being responsive to market conditions in their nondomestic markets and the advantages of integrating their operations across the multiple markets in which they operate.

On the one hand, **local responsiveness** can help firms be successful in addressing the local needs of nondomestic customers, thereby increasing demand for a firm's current products or services. Moreover, local responsiveness enables a firm to expose its traditional core competencies to new competitive situations, thereby increasing the chances that those core competencies will be improved or will be augmented by new core competencies. Finally, detailed local knowledge is essential if firms are going to leverage their traditional competencies in new ways in their nondomestic markets. Honda was able to begin exploiting its power train competencies in the U.S. lawn mower market only because of its detailed knowledge of, and responsiveness to, that market.

On the other hand, the full exploitation of the economies of scale that can be created by selling a firm's current products or services in a nondomestic market often can occur only if there is tight integration across all the markets in which a firm operates. Gaining access to low-cost factors of production can not only help a firm succeed in a nondomestic market but also help it succeed in all its markets— as long as those factors of production are used by many parts of the international firm. Developing new core competencies and using traditional core competencies in new ways can certainly be beneficial in a particular domestic market. However, the full value of these economies of scope is realized only when they are transferred from a particular domestic market into the operations of a firm in all its other markets.

Traditionally, it has been thought that firms have to choose between local responsiveness and international integration. For example, firms like CIBA-Geigy (a Swiss chemical company), Nestlé (a Swiss food company), and Phillips (a Dutch consumer electronics firm) have chosen to emphasize local responsiveness. Nestlé, for example, owns nearly 8,000 brand names worldwide. However, of those 8,000 brands, only 750 are registered in more than one country, and only 80 are registered in more than 10 countries. Nestlé adjusts its product attributes to the needs of local consumers, adopts brand names that resonate with those consumers, and builds its brands for long-run profitability by country. For example, in the United States, Nestlé's condensed milk carries the brand name "Carnation" (obtained through the acquisition of the Carnation Company); in Asia, this same product carries the brand name "Bear Brand." Nestlé delegates brand management authority to country managers, who can (and do) adjust traditional marketing and manufacturing strategies in accordance with local tastes and preferences. For example, Nestlé's Thailand management group dropped traditional coffee-marketing efforts that focused on taste, aroma, and stimulation and instead began selling coffee as a drink that promotes relaxation and romance. This marketing strategy resonated with Thais experiencing urban stress, and it prompted Nestlé coffee sales in Thailand to jump from $25 million to $100 million four years later.[25]

Of course, all this local responsiveness comes at a cost. Firms that emphasize local responsiveness are often unable to realize the full value of the economies of scope and scale that they could realize if their operations across country borders were more integrated. Numerous firms have focused on appropriating this economic value and have pursued a more integrated international strategy. Examples of such firms include IBM, General Electric, Toyota Motor Corporation, and most major pharmaceutical firms, to name just a few.

Internationally integrated firms locate business functions and activities in countries that have a comparative advantage in these functions or activities. For example, the production of components for most consumer electronics is research intensive, capital intensive, and subject to significant economies of scale. To manage component manufacturing successfully, most internationally integrated consumer electronics firms have located their component operations in technologically advanced countries like the United States and Japan. Because the assembly of these components into consumer products is labor intensive, most internationally integrated consumer electronics firms have located their assembly operations in countries with relatively low labor costs, including Mexico and China.

Of course, one of the costs of locating different business functions and activities in different geographic locations is that these different functions and activities must be coordinated and integrated. Operations in one country might very efficiently manufacture certain components. However, if the wrong components are shipped to the assembly location or if the right components are shipped at the wrong time, any advantages that could have been obtained from exploiting the comparative advantages of different countries can be lost. Shipping costs can also reduce the return on international integration.

To ensure that the different operations in an internationally integrated firm are appropriately coordinated, these firms typically manufacture more standardized products, using more standardized components, than do locally responsive firms. Standardization enables these firms to realize substantial economies of scale and scope, but it can limit their ability to respond to the specific needs of individual markets. When international product standards exist, as in the personal computer industry and the semiconductor chip industry, such standardization is not problematic. Also, when local responsiveness requires only a few modifications of a standardized product (for example, changing the shape of the electric plug or changing the color of a product), international integration can be very effective. However, when local responsiveness requires a great deal of local knowledge and product modifications, international integration can create problems for a firm pursuing an international strategy.

The Transnational Strategy

Recently, it has been suggested that the traditional trade-off between international integration and local responsiveness can be replaced by a **transnational strategy** that exploits all the advantages of both international integration and local responsiveness.[26] Firms implementing a transnational strategy treat their international operations as an integrated network of distributed and interdependent resources and capabilities. In this context, a firm's operations in each country are not simply independent activities attempting to respond to local market needs; they are also repositories of ideas, technologies, and management approaches that the firm might be able to use and apply in its other international operations. Put differently, operations in different countries can be thought of as "experiments" in the creation of new core competencies. Some of these experiments will work and generate important new core competencies; others will fail to have such benefits for a firm.

When a particular country operation develops a competence in manufacturing a particular product, providing a particular service, or engaging in a particular activity that can be used by other country operations, the country operation with this competence can achieve international economies of scale by becoming the firm's primary supplier of this product, service, or activity. In this way, local responsiveness is retained as country managers constantly search for new competencies that enable them to maximize profits in their particular markets, and international integration and economies are realized as country operations that have developed unique competencies become suppliers for all other country operations.

Managing a firm that is attempting to be both locally responsive and internationally integrated is not an easy task. Some of these organizational challenges are discussed later in this chapter.

Financial and Political Risks in Pursuing International Strategies

There is little doubt that the realization of the economies of scope listed in Table 11.1 can be a source of economic value for firms pursuing international strategies. However, the nature of international strategies can create significant risks that these economies of scope will never be realized. Beyond the implementation problems (to be discussed later in this chapter), both financial circumstances and political events can significantly reduce the value of international strategies.

Financial Risks: Currency Fluctuation and Inflation

As firms begin to pursue international strategies, they may begin to expose themselves to financial risks that are less obvious within a single domestic market. In particular, currency fluctuations can significantly affect the value of a firm's international investments. Such fluctuations can turn what had been a losing investment into a profitable investment (the good news). They can also turn what had been a profitable investment into a losing investment (the bad news). In addition to currency fluctuations, different rates of inflation across countries can require very different managerial approaches, business strategies, and accounting practices. Certainly, when a firm first begins international operations, these financial risks can seem daunting.

Fortunately, it is now possible for firms to hedge most of these risks through the use of a variety of financial instruments and strategies. The development of money markets, together with growing experience in operating in high-inflation economies, has substantially reduced the threat of these financial risks for firms pursuing international strategies. Of course, the benefits of these financial tools and experience in high-inflation environments do not accrue to firms automatically. Firms seeking to implement international strategies must develop the resources and capabilities they will need to manage these financial risks. Moreover, these hedging strategies can do nothing to reduce the business risks that firms assume when they enter into nondomestic markets. For example, it may be the case that consumers in a nondomestic market simply do not want to purchase a firm's products or services, in which case this economy of scope cannot be realized. Moreover, these financial strategies cannot manage political risks that can exist for firms pursuing an international strategy.

Political Risks

The political environment is an important consideration in all strategic decisions. Changes in the political rules of the game can have the effect of increasing some environmental threats and reducing others, thereby changing the value of a firm's resources and capabilities. However, the political environment can be even more problematic as firms pursue international strategies.

Types of Political Risks

Politics can affect the value of a firm's international strategies at the macro and micro levels. At the macro level, broad changes in the political situation in a country can change the value of an investment. For example, after the Second World War, nationalist governments came to power in many countries in the Middle East. These governments expropriated for little or no compensation many of the assets of oil and gas companies located in their countries. Expropriation of foreign company assets also occurred when the Shah of Iran was overthrown, when a communist government was elected in Chile, and when new governments came to power in Angola, Ethiopia, Peru, Zambia, and, more recently, Venezuela and Bolivia.[27]

Government upheaval and the attendant risks to international firms are facts of life in some countries. Consider, for example, oil-rich Nigeria. From 1960–1999, Nigeria has experienced several successful coups d'états, one civil war, two civil governments, and six military regimes.[28] The prudent course of action for firms engaging in business activities in Nigeria is to expect the current government to change and to plan accordingly.

Quantifying Political Risks

Political scientists have attempted to quantify the political risk that firms seeking to implement international strategies are likely to face in different countries. Although different studies vary in detail, the country attributes listed in Table 11.4

Increments to Country		
Risk If Risk Factor Is:	Low	High
The political economic environment		
1. Stability of the political system	3	14
2. Imminent internal conflicts	0	14
3. External threats to stability	0	12
4. Degree of control of the economic system	5	9
5. Reliability of country as a trade partner	4	12
6. Constitutional guarantees	2	12
7. Effectiveness of public administration	3	12
8. Labor relations and social peace	3	15
Domestic economic conditions		
1. Size of the population	4	8
2. Per capita income	2	10
3. Economic growth over the past five years	2	7
4. Potential growth over the next three years	3	10
5. Inflation over the past two years	2	10
6. Availability of domestic capital markets to outsiders	3	7
7. Availability of high-quality local labor force	2	8
8. Possibility of employing foreign nationals	2	8
9. Availability of energy resources	2	14
10. Environmental pollution legal requirements	4	8
11. Transportation and communication infrastructure	2	14
External economic relations		
1. Import restrictions	2	10
2. Export restrictions	2	10
3. Restrictions on foreign investments	3	9
4. Freedom to set up or engage in partnerships	3	9
5. Legal protection for brands and products	3	9
6. Restrictions on monetary transfers	2	8
7. Revaluation of currency in the past five years	2	7
8. Balance-of-payments situation	2	9
9. Drain on hard currency through energy imports	3	14
10. Financial standing	3	8
11. Restrictions on the exchange of local and foreign currencies	2	8

TABLE 11.4 Quantifying Political Risks from International Operations

Source: Adapted from E. Dichtl and H. G. Koeglmayr (1986). "Country risk ratings." *Management Review*, 26(4), pp. 2–10. Reprinted with permission.

summarize most of the important determinants of political risk for firms pursuing international strategies.[29] Firms can apply the criteria listed in the table by evaluating the political and economic conditions in a country and by adding up the scores associated with these conditions. For example, a country that has a very unstable political system (14 points), a great deal of control of the economic system (9 points), and significant import restrictions (10 points) represents more political risk than a country that does not have these attributes.

Managing Political Risk

Unlike financial risks, there are relatively few tools for managing the political risks associated with pursuing an international strategy. Obviously, one option would be to pursue international opportunities only in countries where political risk is very small. However, it is often the case that significant business opportunities exist in politically risky countries precisely because they are politically risky. Alternatively, firms can limit their investment in politically risky environments. However, these limited investments may not enable a firm to take full advantage of whatever economies of scope might exist by engaging in business in that country.

Another approach to managing political risk is to see each of the determinants of political risk, listed in Table 11.4, as negotiation points as a firm enters into a new country market. In many circumstances, those in a nondomestic market have just as much an interest in seeing a firm begin doing business in a new market as does the firm contemplating entry. International firms can sometimes use this bargaining power to negotiate entry conditions that reduce, or even neutralize, some of the sources of political risk in a country. Of course, no matter how skilled a firm is in negotiating these entry conditions, a change of government or changes in laws can quickly nullify any agreements.

A third approach to managing political risk is to turn this risk from a threat into an opportunity. One firm that has been successful in this way is Schlumberger, an international oil services company. Schlumberger has headquarters in New York, Paris, and the Caribbean; it is a truly international company. Schlumberger management has adopted a policy of strict neutrality in interactions with governments in the developing world. Because of this policy, Schlumberger has been able to avoid political entanglements and continues to do business where many firms find the political risks too great. Put differently, Schlumberger has developed valuable, rare, and costly-to-imitate resources and capabilities in managing political risks and is using these resources to generate high levels of economic performance.[30]

Research on the Value of International Strategies

Overall, research on the economic consequences of implementing international strategies is mixed. Some research has found that the performance of firms pursuing international strategies is superior to the performance of firms operating only in domestic markets.[31] However, most of this work has not examined the particular economies of scope that a firm is attempting to realize through its internationalization efforts. Moreover, several of these studies have attempted to evaluate the impact of international strategies on firm performance by using accounting measures of performance. Other research has found that the risk-adjusted performance of firms pursuing an international strategy is not different from the risk-adjusted performance of firms pursuing purely domestic strategies.[32]

These ambivalent findings are not surprising because the economic value of international strategies depends on whether a firm pursues valuable economies of scope when implementing this strategy. Most of this empirical work fails to examine the economies of scope that a firm's international strategy might be based on. Moreover, even if a firm is able to realize real economies of scope from its international strategies, to be a source of sustained competitive advantage, this economy of scope must also be rare and costly to imitate, and the firm must be organized to fully realize it.

International Strategies and Sustained Competitive Advantage

As suggested earlier in this chapter, much of the discussion of rarity and imitability in strategic alliance, diversification, and merger and acquisition strategies also applies to international strategies. However, some aspects of rarity and imitability are unique to international strategies.

The Rarity of International Strategies

V R I O

In many ways, it seems likely that international strategies are becoming less rare among most competing firms. Consider, for example, the increasingly international strategies of many telephone companies around the world. Through much of the 1980s, telecommunications remained a highly regulated industry around the world. Phone companies rarely ventured beyond their country borders and had few, if any, international aspirations. However, as government restrictions on telecommunications firms around the world began to be lifted, these firms began exploring new business alternatives. For many firms, this originally meant exploring new telecommunications businesses in their domestic markets. Thus, for example, many formerly regulated telecommunications firms in the United States began to explore business opportunities in less-regulated segments of the U.S. telecommunications market, including cellular telephones and paging. Over time, these same firms began to explore business opportunities overseas.

In the past several years, the telecommunications industry has begun to consolidate on a worldwide basis. For example, in the early 1990s, Southwestern Bell (now AT&T) purchased a controlling interest in Mexico's government-owned telecommunications company. Ameritech (now a division of AT&T), Bell Atlantic, U.S. West, BellSouth, and Pacific Telesis (now a division of AT&T) also engaged in various international operations. In the late 1990s, MCI (a U.S. firm) and British Telecom (a British company) merged. In 1999, the Vodafone Group (a British-headquartered telecommunications company) purchased AirTouch Cellular (a U.S. firm) for $60.29 billion, formed a strategic alliance with U.S. West (another U.S. firm), purchased Mannesmann (a German telecommunications firm) for $127.76 billion, and increased its ownership interest in several smaller telecommunications companies around the world. Also, in 1999, Olivetti (the Italian electronics firm) successfully beat back Deutsche Telephone's effort to acquire ItaliaTelecom (the Italian telephone company). And, in 2012, the Japanese mobile phone company Softbank purchased the U.S. phone company SprintNextel. Obviously, international strategies are no longer rare among telecommunications companies.[33]

There are, of course, several reasons for the increased popularity of international strategies. Not the least of these are the substantial economies of scope that internationalizing firms can realize. In addition, several changes in the organization of the international economy have facilitated the growth in popularity of international strategies. For example, the General Agreement on Tariff and Trade (GATT) treaty, in conjunction with the development of the European Community (EC), the Andean Common Market (ANCOM), the Association of Southeast Asian Nations (ASEAN), the North American Free Trade Agreement (NAFTA), and other free-trade zones, has substantially reduced both tariff and nontariff barriers to trade. These changes have helped facilitate trade among countries included in an agreement; they have also spurred firms that wish to take advantage of these opportunities to expand their operations into these countries.

Improvements in the technological infrastructure of business are also important contributors to the growth in the number of firms pursuing international strategies. Transportation (especially air travel) and communication (via computers, fax, telephones, pagers, cellular telephones, and so forth) have evolved to the point where it is now much easier for firms to monitor and integrate their international operations than it was just a few years ago. This infrastructure helps reduce the cost of implementing an international strategy and thus increases the probability that firms will pursue these opportunities.

Finally, the emergence of various communication, technical, and accounting standards is facilitating international strategies. For example, there is currently a de facto world standard in personal computers. Moreover, most of the software that runs off these computers is flexible and interchangeable. Someone can write a report on a PC in India and print that report out on a PC in France with no real difficulties. There is also a world de facto standard business language: English. Although fully understanding a non-English–speaking culture requires managers to learn the native tongue, it is nevertheless possible to manage international business operations by using English.

Even though it seems that more and more firms are pursuing international strategies, it does not follow that these strategies will never be rare among a set of competing firms. Rare international strategies can exist in at least two ways. Given the enormous range of business opportunities that exist around the globe, it may very well be the case that huge numbers of firms can implement international strategies and still not compete head to head when implementing these strategies.

Even if several firms are competing to exploit the same international opportunity, the rarity criterion can still be met if the resources and capabilities that a particular firm brings to this international competition are themselves rare. Examples of these rare resources and capabilities might include unusual marketing skills, highly differentiated products, special technology, superior management talent, and economies of scale.[34] To the extent that a firm pursues one of the economies of scope listed in Table 11.1 using resources and capabilities that are rare among competing firms, that firm can gain at least a temporary competitive advantage, even if its international strategy, per se, is not rare.

VRIO The Imitability of International Strategies

Like all the strategies discussed in this book, both the direct duplication of and substitutes for international strategies are important in evaluating the imitability of these actions.

Direct Duplication of International Strategies

In evaluating the possibility of the direct duplication of international strategies, two questions must be asked: (1) Will firms try to duplicate valuable and rare international strategies? and (2) Will firms be able to duplicate these valuable and rare strategies?

There seems little doubt that, in the absence of artificial barriers, the profits generated by one firm's valuable and rare international strategies will motivate other firms to try to imitate the resources and capabilities required to implement these strategies. This is what has occurred in the international telecommunications industry. This rush to internationalization has occurred in numerous other industries as well. For example, the processed-food industry at one time had a strong home-market orientation. However, because of the success of Nestlé and Procter & Gamble worldwide, most processed-food companies now engage in at least some international operations.

However, simply because competing firms often try to duplicate a successful firm's international strategy does not mean that they are always able to do so. To the extent that a successful firm exploits resources or capabilities that are path dependent, uncertain, or socially complex in its internationalization efforts, direct duplication may be too costly, and thus international strategies can be a source of sustained competitive advantage. Indeed, there is some reason to believe that at least some of the resources and capabilities that enable a firm to pursue an international strategy are likely to be costly to imitate.

For example, the ability to develop detailed local knowledge of nondomestic markets may require firms to have management teams with a great deal of foreign experience. Some firms may have this kind of experience in their top management teams; other firms may not. One survey of 433 chief executive officers from around the world reported that 14 percent of U.S. chief executive officers (CEOs) had no foreign experience and that the foreign experience of 56 percent of U.S. CEOs was limited to vacation travel. Another survey showed that only 22 percent of the CEOs of multinational companies had extensive international experience.[35] Of course, it can take a great deal of time for a firm that does not have much foreign experience in its management team to develop that experience. Firms that lack this kind of experience will have to bring managers in from outside the organization, invest in developing this experience internally, or both. Of course, these activities are costly. The cost of creating this experience base in a firm's management team can be thought of as one of the costs of direct duplication.

Substitutes for International Strategies

Even if direct duplication of a firm's international strategies is costly, substitutes might still exist that limit the ability of that strategy to generate sustained competitive advantages. In particular, because international strategies are just a special case of corporate strategies in general, any of the other corporate strategies discussed in this book—including some types of strategic alliances, diversification, and mergers and acquisitions—can be at least partial substitutes for international strategies.

For example, it may be possible for a firm to gain at least some of the economies of scope listed in Table 11.1 by implementing a corporate diversification strategy within a single country market, especially if that market is large and geographically diverse. One such market, of course, is the United States. A firm that originally conducted business in the northeastern United States can gain many of the benefits of internationalization by beginning business operations in the southern United States, on the West Coast, or in the Pacific Northwest. In this sense, geographic diversification within the United States is at least a partial substitute for internationalization and is one reason why many U.S. firms have lagged behind European and Asian firms in their international efforts.

There are, however, some economies of scope listed in Table 11.1 that can be gained only through international operations. For example, because there are usually few limits on capital flows within most countries, risk management is directly valuable to a firm's equity holders only for firms pursuing business opportunities across countries where barriers to capital flow exist.

VRIO   # The Organization of International Strategies

To realize the full economic potential of a valuable, rare, and costly-to-imitate international strategy, firms must be appropriately organized.

Becoming International: Organizational Options

A firm implements an international strategy when it diversifies its business operations across country boundaries. However, firms can organize their international business operations in a wide variety of ways. Some of the most common, ranging from market forms of governance to manage simple export operations to the use of wholly owned subsidiaries to manage **foreign direct investment**, are listed in Table 11.5.

Market Exchanges and International Strategies

Firms can maintain traditional arm's-length market relationships between themselves and their nondomestic customers and still implement international strategies. They do this by simply exporting their products or services to nondomestic markets and limiting any foreign direct investment into nondomestic markets. Of course, exporting firms generally have to work with some partner or partners to receive, market, and distribute their products in a nondomestic setting. However, it is possible for exporting firms to use contracts to manage their relationship with these foreign partners and thereby maintain arm's-length relationships with them—all the time engaging in international operations.

The advantages of adopting exporting as a way to manage an international strategy include its relatively low cost and the limited risk exposure that firms pursuing international opportunities in this manner face. Firms that are just beginning to consider international strategies can use market-based exporting to test international waters—to find out if there is demand for their current products or services, to develop some experience operating in nondomestic markets, or to begin to develop relationships that could be valuable in subsequent international strategy efforts. If firms discover that there is not much demand for their products or services in a nondomestic market or if they discover that they do not have the resources and capabilities to effectively compete in those markets, they can simply cease their exporting operations. The direct cost of ceasing export operations can be quite low, especially if a firm's volume of exports is small and the firm has not invested in plant and equipment designed to facilitate exporting. Certainly, if a firm has limited its foreign direct investment, it does not risk losing this investment if it ceases export operations.

However, the opportunity costs associated with restricting a firm's international operations to exporting can be significant. Of the economies of scope listed in Table 11.1, only gaining access to new customers for a firm's current products

TABLE 11.5 Organizing Options for Firms Pursuing International Strategies

Market Governance	Intermediate Market Governance	Hierarchical Governance
Exporting	Licensing	Mergers
	Non-equity alliances	Acquisitions
	Equity alliances	Wholly owned subsidiaries
	Joint ventures	

or services can be realized through exporting. Other economies of scope that hold some potential for firms exploring international business operations are out of the reach of firms that restrict their international operations to exporting. For some firms, realizing economies from gaining access to new customers is sufficient, and exporting is a long-run viable strategy. However, to the extent that other economies of scope might exist for a firm, limiting international operations to exporting can limit the firm's economic profit.

Intermediate Market Exchanges and International Strategies

If a firm decides to move beyond exporting in pursuing international strategies, a wide range of **strategic alliances** are available. These alliances range from simple licensing arrangements, where a domestic firm grants a firm in a nondomestic market the right to use its products and brand names to sell products in that nondomestic market, to full-blown joint ventures, where a domestic firm and a nondomestic firm create an independent organizational entity to manage international efforts. As suggested in Chapter 9, the recent growth in the number of firms pursuing strategic alliance strategies is a direct result of the growth in popularity of international strategies. Strategic alliances are one of the most common ways that firms manage their international efforts.

Most of the discussion of the value, rarity, imitability, and organization of strategic alliances in Chapter 9 applies to the analysis of strategic alliances to implement an international strategy. However, many of the opportunities and challenges of managing strategic alliances as cooperative strategies, discussed in Chapter 9, are exacerbated in the context of international strategic alliances.

For example, it was suggested that opportunistic behavior (in the form of adverse selection, moral hazard, or holdup) can threaten the stability of strategic alliances domestically. Opportunistic behavior is a problem because partners in a strategic alliance find it costly to observe and evaluate the performance of alliance partners. Obviously, the costs and difficulty of evaluating the performance of an alliance partner in an international alliance are greater than the costs and difficulty of evaluating the performance of an alliance partner in a purely domestic alliance. Geographic distance, differences in traditional business practices, language barriers, and cultural differences can make it very difficult for firms to accurately evaluate the performance and intentions of international alliance partners.

These challenges can manifest themselves at multiple levels in an international strategic alliance. For example, one study has shown that managers in U.S. organizations, on average, have a negotiation style very different from that of managers in Chinese organizations. Chinese managers tend to interrupt each other and ask many more questions during negotiations than do U.S. managers. As U.S. and Chinese firms begin to negotiate collaborative agreements, it will be difficult for U.S. managers to judge whether the Chinese negotiation style reflects Chinese managers' fundamental distrust of U.S. managers or is simply a manifestation of traditional Chinese business practices and culture.[36]

Similar management style differences have been noted between Western and Japanese managers. One Western manager was quoted:[37]

> Whenever I made a presentation [to our partner], I was one person against 10 or 12. They'd put me in front of a flip chart, and then stop me while they went into a conversation in Japanese for 10 minutes. If I asked them a question they would break into Japanese to first decide what I wanted to know, and then would discuss options in terms of what they might tell me, and finally would come back with an answer.

During those 10-minute breaks in the conversation, it would be very difficult for this manager to know whether the Japanese managers were trying to develop a complete and accurate answer to his question or scheming to provide an incomplete and misleading answer. In this ambiguous setting, to prevent potential opportunism, Western managers might demand greater levels of governance than were actually necessary. In fact, one study has shown that differences in the perceived trustworthiness of international partners have an impact on the kind of governance mechanisms that are put into place when firms begin international operations. If partners are not perceived as being trustworthy, then elaborate governance devices, including joint ventures, are created—even if the partners are in fact trustworthy.[38]

Cultural and style conflicts leading to perceived opportunism problems are not restricted to alliances between Asian and Western organizations. U.S. firms operating with Mexican partners often discover numerous subtle and complex cultural differences. For example, a U.S. firm operating a steel conveyor plant in Puebla, Mexico, implemented a three-stage employee grievance policy. An employee who had a grievance first went to the immediate supervisor and then continued up the chain of command until the grievance was resolved one way or another. U.S. managers were satisfied with this system and pleased that no grievances had been registered—until the day the entire plant walked out on strike. It turns out that there had been numerous grievances, but Mexican workers had felt uncomfortable directly confronting their supervisors with these problems. Such confrontations are considered antisocial in Mexican culture.[39]

Although significant challenges are associated with managing strategic alliances across country boundaries, there are significant opportunities as well. Strategic alliances can enable a firm pursuing an international strategy to realize any of the economies of scope listed in Table 11.1. Moreover, if a firm is able to develop valuable, rare, and costly to imitate resources and capabilities in managing strategic alliances, the use of alliances in an international context can be a source of sustained competitive advantage.

Hierarchical Governance and International Strategies

Firms may decide to integrate their international operations into their organizational hierarchies by acquiring a firm in a nondomestic market or by forming a new wholly owned subsidiary to manage their operations in a nondomestic market. Obviously, both of these international investments involve substantial direct foreign investment by a firm over long periods of time. These investments are subject to both political and economic risks and should be undertaken only if the economy of scope that can be realized through international operations is significant and other ways of realizing this economy of scope are not effective or efficient.

Although full integration in international operations can be expensive and risky, it can have some important advantages for internationalizing firms. First, like strategic alliances, this approach to internationalization can enable a firm to realize any of the economies of scope listed in Table 11.1. Moreover, integration enables managers to use a wider range of organizational controls to limit the threat of opportunism that are normally not available in market forms of international governance or intermediate market forms of international governance. Finally, unlike strategic alliances, where any profits from international operations must be shared with international partners, integrating into international operations enables firms to capture all the economic profits from their international operations.

Managing the Internationally Diversified Firm

Not surprisingly, the management of international operations can be thought of as a special case of managing a diversified firm. Thus, many of the issues discussed in Chapter 8 apply here. However, managing an internationally diversified firm does create some unique challenges and opportunities.

Organizational Structure. Firms pursuing an international strategy have four basic organizational structural alternatives, listed in Table 11.6 and discussed later. Although each of these structures has some special features, they are all special cases of the multidivisional structure first introduced in Chapter 8.[40]

Some firms organize their international operations as a **decentralized federation**. In this organizational structure, each country in which a firm operates is organized as a full profit-and-loss division headed by a division general manager who is typically the president of the company in a particular country. In a decentralized federation, there are very few shared activities or other relationships among different divisions/country companies, and corporate headquarters plays a limited strategic role. Corporate staff functions are generally limited to the collection of accounting and other performance information from divisions/country companies and to reporting this aggregate information to appropriate government officials and to the financial markets. Both strategic and operational decision making are delegated to division general managers/country company presidents in a decentralized federation organizational structure. There are relatively few examples of pure decentralized federations in today's world economy, but firms like Nestlé, CIBA-Geigy, and Electrolux have many of the attributes of this type of structure.[41]

A second structural option for international firms is the **coordinated federation**. In a coordinated federation, each country operation is organized as a full profit-and-loss center, and division general managers can be presidents of country companies. However, unlike the case in a decentralized federation, strategic and operational decisions are not fully delegated to division general managers. Operational decisions are delegated to division general managers/country presidents, but broader strategic decisions are made at corporate headquarters. Moreover, coordinated federations attempt to exploit various shared activities and other relationships among their divisions/country companies. It is

TABLE 11.6 Structural Options for Firms Pursuing International Strategies

Decentralized federation	Strategic and operational decisions are delegated to divisions/country companies.
Coordinated federation	Operational decisions are delegated to divisions/country companies; strategic decisions are retained at corporate headquarters.
Centralized hub	Strategic and operational decisions are retained at corporate headquarters.
Transnational structure	Strategic and operational decisions are delegated to those operational entities that maximize responsiveness to local conditions and international integration.

Source: Adapted from C. A. Bartlett and S. Ghoshal (1989). *Managing across borders: The transnational solution.* Boston: Harvard Business School Press.

not uncommon for coordinated federations to have corporately sponsored central research and development laboratories, corporately sponsored manufacturing and technology development initiatives, and corporately sponsored management training and development operations. There are numerous examples of coordinated federations in today's world economy, including General Electric, General Motors, IBM, and Coca-Cola.

A third structural option for international firms is the **centralized hub**. In centralized hubs, operations in different companies may be organized into profit-and-loss centers, and division general managers may be country company presidents. However, most of the strategic and operational decision making in these firms takes place at the corporate center. The role of divisions/country companies in centralized hubs is simply to implement the strategies, tactics, and policies that have been chosen at headquarters. Of course, divisions/country companies are also a source of information for headquarters staff when these decisions are being made. However, in centralized hubs, strategic and operational decision rights are retained at the corporate center. Many Japanese and Korean firms are managed as centralized hubs, including Toyota, Mitsubishi, and NEC in Japan and Goldstar, Daewoo, and Hyundai in Korea.[42]

A fourth structural option for international firms is the **transnational structure**. This structure is most appropriate for implementing the transnational strategy described earlier in this chapter. In many ways, the transnational structure is similar to the coordinated federation. In both, strategic decision-making responsibility is largely retained at the corporate center, and operational decision making is largely delegated to division general managers/country presidents. However, important differences also exist.

In a coordinated federation structure, shared activities and other cross-divisional/cross-country economies of scope are managed by the corporate center. Thus, for many of these firms, if research and development is seen as a potentially valuable economy of scope, a central research and development laboratory is created and managed by the corporate center. In the transnational structure, these centers of corporate economies of scope may be managed by the corporate center. However, they are more likely to be managed by specific divisions/country companies within the corporation. Thus, for example, if one division/country company develops valuable, rare, and costly-to-imitate research-and-development capabilities in its ongoing business activities in a particular country, that division/country company could become the center of research-and-development activity for the entire corporation. If one division/country company develops valuable, rare, and costly-to-imitate manufacturing technology development skills in its ongoing business activities in a particular country, that division/country company could become the center for manufacturing technology development for the entire corporation.

The role of corporate headquarters in a transnational structure is to constantly scan business operations across different countries for resources and capabilities that might be a source of competitive advantage for other divisions/country companies in the firm. Once these special skills are located, corporate staff must then determine the best way to exploit these economies of scope—whether they should be developed within a single division/country company (to gain economies of scale) and then transferred to other divisions/country companies, or developed through an alliance between two or more divisions/country companies (to gain economies of scale) and then transferred to other divisions/country companies, or developed for the entire firm at corporate headquarters. These options are not available to decentralized federations (which always let individual divisions/country companies develop their own competencies), coordinated federations, or centralized hubs (which always develop corporate-wide economies of scope at the corporate level). Firms that have been successful in adopting this transnational structure include Ford (Ford Europe has become a leader for automobile design in all of the Ford Motor Company) and Ericson (Ericson's Australian subsidiary developed this Swedish company's first electronic telecommunication switch, and corporate headquarters was able to help transfer this technology to other Ericson subsidiaries).[43]

Organizational Structure, Local Responsiveness, and International Integration. It should be clear that the choice among these four approaches to managing international strategies depends on the trade-offs that firms are willing to make between local responsiveness and international integration. Firms that seek to maximize their local responsiveness will tend to choose a decentralized federation structure. Firms that seek to maximize international integration in their operations will typically opt for centralized hub structures. Firms that seek to balance the need for local responsiveness and international integration will typically choose centralized federations. Firms that attempt to optimize both local responsiveness and international integration will choose a transnational organizational structure.

Management Control Systems and Compensation Policies. Like the multidivisional structure discussed in Chapter 8, none of the organizational structures described in Table 11.5 can stand alone without the support of a variety of management control systems and management compensation policies. All the management control processes discussed in Chapter 8, including evaluating the performance of divisions, allocating capital, and managing the exchange of intermediate products among divisions, are also important for firms organizing to implement an international strategy. Moreover, the same management compensation challenges and opportunities discussed in that chapter apply in the organization of international strategies as well.

However, as is often the case when organizing processes originally developed to manage diversification within a domestic market are extended to the management of international diversification, many of the management challenges highlighted in Chapter 8 are exacerbated in an international context. This puts an even greater burden on senior managers in an internationally diversified firm to choose control systems and compensation policies that create incentives for division general managers/country presidents to appropriately cooperate to realize the economies of scope that originally motivated the implementation of an international strategy.

Summary

International strategies can be seen as a special case of diversification strategies. Firms implement international strategies when they pursue business opportunities that cross country borders. Like all diversification strategies, international strategies must exploit real economies of scope that outside investors find too costly to exploit on their own in order to be valuable. Five potentially valuable economies of scope in international strategies are (1) to gain access to new customers for a firm's current products or services, (2) to gain access to low-cost factors of production, (3) to develop new core competencies, (4) to leverage current core competencies in new ways, and (5) to manage corporate risk.

As firms pursue these economies of scope, they must evaluate the extent to which they can be responsive to local market needs and obtain the advantages of international integration. Firms that attempt to accomplish both these objectives are said to be implementing a transnational strategy. Both economic and political risks can affect the value of a firm's international strategies.

To be a source of sustained competitive advantage, a firm's international strategies must be valuable, rare, and costly to imitate, and the firm must be organized to realize the full potential of its international strategies. Even though more and more firms are pursuing international strategies, these strategies can still be rare, for at least two reasons: (1) Given the broad range of international opportunities, firms may not compete head to head with other firms pursuing the same international strategies that they are pursuing; and (2) firms may bring valuable and rare resources and capabilities to the international strategies they pursue. Both direct duplication and substitution can affect the imitability of a firm's international strategy. Direct duplication is not likely when firms bring valuable, rare, and costly to imitate resources and capabilities to bear in their international strategies. Several substitutes for international strategies exist, including some strategic alliances, vertical integration, diversification, and mergers and acquisitions, especially if these strategies are pursued in a large and diverse single country market. However, some potential economies of scope from international strategies can be exploited only by operating across country borders.

Firms have several organizational options as they pursue international strategies, including market forms of exchange (for example, exports), strategic alliances, and vertical integration (for example, wholly owned subsidiaries). Four alternative structures, all special cases of the multidivisional structure introduced in Chapter 8, can be used to manage these international operations: a decentralized federation structure, a coordinated federation structure, a centralized hub structure, and a transnational structure. These structures need to be consistent with a firm's emphasis on being responsive to local markets, on exploiting international integration opportunities, or both.

MyManagementLab®

Go to **mymanagementlab.com** to complete the problems marked with this icon ✪.

Challenge Questions

✪ **11.1.** Are international strategies always just a special case of diversification strategies that a firm might pursue?

11.2. In international expansion, companies are more exposed to currency risks than domestic organizations. Describe the basic mechanics of this

exposure and how firms can guard against it.

11.3. Investing abroad is always risky for companies; external macroenvironmental factors are elements that a firm has little or no control over. When participating in foreign direct investment (FDI) especially in jurisdictions with left wing governments, political

risks can be particularly heightened. Identify and discuss some of these risks.

11.4. The transnational strategy is often seen as one way in which firms can avoid the limitations inherent in the local responsiveness/international integration trade-off. However, given the obvious advantages of being both locally responsive and internationally integrated, why are apparently only a relatively few firms implementing a transnational strategy?

11.5. Can a firm's transnational strategy be a source of sustained competitive advantage?

✪**11.6.** On average, why is the threat of adverse selection and moral hazard in strategic alliances greater for firms pursuing an international strategy or a domestic strategy?

11.7. How are the organizational options for implementing an international strategy related to the M-form structure described in Chapter 8?

11.8. Are international organizational options for implementing an international strategy just special cases of the M-form structure, with slightly different emphases, or are these international organizational options fundamentally different from the M-form structure?

Problem Set

11.9. Countries participate in cross border trade to exchange goods otherwise not available in their own countries, at a price, quality or variety level as demanded by customers. Unless countries are members of the World Trade Organization (WTO), governments may take unilateral steps to frustrate the import of goods, usually for the protection of domestic industries. List the potential actions that governments can take to impede or prevent foreign companies from competing in their country and the reasons, besides protectionism, for doing so.

11.10. Your firm has decided to begin selling its mining machinery products in Ghana. Unfortunately, there is not a highly developed trading market for currency in Ghana. However, Ghana does have significant exports of cocoa. Describe a process by which you would be able to sell your machines in Ghana and still translate your earnings into a tradable currency (e.g., dollars or euros).

11.11. Match the actions of these firms with their sources of potential value.

(a) Tata Motors (India) acquires Jaguar (United Kingdom).
(b) Microsoft (United States) opens four research and development centers in Europe.
(c) Disney opens Disney–Hong Kong.
(d) Merck forms a research and development alliance with an Indian pharmaceutical firm.
(e) Lenovo purchases IBM's laptop computer business.
(f) Honda Motor Company opens an automobile manufacturing plant in southern China. Most of the cars it produces are sold in China.
(g) Honda starts exporting cars made in its China plant to Japan.
(h) A Canadian gold mining company acquires an Australian opal mining company.

1. Managing corporate risk
2. New core competencies
3. Leveraging current core competencies in new ways
4. Gaining access to low-cost factors of production
5. New customers for current products or services

MyManagementLab®

Go to **mymanagementlab.com** for the following Assisted-graded writing questions:

✪ **11.12.** How can we measure the political risks associated with international strategies?

✪ **11.13.** How does internationalization affect product life cycles?

End Notes

1. See Yoshino, M., S. Hall, and T. Malnight. (1991). "Whirlpool Corp." Harvard Business School Case no. 9-391-089.
2. 258marketing.wordpress.com/2008/02/27/bad-ads-nothing-sucks-like-an-electrolux/. Accessed June 17, 2009.
3. See Perry, N. J. (1991). "Will Sony make it in Hollywood?" *Fortune*, September 9, pp. 158–166; and Montgomery, C. (1993). "Marks and Spencer Ltd. (A)," Harvard Business School Case no. 9-391-089.
4. See Rapoport, C. (1994). "Nestlé's brand building machine." *Fortune*, September 19, pp. 147–156.
5. See Yoshino, M. Y., and P. Stoneham. (1992). "Procter & Gamble Japan (A)." Harvard Business School Case no. 9-793-035.
6. See Davis, B. (1995). "U.S. expects goals in pact with Japan to be met even without overt backing." *The Wall Street Journal*, June 30, p. A3; Bounds, W., and B. Davis. (1995). "U.S. to launch new case against Japan over Kodak." *The Wall Street Journal*, June 30, p. A3; Jacob, R. (1992). "India is opening for business." *Fortune*, November 16, pp. 128–130; and Rugman, A., and R. Hodgetts. (1995). *Business: A strategic management approach.* New York: McGraw-Hill.
7. See Jacob, R. (1992). "India is opening for business." *Fortune*, November 16, pp. 128–130; Serwer, A. E. (1994). "McDonald's conquers the world." *Fortune*, October 17, pp. 103–116; and World Bank (1999). *World development report.* Oxford: Oxford University Press.
8. See Jacob, R. (1992). "India is opening for business." *Fortune*, November 16, pp. 128–130; Ignatius, A. (1993). "Commodity giant: Marc Rich & Co. does big deals at big risk in former U.S.S.R." *The Wall Street Journal*, May 13, p. A1; and Kraar, L. (1995). "The risks are rising in China." *Fortune*, March 6, pp. 179–180.
9. The life cycle is described in Utterback, J. M., and W. J. Abernathy. (1975). "A dynamic model of process and product innovation." *Omega*, 3, pp. 639–656; Abernathy, W. J., and J. M. Utterback. (1978). "Patterns of technological innovation." *Technology Review*, 80, pp. 40–47; and Grant, R. M. (1991). *Contemporary strategy analysis.* Cambridge, MA: Basil Blackwell.
10. See Bradley, S. P., and S. Cavanaugh. (1994). "Crown Cork and Seal in 1989." Harvard Business School Case no. 9-793-035; and Hamermesh, R. G., and R. S. Rosenbloom. (1989). "Crown Cork and Seal Co., Inc." Harvard Business School Case no. 9-388-096. Of course, this strategy works only until nondomestic markets mature. This occurred for Crown Cork & Seal during the 1990s. Since then, it has had to search elsewhere for growth opportunities.
11. Porter, M. E. (1986). "Competition in international industries: A conceptual framework." In M. E. Porter (ed.), *Competition in International Industries.* Boston: Harvard Business School Press, p. 43; and Ghoshal, S. (1987). "Global strategy: An organizing framework." *Strategic Management Journal*, 8, p. 436.
12. See Kobrin, S. (1991). "An empirical analysis of the determinants of global integration." *Strategic Management Journal*, 12, pp. 17–31.
13. See Trager, J. (1992). *The people's chronology.* New York: Henry Holt.
14. Kraar, L. (1992). "Korea's tigers keep roaring." *Fortune*, May 4, pp. 108–110.
15. See Collis, D. J. (1991). "A resource-based analysis of international competition: The case of the bearing industry." *Strategic Management Journal*, 12 (Summer Special Issue), pp. 49–68; and Engardio, P. (1993). "Motorola in China: A great leap forward." *Business Week*, May 17, pp. 58–59.
16. Gain, S. (1993). "Korea is overthrown as sneaker champ." *The Wall Street Journal*, October 7, p. A14.
17. See Reibstein, L., and M. Levinson. (1991). "A Mexican miracle?" *Newsweek*, May 20, p. 42; and de Forest, M. E. (1994). "Thinking of a plant in Mexico?" *Academy of Management Executive*, 8(1), pp. 33–40.
18. See Zimmerman, M. (1985). *How to do business with the Japanese.* New York: Random House; and Osborn, R. N., and C. C. Baughn. (1987). "New patterns in the formation of US/Japan cooperative ventures: The role of technology." *Columbia Journal of World Business*, 22, pp. 57–65.
19. Ibid.
20. See Benedict, R. (1946). *The chrysanthemum and the sword.* New York: New American Library; Peterson, R. B., and H. F. Schwind. (1977). "A comparative study of personnel problems in companies and joint ventures in Japan." *Journal of Business Studies*, 8(1), pp. 45–55; Peterson, R. B., and J. Y. Shimada. (1978). "Sources of management problems in Japanese-American joint ventures." *Academy of Management Review*, 3, pp. 796–804; and Hamel, G. (1991). "Competition for competence and inter-partner learning within strategic alliances." *Strategic Management Journal*, 12, pp. 83–103.
21. See Burgleman, R. A. (1983). "A process model of internal corporate venturing in the diversified major firm." *Administrative Science Quarterly*, 28(2), pp. 223–244; Hedberg, B. L. T. (1981). "How organizations learn and unlearn." In P. C. Nystrom and W. H. Starbuck (eds.), *Handbook of Organizational Design.* London: Oxford University Press; Nystrom, P. C., and W. H. Starbuck. (1984). "To avoid organizational crisis, unlearn." *Organizational Dynamics*, 12(4), pp. 53–65; and Argyris, C., and D. A. Schon. (1978). *Organizational learning.* Reading, MA: Addison-Wesley.
22. A problem described in Burgleman, R. A. (1983). "A process model of internal corporate venturing in the diversified major firm." *Administrative Science Quarterly*, 28(2), pp. 223–244.
23. Quoted in Hamel, G. (1991). "Competition for competence and inter-partner learning within strategic alliances." *Strategic Management Journal*, 12, p. 97.
24. See Agmon, T., and D. R. Lessard. (1977). "Investor recognition of corporate diversification." *The Journal of Finance*, 32, pp. 1049–1056.
25. Rapoport, C. (1994). "Nestlé's brand building machine." *Fortune*, September 19, pp. 147–156.
26. See Bartlett, C. A., and S. Ghoshal. (1989). *Managing across borders: The transnational solution.* Boston, MA: Harvard Business School Press.
27. See Rugman, A., and R. Hodgetts. (1995). *International business: A strategic management approach.* New York: McGraw-Hill.
28. Glynn, M. A. (1993). "Strategic planning in Nigeria versus U.S.: A case of anticipating the (next) coup." *Academy of Management Executive*, 7(3), pp. 82–83.
29. Dichtl, E., and H. G. Koeglmayr. (1986). "Country risk ratings." *Management International Review*, 26(4), pp. 2–10.
30. See Auletta, K. (1983). "A certain poetry—Parts I and II." *The New Yorker*, June 6, pp. 46–109; and June 13, pp. 50–91.
31. See, for example, Leftwich, R. B. (1974). "U.S. multinational companies: Profitability, financial leverage and effective income tax rates." *Survey of Current Business*, 54, May, pp. 27–36; Dunning, J. H. (1973). "The determinants of production." *Oxford Economic Papers*, 25, November, pp. 289–336; Errunza, V., and L. W. Senbet. (1981). "The effects of international operations on the market value of the firm: Theory and evidence." *The Journal of Finance*, 36, pp. 401–418; Grant, R. M. (1987). "Multinationality and performance among British manufacturing companies." *Journal of International Business Studies*, 18 (Fall), pp. 78–89; and Rugman, A. (1979). *International diversification and the multinational enterprise.* Lexington, MA: Lexington Books.
32. See, for example, Brewer, H. L. (1981). "Investor benefits from corporate international diversification," *Journal of Financial and Quantitative Analysis*, 16, March, pp. 113–126; and Michel, A., and I. Shaked. (1986). "Multinational corporations vs. domestic corporations: Financial performance and characteristics," *Journal of Business*, 17 (Fall), pp. 89–100.
33. Kirkpatrick, D. (1993). "Could AT&T rule the world?" *Fortune*, May 17, pp. 54–56; Deogun, N. (2000). "Europe catches merger fever as international volume sets record." *The Wall Street Journal*, January 3, p. R8.
34. See Caves, R. E. (1971). "International corporations: The industrial economics of foreign investment." *Economica*, 38, Feb. pp. 1–28; Dunning, J. H. (1973). "The determinants of production." *Oxford Economic Papers*, 25, Nov., pp. 289–336; Hymer, S. (1976). *The international operations of national firms: A study of direct foreign investment.* Cambridge, MA: The MIT Press; Errunza, V., and L. W. Senbet. (1981). "The effects of international operations on the market value of the firm: Theory and evidence." *The Journal of Finance*, 36, pp. 401–418.
35. Anders, G. (1989). "Going global: Vision vs. reality." *The Wall Street Journal*, September 22, p. R21; Carpenter, M., G. Sanders, and H. Gregerson. (2001). "Building human capital with organizational context: The impact of assignment experience on multinational firm performance and CEO pay." *Academy of Management Journal*, vol. 44 no. 3, pp. 493–511.

36. Adler, N., J. R. Brahm, and J. L. Graham. (1992). "Strategy implementation: A comparison of face-to-face negotiations in the People's Republic of China and the United States." *Strategic Management Journal*, 13, pp. 449–466.

37. Hamel, G. (1991). "Competition for competence and inter-partner learning within international strategic alliances." *Strategic Management Journal*, 12, p. 95.

38. Shane, S. (1994). "The effect of national culture on the choice between licensing and direct foreign investment." *Strategic Management Journal*, 15, pp. 627–642.

39. See de Forest, M. E. (1994). "Thinking of a plant in Mexico?" *Academy of Management Executive*, 8(1), pp. 33–40.

40. See Bartlett, C. A. (1986). "Building and managing the transnational: The new organizational challenge." In M. E. Porter (ed.), *Competition in international industries.* Boston: Harvard Business School Press, pp. 367–401; and Bartlett, C. A., and S. Ghoshal. (1989). *Managing across borders; The transnational solution.* Boston: Harvard Business School Press.

41. See Baden-Fuller, C. W. F., and J. M. Stopford. (1991). "Globalization frustrated: The case of white goods." *Strategic Management Journal*, 12, pp. 493–507.

42. See Kraar, L. (1992). "Korea's tigers keep roaring." *Fortune*, May 4, pp. 108–110.

43. Bartlett, C. A., and S. Ghoshal. (1989). *Managing across borders: The transnational solution.* Boston: Harvard Business School Press; Grant, R. M. (1991). *Contemporary strategy analysis.* Cambridge, MA: Basil Blackwell.

Case 3–1: e-Bay's Outsourcing Strategy*

"If we are to continue outsourcing, and even consider expanding it, why should we keep paying someone else to do what we can do for ourselves?"

Kathy Dalton leaned forward in her chair. She read the message on her computer screen and let the words sink in. Why had she not anticipated that? After all, she was adept at asking insightful questions. She felt her heart rate quicken.

She would have stared out her office window and pondered this question, but she didn't have an office. In keeping with a well-established Silicon Valley tradition, everyone at eBay, including CEO Meg Whitman, occupied a cubicle. Dalton, an attractive, 38-year-old executive, had joined eBay in late 2002 after years of call center experience for major long distance carriers. Now, nearly two years later, she couldn't think of doing business any other way. She liked being in the center of the action. Sitting in a transparent cube, surrounded by hundreds of service representatives, added to her already high level of energy and kept her in touch with eBay's internal and external customers.

Dalton reflected on the e-mail she had just received from her boss, Wendy Moss, vice president of Global Customer Support. She knew she would pick up the phone

soon, call Moss, and ask her clarifying questions about her e-mail. Her mind raced through the details of the proposed outsourcing strategy she had submitted to Moss last week. She quizzed herself:

- "Did my team and I make a strong enough case for proposing almost a 100 percent increase in the amount of volume to be outsourced?"
- "Will eBay management concur with our recommendation to begin outsourcing potentially sensitive risk-related inquires for the first time?"
- "How will senior management react to the addition of a second outsourcing vendor?"
- "Did we cover adequately the types of proposed volumes targeted and how these would be transitioned to the outsourcing vendors?"
- "In the event of a major vendor problem, systems issue, or natural disaster, how executable is our back-out plan?"
- "Will the data in our proposal allay the growing concerns among executives about offshore outsourcing altogether?"

She wondered, "How would eBay senior managers react to our proposal to reorganize and expand outsourcing in a new three-tiered approach? And would they even consider expansion in light of recent headlines about companies reducing the amount of work outsourced to India because of quality issues?"

This last question had perplexed her for several months. Not only was it a personal issue for Dalton—she felt her job security at eBay depended largely on the company's continuing commitment to offshore outsourcing—but one she recognized as a business practice whose time perhaps had come and gone. Several leading consultants were claiming that offshoring had lost much of its cachet in recent years as companies were coming to grips with the real costs, logistics, management commitment, and service quality associated with third-party partners in India, the Philippines, and elsewhere. In her proposal, Dalton had

*Professors Scott Newman, Gary Grikscheit, and Rohit Verma and Research Assistant Vivek Malapati prepared this case solely as the basis for class discussion. The information presented in this case is based on publicly available information and insights gained through numerous interactions between University of Utah MBA students, their faculty advisors, and local eBay managers during a field study project (sponsored by the University of Utah and approved by the eBay Salt Lake City Service Center). The case contains writer-compiled, disguised information and is not intended to endorse and/or illustrate effective or ineffective service management practices. Certain sections of the case study have been fabricated based on current service management and customer service literature to provide a realistic and stimulating classroom experience. The numbers in the case are available from public information or estimates or are fictitious. This case was the winner of the 2006 CIBER-Production and Operations Management Society International Case Competition.

reinforced the benefits to eBay of continuing to outsource outside the United States and had woven into her new strategy more "nearshoring" alternatives as well.

Dalton was scheduled to fly to San Jose in just two weeks to present her outsourcing strategy to Whitman and her executive staff. Now, here was Moss's e-mail, questioning why she had not addressed the option of cutting out the middleman and building eBay-owned outsourcing locations in other countries.

A Little History

eBay called itself "The World's Online Marketplace." For the sale of goods and services by a diverse community of individuals and small businesses no venue was more appropriate. eBay's mission was to provide a robust trading platform where practically anyone could trade practically anything. Sellers included individual collectors of the rare and eclectic, as well as major corporations like Microsoft and IBM. Items sold on eBay ranged from collectibles like trading cards, antiques, dolls, and housewares to everyday items like used cars, clothing, books, CDs, and electronics. With 11 million or more items available on eBay at any one time, it was the largest and most popular person-to-person trading community on the Internet.

eBay came a long way from being a pet project for founder Pierre Omidyar and holding its first auction on Labor Day in September 1995. Omidyar developed a program and launched it on a Web site called Auction Web. According to eBay legend, he was trying to help his wife find other people with whom she could trade Pez dispensers. Omidyar found he was continually adding storage space to handle the amount of e-mail generated, reflecting the pent-up demand for an online meeting place for sellers and buyers. The site soon began to outgrow his personal Internet account.

Realizing the potential this Web service could have, he quit his job as a services development engineer at General Magic, a San Jose–based software company, and devoted full-time attention to managing Auction Web. As traffic increased, he also began charging a fee of $0.25 per listing to compensate for the cost involved in maintaining a business Internet account.

In 1996, Jeff Skoll, a Stanford Business School graduate and friend of Omidyar's, joined him to further develop Auction Web. They changed the name to eBay, short for East Bay Technologies. In mid-1997, a Menlo Park–based venture capital firm invested $5 million for a 22 percent stake in eBay. Omidyar knew that the venture capital

would be critical in building infrastructure and attracting top-tier management to the company.

In early 1998, Omidyar and Skoll realized eBay needed an experienced CEO to lead and develop an effective management team as well as to solidify the company's financial position with an IPO. In March of that year, Whitman accepted the position of president and CEO. A graduate of the Harvard Business School, Whitman had learned the importance of branding at companies such as Hasbro and Walt Disney. She hired senior staff from companies like Pepsico and Disney. She built a management team with an average of 20 years of business experience per executive and developed a strong vision for the company. Whitman immediately understood that the eBay community of users was the foundation of the company's business model. A central tenant of eBay's culture was captured in the phrase "The community was not built for eBay, but eBay was built by and for the community." It was not about just selling things on the Internet; it was about bonding people through the Web site.

Business Model and Market Share

Unlike many companies that were born before the Internet and then had to scramble to get online, eBay was born with the Net. Its transaction-based business model was perfectly suited for the Internet. Sellers "listed" items for sale on the Web site. Interested buyers could either bid higher than the previous bid in an auction format or use the "Buy It Now" feature and pay a predetermined price. The seller and buyer worked out the shipping method. Payment was usually made through PayPal, the world's leading online payment company, which eBay acquired in 2002. Because eBay never handled the items being sold, it did not incur warehousing expense and, of course, did not hold any inventory. For a company with almost $8 billion in assets, not a single dollar was invested in inventory (Exhibit 1).

In 2004, eBay reported revenue of nearly $3.3 billion. Revenue was mainly generated from two categories. The first, called the Listing Fee, involved a nominal fee incurred by the seller in posting an item for sale. This fee ranged from $0.25 to $2.00. The second, the Final Value Fee, was charged to the seller as a percentage of the final price when a sale was made. This amounted to between 1.25 percent and 5 percent of the selling price, depending on the price of the item. The Final Value Fee on a $4.00 Beanie Baby would be $0.20, representing a 5 percent fee. The same fee on a mainframe computer selling for $400,000.00 would be 1.25 percent, or $5,000.00.

Exhibit 1   Income Statement and Balance Sheet (abridged)

eBay's Income Statement (in 000s Dollars)	12/31/2004	12/31/2003	12/31/2002
Net revenues	$ 3,271,309	$ 2,165,096	$ 1,214,100
Cost of net revenues	614,415	416,058	213,876
Gross profit (loss)	2,656,894	1,749,038	1,000,224
Sales and marketing expenses	857,874	567,565	349,650
Product development expenses	240,647	159,315	104,636
General and administrative expenses	415,725	302,703	171,785
Patent litigation expense		29,965	
Payroll expense on employee stock options	17,479	9,590	4,015
Amortization of acquired intangible assets	65,927	50,659	15,941
Total operating expenses	1,597,652	1,119,797	646,027
Income (loss) from operations	1,059,242	629,241	354,197
Interest and other income, net	77,867	37,803	49,209
Interest expense	8,879	4,314	1,492
Impairment of certain equity investments		−1,230	−3,781
Income before income tax—United States	820,892		
Income before Income tax—international	307,338		
Net income (loss)	778,223	441,771	249,891
Net income (loss) per share-diluted	0.57	0.335	0.213
Net income (loss)	778,223	441,771	249,891
Cumulative effect of accounting change		5,413	
Provision for doubtful accounts and auth cred	90,942	46,049	25,455
Provision for transaction losses	50,459	36,401	7,832
Depreciation and amortization	253,690	159,003	76,576
Stock-based compensation		5,492	5,953
Amortization of unearned stock-based compens	5,832		
Tax benefit on the exer of employ stock opts	261,983	130,638	91,237
Impairment of certain equity investments		1,230	3,781
Minority interests	6,122		
Minority interest and other net income adj		7,784	1,324
Gain (loss) on sale of assets			−21,378
Accounts receivable	−105,540	−153,373	−54,583
Funds receivable from customers	−44,751	−38,879	−11,819
Other current assets	−312,756	−13,133	10,716
Other non-current assets	−308	−4,111	−1,195
Deferred tax assets, net		69,770	8,134
Deferred tax liabilities, net	28,652		
Accounts payable	−33,975	17,348	14,631
Net cash flows from investing activities	−2,013,220	−1,319,542	−157,759
Proceeds from issuance of common stock, net	650,638	700,817	252,181
Proceeds (principal pmts) on long-term obligs	−2,969	−11,951	−64
Partnership distributions			−50
Net cash flows from financing activities	647,669	688,866	252,067
Eff of exch rate change on cash and cash equivs	28,768	28,757	11,133
Net incr (decr) in cash and cash equivalents	−51,468	272,200	585,344
Cash and cash equivalents, beginning of year	1,381,513	1,109,313	523,969
Cash and cash equivalents, end of year	1,330,045	1,381,513	1,109,313
Cash paid for interest	8,234	3,237	1,492

Source: Case writers' estimates, compilations, and public records.

Being first to market in the e-commerce world was frequently an insurmountable competitive edge. eBay capitalized on being the first online auction house. Early competition came from companies like OnSale, Auction Universe, Amazon, Yahoo!, and Classified2000. These companies battled eBay on a number of fronts, mainly pricing, advertising online, and attempting to lure key eBay employees away to join their ranks. eBay's biggest and most formidable competitive threat came from Amazon.com when it spent more than $12 million launching its person-to-person auction service in 1999. eBay withstood all of these challenges. Amazon's efforts ultimately failed because it could not

Exhibit 2   Online Auction Market Share

	2001		2002		2003		2004	
	U.S.	Int'l	U.S.	Int'l	U.S.	Int'l	U.S.	Int'l
eBay	83%	41%	87%	50%	90%	65%	92%	74%
Yahoo!	7%	28%	6%	25%	4%	16%	3%	11%
Amazon	6%	10%	4%	8%	2%	5%	1%	2%
Overstock	N/A	N/A	1%	1%	2%	2%	2%	2%
uBid	1%	1%	1%	1%	1%	N/A	1%	N/A
All others	3%	20%	1%	15%	1%	12%	1%	11%

Source: Case writers' estimates, compilations, and public records.

generate enough site traffic. Auction buyers went where the most items were available for sale, and sellers went where the most buyers were found for their products. eBay had more buyers, more sellers, and more items—more than 1.4 billion items were listed on the site in 2004! These numbers dwarfed the nearest competitor by a factor of more than 50. eBay enjoyed a dominant 92 percent market share of the domestic online auction business and a 74 percent share of the international market (Exhibit 2).

eBay's Customer Support Organization

In December 2004, Dalton was an operations director in eBay's Customer Support organization. She had several major responsibilities; the most critical one was customer support outsourcing, both domestic and offshore (Exhibit 3). This role occupied approximately 80 percent

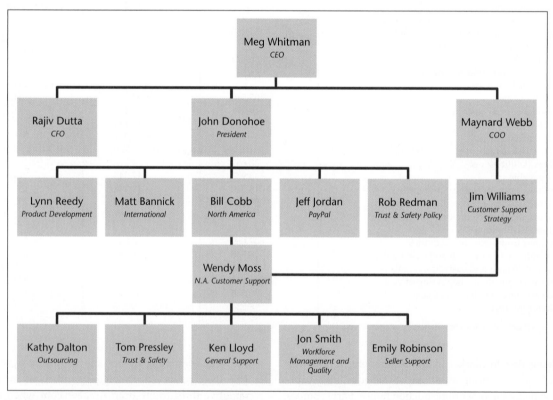

Exhibit 3   eBay Organization Chart

Source: Case writers' compilations and public records.

of her time. Upon joining the company, she had relocated to Salt Lake City, Utah, the site of eBay's largest customer service center. Utah's four seasons and mountainous terrain suited her. She loved to ski knee-deep powder in the winter and navigate forest trails on her mountain bike in summer. While thoughts of early season skiing had entered her mind, she had in fact spent the past three weekends in her cube and in conference rooms with her managers hammering out the strategy she had passed on to Moss for review.

Worldwide, eBay's Customer Support staff consisted of an estimated 3,000 FTE, comprising roughly two-thirds of the corporate workforce. eBay operated major service centers in Salt Lake City, Omaha, Vancouver, Berlin, and Dublin. Smaller company-owned Customer Support groups were located in Sydney, Hong Kong, London, and Seoul. The majority of these employees spent their workdays responding to customer e-mails. In 2004, eBay answered more than 30 million customer inquiries, covering everything from questions about selling, bidding, product categories, billing, and pricing to thornier issues involving illegal or prohibited listings and auction security (Exhibit 4).

The Customer Support organization was made up of two major units: (1) General Support and (2) Trust and Safety. Historically, most of the customer contacts were handled by the General Support unit. The communications consisted of questions regarding bidding on auctions, listing and selling items, and account adjustments. By mid-2004, however, nearly 45 percent of inquiries were directed toward the Trust and Safety function. Here hundreds of employees were responsible for ensuring that the items listed on eBay were legitimate and legal, did not infringe on copyrighted, patented, or original material, and fell within the company's policies (i.e., no firearms, tobacco, alcohol, human body parts, and so on). It also enforced eBay's guidelines for proper member behavior by policing activities such as shill bidding, merchandise misrepresentation, and outright fraud.

PowerSellers

Approximately 94 percent of eBay's customer service volume was e-mail-based. However, live chat and phone inquiries were growing as the company opened up these channels to more customers, based on their profitability. Live chat volume was predicted to increase to 1.5 million communications in 2005, up 50 percent over 2004. Phone calls handled in 2005 were anticipated to reach 1.4 million, almost double the number in the previous year. This phone volume was expected to come primarily from "PowerSellers," who represented less than 7 percent of eBay users but, due to the volume of merchandise they traded on the site, accounted for nearly 90 percent of the company's profit.

Phone and live chat access to Customer Support was designed to enlarge the pool of PowerSellers. Dedicated service representatives received additional training in upsell, cross-sell, and auction display techniques to share with sellers to increase the number of items they sold and qualify them for higher PowerSeller monthly sales volume thresholds (Bronze, Silver, Gold, Platinum, Titanium). Once attained, these thresholds qualified sellers for dedicated phone and chat support as well as for the coveted PowerSeller logo (Exhibit 5).

Trust and Safety

No other company was able to harness the ubiquity of the Web and marry it to the auction concept as successfully as eBay. At the same time, eBay had to confront challenges never faced before, particularly in the arena of auction security and fraud prevention. *Caveat emptor*, "let the buyer beware," had been a rule in the auction world since the middle ages. With the advent of eBay, buyers had to deal with unknown sellers over the Internet, sight unseen, often in a totally different country, without the

Exhibit 4	eBay Customer Support Volumes by Channel (in millions)			
	2001	**2002**	**2003**	**2004**
General Support				
E-mail	8.1	12.1	14.6	16.1
Phone	0.1	0.3	0.4	0.8
Chat	NA	NA	0.4	0.4
Total	8.2	12.4	15.4	17.3
Trust and Safety				
E-mail	4	6.8	9.8	12.6
Phone	0	0	0	0
Chat	NA	NA	0.1	0.6
Total	4	6.8	9.9	13.2
Combined GS and T&S				
E-mail	12.1	18.9	24.4	28.7
Phone	0.1	0.3	0.4	0.8
Chat	NA	NA	0.5	1
Total	12.2	19.2	25.3	30.5

Source: Case writers' estimates, compilations, and public records.

Exhibit 5   PowerSeller Criteria

To qualify, members must:

- Uphold the eBay community values, including honesty, timeliness, and mutual respect
- Average a minimum of $1,000 in sales per month for three consecutive months
- Achieve an overall Feedback rating of 100, of which 98 percent or more is positive
- Have been an active member for 90 days
- Have an account in good financial standing
- Not violate any severe policies in a 60-day period
- Not violate three or more of **any** eBay policies in a 60-day period
- Maintain a minimum of four average monthly listings for the past three months

PowerSeller program eligibility is reviewed every month. To remain PowerSellers, members must:

- Uphold eBay community values, including honesty, timeliness, and mutual respect
- Maintain the minimum average monthly sales amount for your PowerSeller level
- Maintain a 98 percent positive total feedback rating
- Maintain an account in good financial standing
- Comply with all eBay listing and marketplace *policies*—Not violate any severe policies in a 60-day period and not violate three or more of **any** eBay policies in a 60-day period

PowerSeller Levels

There are five tiers that distinguish PowerSellers, based on their gross monthly sales. Some benefits and services vary with each tier. eBay automatically calculates eligibility each month and notifies qualified sellers via e-mail.

Gross Sales Criteria for Each PowerSeller Tier

	Bronze	Silver	Gold	Platinum	Titanium
	$1,000	$3,000	$10,000	$25,000	$150,000

Sources: eBay Web site; case writers' estimates, compilations, and public records.

---

ability to personally examine the goods, and with little information about the seller except some written feedback from other buyers who had previously done business with him or her. It was absolutely critical for eBay's survival to create and nurture an environment of trust where millions of people around the globe could feel secure in trading online. The Trust and Safety Department was given this task. Procedural complexities, the differing legal environments and customs between countries, and the sophistication of online identity theft scams combined to make Trust and Safety a challenging business unit to manage.

Dalton wrestled with a number of questions related to Trust and Safety and its potential for outsourcing:

- "What kind of Trust and Safety volume could be safely outsourced?
- "What kind of Trust and Safety volume could not be outsourced?"
- "How could she and eBay determine the credibility and quality of the potential outsourcing vendors?"

- "How could she guarantee the vendors' ability to safeguard the eBay information entrusted to them?"

A number of eBay's executives had expressed concern and outright hostility to the idea of outsourcing any Trust and Safety volume. Rob Redman headed up the Trust and Safety Policy group in San Jose. He and other executives worried about outside vendors handling the sensitive type of customer inquiries common to this unit, especially when personal information such as Social Security numbers and credit card account numbers could be accessed. In addition, many of the jobs within Trust and Safety required direct and ongoing contact with local, national, and international law enforcement agencies in the hunt for and prosecution of fraudsters. Redman believed outsourcing vendors would never be as skilled at developing and nurturing these key liaisons as eBay's own personnel, and he had made this known to Whitman, Moss, and Dalton on numerous occasions.

Underneath her confident exterior, Dalton worried about these issues as well. She did not have any hands-on background in Trust and Safety herself. Still, she was intrigued by the possibility that several categories of inquiries within the department might be outsourced without undue risk.

Outsourcing Beginnings

By late 1999, eBay had enrolled four million registered members, nearly all in the United States. Five years later, the eBay community had burgeoned to more than 135 million members, living in every country in the world. If eBay were its own country, it would have been the nineth largest on earth, behind Russia.

To stay abreast of the growth of its customer base, eBay significantly increased the resources dedicated to its Customer Support group. In the very early days of 1995–1996, founder Omidyar would reserve part of his Saturday afternoons in a local San Jose park to respond directly to member questions. He soon could not manage the volume himself so the first customer service staff was organized. A measure of the power of the eBay community was the fact that these first service staffers were not employees at all, but members who had shown a penchant for helping other eBayers. These people worked on a contract basis out of their homes responding to customers' e-mails. At one time, there were close to 75 such employees, called "remotes," living in 17 different states across the country, handling an average of five e-mails per hour at all hours of the day and night, often while sitting in their pajamas!

In early 1998, eBay Customer Support took another step to simplify management and improve the consistency and quality of service. The company hired a small corps of "in-house" customer service personnel in the San Jose, California, headquarters to supplement its remote contractors. The "remotes" had been a creative solution for a time, but one that could not be scaled as the technology, logistics, and training requirements of the Customer Support group increased in sophistication.

Kana

One such technological advancement occurred when eBay purchased the Kana e-mail management system later that year to provide service personnel with a variety of "canned" responses and performance statistics similar to an automatic call distributor. Kana allowed representatives to answer common questions, such as "How do I list an item for sale?," "How do I leave feedback?," or "What do I do with an item I received that is damaged in shipment?" with a few quick keystrokes to input the code number of a pre-scripted e-mail reply. The representatives then took a moment to personalize the e-mail with their name and the recipients' names.

The Kana technology enabled service employees to be trained more quickly and effectively. Most importantly, it reduced response time to customer inquiries and increased the accuracy of information the customer received. It doubled the service representatives' e-mail productivity from five responses per hour to 10 and more. Without Kana, there was no way that eBay could have ever considered outsourcing even a portion of its overall Customer Support volume, let alone, as Dalton's new strategy proposed, increasing it to more than 50 percent.

By early 1999, nearly twice as many in-house representatives were employed as compared to the "remotes." This staffing strategy had paid off in improved productivity and in the rising customer satisfaction scores received from the hundreds of customers polled by mail each month (Exhibit 6). More in-house staff was needed, and a search was begun to build a dedicated center for Customer Support outside of California in a more cost-efficient locale. Three potential sites were considered—Salt Lake City, Tucson, and Albuquerque. In the end, the Utah location was selected due to the availability of a ready-made facility as well as a communications infrastructure, generous incentives offered by the state, and the educational level, work ethic, and foreign language capabilities of the potential employees.

Exhibit 6   eBay Customer Support Productivity and Quality

	1998	1999	2000	2001	2002	2003	2004
E-mails Productivity/Hr	4.7	9.5	11.1	13.8	15.3	16	16.1
E-mails per FTE/Month	571	1254	1475	1980	2078	2225	2280
E-mail Quality %	N/A	83%	89%	91%	94%	95%	94%
Customer Satisfaction %	N/A	N/A	84%	86%	87%	88%	88%

Source: Case writers' estimates, compilations, and public records.

Designed originally for about 300 personnel, the Salt Lake facility was enlarged to accommodate more than 1,000 by year-end 2000. In addition, a staff of 125 was added in both the newly opened Berlin and the Sydney locations to handle customer service inquiries. Still, with the worldwide popularity of eBay growing at a rate of 250,000 new members each month, it was apparent by 2001 that eBay could hire only so many of its own service personnel and build only so much of its own brick-and-mortar contact centers and that even trying to do so would not keep up with the demand (Exhibit 7). Alternatives like outsourcing had to be explored.

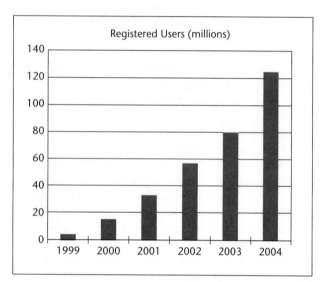

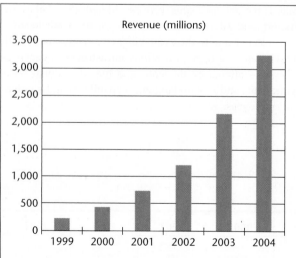

Exhibit 7   Growth in eBay Users and Revenues

Source: Case writers' estimates, compilations, and public records.

Outsourcing Pilot

eBay had made headlines for years for its innovation in the online auction space, its market leadership, its product and technological ingenuity, such as member feedback, the Buy It Now feature, item search capabilities, and Kana, and its irresistible pace and can-do attitude. eBay did not manage itself by "the seat of its pants," contrary to what others may consider to be a trademark of dotcoms. Far from it, the company was thoughtfully led, financially disciplined, and extremely customer conscious. These were the underpinnings of its tremendous success. eBay let others serve as lab mice, test and bleed, stub their toe, and work out the wrinkles. Then, and only then, it stepped in and adopted the "latest and greatest" business practices.

Such was the case with outsourcing the elementary portions of its Customer Support operation. Leading companies like American Express, GE, and Citibank had been outsourcing some of their customer service functions for 10 to 15 years domestically and for at least half that time offshore before eBay felt comfortable in considering outsourcing. By mid-2001, outsourcing surfaced as a viable way for eBay Customer Support to scale to demand, avoid capital outlays, reduce unit costs, and leverage its investment in technology and management talent.

But the senior staff in San Jose, including Whitman, was concerned about the potential reaction of the eBay community. If you traded on eBay, you were not a customer. You were a member of a passionate and vocal community of users, who felt strongly (and rightly so) that eBay's success was directly attributable more to them than to any business savvy of headquarters staff in San Jose. How would the community react to knowing that some customer support inquiries were answered by staff not employed by eBay—or not even residing within the United States?

Another concern at headquarters was the lack of talent inside eBay who had experience with outsourcing. For eBay to uphold its philosophy of "prudent adoption," it needed a team of managers who could thoroughly investigate how other companies had successfully outsourced and then actually run the day-to-day operation.

In December 2001, eBay hired Jim Williams, an executive vice president from Precision Response Corporation (PRC), one of the country's top echelon outsourcing vendors, and gave him responsibility for customer service worldwide. Williams brought instant credibility to the outsourcing initiative. His knowledge of the industry from the providers' point of view reinforced the research already compiled on other companies that had been successfully outsourcing elements of customer service in India and the Philippines

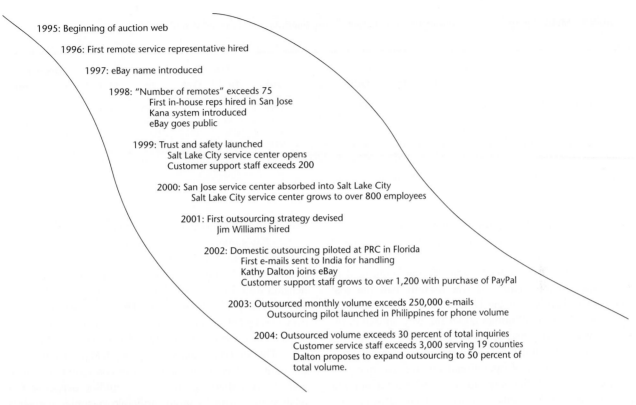

1995: Beginning of auction web

1996: First remote service representative hired

1997: eBay name introduced

1998: "Number of remotes" exceeds 75
First in-house reps hired in San Jose
Kana system introduced
eBay goes public

1999: Trust and safety launched
Salt Lake City service center opens
Customer support staff exceeds 200

2000: San Jose service center absorbed into Salt Lake City
Salt Lake City service center grows to over 800 employees

2001: First outsourcing strategy devised
Jim Williams hired

2002: Domestic outsourcing piloted at PRC in Florida
First e-mails sent to India for handling
Kathy Dalton joins eBay
Customer support staff grows to over 1,200 with purchase of PayPal

2003: Outsourced monthly volume exceeds 250,000 e-mails
Outsourcing pilot launched in Philippines for phone volume

2004: Outsourced volume exceeds 30 percent of total inquiries
Customer service staff exceeds 3,000 serving 19 counties
Dalton proposes to expand outsourcing to 50 percent of
total volume.

Exhibit 8   eBay Customer Support Timeline

Source: Case writers' estimates, compilations, and public records.

for years. Furthermore, his intimate association with PRC, its management team, and its training and technological capabilities made Whitman and her executives comfortable utilizing PRC as eBay's first global outsourcing partner.

When it came to the issue of how the eBay community would react to the new venture, Williams had an answer for that, too. Rather than launch a pilot in India, he proposed beginning with a small test near PRC's domestic headquarters in Fort Lauderdale. He essentially hand-picked the most talented customer service representatives at PRC to handle the eBay business. By February 2002, all preparations for the pilot were completed, and eBay's first-ever outsourcing effort was launched (Exhibit 8).

Expansion of Outsourcing

Dalton reflected on the progress made in outsourcing over the past several years. The outsourcing pilot program begun in Fort Lauderdale in 2002 had been relatively seamless. The plan had been to run the pilot for six months before attempting to route volume offshore to one of PRC's

service centers in Bangalore, India. Yet the service quality and e-mail productivity results from the vendor were on par with eBay's own staff after only three months. Williams and his Customer Support team decided to cut the pilot short and sent the first e-mails to India in June 2002.

The eBay community's reaction to outsourcing portions of its customer service was essentially only a small ripple in a big pond. There had been some issues with the written English of the agents in India. A handful of complaints found their way to Whitman's desk. Still, the service quality and productivity metrics of the outsource providers, both domestic and foreign, rivaled and frequently surpassed the same measurements of eBay's own employees (Exhibit 9).

And who could argue with the cost differential? While eBay honored its community, it was also a publicly traded company with shareholders who were accustomed to a compounded annual growth rate in revenues of more than 65 percent. The domestic outsourcing cost per contact for the volume handled in Fort Lauderdale was not that much less than eBay's own staff results. This was perfectly acceptable because a significant driver for outsourcing to another location within the United States had been, in

Exhibit 9   Metric Comparison for eBay In-house and Outsourcing Vendors (comparison for similar volume types)

	Jul-02		Dec-02		Jul-03		Dec-03		Jul-04		Dec-04	
	In	Out	In	Out	In	Out	In	Out	In	Out	In	Out
E-mails Productivity/Hr	14.8	13.1	15.2	14.7	15.5	15.4	15.7	16.1	15.8	16.3	15.8	16.3
E-mails per FTE/Month	2050	1963	2181	2095	2202	2189	2240	2255	2250	2291	2250	2285
E-mail Quality %	94%	88%	95%	94%	95%	95%	94%	95%	93%	95%	93%	96%
Customer Satisfaction %	87%	83%	87%	86%	87%	88%	88%	88%	87%	88%	87%	89%
E-mail Unit Cost ($)	1.59	0.87	1.55	0.86	1.56	0.85	1.49	0.82	1.48	0.81	1.48	0.81

Source: Case writers' estimates, compilations, and public records.

addition to initially testing the outsourcing model, to avoid the capital outlay of building more plant and equipment for Customer Support.

The unit cost for the e-mail volume being sent to India was another matter. It was literally half the cost per contact handled in the United States. An occasional complaint letter to Whitman about the way an e-mail response was worded by one of the service reps in India was not taken lightly, but it was still considered a small price to pay for the level of operational savings. No question about it, after both the domestic and offshore outsourcing performance of 2002, eBay executives were satisfied that outsourcing would remain a component of its customer support strategy. Dalton wondered, "What are the limits?"

Throughout 2003 and most of 2004, eBay had increased the volume of customer service sent offshore. Through analyses of e-mail complexity and available canned responses in Kana, about 40 percent of the General Support volume, representing close to 500,000 e-mails a month, had been earmarked as "outsourceable." As additional service staff was hired and uptrained in India, the throttle was opened and more e-mail was directed overseas for handling.

Dalton grabbed the hard copy of the strategy document she had submitted to Moss the previous week. She focused on several pages that highlighted the outsourcing expansion since her arrival at eBay. In a business as fluid as eBay's, it was realistic to expect that the original outsourcing strategy devised in 2002 would change over time. Indeed, even with eBay's penchant for hindsight learning from others' mishaps, Dalton's three-tiered strategy had only evolved after some operational missteps and plenty of analysis of test results.

Customer Relationship Management

One such misstep occurred in late 2003, when eBay conducted an outsourcing pilot in the Philippines for phone volumes. Less than 2 percent of eBay's volume arrived via telephone, but it was an expensive piece. The hope had been to cut eBay's phone unit cost in half, to just around $2.00. It did not play out that well in reality. During the pilot, both the accents of the Philippino agents and their language comprehension were issues. Logistical issues with phone lines and data servers plagued the startup. The biggest concern, however, was that eBay at the same time was taking its first major steps into Customer Relationship Management (CRM).

The company's marketing group had just completed a thorough segmentation analysis of its community members and saw potential opportunities in building deeper service relationships with its more profitable customer segments. More than 40 distinct customer segments were identified, and strategies for increasing profitability were then prepared for each segment. One of the proposed strategies was to offer dedicated live phone support to certain segments, particularly PowerSellers and potential PowerSellers.

With its focus on optimizing the phone touch point to generate revenue, senior management wanted to keep its phone support group in-house, rather than outsource it to third parties offshore. Management reasoned that this not only allowed for more efficient rollout of profit-enhancing marketing programs, but also provided job enrichment and new career paths to eBay's own employees. In line with being more accessible by phone to high-value customers, Customer Support shut down its phone outsourcing pilot in the Philippines in early 2004. Whether the pilot could have eventually been successful was unclear.

The same logic was used for eBay's live chat channel, which represented 2 percent of total volume or about 45,000 chat sessions a month. The original plan was to outsource this volume overseas as well. However, with the vision of using the chat channel to cross-sell products and increase seller volume, it was determined to service chat line customers in-house, too. These CRM-led constraints for the phone and chat channels helped fashion the new outsourcing strategy that Dalton had proposed to her boss last week and that she was scheduled to present to Whitman.

New Outsourcing Strategy

When she was given the responsibility for outsourcing in July 2004, Dalton dug deeply into the existing operation to understand the issues as well as the opportunities and threats facing the department. She identified three major opportunities for improvement. She needed to figure out how to analyze each one and implement programs within 12 months, which was the time frame she and Moss had agreed was feasible.

The first opportunity she saw was to increase the percentage of outsourcing from 30 percent of overall volume to at least 50 percent. She calculated that this would save an incremental $3.9 million a year. What made this endeavor particularly difficult, however, was the CRM initiative that required her to keep the growing phone and chat volume with in-house service representatives only.

The second opportunity would help her to accomplish the first. It was to target for the first time specific volume types within Trust and Safety and demonstrate that these could be successfully handled by a third-party outsourcer. Several within Whitman's executive team felt strongly that it was too risky to outsource any of this volume and Dalton knew she would be in for a fight. She deemed it a worthwhile fight because, according to her analysis, between 20 percent and 25 percent of Trust and Safety's monthly volume was straightforward enough to be included in the outsourceable pool.

The third area of opportunity was to seek an outsourcing partner in addition to PRC with which to contract. Dalton was concerned that eBay had for two years used only one outsourcing vendor. She reasoned that adding a second one would benefit eBay by instilling competition both in pricing and performance metrics between the two vendors, as well as providing a measure of redundancy in the event of system outages.

She and her staff had wrestled with these three problems over the ensuing months. Selecting a second vendor that could meet eBay's criteria proved challenging. The candidate company had to have both a domestic and international presence, have a proven track record in servicing large quantities of phone, chat, and e-mail inquiries, and be willing to rival PRC's already attractive per unit pricing. Finding a vendor that had sufficient e-mail experience proved the toughest challenge. Dalton and her team finally settled on I-Sky, a medium-sized vendor, but one that could deliver impressive e-mail results out of its several service centers located in more rural parts of Canada.

Three Tiers

In order to increase the outsourcing to 50 percent of total volume, while at the same time taking advantage of the opportunity for including Trust and Safety volume in the mix, Dalton had devised a strategy made up of three levels or tiers. Each tier represented a progressively more complex type of work, both in terms of the nature of the customer inquiry and the channel through which it accessed Customer Support (Exhibit 10).

■ **TIER ONE:** Was composed of e-mail-only volume involving the most basic of General Support–type questions. These were typically simple bidding and selling questions that could be answered using a template of responses from Kana. Because these were less-complex customer inquiries, training for the service representatives was less demanding and could be conducted over a three-week period. Most of eBay's Tier One volume was already being handled by PRC's two outsourcing facilities in India. Dalton analyzed all remaining inquiry types to find an additional 260,000-plus e-mails

---

Exhibit 10   Proposed Outsourced Volume and Unit Cost by Tiers

	Current (Dec. 2004)			Proposed (Dec. 2004)		
	Monthly Volume	% of Total Volume	Unit Cost	Monthly Volume	% of Total Volume	Unit Cost
Tier One						
Gen'l Support	510000	21.30%	$0.81	775000	32.40%	$0.72
Tier Two						
Gen'l Support	68000	2.80%	$1.45	186000	7.80%	$1.15
Tier Three						
Gen'l Support	20000	0.80%	$1.48	25000	1.04%	$1.33
Trust and Safety	NA	NA	NA	210000	8.80%	$1.33
Total	598000	24.20%		1196000	50.00%	

Source: Case writers' estimates, compilations, and public records.

per month that could be safely offloaded to India as well. If these volumes could be found, she thought she might be able to negotiate with the vendor for a price reduction from $0.81 to $0.72 per e-mail.

- **TIER TWO:** Was designated for General Support e-mail volume that was considered a bit more complex than Tier One work. This accounted for more billing-related and account adjustment questions, where more in-depth training was needed for the service representatives. eBay had outsourced a small portion of this volume, but only to PRC's Florida center, where English was the native language. Now, utilizing I-Sky's locations in Canada, Dalton proposed another option for handling this volume. These locations could satisfy the native English requirement and prove very effective from a cost standpoint. Though not as low-cost an environment as India, the Canadian Tier Two locations were on average 22 percent more economical in cost per e-mail than PRC's domestic facilities and eBay's wholly owned service centers.

- **TIER THREE:** Was reserved for more complex General Support questions, those that required flexibility and some judgment on the part of the service employees. Also, it was in this tier that Dalton proposed that some simple Trust and Safety inquiries be handled. She was careful not to select work that was overly sensitive in terms of customers' personal information or that necessitated detailed investigative work. Types of inquires that qualified included reports from eBay users on spam or potential scam sites and on listing violations or member misbehavior, such as not paying for items received, and shill bidding. This tier consisted mainly of e-mail volume, yet Dalton designed it so that some simple phone and chat inquiries were included as well. While this was contrary to eBay's CRM philosophy that phone calls and chat sessions be kept in-house with experienced eBay service agents, she asserted that top reps at both PRC and I-Sky could be taught to service this volume just as adeptly as eBay's own.

Tier Three was to be handled by outsourcing centers exclusively in the United States, located in close proximity to eBay's own contact centers. This "nearshoring" arrangement ensured that no language barrier existed and that Dalton and her managers were within close proximity if the outsourcer needed extra support and training.

In her recommendations to Moss the previous week, Dalton had made sure her boss understood that the arrangement for Tier Three volume would save the company only about $500,000 per year from a pure cost reduction standpoint, but that it did pay off in keeping Customer

Support from having to invest in additional plant and equipment, as well as reducing the risk of spreading its management talent too thin. Plus, it opened the door to outsourcing approximately 20 percent of Trust and Safety work types, which was essential to meeting the goal of offloading upward of 50 percent of eBay's entire support volume.

Moss had readily acknowledged and appreciated Dalton's explanation on her team's strategy behind the logic for Tiers Two and Three. She was more inquisitive, however, about the Tier One work being serviced in India. The payoffs there in reduced operating expense were impressive, saving the company almost $3 million annually, and Dalton had sensed right away Moss's interest in bringing more dollars to the bottom line. Moss had quizzed her in detail the previous week on PRC's Indian-based operations and I-Sky. How experienced, how financially muscled, how well led, how competitively positioned, how quick to market were these two companies? What kind of presence did Customer Support have in these centers? Were eBay managers always on site in India training new hires, sampling e-mails, admonishing the "eBay way"?

As she recounted these queries in her mind from the meeting, Dalton admitted that the question her boss had posed in her e-mail was really no surprise at all. Customer Support was heavily invested in making the Indian operation a long-term service and financial win. But why line someone else's pockets along the way? What Moss wanted to know, and what she had anticipated that Whitman and her staff would likewise want to know, was the feasibility of doing exactly what Dalton's outsourcing group was doing in India, but doing it without the middleman. "Imagine if Customer Support was saving approximately 45 percent per e-mail by offshore outsourcing. How much more could be saved by running our own sites in India?" Moss's e-mail concluded.

To BOT or Not to BOT

Fortunately, Dalton had done research on the subject of developing eBay-owned and -managed sites offshore, though not in real depth. She had figured that opportunities would exist for her and her staff to still work out the minor kinks with the present outsourcing strategy. "Chalk up another one to the exhilarating eBay pace," she thought to herself.

She wanted to call Moss in San Jose and discuss her e-mail and the next steps in preparing for the upcoming presentation to Whitman. But first she opened her file drawer and pulled out a folder labeled across the top with the letters "BOT." It had been several months since she

Exhibit 11   Dalton's Spreadsheet

		Cost/Hr/Seat (250 seats)	Cost/Hr/Seat (500 seats)	Cost/Hr/Seat (1,000 seats)	Avg. Initial Investment/Seat (one-time cost)	Avg. Transfer Cost/Seat (one-time cost)
Scenario #1: Outsourcing to 3rd party vendors	*e-mail, phone, chat*	$ 10.17	$ 9.56	$ 8.60	N/A	N/A
	e-mail only	$ 6.24	$ 5.38	$ 4.66	N/A	N/A
Scenario #2: Build eBay owned center	*e-mail, phone, chat*	$ 9.73	$ 8.85	$ 7.77	$ 12,000	N/A
	e-mail only	$ 5.30	$ 4.68	$ 4.14	$ 11,000	N/A
Scenario #3: Build, Operate, Transfer (BOT)	*e-mail, phone, chat*	$ 9.88	$ 9.03	$ 8.10	N/A	$ 3,500
	e-mail only	$ 5.34	$ 4.96	$ 4.40	N/A	$ 2,900

Source: Case writers' estimates, compilations, and public records.

gathered the contents. Before she knew it, an hour elapsed and she remained focused on sifting through the packet of information, occasionally pausing to run several scenarios through a quickly composed Excel spreadsheet.

After another 45 minutes of analysis, she was ready. She printed the spreadsheet and quickly surveyed it for clarity. It was not as detailed as it would need to be in the coming days, but it would help her frame a conversation with Moss about the question she asked in her e-mail, the one she asked on behalf of Whitman:

"Why should we keep paying someone else to do what we can do for ourselves?"

In her spreadsheet, Dalton outlined and quantified three alternatives (Exhibit 11). The first alternative was the Tier One of her proposed three-tiered strategy—maintain the relationships with eBay's offshore outsourcing partners, continue to improve the operation in India, and identify incremental volume to outsource in order to drive e-mail costs lower. She viewed this scenario as the least risky of the three alternatives.

The second alternative was to eliminate the outsourcing vendors altogether. In this option, she proposed that Customer Support not renew its contracts with the vendors and instead purchase or lease land or an already established facility in India and build its own operation. Dalton knew this alternative presented the most risks to eBay, including capital outlay, real estate commitments, governmental compliance, communications infrastructure,

and in-country management resources. Yet, according to her spreadsheet assumptions, this alternative promised the biggest potential payoff long-term in unit cost reduction, something that eBay's executive staff prized highly.

She believed her third alternative, called "Build, Operate, and Transfer," or "BOT" for short, was the most creative and represented a hybrid of the first two. She recommended that eBay contract with a third-party vendor that would acquire or build an operations center, staff and manage it, and then, after a specified period of time of perhaps a year or two, transfer full ownership to eBay. This option appealed to her more than the second one because the vendor would bear the initial risks for the startup phase, which she considered the most challenging and expensive. eBay could limit its cost exposure up front until the operation was ramped up and running. She planned to tell Moss that the most critical points of the BOT alternative were to negotiate the appropriate level of management fees with the outsourcing vendor and to work out the intricacies of the actual transfer of ownership down the road.

Dalton's biggest concern, however, was the fact that to date she had not been able to find any example of a domestic company utilizing a BOT approach with a vendor in India. To her knowledge, eBay would be the first customer service operation attempting such a strategy. As she prepared to pick up the phone and dial Moss's number, she was haunted by eBay's well-entrenched mantra of not being on the "bleeding edge" with any new unproven experiments.

Case 3-2: National Hockey League Enterprises Canada: A Retail Proposal

IVEY | Publishing

Elizabeth Gray prepared this case under the supervision of Elizabeth M.A. Grasby solely to provide material for class discussion. The authors do not intend to illustrate either effective or ineffective handling of a managerial situation. The authors may have disguised certain names and other identifying information to protect confidentiality.

Version: (A) 2010-01-08

In July 1998, Glenn Wakefield, vice-president of National Hockey League Enterprises Canada (NHLEC), was faced with an opportunity to pursue the development of a retail outlet solely dedicated to Brand NHL merchandise. If pursued, Wakefield had to select one of three implementation options: NHLEC could retain managerial and financial control of the facility, control could be relinquished to a management firm, or floor space could be rented in a department store where NHLEC would maintain partial control over operations. Opening a flagship store would be a shift in the organization's strategy and Wakefield wondered if it was the right thing to do.

The National Hockey League

The National Hockey League (NHL), a professional hockey organization housing 27 teams in total, was divided into two conferences, each consisting of three divisions (see Exhibit 1). Each team received representation from the

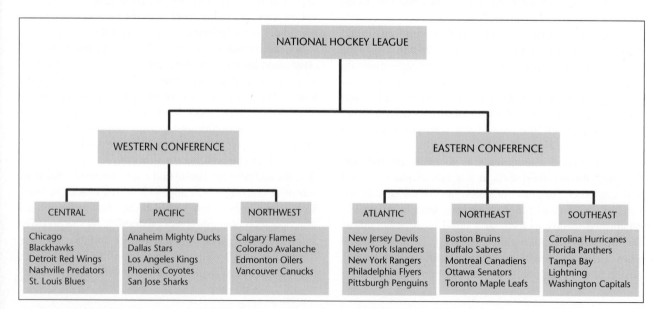

Exhibit 1 National Hockey League

NHL division responsible for officiating, scouting, and public relations as well as the marketing division, National Hockey League Enterprises. Additionally, each NHL team employed its own marketers who were responsible for promoting the team and selling tickets to the team's games.

National Hockey League Enterprises

National Hockey League Enterprises (NHLE) managed the promotion of the game, the licensing of NHL merchandise, and the exploitation of corporate marketing partnerships. NHLE was a large enterprise with job descriptions ranging from "Asia/Pacific Promotions" to "Grassroots Development". NHLE was housed in downtown New York, New York, U.S.A.

National Hockey League Enterprises Canada

NHLE's Canadian counterpart, the National Hockey League Enterprises Canada (NHLEC), was located in Toronto, Ontario, Canada. NHLEC was a relatively small operation under the managerial control of the New York office (an organizational chart is given in Exhibit 2).

One of NHLEC's primary strategic goals was to develop a distinct brand image. The ever-increasing number of licensees and retailers for NHL-branded merchandise was becoming too fragmented. Wakefield wanted the brand's image to be presented consistently to consumers at the retail level. He believed this approach would, in turn, translate into increased sales of NHL-brand merchandise and also increased recognition of the NHL. The greatest obstacle in achieving this goal lay not with the independent retailer, but with the larger department store chains such as Wal-Mart. NHLEC relied on these large retailers to push crucial sales volume but the end result was scattered NHL merchandise and an inconsistent brand image presented to the consumer. Frequent buyer turnover, power struggles and turf wars among the buyers, and the sheer size of these retailers had all contributed to NHLEC's difficulties in developing brand equity at a mass-market consumer level.

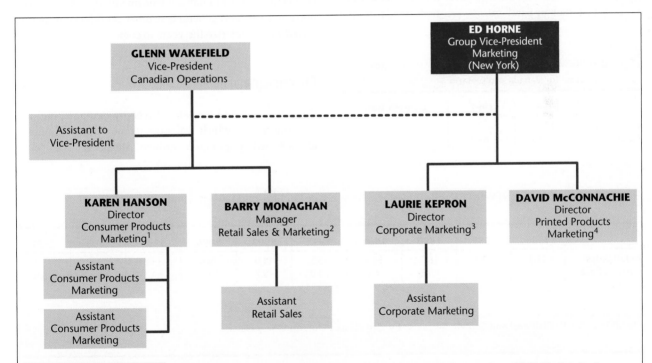

1. Managed the relationship with all manufacturers licensed to print an NHL or member team logo. These manufacturers then paid NHLEC a licensing fee (a percentage of the manufacturers' sales) to produce NHL branded products.
2. Coordination of all retail stores carrying NHL brand merchandise. Activities included the development and maintenance of the relationships with these retailers. These activities included promotional incentives for retailers to boost sales of NHL brand merchandise.
3. Responsible for governing partnerships with large corporations; currently managing relationships with Air Canada and McDonald's Corporation.
4. Governed all printed products related to the NHL, including PowerPlay Magazine™, season schedule pamphlets, trading cards, and corporate sponsor print material.

Exhibit 2   National Hockey League Enterprises Canada Organizational Chart

A New Approach

Wakefield had to find a way to convince large retailers that there was a better way to display and promote NHL product. One potential solution would be to focus NHLEC's selling efforts toward the general merchandise manager, rather than (and one step above) the individual buyer, encouraging a more coordinated purchase and display effort. Another option would be the introduction of the NHL's own store. This flagship store would sell merchandise purchased from NHL licensees. This store would be used to illustrate to these large retailers the positive effects that a consistent NHL brand image could have on sales.

The Industry

While the apparel industry experienced rapid growth throughout the 1980s, the recession in the early 1990s had hurt apparel sales (see Exhibits 3 and 4). Recovery from the recession had been gradual and it was a well-known fact that apparel sales were tied tightly to the overall level of economic activity (see Exhibit 5 for Gross Domestic Product data and Exhibit 6 for Canadian disposable income and expenditure on clothing).

With the introduction of both the Canada-U.S. Free Trade Agreement (FTA) and the North American Free Trade Agreement (NAFTA) in the late 1980s, Canadians had witnessed a multitude of lower priced imports entering the market. Within the last decade, there had been a restructuring of the retail apparel industry. Consolidation and the emergence of U.S.-based retail giants such as Wal-Mart had resulted in a highly concentrated retail industry. These large Canadian retailers had sought to narrow their supplier base and increase their margins. In addition, the Canadian dollar was trading at a record low (around US$0.66).

Although Wakefield wondered what impact all of this would have on small NHL licensees and what the NHL store might do for these retailers, his review of the retail industry convinced him that the timing was right for such a venture. GDP for both Canada and Ontario was expected to grow steadily at a rate of three per cent into the next century. Additionally, lower unemployment, reduced housing costs, and general consumer confidence were predicted to characterize the years to come.

Demographics

Consumer demand was also driven by demographic factors, the first of which was population. Refer to Exhibit 7 for selected population growth statistics. The "baby

Exhibit 3   Retail Sales in 1996–1997 ($Billions) and Growth Rate for Canada and Ontario

	1996	1997	Growth Rate
Canada	217.0	232.7	+7.2
Ontario	78.6	84.4	+7.4

Exhibit 4   Canadian Apparel Retail Sales ($Billions) and Growth Rate (%) 1988–1997

	1988	1989	1990	1991	1992	1993	1994	1995	1996	1997
Retail Sales	14.3	15.5	16.3	14.9	15.5	14.0	14.6	15.2	15.8	16.4
Growth Rate		+8.4	+5.2	−8.6	+4.0	−9.7	+4.3	+4.1	+3.9	+3.8

Exhibit 5   GDP ($Billions) and Growth Rates (%) for Canada and Ontario 1987–1996

	1987	1988	1989	1990	1991	1992	1993	1994	1995	1996
Canada										
GDP	551.5	606.9	650.7	669.5	676.5	690.1	712.9	747.3	776.3	797.8
Growth Rate		+10.0	+7.2	+2.9	+1.0	+2.0	+3.3	+4.8	+3.9	+2.8
Ontario										
GDP	226.8	253.1	276.1	277.6	278.5	282.8	288.6	300.8	314.1	323.0
Growth Rate		+11.6	+9.1	+0.5	+0.3	+1.5	+2.1	+4.2	+4.4	+2.8

Exhibit 6   Canadian Disposable Income ($Billions), Growth Rates (%), and Clothing Expenditure (%) 1994–1997

	1994	1995	1996	1997
Disposable Income	493.6	510.8 +3.5	518.2 +1.4	523.7 +1.1
Expenditure on Clothing	23.0	23.9 +3.9	23.9 0.0	24.7 +3.3
Expenditure on clothing as a percentage of disposable income	4.7	4.7	4.6	4.7

Exhibit 7   Populations and Growth Rates (%) for Canada, Ontario and Toronto

	1981	1991	1996	Growth Rate (Arithmetic)
Canada	24,343,181	27,296,859	28,846,761	9.2%
Ontario	8,625,107	10,084,885	10,753,573	24.6%
Toronto		3,893,046	4,263,757	10.0%

boom" and "baby boom echo[1]" population accounted for 56 per cent of the total population, with this group driving growth in consumer demand. As baby boomers aged, their needs in terms of apparel were likely to include a greater emphasis on quality, comfort, functionality, value, and service; whereas, by 1996, those in the "baby boom echo" phase had entered their teenage years, a time when people were typically more fashion-conscious.

Other Trends

Canadians were spending a greater portion of their disposable income on consumer goods such as computers, electronics, and leisure products—leaving less for apparel. Also, as consumers became more knowledgeable about products, they placed increased importance on the price-value relationship. Today's consumers demanded "value"—high quality merchandise at reasonable prices and had begun to shop at more inexpensive retail stores. Furthermore, today's consumers spent less time shopping for apparel. Since less time was spent shopping, consumers looked for reliable indicators of product quality and service prior to the purchase. In addition to these changes in consumer behavior, there was a trend towards relaxation of the dress code in the work place.

As consumers became more knowledgeable about products and demanded more from retailers, quick response (QR) technologies—such as electronic data interchange (EDI) — were being utilized to provide top-notch service to customers. These technologies allowed retailers to immediately process, store, and forward point-of-sale statistics to the manufacturer who, in turn, could replenish inventory levels.

Alternatives

Wakefield identified three models for establishing a NHLEC retail presence. In the first model, NHLEC would have complete managerial control over the location and operation of the retail store. There were three viable locations to choose from: Vancouver, Toronto and Montreal. Investment funds of $2,200,000 for start-up and approximately $800,000 in working capital would be required. He wondered how NHLEC could raise those kinds of funds. He also knew that if the venture was not profitable, NHLEC would have to absorb the loss and NHLEC's budget was simply not large enough to sustain significant losses. If he decided to pursue this option, Wakefield would have to convince New York to give the go-ahead.

The location would need to be 15,000 square feet in total, with 10,000 of that being retail space. The average lease range for a downtown Toronto location was $50 to $60 per square foot. Wakefield estimated the store could generate $750 revenue per retail square foot per year. Cost of goods sold was estimated to be 50 per cent of sales. Salaries and wages were estimated at 10 per cent and other miscellaneous costs at 15 per cent. Net income would be taxed at 45 per cent and the prime lending rate was currently at 6.5 per cent (borrowers would typically pay an interest rate of prime plus one and a half per cent).

In the second model, NHLEC would hire and relinquish all control to a management firm that would handle all the operational and administrative functions. In turn, NHLEC would collect a licensing fee—15 per cent of gross revenue—from the management firm. Typically, a management firm would rent a much smaller space, likely around 4,000 square feet, and might require NHLEC to invest as much as $500,000 for furnishings and fixtures. While he knew that several of these firms existed, he also knew that it was often a challenge to persuade them to adopt a project. How could he pitch the idea to such a firm?

In the third model, NHLEC could rent floor space in a major department store (i.e., The Bay, Sears, etc.). Wakefield estimated the location would be 200 square feet in size and would generate $200 revenue per square foot per year. The department store usually charged an operating fee of 10 per cent of sales to manage the area and a lease rate equal to 50 per cent of revenues. An initial investment in inventory of $6,000 and another $6,000 would be needed to equip the space with fixtures and signage.

With these three options before him, Wakefield sat down to write out his proposal. He knew each proposal would have to be evaluated based on the following criteria:

- Maintaining sufficient control to present the proper "Brand NHL" image.
- Limiting NHLEC's investments—both financial and human resources.
- Establishing a profitable retail outlet.

Glenn was unsure how important this last criterion was in the face of the project's true objective to increase the exposure of "Brand NHL".

End Note

1. Children of the "baby boom."

Case 3-3: Starbucks: An Alex Poole Strategy Case*

Alex Poole sighed heavily and rubbed his tired eyes. It was the fourth time in the past hour he had read the letter from his grandfather. "I don't know what to do," Alex thought. I wish Gramps could have put someone else in charge of his estate. What if I make a mistake? Then what will Grandma do?" Alex was a senior in college, working on a double major in finance and management and a minor in Chinese. He hoped to land a job with a large, multinational company after graduation and move to Hong Kong or Singapore. He was determined to get his foot in the door at a Fortune 100 company—no matter how hard he had to work. Alex was used to hard work. For the past three years, he had held down a part-time job while attending school full time. His philosophy was that he could afford to go to school only if he earned enough money to cover his expenses, so he would find a way to do it.

Alex shuffled some papers on his grandfather's desk and pulled up the stock chart on Starbucks on his MacBook. "This chart is amazing," he thought. After going public at a split-adjusted $0.53 per share in June 1992, the stock had taken off. A person who had invested $1,000 in Starbucks in the initial public offering would have had shares worth nearly $22,000 on the same day 10 years later. The stock continued its run until late 2006 when the combination of the Great Recession and internal problems caused it to fall from a high of $39.43 per share to a low of $6.80 per share in November 2008. The board brought Howard Schultz, the iconic founder of Starbucks, back as CEO in January 2008 as the company faltered. Schultz engineered a spectacular turnaround of the company. As of November 2013, the stock traded at more than $80 per share.

"Gramps sure was a savvy investor. When everyone else was saying Starbucks was roasted, he bought the stock," Alex thought. "But now what should I do? I could sell it and take profits, but Grandma will end up paying a lot of taxes. I don't know where to put the cash, either. If I hold on to it and the stock goes down a lot, I'll feel terrible." Alex yawned and rubbed his eyes again. "I guess I'd better get some sleep and try to figure it out tomorrow. I think I'll stop by the Starbucks on the corner in the morning and check it out. If it's crowded, I'll feel better."

WRRAANNNN! WRRAANNNN! WRRAANNNN! WRRAANNNN! Alex groaned, rolled over, and tried to hit the snooze button on his Clocky alarm clock. The Clocky expertly evaded his hand, rolled off the night table and on

to the floor. In order to cut off the ear-piercing shriek of the alarm clock, Alex was forced to roll out of bed and chase it around the room. Sarah, Alex's girlfriend, had given him the alarm clock after a couple of close shaves in which Alex slid into his seat next to her their 7:30 a.m. investments class just in time to take the weekly quiz. The professor took missing a quiz as a personal affront and was likely to cold-call the miscreant on multiple occasions to ensure that the point about being prepared and on time for class was hammered home. Students rarely missed more than one quiz.

Once Alex's brain woke up enough to process information, he realized that it was Saturday so he didn't need to rush to class. He took a quick shower, got dressed, and laced up his Asics running shoes. After a brisk three-mile run, he stopped in at the Starbucks on the corner for coffee and a snack. There was a line of customers waiting, but it was moving fairly quickly. Once he made it to the head of the line, the barista at the register greeted him by name with a bright smile and asked how his day was going. Alex ordered a Venti Starbucks Blonde Roast with a slice of iced lemon pound cake. He'd heard a rumor that the chain planned to cut the lemon pound cake from the menu, but it was still available. Prior to the addition of the distinctly lighter flavored Blonde Roast, Alex rarely shopped at Starbucks. He was one of the estimated 40 percent of Americans who felt Starbucks' traditional coffee offerings were too dark and too bitter[1] for their taste. The launch of Starbucks Blonde Roast along with its recent "converts wanted" ad campaign had persuaded Alex to give the new coffee a try. Now, he was hooked on Starbucks and often joked about needing his "Starbucks fix" to make sure he had a good day.

While he sipped his coffee, Alex pulled out his iPhone 4S and began to surf the Internet for recent news on Starbucks. After reading the company's press release on 3Q:13 earnings, he moved over to SeekingAlpha.com to try to gauge investors' reactions to Starbucks' better-than-anticipated earnings. As usual, the opinions on the stock ranged from "buy, buy, buy" to "great company but overvalued stock." "That didn't help a whole lot," Alex thought. "Gramps always said the company's management team, brand franchise, and business model were a lot more important than the stock's valuation or Wall Street sentiment. He thought a company's balance sheet was super important, too. I guess I had better figure out what this company does besides serve a great cup of coffee. I know Gramps thought Howard Schultz was one of the best business leaders of all time, but I sure don't know much about him." Alex waved

---

*This case was prepared by Bonita Austin for the purposes of class discussion. It is reprinted with permission.

good-bye to the barista and headed out the door. He intended to spend the afternoon in his university's library digging up as much information as possible on Starbucks.

Over the next week, Alex had amassed a lot of information on Starbucks. After visiting the library, Alex had gone back to his apartment and pulled out his previously unread copy of Schultz's book, *Onward*. He had been meaning to read it for months but hadn't gotten around to it due to his schoolwork and Gramps's passing. In the course of his research, Alex found out that Schultz was not the founder of the original coffee roasting and retail business named Starbucks. Schultz purchased the six Starbucks stores and the brand name for $3.8 million in 1987 from the company's founders. Alex thought about what he had read about Schultz—how he had joined Starbucks as its head of marketing in 1982 and had fallen in love with Italian coffee bars at a trade show in Italy in 1983. Schultz was enchanted by the connection between the customers and coffee bar employees. "I saw something. Not only the romance of coffee, but…a sense of community. And the connection that people had to coffee—the place and one another," Schultz recalled in a 2013 interview with *The Biography Channel*. "And after a week in Italy, I was so convinced with such unbridled enthusiasm that I couldn't wait to get back to Seattle to talk about the fact that I had seen the future."[2]

Schultz persuaded the owners of Starbucks to let him install a coffee bar in one location. Despite the success of the coffee bar test, Starbucks' founders were not interested in transforming the company into a restaurant. They had served coffee throughout the 1970s and even had an espresso machine in the stores. Nevertheless, Starbucks' founders felt the restaurant industry was an unattractive

one. Schultz reckoned that Italy's 200,000 coffee bars serving a population of just 55 million people meant the U.S. market had huge potential to support his vision of what he called a "third place." The "third place" would be a place outside of the home and the office that would allow people to congregate and gain a sense of community. Schultz left Starbucks to start his own coffee business, Il Giornale, in 1985. Two years later, he purchased Starbucks and merged it with Il Giornale.

"The weird thing about it," Alex thought, "is that anyone would want to be in the coffee business in the 1980s. From what I can tell, it was a pretty unattractive market." Alex glanced down at the chart on U.S. coffee consumption[3] he had put together and shrugged his shoulders. According to the USDA data, Americans consumed about 33 gallons of coffee per capita in 1970. By 1987, annual per capita coffee consumption was down to about 27 gallons. That translated into a large drop in the number of cups of coffee Americans drank per day. The decline had started way back in 1962, when Americans consumed 3.12 cups of coffee per day. By 1980, average per capita coffee consumption was down to about 2.0 cups per day. U.S. average per capita coffee consumption fell to a new all-time low of 1.67 cups per person per day in 1988.[4] "How could someone look at a declining product market—a market in which in one generation usage had fallen to 52 percent of the population from nearly 75 percent of Americans[5]—and see a phenomenal business opportunity?" Alex wondered.

Moreover, the competition at retail was brutal. Three large companies—Procter & Gamble (Folgers), General Foods (Maxwell House, Sanka), and Nestlé (Nescafe, Taster's Choice, Hills Brothers)—dominated the retail coffee business with a combined market share of more than

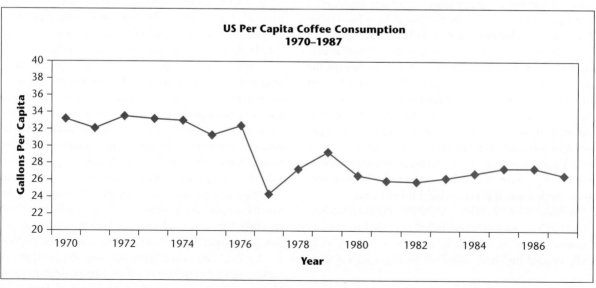

Source: USDA Economic Research Service.

80 percent.[6] As coffee consumption declined, the roasting companies often relied upon promotions and price cuts to stimulate demand. Moreover, retail prices tended to be tied to volatile coffee commodity prices, as roasters were unable to hold off demands by powerful supermarket buyers to cut prices when bean prices fell. To protect margins, roasters hiked retail prices when bean prices soared, but the price hikes hurt demand and were difficult to maintain. Although discerning Americans began to get interested in high-quality coffees at the beginning of the decade, specialty coffee only accounted for about $750 million in sales in 1990 or roughly 10 percent of the market, up from 3 percent of the market or $210 million in 1983[7] and $50 million in 1979.[8]

Against that backdrop, Schultz invented the modern Starbucks—transforming the coffee-roasting company into a retailer that was backward vertically integrated into coffee bean purchasing and roasting. Alex reflected on the incredible success the new concept had enjoyed during its first 20 years. By 1997, Starbucks' revenues had grown to $975 million and the balance sheet showed positive net cash position (cash minus debt) of $42 million. About 86 percent of revenues were derived from the company's 1,325 retail stores. Starbucks tested sales of coffee through 10 West Coast supermarkets—expanding to 4,000 grocery stores the next year. By the end of its next decade, Starbucks

had more than 15,000 company-owned and licensed stores. Revenues for 2007 came in at $9.4 billion accompanied by operating income of more than $1 billion for an operating profit margin of 11.2 percent. Return on invested capital was an impressive 17.7 percent in 2007—despite the company's whopping $282 million in cash. The company's average annual sales growth of 57 percent along with its 65 percent average yearly jump in operating profits over the decade put Starbucks squarely in an elite class of American success stories such as Wal-Mart.

"That's right when things turned sour for Starbucks," Alex thought. Schultz stepped down as CEO in 2000 and took a much less active role in day-to-day operations as the company's chairman. Store traffic began to slow early in 2007. By fall 2007, cracks appeared in Starbucks' business model. The company announced in November 2007 that traffic at its U.S. stores had fallen for the first time. The company also lowered its projected store openings for fiscal 2008 and lowered its estimates on comparable store sales growth (sales growth in stores open 12 months or longer). Starbucks was feeling the effects of the stagnant economy. At the same time, Starbucks was struggling to offset rising dairy and labor costs and trying to fight off strong competitive pressure from McDonald's and Dunkin' Donuts. The stock dropped nearly 50 percent in 2007.

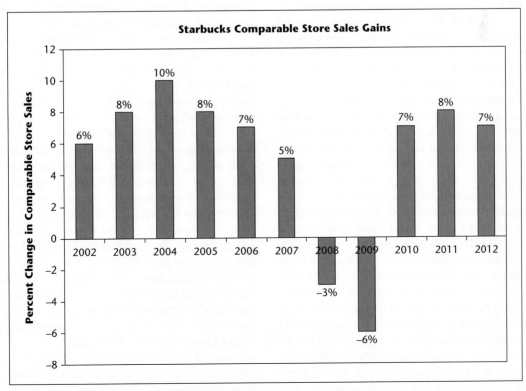

Source: Starbucks 2012 10-K.

"Comps," Alex thought. "Comps were the company's downfall—at least that's what Schultz said in his book." Alex's grandfather had given him a copy of the book last Christmas. He had inscribed, "To Alex, I hope Howard Schultz's extraordinary leadership and his passion will inspire you. Love, Gramps." Alex choked up a bit thinking about Gramps and how much he had tried to stand in for Alex's dad. Alex had lost his dad in a car accident when Alex was in the third grade. Alex cleared his throat and went back to reviewing his notes on Starbucks. "Comps had gotten really ugly in 2008," Alex thought.

Schultz and the Starbucks team spent months diagnosing Starbucks' problems. As Schultz noted in *Onward*, "The more rocks we turned over, the more problems we discovered."[9] Operating margins had slumped from a peak of 12.3 percent in 2005 to 11.2 percent in 2007, but earnings still increased. That all changed in 2008 when operating earnings plunged nearly 27 percent excluding restructuring charges and 52 percent including charges. Schultz went on to say, "From where I sat as CEO, the pieces of our rapid decline were coming together in my mind. Growth had been a carcinogen. When it became our primary operating principle, it diverted attention from revenue and cost-saving opportunities, and we did not effectively manage expenses such as rising construction costs and additional monies spent on new equipment…Then, as customers cut their spending, we faced a lethal combination—rising costs and sinking sales—which meant Starbucks' economic model was no longer viable."[10] Although Starbucks had a sizable presence in international markets, the United States still accounted for 76 percent of company revenues. The United States had to be fixed in order to turn around the company.

Schultz spent the next couple of years refocusing Starbucks on the coffee business. He cut breakfast items from the menu and got managers to think about customer service and selling coffee. Schultz closed all the U.S. stores for a day and retrained baristas on preparing the perfect cup of espresso. He also replaced top management and built up the company's capabilities in supply and logistics. The management team tackled major inefficiencies in the supply chain as well as in the stores. Stores were redesigned to improve efficiency and reduce on-the-job injuries. He also emphasized the Starbucks experience and the importance of being passionate about coffee. Despite significant pressures from Wall Street, Schultz refused to drop health care benefits for part-time employees as he recognized the barista was one of the fundamental drivers of company performance. Starbucks also closed nearly 1,000 underperforming stores and laid off about 12,000 workers. It slowed dramatically the rate of store expansion from about 1,300 per year in the United States to about 300. After a painful few years, the company came roaring back with outstanding results. Schultz vowed never to allow the company to make the same mistakes again.

Alex Meets with His Broker

Two weeks later, Alex pushed his books aside and opened the Starbucks folder on his MacBook. He sipped his Tall Caffe Mocha Espresso and looked around the Starbucks store. There was a steady stream of customers even at 2 in the afternoon on a Monday. Alex had arranged a meeting with his grandfather's stockbroker, and the broker was 10 minutes late. He glanced down at his blue steel ESQ Movado watch, checked the time for the hundredth time, and drummed his pen on the table impatiently. Gramps's broker was an old pro—a self-made man with a flair for stock picking. Gramps and the broker, Harry Wallace, had been close friends. They were both members of the local Rotary Club and avid golfers.

"Alex, how've you been?" Alex looked up and saw Harry walking toward him, hand outstretched. After the two had exchanged greetings and small talk, Alex got down to business. "Harry, I'm trying to sort out Gramps's portfolio. His largest position is in Starbucks, so I started there," Alex said. He went on, "I need to figure out whether to sell the stock or not. I've done quite a bit of research on it already, but it would help if you filled in the details on the company's strategy for me."

"Sure, I'd be happy to," Harry said. "The stock had been hitting all-time highs until it hit a bump in the road when an arbitrator decided that Starbucks would have to pay Kraft $2.23 billion plus $537 million in attorneys' fees to settle a three-year-old fight between the two companies. Starbucks and Kraft had been partners in the packaged coffee business since 1998. Starbucks supplied the coffee and the brand name. Kraft supplied the distribution to mass retail outlets. In 2004, the two companies renegotiated their contract and extended it to 2014. In 2010, Starbucks terminated the agreement, claiming Kraft had not upheld its part of the bargain and had failed to work closely with it on marketing decisions and customer contacts."[11] Harry went on to say, "Starbucks claimed Kraft had hurt the performance of the Starbucks brand at retail, but Kraft pointed out that it had grown the company's packaged coffee business from $50 million in sales to $500 million in sales. Starbucks maintained terminating the Kraft agreement early was the right thing to do to accelerate the growth of its mass retail business." Harry added, "The stock sold off −1.5 percent on the news before rebounding the next day as Starbucks convinced investors that it had ample funds to make the payment."

The company's revenue and earnings growth had been pretty astonishing over the past couple of years as it pulled out of its 2008–2009 slump. In the short term, the risk in the stock was that investors are looking for another positive earnings surprise when the company commented on holiday sales in a few weeks in Harry's opinion.

"I'm not all that interested in the short-term outlook. You know Gramps always focused on a company's long-term prospects," Alex said. "Tell me how things look for Starbucks over the next couple of years."

"Starbucks has approached long-term growth in a unique way. The way I see it, the company's so-called blueprint for growth has a lot of potential to keep the company's growth high," Harry said.

Starbucks' Blueprint for Profitable Growth

In late 2010, Starbucks' management announced plans to create long-term shareholder value through a new "blueprint for profitable growth." Schultz said, "Our next phase of growth will come from extending the *Starbucks Experience* to our customers beyond the third place to every part of their day, through multiple brands and channels. Starbucks' U.S. retail business and our connection with our customers form the foundation on which we build all of our lasting assets, and we will combine that with new capabilities in multiple channels to accelerate the model we've created that no other company can replicate." Starbucks Chief Financial Officer Troy Alstead went on to say, "Starbucks has reached a critical juncture as we move from a high unit growth specialty retailer focused on coffee in our stores, to a global consumer company with diversified growth platforms across multiple channels."[12]

In short, Starbucks intended to introduce new products and brands in its Starbucks retail stores, establish a base of customers for the new items, and later expand distribution to mass-market channels like grocery stores. The company meant to transform itself from a specialty retailer selling a few coffee and tea products through mass outlets into a global consumer products powerhouse. To do so, Starbucks planned to augment its proven model for new brand development with vertical integration and acquisitions. Management was confident it would be able to build a stable of billion-dollar brands by following the model Starbucks developed with two key products: Frappuccino and VIA.

Frappuccino was a coffee blended with ice and milk. The sugary beverage became enormously popular with Starbucks devotees immediately after its summer 1995 introduction. Frappuccino built up a following in Starbucks stores before Starbucks and Pepsi pushed a bottled version of the product into mass retail outlets. Schultz credited a large part of Frappuccino's retail success to Starbucks having the "unique opportunity every single day to reinforce the equity of the Frappuccino blended product in our stores."[13] The $2 billion global brand commanded nearly two-thirds of the U.S. iced coffee category in 2012.

Similarly, Starbucks introduced VIA instant coffee in its stores in 2009. According to Schultz, the product introduction marked the first innovation other than in packaging in the instant coffee market in 50 years.[14] Schultz regarded the category as one that was "ripe for renewal."[15] Although the U.S. market for instant coffee was relatively small at about $700 million in 2009, Schultz regarded the product extension as a critical one for the company. He felt it would spur innovation within the company, put Starbucks into new retail channels like specialty sporting goods stores, and support the company's objective to be the undisputed coffee authority. The instant coffee market accounted for about 40 percent of worldwide coffee consumption and generated an estimated $21 billion per year in sales. Higher-end instant coffees generated less than 20 percent of instant coffee sales globally, which suggested to Schultz the category was a candidate for "premiumization"—just as the U.S. coffee market had been prior to Starbucks' entry into the market.

In addition, instant coffee consumption had grown at a much faster clip in emerging markets than in the United States, where sales of the product were flat. *Global Coffee Review* magazine pegged worldwide instant coffee growth at 7 to 10 percent and 15 to 20 percent in emerging markets from 2000 to 2012.[16] Coffee drinkers in emerging markets favored instant or soluble coffee over brewed coffee because consumers often could not afford special coffee-making equipment. Starbucks' management reckoned that it could establish the VIA brand in the United States in its own stores, expand into mass retailing, and then move the brand into Starbucks stores in the United Kingdom, Japan, and emerging markets. (Instant coffee accounted for about 80 percent of all coffee sales in the United Kingdom and 63 percent of sales in Japan.)

Schultz believed Starbucks could use technology to produce a cup of instant coffee that would taste the same as a cup of Starbucks brewed coffee. The challenge for Starbucks was threefold. First, the company had to overcome the stigma of instant coffee being associated with weak, low-quality, poor-tasting coffee in the United States. Second, Starbucks had to convince consumers to pay a hefty premium for VIA, which retailed for $0.82 to $0.98 per serving. Other instant coffees could be purchased for as little as $0.04 to $0.07 per serving. Folgers Instant Coffee Singles were priced at $0.20 per serving. Third, the company had to overcome substantial competition in the segment once it launched the product into supermarkets and other mass outlets.

In order to change consumer perceptions of instant coffee, the company employed extensive use of sampling in its own stores to encourage consumers to taste VIA side by side with Starbucks brewed coffee. The taste tests continued for a year before Starbucks rolled out the product into grocery and other mass retail stores. The company also sent baristas into its network of 3,000 licensed store-within-a-store Starbucks locations in retailers such as Target and Safeway to give out millions of VIA samples to customers. Starbucks created free publicity for the brand by inviting reporters to participate in blind taste tests comparing Starbucks brewed coffee with VIA instant coffee. The evidence from the taste tests overwhelmingly supported Starbucks' claim that VIA was a convenient, less expensive version of a Starbucks coffee rather than a low-quality, watered-down version of "real" coffee. (An eight-ounce serving of brewed coffee in Starbucks stores cost $1.50 in 2009.) In April 2012, the *Huffington Post* conducted a blind taste test of instant coffees and concluded that VIA Columbia was not only the best instant coffee on the market but was indistinguishable from regular brewed coffee.[17]

Starbucks had to compete against well-established brands in the United States and elsewhere. Nestlé, the worldwide leader in instant coffee and inventor of the product, held about 34 percent of the U.S. instant coffee market in 2010. Kraft General Foods (Maxwell House) was number two in the market with a share of about 26 percent, followed by JM Smacker (Folgers) with about a 21 percent share. Nestle had used its first-mover status to its advantage—holding 51 percent of the global market for instant coffee. In fact, Nestlé was the largest manufacturer of packaged coffee in the world with nearly a 22 percent global share due largely to its huge presence in the instant coffee market. Nevertheless, Starbucks grabbed more than 10 percent of the U.S. instant coffee market in VIA's first year on the market.

Starbucks aimed to turn VIA into a $1 billion dollar brand by leveraging its international presence and taking on Nestlé head to head. The company launched VIA in the Chinese market in April 2011 where Nestle controlled 75 percent of the instant coffee market. Instant coffee accounted for 80 to 90 percent of coffee consumption in the $11.3 billion Chinese coffee market.[18] Still, by 2012, VIA had generated $300 million in annual worldwide revenues through 80,000 distribution points in 14 countries.

Evolution Fresh

Starbucks acquired premium juice brand Evolution Fresh for $30 million in cash in late 2011. The acquisition was Starbucks' first major plank in a new health and wellness platform for the company. Starbucks intended to expand the brand by launching a chain of juice bars, selling the line through Starbucks coffeehouses, and expanding the brand's retail distribution. Schultz commented, "This is the first of many things we're going to do around health and wellness...We're not only acquiring a juice company, but we're using this acquisition to build a broad-based, multi-million-dollar health and wellness business over time."[19] As it had done in the coffee and instant coffee markets, Starbucks aimed to "reinvent the $1.6 billion super-premium juice segment." Starbucks claimed the company would be able to take "a currently undifferentiated, commoditized product segment and introduce a unique, high-quality product to redefine and grow the super-premium juice market."[20] According to Schultz, "Our intent is to build a national Health and Wellness brand leveraging our scale, resources and premium product expertise. Bringing Evolution Fresh into the Starbucks family marks an important step forward in this pursuit."[21] By October 2013, Evolution Fresh juice was sold in 8,000 retail locations—up from 2,000 in 2012—as well as in four standalone Evolution Fresh stores. The company opened a $70 million factory in Rancho Cucamonga, California, in late 2013 to support the rollout of Evolution Fresh products across the United States.

Sales of fruit and vegetable juices and juice drinks generated an estimated $20 billion in annual revenues in 2012. Industry sales had not grown appreciably for more than five years. Moreover, per capita juice consumption had declined as Americans turned to other beverages like energy drinks and fortified waters to slake their thirst. Per capita juice consumption declined from 6.1 gallons in 2006 to 5.17 gallons in 2011.[22] In contrast, the super premium juice segment had boomed, and sales jumped to an estimated $2.25 billion in 2013 as "juice cleanses" gained popularity and manufacturers touted the health benefits of cold-pressed juices.

Norman Walker, supposed "health expert" and sometime mountebank, invented cold pressing in 1910. His Norwalk hydraulic juicer was still considered by many to be the best on the market in 2013 and retailed for a whopping $2,000. Cold pressing pulverized fresh fruits and vegetables in order to extract all of the juice from the produce. Evolution Fresh and others placed cold-pressed juices in bottles and then subjected the filled bottles to high pressure while floating in water. The high-pressure pascalization (HPP) process stunted the growth of pathogens and extended the shelf life of the juice from a few days to about three weeks. Mass-market brands such as Tropicana relied on high-heat pasteurization to kill pathogens in juice. Fans of cold-pressed juice claimed it was healthier than pasteurized juices. While there was little scientific evidence to support manufacturers' claims of superior health benefits, so-called juicers asserted the flavor of cold-pressed juice was "closer to fresh" than mass-market stalwarts like Minute Maid or Tropicana. Critics of cold pressing were concerned about the product's safety. They noted that Odawalla juice, a leader in the cold-pressed juice category, introduced flash pasteurization after a batch of apple juice was contaminated with E. coli in 1996. The contaminated apple juice had caused illness in at least 66 people and reportedly led to the death of a 16-month-old child. In fact, the FDA had begun to push cold-pressed juice makers to include HPP or an alternative process as a way to increase the product's safety. Given that each HPP machine cost $800,000 to $2 million, it was difficult for small juicers to jump on the HPP bandwagon.[23] Nevertheless, an E. coli outbreak could generate a consumer backlash against all cold-pressed juices.

Despite Starbucks' ambitious plans, it was not clear that the juice market could be characterized as "commoditized." The category was bombarded annually with product introductions touting new flavor combinations and health benefits. Some of the more exotic juices introduced into the mass market in recent years included coconut water, acai, beet juice, and Suavva Cacao. Ironically, health concerns had stymied growth in the mass market as consumers became concerned about the high sugar content in juices. While whole fruits had been shown to reduce the risk of type 2 diabetes, the high sugar content in fruit juices had some consumers shying away from the product due to concerns over obesity. PepsiCo had scrambled to find a solution to the sugar problem. While the company continued to experiment with new sugar-free sweeteners, it launched Tropicana Light and Trop50 products under the $6.2 billion Tropicana brand. Tropicana Light was sweetened with sucralose, and Trop50 was sweetened with stevia. Trop50 products also contained only 42 to 43 percent juice as the liberal additional of water allowed PepsiCo to bring down calorie count significantly and increase gross margins. While consumers responded favorably to the new products, PepsiCo management knew the secret to long-term success lay in continued product innovation in sugar replacement. PepsiCo was determined to find a natural sugar replacement to protect its enormous global beverage business.

Juice prices ranged from a few cents per ounce for mass brands to well over $1 per ounce for super premium products. In the super premium segment, large food and beverage companies trying to capitalize on the higher growth in the segment owned by the top four brands. Odawalla (acquired by Coca-Cola in 2001), Naked Juice (PepsiCo), Bolthouse Farms (Campbell Soup), and BluePrint (Hain Celestial Seasonings) together controlled an estimated 51 percent of the super premium market.

The juice bar business also was crowded with competitors trying to take cash in on demand for healthy foods. Sales at juice bars and smoothie chains nearly doubled between 2004 and 2012, according to *Barron's* magazine. Barron's pegged sales at the 6,200 juice bars and smoothie operations at about $2 billion. The top five juice and smoothie chains—Jamba Juice, Freshens, Maui Wowi, Smoothie King, and Orange Julius—accounted for more than 50 percent of all of the juice and smoothie retail locations in the United States in 2012. The top 10 operators owned or had franchised about two-thirds of the industry locations.[24] Rivalry appeared to be fierce as the large chains attempted to fight off small local competitors who often positioned themselves as the most "authentic" purveyor of juices. Marcus Antebi, CEO of Manhattan's trendy Juice Press, commenting on Organic Avenue's appointment of a non-vegan CEO to the *New York Daily News* said, "They'll no longer represent the glossy, sexy brand that they were five years ago, before Juice Press smothered them. I actually water boarded them with green juice."[25]

U.S. Tea Market

Quick as thought the ships were boarded
Hatches bust and chests displayed;
Axe and hammers help afforded,
What a glorious crash they made.

Quick into the deep descended,
Cursed weed of China's coast;
Thus at once our fears were ended
Freemen's rights shall ne'er be lost.

—anonymous American balladeer
commemorating the Boston Tea Party[26]

According to some sources, coffee's popularity in the United States relative to tea stretches back to the Revolutionary War and the Boston Tea Party. In protest to unfair taxation and the granting of a tea monopoly to the East India Company by British Parliament, colonists snuck on board three tea ships (the Dartmouth, the Eleanor, and the Beaver) on December 16, 1773, and dumped 90,000 pounds of tea into Boston Harbor. Colonists went on to boycott British imports, including tea, for many years.

Coffee and herbal teas supposedly became popular due to the boycott as substitutes for the colonists' favorite beverage.

Retail and food-service sales of tea generated about $6.5 billion in revenues in the United States and $40 billion worldwide in 2011. Tea was the second-most consumed beverage worldwide, behind water. However, tea remained distinctly less popular with Americans than coffee. The beverage came in at a distant number six among American favorites behind soft drinks, water, coffee, milk, and beer (in that order). Nevertheless, per capita consumption of tea grew about 5 percent from 2001 to 2011 as Americans sipped slightly more than seven gallons of tea per person. In contrast, per capita coffee consumption fell 1 percent, and carbonated soft drink consumption plunged 16 percent over the period.[27] As tea consumption increased, the number of U.S. tea shops jumped from about 1,500 in 2009 to approximately 4,000 in 2011. Costs to open a single tea shop were relatively low with some tea shop owners estimating it cost $10,000 to $25,000 (comparable with opening a non-franchised pizza place) and others coming in at $100,000 to $250,000 (a bit lower than opening a franchised pizza restaurant).[28]

Starbucks had long been a player in the tea market with its Tazo tea brand, which it had acquired in 1999 for $8.1 million. The company sold Tazo tea in grocery stores and other mass outlets as well as in Starbucks coffeehouses. By 2012, Tazo overall was a $1.4 billion brand for Starbucks. Although the company had been successful in establishing a large tea brand, tea had never been a focal point for Starbucks until it acquired Teavana Holdings. Starbucks announced it would purchase Teavana Holdings for $620 million in cash in November 2012. Teavana was the largest tea shop operator in the United States with 300 retail stores mainly in shopping malls. Founded in Atlanta in 1997, Teavana sold high-end loose-leaf teas exclusively through its own stores.

Teavana's mission was to establish its brand "as the most recognized and respected brand in the tea industry by expanding the culture of tea across the world."[29] As noted by Seattle's Crosscut.com reporter Ronald Holden "Just as a wine aficionado can wax on (and on and on) about grape varieties and legendary vintages, a devotee of tea can cite literally hundreds of varieties of *camellia sinensis* leaves (white, green, oolong, black), and their methods of 'withering' (steaming, pan-firing, shaking, bruising, rolling, drying, oxidizing). Then there are the tea-like drinks that don't contain *Camillia sinensis*, like prepared herbal infusions, rooibos (red teas) and the green-powdered matés."[30]

Teavana management identified the key elements of its strategy as developing and sourcing the world's finest assortment of premium loose-leaf teas and tea-related merchandise, locating stores in high-traffic areas primarily in shopping malls and lifestyle centers, and creating a "Heaven of Tea" retail experience for customers. Teavana's emphasis on training "passionate and knowledgeable teaologists" to "engage and educate customers about the ritual and enjoyment of tea"[31] allowed it to charge premium prices and develop a loyal following in the United States.

Indeed, Teavana's approach to the market had been a very successful and profitable one with sales soaring to $168.1 million and operating profits of $32.6 million. Teavana's highly productive stores generated nearly $1,000 per square foot in sales and comparable store sales growth of nearly 9 percent in 2011 and more than 11 percent in 2010. New stores had an average cash payback period of just a year and a half. The retailer believed it could drive tea category growth in the United States by educating consumers about the health benefits of tea and the culture of tea drinking. Each Teavana store included the "Wall of Tea," which allowed customers to "experience the aroma, color, and texture" of any of the store's approximately 100 different varieties of single-estate and specially blended teas.[32] Like Starbucks and its coffee culture, Teavana emphasized a company culture that celebrated a passion for tea. To that end, Teavana had a policy of promoting from within company ranks, extensive employee training, and teaologist career development. Management recognized that retail success was heavily dependent upon teaologists in the same way Starbucks' success rested upon the barista.

Starbucks intended to develop Teavana as a major growth platform beginning with the U.S. market. In late October 2013, Starbucks opened the first Teavana tea bar on Manhattan's ultra-wealthy Upper East Side. Schultz told reporters the company expected 1,000 tea bars in the United States over the next five years.[33] Schultz was confident that Starbucks could transform the U.S. tea market with Teavana in the same way it had transformed the coffee market. Some industry observers were not as sanguine about Teavana's prospects.

Brian Sozzi of Belus Capital Advisers noted to *Forbes* magazine, "I don't believe Teavana will ever grow into what the Starbucks brand has become for one simple reason: tea lacks the major caffeine count." He added, "That sounds silly, but the bottom line is that in this day and age of frantic tech-driven lifestyles, people want to run on 100 mg of caffeine, and they will trade taste to make that happen."[34] In fact, the contrast between Teavana and Starbucks products was stark at the cultural level. Coffee typically was associated with early-morning commutes and midday pick-me-ups. While Starbucks had done a great job creating a welcoming atmosphere in its coffeehouses, the pace of each shop was quick and energetic, particularly during the morning rush hour. Tea culture was one associated with tranquility and relaxation. Teavana's new tea shop invited customers to slow down and find some quiet time while their tea brewed. According to a University of Northumberland study consisting of 180 hours of testing and 285 cups of tea, it took eight minutes to brew the perfect cup of tea—two minutes of soaking the tea bag in boiling water (100°C or 212°F), removal of the tea bag, addition of milk, and a six-minute wait for the temperature to drop to 60°C or 140°F.[35]

La Boulange Café & Bakery

Starbucks acquired a small chain of San Francisco bakeries for $100 million in the third quarter of 2012. The chain, La Boulange, included 19 store locations. Starbucks intended to roll out La Boulange products to 17,000 Starbucks coffeehouses by the end of 2013. La Boulange Café's major investor commented in a release about the sale: "We have confidence that Starbucks will stay true to the La Boulange brand while bringing the romance of an authentic French bakery to consumers across the United States."[36] Long criticized for having mediocre food, Starbucks nonetheless sold $1.5 billion in food items annually. About one-third of purchases in the United States included a food item.[37] According to Pascal Rigo, vice president of Starbucks' food division and former owner of La Boulange, food had been an afterthought at Starbucks.[38] The company planned to significantly upgrade the quality of its food and add lunch items to the menu under the La Boulange banner. Baked items were to be displayed on pink paper in the coffeehouse's glass cases and served warm. About 25 percent of La Boulange items would be customized for local markets. Starbucks hoped to both take a bigger slice of the lunch business and compete more aggressively with fast-growing Panera Bread in the United States.

Starbucks' Loyalty Card

Starbucks launched "My Starbucks Rewards" in 2009 as a way to create value for its most loyal customers. Customers received points for each purchase regardless of the amount they spent. Points were redeemable for free Starbucks drinks and food. By early 2013, Starbucks had 4.5 million rewards program members. The company intended to double its reward program membership to 9 million members by fall 2013. To that end, Starbucks announced Teavana shoppers were eligible for My Starbucks

Rewards beginning in April 2013. Starbucks customers who purchased Starbucks packaged products in grocery stores and other retail outlets also were eligible for My Starbucks Rewards by registering for the program and entering product codes on the Internet. Starbucks hoped to create value across its brands and distribution channels through its unique loyalty program.

That evening, Alex sat down and thought about what he had learned about Starbucks over the past few weeks. "Well, at least midterms are over," Alex thought. He sighed wearily. The past few days had gone by in a blur of exams, studying, and not enough sleep. His girlfriend, Sarah, had gotten exasperated with him for waiting until the last minute to study for their investments midterm. He was sure she had aced the exam but was less confident about his own score. Alex had gotten bogged down studying for his midterm in his third-year Mandarin course and hadn't spent much time studying for investments. The Mandarin class was a lot harder for Alex than his finance courses, but the investments class was a tough one. "Sarah was right. I shouldn't have put studying off for so long." To top it off, his strategy midterm also had been a difficult one. His strategy professor put a lot of emphasis on applying concepts to real company situations. "It was tough to apply concepts on a couple of hours of sleep," Alex thought ruefully. "Well, there's nothing I can do about it now. I need to focus on finishing this Starbucks analysis because I am just going to get busier as the term goes on. I haven't even thought about the competition. I need to figure out what McDonald's and Dunkin' Donuts are up to."

Bitter Dregs: Starbucks' Rivalry with McDonald's

With $35.6 billion in U.S. sales in 2012, McDonald's was the largest quick-service restaurant in America and nearly three times larger than the number two fast food operator, Subway. Coffee accounted for an estimated 6 to 7 percent of McDonald's U.S. sales or $2.1 to $2.5 billion in annual revenues. Despite its substantial coffee sales, Starbucks' management did not publicly acknowledge McDonald's as a competitor. On the surface, the world's largest fast-food franchise had little in common with Starbucks. Known for efficiency and low costs, McDonald's was the Wal-Mart of fast food. Starbucks was a premium purveyor of specialty coffees. McDonald's empire was built on standardization. Starbucks ran on customization.

Nevertheless, McDonald's was long known for serving good, inexpensive drip coffee. Moreover, McDonald's dominated the breakfast market with more than a 25 percent share. The company announced in mid-2009 the rollout of McCafe specialty coffee shops within 11,000 of its 14,000 U.S. locations. Developed in Australia in 2001, the McCafe brand and McCafe shops gave McDonald's an entry into the pricey and profitable premium coffee segment just as consumers felt the pinch of the Great Recession.

As McDonald's gained momentum in the U.S. coffee market, Starbucks retaliated by announcing it would expand distribution of Seattle's Best Coffee to Burger King and Subway restaurants as well as AMC movie theaters and other mass-market outlets. Starbucks had acquired the brand for $72 million in 2003 but had done little to expand Seattle's Best's market presence since the acquisition. Starbucks' management commented that the move into fast food enabled the company to further its objective to offer great coffee everywhere. Industry observers saw the move as a direct response to McDonald's market share inroads. Morgan Stanley's John Glass noted to *Time* magazine: "… it makes sense to partner with Burger King and Subway against a common enemy: McDonald's."[39] At the time of the rollout announcement, McDonald's also announced its intentions to launch frozen coffee drinks in its restaurants during summer 2010. The Frappe retailed for $2.29 to $3.29 compared with $3.00 to $5.00 for Starbucks' Frappuccino.[40] Whether Starbucks wanted to admit it or not, McDonald's new product introductions placed it squarely in competition with Starbucks in multiple segments of the coffee market.

In fact, McDonald's had garnered close to 13 percent of the U.S. coffee market by 2012. McDonald's U.S. coffee sales had soared 70 percent since the introduction of McCafe. The company introduced a pumpkin spice latte in fall 2013 and announced it would introduce a white chocolate-flavored mocha at the end of November 2013. Both product launches were aimed directly at Starbucks where the pumpkin spice latte was a perennial customer favorite. McDonald's had struggled with execution in the lucrative specialty coffee market with many McDonald's customers complaining about lengthy waits in the drive-through line resulting from the increased time to make the customized drinks. Nevertheless, the coffee business remained a bright spot in McDonald's otherwise lackluster U.S. operations.

In November 2013, McDonald's announced it would partner with Kraft to bring a McCafe line of packaged coffees to supermarkets and other mass retail outlets. McDonald's CEO Don Thompson told investors that coffee was one of the fastest-growing product categories in its worldwide beverages business. Thompson also told investors that McDonald's did not yet have what he called "its fair share" of the business. Kevin Newell, chief brand and strategy officer for McDonald's U.S., noted that 70 percent of U.S. coffee consumption occurred at home. He characterized the move into supermarkets with Kraft as a way to build awareness of the McCafe brand and drive sales in McDonald's restaurants.[41] Analysts noted that McDonald's had 4,200 McCafe shops in international markets—including standalone locations as well as those inside McDonald's restaurants—and intended to add another 350 to 400 locations in 2014 alone.

Death of the Doughnut: Dunkin' Donuts—A Beverage Company

Dunkin' Donuts CFO Paul Carbone told investors in mid-2013 that Dunkin' Donuts had moved to acknowledge publicly that the chain was no longer a doughnut company. Carbone told analysts, "We're a beverage company."[42] Dunkin' Donuts reported that 58 percent of its franchise revenues were derived from espressos, Duncacinnos, Coolattas, and about two dozen other beverages. The shift away from doughnuts to coffee and coffee drinks began in about 1995. Dunkin' Donuts launched a line of flavored coffees to respond to Starbucks' expansion into its home market: Boston. At the time, Dunkin' Donuts was known primarily for its doughnuts and an ad campaign that featured "Fred the Baker." Fred's catch phrase was "It's time to make the doughnuts." According to *Time* magazine, Dunkin' Donuts kicked off in 2006 "the most significant repositioning effort in the company's 55-year history." Its new ad slogan was "America Runs on Dunkin'." *Time* noted in the same article that Dunkin' Donuts had positioned its mostly East Coast coffee business as "fuel" for America rather than a lifestyle choice like Starbucks.[43] With lower prices and an emphasis on practicality, Dunkin' Donuts appealed to the every man in a hurry. Dunkin' Donuts' share of the U.S. coffee and snack shop market was about 25 percent in 2012 compared with Starbucks' share of about 33 percent.

Nevertheless, Dunkin's core business remained in the East. Very few of Dunkin's 7,300 U.S. locations were east of the Mississippi in 2012. However, Dunkin' Donuts management aimed to change that by moving into California with 1,000 Dunkin' Donuts shops. (Starbucks had more than 2,000 locations in California in 2013, its largest market by far.) Overall, Dunkin' Donuts also planned to increase the number of Dunkin' locations in the United States to about 15,000 by 2020. Dunkin' Donuts' overall expansion plans were likely to put it increasingly in head-to-head competition with Starbucks. Starbucks planned to add about 1,500 stores to its U.S. store base of about 11,000 coffeehouses. Industry observers noted that Dunkin'

Donuts' expansion into California marked its third attempt to crack the market in the past 30 years. The chain had about a dozen stores in California until the late 1990s, according to *Bloomberg BusinessWeek*.[44] Dunkin' tried to reenter the Sacramento market in 2002 but pulled out quickly.[45]

Conclusion

Alex realized that he hadn't spent enough time thinking about the questions that needed to be answered in order for him to make a decision on the stock. He spent an hour compiling questions, scratching them out and condensing them into their most fundamental elements. At the end of the exercise, Alex realized that he needed to answer three questions in order to make a decision about whether to sell the stock. Could Starbucks successfully expand beyond the coffee shop business in a meaningful way without destroying its core business? Could the company create value through its diversification strategy? Would McDonald's and Dunkin' Donuts eat into Starbucks' business enough to slow the company's growth rate?

Reference

Miller, C. (2009). "Starbucks coffee, now in instant. *New York Times*, February 18.

End Notes

1. (2013). "Free Starbucks Blonde samples aim to sway light-roast coffee drinkers [update]." www.huffingtonpost.com/2013/01/08/free-starbucks-blonde-samples_n_2431793.html#slide=873948. Accessed October 15, 2013.
2. (2013). "Howard Schultz." *The Biography Channel*. October 16, www.biography.com/people/howard-schultz-21166227.
3. (2013). "Beverages: Per capita availability." USDA Economic Research Service, October 16, www.ers.usda.gov/data-products/food-availability-%28per-capita%29-data-system/.aspx#.UmA9oYX5AYs.
4. Roseberry, W. (1996). "The rise of yuppie coffees and the reimagination of class in the United States." *American Anthropologist, New Series*, 98(4), p. 765.
5. Ibid., p. 765.
6. Samuelson, R. J. (1989). "The coffee cartel: Brewing up trouble." *The Washington Post*, July 26.
7. Sturdivant, S. (1990). "Coffee in the next decade: Upcoming trends (coffee in the 1990s)." *Tea & Coffee Trade Journal*, January 1.
8. Van Vynckt, V. (1986). "Coffee: A treat for the 'buds: 'Specialties' perk up market." *Chicago Sun-Times*, April 3.
9. Schultz, H., with Gordon, J. (2011). *Onward: How Starbucks fought for its life without losing its soul*. Rodale Books, Kindle Edition, p. 150.
10. Ibid., pp. 152–153.
11. D'Innocenzio, A. (2013). "Starbucks Kraft lawsuit: Coffee chain must pay $2.76 billion to settle dispute." *Huffington Post*, November 12.
12. (2010). "Starbucks outlines blueprint for multi-channel growth." Starbucks press release. *Business Wire*, December 1.
13. Schultz, H. (2012). "Starbucks CEO hosts biennial investor conference (transcript)." December 5, p. 7. www.seekingalpha.com. Accessed November 1, 2013.
14. Ibid.
15. Schultz, H., with Gordon, J. (2011). *Onward: How Starbucks fought for its life without losing its soul*. Rodale Books, Kindle Edition, p. 252.
16. (2013). "Instant coffee consumption in emerging markets." *Global Coffee Review*, March. globalcoffeereview.com/market-reports/view/instant-coffee-consumption-in-emerging-markets. Accessed November 18, 2013.

17. (2012). "Taste test: The best instant coffee." Huff Taste, *The Huffington Post*, April 5.

18. O'Brian, R. (2013). "Starbucks, Nestlé square off in bid for dominance of China's coffee market." *Context China.* contextchina.com/2013/05/starbucks-nestle-square-off-in-bid-for-dominance-of-chinas-coffee-market. Accessed November 17, 2013.

19. (2011). "Starbucks acquires Evolution Fresh to establish national retail and grocery health and wellness brand." Starbucks press release, November 10.

20. Ibid.

21. Ibid.

22. Fottrell, Q. (2013). "Graphic: Tea up 5%. Milk: Out. Wine: In. Plus 8 other drink trends. How the nation's thirsts have shifted over the past decade." Marketwatch.com, February 15 Accessed October 15, 2013.

23. Latif, R. (2013). "The juice uprising." *BevNET Magazine*, September 12.

24. Blumenthal, R. (2012). "Drink up!" *Barron's*, July 23.

25. Friedman, M. (2013). "Juice makers battle over market share and product purity as sales surge." *New York Daily News*, May 22.

26. "The Boston Tea Party." United Kingdom Tea Council, www.tea.co.uk/the-boston-tea-party. Accessed October 26, 2013.

27. Fottrell, Q. (2013). "Graphic: Tea up 5%. Milk: Out. Wine: In. Plus 8 other drink trends. How the nation's thirsts have shifted over the past decade." Marketwatch.com, February 15 Accessed October 15, 2013.

28. Simrany, J. "The state of the U.S. tea industry." Specialty Tea Institute and Tea Council USA.

29. (2011). Teavana prospectus form 424, July 28, p. 1.

30. Holden, R. (2013). "Cuppa inner peace? U Village Teavana expands Starbucks empire." Crosscut.com, Crosscut PublicMedia. November 21, crosscut.com/2013/11/21/business/117566/starbucks-tea-volution-slinging-u-village-enlighte. Accessed November 23, 2013.

31. (2011). Teavana prospectus form 424, July 28, p. 1.

32. Ibid.

33. O'Connor, C. (2013). "Starbucks opens its first tea bar as CEO Schultz bets on $90 billion market." *Forbes*, October 23.

34. Ibid.

35. Alleyne, R. (2011). "How to make the perfect cup of tea: Be patient." *The Telegraph*, June 15.

36. Wilkey, R. (2012). "Starbucks La Boulange acquisition: Coffee giant buys local patisserie for $100 million." Huff Post San Francisco. *Huffington Post*, June 4, www.huffingtonpost.com/2012/06/04/la-boulange-starbucks_n_1569522.html. Accessed November 23, 2013.

37. Choi, C. (2012). "Starbucks buys La Boulange bakery for $100 million to improve food offerings."AP Newswire, June 4.

38. Tepper, R. (2013). "Starbucks' new La Boulange menu is its largest-ever investment in food." *Huffington Post*, September 19, www.huffingtonpost.com/2013/09/19/starbucks-la-boulange_n_3954803.html. Accessed November 23, 2013.

39. Gregory, S. (2010). "Starbucks aims at McDonald's with Seattle's Best Coffee." *Time*, May 25, content.time.com/time/business/article/0,8599,1990813,00.html#ixzz2lafvjXPz. Accessed November 23, 2013.

40. Ibid.

41. Choi, C. (2013). "McDonald's eyes bigger share of coffee market."AP Newswire, *ABC News*, November 14, abcnews.go.com/Business/wireStory/mcdonalds-eyes-global-coffee-growth-20891507. Accessed November 23, 2013.

42. O'Connor, C. (2013). "Dunkin' Donuts now class itself a 'beverage company' as it aims for Starbucks and heads west." *Forbes*, June 20, www.forbes.com/sites/clareoconnor/2013/06/20/dunkin-donuts-now-calls-itself-a-beverage-company-as-it-aims-for-starbucks-and-heads-west. Accessed November 23, 2013.

43. Sanborn, J. (2013). "Don't call Dunkin' Donuts a donut company." *Time*. June 26, business.time.com/2013/06/26/dont-call-dunkin-donuts-a-donut-company/#ixzz2lbRdWNqb. Accessed November 23, 2013.
44. Wong, V. (2013). "America: Dunkin' Donuts' next frontier." *Bloomberg BusinessWeek*, April 11, www.businessweek.com/articles/2013-04-11/america-dunkin-donuts-next-frontier. Accessed November 23, 2013.
45. Ibid.

Case 3–4: Rayovac Corporation: International Growth and Diversification Through Acquisitions[1]

IVEY | Publishing

School of Business
D'Amore-McKim
Northeastern University

David T.A. Wesley prepared this case under the supervision of Professor Ravi Sarathy solely to provide material for class discussion. The authors do not intend to illustrate either effective or ineffective handling of a managerial situation. The authors may have disguised certain names and other identifying information to protect confidentiality.

Copyright © 2006, Northeastern University, College of Business Administration

Version: (A) 2009-09-21

In 2005, Rayovac announced acquisitions totalling $1.5 billion, which encompassed the purchases of United Industries and of Tetra Holdings and aimed at making Rayovac the most "significant global player in the pet supplies industry."[2] These acquisitions were the latest in a series, going back to 1999, that gave Rayovac significant market presence in new product categories, including lawn and garden care, household insecticides and pet foods (see Exhibit 1). Through such acquisitions, Rayovac grew from $400 million in sales in 1996 to approximately $2.8 billion in 2005. In recognition of this major shift in both composition and direction, the company changed its name from Rayovac to Spectrum Brands.

Company Background[3]

Rayovac was established in Madison, Wisconsin, in 1906 as the French Dry Battery Company. After changing its name to Rayovac in 1921, the company became one of the best known battery brands in the United States and quickly established itself as the leading marketer of value-brand batteries in North America.

In 1996, after seeing its market share steadily eroded by Duracell, Energizer and Panasonic (owned by Matsushita), the company was purchased by private equity firm Thomas H. Lee Partners (THL). At the time, revenues were approximately $400 million. THL sought to revive the Rayovac brand name by growing the company

through acquisitions. Initially, acquisitions focused on the battery business, but later included businesses focused on shaving products and personal care. This strategy met with some success as Rayovac increased its U.S. market share from 27 per cent to 34 per cent between 1996 and 2001.

Historically, most of the company's growth had been in North America. However, beginning in 2002, the company began to selectively acquire battery manufacturers and distributors in key foreign markets in an effort to establish a strong global presence. Then in 2003, the company acquired Remington Products in its first move to diversify away from consumer batteries.

According to David A. Jones, chief executive officer (CEO) of Rayovac Corporation, the company's diversification efforts had only begun. He explained,

> We set out consciously for the first five or six years to globalize the battery and lighting business, which we've done, and we have consciously now, for some period of time, been looking for the right diversification moves....There are other things that, over time, we'll become interested in and you'll probably see us move towards.[4]

The Global Battery Business

In 2003, the global battery market was worth approximately $24 billion, with the United States accounting for about one-third of total consumption. Between 1990

Exhibit 1	Rayovac Acquisitions (1999 to 2005) (in $ millions)			
Year	**Company Acquired**	**Price Paid**	**EBITDA**	**Key characteristics of acquired company**
1999	ROV Ltd.	155	41.0	Leading Latin-American battery manufacturer (except Brazil)
Oct. 2002	Varta	258	41.2	Leading Europe-based battery manufacturer of general batteries and the market leader in Germany and Latin America
Sept. 2003	Remington Products	322	48.8	Largest selling brand in the United States in the combined dry shaving and personal-grooming products categories, on the basis of units sold; share similar distribution channels, sales outlets. Mid-tier brand competes with Braun, not wet shavers.
Jan. 2004	Ningbo Baowang Battery Co., China	31 (for 85% stake)	3.4	Manufactures alkaline and heavy-duty batteries in China
June 2004	Microlite Brazil	38	(6.4)	Owned Rayovac brand name in Brazil; leading Brazilian brand with 49% market share in alkaline and zinc carbon segments.
Jan. 2005	United Industries	1,504	150.0	Significant presence in lawn and garden care products, and pet supplies
April 2005	Tetra Holding	555	52.9	Pet food for fish and reptiles, aquarium accessories; No. 1 or No. 2 in market share in every major segment and market—United States, Japan, Germany, United Kingdom and France

Source: Company files.

and 2000, the United States achieved an annual growth rate of 7.4 per cent in alkaline battery products. Rayovac Corporation accompanied this trend but lagged behind Duracell and Energizer in the United States. The intensely competitive U.S. battery market led to considerable price discounting and required significant advertising and promotion expenditures. Rayovac, as the No. 3 player, had to carefully choose its competitive strategy, its product line composition and features, its price points, its cost position, its distribution channels and its advertising strategy in order to be able to close the competitive gap.

Gillette, owner of the Duracell brand, had annual revenues of $9 billion, followed by Energizer Holdings, with revenues of $1.7 billion. Although Rayovac was in third place in the United States, globally, it was the worldwide leader in hearing aid batteries, the leading manufacturer of zinc carbon household batteries in North America and Latin America, and the leading marketer of rechargeable batteries and batterypowered lights in the United States.

Both Energizer and Duracell produced premium brands that sold for approximately 15 per cent above comparable Rayovac products. Jones believed that Rayovac's value position distinguished it from its premium brand competitors. He explained,

For any brand, whether it's a value brand or premium brand, you have to have high quality products. And the facts are on our side. Our products are very good, high quality products. But once you have that, certainly our point of differentiation is value. You can buy our products for 10 per cent to 15 per cent lower than our competitors.... We're actively outselling our value proposition, because we've tried to create a business model and a business plan different from Duracell and Energizer. Our products are as good as those two fine companies but sell at value price.[5]

For several years, battery manufacturers experienced strong growth worldwide due to the increased use of personal electronic devices, such as portable music players, fitness monitors, handheld computers (PDAs) and gaming devices. Portable lighting was another significant Rayovac product category, with 2003 global sales approaching $3 billion, of which flashlights represented about half of the market.

With the proliferation of personal electronic devices, average household battery consumption increased from approximately 23 batteries per year in 1986 to 44 batteries per year in 2000. As incomes grew, consumption in developed countries switched from zinc carbon to the better performing and higher-priced alkaline batteries, a trend that Rayovac expected to be duplicated in emerging markets. According to

Rayovac, the company's strategy of raising brand awareness and increasing the number of distribution channels allowed it to take better advantage of market growth than its competitors. Kent Hussey, Rayovac chief operating officer (COO), underlined the central role of brands, noting,

We believe that brands are very important. Being able to easily identify high-quality products that deliver on the value proposition and have recognizable brand names is very important in terms of marketing to consumers. Having that brand name that the consumer can identify and find on the shelf is key. We think that one of Rayovac's core competencies is our expertise in marketing branded consumer products, and it's really the focus of our entire business.[6]

From the 12 months ended September 30, 1996, through the 12 months ended April 1, 2001, Rayovac grew net sales and adjusted income from operations from $417.9 million to $675.3 million and from $27 million to $83.3 million, respectively. This represented an 11.3 per cent and 28.4 per cent compound annual growth rate in net sales and adjusted income from operations, respectively. In addition, adjusted income from operations margins improved from 6.5 per cent for the 12 months ended September 30, 1996, to 12.3 per cent for the 12 months ended April 1, 2001 (see Exhibits 2 to 5).

Rayovac's ability to distribute its products to customers was constrained to some extent by the emergence of large retailers that controlled access to large numbers of consumers. Wal-Mart Stores, Inc., alone accounted for 21 per cent of Rayovac's annual sales. Other significant outlets were Home Depot, Lowe's and Target. Rayovac also sold through discount channels such as "dollar stores."

Acquisitions

Varta AG (Germany)

In 2002, Rayovac acquired the consumer battery business of Varta AG of Germany for $258 million.[7] Varta was the leading European-based manufacturer of general batteries with 2001 revenues of $390 million. Prior to the acquisition, 73 per cent of Rayovac's revenues came from North America while 86 per cent of Varta's revenues came from Europe. The largest overlap was in Latin America where combined operations solidified Rayovac's market lead, excluding Brazil. The acquisition allowed the two companies to consolidate production and distribution in Latin America and to close redundant manufacturing plants.

The complementary geographic distribution of the two companies' production facilities and distribution

Exhibit 2 Rayovac Financial Summary (for years ending September 30) (in $ millions)

	2004	2003	2002	2001	2000
Income Statement					
Net Sales	1,417.19	922.12	572.74	616.17	630.91
Cost of Goods Sold	811.89	549.51	334.15	361.17	371.47
Pretax Income	90.53	23.04	45.68	17.50	57.95
Net Income	55.78	15.48	29.24	11.53	38.35
Balance Sheet					
Assets					
Total Current Assets	650.51	666.82	259.32	303.09	291.17
Net PP&E	182.40	150.61	102.59	107.26	111.90
Total Assets	1,635.97	1,545.29	533.23	566.50	569.02
Liabilities and Shareholders' Equity					
Total Current Liabilities	398.66	397.01	118.78	144.54	186.48
Long-Term Debt	806.00	870.54	188.47	233.54	272.82
Total Liabilities	1,318.55	1,343.29	358.44	408.91	488.32
Total Shareholders' Equity	316.04	202.00	174.79	157.59	80.70
Total Liabilities and Shareholders' Equity	1,635.97	1,545.29	533.23	566.50	569.02
Cash Flow Statement					
Net Cash Flows from Operations	104.86	76.21	66.83	18.05	32.84
Net Cash Flows from Investing	(68.58)	(446.40)	(15.47)	(18.27)	(17.95)
Net Cash Flows from Financing	(131.02)	471.85	(56.71)	1.67	(16.00)

Source: Company 2004 Annual Report.

Exhibit 3   Rayovac Corporation and Subsidiaries Consolidated Balance Sheets
(for years ending September 30) (in $ millions)

	2004	2003	2002	2001	2000
Assets					
Cash	15.79	107.77	9.88	11.36	9.76
Receivables	269.98	255.21	128.93	160.94	147.77
Total Inventories	264.73	219.25	84.28	91.31	100.68
Other Current Assets	100.02	84.58	36.24	39.48	32.97
Total Current Assets	650.51	666.82	259.32	303.09	291.17
Property, Plant and Equipment	182.40	150.61	102.59	107.26	111.90
Deferred Charges	60.38	76.61	51.90	37.08	43.84
Intangibles	742.68	651.25	119.43	119.07	122.11
Total Assets	1,635.97	1,545.29	533.23	566.50	569.02
Liabilities					
Accounts Payable	228.05	172.63	76.16	81.99	97.86
Current Long-Term Debt	23.90	72.85	13.40	24.44	44.82
Accrued Expense	56.44	41.47	22.09	38.12	43.81
Income Taxes	21.67	20.57	7.14	n/a	n/a
Other Current Liabilities	68.60	89.49	n/a	n/a	n/a
Total Current Liabilities	398.66	397.01	118.78	144.54	186.48
Deferred Charges/Inc.	7.27	n/a	20.96	7.43	8.24
Long-Term Debt	806.00	870.54	188.47	233.54	272.82
Other Long-Term Liabilities	106.61	75.73	30.23	23.40	20.78
Total Liabilities	1,318.55	1,343.29	358.44	408.91	488.32
Shareholders' Equity					
Minority Interest	1.38	n/a	n/a	n/a	n/a
Common Stock	0.64	0.62	0.62	0.62	0.57
Capital Surplus	224.96	185.56	180.82	180.75	104.20
Retained Earnings	220.48	164.70	149.22	119.98	108.45
Treasury Stock	130.07	130.07	130.07	130.07	129.98
Total Shareholders' Equity	316.04	202.00	174.79	157.59	80.70
Total Liabilities and Shareholders' Equity	1,635.97	1,545.29	533.23	566.50	569.02

Source: Company 2004 Annual Report.

channels was expected to give greater access to global sourcing and distribution opportunities and generate cost savings of between $30 million and $40 million through the consolidation of production plants and administration. As a direct result of the Varta acquisition, Rayovac became the market leader in consumer batteries in Germany and Austria and the second leading producer in Europe.

ROV Ltd. and Microlite (Latin America)

Rayovac was the leading producer of zinc carbon batteries in Latin America, a region where the company enjoyed strong brand recognition. However, Latin America was plagued by frequent economic downturns, and consumers had relatively low purchasing power. Despite the region's volatility, Latin America played an important role in the company's geographic diversification strategy.

In the late 1990s, Latin America was one of Rayovac's fastest growing markets, where it had distribution

agreements with Ahold, Woolworths, Makro and several other large supermarket and box-store chains. A large part of the company's growth came from its 1999 acquisition of Miami-based ROV Limited for $155 million. ROV, which was spun off from Rayovac in 1982, was Rayovac's largest distributor of batteries in Latin America, with approximately $100 million in revenues, compared to Rayovac's regional preacquisition revenues of less than $20 million.

However, shortly after the ROV Limited acquisition, Latin America sales took a turn for the worse. All three major manufacturers saw declines of approximately 30 per cent. Rayovac also saw delinquent accounts increase to nearly $5 million, which Rayovac attempted to mitigate by withholding future product shipments. As a result, Rayovac decreased receivables for Latin America from $50 million to $41 million. Fixed costs were also reduced by $12 million, including process rationalization and a reduction in staff by 120 people.

Exhibit 4   Rayovac Corporation and Subsidiaries Statement of Operations Data
(for years ending September 30) (in $ millions)

	2004	2003	2002	2001	2000	1999	1998
Net sales	1,417.2	922.1	572.7	616.2	703.9	564.3	495.7
Cost of goods sold	811.9	549.5	334.1	361.2	358.2	293.9	258.3
Other special charges[1]	(0.8)	21.1	1.2	22.1	-	1.3	-
Gross profit	606.1	351.5	237.4	232.9	345.7	269.1	237.4
Operating expenses:							
Selling expense	293.1	185.2	104.4	119.6	195.1	160.2	148.9
General and administrative expense	121.3	80.9	56.9	46.6	50.5	37.4	32.4
Research and development expense	23.2	14.4	13.1	12.2	10.8	9.8	9.4
Other special charges[2]	12.2	11.5	-	0.2	-	8.1	6.2
	449.9	291.9	174.4	178.6	256.4	215.5	196.9
Income from operations	156.2	59.6	63.0	54.4	89.3	53.6	40.5
Interest expense	65.7	37.2	16.0	27.2	30.6	16.3	15.7
Non-operating expense	-	3.1	-	8.6	-	-	-
Other (income) expense, net	0.1	(3.6)	1.3	1.1	0.7	(0.3)	(0.2)
Income before income taxes and extraordinary item	90.5	23.0	45.7	17.5	58.0	37.6	25.0
Income tax expense	34.3	7.6	16.4	6.0	19.6	13.5	8.6
Income before extraordinary item	56.2	15.5	29.2	11.5	38.4	24.1	16.4
Extraordinary item[3]	(0.4)	-	-	-	-	-	(2.0)
Net income	55.8	15.5	29.2	11.5	38.4	24.1	14.4

Notes:
[1] Related to plant closings, restructuring, process rationalization and severance pay.
[2] Ibid.
[3] Loss from discontinued operations (2004) and expense associated with the repurchase of shares (1998).
Source: Company 2004 Annual Report

Exhibit 5   Rayovac Corporation and Subsidiaries Consolidated Statements of Cash Flows
(for years ending September 30) (in $ millions)

	2004	2003	2002	2001	2000
Net Income (Loss)	55.78	15.48	29.24	11.53	38.35
Depreciation/Amortization	44.75	36.95	22.05	24.86	22.33
Net Increase (Decrease) in Assets/Liabilities	(13.12)	14.38	10.48	(37.67)	(30.07)
Cash Flow from Discontinued Operations	0.38	n/a	n/a	8.59	n/a
Other Adjustments-Net	17.08	9.39	5.06	10.74	2.23
Net Cash Flow from Operations	104.86	76.21	66.83	18.05	32.84
Increase (Decrease) in Prop. Plant and Equip	(26.86)	(25.99)	(15.47)	(18.83)	(17.95)
(Acquisition) Disposal of Subsidiary. Business	(41.71)	(420.40)	n/a	n/a	n/a
Increase (Decrease) in Securities Investments	n/a	n/a	n/a	0.56	n/a
Other Cash Flow from Investing	(0.34)	n/a	(0.24)	(69.65	n/a
Net Cash Flow from Investing	(68.58)	(446.40)	(15.47)	(18.27)	(17.95)
Issue (Repayment) of Debt	(1.35)	(29.93)	n/a	n/a	n/a
Increase (Decrease) in Borrowing	(150.46)	501.61	(56.22)	3.90	(15.74)
Net Cash Flow from Financing	(131.02)	471.85	(56.71)	1.67	(16.00)
Effect of Exchange Rate on Cash	2.75	(3.77)	3.88	0.16	(0.20)
Cash or Equivalents at Year Start	107.77	9.88	11.36	9.76	11.07
Cash or Equivalents at Year End	15.79	107.77	9.88	11.36	9.76
Net Change in Cash or Equivalent	(91.99)	97.89	(1.48)	1.60	(1.31)

In 2004, the company was able to offset this decline through its acquisition of Microlite S.A., the largest producer of consumer batteries in Brazil and owner of the Rayovac brand name in Brazil, for $38 million.[8] The Microlite acquisition allowed Rayovac to immediately realize a 50 per cent market share in Latin America's largest consumer market.[9] Rayovac replaced Microlite's management team with Rayovac veterans who proceeded to reduce costs, increase efficiency and improve product packaging. The latter allowed Rayovac to increase prices by 16 per cent. Regional competitors, following Rayovac's lead, also raised prices.

When Rayovac acquired Microlite, the business was undercapitalized and losing money. Its precarious situation made it a high risk for lenders who, in turn, charged very high interest rates. Rayovac immediately proceeded to recapitalize the business and to replace high-rate debt with Rayovac-backed debentures. The reduction in interest payments immediately improved the acquired company's financial results. According to Chief Executive Officer David A. Jones, the results exceeded company expectations.

> We were frankly surprised by how fast the actions took hold. It didn't surprise us that we were going to make it profitable. I think in the future it's going to be a star performer. Our numerical distribution is high because of the dominance of the brand in the marketplace.[10]

As a result of the Microlite acquisition, Rayovac expected to increase total Latin American revenues by approximately 50 per cent in 2005.

China

In the same year that Rayovac acquired Microlite, the company acquired 85 per cent of Ningbo Baowang for $24 million. Located in Ninghai, China, Ningbo Baowang was a major exporter of private label branded batteries with annual revenues of $6.4 million. The company also sold its own Baowang brand throughout China.

By acquiring a Chinese manufacturer, Rayovac hoped to both increase its presence in the rapidly growing Asia market and to add a low-cost manufacturing subsidiary from which to export Rayovac and Varta branded batteries to its global markets. Rayovac replaced Ningbo Baowang's existing management with its own company managers in order to implement Rayovac process controls and management policies more efficiently. It also installed new manufacturing equipment that would allow it to produce one billion Rayovac branded batteries a year beginning in 2005.[11] Explained Jones,

> China is going to be the growth vehicle for all the alkaline capacity needs in the future. We have a very large plant in Fennimore; we have a very large plant

> in Dischingen in Germany (see Exhibit 6). Those plants are running near capacity and so, as alkaline grows around the world, all the future capacity needs are going to come out of that China plant.[12]

Remington Products Company

In 2003, Rayovac diversified its product offering by acquiring Remington Products for $322 million.[13] Remington was established in 1816 and was recognized as one of America's oldest consumer brands. The company focused on personal care products but was best known for its electric shavers. In this category, Remington was the No. 2 brand in North America with 35 per cent market share, compared with 40 per cent for Norelco and less than 20 per cent for Braun. Other "personal grooming" products included hair dryers, curling irons and hot air brushes. In the four years leading up to its acquisition, Remington experienced a compound annual growth rate in excess of 10 per cent.

In 2003, global sales of electric shaving and grooming products were around $3 billion, growing at about three per cent annually. The global market for other electric personal case products, such as hair dryers, curling irons, hot air brushes and lighted mirrors, was estimated at $2 billion, with annual unit sales growth also at three per cent.

Remington was considered a low-cost producer with capital expenditures of approximately one per cent of revenues. Production was mainly outsourced to low-cost Far East suppliers, particularly in mainland China. Therefore, any synergies between the two companies would be limited to administration, purchasing and distribution, with estimated annual savings of approximately $23 million. Rayovac also planned to use its established international distribution network to expand the presence of Remington products outside North America, which accounted for 64 per cent of that company's sales in 2002. The Varta distribution network in particular would be used to increase the presence of Remington products in Europe. According to Jones,

> In 1996, we were selling our products in 36,000 stores principally the U.S. We are now selling in over a million stores. Remington is selling in 20,000 stores in the U.S. There are a lot more in the U.S. and a lot of retailers around the world that we currently do business with. We think some of the Remington product line is applicable, and we think because our sales organizations are on the ground and have strong relationships with retailers, we could build the Remington brand name globally.
>
> Remington represents a very logical diversification for Rayovac due to its product offerings, brand

Exhibit 6 Rayovac Corporation and Subsidiaries Manufacturing and Distribution Centers 2004

Facility	Function	Ft^2
North America		
Fennimore, Wisconsin[1]	Alkaline Battery Manufacturing	176,000
Portage, Wisconsin[1]	Zinc Air Button Cell and Lithium Coin Cell Battery Manufacturing and Foil Shaver Component Manufacturing	101,000
Dixon, Illinois[2]	Packaging and Distribution of Batteries and Lighting Devices and Distribution of Electric Shaver and Personal Care Devices	576,000
Nashville, Tennessee[2]	Distribution of Batteries, Lighting Devices, Electric Shaver and Personal Care Devices	266,700
Bridgeport, Connecticut[1, 3]	Foil Cutting Systems and Accessories Manufacturing	167,000
Asia		
Ninghai, China[1]	Zinc Carbon and Alkaline Battery Manufacturing & Distribution	274,000
Europe		
Dischingen, Germany[2]	Alkaline Battery Manufacturing	186,000
Breitenbach, France[1]	Zinc Carbon Battery Manufacturing	165,000
Washington, UK[2]	Zinc Air Button Cell Battery Manufacturing & Distribution	63,000
Ellwangen, Germany[2]	Battery Packaging and Distribution	312,000
Latin America		
Guatemala City, Guatemala[1]	Zinc Carbon Battery Manufacturing	105,000
Ipojuca, Brazil[1]	Zinc Carbon Battery Component Manufacturing	100,000
Jaboatoa, Brazil[1]	Zinc Carbon and Alkaline Battery Manufacturing	516,000
Manizales, Colombia[1]	Zinc Carbon Battery Manufacturing	91,000

[1]Facility is owned.
[2]Facility is leased.
[3]Facility closed September 30, 2004.

positioning and customer similarities, and represents the first step of hopefully several other diversification moves over the next few years as we build Rayovac into a much larger, more diversified consumer products company.[14]

Integrating Remington into Rayovac involved closing several Remington manufacturing and distribution facilities, integrating all functional departments of the two companies and absorbing Remington's worldwide operations into Rayovac's existing North American and European operations, thereby creating a global organization and infrastructure. This included merging sales management, marketing and field sales of the two companies into a single North American sales and marketing organization. Similarly, research and development (R&A) would be merged into Rayovac's research facility at the company's headquarters in Wisconsin. From a total of 20 plants in 1996, Rayovac reduced its plants to nine by the end of 2004 while still quadrupling sales and unit volume. The number of suppliers was reduced to 40 per cent of 1996

levels, while average procurement per supplier rose tenfold. Remington also focused on matching the product performance of its two major rivals, Braun and Norelco, in terms of consumer attributes, features, functionality and overall quality.

Following these acquisitions, Rayovac products were sold by 19 of the world's top 20 retailers and were available in over one million stores in 120 countries. Company revenues increased to approximately $1.5 billion, and employees numbered more than 6,500 worldwide. The company also realized annual cost savings of more than three per cent of cost of goods sold.

Lawn and Garden Care, Insecticides and Pet Supplies

In 2005, Rayovac announced its intention to acquire two pet supply companies for more than $2 billion and to change its name to Spectrum Brands. The first of these acquisitions was United Industries Corporation, which Rayovac acquired for $1.5 billion, funded with cash payments of $1 billion, stock issued from Treasury totalling $439 million with acquisition related expenses, and assumed debt totalling $36 million. To fund the acquisition, Rayovac issued $1.03 billion in new long-term debt.[15]

United Industries

United Industries was the leading North American producer of consumer lawn and garden care products, household insect control products and specialty pet supplies. The company had about 24 per cent market share in lawn products, such as fertilizers and pesticides, which it sold under the brand name Spectrum. In insect control (mosquito repellents), it had an 18 per cent market share. Retails sales of household insect control products in the United States was approximately $1 billion in 2003, growing at four per cent a year, with sales likely to increase as public awareness increased of insect-borne diseases such as the West Nile virus.

The U.S. pet supplies market was estimated at $8 billion in 2004, while the European market was about $4 billion. Annual growth in the pet supplies category was between six per cent and eight per cent. With increased incomes, more households were likely to have pets and to treat them as household members, spending increasing amounts on feeding and care. The U.S. pet supplies industry was highly fragmented, with over 500 manufacturers, primarily small firms. The industry was not significantly affected by business cycles. The rise of pet superstores, such as Petco and Pet Smart, provided a competitive opportunity for larger companies, such as Rayovac, with strong distribution channels.

The lawn and garden segment also enjoyed favorable demographic trends. People over age 45 were more likely to pursue gardening compared to the general population, a group whose cohort was increasing as the North American, European and Japanese populations increased in average age. About 80 per cent of U.S. households participated in some form of lawn and garden activity. In 2003, North American industry revenues were approximately $3.2 billion, growing at approximately four per cent annually. Lawn and garden care product sales, as well as insecticide sales, were seasonal. Garden product sales typically fell off when the weather was wet and cold.[16]

The Scotts Miracle-Gro Company was the largest producer of home gardening supplies, with annual net sales of $2 billion. Scotts led the market in almost every product category and every region in which it conducted business. Its major brands included Scotts, Miracle-Gro and Ortho fertilizers and herbicides. It was also the sole distributor in the home gardening segment for Monsanto's Roundup brand herbicides.[17]

Central Garden and Pet Company was a distant third, with $1.2 billion in annual revenues. Central Garden's pet products included pet food, aquarium products, pest control products, cages, pet books and other small animal products. Lawn and garden products included grass seed, wild bird food, herbicides, insecticides and outdoor patio furniture. The company's products were sold under more than 16 different brand names.[18]

United itself had just completed two significant acquisitions in 2004 as it expanded geographically and diversified away from its roots in pesticides. In 2004, it entered the pet supply business with its acquisition of United Pet Group, Inc. (UPG) for $360 million. UPG derived approximately half its sales from aquarium supplies, while the remainder consisted of a variety of supplies for small household pets, excluding pet food. As United was still in the process of integrating UPG when it was acquired by Rayovac, Jones expected its integration to be considerably more complicated than previous acquisitions, taking up to three years to complete (compared to less than one year for Remington and Varta). Nevertheless, Jones reasoned that any company that sold its products through major retail chains, such as Wal-Mart, was a fair acquisition target. He explained,

> As a larger and more significant supplier of consumer products, we believe the postacquisition Rayovac will enjoy stronger relationships with our most important global retailer customers. For instance, United does a substantial business with Wal-Mart, Home Depot and Lowe's, all of whom are important relationships for Rayovac today and all of whom will become even more significant.[19]

Many of the cost savings associated with the integration of United Industries were expected in marketing and distribution, as existing networks increased cross-selling to department store customers. Other savings were expected in administration and purchasing.[20] According to Rayovac Chief Operating Officer Kent Hussey, his company's strong presence in Asia and Europe provided it with more sophisticated sourcing and distribution opportunities than those available to United, which had a limited presence outside of North America. Hussey explained,

> Rayovac operates on a global scale. From a purchasing perspective, significant sourcing capabilities exist in the Far East. I think, with our experience and our infrastructure, we can accelerate dramatically, purchasing leverage and sourcing in the Far East. And then finally, in manufacturing in distribution, we can use our expertise very quickly to help rationalize, eliminate redundancies and improve the efficiency of the overall supply chain. It really is very much operationally driven. There are clearly some administrative

synergies here in IT and finance and administration, but the bulk of this is really operationally focused.[21]

Jones added that Rayovac also planned to use its global network to expand United Industries' distribution beyond North America.

While United is a North American business now, that is not to say it will be only a North American business in the future. Our European teams are actively looking at the categories that United participates in and looking at where we can potentially expand there or in Latin America by taking advantage of obvious distribution opportunities and customer relationships that we have in regions other than North America.[22]

Rayovac further argued that industry consolidation in pet supplies was needed "in order to meet the requirements of global retailers." According to Jones, pet supplies was the fastest growing retail category but one that was highly fragmented. Rayovac intended to increase its participation by further acquiring and consolidating pet supply companies. "We think we can actually accelerate consolidation," he noted. "Pet is going to be a major growth platform and opportunity for further acquisitions." [23]

United's 2004 revenues of around $950 million came mainly from major chains, such as Home Depot, Lowe's, Wal-Mart, Petco and PetSmart. Through increased sales and cost savings, Rayovac anticipated "gross synergies" of

between $70 million and $75 million over the first three years. Boston-based private equity firm Thomas Lee Partners, which had acquired United in 1999, would end up with nearly 25 per cent ownership in Rayovac, as well as two seats on Rayovac's 10-member board of directors. Thomas H. Lee Partners had previously invested in Rayovac in 1995, and helped take it public in 1997. In addition, David Jones, Rayovac chairman and CEO, had served on United's board between 1999 and 2003. THL acquired significant stakes in growth companies, and at the time of the United acquisition, managed over $12 billion of committed capital. Some of its major deals include Warner Music, Houghton Mifflin Co., Snapple Beverage and Fisher Scientific.

Tetra Holdings

Rayovac's interest in pet supplies was further realized with the acquisition of Tetra Holdings of Germany less than two months after the United deal for $555 million (see Exhibit 7), of which $500 million was financed with long-term debt (Table 1 summarizes Rayovac debt as of July 2005, following the United and Tetra acquisitions).[24] Tetra was founded in 1955 by Dr. Ulrich Baensch, the inventor of flaked fish food. The company supplied pet fish and reptile products in 90 countries and had annual sales of $233 million in 2004 (compared to $179 million in 2001). Tetra was purchased by Warner-Lambert in 1974 and was later spun off when Warner

Exhibit 7	Pre and Post 2005 Acquisitions Consolidated Balance Sheets (in $ millions)	
	Period ending Jul 3, 2005	Period ending Sep 30, 2004
Cash	27.0	15.8
Receivables	462.6	289.6
Inventories	470.3	264.7
Prepaid Expenses	99.6	80.4
Total Current Assets	1,059.4	650.5
Net Plant and Equipment	310.7	182.4
Goodwill	1,432.6	320.6
Net intangible Assets	1,169.7	422.1
Other assets	83.7	60.4
Total assets	4,056.1	1,636.0
Accounts Payable	280.2	228.1
Accrued Liabilities	261.2	146.7
Current L-T debt	38.8	23.9
Total Current Liabilities	580.2	398.7
Long-term Debt	2,298.0	806.0
Employee benefits	73.8	69.2
Other Liabilities	259.2	44.6
Shareholders' Equity	845.0	316.0
Total Liabilities and Equity	4,056.1	1,636.0

Table 1   Rayovac Debt (as of July 2005)

Debt	Amount $ Millions	Interest Rate %
Senior Subordinated Notes, due February 1, 2015	700.0	7.4
Senior Subordinated Notes, due October 1, 2013 *(pre-existing)*	350.0	8.5
Term Loan, U.S. dollar, expiring February 6, 2012	653.7	5.3
Term Loan, Canadian dollar, expiring February 6, 2012	71.0	4.7
Term Loan, Euro expiring February 6, 2012	138.0	4.7
Term Loan, Euro Tranche B, expiring February 6, 2012	340.4	4.4
Revolving Credit Facility, expiring February 6, 2011	28.3	7.3
Euro Revolving Credit Facility, expiring February 6, 2011	3.6	4.4

Lambert was acquired by Pfizer in 2000, and Pfizer decided to shed "poorer performing consumer brands."[25] Jones justified his company's latest acquisition by noting,

> The combination of Tetra with United Pet Group means Rayovac will become the world's largest manufacturer of pet supplies, a position with which we can leverage our company's worldwide operations.

Commenting on the Tetra acquisition, Kent Hussey remarked,

> Tetra is a globally recognized brand name in the pet supplies category, one that consumers know and trust. It gives us entry into the pet supplies category literally around the world, and it's a brand that virtually every pet supply retailer considers a must-have brand in terms of consumer loyalty. If the retailer doesn't have that product on the shelf, he is missing significant sales opportunities. That makes Tetra a very attractive asset for us."[26]

Throughout its history, Rayovac had been primarily a battery company. After the Tetra and United acquisitions,

for the first time in its history, Rayovac's battery division accounted for only slightly more than a third of total sales, significantly less than the combined sales for lawn, garden and pet care products (see Table 2 and Exhibit 8). Furthermore, with the United and Tetra acquisitions, more than a third of total sales came from international sources. Tetra, for example, obtained 40 per cent of its sales from Europe, 40 per cent from the United States and 20 per cent from Japan. Correspondingly, the company incurred a third of its total operating expenses in foreign currencies.

Investment analyst Alyce Lomax described Rayovac's move into pet supplies as "diworseification,"[27] a term that described "companies that lose their primary focus in their quest to jumpstart growth through diversification."[28] Even so, most analysts hailed the deal, while investors sent the company's stock up nearly 10 per cent immediately following the announcement. Overall, the company's stock had risen from about $15 to around $45 in the two years since its acquisition of Remington (see Exhibit 9).

Table 2   Rayovac: Percentage of Sales from Major Product Lines

% of Sales	October 2004	June 2005
Batteries	65	35
Shaving	21	11
Personal care	8	5
Lighting	6	3
Pet Supplies		20
Lawn & Garden		20
Household Insecticides		6

Exhibit 8   Rayovac And Its Competitors, Percentage of Market Share by Major Product Line (as of 2005)

Brand	Batteries			U.S. Shaving and Grooming	U.S. Lawn and Garden	U.S. Household Insecticide	U.S. Pet Supplies
	U.S.	L.A	Europe				
Duracell	37	9	28	24 (Braun)			
Energizer	26	19	22				
Rayovac/ Spectrum Brands	21	41	26 (Varta)	29 (Remington)	24	18	7
Panasonic		20					
Norelco				43			
Scotts					49		
Central Garden					8		8
S C Johnson						42	

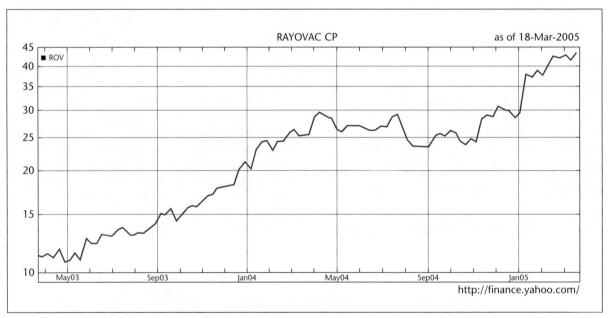

Exhibit 9   Rayovac Corporation Stock Chart

Note: The chart includes data up to and including the announced acquisition of Tetra Holdings on March 15, 2005.

End Notes

1. This case has been written on the basis of published sources only. Consequently, the interpretation and perspectives presented in this case are not necessarily those of Rayovac Corporation or any of its employees.
2. Rayovac Buys Pet Supplies Company, *Reuters*, March 15, 2005.
3. Portions adapted from Rayovac Corporation, Prospectus Supplement, June 20, 2001.

4. "Rayovac to Acquire Remington Products," Company Conference Call, *Fair Disclosure Wire*, August 22, 2003.
5. Transcript "In The Game," *CNNfn*, March 9, 1999.
6. SunTrust Robinson Humphrey Conference, Interview with Kent Hussey, Rayovac Corporation, *Wall Street Transcript*, April 2005.
7. The acquisition did not include Microlite, SA, a Brazilian joint venture that Rayovac acquired separately in 2004. It also excluded Varta's automotive and micro-power divisions.
8. "Rayovac Gains Worldwide Rights to Brand Name, " *Atlanta Business Chronicle*, June 1, 2004.
9. Brazil represented 30 per cent of total Latin American market for consumer goods.
10. "Event Brief of Q1 2005 Rayovac Earnings, " Conference Call, *Fair Disclosure Wire*, January 25, 2005.
11. "Rayovac to Acquire 85% of Ningbo Baowang China Battery Company, " *PR Newswire*, January 19, 2004.
12. Ibid.
13. The purchase price represented 6.9 times Remington's 2002 EBITDA of $47 million.
14. "Rayovac to Acquire Remington Products, " Company Conference Call, *Fair Disclosure Wire*, August 22, 2003.
15. "Rayovac Taps BofA, Citigroup For Add-On To Back Tetra Buy, " *Bank Loan Report*, April 4, 2005.
16. Seasonality also affected Rayovac's other products, such as batteries and electric shavers, sales of which surged during the holiday season (quarter ending December 31).
17. Background information on Scotts Miracle-Gro Company was adapted from the company's investor relations website, *investor.scotts.com*, August 30, 2005.
18. Background information on Central Garden and Pet Company was adapted from the company's investor relations website, *www.centralgardenandpet.com*, August 30, 2005.
19. "Rayovac Acquisition Update," *Fair Disclosure Wire*, January 4, 2005.
20. Rayovac anticipated $75 million in cost savings during the first three years.
21. "Rayovac Acquisition Update," *Fair Disclosure Wire*, January 4, 2005.
22. Ibid.
23. Ibid.
24. "Rayovac Taps BofA, Citigroup For Add-On To Back Tetra Buy," *Bank Loan Report*, April 4, 2005.
25. "Tetra Under The Hammer?" *UK Pets*, December 17, 2001.
26. Rayovac Corporation, *The Wall Street Transcript*, April 2005.
27. "Will Pets Juice Rayovac?" *Motley Fool*, March 16, 2005.
28. "Diworseification" was first coined by mutual fund manager Peter Lynch in his book "One Up On Wall Street : How To Use What You Already Know To Make Money In The Market" (Simon & Schuster; 2000).

Case 3–5: Aegis Analytical Corporation's Strategic Alliances*

Paul Olk

Joan Winn

—*University of Denver*

As Gretchen Jahn, cofounder and executive vice president of Corporate Development of Aegis Analytical Corporation, looked over the financial statements for the first half of 2003, she tried to muster the enthusiasm she had had the previous spring when Aegis entered into alliances with two leading pharmaceutical manufacturing distributors. Jahn had expected that the increased visibility in the market would buoy Aegis's lagging sales. Meanwhile, Justin Neway, cofounder of the company, carefully prepared a presentation to potential investors, as they both knew that this round of funding was needed to support Aegis's growth plan and achieve positive cash flow in late 2004.

Gretchen L. Jahn and Justin O. Neway formed Aegis Analytical Corporation in 1995 to provide process manufacturing software and consulting services to pharmaceutical and biotech manufacturers. The product, called "Discoverant," helped managers see what was happening during the manufacturing process. It allowed users to connect to multiple databases simultaneously—including electronic data formats and manual inputs taken from paper records—and assemble the data. The user could then develop models to evaluate the performance of specific manufacturing processes. The product greatly reduced the time and effort needed to identify problems in a company's manufacturing processes.

In March 2002, Aegis formed an alliance with Honeywell POMS that made POMS a reseller of the Aegis Discoverant product. As an add-on product to the POMS software that monitored manufacturing plant activities, Honeywell agreed to sell the product under the name "POMS Explorer, powered by Aegis." Jahn and Neway believed that combining the products would enhance the sales of each and that Honeywell's name recognition in the pharmaceutical market would help Aegis gain credibility and visibility.

Later that spring, Aegis entered into an agreement with Rockwell Automation to market Aegis's Discoverant with Rockwell's ProPack Data manufacturing software, designed to help companies monitor production operations. Again, because a customer could use the ProPack Data system with Discoverant, both companies hoped the collaboration would increase the sales of each product.

Neither relationship had yet produced a single sale, and Aegis began questioning the wisdom of this strategy. Strategic alliances were integral to the company's sales efforts, and after Jahn reflected upon the disappointments of the past year, she and Neway debated what actions the much smaller Aegis should take to improve these alliances with the larger companies.

History of Aegis Analytical

In 1995, Jahn and Neway cofounded Aegis Analytical Corporation in Lafayette, Colorado. Jahn had 20 years of experience in information technology and integrated resources management prior to starting Aegis. She had recently sold her software consulting company and was working as an independent information technology and management consultant. Neway, a biochemist, had 20 years of experience in pharmaceutical and biotechnology manufacturing. He had moved to Colorado from California in 1990 and taken a job as director of manufacturing for Somatogen, a biotech research company. (Exhibit 1 shows management team profiles.) Both had worked closely with the regulatory, quality-control, and operational issues that plagued pharmaceutical manufacturing processes.

*The authors wish to thank Gretchen Jahn, Justin Neway, and the employees of the Aegis Analytical Corporation for their cooperation in the preparation of this case. The authors also thank Chooch Jewel and Brian Swenson for research assistance and insights. This case is intended to stimulate class discussion rather than to illustrate the effective or ineffective handling of a managerial situation. All events and individuals in this case are real.

Exhibit 1   Aegis Management Team, 2003

Gretchen L. Jahn, cofounder, executive vice president, Corporate Development, has more than 20 years' experience in IT. Ms. Jahn most recently led the turnaround of the software development of a CEO-less venture-backed startup company. Previously, Ms. Jahn was a principal and vice president at Mile-High Information Services, a consulting, software development, and product sales company. She has prior experience as a data processing manager and a software specialist for Digital Equipment Corporation. Ms. Jahn received her BA in 1973 from Lawrence University and her MA in 1975 from the University of Colorado.

Justin O. Neway, PhD, cofounder, executive vice president, and chief science officer, has more than 19 years' experience in pharmaceutical and biotechnology manufacturing and in software marketing and applications. Prior to joining Aegis, Dr. Neway was director of fermentation R&D at Somatogen, a biotechnology manufacturer. He was the project leader for several technical teams, one of which developed a demonstration system for data analysis and visualization of batch process information. Dr. Neway received his BSc (microbiology, 1975) and MSc (biochemistry, 1977) from the University of Calgary and his PhD in biochemistry from the University of Illinois in 1982.

John M. Darcy, president and CEO, has more than 25 years in proven management and leadership in *Fortune* 50 companies, turnarounds, and startups. Mr. Darcy has been an advisor to Aegis and is providing significant marketing assistance for the Discoverant product launch as director of marketing. Most recently he built three separate startup companies in the food, agricultural chemicals, and Web imaging businesses. Prior to this, Mr. Darcy was

president and chief operating officer at Avis Enterprises, a $2 billion private investment company with majority equity positions in several industries including automobile rentals and dealerships and has held management positions at Carnation/Nestlé and Pillsbury. Mr. Darcy received his BA in 1967 and his MA in 1969 from the University of California, Los Angeles.

Geri L. Studebaker, vice president, Marketing, has more than 12 years of experience in software marketing and applications. Prior to Aegis, Ms. Studebaker was senior director of worldwide marketing for Webb Interactive, an e-business software provider for small to medium-sized businesses. There she successfully managed overall product redesign and company positioning efforts. Prior to Webb, Ms. Studebaker held several positions with JD Edwards, the most recent being senior marketing manager.

Cheryl M. Boeckman, vice president, Sales, has more than 17 years of experience in executive-level sales. Ms. Boeckman was vice president of sales with SoftBrands Manufacturing/Fourth Shift, where she managed a team selling enterprise resource planning and supply chain management software to tier-one through tier-three manufacturing companies focusing on multiple industries including medical device and pharmaceuticals.

Steve C. Sills, director, Business Development, has more than 10 years of experience in software marketing and business development. Mr. Sills joins Aegis with a broad range of experience in the software industry. Prior to joining Aegis, he was a business development manager with Vitria Technology, a leading enterprise application integration (EAI) vendor.

Finding Development Partners

Jahn, a self-described "serial entrepreneur," had started two companies before Aegis. She had experience with software development and implementation and understood the importance of manufacturing efficiencies and process improvements in getting drugs through the regulatory process. Neway's experiences in biotech and pharmaceutical manufacturing gave him an in-depth understanding of the difficulties in accessing data from a variety of sources and across many different products and then putting them into a unified format. Originally, Jahn and Neway had hoped to use Somatogen's name as a launching pad for their product. However, when Somatogen began negotiations for its eventual sale to the pharmaceutical company Baxter, they recognized they would need to find an alternative. Neway focused his efforts on courting potential development partners. Jahn recalled,

> We spent several years working out of our respective basements, using our own funds to make invited

> technical presentations. We made 23 presentations in the United States and Europe to major pharmaceutical companies to demonstrate our product and to get feedback to improve the product and also to see if we could find someone who would be an initial development partner. Eventually Aventis gave us a contract worth $1.3 million to jointly develop our software product with them. This was in 1999. In May and July of 1999, we received our first funding—seed investments of $400,000 and $500,000—from angel investors and Sandlot Capital. We were three people at that time.

> So we built this first version and we got office space and then graduated to other office space once we were all sitting on top of each other. And we hired people and subcontracted all kinds of nifty stuff and then we went out for the next round of funding. We closed on that in 2000—right around 41/2 million—from GlaxoSmithKline's investment arm, SR One, and Aventis's investment arm, Future Capital, which is in Frankfurt, Germany, as well as Viscardi Ventures, a financial investment firm in Munich, Germany.

Growing the Organization

Aegis had been successful in getting enough financing to develop and test its manufacturing software product and set up a team of applications and technical specialists, a management team, and an advisory board of industry and regulatory experts. It had organized research seminars and conferences with leaders in biotech research and application and successfully sold and implemented its first product in July 2000. Jahn continued,

> Our next funding in 2001 just about destroyed me. We brought in $14.5 million in October 2001, after the bubble had burst. What's funny is that Aegis is not a dot-com. So during the boom we were discounted because we weren't a dot-com. After the boom, we were discounted because every software company was. The Friday before September 11 (2001), I turned down $4 million because our valuation was so low. Then September 11th happened. We were supposed to have a board meeting on the 14th over in Munich, which we ended up having over the phone, and I said, "Look guys, we don't know what is going to happen ... we just better get through this." We were one of the few people whose funding got bigger. Everybody else that I talked to that was raising money at that time had their investors dry up and go away.

By 2002, the company had grown to 35 employees. Aegis had entered into sales agreements with eight corporate customers and had 25 sales in the pipeline by the end of that year. Exhibit 2 reports Aegis's financial performance over the previous several years. Also in 2002, Jahn hired John M. Darcy, former Avis CEO, as president and CEO to reposition the company with a sales and marketing focus rather than a development focus. Jahn moved into a corporate development role to pursue new markets for the product and develop alliances and market awareness. Because of its small size, Aegis was able to share information within the organization quickly and did not need to spend a lot of time making decisions. Aegis also prided itself on having an organization that emphasized precision in its work as well as honesty and integrity when dealing with others. Management believed that understanding and concern for customers would be a key to Aegis's success.

The Discoverant Product

Aegis positioned Discoverant as a manufacturing performance management software system that fulfilled three critical requirements: practical data access, useful data analysis, and ability to communicate results to nonexperts.

Aegis's Discoverant enabled manufacturing employees and managers to analyze specific manufacturing processes that crossed database boundaries. Exhibit 3 shows the relationship of Discoverant to disparate data sources and to analysis and results reporting. The software did not require that every piece of corporate data be stored and controlled in a single location. In developing Discoverant, Aegis's developers had incorporated existing software engines, both as a cost savings and implementation aid, building only those parts of the product that were needed to fill the gap and integrate the various systems. Jahn and Neway explained that companies without Aegis's product would have to go through a lot of time and effort to get the same information. Without Discoverant, it was common for a company's information technology (IT) department to spend two to four weeks to get appropriate data from multiple systems. After company employees collected the data, it would take them another week to interpret and analyze the data. Discoverant took minutes to perform the same steps. The cost savings became significant when a company that manufactured a defective product or ran invalid experiments searched for the errors in the manufacturing process.

The company emphasized Discoverant's ability to "easily access millions of data values from diverse sources, drill down on any operation, make informed proactive decisions by identifying critical process parameters, and enable manufacturing enterprise compliance strategies." A simple point-and-click feature allowed the user to select the relevant data and produce desired statistical analyses, charts, or graphs. A major advantage was the fact that the person running the analyses and reports did not have to have a programming background. Aegis would help the company install the system and develop the data models. Aegis's implementation process required staff from the client company to be active participants. Aegis provided a two-day user-training session for its customers so that they understood the product's basic functions and tools and how to use it to evaluate the various manufacturing systems. This included a basic course on statistics so nonstatisticians could use the software. Postimplementation customer support was provided via phone, fax, e-mail, and Internet. Aegis wanted to make sure that everyone in the company who used the software had a complete understanding of Discoverant.

Aegis also offered additional consulting services, including follow-up, validation, and advanced technical and user training. These services were offered to companies who needed more assistance or wanted additional advice for improving their manufacturing systems.

Exhibit 2   Five-Year Financial Performance, 1998–2003[a]

Income Statement Summaries

Calendar Year Ending:	1998	1999	2000	2001	2002	2003 Jan–June	Cumulative 1998–2003
Revenues	$8,053	$814,001	$670,754	$562,741	$2,513,267	$352,847	$4,921,663
Operating Expenses	152,189	1,239,510	3,417,575	5,128,508	7,779,047	3,446,349	21,163,178
Net Operating Income	(144,136)	(425,509)	(2,746,821)	(4,565,767)	(5,265,780)	(3,093,502)	(16,241,515)

Consolidated Balance Sheet Summaries (at December 31)

	1998	1999	2000	2001	2002
ASSETS					
Current Assets					
Cash Equivalent	$ 2,732	$ 193,481	$1,393,732	$12,268,918	$ 6,210,001
Accounts Receivable	3,774	248,267	397,581	158,381	364,613
Other Current Assets		25,151	122,732	146,494	406,589
Total Current Assets	6,506	466,899	1,914,045	12,573,793	6,981,203
Long-Term Assets					
Furniture and Equipment (net)[b]	15,103	102,960	340,679	523,743	378,162
Capitalized Lease and Improvements	182,468	38,261	40,061	40,061	
Other Assets (Net)[c]	1,632	227,524	533,581	661,249	297,832
Total Long-Term Assets	16,735	512,952	912,521	1,225,053	716,055
Total Assets	23,241	979,851	2,826,566	13,798,846	7,697,258
LIABILITIES AND EQUITY					
Liabilities					
Accounts Payable	89,941	360,716	255,024	491,971	572,740
Deferred Revenue			291,700	1,580,040	799,000
Capitalized Lease obligation	4,808	173,760	225,318	252,837	111,753
Total Liabilities	94,749	534,476	772,042	2,324,848	1,483,493
Equity					
Stock and Paid-In Capital	104,313	1,053,474	5,495,757	20,498,977	28,095,497
Retained Earnings	(38,840)	(183,017)	(694,412)	(4,459,213)	(16,615,952)
Net Income	(136,981)	(425,509)	(2,746,821)	(4,565,767)	(5,265,780)
Total Equity	(71,508)	444,948	2,054,524	11,473,997	6,213,765
Total Liabilities and Equity	$ 23,241	$ 979,424	$2,826,566	$13,798,845	$ 7,697,258

[a] Some figures may be disguised.
[b] Furniture and Equipment is net of depreciation.
[c] Other Assets includes trademarks and patent costs, capitalized software development costs, and Web site development.

Source: Aegis Analytical Corporation documents, 2003.

Sales Efforts

The keys to selling such a sophisticated product were having a simple way to communicate the benefits of the product, a knowledgeable sales force, and skilled consultants to implement the software for the client. Neway understood that his audience—research scientists who used mathematics and statistics but were not programmers themselves—needed an image of the numeric processes. He worked to put together a visual representation that showed the manufacturing data in a three-dimensional image. This eventually became Aegis's "visual process signature" used for both sales presentations and actual data tracking.

To help convey the Discoverant product, Aegis developed a short video clip based on a case study. Aegis management made the video available to potential customers via a CD-ROM and posted it on the company's Web site. The scenario depicted a manager preparing for a meeting the next day where she would need to explain to her superiors why there were batch failures in a drug's tablet dissolution rate. Even though she had all the data she had requested on the manufacturing processes, she did not have weeks to

Exhibit 3   The Discoverant Connectivity Link Between Disparate Data Sources and Reports

Source: Adapted from Aegis material.

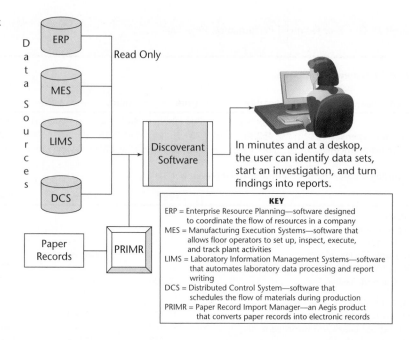

KEY

ERP = Enterprise Resource Planning—software designed to coordinate the flow of resources in a company

MES = Manufacturing Execution Systems—software that allows floor operators to set up, inspect, execute, and track plant activities

LIMS = Laboratory Information Management Systems—software that automates laboratory data processing and report writing

DCS = Distributed Control System—software that schedules the flow of materials during production

PRIMR = Paper Record Import Manager—an Aegis product that converts paper records into electronic records

analyze the data and expected that she would have to spend more time collecting additional data. What she needed was immediate access to all of the company's manufacturing data and a program that would help with the analysis. A colleague introduces her to Discoverant. With this program, she has direct access to the raw data stored in the various databases (e.g., Laboratory Information Management Systems [LIMS], enterprise resource planning [ERP]) and can begin analyzing the manufacturing conditions associated with the batch failures. Discoverant revealed that the failures appeared to be related to the drying process—particularly, to lower dryer air temperature. Through Discoverant's statistical tools, she is able to analyze the relationship and reveal that it is highly significant. Discoverant's reporting tools—including the visual process signature—then enable her to illustrate the relationship between temperature variations and batch variations. Within minutes she has her answer and feels very prepared for the next day's meeting.

Beyond these promotional efforts, Aegis set up sales teams to provide long-term consultative relationships that would help customize the product for each customer. A sales account manager led a specialized team of applications and technical specialists organized for each sales and market effort and was responsible for the relationship with each customer. Full installation and implementation of the product was expected to take between six and nine months. The standard purchase cycle for enterprise software within the pharmaceutical industry started with an evaluation in one facility or production line followed by expansion to other facilities on a global scale. A contract

often was negotiated for the full expansion up front in the purchase process. Specific sites were identified and a timeline established. This enabled Aegis to understand the total potential value of a customer at the time of initial phase.

The sales cycle itself varied from seven months to more than two years. The delay was due to the multiple sales cycles involved in selling the product. In its initial efforts, Aegis sales teams quickly found that there were really three selling cycles, each requiring multiple visits. Aegis thought it would only have to make the first sale, to the individuals in the company who would actually use the product. The sales team typically started with the head of manufacturing but also spoke with the head of quality and process scientists. Although this effort often took from three to nine months, the product was generally well received, particularly by the IT departments, because it eliminated their having to write numerous queries. After getting commitment by these users, however, Aegis discovered two more cycles. First, Aegis had to help convince upper management to purchase the software. Aegis found that upper management would spend as much time conducting due diligence on the decision to spend an estimated $0.5 to $1.5 million on Discoverant as they would on a $15 million software installation. This cycle typically took between three months and a year. After getting approval from upper management, Aegis would then have to work with the company's purchasing and legal department to complete the sale, which could take another one to six months. This lengthy three-tier sales cycle process increased the amount of time and effort required by Aegis's sales team.

Aegis planned to set up direct sales teams in key geographic areas where there were high concentrations of potential customers. Aegis had already set up a team in Frankfurt, Germany, to provide sales and marketing support for the European market. In geographic areas of lower customer concentration, Aegis planned to use sales agents and alliances to leverage the direct sales force and to provide local coverage and first-line support. Strategic partners would help expand sales and implementation capabilities.

Demand for Manufacturing Process Software in the Pharmaceutical Industry

To succeed in a global context, pharmaceutical companies continually needed to reduce costs while increasing efficiency, responsiveness, and customer satisfaction. Improving profitability in the manufacturing process depended on reducing the cost of raw materials, energy, and capital and on increasing the yield from their assets. Profitability also depended upon demonstrating that they could meet quality standards in producing the drug. To meet such regulations, manufacturers made significant investments in software systems to collect information that revealed where, if any, manufacturing problems existed and, after correcting the problems, demonstrated compliance to the regulators. Initially, production processes were automated through distributed control systems (DCS) that used hardware, software, and industrial instruments to measure, record, and automatically control process variables. More recently, process manufacturers had begun to automate key business processes by implementing ERP and manufacturing execution system (MES) software solutions to enhance the flow of business information across the enterprise, as well as other software programs such as LIMS (Exhibit 3).

The implementation of each of these systems led to an accumulation of large amounts of raw data that recorded in detail the performance of each manufacturing process at full commercial scale over extended periods of time. The proliferation of software products resulted in companies having mountains of data scattered across numerous disparate data sources. Collectively, these held a great deal of information about how to improve manufacturing performance. Prior to 2000, there was no simple way to access all the data and extract the big picture about the manufacturing process. Aegis wanted to become the recognized leader in process manufacturing technology by providing software that could be used to integrate all major functions and provide system-wide information.

The demand for Aegis's product was not driven solely by pharmaceutical companies' interest in reducing costs. Increasing pressure from consumer groups and the federal government's Food and Drug Administration (FDA) led Aegis to believe that this market would be highly receptive to any product that shortened and improved the product-to-market cycle time. In 2002 alone, the FDA had issued 755 warning letters about product quality—an increase of more than 40 percent from 1998. The FDA had also increased the number and severity of penalties levied against pharmaceutical manufacturers, including criminal convictions and fines as high as $500 million.

Discoverant had no direct competitors. Other companies had products that performed parts of what Discoverant did, but no one besides Aegis had a product that did it all. In 2003, there were several commercial vendors of general statistical and visualization tools such as Mathsoft, Statistica, MatLab, IMSL, SAS, Visual Numerics, and AVS. These tools permitted the analysis of already collected data but did not help in accessing the various databases. Other software companies, such as Aspen Technology, OSI, and Lighthammer, provided process manufacturing software that captured shop floor data for process control and data management, but typically the data had to be inside a single database. These products could not combine data from dissimilar databases. Finally, Spotfire and Aspen Technology had recently announced an alliance to develop data analysis capabilities for manufacturing systems, but the product was not yet available. Although some large pharmaceutical and food production companies had custom in-house systems developed by internal IT departments or third-party consultants, most companies' systems were limited in use and required a team of experts to interpret the disparate data that the systems generated. Someone who was not a programmer could use Discoverant.

Aegis had identified a number of pharmaceutical manufacturing companies that would benefit by an integrated manufacturing information system. Though many pharmaceutical manufacturing companies in 2002 were quite small, with annual revenues of less than $250 million, targeting only those pharmaceutical companies with annual revenues of more than $250 million would give Aegis access to a potential market of $604 million in license, service, and maintenance fees. Pharmaceutical manufacturers with annual revenues in excess of $1 billion had the largest IT budget and were therefore most likely to implement manufacturing enterprise software solutions like Discoverant. Importantly, companies of this size accounted for approximately 77 percent, or $464 million, of the total potential market for Aegis's products (Exhibit 4).

Exhibit 4	Market Projections for 2003

(dollar values are in thousands)

Annual Revenues	Number of Companies	Mfg. Sites	Total Cells	Licenses $250K	Services at 50%	Maint. at 15%	TOTAL VALUE
$1B+	52	225	1,125	281,250	140,065	42,188	$464,063
$500M–$1B	41	62	186	46,500	23,350	6,975	76,225
$250M–$500M	71	77	154	38,500	19,250	5,775	63,225
Opportunity	164	364	1,465	$366,250	$183,125	$54,938	$604,313

Note: The standard purchase cycle for enterprise software within the pharmaceutical industry starts with an evaluation in one facility or production line followed by expansion to other facilities on a global scale. A contract often is negotiated for the full expansion up front in the purchase process. Specific sites are identified and a timeline established. Therefore, Aegis understands the total potential value of a customer at the time of initial phase. Even under present (sluggish) market conditions, Aegis believed that sales to new pharma accounts could be expected to result in large total sales in the same accounts in the following 18 to 24 months as the initial projects showed good results and decisions were made to proceed with wider deployments.

Source: Aegis Analytical Corporation documents, 2003.

Aegis's Alliance Strategy

Jahn and Neway understood the power of brand recognition and company reputation in reaching their target market. They developed research partnerships with top-tier pharmaceutical manufacturing companies such as Merck, Genentech, and Aventis and invited representatives from Abbott, Amgen, Aventis, Merck, Novartis, GlaxoSmithKline, Eli Lilly, Roche, and Wyeth to join discussions at Aegis-hosted conferences in Colorado. Contacts at the University of Newcastle and University College London, two of the top universities in the world known for software technology applicable to manufacturing processes, joined Aegis's Scientific Advisory Board. These relationships fostered an exchange of technical information and ideas and gave Aegis professional connections and sales leads.

In their initial efforts to sell Discoverant, Neway and a small team of sales and technical people made direct calls to large pharmaceutical and biotech manufacturers. Believing that alliances with well-known service providers would give them credibility and visibility in the marketplace and also permit them to reach more companies than they could alone, they focused Aegis's growth strategy on finding partners. Aegis's first partners were client-investors, pharmaceutical companies like Merck and GlaxoSmithKline in California and Hoechst Marion Roussel in Kansas City. Having big company names as successful users of Aegis's Discoverant product provided important testimonials for Discoverant's features. This networking helped form the research and technical partnerships that Aegis used to get its first contracts and secure venture funding.

The focus in 2002 was on creating alliances that would enhance sales. Although Aegis had made some sales of Discoverant, as top managers began to understand that the three-part sales process was the norm, they realized they did not have enough internal resources. Their sales staff could continue to pursue direct sales, but sales might benefit from partners who could help persuade top management to purchase Discoverant. These alliances were considered an integral part of the sales force. In choosing sales partners, then, Aegis sought out companies that had complementary products and would agree to promote the Discoverant brand using the Aegis name to distinguish it from perceived competition. While it had started screening potential candidates, in 2002, Aegis was approached by two companies that seemed to be the best candidates with which to partner. In that year, Aegis formed a relationship with Honeywell POMS and another with Rockwell Automation.

Honeywell POMS Alliance

In 1999, Honeywell acquired the POMS Corporation, a leader in providing manufacturing execution systems (MES) for the pharmaceutical as well as for other industries. POMS had sold more than 70 systems to nine of the top 10 pharmaceutical companies in the world. POMS employed 150 people and was headquartered in Herndon, Virginia. Prior to the acquisition, POMS was strictly a reseller of software and, according to an Aegis manager, had a spotty record of implementing and supporting its software offerings.

On March 13, 2002, Aegis formed an alliance with Honeywell POMS that made it a reseller of the Aegis Discoverant product in combination with POMS's manufacturing system. Honeywell approached Aegis after a potential customer asked if POMS was compatible with Discoverant. This interest helped Aegis during negotiations. Although Honeywell initially requested an exclusive relationship, Aegis thought that it was not in the company's best interests. Eventually the two sides did come to an agreement that Aegis's product would be packaged and resold under the name "POMS Explorer, powered by Aegis." According to Chris Lyden, vice president and general manager of Honeywell's Industry Solutions Business for Chemicals, Life Sciences, and Consumer Goods,

> By combining Aegis's Discoverant with our the flagship POMS MES product, we will be able to provide added benefits to our customers and further enhance the way they manage their manufacturing systems. Honeywell's new POMS Explorer module, powered by Aegis, can save significant cost for our customers by reducing batch failures, stabilizing the manufacturing operations, and getting products to market faster.

Both companies recognized the mutual benefits from the alliance. Aegis believed this alliance was a significant step toward gaining both credibility and visibility within the Life Sciences market. With Honeywell, Aegis aligned itself with an organization that had $24 billion in sales, more than 120,000 employees, and operations in 95 countries throughout the world.

Aegis was banking on POMS's name recognition and reputation to build market awareness for Aegis and Discoverant. Honeywell POMS, located in the Automation and Control Solutions division, one of four major strategic business units in Honeywell (besides Aerospace, Specialty Materials and Transportation, and Power Systems), viewed Discoverant as an additional software offering that would expand the capability of its MES product. The Aegis software provided POMS customers with the software needed to visually see and analyze the manufacturing data. To help reach these expectations, the two companies put together a relatively standard contract that included the following:

■ Honeywell POMS had a nonexclusive, nontransferable, non-sublicensable license to resell Aegis's product.

■ The agreement would initially run for two years with an additional one-year automatic renewal, unless either party wished to terminate the agreement at least 90 days before the end of the two-year period.

■ Aegis and Honeywell POMS agreed to appoint one sales professional to act as the primary representative to the other. The agreement specified that the representatives shall meet in person at least once per calendar quarter to discuss the status of the sales effort and other questions about selling the software. These meetings will alternate between Aegis's and Honeywell

POMS's facilities, unless both parties agree to talk telephonically or at another location.

■ Aegis would provide training sessions for Honeywell POMS sales personnel within 90 days of the start date of the contract.

■ Honeywell POMS was responsible for the point-of-contact sales support for users. If Honeywell POMS was not able to solve the problem, it would contact Aegis for support. Provisions were provided for the time by which Aegis had to respond.

■ The parties agreed to prepare mutually agreed press releases to promote the relationship. They also agreed to collaborate on marketing events, on distributing promotional materials, and on promotion of the other's product on their Web sites.

■ Honeywell POMS would receive a discount on the licensing fees Aegis charged. This was a reduced price on what Aegis would charge Honeywell POMS to resell Discoverant. The more sales Honeywell POMS recorded, the greater the discount.

■ Termination clauses permitted each party to end the relationship if the other went out of business or if there was a breach of any provisions within the agreement.

In considering the agreement, Jahn acknowledged that it had provisions for Honeywell to "make sure that their sales reps would get enough of a commission so that they would be motivated to sell it and also that our sales reps would not be disadvantaged by selling through our partner instead of selling direct.... There are lots of ways of arranging [sales incentives plans] and we had lots of conversation with Honeywell to determine what would work best in this particular environment." Aegis's VP of sales also was involved in making sure both sides were aware of the selling message and pricing structures and were present at the training sessions. He had numerous face-to-face meetings with his Honeywell counterparts to discuss the product. They focused on building a relationship first and did that successfully. Further, the Honeywell relationships benefited from Jahn having personal contact with Honeywell's director of business development.

However, from her experience in larger companies, Jahn was concerned about Honeywell's commitment to promoting the Discoverant product, and the VP of sales spent much of his time convincing his counterparts of the value of this add-on product. "For Honeywell, we're a line item in their sales catalogue," Jahn later observed. "When the market fell out, their sales reps were concentrating on how to get people to buy their own products, much less other things in the catalogue."

Rockwell Automation Agreement

Rockwell Automation purchased ProPack Data in April 2002. ProPack Data, a German company established in 1984, was a market leader of MES and electronic batch record systems (EBRS) for the pharmaceutical and other regulated industries. The company employed 230 people and became a part of Rockwell's Process Solutions business. Rockwell Automation had revenues of $4.3 billion, employed 23,000 individuals, and had operations in 80 different countries.

Aegis had been approached by ProPack—and had already begun negotiations with them—before the Rockwell acquisition. The ProPack Data manufacturing execution system PMX was designed to help customers reduce operating costs, shorten cycle times, and improve product quality in production operations. The software solution provided by Aegis provided connectivity and visibility to the manufacturing processes that PMX was managing.

As with the Honeywell alliance, the relationship with ProPack was designed to make Aegis visible to much larger organizations. The addition of Rockwell into the ProPack equation was a double-edged sword for Aegis's managemers. On one hand, they were excited by the large size of Rockwell and the possibility to leverage that size to their advantage. However, Jahn was concerned that those advantages might be offset by increased bureaucracy and added delays.

Aegis and ProPack Data set up a sales and marketing agreement for lead generation that was simpler than the Honeywell POMS agreement. If a company's referral led to a sale for the partner, the company would receive a finder's fee. The agreement's primary function was to increase access to new sales territory. Aegis hoped to increase the number of sales leads, thus generating a higher number of sales opportunities. According to Bernhard Thurnbauer, senior vice president of strategic marketing of ProPack Data,

> We are excited about this agreement with Aegis. We feel that this [arrangement] will give ProPack Data a significant edge in providing a true value added solution. Aegis's Discoverant Manufacturing Informatics system meets the need of leading pharmaceutical manufacturers to analyze and visualize all their data in a multitude of disparate sources. Using Discoverant, manufacturers can find and control the key process drivers across their entire manufacturing processes, all the way from raw materials to final product.

Each company intended to use the partner's strengths to build interest in its own products and services and committed its sales representatives to prospect for the partner. Once opportunities were identified, various strategies would be employed to close the sale. The sales opportunity itself would dictate how the two companies would work together and who would take the dominant role in the sales process. Each sale would be governed by a separate agreement, which would include a finder's fee for the partner that developed the sale. Additional highlights of the agreement included:

- The agreement committed both Aegis and Propack Data to explore mutually beneficial ways in which they could complement one another's sales and marketing activities.
- Both Aegis and Propack Data agreed this was an important relationship and would seek to communicate ideas for improving the relationship.
- Each party would assign a person to act as the primary liaison to the other party.
- Each party would independently market its respective products and services, but the two companies would prepare mutually agreed press releases to promote the relationship, provide marketing and sales support to each other, and spread the word about the relationship within their respective organizations.
- The liaisons were to attend quarterly meetings to discuss comarketing of their products and customer leads. The location of the meetings would alternate between Aegis and Propack Data facilities.
- Unless there was a sale, there would be no commissions or other type of remuneration owed by one party to the other.
- Upon request, each party agreed to provide on-site product training to the other party's employees up to once a year.
- A separate agreement would be written up when both parties decided to pursue jointly a product installation and implementation.
- The agreement could be terminated at any time without cause with 90 days' written notification.

Effectiveness of the Partnerships

When, by 2003, neither the Honeywell nor Rockwell relationship had produced a single sale, Jahn began to question the value of these alliances. With sales as the major focus in the alliances and the primary criterion for evaluating the success of the alliance, Jahn tried to understand possible reasons for the lack of sales. It was easy to blame lagging sales on the struggling economy. With the drug manufacturing industry not experiencing consistent growth, companies were not able to spend money on improving their processes, upgrading software, or revamping production. Budgets cuts and purchasing managers following orders to reduce expenses led to a shrinking market. Unfortunately, the products that Aegis and its alliance partners were selling fell into the category of items that were not essential to current operations. In fact, Honeywell's POMS division, while having some success with other software products, overall had low sales and had recently laid off 25 percent of its sales force, including individuals with whom Aegis had worked. Aegis had also lost some its original sales team. During lean times, the companies that normally would be interested in purchasing Aegis software solutions were looking internally to make incremental improvements.

Another reason for the absence of sales might have been the characteristics of the relationships and the partner communication systems and performance metrics that were set up. Effective communication between alliance partners was essential. Was Aegis effectively communicating with either alliance partner? Although there were contractual specifications about how often they had to meet, communication appeared to be confined to situations when either side had a question or needed clarification on an issue. Communications between Honeywell POMS and ProPack Data had been cordial, but there was no evidence that the partners had a free flow of communication beyond the "need to know" when problems arose.

For Honeywell POMS, the Aegis director of business development handled all direct communications. The current agreement allowed the companies to set agendas and develop sales opportunities at a level that met the alliance's needs. Group phone calls, sales calls, and bi-yearly face-to-face meetings were designed to keep the companies in contact with each other. Though initially there was contact between engineers to make sure the technologies were compatible, most communication occurred between the companies' sales teams and corporate management. Communication between sales teams occurred when they were working the same sales together, which they had done on several occasions; then there was frequent communication. The loss of key personnel in both companies required the new managers to begin to rebuild the communication level and the overall interest in the relationship. At the corporate level, they communicated weekly. Though more frequent communication would perhaps be better, Jahn believed the current level allowed the companies to set agendas and develop sales opportunities at a level that met the alliance's needs. As the alliance developed, Aegis

realized it had a good cultural fit with Honeywell POMS and noted very few communication problems. Aegis believed it could share information with Honeywell.

The Aegis and ProPack Data agreement was hindered when Aegis's primary contact left ProPack Data, handing off responsibility to someone who did not take an active role, thereby frustrating the Aegis team. On both sides, communication had not extended beyond the contact persons, and the relationship suffered. The two companies had been trying to move beyond these events and had taken steps to improve the channels of communication between the firms.

A Difficult Decision

As Jahn reflected upon the development of the company and these relationships, she wondered about Aegis's alliance strategy and what actions to take. Perhaps it was too early to make changes—these were difficult economic times and Aegis might not have given the relationships enough time to produce sales. Jahn and Neway knew that communication and trust were important to keeping a relationship going through troubled times. Their comfort level and trust increased with each partner as time went on. On the other hand, one could argue that these relationships had already had sufficient time to prove themselves and it did not appear that either would be successful. If Aegis terminated one or both of these relationships, it would need to focus its time and energy on more productive sales options. But what would these be?

Relationships with other partners large enough to get the attention of main pharmaceutical companies would likely have some of the same problems as these two relationships and would take time to develop. Rather than terminate these alliances, a more reasonable solution might be to restructure the relationships. This could include changes in the contract with either Rockwell or Honeywell or in their interactions with one another. Believing they had put together contracts with appropriate incentives to encourage sales, their thoughts turned to improving the relationships with each company. But how would a company of fewer than 40 employees influence either of these large corporations? Further, as a small company between rounds of financing, Aegis did not have a lot of extra financial or staffing resources. Any solution would have to be a low-cost one. Each path was filled with risk and difficulties in implementation, but Jahn and Neway knew that for Aegis to attract investments and to succeed would require a quick but thoughtful decision.

Case 3–6: McDonald's and KFC: Recipes for Success in China

Quick Service Restaurant Giants in the Middle Kingdom

In 2008, McDonald's and KFC were the two largest quick-service restaurants (QSR) in the world, with 31,999 and 15,580 outlets, respectively.[1] Both chains were renowned for their broad spectrum of consumers on a global basis.

McDonald's appeared to be a clear winner in international expansion. It had over 17,500 international outlets and was the first corporation to set up a solid foundation for international franchising. It spearheaded global expansion with its first overseas outlet in Canada in 1967, and entered Japan in 1971.[2] McDonald's outlets had tremendous success in Japan—despite the difference in culture—with record-breaking daily sales and speed of expansion in the initial stage.[3]

KFC also started international expansion early, opening its first overseas outlet in England in 1964. However, it was given a bumpy ride when it began to penetrate the market in Asia. The Japanese outlets were far less successful than McDonald's and only started to make a profit in 1976, six years after KFC entered Japan. KFC outlets opened in Hong Kong in 1973 but were all closed down within two years. The company would eventually win the confidence of Hong Kong customers ten years after its first entry. In Taiwan it experienced relatively smoother development, although KFC headquarters was to spend a huge amount of money and effort in order to get the ownership back from its joint venture partners at a later stage.[4]

This case was written by Gabriel Szulanski, Professor of Strategy at INSEAD, Weiru Chen, Assistant Professor of Strategy, and Jennifer Lee, Research Associate. It is intended to be used as a basis for class discussion rather than to illustrate either effective or ineffective handling of an administrative situation. The authors gratefully acknowledge funding from INSEAD R&D.

It was a totally different picture in China. In the 'Middle Kingdom,' KFC was not only recognised as the leader in foreign quick-service restaurants but was also a significant player in the Chinese restaurant industry as a whole, alone contributing 1% of the country's total food and beverage industry revenues in 2005.[5] In 2005, KFC's outlets in China recorded an average of US$1.2 million in annual sales per store, compared with just US$900,000 for similar stores in the US.[6] According to the 2008 figures, KFC had over 2,300 outlets in China, with an average profit margin of nearly 20.1%.[7]

In contrast, at 1,000 outlets, McDonald's presence in China was less than half of KFC's, with an estimated profit margin significantly below that of its leading competitor. Many people attributed KFC's success in China to its early entry—three years earlier than McDonald's—and its natural advantage in menu selection which corresponded to the typical consumer's preference for chicken over beef. However, were these reasons enough to explain KFC's continued growth and the extension of its lead over its rival? How could McDonald's as a latecomer and the second-largest QSR player in China, capitalize upon its global dominance and resources to catch up with KFC?

Replicate or Adapt?

The Inherent Challenge for International Franchisors

International franchising is frequently associated with service firms, such as hotels, retail outlets and quick service restaurants. These firms often have strongly identifiable trademarks and try to guarantee the customer a uniform and consistent level of service and product quality across different locations and over time. However, the high degree of standardised operations makes the replication of the format across diverse markets difficult. Differences in things such as ingredients, labour and physical space can mean significant modifications to the service formula. Consequently, the basic service may be similar to that of the home country, but details in the delivery of the service are often altered.[8]

Many foreign enterprises found China very different in culture and consumer behaviour. Franchise restaurants faced several major hurdles, including a different labour force structure, difficulty in recruiting technically competent and culturally sensitive managers, tough technological problems and a less than satisfactory legal environment and enforcement.[9] So the challenge for international franchisors like McDonald's and KFC was to decide whether to comply strictly with their original models, and if adaptation was required, when and how to make adaptations in order to deliver globally consistent standards while catering to local consumer needs.

Potential of China's Restaurant Industry

Chinese consumers' spending on eating out had increased tremendously along with the country's economic boom in the past decade. Retail revenues of the restaurant industry increased from 5.2% in 1991 to 14% in 2007 as a portion of total retail revenues from consumer goods.[10] According to annual statistics from the Ministry of Commerce of the People's Republic of China, the retail revenue of the hotel and restaurant industry reached 1,235.2 billion RMB in 2007, representing 19.4% growth over the previous year; foreign franchises were the main driver of food and beverage revenue growth as foreign direct investment in the hotel and restaurant industry totaled US$10.4 billion, an increase of 25.8% on the previous year.[11] China was the world's largest consumer of meat. The Economist Intelligence Unit forecast that annual meat consumption in China would jump from 59 kg per head in 2005 to 74 kg per head in 2009.[12] With US meat consumption at 128 kg a head, there seemed plenty of scope for the Western fast-food industry to expand in China.[13]

Foreign quick service restaurants played a significant role in China's restaurant industry. The share of fast food in the retail industry was expected to reach 9.3% by 2011 from 74% in 2007. China's fast-food industry was expected to grow at a CAGR of around 25% during 2008–2011.[14]

The first comprehensive franchising regulations, which came into effect in February 2005, made it easier for foreign fast-food operators to open branches and roll out the franchising model, which had proven to be such a sure path for fast-track growth in the US and Europe.[15] The new

Law on Franchise Regulations, passed in February 2007, helped clear up the ambiguity surrounding franchisor's disclosure duty.[16] Thenceforth, the rights of both franchisors and franchisees were better protected.

Quick Service Restaurant Chains: A New Experience for China

Foreign quick service restaurants began to surface in China with the opening of KFC's first store in 1987, followed by McDonald's entry three years later. The timing was propitious for foreign enterprises as it had been nine years since China embarked upon a policy of opening up and reform in 1978 and Chinese curiosity about the West was at a peak.

Although GDP growth in China had averaged well over 9% per year since 1978, per capita GDP at the time of KFC's entry was a mere US$621.05.[17] Given the 120 to 130 yuan monthly salary of Beijing urban residents at that time, KFC prices were unaffordable to most, but many still flocked to the store to purchase the 12-yuan KFC hamburger or 8-yuan fried chicken. The most frequent customers were foreigners living in China. Despite the attractiveness of fast food chains, local consumers in those early days could seldom afford to eat at KFC, McDonald's or Pizza Hut. Dining at these establishments was considered such a luxury that some couples chose to hold their wedding banquets there.[18]

Behind the 'dream market' with a vast land area and 1.3 billion people, the complexity of China's population, geography and history presented major challenges for foreign players. Population density, economic development and wealth distribution varied greatly from east to west and from south to north. Foreign invested enterprises usually focused on the populous, more affluent eastern China. The western regions were beyond the reach of even domestic businesses without an effective national transportation system.

Chinese-style fast food had existed prior to the entry of western quick service restaurants but represented a totally different concept and ambience compared with modern chains. Most of the catering units for Chinese fast food were small in scale, serving pre-made appetizers such as congee, buns and fritters of twisted dough (yiu-tiao). They lacked funding, trained employees and a well-maintained dining environment.[19] As restaurant staff required at least five years of experience, western food chains could not find a sufficient number of internal candidates to meet growth-driven demand and had to import skilled managers from neighbouring markets such as Taiwan and Hong Kong, and even from headquarters in the US.

KFC in China

The Very First Western Restaurant Chain

Yum!'s KFC brand was the first foreign quick-service restaurant chain to enter China.[20] On 12 November 1987, the first KFC in China was officially opened at Beijing Qianmen, within walking distance of Tiananmen. In 2002, KFC opened the first ever drive-through restaurant in the country. In 2004, the 1,000th KFC restaurant was opened in China (Beijing), only a few kilometres from the site of its first restaurant. From the beginning of 2005, the Yum! China Division (including Mainland China, Thailand and KFC Taiwan), based in Shanghai, reported directly to Yum! headquarter instead of to its international division, reflecting China's market size, unique strength and importance.[21] From 1987 to 2005, the number of KFC outlets in China grew by 50% annually, growth which was considered exponential outside its parent market in the US,[22] particularly in a country known for its culinary sophistication developed over thousands of years. Today, KFC is the number one quick-service restaurant brand in China. Yum! China has more than 2,300 KFC restaurants in nearly 500 cities in Mainland China (Q3 2008).[23]

Initial Stage—Replication with Localisation in Mind

In 1987, KFC set up a joint venture, B-KFC, with Beijing Animal Production Company and Beijing Tourism Board in order to gain access to better product supply and F&B management authority. Sim Kay Soon, a Singaporean who had held area manager and training officer positions within KFC system since the 1980s, was appointed to be its the first general manager, responsible for day-to-day operations.[24] Positions below (and including) assistant managers were all held by Chinese nationals. The company started using local food ingredients from day one. Chicken was purchased from Beijing Animal Production, and potatoes, cabbage and carrots were all purchased locally. However, cooking equipment was mostly imported, such as blenders, heating racks and even cash registers.

The first Beijing outlet represented KFC's largest restaurant worldwide with 1,400 square metres of space allowing for a capacity of 500 seats and considerable office space for B-KFC staff. Only four months after opening, the Beijing restaurant had become the highest-selling single KFC store in the world.

The response to B-KFC's recruitment was overwhelming as the base salary offered was set at 140 RMB per month, about 40% more than could be earned by associate professors at the country's universities at that time. So attractive was the compensation package that a ratio of 20 to 1 people applied for every opening. In the end, B-KFC hired those applicants who were high school graduates, could speak some English, did not have previous restaurant work experience, and had demonstrated a willingness to work hard.[25]

A Management Team Familiar with Local Culture

From the beginning, KFC hired elites from overseas—Hong Kong, Taiwan and other Asian countries—some with decades of experiences in the QSR industry, and most with a deep understanding of the language, culture, habits and customs of China. As many of the management team members were associated with Taiwan, they were nicknamed the "Taiwanese gang."[26]

Other than the top management team which was composed of almost all overseas Chinese, KFC was keen on developing local talent from day one. The company paid well to hire highly educated and motivated restaurant staff, and used its training system to develop those staff into future restaurant managers or even district general managers. 80% of China KFC's district general managers were university graduates, some from top schools. This strategy paid off when the company decided to expand aggressively after 10 years in China. Joseph Han, Operating Vice President of Yum! Brands in greater China from 1996 to 2003, described KFC China's people strategy:

> …in China, KFC understands the importance of people's talent…. In the United States, in the fast-food chains, it is very difficult to hire very high-quality people, especially on the cook labour side. So in China, KFC built very aggressive talent recruitment projects. It went to universities to hire university students. KFC hired management trainees with very qualified university graduates…. There are a total of 22 branch offices for Yum! Brands in China and the general managers are now already 90% localised. Those people actually, 20 years ago, started at the restaurants as the cook person, or as a management trainee. This talent pool has become their great asset for the future development.[27]

Takeoff during Time of Crisis

KFC chose to put down roots in big eastern cities along the coast in the 1980s and to go west in the 1990s. Like many foreign enterprises, KFC's expansion route was from east to west, from cities to towns, and blanketed China with wider coverage by linking outlet presence in cities and towns.

Within 10 years of its entry into China, KFC has basically covered the main cities in the populated areas, with only the sparsely populated and low purchasing-powered south-western and north-western districts yet to be penetrated.

During the Asia economic downturn in 1997, KFC faced the challenge of a thinning bottom line. It had two alternatives, either to cut costs or to increase sales. It chose to aggressively expand the number of outlets at a time when most competitors were holding back. The same strategy was applied in other times of crisis, for example, during the SARS epidemic in 2003—that year KFC added more than 300 new outlets, even more than in the previous year.[28]

Self-Developed Logistic and Distribution System

Along with the aggressive expansion plan, a well-connected supply chain was needed before any new KFC outlet could be opened in any city. KFC expected to establish a logistics system to supply neighbouring KFC outlets. If it took more than one day to reach any new KFC restaurant, the logistics team would start finding a new warehouse closer to the outlet.

What was different about the global KFC system was that Yum! Brands established its own logistics system by working closely with local partners rather than simply outsourcing its supply to a third party. KFC established the "STAR System" for its China partners, and suppliers who passed the STAR test could also easily achieve national ISO9002 and HACCP[29] certification. Yum! Brands later consolidated a separate supply system in China—which saved the company nearly 100 million RMB in costs in 1998.[30] It set up Asia's largest logistics and distribution centre in Beijing in October 2004 for its groups of restaurants in China, a move that was the first and only for Yum! Brands Global companies, and which allowed another 10% cost reduction.[31] Warren K. Liu, Vice President of Yum! Brands Greater China from 1997 to 2000, later recalled that he was challenged again and again by headquarters on the decision to invest in its own warehouse, logistics and distribution system, which didn't exist in other parts of the world where Yum! Brands was present:

> What we faced in China were an inefficient and frag-
> mented distribution network, an inadequate highway
> system, local protectionism that lead to fragmentation
> in the supply chain, and inter-provincial trade barriers
> such as excessive tolls. In such an infrastructure-
> deficient market environment, direct control over
> supply storage and distribution complements KFC's
> rapid growth strategy; allowing KFC to penetrate new
> markets further, sooner, faster, at lower unit cost than
> its competitors.[32]

Menu Selection—an American Brand with Chinese Characteristics

KFC has followed the principle of menu localization, striving to become an 'American brand with Chinese characteristics' since its entry.[33] Even in the earliest days, KFC China's most popular items were the spicy chicken wings and spicy chicken thigh burger, rather than its signature Colonel Sanders Original Recipe chicken.

Large-scale menu localisation started in 1998[34] when a local food R&D team and a test kitchen were set up in Shanghai. Since then, KFC has introduced many Chinese items onto their menus. Preserved Sichuan pickle and shredded pork soup was one of the first. The soup proved a success, and mushroom rice, tomato and egg soup, and Dragon Twister (traditional Peking chicken roll) were soon added to the menu. KFC also serves packets of Happy French Fry Shakes that contain beef, orange and Uygur barbecue spices.[35] Chinese consumers received those localised food items very well. While some global companies might have second thoughts about launching a food item containing bones for family consumers, as it might potentially create food safety concerns, KFC's chicken kebab is made of soft bones and meat (see Exhibit 1), and has become one of the most popular items among children and teenagers. Chinese consumers can find preserved egg with pork porridge, egg and pork floss roll, and Hong Kong milk tea for breakfast, egg and vegetable soup as a side dish, Dragon Twister for a main meal, and Portuguese egg tart for dessert on the menu.

In an interview, Joseph Han talked about why KFC China was determined to provide a localised menu, one of the keys to successfully penetrating into fourth and fifth tier cities in rural areas:

> I think McDonald's and KFC do bring in the dining
> environment, and they bring in their working concept
> to change people's lifestyle. But product-wise, you can
> see Chinese are still Chinese. When Chinese students
> go to the United States to study, they still choose the
> kind of food they feel is close to their life. Even though
> they admire the Western lifestyle, I think they still
> need time to change their dietary habits. Especially
> breakfast. In the three meals, breakfast is usually
> cooked by your mother. Your mother always cooks
> traditional food. So that's why now even McDonald's
> in China created its own breakfast menu. Every-
> where in the world you don't change, but when you
> came to China and India, I can guarantee you have
> to change, because maybe you can change younger
> people's lifestyle, but you cannot change some of their
> dietary habits.[36]

China
KFC China Print Advertisement

Chicken Kebab—*"Bone and flesh Relations"*

KFC China TV Advertisement

Exhibit 1 KFC Advertisement

Franchised or Not?

KFC's aggressive expansion through franchising did not get off to a good start in China. In 1993, it signed its first regional franchise agreement for the Xian area in the northwest of China with a Taiwanese entrepreneur.[37] This served the purpose at that time for KFC China headquarters to focus on more strategically important coastal cities. However, due to a slower-than-expected development pace in Xian, KFC China had to go down the same path as

in Taiwan during the 1990s, launch new outlets separately and independently from those operated by the franchisee, and finally bought back restaurant ownership in Xian.

The KFC team in China decided not to authorise any franchise agreements with entrepreneurs in any city or region to avoid making the same mistake as in Taiwan or Xian, no matter how small or remote that city or region might be. In August 2000, KFC authorised the first individual franchisee in Changzhou. By paying a one-time transfer fee of 8 million RMB, the franchisee could own an operating KFC outlet which was already in profit. The franchising strategy was limited to townships with a population of between 150,000 and 400,000, and which achieved more than 6,000 RMB in per capita annual consumption.[38] By the end of 2007, there were 228 franchised KFC outlets, 8.7% of its total number of outlets in China.[39]

McDonald's in China

Entry into China

On 8th October 1990, nearly three years after KFC set up its first outlet near Tiananmen Square, McDonald's opened its first outlet in China in Shenzhen[40] and it was warmly welcomed by the local consumers. It continued to extend in the southern cities of China, and in April 1992, the Golden Arches could finally be seen in McDonald's Wangfujing outlet in Beijing. This outlet was formed with an unlisted investment unit of the Beijing municipal government. Overtaking the Moscow outlet in size, it became the largest McDonald's restaurant in the world, attracting 13,000 customers on its very first day.[41]

By September 2003, McDonald's had 566 outlets in 94 cities across 19 provinces and China had become McDonald's third largest Asian market behind Japan and Australia. In 2004, China became one of its top ten markets—making the country McDonald's Corp's fastest-growing market worldwide.[42]

However, although the number of McDonald's outlets was on a par with that of KFC in the first six years after its entry, it had started to lag behind KFC since 1997. While KFC celebrated the opening of its 1,500th outlet in China (Shanghai) in 2005, McDonald's had around 600.[43] What had McDonald's done differently in China to explain this?

Consistent Global Supply Chain Partners

McDonald's developed its supply chain partners along with its global business growth. HAVI Food, its global logistics partner, would enter any new market to invest and set up the logistics system even before the first McDonald's outlet opened in that market. In China, HAVI Food also established a logistics centre exclusively for McDonald's, and there were three major distribution centres in Beijing, Shanghai, Guangzhou, and satellite dispatch centres in other smaller cities.

McDonald's also tried to work with its global food suppliers as much as possible. There were 43 suppliers for McDonald's in China, 70% of which were its global partners. For example, J.R. Simplot Co., which supplied frozen French fries to McDonald's, had founded a joint venture company in Beijing in 1993, surveying the varieties of potatoes before McDonald's entry; McDonald's vegetable supplier set up a branch in Guangzhou in 1997 in order to satisfy McDonald's intention to source locally, and 100% of its facility and equipment were imported from overseas. Likewise, the global suppliers of McDonald's buns and seasonings had all set up branches in China to strengthen the supply chain network for McDonald's in China.[44]

Why did McDonald's insist on bringing their global partners to China? Peter Tan, former Senior Vice President and President of McDonald's Greater China, summed it up:

> McDonald's in China today reflects the attitude that they are a global brand, hence the need to set standards that are globally consistent, be it in Oakbrook, USA, or Xian, China…McDonald's is saying that 'we are in this emerging country, but because we are a global brand, we need to give them first world standards…' McDonald's had fewer than five chicken suppliers up in the northeast, and the reason for this is that McDonald's is very concerned about quality consistency.[45]

Catching Up with Cautiously Aggressive Expansion

Although McDonald's came in late, its expansion in China was still aggressive, especially in the earlier years. Its strategy was to start in the foreign influenced and economically affluent southern cities and then expand to cities in north and central China.

However, compared with KFC, McDonald's did not successfully penetrate as many third and fourth tier cities as its rival (see Exhibits 2 and 3). By September 2003, McDonald's had 566 outlets in 94 cities across 19 provinces. The bulk of the restaurants were concentrated in over 40 cities on China's east coast where incomes were higher. The bulk of

Exhibit 2	KFC's penetration in China in the first ten years

Year of Entry	Coverage
1987	Beijing
1989	Shanghai
1992	Nanjing
1993	Suzhou, Hangzhou, Wuxi, Guangzhou, Qingdao, Xian (franchised)
1994	Fuzhou, Tianjin, Shenyang
1995	Chendu, Dalian, Wuhan
1996	Shenzhen, Xiamen
1997	Changsha, Chongqing

Source: Warren K. Liu, *KFC in China—Secret Recipe for Success*, John Wiley & Sons (Asia) Pte Ltd., 2008.

Exhibit 3   McDonald's penetration in China in the first 10 years

Year of Entry	Coverage
1990	Shenzhen
1992	Beijing
1993	Guangzhou
1994	Tianjin, Shanghai, Nangjing, Wuhan, Chendu, Chongqing
2001	Xian

Source: McDonald's and KFC edited by B.Q. Chen, China Economy Publishing, 2005.

McDonald's sales in China came through its restaurants in Beijing, Shanghai, Shenzhen and Guangzhou. In September 2003, it was reported that McDonald's planned to open 100 new stores per year in China over the next couple of years. A majority of the proposed outlets would be opened in developed markets such as Beijing, Shanghai and Guangzhou. The remainder would be located in Inner Mongolia and other less developed regions of China. The company also planned to expand in Western China.[46] By January 2007, McDonald's had penetrated into more than 120 cities across China,[47] and in November 2008, it finally crossed the 1,000 outlets threshold, with plans to add another 175 in 2009.[48]

However, unlike KFC, McDonald's did not take bold steps in expanding its territory in China. The number of outlets in China began to dwindle from 2002 onwards. In order to strengthen its foothold in China, McDonald's moved its Asia headquarters from Hong Kong to Shanghai in January 2005, signaling its determination to intensify its aggressive expansion in China.

Standardised Global Menu with Local Selections

McDonald's was known for its quality of food and consistency in food preparation processes. In order to maintain quality and consistency, McDonald's imposed standardisation in three domains—ingredient procurement, food preparation and food quality. The same consistency could be seen in their food menu; Big Mac remained their signature product, although chicken varieties were added to suit local consumers' tastes and accounted for an estimated 60% of food sales in McDonald's China.[49]

The McDonald's menu in China was essentially the same as in the US. Its use of local food selection was apparently not as varied as KFC's. However, not content to lag behind KFC, McDonald's introduced Vegetable and Seafood Soup and Corn Soup in 2004,[50] and other Chinese-style menu items such as red bean sundaes and taro pies, which also became popular. McDonald's gradually recognised the importance of catering to local consumers' tastes. Jeffrey Schwartz, newly-appointed President of McDonald's China in 2005, said that 80% of the menu in China would be the same and the other 20% would be allowed to be different in order to reflect regional tastes. He also said that McDonald's would open outlets in more areas in the future to make McDonald's food accessible to more customers.[51]

McDonald's detail-oriented approach was also extended to their China operations. Every aspect of food preparation was done according to the operating manual. Packaging such as Happy Meal boxes and apple pie wrappers were produced to exactly the same global standards. In an interview, Peter Tan commented on the balance between production innovation and global consistency:

> For a global brand to maintain brand consistency, it is important to ensure that the icon products remain an integral part of the menu offering. But then the question arises as to how you penetrate into emerging countries where you need to balance between what the brand stands for versus local tastes. That's where I think product innovation done strategically plays a vital role.[52]

Today, McDonald's menu in China has grown to include foods tweaked for local tastes to satisfy consumers, such as spicy chicken fillet and pineapple sundae. Some of the menu ideas, such as the corn cup developed in China, have been exported to other markets around the world. However, according to CEO Jeffrey Schwartz, the hamburger and fries Western-style are still at the heart of the Chinese menus.[53]

Franchised or Not?

McDonald's has always been a franchising company and franchisees have played a significant role in its success. About three-quarters of McDonald's outlets worldwide have been franchised.[54] However, due to ambiguity in China's legal environment, up until 2003 McDonald's China had established all of its 566 outlets by joint venture or sole proprietor, rather than using its global franchising model. It announced in 2003 that it would open ten franchised outlets in China by June 2006, with a loyalty fee of 2.5 to 3.2 million RMB. The requirements that individuals must meet before being granted a franchise were the same in China as they are worldwide. The first pilot franchise was launched in Tianjin in September 2003. The licence was awarded to Meng Sun on the basis of her business acumen and understanding of the Tianjin market.[55] In 2007, McDonald's had fewer than 0.5% outlets in China that were franchised[56] while the percentage was 78% worldwide.[57]

The Challenges Ahead

McDonald's

2004 was a year of tragedy and loss for the company. The CEO who had put McDonald's on the road to revitalization, Jim Cantalupo, died on the eve of the company's global convention. His successor, Charlie Bell, was diagnosed with cancer soon after taking the helm. He resigned in November of that same year, and passed away in January 2005.[58] The China management team saw a high level of turnover: McDonald's Greater China President, Peter Tan, left in June 2005. His post was filled by Guy Russo, who was originally President of McDonald's Australia. In October the same year, the Managing Director of McDonald's North region and the General Manager of McDonald's Beijing both left the company.[59]

Despite the general perception that McDonald's would try to catch up with KFC in China using franchising, a report in 2007 revealed that they were cautious about franchises. China Vice President, Gary Rosen, commented: "The franchise business requires a lot of effort and right now we have other priorities in China." The company would open at least 100 new stores in the country annually and half of them would be wholly owned drive-through outlets.[60] McDonald's took a strategic move to link with China's SinoPec in 2006, giving McDonald's the rights to build drive-through outlets at the oil company's 30,000 gas stations.[61] Up until November 2008, it owned 81 drive-through restaurants in China. Another expansion direction for McDonald's China was to convert its restaurants into 24-hour operations. By the end of 2008, 80% of its 1,000 outlets in China already provided service round the clock.[62] All these efforts were consistent with its global strategy of making McDonald's a convenient choice for customers.[63]

> We have a business model of getting better versus getting bigger. It's not about how many restaurants you have, it's about how many restaurants that serve your customers well. It's not about how big, it's about how good and how you run your business.[64]

—Jeffrey Schwartz, CEO, McDonald's China, 2008

KFC

Despite its success in China, KFC Global was struggling to overcome weak performance in the homeland. Data showed that in 2008 Yum's overall second-quarter profit rose 4%; it achieved 38% growth in operating profit in its China division and 18% growth in its international division. These figures offset a 12% drop in US operating profit for that quarter. Yum! CEO, David C. Novak, singled out KFC in the US as "our only major soft spot."[65]

On the road of aggressive expansion, KFC China ran up against the issue of consumer confidence in its food safety standards. Sudan I, a red chemical dye thought to cause cancer, was discovered in two products sold in China: KFC's New Orleans Roast Chicken Wings and New Orleans Roast Chicken Legs.[66] KFC took the dishes off the menu, but Chinese consumers were still angry because a large amount of the consumption was made by children.[67]

Other Competition

Burger King, the second-largest United States hamburger chain, entered China in 2005, planning to open ten stores in China in 12 months with a view to participating in the large and fast-growing eating out market.[68] It signed a regional franchisee agreement with a company in Fujian, a populous province in southern China, in order to expand its territory.

Faced with increasing competition, how could McDonald's strengthen its position in China? Should it aggressively increase its number of outlets by taking bold steps like KFC, or gradually expand its presence by strictly following its global strategy and procedures? Could KFC sustain its leading edge while ensuring expansion and quality at the same time? Would the success of China KFC be carried over to its US base and bring changes to the business model in order to compete with McDonald's Global?

McDonald's and KFC Worldwide

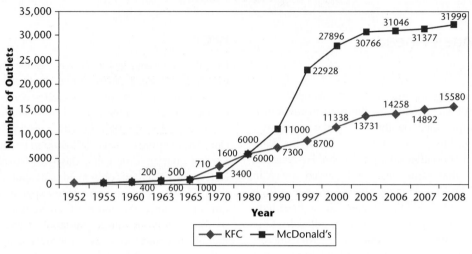

Exhibit 4 Historical Store Count

Source: McDonald's and Yum website. Various press releases and web articles.

Exhibit 5 KFC Top 25 Markets by Unit Count

For Full Year 2007	
2007 Top 25 Markets	**KFC**
United States	**5,273**
China Mainland	2,140
Japan	1,152
Canada	720
Great Britain	664
Australia	559
South Africa	479
Malaysia	402
Mexico	323
Thailand	314
Indonesia	300
Philippines	165
Korea	158
Taiwan	138
Saudi Arabia	97
New Zealand	95
Puerto Rico	86
Poland	83
Egypt	81
Singapore	70
Hong Kong	69
France	57
Germany	51
Spain	47
India	31

Source: www.yum.com

Exhibit 6   Yum Worldwide System Units

Year end	2008	2007	2006	2005	2004	2003
Company Owned	7,568	7,625	7,736	7,587	7,743	7,854
Franchisees	25,911	24,297	23,516	22,666	21,858	21,471
Licensees	2,168	2,109	2,137	2,376	2,345	2,362
Total[a]	36,292	35,345	34,595	34,277	33,608	33,199

Year end	2008	2007	2006	2005	2004	2003
United States						
KFC	5,253	5,358	5,394	5,443	5,525	5,524
Pizza Hut	7,564	7,515	7,532	7,566	7,500	7,523
Taco Bell	5,588	5,580	5,608	5,845	5,900	5,989
Long John Silver's	1,022	1,081	1,121	1,169	1,200	1,204
A & W	363	371	406	449	485	576
Total Us	19,790	19,905	20,061	20,472	20,610	20,822

International	2008	2007	2006	2005	2004	2003
KFC	7,347	6,942	6,606	6,307	6,084	5,944
Pizza Hut	5,026	4,882	4,788	4,701	4,528	4,357
Taco Bell	245	238	236	243	237	247
Long John Silver's	38	38	35	34	34	31
A & W	264	254	238	229	210	183
Total International	12,920	12,354	11,903	11,514	11,093	10,762

China	2008	2007	2006	2005	2004	2003
KFC	2,980	2,592	2,258	1,981	1,657	1,410
Pizza Hut	585	480	365	305	246	204
Taco Bell	0	2	2	2	1	1
A & W	0	0	0	0	0	0
Total China[b]	3,582	3,086	2,631	2,291	1,905	1,615

[a] Includes unconsolidated affiliates.
[b] Includes East Dawning units for China.

Source: www.yum.com

Exhibit 7 Yum China Division Operating Results (in millions)

	2001	2002	2003	2004	2005	2006	2007
Company sales	$569	$722	$871	$1,082	$1,255	$1,587	$2,075
Franchise and licence fees	18	22	30	38	41	51	69
Revenues	587	744	901	1,120	1,296	1,638	2,144
Food and paper	244	289	331	401	454	562	756
Payroll and employee benefits	61	77	93	125	167	205	273
Occupancy and other operating expenses	179	217	275	337	415	497	629
Company restaurant expenses	484	583	699	863	1,036	1,264	1,658
General and administrative expenses	46	51	62	80	92	119	151
Franchise and licence expenses	-	-	-	-	-	-	-
Closures and impairment expenses	6	6	6	4	7	6	7
Other (income) expenses	(12)	(16)	(27)	(32)	(50)	(41)	(47)
	524	624	740	915	1,085	1,348	1,769
Operating profit	$63	$120	$161	$205	$211	$290	$375
Company sales	100%	100%	100%	100%	100%	100%	100%
Food and paper	42.9	40.0	38.0	37.1	36.2	35.4	36.4
Payroll and employee benefits	10.7	10.6	10.7	11.5	13.3	12.9	13.2
Occupancy and other operating expenses	31.5	30.1	31.5	31.1	33.1	31.3	30.3
Restaurant margin	14.9%	19.3%	19.8%	20.3%	17.4%	20.4%	20.1%
	$	$	$	$	$	$	$
Company sales	569	722	871	1,082	1,255	1,587	2,075
Franchisee sales	328	397	510	619	665	840	1,098
System sales growth							
Local currency	17%	25%	23%	23%	11%	23%	24%
U.S. dollars	14%	25%	23%	23%	13%	26%	31%

Source: www.yum.com

Exhibit 8   Yum U.S. Division Operating Results (in millions)

	2001	2002	2003	2004	2005	2006	2007
Company sales	$4,287	$4,778	$5,081	$5,163	$5,294	$4,952	$4,518
Franchise and licence fees	540	569	574	600	635	651	679
Revenues	4,827	5,347	5,655	5,763	5,929	5,603	5,197
Food and paper	1,225	1,346	1,463	1,546	1,576	1,399	1,317
Payroll and employee benefits	1,313	1,479	1,576	1,573	1,600	1,489	1,377
Occupancy and other operating expenses	1,100	1,189	1,303	1,333	1,385	1,340	1,221
Company restaurant expenses	3,638	4,014	4,342	4,452	4,561	4,228	3,915
General and administrative expenses	418	469	469	501	536	546	510
Franchise and licence expenses	49	39	16	19	26	23	29
Closures and impairment expenses	27	23	16	14	46	37	14
Other income	-	-	-	-	-	6	(10)
	4,132	4,545	4,843	4,986	5,169	4,840	4,458
Operating profit	$695	$802	$812	$777	$760	$763	$739
Company sales	100%	100%	100%	100%	100%	100%	100%
Food and paper	28.6	28.2	28.8	29.9	29.8	28.2	29.2
Payroll and employee benefits	30.6	30.9	31.0	30.5	30.2	30.1	30.5
Occupancy and other operating expenses	25.6	24.9	25.6	25.8	26.2	27.1	27.0
Restaurant margin	15.2%	16.0%	14.6%	13.8%	13.8%	14.6%	13.3%
Company same store sales growth	1%	2%	0%	3%	4%	0%	(3)%
Company sales	$4,287	$4,778	$5,081	$5,163	$5,294	$4,952	$4,518
Franchise sales	10,309	11,061	11,257	11,724	12,428	12,804	13,304

Source: www.yum.com

Exhibit 9   Yum Division Historical Sales Growth (in %)

CHINA DIVISION
(Mainland China, Thailand, KFC Taiwan)

	2008	2007	2006	2005	2004
1st Quarter	28%	19%	14%	26%	17%
2nd Quarter	28%	19%	29%	2%	34%
3rd Quarter		23%	25%	11%	20%
4th Quarter		30%	23%	6%	21%
Full Year		24%	23%	10%	23%

INTERNATIONAL DIVISION
(Excludes China Division)

	2008	2007	2006	2005	2004
1st Quarter	9%	10%	6%	7%	5%
2nd Quarter	8%	11%	8%	6%	6%
3rd Quarter		11%	9%	4%	9%
4th Quarter		9%	11%	4%	6%
Full Year		10%	9%	5%	6%

U.S. COMPANY SAME-STORE

	2008	2007	2006	2005	2004
1st Quarter	3%	−6%	4%	4%	3%
2nd Quarter	4%	−3%	0	5%	2%
3rd Quarter		−1%	−2%	4%	4%
4th Quarter		−1%	−2%	4%	2%
Full Year		−3%	0	4%	3%

Source: www.yum.com

Exhibit 10   McDonald's Number of Restaurants Top 25 Market by unit count

(at year-end 2007 and 2002)	2007	2002
Total	31,377	31,108
United States	13,862	13,491
Japan	3,746	3,891
Canada	1,401	1,304
Germany	1,302	1,211
United Kingdom	1,191	1,231
France	1,108	973
England	1,019	1,055
China Mainland	876	546
Australia	761	726
Brazil*	551	584
Spain	378	333
Mexico*	364	261
Italy	361	329
Taiwan	348	350
Philippines*	273	236
South Korea	233	357
Sweden	230	245
Netherlands	220	220
Poland	213	200
Hong Kong	207	216
Russia	189	94
Argentina*	183	203
Malaysia	176	149
Austria	163	157

*Developmental Licensee market as of December 31, 2007.

Source: www.mcdonalds.com.

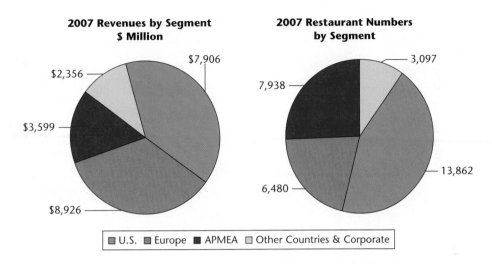

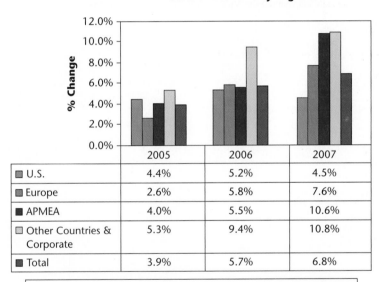

	2005	2006	2007
■ U.S.	4.4%	5.2%	4.5%
■ Europe	2.6%	5.8%	7.6%
■ APMEA	4.0%	5.5%	10.6%
□ Other Countries & Corporate	5.3%	9.4%	10.8%
■ Total	3.9%	5.7%	6.8%

■ U.S.   ■ Europe   ■ APMEA   □ Other Countries & Corporate   ■ Total

Exhibit 11   McDonald's Financial Results by Segment
APMEA: Asia/Pacific, Middle East and Africa.

Source: www.mcdonalds.com

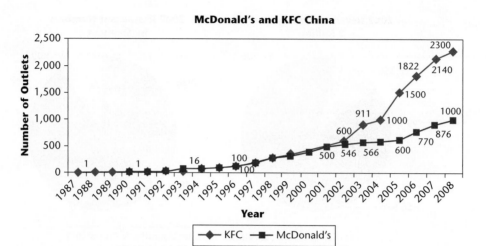

Exhibit 12 Historical Store Count

Source: McDonald's and Yum website. Various press releases and web articles.

Exhibit 13   Comparsion of McDonald's and KFC in-store Menu

	China	
	McDonald's	**KFC**
Main Meal	Big Mac Double Cheese Burger Hamburger Cheese Burger Beef 'N' Egg Burger McSpicy Chicken Burger McChicken Burger Fillet-O-Fish Vegetable Beef Burger McSpicy Chicken Twister Curry Chicken Burger Teriyaki Chicken Burger Double Mala Chicken Burger Spicy Teriyaki Chicken Burger	Buckets of Chicken New Orleans BBQ Chicken Burger Spicy Chicken Burger Crispy Chicken Burger Garden Crispy Chicken Burger Cod Fish Burger Mexican Chicken Twister Dragon Twister Spicy 'Saliva' Chicken Burger
Side Dishes/ Light Snacks	McNugget McSpicy Chicken Wings Sweet Corn in a Cup French Fries	Corn on a cob Mashed Potato Egg 'N' Vegetable Soup Vegetable Salad Corn Salad Carrot Bread Roll Chicken Kebab French Fries Chicken Nuggets Popcorn Chicken New Orleans BBQ Chicken Wings Original Recipe Chicken Spicy Chicken Wings Cod Fish Sticks
Breakfast	Big Breakfast Pancake Cheese'N'Egg Burger Pork McMuffin Orange Juice Fresh Milk	Crispy Chicken Burger (with egg) Cheese'N' Egg Burger Pork'N' Egg Burger Beef'N' Egg Porridge Chicken'N' Mushroom Porridge Preserved Egg'N' Lean Pork Porridge Egg'N' Pork Floss Twister Egg'N' Pork Twister Shrimp'N' Egg Twister Hong Kong Milk Tea Shrimp Spring Roll Orange Juice
Dessert	Sundae (Chocolate/Pineapple/Strawberry) Ice Cream Cone (Vanilla/Chocolate/Mixed/Crunchy) Milkshake (Chocolate/Strawberry)	Portuguese Egg Tart Sundae Ice Cream Cone Coffee/Irish Coffee Lemon Cola Pomelo Honey Tea

Shaded areas: local specialities.

Source: McDonald's and KFC China websites.

China
McDonald's China Print Advertisement

I just love not having a backbone   **I just love being sissy**

I just love fighting my teacher

McDonald's China TV Advertisement

Exhibit 14   McDonald's Advertisement

Appendix: KFC and McDonald's Global Milestones

KFC

At the start of the Great Depression in 1930, Harland Sanders opened his first restaurant in the small front room of a gas station in Corbin, Kentucky. He was made an honorary Kentucky colonel six years later in recognition of his contribution to the state's cuisine. The Original Recipe chicken, which was deep fried in a pressure cooker with 11 herbs and spices, was created in 1940. In 1969, the Kentucky Fried Chicken Corporation was listed on the New York Stock Exchange. In 1986, PepsiCo, Inc. acquired KFC from RJR Nabisco, Inc., and 11 years later, in 1997, PepsiCo, Inc. announced the spin-off of its quick service restaurants—KFC, Taco Bell and Pizza Hut. In 2002, the world's largest restaurant company changed its corporate name to Yum! Brands, Inc. In addition to KFC, the company owns A&W® All-American Food® Restaurants, Long John Silver's®, Pizza Hut® and Taco Bell® restaurants.

Management Philosophy

KFC's parent company, Yum! Brands, runs a multi-brand strategy and is proud of its customer focus approach. Its restaurant management philosophy is summarized by the acronym "CHAMPS"—cleanness, hospitality, accuracy, maintenance, product quality, and speed. After the first successful ten years, Yum! began looking to sustain long-term growth, especially on an international level. According to the Yum! 2008 management presentation, its four key growth strategies are to build leading brands in China in every significant category; drive aggressive international expansion and build strong brands everywhere; dramatically improve US brand positions, consistency and returns, and drive industry-leading, long-term shareholder and franchisee value.[69]

International Expansion

KFC's penetration of Asia started with Japan in 1970. In 1984, it entered Taiwan, awarding the franchise to a joint venture company formed by two Japanese companies and a local entity. A year later, it re-entered Hong Kong after a 10-year gap, by giving franchise rights to Birdland, which later acquired the franchisee in Taiwan. From 1996 to 2001, Yum! Brands tried to win back ownership in the Greater China area by launching new KFC outlets in Taiwan in tandem with Birdland's operations, until finally in 2001, Birdland agreed to sell its KFC outlets in Taiwan to Yum! Brands. These experiences in Asian markets prepared Yum! Brands for its entry in 1987 into the largest and most exciting market in the world—China.[70]

McDonald's

The McDonald's concept was introduced in Southern California by Dick and Mac McDonald in 1937. In 1953, the McDonald brothers franchised their restaurant to Neil Fox, the first franchisee. The second McDonald's opened in Fresno, California—the first to feature the Golden Arches design. The fast-food idea was modified and expanded by their business partner Ray Kroc, of Oak Park, Illinois, who later bought out business interest of the McDonald brothers in the concept and went on to found McDonald's Corporation in 1955. In 1965, McDonald's went public with the company's first offering on the stock exchange. Twenty years later, in 1985, McDonald's was added to the 30-company Dow Jones Industrial Average.

The signature product, the Big Mac, was added to the product line in 1968 and was the brainchild of Jim Delligatti, one of Ray Kroc's earliest franchisees. Another popular product—the Happy Meal—has been making children's visits special since 1979.[71] McDonald's has become a global phenomenon, with more than 31,000 outlets operating in over 100 countries today.

Management Philosophy

Like KFC, McDonald's values were consumer driven. Its principles were summarized by QSCV. Quality, Service, Cleanness and Value. McDonald's was also known for the consistency of its procedures and quality, and its powerful global marketing campaigns. Its recent advertising campaign "i'm lovin' it",™ launched in every country in the world by September 2005, featured sports, entertainment, music, and fashion. Pop icons such as Justin Timberlake, Destiny's Child, and Wang Lee Hom for Asia were central to the campaign.

McDonald's was also known for its detail-oriented insistence on food preparation. Fred Turner, Senior

Chairman of McDonald's, developed the first operations manual in 1957. By 1991, it counted 750 detailed pages, setting out exact cooking times, proper temperature settings, and precise portions for all food items. For example, French fries were to be 9/32 of an inch; to ensure quality and taste, no products were to be held more than 10 minutes in the transfer bin.[72]

Peter Tan, former Senior Vice President and President of McDonald's Corporation Greater China, attributed McDonald's success to the fact that it provided consistency, convenience in terms of location, and good pricing. Great advertising, great taste in signature products such as Big Mac and French fries, and retail excitement such as Happy Meal promotions also played important roles.[73]

International Expansion

In 1967, the first McDonald's restaurant outside the United States opened in Richmond, British Columbia. In 1971, the first Asian McDonald's opened in Japan, in Tokyo's Ginza district. Although McDonald's opened its first outlet in greater China in Hong Kong as early as 1975, and Taiwan opened its first McDonald's in 1984, the first Mainland China McDonald's outlet was only introduced in October 1990 in Shenzhen. On 23 April 1992, the world's largest McDonald's opened in Beijing, China with over 700 seats.[74] In 1994, McDonald's made an historical debut in Kuwait City, and in 1996 the fast-food giant entered India.

Bibliography

1. *Transcript: Interview with Joseph Han, former Operating Vice President of Yum! Brands, greater China*, 2 November, 2007.
2. *Transcript: Interview with Peter Tan, former Senior Vice President and President of McDonald's Corporation*, Greater China, 20 March 2008 and 18 July 2008.
3. *KFC in China Secret Recipe for Success*, by Warren K. Liu, 2008, John Wiley & Sons (Asia) Pte Ltd.
4. *McDonald's and KFC*, edited by B.Q. Chen, China Economy Publishing, 2005.
5. *Globalization of Services: Some Implications for Theory and Practice*, Yair Aharoni, Lilach Nachum. Routledge, 2000.
6. *Kentucky Fried Chicken in China*, Professor Allen J. Morrison and Paul W. Beamish, Richard Ivey School of Business, The University of Western Ontario, Version(A) 1993-08-18.
7. www.mcdonalds.com.
8. www.yum.com.
9. *Shantel Wong; McDonald's China Development Co.*, Advertising Age, January, 2004.
10. *KFC and McDonald's—a model of blended culture*, China Today, June 2004.
11. *Hamburger heaven*, Economist, February 2005.
12. *McDonald's China Development Co.*, Advertising Age, 00018899, 1/26/2004, Vol. 75, Issue 4.
13. *McDonald's considers reform to adapt to Chinese tastes*, Xinhuanet, November 9, 2005.
14. *Fast Food Domination*, Chinese International Business, April 2007.
15. *Adapt Franchise to China's Soil: China's Regulations on Franchise in the Past Ten Years*, The Illinois Business Law Journal, 29 March 2007.
16. *McDonald's in China*, ICFAI Business School, 2003.
17. *McDonald's enter into puzzledom, what's its outlet?* December 2005, Chinese and Foreign Corporate Culture.
18. *McDonald's*, Harvard Business School Review: April 3, 2008.
19. *SW China begins dialogues with UK on food safety*, People's Daily online, March 23, 2005.
20. *Franchising Opportunities in China for American Fast Food Restaurants*, Zerong Yu, Karl Titz, Asia Pacific Journal of Tourism Research, Volume 5 Issue 1, 2000.
21. *2007 National Economic and Social Development Statistic Report*, Ministry of Commerce, People's Republic of China, http://provincedata.mofcom.gov.cn/communique/disp.asp?pid=43705.
22. *Rivals to feel bite from Burger King*, Janet Ong, June 28, 2005, Bloomberg.
23. *McDonald's Corporation (Abridged)*, Harvard Business School, Rev: June 16, 2005.

24. *Yum Brands CEO says poor performance at KFC, higher costs have taken 'fun' from US business*, Bruce Schreiner, July 17, 2008, Canadian Business Online.
25. *China Fast Food Analysis*, Just-food.com, Aroq Ltd., 2007.
26. *McDonald's opens 100th China store, sees 175 more in 2009*, http://www.forbes.com/feeds/afx/2008/ll/14/afx5693724.html.
27. *McDonald's Growing in China*, Liu Jie, China Daily, 2008-09-08 10:27, http://www.chinadaily.com.cn/bizchina/2008-09/08/content_7007412.htm.
28. Fast food nation, Ding Qing-Fen, China Daily, 30th June 2008.

End Notes

1. www.mcdonalds.com, www.yum.com, end of 2008 data.
2. www.mcdonalds.com.
3. McDonald's and KFC, edited by B.Q. Chen, China Economy Publishing, 2005.
4. Warren K. Liu, KFC in China—Secret Recipe for Success, John Wiley & Sons (Asia) pte Ltd., 2008.
5. Ibid.
6. Hamburger heaven, *Economist*, February 2005.
7. www.yum.com, Q3 2008.
8. Yair Aharoni, Lilach Nachum. Routledge, *Globalization of Services: Some Implication for Theory and Practice*, 2000.
9. Zerong Yu, Karl Titz, Franchising Opportunities in China for American Fast Food Restaurant, *Asia Pacific Journal of Tourism Research*, Volume 5 Issue 1, 2000.
10. China National Statistics Bureau, 2007.
11. 2007 National Economic and Social Development Statistics Report. Ministry of Commerce, People's Republic of China, http://provincedata.mofcom.gov.cn/communique/disp.asp?pid=43705.
12. Op Cit. Hamburger heaven.
13. Ibid.
14. China Fast Food Analysis, Just-food.com, Aroq.Ltd., 2007.
15. Fast Food Domination, *Chinese International Business*, April 2007.
16. Adapt Franchise to China's Soil: China's Regulations on Franchise in the Past Ten Years, *The Illinois Business Law Journal*, 29th March 2007.
17. International Monetary Fund—2008 World Economic Outlook.
18. Fast food nation, Ding Qing-Fen, *China Daily*, 30th June 2008.
19. Op Cit. KFC in China—Secret Recipe for Success.
20. Ibid.
21. www.yum.com.
22. Op Cit. KFC in China—Secret Recipe for Success.
23. www.yum.com.
24. Kentucky Fried Chicken in China, Professor Allen J. Morrison and Paul W. Beamish, Richard Ivey School of Business, The University of Western Ontario, 1993.
25. Op Cit. Kentucky Fried Chicken in China.
26. Op Cit. KFC in China—Secret Recipe for Success.
27. Interview with Joseph Han, former operating Vice President of Yum! Brands, Greater China, 2 November, 2007.
28. Op Cit. KFC China—Secret Recipe for Success.
29. Hazard Analysis and Critical Control Points, a systematic preventive approach to food safety and pharmaceutical safety. The Food and Drug Administration (FDA) and the United States Department of Agriculture (USDA) use mandatory juice, seafood, meat and poultry HACCP programmes as an effective approach to food safety and protecting public health.
30. Op Cit. KFC in China—Secret Recipe for Success.
31. Ibid.

32. Interview with Warren Liu, former Vice President of Yum! Brands, Greater China, 30 January, 2009.
33. Op Cit. KFC in China—Secret Recipe for Success.
34. Ibid.
35. Op Cit. KFC and McDonald's—a model of blended culture.
36. Op Cit. Interview with Joseph Han.
37. Op Cit. KFC in China—Secret Recipe for Success.
38. Op Cit. McDonald's and KFC.
39. www.yum.com.
40. Op Cit. McDonald's and KFC.
41. Op Cit. McDonald's in China.
42. Shantel Wong; McDonald's China Development Co., *Advertising Age*, January 2004.
43. McDonald's enters into puzzledom, what's its outlet? December 2005, Chinese and Foreign Corporate Culture.
44. Op Cit. McDonald's and KFC.
45. Interview with Peter Tan, former senior vice president and president of McDonald's Corporation, Greater China, 20 March 2008.
46. Op Cit. McDonald's in China.
47. McD's Preps for China Drive-Thru Boom, The Associated Press, January 19, 2007.
48. McDonald's opens 1,000th China store, sees 175 more in 2009, Thomson Financial News, http://www.forbes.com/feeds/afx/2008/11/14/afx5693724.html.
49. Op Cit. McDonald's in China.
50. Op Cit. KFC and McDonald's—a model of blended culture.
51. McDonald's considers reform to adapt to Chinese tastes, *Xinhuanet*, November 9, 2005.
52. Op Cit. Interview with Peter Tan.
53. McDonald's Growing in China, Liu Jie, *China Daily*, September 8, 2008, http://www.chinadaily.com.cn/bizchina/2008-09/08/content_7007412.htm.
54. Op Cit. McDonald's in China.
55. Ibid.
56. McDonalds's goes slow in China franchising, *International Herald Tribune*. February 7, 2007.
57. McDonald's Corporation Annual Report 2007.
58. McDonald's, Harvard Business School, Rev: April 3, 2008.
59. Op Cit. McDonald's enters into puzzledom, what's its outlet?
60. McDonald's to issue franchise licenses slowly, *Shenzhen Daily*, February 9, 2007.
61. McDonald's Press Release, December 10, 2005.
62. http://www.mcdonalds.com.cn/news/news_content.aspx?id=123.
63. McDonald's Corporation Annual Report 2007.
64. McDonald's growing in China, *China Daily*, September 8, 2008.
65. Yum Brands CEO says poor performance at KFC, higher costs have taken "fun" from US business, Bruce Schreiner, July 17, 2008, *Canadian Business Online*.
66. Stricter standards needed, Liu Jie, *China Daily*, 2006-03-16 http://www.chinadaily.com.cn/bizchina/2006-03/16/content_539721.htm.
67. SW China begins dialogues with UK on food safety, *People's Daily Online*, March 23, 2005.
68. Rivals to feel bite from Burger King, Janet Ong, June 28, 2005, Bloomberg.
69. Presentations for Investor and Analysts Conference, May 2008, www.yum.com.
70. Op Cit. KFC in China—Secret Recipe for Success.
71. www.mcdonalds.com.
72. McDonald's Corporation (Abridged), Harvard Business School Review: June 16, 2005.
73. Interview with Peter Tan, former senior vice president and president of McDonald's Corporation, Greater China, 20 March 2008.
74. McDonald's In China, ICFAI Business School, Case Development Center.

Appendix

Analyzing Cases and Preparing for Class Discussions

This book, properly understood, is really about how to analyze cases. Just reading the book, however, is no more likely to fully develop one's skills as a strategist than reading a book about golf will make one a golfer. Practice in applying the concepts and tools is essential. Cases provide the opportunity for this necessary practice.

Why the Case Method?

The core of many strategic management courses is the case method of instruction. Under the case method, you will study and discuss the real-world challenges and dilemmas that face managers in firms. Cases are typically accounts of situations that a firm or manager has faced at a given point in time. By necessity, cases do not possess the same degree of complexity that a manager faces in the real world, but they do provide a concrete set of facts that suggest challenges and opportunities that real managers have faced. Very few cases have clear answers. The case method encourages you to engage problems directly and propose solutions or strategies in the face of incomplete information. To succeed at the case method, you must develop the capability to analyze and synthesize data that are sometimes ambiguous and conflicting. You must be able to prioritize issues and opportunities and make decisions in the face of ambiguous and incomplete information. Finally, you must be able to persuade others to adopt your point of view.

In an applied field like strategic management, the real test of learning is how well you can apply knowledge to real-world situations. Strategic management cases offer you the opportunity to develop judgment and wisdom in applying your conceptual knowledge. By applying the concepts you have learned to the relatively unstructured information in a case, you develop judgment in applying concepts. Alfred North Whitehead discussed the importance of application to knowledge:

> *This discussion rejects the doctrine that students should first learn passively, and then, having learned, should apply knowledge.... For the very meaning of the things known is wrapped up in their relationship beyond themselves. This unapplied knowledge is knowledge shorn of its meaning.*

Alfred North Whitehead (1947). *Essays in Science and Philosophy*. New York: Philosophical Library, Inc. pp. 218–219.

Thus, you gain knowledge as you apply concepts. With the case method, you do not passively absorb wisdom imparted from your instructor, but actively develop it as you wrestle with the real-world situations described in the cases.

How to Analyze Cases

Before discussing how to analyze a case, it may be useful to comment on how *not* to prepare a case. We see two common failings in case preparation that often go hand-in-hand. First, students often do not apply conceptual frameworks in a rigorous and systematic manner. Second, many students do not devote sufficient time to reading, analyzing, and discussing a case before class. Many students succumb to the temptation to quickly read a case and latch on to the most visible issues that present themselves. Thus, they come to class prepared to make only a few superficial observations about a case. Often, they entirely miss the deeper issues around why a firm is in the situation that it is in and how it can better its performance. Applying the frameworks systematically may take more time and effort in the beginning, but it will generally lead to deeper insights about the cases and a more profound understanding of the concepts in the chapters. As you gain experience in this systematic approach to analyzing cases, many of you will find that your preparation time will decrease. This appendix offers a framework that will assist you as you analyze cases. The framework is important, but no framework can substitute for hard work. There are no great shortcuts to analyzing cases, and there is no single right method for preparing a case. The following approach, however, may help you develop your ability to analyze cases.

1. **Skim through the case very quickly.** Pay particular attention to the exhibits. The objective in this step is to gain familiarity with the broad facts of the case. What apparent challenges or opportunities does the company face? What information is provided? You may find it especially useful to focus on the first and last few paragraphs of the case in this step.

2. **Read the case more carefully and make notes, underline, etc.** What appear to be important facts? The conceptual frameworks in the chapters will be essential in helping you identify the key facts. Throughout the course, you will want to address central questions such as the following:

   - What is the firm's performance?
   - What is the firm's mission? strategy? goals?
   - What are the resources involved in the firm's value chain? How do they compare to competitors on cost and differentiation?
   - Does the firm have a competitive advantage?
   - Are the firm's advantages and disadvantages temporary or sustainable?
   - What is the value of the firm's resources?
   - Are the firm's resources rare?
   - Are the firm's resources costly to imitate?
   - Is the firm organized sufficiently to exploit its resources?

Depending on the case, you may also want to consider other frameworks and questions, where appropriate. Each chapter provides concepts and frameworks that you may want to consider. For example:

- What are the five forces? How do they influence industry opportunities and threats? (Chapter 2)
- What are the sources of cost differences in an industry? (Chapter 4)
- What are the bases and potential bases for product differentiation in an industry? (Chapter 5)

Each chapter suggests more specific questions and concepts than those above. You will want to consider these concepts in detail. In some cases, the instructor may offer direction about which concepts to apply to a given case. In other instances, you may be left to use your judgment in choosing which concepts to focus on in analyzing a case.

3. **Define the basic issues.** This is perhaps the most important step and also the stage of analysis that requires the most wisdom and judgment. Cases are rarely like tidy problem sets where the issues or problems are explicitly stated and the tools needed to address those issues are prescribed. Generally, you need to determine what the key issues are. In doing this, it may help for you to begin by asking: What are the fundamental issues in the case? Which concepts matter most in providing insight into those issues? One trap to avoid in defining basic issues is doing what some decision-making scholars label "plunging-in," which is drawing conclusions without first thinking about the crux of the issues involved in a decision.[1] Many students have a tendency to seize the first issues that are prominently mentioned in a case. As an antidote to this trap, you may want to consider a case from the perspective of different conceptual frames.

4. **Develop and elaborate your analysis of the key issues.** As with all of the steps, there is no substitute for painstaking work in this stage. You need to take the key issues you have defined in Step 3, examine the facts that you have noted in Step 2, and assess what are the key facts. What does quantitative analysis reveal? Here it is not just ratio analysis that we are concerned with. Just as body temperature, blood pressure, and pulse rate may reveal something about a person's health but little about the causes of a sickness, ratio analysis typically tells us more about the health of a company than the causes of its performance. You should assemble facts and analysis to support your point of view. Opinions unsupported by factual evidence and analysis are generally not persuasive. This stage of the analysis involves organizing the facts in the case. You will want to develop specific hypotheses about what factors relate to success in a particular setting. Often, you will find it helpful to draw diagrams to clarify your thinking.

5. **Draw conclusions and formulate a set of recommendations.** You may be uncomfortable drawing conclusions and making recommendations because you do not have complete information. This is an eternal dilemma for managers. Managers who wait for complete information to do something, however, usually act too late. Nevertheless, you should strive to do the most complete analysis that you can under reasonable time constraints. Recommendations should also

---

[1] J. E. Russo and P. J. H. Schoemaker (1989). *Decision Traps: The Ten Barriers to Brilliant Decision-Making and How to Overcome Them*. New York: Fireside.

flow naturally from your analysis. Too often, students formulate their recommendations in an ad hoc way. In formulating recommendations, you should be clear about priorities and the sequence of actions that you recommend.

6. **Prepare for class discussion.** Students who diligently work through the first five steps and rigorously examine a case should be well prepared for class discussion. You may find it helpful to make some notes and bring them to class. Over the years, we have observed that many of the students who are low contributors to class discussions bring few or no notes to class. Once in class, a case discussion usually begins with a provocative question from the instructor. Many instructors will "cold call"—direct a question to a specific student who has not been forewarned. Students who have thoroughly analyzed and discussed the case before coming to class will be much better prepared for these surprise calls. They will also be better prepared to contribute to the analysis, argument, and persuasion that will take place in the class discussion. Discussions can move rapidly. You will hear new insights from fellow students. Preparation helps you to absorb, learn, and contribute to the insights that emerge from class discussion.

Summary

Students who embark in the case method soon learn that analyzing cases is a complex process. Having a clear conceptual approach such as the VRIO framework does not eliminate the complexity. This systematic approach, however, does allow the analyst to manage the complexity of real-world business situations. In the end, though, neither cases nor real-world businesses conclude their analyses with tidy solutions that resolve all the uncertainties and ambiguities a business faces. However, the case method coupled with a good theory such as the VRIO approach and hard work do make it more likely that you will generate valuable insights into the strategic challenges of firms and develop the strategic skills needed to lead a firm.

Glossary

above average accounting performance when a firm's accounting performance is greater than the industry average

above normal economic performance when a firm earns above its cost of capital

absorptive capacity the ability of firms to learn

accounting performance a measure of a firm's competitive advantage; calculated from information in the firm's published profit and loss and balance sheet statements

accounting ratios numbers taken from a firm's financial statements that are manipulated in ways that describe various aspects of the firm's performance

acquisition a firm purchases another firm

acquisition premium the difference between the current market price of a target firm's shares and the price a potential acquirer offers to pay for those shares

activity ratios accounting ratios that focus on the level of activity in a firm's business

adverse selection an alliance partner promises to bring to an alliance certain resources that it either does not control or cannot acquire

agency problems parties in an agency relationship differ in their decision-making objectives

agency relationship one party to an exchange delegates decision-making authority to a second party

agent a party to whom decision-making authority is delegated

architectural competence the ability of a firm to use organizational structure and other organizing mechanisms to facilitate coordination among scientific disciplines to conduct research

auction in mergers and acquisitions, a mechanism for establishing the price of an asset when multiple firms bid for a single target firm

audit committee subgroup of the board of directors responsible for ensuring the accuracy of accounting and financial statements

average accounting performance when a firm's accounting performance is equal to the industry average

backward vertical integration a firm incorporates more stages of the value chain within its boundaries and those stages bring it closer to gaining access to raw materials

barriers to entry attributes of an industry's structure that increase the cost of entry

below average accounting performance when a firm's accounting performance is less than the industry average

below normal economic performance when a firm earns less than its cost of capital

board chair the person who presides over the board of directors; may or may not be the same person as a firm's senior executive also known as Chairman of the Board

board of directors a group of 10 to 15 individuals drawn from a firm's top management and from people outside the firm whose primary responsibilities are to monitor decisions made in the firm and to ensure that they are consistent with the interests of outside equity holders

business angels wealthy individuals who act as outside investors typically in an entrepreneurial firm

business cycle the alternating pattern of prosperity followed by recession followed by prosperity

business-level strategies actions firms take to gain competitive advantages in a single market or industry

business model the set of activities that a firm engages in to create and appropriate economic value

business plan a document that summarizes how an entrepreneur will organize a firm to exploit an opportunity, along with the economic implications of exploiting that opportunity

business strategy a firm's theory of how to gain competitive advantage in a single business or industry

buyers those who purchase a firm's products or services

capabilities a subset of a firm's resources, defined as tangible and intangible assets, that enable a firm to take full advantage of other resources it controls

cashing out the compensation paid to an entrepreneur for risk-taking associated with starting a firm

causally ambiguous imitating firms do not understand the relationship between the resources and capabilities controlled by a firm and that firm's competitive advantage

centralized hub each country in which a firm operates is organized as a full profit-and-loss division headed by a division general manager; strategic and operational decisions are retained at headquarters

chairman of the board the person who presides over the board of directors; may or may not be the same person as a firm's senior executive

chief executive officer (CEO) person to whom all functional managers report in a U-form organization; the person to whom all divisional personal and corporate staff report to in an M-form organization: responsible for strategy formulation and implementation

chief operating officer (COO) reports to CEO; primary responsibility is strategy implementation

closely held firm a firm that has not sold many of its shares on the public stock market

collusion two or more firms in an industry coordinate their strategic choices to reduce competition in that industry

compensation policies the ways that firms pay employees

competitive advantage a firm creates more economic value than rival firms

competitive disadvantage a firm generates less economic value than rival firms

competitive dynamics how one firm responds to the strategic actions of competing firms

competitive parity a firm creates the same economic value as rival firms

competitor any firm, group, or individual trying to reduce a firm's competitive advantage

complementary resources and capabilities resources and capabilities that have limited ability to generate competitive advantage in isolation but in combination with other resources can enable a firm to realize its full potential for competitive advantage

complementor when the value of a firm's products increases in the presence of another firm's products

conduct (as in structured conduct performance model) the strategies that firms in an industry implement

conglomerate merger a merger or acquisition where there are no vertical, horizontal, product extension, or market extension links between the firms

consolidation strategy strategy that reduces the number of firms in an industry by exploiting economies of scale

controlling share when an acquiring firm purchases enough of a target firm's assets to be able to make all the management and strategic decisions in the target firm

coordinated federation each country in which a firm operates is organized as a full profit-and-loss division headed by a division general manager; operational decisions are delegated to these divisions or countries, but strategic decisions are retained at headquarters

core competence the collective learning in an organization, especially how to coordinate diverse production skills and integrate multiple streams of technologies

corporate diversification strategy when a firm operates in multiple industries or markets simultaneously

corporate-level strategies actions firms take to gain competitive advantages by operating in multiple markets or industries simultaneously

corporate spin-off exists when a large, typically diversified firm divests itself of a business in which it has historically been operating and the divested business operates as an independent entity

corporate staff upper-level managers who provide information about a firm's external and internal environments to the firm's senior executive

corporate strategy a firm's theory of how to gain competitive advantage by operating in several businesses simultaneously

cost centers divisions are assigned a budget and manage their operations to that budget

cost leadership business strategy focuses on gaining advantages by reducing costs below those of competitors

cost of capital the rate of return that a firm promises to pay its suppliers of capital to induce them to invest in a firm

cost of debt the interest that a firm must pay its debt holders to induce them to lend money to the firm

cost of equity the rate of return a firm must promise its equity holders to induce them to invest in the firm

countertrade international firms receiving payment for the products or services they sell into a country not in the form of currency, but in the form of other products or services that they can sell on the world market

crown jewel sale a bidding firm is interested in just a few of the most highly regarded businesses being operated by the target firm, known as its *crown jewels*, and the target firm sells these businesses

culture the values, beliefs, and norms that guide behavior in a society and in a firm

cumulative abnormal return (CAR) performance that is greater (or less) than what was expected in a short period of time around when an acquisition is announced

current market value the price of each of a firm's shares multiplied by the number of shares outstanding

customer-switching costs customers make investments in order to use a firm's particular products or services that are not useful in using other firms' products

debt capital from banks and bondholders

decentralized federation each country in which a firm operates is organized as a full profit-and-loss division headed by a division general manager and strategic and operational decisions are delegated to these country managers

decline the final phase of the product life cycle during which demand drops off when a technologically superior product or service is introduced

declining industry an industry that has experienced an absolute decline in unit sales over a sustained period of time

deep-pockets model a firm that takes advantage of its monopoly power in one business to subsidize several different businesses

demographics the distribution of individuals in a society in terms of age, sex, marital status, income, ethnicity, and other personal attributes that may determine their buying patterns

depression a severe recession that lasts for several years

direct duplication the attempt to imitate other firms by developing resources that have the same strategic effects as the resources controlled by those other firms

diseconomies of scale a firm's costs begin to rise as a function of the volume of production

distinctive competence a valuable and rare resource or capability

distribution agreement one firm agrees to distribute the products of others

diversification economies sources of relatedness in a diversified firm

divestment a firm sells a business in which it had been operating

division   each business that a firm engages in, also called a strategic business unit (SBU)

dominant-business firms   firms with between 70 percent and 95 percent of their total sales in a single product market

dominant logic   common theory of how to gain competitive advantages shared by each business in a diversified firm

economic climate   the overall health of the economic systems within which a firm operates

economic measures of competitive advantage   measures that compare a firm's level of return to its cost of capital instead of to the average level of return in the industry

economic value   the difference between the perceived benefits gained by a customer who purchases a firm's products or services and the full economic cost of these products or services

economic value added (EVA)   worth calculated by subtracting the cost of the capital employed in a division from that division's earnings

economies of scale   the per-unit cost of production falls as the volume of production increases

economies of scope   the value of a firm's products or services increases as a function of the number of different businesses in which that firm operates

emerging industries   newly created or newly re-created industries formed by technological innovations, change in demand, or the emergence of new customer needs

emergent strategies   theories of how to gain competitive advantage in an industry that emerge over time or have been radically reshaped once they are initially implemented

environmental threat   any individual, group, or organization outside a firm that seeks to reduce the level of that firm's performance

equity   capital from individuals and institutions that purchase a firm's stocks

equity alliance   cooperating firms supplement contracts with equity holdings in alliance partners

escalation of commitment   an increased commitment by managers to an incorrect course of action, even as its limitations become manifest

event study analysis   evaluates the performance effects of acquisitions for bidding firms

executive committee   typically consists of the CEO and two or three functional senior managers

explicit collusion   firms directly communicate with each other to coordinate levels of production, prices, and so forth (illegal in most countries)

external analysis   identification and examination of the critical threats and opportunities in a firm's competitive environment

finance committee   subgroup of the board of directors that maintains the relationship between the firm and external capital markets

financial resources   all the money, from whatever source, that firms use to conceive and implement strategies

firm-specific human capital investments   investments made by employees in a particular firm over time, including understanding the culture, policies, and procedures and knowing the people to contact to complete a task, that have limited value in other firms

firm-specific investments   the value of stakeholders' investments in a particular firm is much greater than the value those same investments would be in other firms

first-mover advantages   advantages that come to firms that make important strategic and technological decisions early in the development of an industry

flexibility   how costly it is for a firm to alter its strategic and organizational decisions

foreign direct investment   investing in operations located in a foreign country

formal management controls   a firm's budgeting and reporting activities that keep people higher up in a firm's organizational chart informed about the actions taken by people lower down in the organizational chart

formal reporting structure   a description of who in the organization reports to whom

forward vertical integration   a firm incorporates more stages of the value chain within its boundaries and those stages bring it closer to interacting directly with final customers

fragmented industries   industries in which a large number of small or medium-sized firms operate and no small set of firms has dominant market share or creates dominant technologies

free cash flow   the amount of cash a firm has to invest after all positive net present-value investments in its ongoing businesses have been funded

friendly acquisition   the management of a target firm wants the firm to be acquired

functional manager   a manager who leads a particular function within a firm, such as manufacturing, marketing, finance, accounting, or sales

functional organizational structure   the structure a firm uses to implement business-level strategies it might pursue where each function in the firm reports to the CEO

general environment   broad trends in the context within which a firm operates that can have an impact on a firm's strategic choices

generic business strategies   another name for business-level strategies, which are cost leadership and product differentiation

geographic market diversification strategy   when a firm operates in multiple geographic markets simultaneously

golden parachutes   incentive compensation paid to senior managers if the firm they manage is acquired

greenmail   a target firm's management purchases any of the target firm's stock owned by a bidder for a price that is greater than its current market value

growth   the second stage of the product life cycle during which demand increases rapidly and many new firms enter to begin producing the product or service

hard currencies   currencies that are traded globally and thus have value on international money markets

harvest strategy   a firm engages in a long, systematic, phased withdrawal from a declining industry, extracting as much value as possible

hedonic price   that part of the price of a product or service that is attributable to a particular characteristic of that product or service

holdup   one firm makes more transaction-specific investments in an exchange than partner firms make and the firm that has not made these investments tries to exploit the firm that has made the investments

horizontal merger   a firm acquires a former competitor

hostile takeover   the management of a target firm does not want the firm to be acquired

human capital resources   the training, experience, judgment, intelligence, relationships, and insight of individual managers and workers in a firm

imperfectly imitable   resources and capabilities that are more costly for other firms to imitate, compared to firms that already possess them

increasing returns to scale   in network industries, the value of a product or service increases as the number of people using those products or services increases

inelastic in supply   the quantity of supply is fixed and does not respond to price increases, such as the total supply of land, which is relatively fixed and cannot be significantly increased in response to higher demand and prices

informal management controls   include a firm's culture and the willingness of employees to monitor each other's behavior

initial public offering (IPO)   the initial sale of stock of a privately held firm or a division of a corporation to the general public

institutional owners   pension funds, corporations, and others that invest other peoples' money in firm equities

intermediate products or services   products or services produced in one division that are used as inputs for products or services produced by a second division

internal analysis   identification of a firm's organizational strengths and weaknesses and of the resources and capabilities that are likely to be sources of competitive advantage

internal capital market   when businesses in a diversified firm compete for corporate capital

international strategies   operations in multiple geographic markets: vertical integration, diversification, the formation of strategic alliances, or implementation of mergers and acquisitions, all across national borders

introduction   the first stage of a product's life cycle when relatively few firms are producing a product, there are relatively few customers, and the rate of growth in demand for the product is relatively low

invented competencies   illusory inventions by creative managers to justify poor diversification moves by linking intangible core competencies to completely unrelated businesses

joint venture   cooperating firms create a legally independent firm in which they invest and from which they share any profits that are created

learning curve   a concept that formalizes the relationship between cumulative volumes of production and falling per-unit costs

learning race   both parties to an alliance seek to learn from each other, but the rate at which these two firms learn varies; the first party to learn "wins" the race and may withdraw from the alliance

legal and political conditions   the laws and the legal system's impact on business, together with the general nature of the relationship between government and business

leverage ratios   accounting ratios that focus on the level of a firm's financial flexibility

licensing agreement   one firm allows others to use its brand name to sell products in return for some fee or percentage of profits

limited corporate diversification   all or most of a firm's business activities fall within a single industry and geographic market

liquidity ratios   accounting ratios that focus on the ability of a firm to meet its short-term financial obligations

local responsiveness   in an international strategy, the ability a firm has to respond to the consumer preferences in a particular geographic market

management control systems   a range of formal and informal mechanisms to ensure that managers are behaving in ways consistent with a firm's strategies

managerial hubris   the unrealistic belief held by managers in bidding firms that they can manage the assets of a target firm more efficiently than the target firm's current management

managerial know-how   the often-taken-for-granted knowledge and information that are needed to compete in an industry on a day-to-day basis

managerial perquisites   activities that do not add economic value to the firm but directly benefit the managers who make them

managerial risk aversion   managers unable to diversify their firm-specific human capital investments may engage in less risky business decisions than what would be preferred by equity holders

market extension merger   firms make acquisitions in new geographical markets

market for corporate control   the market that is created when multiple firms actively seek to acquire one or several firms

market leader   the firm with the largest market share in an industry

matrix structures   one employee reports to two or more people

mature industries   an industry in which, over time, ways of doing business have become widely understood, technologies have diffused through competitors, and the rate of innovation in new products and technologies drops

maturity   third phase of the product life cycle during which the number of firms producing a product or service remains stable, demand growth levels off, and firms direct their investment efforts toward refining the process by which a product or service is created and away from developing entirely new products

merger   the assets of two similar-sized firms are combined

M-form (multidivisional form)   an organizational structure for implementing a corporate diversification strategy whereby each business a firm engages in is managed through a separate profit-and-loss division

mission   a firm's long-term purpose

mission statement   written statement defining both what a firm aspires to be in the long run and what it wants to avoid in the meantime

monopolistic competition   a market structure where within the market niche defined by a firm's differentiated product, a firm possesses a monopoly

monopolistic industries   industries that consist of only a single firm

monopolistically competitive industries   industries in which there are large numbers of competing firms and low-cost entry and exit, but products are not homogeneous with respect to cost or product attributes; firms are said to enjoy a "monopoly" in that part of the market they dominate

moral hazard   partners in an exchange possess high-quality resources and capabilities of significant value to the exchange but fail to make them available to the other partners

mutual forbearance   a form of tacit collusion whereby firms tacitly agree to not compete in one industry in order to avoid competition in a second industry

network industries   industries in which a single technical standard and increasing returns to scale tend to dominate; competition in these industries tends to focus on which of several competing standards will be chosen

new competitors   firms that have either recently started operating in an industry or that threaten to begin operations in an industry soon

niche strategy   a firm reduces its scope of operations and focuses on narrow segments of a declining industry

nominating committee   subgroup of the board of directors that nominates new board members

nonequity alliance   cooperating firms agree to work together to develop, manufacture, or sell products or services, but they do not take equity positions in each other or form an independent organizational unit to manage the cooperative efforts

normal economic performance   a firm earns its cost of capital

objectives   specific, measurable targets a firm can use to evaluate the extent to which it is realizing its mission

office of the president   together, the roles of chairman of the board, CEO, and COO

oligopolies   industries characterized by a small number of competing firms, by homogeneous products, and by costly entry and exit

operational economies of scope   shared activities and shared core competencies in a diversified firm

operations committee   typically meets monthly and usually consists of the CEO and each of the heads of the functional areas included in the firm

opportunism   a firm is unfairly exploited in an exchange

organizational chart   a depiction of the formal reporting structure within a firm

organizational resources   a firm's formal reporting structure; its formal and informal planning, controlling, and coordinating systems; its culture and reputation; and informal relations among groups within a firm and between a firm and those in its environment

Pac Man defense   fending off an acquisition by a firm acquiring the firm or firms bidding for it

path dependence   events early in the evolution of a process have significant effects on subsequent events

pecuniary economies   sources of relatedness in market power between bidding and target firms

perfectly competitive industry   when there are large numbers of competing firms, the products being sold are homogeneous with respect to cost and product attributes, and entry and exit costs are very low

performance   (in the structure-conduct-performance model) performance of individual firms and performance of the industry

personnel and compensation committee   subgroup of the board of directors that evaluates and compensates the performance of a firm's senior executive and other senior managers

physical resources   all the physical technology used in a firm

poison pills   a variety of actions that target firm managers can take to make the acquisition of the target prohibitively expensive

policy choices   choices firms make about the kinds of products or services they will sell—choices that have an impact on relative cost and product differentiation position

policy of experimentation   exists when firms are committed to engage in several related product differentiation efforts simultaneously

predatory pricing   setting prices so that they are less than a business's costs

price takers   where the price of the products or services a firm sells is determined by market conditions and not by the decisions of firms

principal   the party who delegates the decision-making authority

privately held   a firm that has stock that is not traded on public stock markets and that is not a division of a larger company

processes   the activities a firm engages in to design, produce, and sell its products or services

process innovation   a firm's effort to refine and improve its current processes

process manufacturing   when manufacturing is accomplished in a continuous system; examples include manufacturing in chemical, oil refining, and paper and pulp industries

product differentiation   a business strategy whereby firms attempt to gain a competitive advantage by increasing the perceived value of their products or services relative to the perceived value of other firms' products or services

product diversification strategy   a firm operates in multiple industries simultaneously

product extension merger   firms acquire complementary products through merger and acquisition activities

product life cycle   naturally occurring process that occurs when firms begin offering a product or service; the stages consist of introduction, growth, maturity, and decline

productive inputs   any supplies used by a firm in conducting its business activities, such as labor, capital, land, and raw materials, among others

product-market diversification strategy   a firm implements both product and geographic market diversification simultaneously

profitability ratios   accounting ratios with some measure of profit in the numerator and some measure of firm size or assets in the denominator

profit-and-loss centers   profits and losses are calculated at the level of the division in a firm

proprietary technology   secret or patented technology that gives incumbent firms important advantages over potential entrants

question of imitability   "Do firms without a resource or capability face a cost disadvantage in obtaining or developing it compared to firms that already possess it?"

question of organization   "Is a firm organized to exploit the full competitive potential of its resources and capabilities?"

question of rarity   "How many competing firms already possess particular valuable resources and capabilities?"

question of value   "Does a resource enable a firm to exploit an external opportunity or neutralize an external threat?"

real options   investments in real assets that create the opportunity for additional investments in the future

recession   a period of relatively low prosperity; demand for goods and services is low and unemployment is high

related-constrained diversification   all the businesses in which a firm operates share a significant number of inputs, product technologies, distribution channels, similar customers, and so forth

related corporate diversification   less than 70 percent of a firm's revenue comes from a single product market and its multiple lines of business are linked

related-linked diversification strategy   the different businesses that a single firm pursues are linked on only a couple of dimensions or different sets of businesses are linked along very different dimensions

reputation   beliefs customers hold about a firm

resource-based view (RBV)   a model of firm performance that focuses on the resources and capabilities controlled by a firm as sources of competitive advantage

resource heterogeneity   for a given business activity, some firms may be more skilled in accomplishing the activity than other firms

resource immobility   resources controlled by some firms may not diffuse to other firms

resources   the tangible and intangible assets that a firm controls, which it can use to conceive and implement its strategies

retained earnings   capital generated from a firm's ongoing operations that is retained by a firm

seemingly unrelated diversified   diversified firms that exploit core competencies as an economy of scope, but are not doing so with any shared activities

senior executive   the president or CEO of a firm

shakeout period   period during which the total supply in an industry is reduced by bankruptcies, acquisitions, and business closings

shared activities   potential sources of operational economies of scope for diversified firms

shark repellents   a variety of relatively minor corporate governance changes that, in principle, are supposed to make it somewhat more difficult to acquire a target firm

single-business firms   firms with greater than 95 percent of their total sales in a single product market

"skunk works"   temporary teams whose creative efforts are intensive and focused

socially complex   resources and capabilities that involve interpersonal, social, or cultural links among individuals

social welfare   the overall good of society

specific international events   events such as civil wars, political coups, terrorism, wars between countries, famines, and country or regional economic recessions, all of which can have an enormous impact on the ability of a firm's strategies to generate competitive advantage

stakeholders   all groups and individuals who have an interest in how a firm performs

standstill agreement   contract between a target and a bidding firm wherein the bidding firm agrees not to attempt to take over the target for some period of time

stock grants   payments to employees in a firm's stock

stock options   employees are given the right, but not the obligation, to purchase a firm's stock at predetermined prices

strategic alliance   whenever two or more independent organizations cooperate in the development, manufacture, or sale of products or services; a form of exchange governance between market exchanges and hierarchical exchanges; examples include licensing arrangements, manufacturing agreements, and joint ventures

strategic management process   a sequential set of analyses that can increase the likelihood of a firm's choosing a strategy that generates competitive advantages

strategically valuable assets   resources required to successfully compete in an industry, including access to raw materials, particularly favorable geographic locations, and particularly valuable product market positions

strategy   a firm's theory about how to gain competitive advantage

strategy implementation   a firm adopting organizational policies and practices that are consistent with its strategy

structure   (in the structure-conduct-performance model) industry structure measured by such factors as the number of competitors in an industry, the heterogeneity of products in an industry, the cost of entry and exit in an industry, and so forth

structure-conduct-performance model (S-C-P)   theory suggesting that industry structure determines a firm's conduct, which in turn determines its performance

substitutes   products or services that meet approximately the same customer needs but do so in different ways

substitution   developing or acquiring strategically equivalent, but different, resources as a competing firm

supermajority voting rules   an example of a shark repellent that specifies that more than 50 percent of the target firm's board of directors must approve a takeover

suppliers   firms that make a wide variety of raw materials, labor, and other critical assets available to firms

supply agreements   one firm agrees to supply others

sustainable distinctive competencies   valuable, rare, and costly-to-imitate resources or capabilities

sustained competitive advantage   a competitive advantage that lasts for a long period of time; an advantage that is not competed away through strategic imitation

tacit collusion   firms coordinate their production and pricing decisions not by directly communicating with each other, but by exchanging signals with other firms about their intent to cooperate; special case of tacit cooperation

tacit cooperation   actions a firm takes that have the effect of reducing the level of rivalry in an industry and that do not require firms in an industry to directly communicate or negotiate with each other

tactics   the specific actions a firm takes to implement its strategies

technical economies   sources of relatedness in marketing, production, and similar activities between bidding and target firms

technological hardware   the machines and other hardware used by firms

technological leadership strategy   firms make early investments in particular technologies in an industry

technological software   the quality of labor–management relations, an organization's culture, and the quality of managerial controls in a firm

temporary competitive advantage   a competitive advantage that lasts for a short period of time

tender offer   a bidding firm offers to purchase the shares of a target firm directly by offering a higher-than-market price for those shares to current shareholders

thinly traded market   a market where there are only a small number of buyers and sellers, where information about opportunities in this market is not widely known, and where interests besides purely maximizing the value of a firm can be important

transaction-specific investment   the value of an investment in its first-best use is much greater than its value in its second-best use; any investment in an exchange that has significantly more value in the current exchange than it does in alternative exchanges

transfer-pricing system   using internally administered "prices" to manage the movement of intermediate products or services among divisions within a firm

transnational strategy   actions in which a firm engages to gain competitive advantages by investing in technology across borders

transnational structure   each country in which a firm operates is organized as a full profit-and-loss division headed by a division general manager and strategic and operational decisions are delegated to operational entities that maximize local responsiveness and international integration

transparent business partners   international business partners that are open and accessible

U-form structure   organization where different functional heads report directly to CEO; used to implement business-level strategies

uncertainty   the future value of an exchange cannot be known when investments in that exchange are being made

unfriendly acquisition   the management of the target firm does not want the firm to be acquired

unlearning   when a firm tries to modify or abandon traditional ways of engaging in business

unrelated corporate diversification   less than 70 percent of a firm's revenues is generated in a single product market and a firm's businesses share few, if any, common attributes

value added as a percentage of sales   measures the percentage of a firm's sales that are generated by activities done within the boundaries of a firm; a measure of vertical integration

value chain that set of activities that must be accomplished to bring a product or service from raw materials to the point that it can be sold to a final customer

venture capital firms outside investment firms looking to invest in entrepreneurial ventures

vertical integration the number of steps in the value chain that a firm accomplishes within its boundaries

vertical merger when a firm vertically integrates, either forward or backward, through its acquisition efforts

visionary firms firms whose mission is central to all they do

VRIO framework four questions that must be asked about a resource or capability to determine its competitive potential: the questions of value, rarity, imitability, and organization

weighted average cost of capital (WACC) the percentage of a firm's total capital that is debt multiplied by the cost of debt plus the percentage of a firm's total capital; that is, equity times the cost of equity

white knight another bidding firm that agrees to acquire a particular target in place of the original bidding firm

zero-based budgeting corporate executives create a list of all capital allocation requests from divisions in a firm, rank them from most important to least important, and then fund all the projects the firm can afford, given the amount of capital it has available

Company Index

In the page references, the number after "n" refers to the number of the end note in which the name is cited.

Name Index

In the page references, the number after "n" refers to the number of the end note in which the name is cited.

A

Abernathy, W. J., 337n9
Adler, N., 355n36
Agins, T., 177n30
Agmon, T., 344n24
Aguilar, F. J., 77n50, 263n25
Alchian, A., 187n2, 280n14
Allen, M., 62n22
Alley, J., 98n15
Alvarez, S., 43n, 91n, 274n
Amit, R., 34n, 102n26, 231n33, 233n
Anders, G., 90n7, 353n35
Angwin, J., 163n
Ansoff, H. I., 217n
Ante, S., 297n
Applebaum, A., 28n7
Argyris, C., 342n21
Arikan, A., 308n
Armour, H. O., 242n1
Armstrong, L., 168n17
Arthur, W. B., 97n13, 98n15
Artz, K. W., 86n1
Auletta, K., 350n30
Axelrod, R. M., 284n

B

Badaracco, J. L., 270n2, 283n16
Baden-Fuller, C.W.F., 357n41
Bain, J. S., 53n7, 58n10
Balakrishnan, S., 278n9
Balmer, S., 75
Barnes, B., 52n5
Barnett, W. P., 86n1
Barney, B., 57n
Barney, J., 43n, 88n5, 91n, 215, 215n, 233n
Barney, J. B., 30n8, 53n7, 54n, 86n1, 95n9, 97n12, 99n18, 99n21, 101n, 139n19, 189n4, 202n9, 225n18, 233n, 274n, 277, 277n, 278n11, 283n17, 286n21, 286n22, 288n23, 289n24, 291n29, 300n4, 310n16
Barrett, A., 344n
Bartlett, C., 253n11, 283n19
Bartlett, C. A., 277n7, 347n26, 357n, 357n40, 359n43
Baughn, C. C., 278n11, 340n18, 341n19
Baum, J.A.C., 227n24
Beane, W. L., 142
Beatty, R., 290n25
Becker, G. S., 86n3, 201n8
Benedict, R., 342n20
Bennett, T., 199
Bennis, W. G., 113n34
Berg, N. A., 126n2
Berg, P. O., 99n20
Berger, P., 225n21, 252n9, 261n
Bergh, D., 248n6
Bernheim, R. D., 227n24
Besanko D., 30n8
Bethel, J., 225n19, 248n6, 254n13

Bettis, R. A., 222n15
Bhambri, A., 263n25
Bhide, A., 91, 91n
Bigelow, L. S., 231n33
Bleeke, J., 278n10, 283n17, 283n18, 284n, 291–292n30, 291n29
Blois, K. J., 291n29
Bock, A. J., 34n
Bond, R. S., 72n42
Bounds, W., 335n6
Bower, J., 312n18
Bower, J. L., 77n50
Boyd, B., 247, 247n
Bradey, M., 322n
Bradley, S. P., 338n10
Brahm, J. R., 355n36
Brandenburger, A., 30n8, 67, 67n31, 68
Branson, R., 222
Breen, B., 96n11, 98n14
Brennan, M., 226n23
Bresnahan, T. F., 71n38
Bresser, R. K., 279n12
Brewer, H. L., 350n32
Brickley, J., 258n20
Bright, A. A., 71n38
Brin, S., 85
Bromiley, P., 86n1
Brown, S. J., 308n
Brush, T. H., 86n1
Buffett, W., 241, 241n, 263
Burgers, W. P., 275n4, 278n8
Burgleman, R. A., 342n21, 342n22
Butler, J. K., Jr., 291n29
Buzzell, R. D., 131n

C

Camerer, C., 289n24
Cameron, K. S., 307n13
Campbell, E., 289n
Cantrell, R. S., 291n29
Capell, K., 123n
Carlisle, K., 133n
Carnevale, M. L., 228n30
Carney, M., 291n29
Carpenter, M., 353n35
Carroll, G. R., 231n33
Carroll, P., 154n4
Cartwright, S., 319n21
Cauley, L., 63n26
Cavanaugh, S., 338n10
Caves, R. E., 153n, 153n2, 352n34
Chamberlin, E., 160, 161, 161n
Chandler, A., 242n1
Chartier, J., 62n23, 73–74n44, 74n46
Chatterjee, S., 219n12, 319n21
Chen, M.-J., 227n24
Chew, D., 255n15
Chiles, T. H., 291n29
Christensen, C., 78n52

Christensen, C. R., 126n2
Coase, R., 185, 185n1, 187
Cockburn, I., 61n20, 86n1, 99n18, 157n9
Cohen, B., 28
Cohen, W., 274n
Collins, J., 113n34
Collins, J. C., 27n5, 27n6, 41n11
Collis, D. J., 340n15
Comment, R., 214, 215n, 225n21
Conner, K. R., 86n1, 189n4
Cool, K., 61n18, 86n1, 97n12, 97n13
Cooper, C., 319n21
Copeland, T., 42n
Cowling, K., 155n
Cox, J., 226n23
Cox, M., 63n26
Coyne, W., 173n
Crawford, R., 187n2, 280n14
Crowe, J., 262
Cubbin, J., 155n
Cyert, R., 259n21

D

Dalton, D., 247n
Dann, L. Y., 322n
D'Aveni, R., 244n2, 247n
Davidson, J. H., 72n42
Davis, B., 335n6
Davis, S. M., 144n22
Dawley, H., 133n
DeAngelo, H., 322n
DeFillippi, R. J., 98n16
de Forest, M. E., 340n17, 356n39
DeGeorge, R., 133n
Delaney, K. J., 183n
Delmar, F., 91, 91n
Demetrakakes, P., 74n45
Demick, B., 329n
Demsetz, H., 54n, 230n
Dent-Micallef, A., 86n1
Deogun, N., 306n11, 351n33
Der Hovanseian, M., 308n
Deutsch, C. H., 168n17
Devinney, T. M., 231n33
DeWitt, W., 65n28
Dial, J., 78n54, 263n25
Dichtl, E., 348–349n29, 349n
Dierickx, I., 61n18, 86n1, 97n12, 97n13
Dobie, A., 61n16
Dodd, P., 309n15
Donaldson, L., 42n
Dranove, D., 30n8
Drucker, P., 26n1, 27n2
Duell, C. H., 50
Duffy, M., 254n14
Dumaine, B., 251n8
Dunning, J. H., 350n31, 352n34
Dyer, J. H., 99n18

Subject Index

In the page references, the number after "n" refers to the number of the end note in which the name is cited.